Method
AND
Madness

Method
AND
Madness

THE MAKING OF A STORY

Alice LaPlante

San Francisco State University

W. W. Norton & Company

New York • London

Previous trade edition published as THE MAKING OF A STORY: A Norton Guide to
Creative Writing

The text of this book is composed in Palatino
with the display set in Kallos.
Book design by Charlotte Staub
Composition by Sue Carlson and Matrix
Manufacturing by R. R. Donnelley & Sons—Haddon Division
Editor: Marilyn Moller
Managing Editor, College: Marian Johnson
Production Manager: Benjamin Reynolds
Project Editor: Melissa Atkin
Editorial Assistant: Ana Cooke
Copyeditor: Alice Vigliani

Library of Congress Cataloging-in-Publication Data
LaPlante, Alice, 1958–
    Method and madness : the making of a story / Alice LaPlante.
        p. cm.
    Rev. ed. of: The making of a story. 2007
    Includes bibliographical references and index.
    ISBN 978-0-393-92817-4 (pbk.)
1. English language—Rhetoric—Study and teaching (Higher) 2. Creative writing
(Higher education) 3. English language—Style—Handbooks, manuals, etc.
I. LaPlante, Alice, 1958– Making of a story. II. Title.
    PE1408.L31887 2008
    808′.042—dc22

                                                                2008015539

ISBN 978-0-393-92817-4

W. W. Norton & Company, Inc., 500 Fifth Avenue, New York, N.Y. 10110
                        www.wwnorton.com

W. W. Norton & Company Ltd., Castle House, 75/76 Wells Street, London W1T 3QT

  3 4 5 6 7 8 9 0

Though this be madness,
yet there is method in't.

—*Hamlet* (Act 2, Scene 2)

For Sarah and David,
who continue to teach me
everything I need to know

Contents

List of Readings XVII
Acknowledgments XIX

CHAPTER

1. What Is This Thing Called Creative Writing? 1
The Basics

Reconciling the Method with the Madness 1
Some Basic Definitions 3
Writing That Is Surprising Yet Convincing 3
Resisting Paraphrase 4
Sentiment, Not Sentimentality 5
Our First Job as Writers: To Notice 9
Avoiding the "Writerly" Voice 10

EXERCISES 11
1. "I Don't Know Why I Remember . . ." 11
2. "I Am a Camera . . ." 12

READINGS 13
DENIS JOHNSON *Emergency* 13
AMY BLOOM *Silver Water* 21

CHAPTER

2. The Gift of Not Knowing 29
Writing as Discovery

What Do You Know? 30
What You Don't Know (about What You Know) 32
On Rendering the Mysteries That Surround Us 33

Moving from "Triggering" to Real Subject 35
Surprise Yourself, Interest Others 36
Obsession as a Creative Virtue 37

EXERCISES 38
1. Things I Was Taught / Things I Was Not Taught 38
2. I Want to Know Why 39

READINGS 40
JOYCE CAROL OATES *Where Are You Going, Where Have You Been?* 40
SANDRA CISNEROS *Woman Hollering Creek* 53

CHAPTER

3. Details, Details 61
The Basic Building Blocks

On Thinking Small 61
Defining "Image" within a Literary Context 63
Imagery That Works on Two Levels 64
On Seeing the General in the Particular 66
On Crowding Out the Reader 68
Don't Lose Any of Your Senses 69
Use and Abuse of Metaphor 69
When Should You Use Metaphor? 72
The "S" Word: Avoiding Conscious Symbols 72
Imagery as Creative Source 73

EXERCISES 75
1. *Harper's* Index on a Personal Level 75
2. Render a Tree, Capture the Forest 78

READINGS 79
TIM O'BRIEN *The Things They Carried* 79
RON HANSEN *Nebraska* 92

CHAPTER

4. The Short Story 96
Defining and Shaping

Some Basic Definitions 96
The Conflict–Crisis–Resolution Model 98
Linear versus Modular Stories 101

To Epiphany or Not to Epiphany? 102
Is Change Necessary? (The Debate Continues) 104
On Not Becoming Slaves to Theory 105

EXERCISES 107

1. False Epiphanies I Have Had 107
2. Opportunities Not Taken 108

READINGS 109

FRANCINE PROSE *What Makes a Short Story?* 109
JOHN EDGAR WIDEMAN *Fever* 118
JUNOT DÍAZ *Fiesta, 1980* 137

CHAPTER

5. **Why You Need to Show and Tell** 147
Dramatizing and Narrating

Some Basic Definitions 147
Why "Show, Not Tell" Is Such Common Advice 148
The Show-and-Tell Balancing Act 150
Traditional Uses of Narration (Telling) 153
Why Narration Is Such an Important Tool 154
How Showing and Telling Complement Each Other 156
Good Intentions, Bad Advice 156
The Showing-Telling Continuum 157

EXERCISES 161

1. Tell Me a Story 161
2. What Everyone Knows / What I Know 162

READINGS 163

ZZ PACKER *Brownies* 163
FLANNERY O'CONNOR *Everything That Rises Must Converge* 178

CHAPTER

6. **Who's Telling This Story?** 190
Point of View

Some Basic Definitions 190
First Person 191
Whose Story Is It? 192
Second Person 194

Third Person 196
A Word about Attitude 200
Distance and Point of View 200
Shifts in Narrative Distance 202
Choosing a Point of View 203
Common Point of View Problems 205

EXERCISES 206

1. Changing Point of View: Experiments in Narration 206
2. Using Point of View as a Way "In" to Difficult Material 207

READINGS 208

ANTON CHEKHOV *The Lady with the Little Dog* 208
DAN CHAON *The Bees* 220

CHAPTER
7. **How Reliable Is This Narrator?** 234
How Point of View Affects Our Understanding

How We Judge the Integrity of Stories 234
First Person Point of View and Reliability 234
Third Person Point of View and Reliability 238

EXERCISES 241

1. The Way I See It 241
2. See What I See, Hear What I Hear 242

READINGS 243

ROBERT OLEN BUTLER *A Good Scent from a Strange Mountain* 243
GABRIEL GARCÍA MÁRQUEZ *A Very Old Man with Enormous Wings* 252

CHAPTER
8. **He Said, She Said** 257
Crafting Effective Dialogue

What Dialogue Is Good For 257
What Dialogue Is Not 258
A Word about Attribution 260
Five Important Things to Remember about Dialogue 260
On Subtext 264
A Word about Dialect 265
Using Placeholders 266

EXERCISES 267

1. Nonverbal Communication 267
2. Them's Fighting Words 268

READINGS 269

ERNEST HEMINGWAY *Hills Like White Elephants* 269
TONI CADE BAMBARA *My Man Bovanne* 273

CHAPTER

9. **What Happens Next?** 278
Figuring the Plot

Story versus Plot: Some Basic Definitions 278
A Word about Causality 279
Render *How*—Don't Try to Answer *Why* 280
On Metafiction 281
Character-Based Plotting 282
On Conflict 282
Analyzing Plot Points 284
Avoiding *Scènes à Faire:* Recognizing Clichéd Plot Twists 287

EXERCISES 288

1. What's Behind the Door of Room 101? 288
2. "By the Time You Read This . . ." 289

READINGS 290

JAMES BALDWIN *Sonny's Blues* 290
MICHAEL CUNNINGHAM *White Angel* 313

CHAPTER

10. **Recognizable People** 326
Crafting Characters

Flat versus Round Characters 326
Eschewing the General in Favor of the Particular 328
Consistent Characters? 329
Ways of Defining Character 329
Character and Plot 333
Wants and Needs 335
Characters in Relationships 336

EXERCISES 338

1. Emptying Pockets 338
2. Sins of Commission, Sins of Omission 339
3. Seven or Eight Things I Know about Him / Her 340

READINGS 342

AKHIL SHARMA *Surrounded by Sleep* 342
BHARATI MUKHERJEE *The Management of Grief* 353

CHAPTER

11. Raising the Curtain 366
Beginning Your Story

Your Contract with the Reader 366
Characteristics of a Good Opening 367
Unbalancing Acts 368
Starting in the Middle 369
Beginning with Action 371
Beginning with Inaction 372
On the Nature of Suspense 373

EXERCISES 374

1. Give It Your Best Shot 374
2. Start in the Middle 374
3. Make Them Squirm 375

READINGS 376

MADISON SMARTT BELL *Customs of the Country* 376
MARY YUKARI WATERS *Aftermath* 388

CHAPTER

12. What's This Story Really About? 397
True Emotions, Sensory Events

Many Different Answers to the Same Question 397
Writing about What Matters 398
Transference: Borrowing from Freud 399
"We Are Made of Dust" 399
The Road to Universality 400
But It's the Truth! 401
Making Things Carry More Emotional Weight than They Logically
    Should 401

EXERCISES 404

1. Getting an Image to Spill Its Secrets 404
2. What I Lost 405

READINGS 406

FREDERICK BUSCH *Ralph the Duck* 406
STACEY RICHTER *My Date with Satan* 417

CHAPTER

13. **Learning to Fail Better** 427
On Revision

Advice for Writers from Writers 428
Perfection Is Our Enemy 429
The Workshop Method 429
Undue Influence: A Cautionary Tale 432
The Developmental Stages of a Creative Work 433
"Hot Spots" and Other Noteworthy Aspects of an Early Draft 434
An Exercise-Based Approach to Deep Revision 434
A Word about Constraints 435

EXERCISES 436

1. Analytical / Mechanical Exercises 436
2. Creative Exercises 437
3. Research-Based Exercises 438
4. Chance-Based Exercises 438
5. Revision Example 439
   JAN ELLISON *The Company of Men* 444

READINGS 455

ANNE LAMOTT *Shitty First Drafts* 455
RAYMOND CARVER *The Bath* 458
RAYMOND CARVER *A Small, Good Thing* 463

CHAPTER

14. **Getting Published** 481
A Guide to Starting Out

The Lowdown on Literary Magazines 481
Preparing Your Manuscript 482
Choosing Your Target Publications—and Following Directions
   Carefully 482

Sending It Off 484
Simultaneous Submissions 484
Patience, Patience 485
All Rejections Are Not Equal 486
Success! 486
Publishing: A Case History 486

Anthology of Stories 489

DONALD BARTHELME *Me and Miss Mandible* 491
RICK BASS *Wild Horses* 499
ANGELA CARTER *The Company of Wolves* 512
BARBARA GOWDY *Disneyland* 519
AMY HEMPEL *In the Cemetery Where Al Jolson Is Buried* 529
JAMES ALAN MCPHERSON *A Loaf of Bread* 535
RICK MOODY *Boys* 549
ALICE MUNRO *Save the Reaper* 552
PETER ORNER *The Raft* 567
TOBIAS WOLFF *Bullet in the Brain* 570

Authors 575
Glossary 591
Bibliography 595
Permissions 603
Index 609

List of Readings

JAMES BALDWIN *Sonny's Blues* 290

TONI CADE BAMBARA *My Man Bovanne* 273

DONALD BARTHELME *Me and Miss Mandible* 491

RICK BASS *Wild Horses* 499

MADISON SMARTT BELL *Customs of the Country* 376

AMY BLOOM *Silver Water* 21

FREDERICK BUSCH *Ralph the Duck* 406

ROBERT OLEN BUTLER *A Good Scent from a Strange Mountain* 243

ANGELA CARTER *The Company of Wolves* 512

RAYMOND CARVER *The Bath* 458

RAYMOND CARVER *A Small, Good Thing* 463

DAN CHAON *The Bees* 220

ANTON CHEKHOV *The Lady with the Little Dog* 208

SANDRA CISNEROS *Woman Hollering Creek* 53

MICHAEL CUNNINGHAM *White Angel* 313

JUNOT DÍAZ *Fiesta, 1980* 137

JAN ELLISON *The Company of Men* 444

BARBARA GOWDY *Disneyland* 519

RON HANSEN *Nebraska* 92

ERNEST HEMINGWAY *Hills Like White Elephants* 269

AMY HEMPEL *In the Cemetery Where Al Jolson Is Buried* 529

DENIS JOHNSON *Emergency* 13

ANNE LAMOTT *Shitty First Drafts* 455

GABRIEL GARCÍA MÁRQUEZ *A Very Old Man with Enormous Wings* 252

JAMES ALAN MCPHERSON *A Loaf of Bread* 535

RICK MOODY *Boys* 549

BHARATI MUKHERJEE *The Management of Grief* 353

ALICE MUNRO *Save the Reaper* 552

JOYCE CAROL OATES *Where Are You Going, Where Have You Been?* 40

TIM O'BRIEN *The Things They Carried* 79

FLANNERY O'CONNOR *Everything That Rises Must Converge* 178

PETER ORNER *The Raft* 567

ZZ PACKER *Brownies* 163

FRANCINE PROSE *What Makes A Short Story?* 109

STACEY RICHTER *My Date with Satan* 417

AKHIL SHARMA *Surrounded by Sleep* 342

MARY YUKARI WATERS *Aftermath* 388

JOHN EDGAR WIDEMAN *Fever* 118

TOBIAS WOLFF *Bullet in the Brain* 570

Acknowledgments

It would be impossible to thank everyone who has helped in the making of this book, but special thanks go to Sarah Seidner, David Renton, Rich Seidner, Lovinda Beale, Mary Petrosky, Liza Julian, Christie Cochrell, Teresa Heger, Jan Ellison, Ann Packer, Susan Weinberg, Clare LaPlante, Maxine Chernoff, Michelle Carter, and all the faculty in the Creative Writing Department at San Francisco State University, the faculty and staff at Stanford University's Creative Writing Department, especially Nancy Huddleston Packer and John L'Heureux, and all my students who have so graced me with their presence over the years. I'd also like to thank the teachers who reviewed for this college edition: Lee K. Abbot, Ohio State University; Tracy Heinlein, Seattle Community College; Daryl Herring, Blinn College at Brenham; James Papa, York College, City University of New York; Caroline Pruett, J. Sargeant Reynolds Community College; Jim Sanderson, Lamar University; Susan Spraker, University of Central Florida; Les Standiford, Florida International University; Brad Vice, Mississippi State University; and Janice Zerfas, Lake Michigan College. I am, as always, eternally grateful to my agent, Arielle Eckstut, and her boss, James Levine, of the Levine-Greenberg Literary Agency. This book could never have come into being without the incomparable editorial team at W. W. Norton, including Jill Bialosky, Nancy Rodwan, and Evan Carver; for work on the college edition, thanks go to Marian Johnson, Marilyn Moller, Erin Granville, Melissa Atkin, Cat Spencer, and Ana Cooke.

CHAPTER ONE

What Is This Thing Called Creative Writing?
The Basics

So you want to write. Perhaps you want to try short stories, or you have a dream to write a novel. Perhaps you have some ideas; perhaps you merely have an inexplicable urge to write *something*. You must have a certain amount of motivation, because you've acquired this book, or are enrolled in a class, or are participating in a writers' group. But you don't know where to start. You may worry that you don't have enough experience. You don't know what a short story is, can't imagine starting a novel, and feel you lack the skills to embark upon writing even a short piece of fiction.

This book is designed to help. It will walk you through all aspects of the creative process, from generating the kind of exciting ideas that spark the beginnings of novels and short stories; to learning and practicing all aspects of the craft; to acquiring revision techniques to use once you have finished the first draft of a piece.

In this chapter we'll talk about the basic definitions of fiction and provide insight into some of the key characteristics that make up compelling creative writing. The next section gives you some exercises to prompt fresh and original work that may be the germs of good ideas for stories. Included here (and in similar sections throughout the book) are student samples, so you can get ideas on how to complete the exercises. Finally, two stories underscore all we've talked about in this chapter.

Reconciling the Method with the Madness

The first questions that we have to address in this book are very basic: Can writing be taught? With all the creative writing instruction going on in classes and books, are we producing better writers? Are we doing a good job of helping writers come into their own? The answer is both yes and no.

It's important to understand that there are two aspects to creating truly compelling writing. As the book's epigraph (from William Shakespeare's *Hamlet*) states, what's needed is both method *and* madness. The method can be learned in an academically rigorous, systematic manner. In many ways, writing is a craft, like woodworking or painting, that can be acquired, practiced, mastered. Just as artists learn how to work with the human form or experiment with color, beginning writers can learn about imagery, dialogue, narrative, and scene-building. You can master how to characterize people on the page. You can take apart story structure and learn how to build a solid plot.

But then there's the madness—what is more frequently called the inspiration. "The chief enemy of creativity is good sense," said the painter Pablo Picasso, and that leaves us, as writers, in a quandary. How can we simultaneously be creative—wild, free, chaotic—and yet have sufficient presence of mind to shape all the lovely raw messy material that bubbles inside us into something coherent? How do we reconcile the method with the madness?

Many students of writing simply don't. At one end of the spectrum are those writers who work hard at mastering craft and turn out exquisitely crafted stories that are utterly dead and boring. At the other end are the writers who generate exciting and profound initial drafts—but have no control, no way of shaping them into something that can speak to others.

A contemporary way of talking about this dichotomy between craft and inspiration is by referring to right-brain and left-brain capabilities. According to this theory of how the brain works, its two sides control two modes of thinking. Left brain: logical, sequential, rational. Right brain: random, intuitive, holistic. In today's creative writing workshops (which reflect the way creative writing is taught in most colleges and universities) we are largely using our left-brain, analytical skills to read and take apart a story or poem while trying to figure out why it does or doesn't work. We're being trained to favor our left brains over our right brains, something that can be deadly in the creative process—especially when trying to generate new material.

Of course, some people have no trouble getting the left brain and right brain to work together harmoniously. But one very common thing that happens after you have begun to acquire some craft knowledge (and the vocabulary that goes with it) is that you find it hard to turn your analytical "editor" off when trying to generate new material. The sad fact is that the more you know, the more likely you are to censor yourself at the very time that you should be giving yourself the most creative leeway. Unfortunately, the workshop method of teaching creative writing has no way of helping people access their deepest and most profound material.

So can this ability to tune in to our private material be taught? Not exactly, but it certainly can be nurtured. And within a classroom setting, no less. Writing teachers have known for decades that certain exercises, prompts, and "constraints" take beginning writers out of themselves and push them toward writing truly inspired things. The exercises at the end of each chapter of this book are thus designed to help you put aside your logical sense and immerse yourself in the intuitive creative process. The hope is that you may then take these raw, early pieces and shape them into something meaningful as you continue to learn about the craft. So the whole thing comes full circle: craft and creativity, method and madness.

Are some people more talented than others? Does it come easier to some than to others? Sure. But in my years of teaching I have seen creative breakthroughs that have astounded and humbled me. Perseverance, dedication, and just plain obstinacy count for more than you can imagine. Everyone has *something* within them to express; it's just a question of giving them the *process* tools to discover it and the *craft* tools to express it coherently.

Some Basic Definitions

The word "fiction" comes from the Latin *fictio*, the act of fashioning, and from the Latin *fingere*, to shape, fashion, "feign." *Merriam-Webster's Collegiate Dictionary* says it is "something invented by the imagination."

So fiction is something made up—not factual. We assert as if true something that is not factually real in order to *make* it true. "Poetry lies its way to the truth," said John Ciardi, an American poet. Similarly, Picasso (one of the keenest commentators on the creative process) said, "Art is a lie that makes us realize the truth."

So if you want to write fiction, you are someone who thinks that you can speak the truth primarily through lying. Good. Then the purpose of this book is to teach you how to be the best liar you can be.

Writing That Is Surprising Yet Convincing

What is *good* fiction? What makes something worth reading? One answer, to paraphrase E. M. Forster, in his landmark book *Aspects of the Novel*, is that good writing is that which is *surprising yet convincing*.

Notice the coupling of these two words: *surprising*—something unexpected happens. Equally important, we are *convinced* by the surprise: it is not gratuitously startling; we get a jolt, and then a sense of the rightness of it all.

This is true of all good literature. To demonstrate this quality, here's a poem by Elizabeth Bishop, "Letter to NY (for Louise Crane)":

> In your next letter I wish you'd say
> where you are going and what you are doing;
> how are the plays, and after the plays
> what other pleasures you're pursuing:

This first stanza starts out innocuously—someone is writing a letter to a loved one asking how the trip is going. But some of the declarations in this second stanza surprise us:

> taking cabs in the middle of the night,
> driving as if to save your soul
> where the road goes round and round the park
> and the meter glares like a moral owl,

The writer of the letter starts imagining the things that are happening to the traveler, and they seem ominous. "Driving as if to save your soul"? "The meter glaring like a moral owl"? So the letter writer isn't just missing the person or asking for news; there's a sense of judgment—or perhaps of wishing to believe that the traveler is not having a carefree good time. The poem continues in this vein:

> and the trees look so queer and green
> standing alone in big black caves
> and suddenly you're in a different place
> where everything seems to happen in waves,
>
> and most of the jokes you just can't catch,
> like dirty words rubbed off a slate,
> and the songs are loud but somehow dim
> and it gets so terribly late,
>
> and coming out of the brownstone house
> to the gray sidewalk, the watered street,
> one side of the buildings rises with the sun
> like a glistening field of wheat.
>
> —Wheat, not oats, dear. I'm afraid
> if it's wheat it's none of your sowing,
> nevertheless I'd like to know
> what you are doing and where you are going.

The odd, distressing images then fade into the calming imagery of the morning before the final, almost shocking stanza, with its patronizing accusation that sowing wheat would be none of "your" doing. And we realize that this is *not* a typical letter to a loved one, but almost a taunt, with hints of cruelty (that "dear" in the last stanza stings) and barely suppressed rancor. The poem keeps surprising us—yet we are also convinced by this rendering. We believe (very much) in these two women and in their emotionally intense but seemingly ambivalent relationship.

Resisting Paraphrase

Flannery O'Connor said that a good story "resisted paraphrase," by which she meant that a simple summary of a plot or story line would not have the same emotional impact as the whole story. To understand what she meant, think about trying to paraphrase, or describe, a Chopin sonata without actually playing any music. It's impossible, because nothing can substitute for it with the same effect—not the notes on the page, not a verbal description of the melody and harmony, not even a playing of a simplified version of the main theme. This is also true of the kind of fiction we are trying to write: simply stating what the piece "is about" should not be able to convey the complexity and subtlety of the piece as a whole. Some essential mystery, or emotional subtlety, will be lost in the paraphrase.

Here are some examples of passages from stories that resist paraphrase:

"Well," Jewel says, "you can quit now, if you got a-plenty."

Inside the barn Jewel slides running to the ground before the horse stops. The horse enters the stall, Jewel following. Without looking back the horse kicks at him, slamming a single hoof into the wall with a pistol-like report. Jewel kicks him in the stomach; the horse arches his neck back, crop-toothed; Jewel strikes him across the face with his fist and slides on to the trough and mounts upon it. Clinging to the hay-rack he lowers his head and peers out across the stall tops and through the doorway. The path is empty; from here he cannot even hear Cash sawing. He reaches up and drags down hay in hurried armsful and crams it into the rack.

"Eat," he says. "Get the goddamn stuff out of sight while you got a chance, you pussel-gutted bastard. You sweet son of a bitch," he says.

—WILLIAM FAULKNER, *As I Lay Dying*

How does this passage resist paraphrase? It's not *just* a boy being cruel to a horse. He *is* cruel, even sadistic—we get the impression that the violence to the horse is gratuitous, not necessary to keep the horse in line—but then he feeds the horse, apparently against the will of the caretaker, and calls him a "sweet son of a bitch." Affection and violence are married together in a surprising yet convincing way.

In December Ennis married Alma Beers and had her pregnant by mid-January. He picked up a few short-lived ranch jobs, then settled in as a wrangler on the old Elwood Hi-Top place north of Lost Cabin in Washakie County. He was still working there in September when Alma Jr., as he called his daughter, was born and their bedroom was full of the smell of old blood and milk and baby shit, and the sounds were of squalling and sucking and Alma's sleepy groans, all reassuring of fecundity and life's continuance to one who worked with livestock.   —ANNIE PROULX, "Brokeback Mountain"

This passage captures the ambiguous emotions a man experiences as he settles down and starts a family with someone who is not the love of his life. Nevertheless, we see how these events center him around the things of this earth and reassure him at a deep, emotionally resonant level. Could you paraphrase this and get the same effect? What would you say: "A man without roots finally settles down"? "A cowboy has his first child"? Neither of these paraphrases—or any other—can do it justice. The passage speaks for itself.

Sentiment, Not Sentimentality

By being both surprising and convincing, and by choosing to render things that resist easy summary, we may avoid two problems that often haunt creative writers: sentimentality and melodrama. These words are bandied about in writing classes and workshops, so let's define them precisely:

A work that is *melodramatic* is characterized by extravagant theatricality and the predominance of plot and physical action over characterization. The reader's emotions are evoked through the sensational nature of events and/or actions making up the plot rather than through more subtle elements, such as characterization.

A work that is *sentimental* is falsely emotional in a maudlin way. It occurs when a work exhibits an excess of emotion that doesn't feel "earned" by the piece, or when a piece is imbued with sentiment (feeling) independent of a meaningful context. The writer who succumbs to sentimentality depends on a reader's stock emotional response derived from *general* cultural or human experience, rather than creating a believable context for that response within the story.

We tend to associate the word "sentimental" with things that are precious, mawkish: squishy, "soft" subjects such as babies and kittens and whatnot. But that's only a small part of what can be sentimental. Something is sentimental if it attempts to induce an emotional response in a reader that exceeds what the situation warrants. And this can happen with so-called "hard" subjects like war or death as much as with ruminations on love and ducklings and flowers.

The best illustrations of what we mean by "sentimental" come from advertisements—certainly print, but especially television. These ads deliberately try to provoke an emotional response with a thirty- or sixty-second video clip. Ads for camera equipment, for example, try to tap into our fear that life is passing us by and that we need to capture precious moments on film (or in electronic form) in order to remember them. Telephone companies mine our fears with ads of grown children calling their aged mothers or "reaching out and touching someone." What these advertisements *don't* want is complexity: they don't want us to think that many moments of family life can be painful or tedious or frustrating. They're after the knee-jerk responses that are already fully prepared in our minds.

Sentiment, however, is not bad. Sentiment is variously defined as a "refined feeling"; a "delicate sensing of emotion"; "an idea colored by emotion." If we don't strive for true sentiment, we will never achieve truly moving work. But if a piece is *sentimental,* this basic "good" thing has been overextended or misapplied. As I. M. Richards says:

> A response is sentimental when, either through the over-persistence of tendencies or through the interaction of sentiments, *it is inappropriate to the situation that calls it forth* [emphasis mine]. What is bad in these sentimental responses is their confinement to one stereotyped, unrepresentative aspect of the prompting situation.   —I. M. RICHARDS, *Practical Criticism*

In other words, marriages and births are always happy, funerals are sad, old people are lonely and waiting at home for phone calls. These are stereotyped and *unrepresentative* depictions in that they do not represent the range of emotion, feeling, and complexity that such situations frequently evoke. We all know of births and deaths that conjure up more ambiguous emotions: reluctance to become parents, relief that someone has finally died.

Sentimental writing tends to trigger what Richards calls "stock responses" in the reader. As he goes on to say:

> [Stock responses] have their opportunity whenever a poem invokes views and emotions already fully prepared in the reader's mind, *so that what happens is more of the reader's doing than the poet's* [emphasis mine]. The button is pressed, and then the author's work is done, for immediately the record starts playing in quasi- (or total) independence of the poem which is supposed to be its origin or instrument.

William Shakespeare was a master of avoiding the sentimental. Here, in Sonnet 130, he thumbs his nose at sentimental notions of love and beauty:

> My mistress' eyes are nothing like the sun;
> Coral is far more red than her lips' red;
> If snow be white, why then her breasts are dun;
> If hairs be wires, black wires grow on her head.
> I have seen roses damask'd, red and white,
> But no such roses see I in her cheeks,
> And in some perfumes is there more delight
> Than in the breath that from my mistress reeks.
> I love to hear her speak, yet well I know
> That music hath a far more pleasing sound;
> I grant I never saw a goddess go,
> My mistress when she walks treads on the ground.
> And yet, by heaven, I think my love as rare
> As any she belied with false compare.

This poem contradicts our stock responses. The piece doesn't let us fall back on sentimental or simplistic or prepackaged notions of love or romance; rather, it says that his love for his mistress confounds all the usual expectations. We are adamantly pushed away from any sentimental interpretation of this love song by its bold declarations of all the "negative" qualities of the beloved.

Sentimentality can also infest the opposite end of the spectrum from treacly sweetness. Rather than trying to make everything too "nice," it can represent things as stereotypically bleak or sordid. Again from I. M. Richards:

> The man, in reaction to the commoner naive forms of sentimentality, [who] prides himself upon his hard-headedness and hard-heartedness, his hard-boiledness generally, and who seeks out or invents aspects with a bitter or squalid character, for no better reason than this, is only displaying a more sophisticated form of sentimentality.   —I. M. RICHARDS, *Practical Criticism*

So the writer who decides "No sentimentality for me!" and puts her characters in a trailer park, shouting at each other, drinking whiskey, and generally living a life of degradation and emotional ruin, can be making the same mistake as the writer who writes chirpily about his pet cat: it is still narrow, nonrepresentative, stereotypical, and lacking complexity.

Some writers are so afraid of being called sentimental that they fail to take emotional risks with their pieces—they shut them down and fail to push them to the limit. Yet to avoid real emotion is to avoid the reason that most of us write to begin with: to put complex, urgent emotion down on the page.

Here's a passage that risks sentimentality because it deals with death; it's a deathbed scene, in fact, between a mother and her two sons:

> "First of all, troops, you both need a haircut," Emma said. "Don't let your bangs get so long. You have beautiful eyes and very nice faces and I want people to see them. I don't care how long it gets in back, just keep it out of your eyes, please."
>
> "That's not important, that's just a matter of opinion," Tommy said. "Are you getting well?"
>
> "No," Emma said. "I have a million cancers. I can't get well."
>
> "Oh, I don't know what to do," Teddy said.
>
> "Well, both of you better make some friends," Emma said. "I'm sorry about this, but I can't help it. I can't talk to you too much longer either, or I'll get too upset. Fortunately we had ten or twelve years and we did a lot of talking, and that's more than a lot of people get. Make some friends and be good to them. Don't be afraid of girls, either."
>
> "We're not afraid of girls," Tommy said. "What makes you think that?"
>
> "You might get to be later," Emma said.
>
> "I doubt it," Tommy said, very tense.
>
> When they came to hug her, Teddy fell apart and Tommy remained stiff.
>
> "Tommy, be sweet," Emma said. "Be sweet, please. Don't keep pretending you dislike me. That's silly."
>
> "I *like* you," Tommy said, shrugging tightly.
>
> "I know that, but for the last year or two you've been pretending you hate me," Emma said. "I know I love you more than anybody in the world except your brother and sister, and I'm not going to be around long enough to change my mind about you. But you're going to live a long time, and in a year or two when I'm not around to irritate you you're going to change your mind and remember that I read you a lot of stories and made you a lot of milkshakes and allowed you to goof off a lot when I could have been forcing you to mow the lawn."
>
> Both boys looked away, shocked that their mother was saying these things.
>
> "In other words, you're going to remember that you love me," Emma said. "I imagine you'll wish you could tell me that you've changed your mind, but you won't be able to, so I'm telling you now I already know you love me, just so you won't be in doubt about that later. Okay?"
>
> "Okay," Tommy said quickly, a little gratefully.
>
> —LARRY MCMURTRY, *Terms of Endearment*

Though the situation is rife with pitfalls of sentimentality, McMurtry avoids giving us any "expected" or overly familiar dialogue. Instead, he grounds us thoroughly in the world of the story, in the characters and their relationships, and we pull through this difficult moment relieved—and definitely moved.

Our First Job as Writers: To Notice

How do we manage to write things that are neither melodramatic nor sentimental? Simple. By *really* noticing things. That is our first job.

Whether you realize it or not, you've always noticed. There have always been things that caught your attention, piqued your interest, or otherwise caused you to pay closer attention to something than someone else would. Indeed, the very individual nature of noticing is your greatest strength as a writer.

If you took a walk around your town with a friend, you and your friend would have, in effect, two different experiences. You'd remember different things about the walk, about what you saw, what you talked about, what happened. One of you might comment on the cold, while the other might note the homeless person on the corner. There's no right or wrong, no "correct" thing to have noticed; you're just making observations based on your individual experience of the walk.

Now, though, notice what you noticed. No, go further: tell yourself the audacious thing that because you noticed it, it matters. That man on the corner of 5th and Vine with the black umbrella and navy overcoat? You noticed him. You noticed the way he was standing, the expression on his face—sad? no, wistful—and the remarkable orderliness of his dress. That's a beginning.

Here's the important thing: creative work comes from noticing. You are being given a warning, an intimation of something, and that something is the creative urge, sometimes buried quite deep in your subconscious, telling you that something matters, there's information and *intelligence* there to be considered, material to uncover, memories and associations to explore.

Here is a passage that illustrates this point well. The author talks about his neighborhood in prewar Berlin, and about *noticing*:

> From my window, the deep solemn massive street. Cellar-shops where the lamps burn all day, under the shadow of top-heavy balconied façades, dirty plaster frontages embossed with scroll-work and heraldic devices. The whole district is like this: street leading into street of houses like shabby monumental safes crammed with the tarnished valuables and second-hand furniture of a bankrupt middle class.
>
> I am a camera with its shutter open, quite passive, recording, not thinking. Recording the man shaving at the window opposite and the woman in the kimono washing her hair. Some day, all this will have to be developed, carefully printed, fixed.   —CHRISTOPHER ISHERWOOD, "Goodbye to Berlin"

So your first job is to turn your "camera" on, to notice as you walk. You can worry about "developing" it later—all that matters is that the camera is on.

Avoiding the "Writerly" Voice

Something happens sometimes when we sit down to write. We want what we write to be Important, we want it to Matter, and so we can get pompous. We can sound like we're making proclamations instead of observations. Or we can try so hard to make the language sound sophisticated that it comes off flowery and overwrought. I've often scrawled on students' early papers: "This feels too 'written.'"

Consider the following as an example of what *not* to do, from a letter that Anton Chekhov wrote to the novelist Maxim Gorki:

> It is intelligible when I write, "The man sat down on the grass"; it is intelligible because it is clear and does not impede the reader's attention. Conversely, I will be unintelligible and tax the reader's brain if I write: "The tall, narrow-chested man of average build, who had a short, red beard, sat down on the green grass, already trampled by passersby; sat down noiselessly, timidly, and fearfully glancing around him." One's brain cannot grasp this at once, yet fiction must be grasped at once, on the spot.

Often one of the hardest things for beginning fiction writers to grasp is that they must develop a voice that is unique, and natural to them. One of your main jobs, throughout your writing life (it doesn't necessarily come easy, or soon, or ever stop changing) is to discover and/or develop that voice. It might not be the same as your speaking voice. It is the unique way you have of expressing yourself in the written word, and the more straightforward and honest you are in the words and sentences you put on the page, the more your voice will shine through. For the most part, this means forgetting about using big words, complex sentence structures, and ornate language, *unless that comes naturally to you*. If you're a natural user of metaphor, or have a strong sense of imagery, great. Use your gifts. But one of the operative words is "honest." We try to be honest not just in *what* we say (even if we are lying through fiction) but in *how* we say it.

The goal is to find *your* voice, the voice that isn't like everyone else's. And this is very difficult to do, for the plain reason that we have mostly spent our lives trying to fit in. We want to make sure that we dress appropriately, speak appropriately, act appropriately. Well, creative writing is the one area where you don't want to be "appropriate." Appropriate is for dinner parties. This is the place where the things that make you weird, the things about yourself that you *know* are different and even difficult, count the most.

In the following passage, the narrator gives some very wise advice about writing:

> "You are writing a letter to a friend," was the sort of thing I used to say. "And this is a dear and close friend, real—or better—invented in your mind like a fix-ation. Write privately, not publicly; without fear or timidity, right to the end of the letter, as if it was never going to be published, so that your true friend will read it over and over, and then want more enchanting letters from you. Now, you are not writing about the relationship between your friend and yourself;

you take that for granted. You are only confiding an experience that you think only he will enjoy reading. What you have to say will come out more spontaneously and honestly than if you are thinking of numerous readers. Before starting the letter rehearse in your mind what you are going to tell; something interesting, your story. But don't rehearse too much, the story will develop as you go along, especially if you write to a special friend, man or woman, to make them smile or laugh or cry, or anything you like so long as you know it will interest. Remember not to think of the reading public, it will put you off."

—MURIEL SPARK, *A Far Cry from Kensington*

EXERCISES

The following exercises are meant to be used to supplement the text and readings so that you can practice the underlying concepts presented in this chapter. These exercises can be done in the classroom, assigned as homework, or performed independently of a formal class.

Especially designed to help you "let go" and stop thinking logically, these prompts should open things up emotionally for you as a natural part of the process.

Exercise 1: I Don't Know Why I Remember . . .

GOAL: To pinpoint some previously unexplored material that remains "hot" for you in an important emotional way.

1. "Scan" back over your life and think of things that have stuck in your mind, but for no obvious reason. (No births or deaths or other "important" moments, please. Go for the small ones.)

2. Render them precisely on the page using concrete details, beginning each one with the phrase, "I don't know why I remember."

3. Don't try to explain why they stuck with you; don't interpret their meaning. Just put your reader *there*.

Here's how student Steven Thomas did this exercise:

I don't know why I remember going fishing with my father. He'd come over to the apartment where my mother and I were living since the divorce, bringing a cup of coffee sweetened to the point of making me choke when I sipped it. Dawn would still be an hour or so away, but he insisted on getting started early because that's when the fish would bite, he said. We'd drive from the grimy streets of Oakland out through the lush rolling hills of Alamo and Walnut Creek, and into the dry dusty Sacramento valley where there existed a man-made reservoir. The water was a dull grey reflecting the dirty earth that rose, raw and bleak, from its edges. We'd join the band of early fishermen who were always there, standing on the edge of the gravelly beach, waiting patiently with their lines in the water. Most of them were drinking beer even though it was so early, crushing the cans and throwing them into a pile when they were emptied. My dad would drink two beers during the four hours we would fish, never more, never less. We never caught anything. As far as I remember, no one did. But we stood there, in wordless camaraderie, Saturday after Saturday, for the two long years until my father moved to Arizona without me.

Exercise 2: "I Am a Camera . . ."

GOAL: To notice what you notice—and to render it without trying to explain or interpret it.

1. In the manner of Christopher Isherwood's famous passage (see p. 9), turn on your "camera" (the part of your brain that notices things).

2. Take a walk or go someplace where you can have a rich sensory experience—preferably someplace where other people are present.

3. Record everything precisely on the page, using as many senses as possible.

4. Don't try to interpret it or tell us what it means; everything will get "developed" and "fixed" later. For now, just record.

Student Janis Turin wrote the following in response to this exercise:

As the No. 17 bus passes by the corner of Mission and 17th, an elderly man carrying a brown paper bag filled with groceries trips. A tattooed young man with pink hair rushes over to help. The food of babies: Cheerios, rice cereal, tiny jars of apricot and pears and fruits. The sky grows dim as the bus heaves its way down the crowded street. Opposite me is one of the most beautiful girls I have ever seen. Her heavy hair, dyed a dead black, hangs in braids down her shoulders. She has white skin and the most luminous neck I have ever seen. She is carrying nothing: not a backpack, purse, briefcase. She is dressed casually except for her high heels, absurdly high stiletto heels.

The following response was written by student Christie Cochrell:

The hospital. The dirty carpet in the hospital elevator. The whole institution stank of soap and urine and looked overly clean and shabby at the same time, and I don't know why that little bit of mud on the orange carpet bothered me so much. But it did. Every day, every day I'd go to the fifth floor, riding with all of the happy grandmas and aunties and new daddies carrying stuffed toys and pink or blue flower bouquets and when they would get off on the third floor maternity wing I would be left alone—alone or with one or two other silent souls who were making the longer and darker and ever so much heavier journey with me to the fifth floor—and every day I'd look down and notice in the few moments between third and fifth, between the level of birth and the floor of departure—every day I'd notice those same damn mud stains made by some visitor's shoes long ago. I would think of the mud those shoes had walked through in some past wet season, mud that had been rain-soaked and probably cold, and I thought of how the person who wore those shoes must have greeted and hugged and encouraged the patient at the end of this elevator's ride. I thought of the mud on those shoes and the murky, brown trail it left behind, and I wondered if that was all that was left, all that was left to remember of that day, of that owner of dirty shoes or his love for the one whom he had come to visit. I thought of the ashes-to-ashes, dust-to-dust of that damn dried mud stain and I wondered why no one ever cleaned out that germ-infested metal cage, that moving basket of human contagion.

I wondered about that and other things as the little cell moved up and then the doors would slide open. I'd walk off the elevator platform onto the relative terra firma of the fifth floor and then I would forget the mud and the dirt and the bacteria. I would step off of the elevator and be confronted with all of the other things that I really don't want to remember, like *how much longer* and *no extreme measures* and *how can I ever go on after this?*

READINGS

DENIS JOHNSON

Emergency

I'D BEEN WORKING IN THE EMERGENCY ROOM for about three weeks, I guess. This was in 1973, before the summer ended. With nothing to do on the overnight shift but batch the insurance reports from the daytime shifts, I just started wandering around, over to the coronary-care unit, down to the cafeteria, et cetera, looking for Georgie, the orderly, a pretty good friend of mine. He often stole pills from the cabinets.

He was running over the tiled floor of the operating room with a mop. "Are you still doing that?" I said.

"Jesus, there's a lot of blood here," he complained.

"Where?" The floor looked clean enough to me.

"What the hell were they doing in here?" he asked me.

"They were performing surgery, Georgie," I told him.

"There's so much goop inside of us, man," he said, "and it all wants to get out." He leaned his mop against a cabinet.

"What are you crying for?" I didn't understand.

He stood still, raised both arms slowly behind his head, and tightened his pony-tail. Then he grabbed the mop and started making broad random arcs with it, trembling and weeping and moving all around the place really fast.

"What am I *crying* for?" he said. "Jesus. Wow, oh boy, perfect."

I was hanging out in the E.R. with fat, quivering Nurse. One of the Family Service doctors that nobody liked came in looking for Georgie to wipe up after him. "Where's Georgie?" this guy asked.

"Georgie's in O.R.," Nurse said.

"Again?"

"No," Nurse said. "Still."

"Still? Doing what?"

"Cleaning the floor."

"Again?"

"No," Nurse said again. "Still."

Back in O.R., Georgie dropped his mop and bent over in the posture of child soiling its diapers. He stared down with his mouth open in terror.

He said, "What am I going to do about these fucking *shoes*, man?"

"Whatever you stole," I said, "I guess you already ate it all, right?"

"Listen to how they squish," he said, walking around carefully on his heels.

"Let me check your pockets, man."

He stood still a minute, and I found his stash. I left him two of each, whatever they were. "Shift is about half over," I told him.

"Good. Because I really, really, really need a drink," he said. "Will you please help me get this blood mopped up?"

Around 3:30 a.m. a guy with a knife in his eye came in, led by Georgie.

"I hope *you* didn't do that to him," Nurse said.

"Me?" Georgie said. "No. He was like this."

"My wife did it," the man said. The blade was buried to the hilt in the outside corner of his left eye. It was a hunting knife kind of thing.

"Who brought you in?" Nurse said.

"Nobody. I just walked down. It's only three blocks," the man said.

Nurse peered at him. "We'd better get you lying down."

"Okay, I'm certainly ready for something like that," the man said.

She peered a bit longer into his face.

"Is your other eye," she said, "a glass eye?"

"It's plastic, or something artificial like that," he said.

"And you can see out of *this* eye?" she asked, meaning the wounded one.

"I can see. But I can't make a fist out of my left hand because this knife is doing something to my brain."

"My God," Nurse said.

"I guess I'd better get the doctor," I said.

"There you go," Nurse agreed.

They got him lying down, and Georgie says to the patient, "Name?"

"Terrence Weber."

"Your face is dark. I can't see what you're saying."

"Georgie," I said.

"What are you saying, man? I can't see."

Nurse came over, and Georgie said to her, "His face is dark."

She leaned over the patient. "How long ago did this happen, Terry?" she shouted down into his face.

"Just a while ago. My wife did it. I was asleep," the patient said.

"Do you want the police?"

He thought about it and finally said, "Not unless I die."

Nurse went to the wall intercom and buzzed the doctor on duty, the Family Service person. "Got a surprise for you," she said over the intercom. He took his time getting down the hall to her, because he knew she hated Family Service and her happy tone of voice could only mean something beyond his competence and potentially humiliating.

He peeked into the trauma room and saw the situation: the clerk—that is, me—standing next to the orderly, Georgie, both of us on drugs, looking down at a patient with a knife sticking up out of his face.

"What seems to be the trouble?" he said.

The doctor gathered the three of us around him in the office and said, "Here's the situation. We've got to get a team here, an entire team. I want a good eye man. A great eye man. The best eye man. I want a brain surgeon. And I want a really good gas man, get me a genius. I'm not touching that head. I'm just going to watch this one. I know my limits. We'll just get him prepped and sit tight. Orderly!"

"Do you mean me?" Georgie said. "Should I get him prepped?"

"Is this a hospital?" the doctor asked. "Is this the emergency room? Is that a patient? Are you the orderly?"

I dialed the hospital operator and told her to get me the eye man and the brain and the gas man.

Georgie could be heard across the hall, washing his hands and singing a Neil Young song that went "Hello, cowgirl in the sand. Is this place at your command?"

"That person is not right, not at all, not one bit," the doctor said.

"As long as my instructions are audible to him it doesn't concern me," Nurse insisted, spooning stuff up out of a little Dixie cup. "I've got my own life and the protection of my family to think of."

"Well, okay, okay. Don't chew my head off," the doctor said.

The eye man was on vacation or something. While the hospital's operator called around to find someone else just as good, the other specialists were hurrying through the night to join us. I stood around looking at charts and chewing up more of Georgie's pills. Some of them tasted the way urine smells, some of them burned, some of them tasted like chalk. Various nurses, and two physicians who'd been tending somebody in I.C.U., were hanging out down here with us now.

Everybody had a different idea about exactly how to approach the problem of removing the knife from Terrence Weber's brain. But when Georgie came in from prepping the patient—from shaving the patient's eyebrow and disinfecting the area around the wound, and so on—he seemed to be holding the hunting knife in his left hand.

The talk just dropped off a cliff.

"Where," the doctor asked finally, "did you get that?"

Nobody said one thing more, not for quite a long time.

After a while, one of the I.C.U. nurses said, "Your shoelace is untied." Georgie laid the knife on a chart and bent down to fix his shoe.

There were twenty more minutes left to get through.

"How's the guy doing?" I asked.

"Who?" Georgie said.

It turned out that Terrence Weber still had excellent vision in the one good eye, and acceptable motor and reflex, despite his earlier motor complaint. "His vitals are normal," Nurse said. "There's nothing wrong with the guy. It's one of those things."

After a while you forget it's summer. You don't remember what the morning is. I'd worked two doubles with eight hours off in between, which I'd spent sleeping on a gurney in the nurse's station. Georgie's pills were making me feel like a giant helium-filled balloon, but I was wide awake. Georgie and I went out to the lot, to his orange pickup.

We lay down on a stretch of dusty plywood in the back of the truck with the day-light knocking against our eyelids and the fragrance of alfalfa thickening on our tongues.

"I want to go to church," Georgie said.

"Let's go to the county fair."

"I'd like to worship. I would."

"They have these injured hawks and eagles there. From the Humane Society," I said.

"I need a quiet chapel about now."

Georgie and I had a terrific time driving around. For a while the day was clear and peaceful. It was one of the moments you stay in, to hell with all the troubles of before and after. The sky is blue and the dead are coming back. Later in the afternoon, with sad resignation, the county fair bares its breasts. A champion of the drug LSD, a very famous guru of the love generation, is being interviewed amid a TV crew off to the left of the poultry cages. His eyeballs look like he bought them in a joke shop. It doesn't occur to me, as I pity this extraterrestrial, that in my life I've taken as much as he has.

After that, we got lost. We drove for hours, literally hours, but we couldn't find the road back to town.

Georgie started to complain. "That was the worst fair I've been to. Where were the rides?"

"They had rides," I said.

"I didn't see one ride."

A jackrabbit scurried out in front of us, and we hit it.

"There was a merry-go-round, a Ferris wheel, and a thing called the Hammer that people were bent over vomiting from after they got off," I said. "Are you completely blind?"

"What was that?"

"A rabbit."

"Something thumped."

"You hit him. *He* thumped."

Georgie stood on the brake pedal. "Rabbit stew."

He threw the truck in reverse and zigzagged back toward the rabbit. "Where's my hunting knife?" He almost ran over the poor animal a second time.

"We'll camp in the wilderness," he said. "In the morning we'll breakfast on its haunches." He was waving Terrence Weber's hunting knife around in what I was sure was a dangerous way.

In a minute he was standing at the edge of the fields, cutting the scrawny little thing up, tossing away its organs. "I should have been a doctor," he cried.

A family in a big Dodge, the only car we'd seen for a long time, slowed down and gawked out the windows as they passed by. The father said, "What is it, a snake?"

"No, it's not a snake," Georgie said. "It's a rabbit with babies inside it."

"Babies!" the mother said, and the father sped the car forward, over the protests of several little kids in the back.

Georgie came back to my side of the truck with his shirtfront stretched out in front of him as if he were carrying apples in it, or some such, but they were, in fact, slimy miniature bunnies. "No way I'm eating those things," I told him.

"Take them, take them. I gotta drive, take them," he said, dumping them in my lap and getting in on his side of the truck. He started driving along faster and faster, with a look of glory on his face. "We killed the mother and saved the children," he said.

"It's getting late," I said. "Let's get back to town."

"You bet." Sixty, seventy, eighty-five, just topping ninety.

"These rabbits better be kept warm." One at a time I slid the little things in between my shirt buttons and nestled them against my belly. "They're hardly moving," I told Georgie.

"We'll get some milk and sugar and all that, and we'll raise them up ourselves. They'll get as big as gorillas."

The road we were lost on cut straight through the middle of the world. It was still daytime, but the sun had no more power than an ornament or a sponge. In this light the truck's hood, which had been bright orange, had turned a deep blue.

Georgie let us drift to the shoulder of the road, slowly, slowly, as if he'd fallen asleep or given up trying to find his way.

"What is it?"

"We can't go on. I don't have any headlights," Georgie said.

We parked under a strange sky with a faint image of a quarter-moon superimposed on it.

There was a little woods beside us. This day had been dry and hot, the buck pines and whatall simmering patiently, but as we sat there smoking cigarettes it started to get very cold.

"The summer's over," I said.

That was the year when arctic clouds moved down over the Midwest and we had two weeks of winter in September.

"Do you realize it's going to snow?" Georgie asked me.

He was right, a gun-blue storm was shaping up. We got out and walked around idiotically. The beautiful chill! That sudden crispness, and the tang of evergreen stabbing us!

The gusts of snow twisted themselves around our heads while the night fell. I couldn't find the truck. We just kept getting more and more lost. I kept calling, "Georgie, can you see?" and he kept saying, "See what? See what?"

The only light visible was a streak of sunset flickering below the hem of the clouds. We headed that way.

We bumped softly down a hill toward an open field that seemed to be a military graveyard, filled with rows and rows of austere, identical markers over soldiers' graves. I'd never before come across this cemetery. On the farther side of the field, just beyond the curtains of snow, the sky was torn away and the angels were descending out of a brilliant blue summer, their huge faces streaked with light and full of pity. The sight of them cut through my heart and down the knuckles of my spine, and if there'd been anything in my bowels I would have messed my pants from fear.

Georgie opened his arms and cried out, "It's the drive-in, man!"

"The drive-in . . ." I wasn't sure what these words meant.

"They're showing movies in a fucking blizzard!" Georgie screamed.

"I see. I thought it was something else," I said.

We walked carefully down there and climbed through the busted fence and stood in the very back. The speakers, which I'd mistaken for grave markers, muttered in unison. Then there was tinkly music, of which I could very nearly make out the tune. Famous movie stars rode bicycles beside a river, laughing out of their gigantic, lovely mouths. If anybody had come to see this show, they'd left when the weather started. Not one car remained, not even a broken-down one from last week, or one left here because it was out of gas. In a couple of minutes, in the middle of a whirling square dance, the screen turned black, the cinematic summer ended, the snow went dark, there was nothing but my breath.

"I'm starting to get my eyes back," Georgie said in another minute.

A general greyness was giving birth to various shapes, it was true. "But which ones are close and which ones are far off?" I begged him to tell me.

By trial and error, with a lot of walking back and forth in wet shoes, we found the truck and sat inside it shivering.

"Let's get out of here," I said.

"We can't go anywhere without headlights."

"We've gotta get back. We're a long way from home."

"No, we're not."

"We must have come three hundred miles."

"We're right outside town, Fuckhead. We've just been driving around and around."

"This is no place to camp. I hear the Interstate over there."

"We'll just stay here till it gets late. We can drive home late. We'll be invisible."

We listened to the big rigs going from San Francisco to Pennsylvania along the Interstate, like shudders down a long hacksaw blade, while the snow buried us.

Eventually Georgie said, "We better get some milk for those bunnies."

"We don't have *milk*," I said.

"We'll mix sugar up with it."

"Will you forget about this milk all of a sudden?"

"They're mammals, man."

"Forget about those rabbits."

"Where are they, anyway?"

"You're not listening to me. I said, 'Forget the rabbits.'"

"Where are they?"

The truth was I'd forgotten all about them, and they were dead.

"They slid around behind me and got squashed," I said tearfully.

"They slid around *behind?*"

He watched while I pried them out from behind my back.

I picked them out one at a time and held them in my hands and we looked at them. There were eight. They weren't any bigger than my fingers, but everything was there. Little feet! Eyelids! Even whiskers! "Deceased," I said.

Georgie asked, "Does everything you touch turn to shit? Does this happen to you every time?"

"No wonder they call me Fuckhead."

"It's a name that's going to stick."

"I realize that."

"'Fuckhead' is gonna ride you to your grave."

"I just said so. I agreed with you in advance," I said.

Or maybe that wasn't the time it snowed. Maybe it was the time we slept in the truck and I rolled over on the bunnies and flattened them. It doesn't matter. What's important for me to remember now is that early the next morning the snow was melted off the windshield and the daylight woke me up. A mist covered everything and, with the sunshine, was beginning to grow sharp and strange. The bunnies weren't a problem yet, or they'd already been a problem and were already forgotten, and there was nothing on my mind. I felt the beauty of the morning. I could understand how a drowning man might suddenly feel a deep thirst being quenched. Or how the slave might become a friend to his master. Georgie slept with his face right on the steering wheel.

I saw bits of snow resembling an abundance of blossoms on the stems of the drive-in speakers—no, revealing the blossoms that were always there. A bull elk stood still in the pasture beyond the fence, giving off an air of authority and stupidity. And a coyote jogged across the pasture and faded away among the saplings.

That afternoon we got back to work in time to resume everything as if it had never stopped happening and we'd never been anywhere else.

"The Lord," the intercom said, "is my shepherd." It did that each evening because this was a Catholic hospital. "Our Father, who art in Heaven," and so on.

"Yeah, yeah," Nurse said.

The man with the knife in his head, Terrence Weber, was released around supper-time. They'd kept him overnight and given him an eyepatch—all for no reason, really.

He stopped off at E.R. to say goodbye. "Well, those pills they gave me make every-thing taste terrible," he said.

"It could have been worse," Nurse said.

"Even my tongue."

"It's just a miracle you didn't end up sightless or at least dead," she reminded him.

The patient recognized me. He acknowledged me with a smile. "I was peeping on the lady next door while she was out there sunbathing," he said. "My wife decided to blind me."

He shook Georgie's hand. Georgie didn't know him. "Who are you supposed to be?" he asked Terrence Weber.

Some hours before that, Georgie had said something that had suddenly and com-pletely explained the difference between us. We'd been driving back toward town, along the Old Highway, through the flatness. We picked up a hitchhiker, a boy I knew. We stopped the truck and the boy climbed slowly up out of the fields as out of the mouth of a volcano. His name was Hardee. He looked even worse than we prob-ably did.

"We got messed up and slept in the truck all night," I told Hardee.

"I had a feeling," Hardee said. "Either that or, you know, driving a thousand miles."

"That too," I said.

"Or you're sick or diseased or something."

"Who's this guy?" Georgie asked.

"This is Hardee. He lived with me last summer. I found him on the doorstep. What happened to your dog?" I asked Hardee.

"He's still down there."

"Yeah, I heard you went to Texas."

"I was working on a bee farm," Hardee said.

"Wow. Do those things sting you?"

"Not like you'd think," Hardee said. "You're part of their daily drill. It's all part of a harmony."

Outside, the same identical stretch of grass repeatedly rolled past our faces. The day was cloudless, blinding. But Georgie said, "Look at that," pointing straight ahead of us.

One star was so hot it showed, bright and blue in the empty sky.

"I recognized you right away," I told Hardee. "But what happened to your hair? Who chopped it off?"

"I hate to say."

"Don't tell me."

"They drafted me."

"Oh no."

"Oh yeah. I'm AWOL. I'm bad AWOL. I got to get to Canada."

"Oh, that's terrible," I said to Hardee.

"Don't worry," Georgie said. "We'll get you there."

"How?"

"Somehow. I think I know some people. Don't worry. You're on your way to Canada."

That world! These days it's all been erased and they've rolled it up like a scroll and put it away somewhere. Yes, I can touch it with my fingers. But where is it?

After a while Hardee asked Georgie, "What do you do for a job," and Georgie said, "I save lives."

Reading as a Writer

1. Can you point out the ways that Johnson keeps surprising us? How does he play with our expectations and deliver something that feels fresh and urgent?

2. What purpose does Georgie play in the story? How would it be a completely different story if he weren't in it?

3. What is this story ultimately about? What is the general *feeling* you take away from the story?

AMY BLOOM

Silver Water

MY SISTER'S VOICE was like mountain water in a silver pitcher; the clear blue beauty of it cools you and lifts you up beyond your heat, beyond your body. After we went to see *La Traviata*, when she was fourteen and I was twelve, she elbowed me in the parking lot and said, "Check this out." And she opened her mouth unnaturally wide and her voice came out, so crystalline and bright that all the departing operagoers stood frozen by their cars, unable to take out their keys or open their doors until she had finished, and then they cheered like hell.

That's what I like to remember, and that's the story I told to all of her therapists. I wanted them to know her, to know that who they saw was not all there was to see. That before her constant tinkling of commercials and fast-food jingles there had been Puccini and Mozart and hymns so sweet and mighty you expected Jesus to come down off his cross and clap. That before there was a mountain of Thorazined fat, swaying down the halls in nylon maternity tops and sweatpants, there had been the prettiest girl in Arrandale Elementary School, the belle of Landmark Junior High. Maybe there were other pretty girls, but I didn't see them. To me, Rose, my beautiful blond defender, my guide to Tampax and my mother's moods, was perfect.

She had her first psychotic break when she was fifteen. She had been coming home moody and tearful, then quietly beaming, then she stopped coming home. She would go out into the woods behind our house and not come in until my mother went after her at dusk, and stepped gently into the briars and saplings and pulled her out, blank-faced, her pale blue sweater covered with crumbled leaves, her white jeans smeared with dirt. After three weeks of this, my mother, who is a musician and widely regarded as eccentric, said to my father, who is a psychiatrist and a kind, sad man, "She's going off."

"What is that, your professional opinion?" He picked up the newspaper and put it down again, sighing. "I'm sorry, I didn't mean to snap at you. I know something's bothering her. Have you talked to her?"

"What's there to say? David, she's going crazy. She doesn't need a heart-to-heart talk with Mom, she needs a hospital."

They went back and forth, and my father sat down with Rose for a few hours, and she sat there licking the hairs on her forearm, first one way, then the other. My mother stood in the hallway, dry-eyed and pale, watching the two of them. She had already packed, and when three of my father's friends dropped by to offer free consultations and recommendations, my mother and Rose's suitcase were already in the car. My mother hugged me and told me that they would be back that night, but not with Rose. She also said, divining my worst fear, "It won't happen to you, honey. Some people go crazy and some people never do. You never will." She smiled and stroked my hair. "Not even when you want to."

Rose was in hospitals, great and small, for the next ten years. She had lots of terrible therapists and a few good ones. One place had no pictures on the walls, no windows, and the patients all wore slippers with the hospital crest on them. My mother didn't even bother to go to Admissions. She turned Rose around and the two of them marched out, my father walking behind them, apologizing to his colleagues. My mother ignored the psychiatrists, the social workers, and the nurses, and played Handel and Bessie Smith for the patients on whatever was available. At some places, she had a Steinway donated by a grateful, or optimistic, family; at others, she banged out "Gimme a Pigfoot and a Bottle of Beer" on an old, scarred box that hadn't been tuned since there'd been English-speaking physicians on the grounds. My father talked in serious, appreciative tones to the administrators and unit chiefs and tried to be friendly with whoever was managing Rose's case. We all hated the family therapists.

The worst family therapist we ever had sat in a pale green room with us, visibly taking stock of my mother's ethereal beauty and her faded blue t-shirt and girl-sized jeans, my father's rumpled suit and stained tie, and my own unreadable seventeen-year-old fashion statement. Rose was beyond fashion that year, in one of her dancing teddybear smocks and extra-extra-large Celtics sweatpants. Mr. Walker read Rose's file in front of us and then watched in alarm as Rose began crooning, beautifully, and slowly massaging her breasts. My mother and I laughed, and even my father started to smile. This was Rose's usual opening salvo for new therapists.

Mr. Walker said, "I wonder why it is that everyone is so entertained by Rose behaving inappropriately."

Rose burped, and then we all laughed. This was the seventh family therapist we had seen, and none of them had lasted very long. Mr. Walker, unfortunately, was determined to do right by us.

"What do you think of Rose's behavior, Violet?" They did this sometimes. In their manual it must say, If you think the parents are too weird, try talking to the sister.

"I don't know. Maybe she's trying to get you to stop talking about her in the third person."

"Nicely put," my mother said.

"Indeed," my father said.

"Fuckin' A," Rose said.

"Well, this is something that the whole family agrees upon," Mr. Walker said, trying to act as if he understood or even liked us.

"That was not a successful intervention, Ferret Face." Rose tended to function better when she was angry. He did look like a blond ferret, and we all laughed again. Even my father, who tried to give these people a chance, out of some sense of collegiality, had given it up.

After fourteen minutes, Mr. Walker decided that our time was up and walked out, leaving us grinning at each other. Rose was still nuts, but at least we'd all had a little fun.

The day we met our best family therapist started out almost as badly. We scared off a resident and then scared off her supervisor, who sent us Dr. Thorne. Three hundred pounds of Texas chili, cornbread, and Lone Star beer, finished off with big black cowboy boots and a small string tie around the area of his neck.

"O frabjous day, it's Big Nut." Rose was in heaven and stopped massaging her breasts immediately.

"Hey, Little Nut," You have to understand how big a man would have to be to call my sister "little." He christened us all, right away. "And it's the good Doctor Nut, and Madame Hickory Nut, 'cause they are the hardest damn nuts to crack, and over here in the overalls and not much else is No One's Nut"—a name that summed up both my sanity and my loneliness. We all relaxed.

Dr. Thorne was good for us. Rose moved into a halfway house whose director loved Big Nut so much that she kept Rose even when Rose went through a period of having sex with everyone who passed her door. She was in a fever for a while, trying to still the voices by fucking her brains out.

Big Nut said, "Darlin', I can't. I cannot make love to every beautiful woman I meet, and furthermore, I can't do that and be your therapist too. It's a great shame, but I think you might be able to find a really nice guy, someone who treats you just as sweet and kind as I would if I were lucky enough to be your beau. I don't want you to settle for less." And she stopped propositioning the crack addicts and the alcoholics and the guys at the shelter. We loved Dr. Thorne.

My father went back to seeing rich neurotics and helped out one day a week at Dr. Thorne's Walk-In Clinic. My mother finished a recording of Mozart concerti and played at fund-raisers for Rose's halfway house. I went back to college and found a wonderful linebacker from Texas to sleep with. In the dark, I would make him call me "darlin'." Rose took her meds, lost about fifty pounds, and began singing at the A. M. E. Zion Church, down the street from the halfway house.

At first they didn't know what to do with this big blond lady, dressed funny and hovering wistfully in the doorway during their rehearsals, but she gave them a few bars of "Precious Lord" and the choir director felt God's hand and saw that with the help of His sweet child Rose, the Prospect Street Choir was going all the way to the Gospel Olympics.

Amidst a sea of beige, umber, cinnamon, and espresso faces, there was Rose, bigger, blonder, and pinker than any two white women could be. And Rose and the choir's contralto, Addie Robicheaux, laid out their gold and silver voices and wove them together in strands as fine as silk, as strong as steel. And we wept as Rose and Addie, in their billowing garnet robes, swayed together, clasping hands until the last perfect note floated up to God, and then they smiled down at us.

Rose would still go off from time to time and the voices would tell her to do bad things, but Dr. Thorne or Addie or my mother could usually bring her back. After five good years, Big Nut died. Stuffing his face with a chili dog, sitting in his unair-conditioned office in the middle of July, he had one big, Texas-sized aneurysm and died.

Rose held on tight for seven days; she took her meds, went to choir practice, and rearranged her room about a hundred times. His funeral was like a Lourdes for the mentally ill. If you were psychotic, borderline, bad-off neurotic, or just very hard to get along with, you were there. People shaking so bad from years of heavy meds that they fell out of the pews. People holding hands, crying, moaning, talking to themselves. The crazy people and the not-so-crazy people were all huddled together, like puppies at the pound.

Rose stopped taking her meds, and the halfway house wouldn't keep her after she pitched another patient down the stairs. My father called the insurance company and found out that Rose's new, improved psychiatric coverage wouldn't begin for forty-five days. I put all of her stuff in a garbage bag, and we walked out of the halfway house, Rose winking at the poor drooling boy on the couch.

"This is going to be difficult—not all bad, but difficult—for the whole family, and I thought we should discuss everybody's expectations. I know I have some concerns." My father had convened a family meeting as soon as Rose finished putting each one of her thirty stuffed bears in its own special place.

"No meds," Rose said, her eyes lowered, her stubby fingers, those fingers that had braided my hair and painted tulips on my cheeks, pulling hard on the hem of her dirty smock.

My father looked in despair at my mother.

"Rosie, do you want to drive the new car?" my mother asked.

Rose's face lit up. "I'd love to drive that car. I'd drive to California, I'd go see the bears at the San Diego Zoo. I would take you, Violet, but you always hated the zoo. Remember how she cried at the Bronx Zoo when she found out that the animals didn't get to go home at closing?" Rose put her damp hand on mine and squeezed it sympathetically. "Poor Vi."

"If you take your medication, after a while you'll be able to drive the car. That's the deal. Meds, car." My mother sounded accommodating but unenthusiastic, careful not to heat up Rose's paranoia.

"You got yourself a deal, darlin'."

I was living about an hour away then, teaching English during the day, writing poetry at night. I went home every few days for dinner. I called every night.

My father said, quietly, "It's very hard. We're doing all right, I think. Rose has been walking in the mornings with your mother, and she watches a lot of TV. She won't go to the day hospital, and she won't go back to the choir. Her friend Mrs. Robicheaux came by a couple of times. What a sweet woman. Rose wouldn't even talk to her. She just sat there, staring at the wall and humming. We're not doing all that well, actually, but I guess we're getting by. I'm sorry, sweetheart, I don't mean to depress you."

My mother said, emphatically, "We're doing fine. We've got our routine and we stick to it and we're fine. You don't need to come home so often, you know. Wait 'til Sunday, just come for the day. Lead your life, Vi. She's leading hers."

I stayed away all week, afraid to pick up my phone, grateful to my mother for her harsh calm and her reticence, the qualities that had enraged me throughout my childhood.

I came on Sunday, in the early afternoon, to help my father garden, something we had always enjoyed together. We weeded and staked tomatoes and killed aphids while my mother and Rose were down at the lake. I didn't even go into the house until four, when I needed a glass of water.

Someone had broken the piano bench into five neatly stacked pieces and placed them where the piano bench usually was.

"We were having such a nice time, I couldn't bear to bring it up," my father said, standing in the doorway, carefully keeping his gardening boots out of the kitchen.

"What did Mommy say?"

"She said, 'Better the bench than the piano.' And your sister lay down on the floor and just wept. Then your mother took her down to the lake. This can't go on, Vi. We have twenty-seven days left, your mother gets no sleep because Rose doesn't sleep, and if I could just pay twenty-seven thousand dollars to keep her in the hospital until the insurance takes over, I'd do it."

"All right. Do it. Pay the money and take her back to Hartley-Rees. It was the prettiest place, and she liked the art therapy there."

"I would if I could. The policy states that she must be symptom-free for at least forty-five days before her coverage begins. Symptom-free means no hospitalization."

"Jesus, Daddy, how could you get that kind of policy? She hasn't been symptom-free for forty-five minutes."

"It's the only one I could get for long-term psychiatric." He put his hand over his mouth, to block whatever he was about to say, and went back out to the garden. I couldn't see if he was crying.

He stayed outside and I stayed inside until Rose and my mother came home from the lake. Rose's soggy sweatpants were rolled up to her knees, and she had a bucket-ful of shells and seaweed, which my mother persuaded her to leave on the back porch. My mother kissed me lightly and told Rose to go up to her room and change out of her wet pants.

Rose's eyes grew very wide. "Never. I will never . . ." She knelt down and began banging her head on the kitchen floor with rhythmic intensity, throwing all her weight behind each attack. My mother put her arms around Rose's waist and tried to hold her back. Rose shook her off, not even looking around to see what was slowing her down. My mother lay up against the refrigerator.

"Violet, please . . ."

I threw myself onto the kitchen floor, becoming the spot that Rose was smacking her head against. She stopped a fraction of an inch short of my stomach.

"Oh, Vi, Mommy, I'm sorry. I'm sorry, don't hate me." She staggered to her feet and ran wailing to her room.

My mother got up and washed her face brusquely, rubbing it dry with a dishcloth. My father heard the wailing and came running in, slipping his long bare feet out of his rubber boots.

"Galen, Galen, let me see." He held her head and looked closely for bruises on her pale, small face. "What happened?" My mother looked at me. "Violet, what happened? Where's Rose?"

"Rose got upset, and when she went running upstairs she pushed Mommy out of the way." I've only told three lies in my life, and that was my second.

"She must feel terrible, pushing you, of all people. It would have to be you, but I know she didn't want it to be." He made my mother a cup of tea, and all the love he had for her, despite her silent rages and her vague stares, came pouring through the teapot, warming her cup, filling her small, long-fingered hands. She rested her head against his hip, and I looked away.

"Let's make dinner, then I'll call her. Or you call her, David, maybe she'd rather see your face first."

Dinner was filled with all of our starts and stops and Rose's desperate efforts to control herself. She could barely eat and hummed the McDonald's theme song over and over again, pausing only to spill her juice down the front of her smock and begin weeping. My father looked at my mother and handed Rose his napkin. She dabbed at herself listlessly, but the tears stopped.

"I want to go to bed. I want to go to bed and be in my head. I want to go to bed and be in my bed and in my head and just wear red. For red is the color that my baby wore and once more, it's true, yes, it is, it's true. Please don't wear red tonight, oh, oh, please don't wear red tonight, for red is the color—"

"Okay, okay, Rose. It's okay. I'll go upstairs with you and you can get ready for bed. Then Mommy will come up and say good night too. It's okay, Rose." My father reached out his hand and Rose grasped it, and they walked out of the dining room together, his long arm around her middle.

My mother sat at the table for a moment, her face in her hands, and then she began clearing the plates. We cleared without talking, my mother humming Schubert's "Schlummerlied," a lullaby about the woods and the river calling to the child to go to sleep. She sang it to us every night when we were small.

My father came into the kitchen and signaled to my mother. They went upstairs and came back down together a few minutes later.

"She's asleep," they said, and we went to sit on the porch and listen to the crickets. I don't remember the rest of the evening, but I remember it as quietly sad, and I remember the rare sight of my parents holding hands, sitting on the picnic table, watching the sunset.

I woke up at three o'clock in the morning, feeling the cool night air through my sheet. I went down the hall for a blanket and looked into Rose's room, for no reason. She wasn't there. I put on my jeans and a sweater and went downstairs. I could feel her absence. I went outside and saw her wide, draggy footprints darkening the wet grass into the woods.

"Rosie," I called, too softly, not wanting to wake my parents, not wanting to startle Rose. "Rosie, it's me. Are you here? Are you all right?"

I almost fell over her. Huge and white in the moonlight, her flowered smock bleached in the light and shadow, her sweatpants now completely wet. Her head was flung back, her white, white neck exposed like a lost Greek column.

"Rosie, Rosie—" Her breathing was very slow, and her lips were not as pink as they usually were. Her eyelids fluttered.

"Closing time," she whispered. I believe that's what she said.

I sat with her, uncovering the bottle of Seconal by her hand, and watched the stars fade.

When the stars were invisible and the sun was warming the air, I went back to the house. My mother was standing on the porch, wrapped in a blanket, watching me. Every step I took overwhelmed me; I could picture my mother slapping me, shooting me for letting her favorite die.

"Warrior queens," she said, wrapping her thin strong arms around me. "I raised warrior queens." She kissed me fiercely and went into the woods by herself.

Later in the morning she woke my father, who could not go into the woods, and still later she called the police and the funeral parlor. She hung up the phone, lay down, and didn't get back out of bed until the day of the funeral. My father fed us both and called the people who needed to be called and picked out Rose's coffin by himself.

My mother played the piano and Addie sang her pure gold notes and I closed my eyes and saw my sister, fourteen years old, lion's mane thrown back and eyes tightly closed against the glare of the parking lot lights. That sweet sound held us tight, flowing around us, eddying through our hearts, rising, still rising.

Reading as a Writer

1. How does Bloom's treatment of mental illness avoid being clichéd or sentimental?

2. How does Bloom avoid stereotyping the members of the family in her portrayal of the ways they deal with Rose's illness?

3. Which character are you most interested in, ultimately? Why? What do you understand or learn about this character by the end of the story? How does this *surprise* you?

CHAPTER TWO

The Gift of Not Knowing

Writing as Discovery

"I DON'T HAVE ANY GOOD IDEAS." So goes one of the most common fears expressed by beginning writing students. It can be accompanied by "I don't have anything to write about" and "Nothing interesting has ever happened to me." And although older or more experienced writers might not say these things publicly, many of the most accomplished authors in the world openly acknowledge the uncertainty, anxiety, and dread that can arise when facing a blank piece of paper or the blinking cursor on a computer screen.

Indeed, one of the most difficult lessons a writer must learn is that uncertainty— sometimes *painful* uncertainty—is an integral part of the writing process. It does not go away with age, experience, or praise, although all of these things—particularly critical success—can provide a writer with sufficient confidence in his or her abilities to endure the sometimes extreme discomfort of uncertainty with relative equanimity.

Yet, as frightening as it is, *not* knowing what to write about is often a creative advantage. Not having any "ideas" can be an excellent beginning to generating creative work that is truly fresh and original and exciting precisely because the writer has ventured out of familiar (and comfortable) territory. He or she is exploring, not retelling an old tale. He or she is learning, not teaching. And the things that make exploration and encountering the new so riveting to the writer can, under the best of circumstances, carry over to the reader. As Robert Frost so famously wrote, "No tears in the writer, no tears in the reader."

In this chapter we'll explore ways writers can harness the inherent doubt and uncertainty of the creative process in order to begin discovering their own voices and material. In addition, carefully targeted writing exercises give you a chance to practice some of the techniques discussed. Finally, two classics of contemporary short fiction effectively dramatize how the best creative work consistently engages and surprises us—and how difficult it is, even in retrospect, to summarize or paraphrase the experience we've just read our way through.

What Do You Know?

"Write about what you know" is the first solid piece of writing advice most of us are told, and we usually hear it at a fairly early age. If your primary school teacher didn't tell you this, then almost certainly you encountered it before enrolling in a college-level writing class. And it can be excellent advice for children, or for beginning writers who lack the confidence to believe that anything they know would be of interest to others. It's less helpful for older or more sophisticated students, for reasons that will be explained later in this chapter. But for now, let's accept it as a basic truth that we should write about the things we know.

Why is this good advice? Because it simultaneously grounds you in the concrete sensory world that is all around you and discourages you from clichéd rumination on abstract topics. By emphasizing that there can be infinite value, and beauty, and meaning in the ordinary, this advice helps beginning writers avoid the trap of writing about "love" or "despair" and heroic, exotic, or sensational topics that reflect popular culture (or the desire to impress) more than honest human experience. To write a coming-of-age story about a native of Bora-Bora might seem like a great idea in theory, but when you sit down to actually write it, you'll probably find that your lack of understanding of the everyday world of a thirteen-year-old Bora-Bora girl might hamper you from producing the thrilling results you'd hoped for.

This is not to say that you must avoid large or meaningful (to you) topics; neither is this an admonition to limit use of the imagination or stick solely to a realistic rendering of the world—what a sad and lean literary heritage we would have if this were so! Rather, one of the first difficult lessons any writer must learn is how to trust his or her own personal insight and unique skills of observation, even when these conflict with accepted wisdom and the mass-produced images that bombard all of us daily.

Here's a poem to illustrate how a writer can take an ordinary moment and, through brutally honest insight, transform it into the extraordinary:

Forty-One, Alone, No Gerbil

In the strange quiet, I realize
there's no one else in the house. No bucktooth
mouth pulls at a stainless-steel teat, no
hairy mammal runs on a treadmill—
Charlie is dead, the last of our children's half-children.
When our daughter found him lying in the shavings, transmogrified
         backward from a living body
into a bolt of rodent bread
she turned her back on early motherhood
and went on single, with nothing. Crackers,
Fluffy, Pretzel, Biscuit, Charlie,
buried on the old farm we bought where she could know nature. Well,
         now she knows it

and it sucks. Creatures she loved, mobile and
needy, have gone down stiff and indifferent,
she will not adopt again though she cannot
have children yet, her body like a blueprint
of the understructure for a woman's body,
so now everything stops for a while,
now I must wait many years
to hear in this house again the faint
powerful call of a young animal.

—SHARON OLDS

Even the title pushes us away from expectations of anything "poetic" or "meaning-ful" (which beginning writers often try too hard to provide); the use of slang and informal diction reinforces the impression of spontaneously musing on what is, for parents of young children, a familiar scene. Yet Olds takes us beyond the seemingly trivial scene and folds us into an extraordinarily powerful moment of personal grief and longing. The concrete details anchor us in the specific moment at the same time that the images evoke deep, visceral, and—arguably—universal emotion.

It is precisely because complex and ambiguous emotions like this can only be ren-dered and sustained by specific concrete details that "Write about what you know" advice can still be considered valid.

When Raymond Carver gives advice to other writers, he starts out by saying that talent is commonplace—that he doesn't know many writers who are without it. What *does* distinguish certain writers as being above the crowd, he says, is a "unique and exact way of looking at things," as well as a way of expressing that way of look-ing. In Carver's own words:

> *The World According to Garp* is, of course, the marvelous world according to John Irving. There is another world according to Flannery O'Connor, and others according to William Faulkner and Ernest Hemingway. There are worlds according to Cheever, Updike, Singer, Stanley Elkin, Ann Beattie, Cynthia Ozick, Donald Barthelme. [. . .] Every great or even every very good writer makes the world over according to his own specifications.
>
> —RAYMOND CARVER, *Fires*

Later in the essay, Carver talks about the need to "carry news" from your world to that of your readers. So what do you know? What "news"—about events, people, emotions, thoughts—within your personal experience is worth exploring creatively and telling others about?

But wait a minute. Aren't we back to our starting point: that you might not have lived that exciting of a life to begin writing—yet? That you should perhaps accumu-late more "experience" before trying?

Absolutely not. The kind of experience worth writing about is not necessarily a matter of what you've done or experienced, but rather the depth and breadth of what you've noticed—and your emotional response to what you've taken note of. Consider this advice:

> Experience is not a matter of having actually swum the Hellespont, or danced with the dervishes, or slept in a doss-house. It is a matter of sensibility and intuition, of seeing and hearing the significant things, of paying attention at the right moments, of understanding and coordinating. Experience is not what happens to a man; it is what a man does with what happens to him.
> —ALDOUS HUXLEY, *Texts and Pretexts*

Indeed, the most timid, naive, and protected adolescent has felt terror, known exploitation and betrayal. Because the events that call forth these emotions are not necessarily dramatic, we perhaps dismiss the intensity of these emotional experiences as inauthentic or overwrought. We do not think we have the right to claim these emotions. Yet we do. And what's more, our ability to write truly moving fiction ultimately derives from our ability to transform these very deep and very true experiences into language that effectively arouses deep, true emotions in others.

What You Don't Know (about What You Know)

Now that we've explained how writing about what you know can be helpful advice, we need to talk about the ways it can be limiting, and even detrimental, to your creative efforts.

Eudora Welty had it right: "Write about what you *don't* know about what you know," she advised. And with this, we can begin to put together a basic understanding of what we, as fiction writers, are trying to accomplish.

What Welty is saying, in effect, is that yes, it can make sense to work with material that you feel closest to (both emotionally and physically). Yet there must be a sense of mystery in the material. We don't just write about contemporary urban family life because we're familiar with it. We write about it because it *interests* us, because despite its familiarity there are aspects of it that remain mysterious, unknowable, *worth exploring further*. We're interested in what we *don't* know about very familiar and (to us) ordinary scenes. So just possessing knowledge about a particular topic, or place, or person isn't going to take you very far, creatively. You won't really claim this material the way Sherwood Anderson claimed small-town Ohio life in *Winesburg, Ohio*, for instance—not unless there are things that you don't know about this topic, place, or person, and not unless you are interested to the point of obsession in finding out more.

Jane Kenyon put it this way in her diaries:

> Why do we want to write? What is behind this crazy impulse? The wish to connect with others, on a deep level, about inward things. The pressure of emotion, which many people prefer to ignore, but which, for you, is the very substance of your work, your *clay*. *There's the need to make sense of life behind the impulse to write* [emphasis mine].
> —JANE KENYON

As an example of using not-knowing as the basis for creative exploration, let's look at a poem by Czeslaw Milosz, translated from the Polish by the author and poet Robert Hass. Titled "In the Parish," the poem begins with the narrator's spontaneous visit to a cemetery:

> Were I not frail and half broken inside,
> I wouldn't be thinking of them, who are, like me, half broken inside.
> I would not climb the cemetery hill by the church
> To get rid of my self-pity.

Milosz goes on to comment on the fragility of the physical remains, coupled with notions of what happens after death:

> And eternity close by. Improper. Indecent.
> Like a doll house crushed by wheels, like
> An elephant trampling a beetle, an ocean drowning an island.
> Our stupidity and childishness do nothing to fit us
> For the sobriety of last things.

He is not lecturing so much as talking out his feelings—rage and sorrow, and the sense that these thoughts and emotions are only now being grasped and processed. The poem takes us along with him as he continues to explore what isn't known but begs to be understood within this unremarkable small parish cemetery.

> They had no time to grasp anything
> Of their individual lives,
> Any *principium individuationis*.
> Nor do I grasp it, yet what can I do?
> Enclosed all my life in a nutshell,
> Trying in vain to become something
> Completely different from what I was.

From there he returns to the introspection that began the poem—what he calls "self-pity," which he hoped to dispel by taking this walk. Instead, we see how he has deepened his misery and frustration with his place in the world.

The poem has another stanza, but this is enough to show the movement in the poem—how it is not a set of static statements about the world, but an obviously painful effort to push through bitterness and fear to a more comfortable state—better understanding, perhaps, or acceptance of mortality.

On Rendering the Mysteries That Surround Us

"It is the business of fiction to embody mystery through manners, and mystery is a great embarrassment to the modern mind," Flannery O'Connor told a group of college students (the text of the speech can be found in *Mystery and Manners*, a collection of her essays on writing).

The mystery O'Connor is referring to is "the mystery of our position on earth," she says. What does that mean? That every hour in every day we are confronted by mysteries: by things we don't know, by things we don't understand. Although O'Connor herself viewed the world (and wrote about it) through the prism of a deep religious faith, her point is also valid from a secular perspective. The "mystery" in that case would encompass all the things in the world that we don't fully understand—not just large philosophical issues, but such questions as why your mother was so irritable at dinner or what motivated your girlfriend to suddenly drop out of school.

We are surrounded by such mysteries, large and small, and our first responsibility as writers is simply to *notice* them. Everything follows from that.

All this, of course, is another way to say that we should write about what we *don't* know about what we know. Without using this sense of not-knowingness, or mystery, as a starting point, anything we write will be lifeless and predictable.

The following untitled piece by Tobias Wolff illustrates this point. Written as an essay for an anthology of "short short fiction," it was Wolff's attempt to define this hybrid genre of writing that falls somewhere between short fiction and poetry.

I was on a bus to Washington, D.C. Two days I'd been traveling and I was tired, tired, tired. The woman sitting next to me, a German with a ticket good for anywhere, never stopped yakking. I understood little of what she said but what I did understand led me to believe that she was utterly deranged.

She finally took a breather when we hit Richmond. It was late at night. The bus threaded its way through dismal streets toward the bus station. We rounded a corner and there beneath a street light stood a white man and a black woman. The woman wore a yellow dress and held a baby. Her head was thrown back in laughter. The man was red-haired, rough-looking, naked to the waist. His skin seemed luminous. He was grinning at the woman, who watched him closely even as she laughed. Broken glass glittered at their feet.

There is something between them, something in the instant itself, that makes me sit up and stare. What is it, what's going on here? Why can't I ever forget them?

Tell me, for God's sake, but make it snappy—I'm tired, and the bus is picking up speed, and the lunatic beside me is getting ready to say something.

—TOBIAS WOLFF, untitled

Another point O'Connor stresses, which Wolff also touches on, is the question of *what next*? Okay, you've identified a mystery, a gap in your knowledge of a situation that you feel is worth exploring. What then?

Here's what *not* to do: Don't try to *solve* these mysteries. As writers, we're not looking to provide a lesson or a moral; we're not therapists looking to cure our characters of pain or neurosis. Our job, as writers, is simply to render what *is* by using precise, concrete detail.

Don't give easy answers. Rather, help your readers understand the precise nature of the questions.

Moving from "Triggering" to Real Subject

We've now covered the single most important step a writer must take when gener-ating new work: to identify potential material by paying attention to surrounding mysteries and seeking out those mysteries that resonate loudest for him or her.

The most articulate explanation of the next stage in the creative process can be found in Chapter 1 of Richard Hugo's book *The Triggering Town*. This chapter first underscores the notion that a poem is a process of discovery, not an archive of resolved emotion. Hugo has described this process as moving from the "triggering" subject to the "real" subject. Here is an excerpt:

> A poem can be said to have two subjects, the initiating or triggering subject, which starts the poem or "causes" the poem to be written, and the real or generated sub-ject, which the poem comes to say or mean, and which is generated or discovered in the poem during the writing. That's not quite right because it suggests that the poet recognizes the real subject. The poet may not be aware of what the real sub-ject is but only have some instinctive feeling that the poem is done.
>
> Young poets find it difficult to free themselves from the initiating subject. The poet puts down the title: "Autumn Rain." He finds two or three good lines about Autumn Rain. Then things start to break down. He cannot find anything more to say about Autumn Rain so he starts making up things, he strains, he goes abstract, he starts telling us the meaning of what he has already said. The mistake he is making, of course, is that he feels obligated to go on talking about Autumn Rain, because that, he feels, is the subject. Well, it isn't the subject. You don't know what the subject is, and the moment you run out of things to say about Autumn Rain start talking about something else. In fact, it's a good idea to talk about something else before you run out of things to say about Autumn Rain.   —RICHARD HUGO, "Writing Off the Subject"

Hugo is saying that the very uncertainty we began this chapter discussing is the driv-ing force behind a creative work; that rather than attempting to avoid uncertainty, the writer needs to embrace it—even to the point of changing the "subject" from one line to another. Because it is the writer's imagination that is choosing the next topic, because there must be some connection in the writer's brain (conscious or unconscious) that leads from one subject to another, then the sequence must be meaningful.

Although Hugo is talking about poetry, the *process* he is discussing is equally true when writing fiction. We are always on a path of discovery—if not, the result will be absolute dullness for the reader.

Here's a poem that dramatizes the notion of a triggering subject that leads to a real subject:

Why I Am Not a Painter

I am not a painter, I am a poet
Why? I think I would rather be
a painter, but I am not. Well,

for instance, Mike Goldberg
is starting a painting. I drop in.
"Sit down and have a drink" he
says. I drink; we drink. I look
up. "You have SARDINES in it."
"Yes, it needed something there."
"Oh." I go and the days go by
and I drop in again. The painting
is going on, and I go, and the days
go by. I drop in. The painting is
finished. "Where's SARDINES?"
All that's left is just
letters. "It was too much," Mike says.

But me? One day I am thinking of
a color: orange. I write a line
about orange. Pretty soon it is a
whole page of words, not lines.
Then another page. There should be
so much more, not of orange, of
words, of how terrible orange is
and life. Days go by. It is even in
prose, I am a real poet. My poem
is finished and I haven't mentioned
orange yet. It's twelve poems, I call
it ORANGES. And one day in a gallery
I see Mike's painting, called SARDINES.
                                                    —FRANK O'HARA

Surprise Yourself, Interest Others

"Bad books are about things the writer already knew before he wrote them," the Mexican writer Carlos Fuentes says. What does he mean? Exactly what we have been discussing: that without a sense of discovery, a creative piece will lack urgency and interest. To paraphrase Margaret, the heroine of E. M. Forster's great novel *Howards End*, how do you know what you think until you read what you've written? Even B. F. Skinner, the father of what we know as behavioral psychology, subscribed to this theory. In an essay titled "How to Discover What You Have to Say: A Talk to Students," Skinner asserts that writing is a much more complex act than simply transcribing thoughts into words as accurately as possible. If this were the case, the writer would be doing little more than serving as a "reporter" of past thoughts and experiences already processed by the brain. Instead, Skinner argues that the physical act of writing is the cause, not the effect, of new and original thought, and that any creative work that is not a journey of discovery for the writer will, in turn, bore readers. "It's like driving a car at night," said novelist Robert Stone about how he copes with this uncertainty when writing longer pieces; "you can only see as far ahead as your headlights, but you can make the entire journey that way."

Beginning writers find it difficult to tolerate this state of not-knowing. Yet accepting it, embracing it even, represents an important step in a writer's creative development. Good creative writing is almost always conceived in doubt and fueled by an urgent desire to understand something that eludes understanding. Thus the best writing is less about dispelling than about acquiring wisdom, less about explaining the point of a given experience to others than about exploring and learning about it oneself.

Obsession as a Creative Virtue

But it's not enough just not to know or understand something. You have to be *interested*. If possible, you should go beyond interest to obsession, as the poet Philip Larkin says. A successful creative work has three distinct stages, according to Larkin:

1. A person becomes obsessed with something to the degree that he or she is "compelled to do something about it"—that is, write.

2. The person writes down words (a "verbal device") that attempt to reproduce the original emotion in "anyone who cares to read it."

3. Other people, from all places and all walks of life, read the words and "set off" a device that re-creates what the writer originally felt and/or thought.

Notice how Larkin distinguishes inspiration (Stage 1) from craft (Stage 2). It doesn't matter how inspired or obsessed you are if you do not possess the skills that allow you to get your emotional experience down on paper. However, all the skill in the world won't help you produce a truly moving story if you aren't all that interested in the idea to begin with. And the whole effort will fail if there is no successful reading by an intelligent and interested third party.

As Larkin says:

> If there has been no preliminary feeling, the device has nothing to reproduce and the reader will experience nothing. If the second stage has not been well done, the device will not deliver the goods, or will deliver only a few goods to a few people, or will stop delivering them after an absurdly short while. And if there is no third stage, no successful reading, the [creative work] can hardly be said to exist in a practical sense at all.
>
> —PHILIP LARKIN, "The Pleasure Principle"

Finally, here is what Rick Bass wrote about how an oilman feels about "getting oil." The excitement and danger that he writes about is precisely what happens when, as the Greeks put it, the muse descends.

> Finding oil is sometimes like the feeling you get driving a little over the recommended speed limit on that sharp turn on the interstate outside Baton Rouge en

route to Lafayette, when you come around that climbing corner pulling Gs and truck blast a little too fast and then after that whip of a turn find yourself looking up at that space-age takeoff ramp they call a bridge that spans, after the vertical climb, the Mississippi River. You've been driving along all morning on this pretty but bland interstate, humming along into predictability and all of a sudden there are all these surprise marks on the landscape: intense abruptions, challenges to the spirit. You find yourself almost racing up that bridge even before you've fully acknowledged its existence. You look down and see water. It makes the backs of your hamstrings, and a wide zone across your chest, tingle. That is what finding oil is like.   —RICK BASS, "AN OILMAN'S NOTEBOOK"

EXERCISES

What does one do with this information, that not-knowing and paying attention to personal mysteries leads to good creative writing? First, one learns how to recognize mystery. Learn to understand when you don't understand. Take note of it—if possible, literally, by carrying a notebook with you. So when you see that guy at the coffee shop stare into his cup for ten minutes as if the secret of the universe lay within, or when you see that old woman totter across the street, look alarmed, and totter back again, you can realize you have some potential material in front of you. Second, one learns how to mine that material.

Exercise 1: Things I Was Taught / Things I Was Not Taught

GOAL: To elicit fresh and surprising insights into your relationship to family, friends, community, and the world.

1. Choose an individual who has been enormously influential in your life (usually a parent, sometimes a sibling or a friend).
2. Create a list of the things that person has taught you. The list should be entitled: "Things That X Taught Me."
3. Create a list of the things that same person did not teach you. The list should be entitled, "Things That X Did Not Teach Me."

The following piece was written as a response to this exercise by Clare Dornan:

Things my father taught me

- How if you're sick, it's your special day. Your mother makes tea with lemon and a dash of the whiskey that she hides in her bedroom closet, and your father unplugs the small black-and-white television he keeps in his workroom and allows you to watch cartoons in bed.
- How to walk in the woods after a rain and think of nothing but the smell of eucalyptus and pine.

- How to let the mud dry on your shoes so you can knock it off with a stick the next day.
- That you're allowed to make an absolute pigsty of your car, and throw coffee cups, candy wrappers, half-eaten apples on the floor with abandon. When it gets too disgusting, you take it to the car wash and pay extra for the attendants to haul away the garbage and deodorize the moldy carpet.
- How to drive to Half Moon Bay and choose the best live crabs and lobsters from the tank. You let them crawl around on the back seat, because they don't have long to live, and must be allowed to enjoy the little time left to them. You listen to them scream when you throw them into boiling salted water, then you crack them open and eat them with melted butter and lemon, but only when your father is out of town, because why go to all that trouble for something so tasteless? You must have Hostess Hohos washed down with milk for dessert after you eat a freshly killed lobster.

Things my father didn't teach me

- When it's best to ignore that your wife is deeply unhappy; when you should bring her a glass of water, but be careful not to touch her; how to sit in the same room as her, but not so she has to look directly at you; that you shouldn't notice tears, or muffled phone conversations at 3 a.m., or whether the other side of the bed has been slept in when you wake up in the morning.
- When it's appropriate to continue to embrace your wife even though she struggles at first; when you should not allow her to watch David Letterman because she gets too depressed at how heartily the audience laughs when he mocks his guests; when it's okay to get in the car next to her and let her drive 100 miles north, then 75 miles east before turning the car toward home, all without saying a word.
- How to stop drinking before you have to spend the night on the couch of people you barely know and who don't like you.
- How to keep spare light bulbs around the house so when one goes out you can replace it immediately.
- How to wash your infant son's genitals in the bathtub without feeling ashamed.
- How to cheer with just the right balance of enthusiasm and irony from the bleachers at Wrigley Field when Ernie Banks hits a homer.

Exercise 2: I Want to Know Why

GOAL: To identify interesting gaps in your understanding or knowledge in order to generate raw material for short stories.

1. Create a list of at least ten items that fit into the category of things not known: "I want to know why." Important: impose constraints to avoid abstraction or otherwise "large" topics. For example, you might want to limit the things not known to the events of that week, or to family encounters.

2. Take one item from this list and write half a page of prose.

The following exercise was written by John Sark:

I want to know why:

- I always see the same elderly woman at the bus stop but I've never seen her actually get on a bus.
- Sometimes I just have to have curry for breakfast!
- When my mother calls, she sounds angry even if she isn't.
- My roommate buys milk by the gallon, but it always goes sour before it is even halfway gone.
- That man who works at the coffeehouse never smiles.
- I never seem to win anything—never.
- None of the girls I really like will go out with me.
- My English instructor always looks right at me when asking for comments about whatever it is we're reading.
- Whenever I need to go someplace, I'm out of gas.
- Whenever I want to cook something, I don't have the right ingredients.

Whenever I want to cook something, I don't have the right ingredients. Take last night. Mary was over, and it was a chance to impress her, to show her that I wasn't the usual kind of guy that lives in the undergraduate dorms, that in addition to living in a *real apartment* I was mature enough, etc. to cook for myself, and even for others. Anyway, I had intended to cook some chicken and some corn on the cob, and I thought I had everything I needed, but realized when the chicken was in the oven and the corn was in the boiling water that I was completely out of salt. Corn on the cob without salt! Then of course, I checked, and I didn't have any butter, either. Not a slice. More mortifying, I went to the bathroom and discovered I was out of toilet paper. Some impressive guy I was turning out to be: fulfilling all the usual stereotypes.

READINGS

Joyce Carol Oates

Where Are You Going, Where Have You Been?

For Bob Dylan

HER NAME WAS CONNIE. She was fifteen and she had a quick nervous giggling habit of craning her neck to glance into mirrors, or checking other people's faces to make sure her own was all right. Her mother, who noticed everything and knew everything and who hadn't much reason any longer to look at her own face, always scolded Connie about it. "Stop gawking at yourself, who are you? You think you're so pretty?" she would say. Connie would raise her eyebrows at these familiar complaints and look right through her mother, into a shadowy vision of herself as she was right at that moment: she knew she was pretty and that was everything. Her mother had been pretty once too, if you could believe those old snapshots in the album, but now her looks were gone and that was why she was always after Connie.

"Why don't you keep your room clean like your sister? How've you got your hair fixed—what the hell stinks? Hair spray? You don't see your sister using that junk."

Her sister June was twenty-four and still lived at home. She was a secretary in the high school Connie attended, and if that wasn't bad enough—with her in the same building—she was so plain and chunky and steady that Connie had to hear her praised all the time by her mother and her mother's sisters. June did this, June did that, she saved money and helped clean the house and cooked and Connie couldn't do a thing, her mind was all filled with trashy daydreams. Their father was away at work most of the time and when he came home he wanted supper and he read the newspaper at supper and after supper he went to bed. He didn't bother talking much to them, but around his bent head Connie's mother kept picking at her until Connie wished her mother was dead and she herself was dead and it was all over. "She makes me want to throw up sometimes," she complained to her friends. She had a high, breathless, amused voice which made everything she said a little forced, whether it was sincere or not.

There was one good thing: June went places with girl friends of hers, girls who were just as plain and steady as she, and so when Connie wanted to do that her mother had no objections. The father of Connie's best girl friend drove the girls the three miles to town and left them off at a shopping plaza, so that they could walk through the stores or go to a movie, and when he came to pick them up again at eleven he never bothered to ask what they had done.

They must have been familiar sights, walking around that shopping plaza in their shorts and flat ballerina slippers that always scuffed the sidewalk, with charm bracelets jingling on their thin wrists; they would lean together to whisper and laugh secretly if someone passed by who amused or interested them. Connie had long dark blond hair that drew anyone's eye to it, and she wore part of it pulled up on her head and puffed out and the rest of it she let fall down her back. She wore a pullover jersey blouse that looked one way when she was at home and another way when she was away from home. Everything about her had two sides to it, one for home and one for anywhere that was not home: her walk that could be childlike and bobbing, or languid enough to make anyone think she was hearing music in her head, her mouth which was pale and smirking most of the time, but bright and pink on these evenings out, her laugh which was cynical and drawling at home—"Ha, ha, very funny"—but high-pitched and nervous anywhere else, like the jingling of the charms on her bracelet.

Sometimes they did go shopping or to a movie, but sometimes they went across the highway, ducking fast across the busy road, to a drive-in restaurant where older kids hung out. The restaurant was shaped like a big bottle, though squatter than a real bottle, and on its cap was a revolving figure of a grinning boy who held a hamburger aloft. One night in midsummer they ran across, breathless with daring, and right away someone leaned out a car window and invited them over, but it was just a boy from high school they didn't like. It made them feel good to be able to ignore him. They went up through the maze of parked and cruising cars to the bright-lit, fly-infested restaurant, their faces pleased and expectant as if they were entering a sacred building that loomed out of the night to give them what haven and what blessing they yearned for. They sat at the counter and crossed their legs at the ankles, their thin shoulders rigid with excitement and listened to the music that made everything so good: the music was always in the background like music at a church service, it was something to depend upon.

A boy named Eddie came in to talk with them. He sat backwards on his stool, turning himself jerkily around in semicircles and then stopping and turning again, and after a while he asked Connie if she would like something to eat. She said she did and so she tapped her friend's arm on her way out—her friend pulled her face up into a brave droll look—and Connie said she would meet her at eleven, across the way. "I just hate to leave her like that," Connie said earnestly, but the boy said that she wouldn't be alone for long. So they went out to his car and on the way Connie couldn't help but let her eyes wander over the windshields and faces all around her, her face gleaming with the joy that had nothing to do with Eddie or even this place; it might have been the music. She drew her shoulders up and sucked in her breath with the pure pleasure of being alive, and just at that moment she happened to glance at a face just a few feet from hers. It was a boy with shaggy black hair, in a convertible jalopy painted gold. He stared at her and then his lips widened into a grin. Connie slit her eyes at him and turned away, but she couldn't help glancing back and there he was still watching her. He wagged a finger and laughed and said, "Gonna get you, baby," and Connie turned away again without Eddie noticing anything.

She spent three hours with him, at the restaurant where they ate hamburgers and drank Cokes in wax cups that were always sweating, and then down an alley a mile or so away, and when he left her off at five to eleven only the movie house was still open at the plaza. Her girl friend was there, talking with a boy. When Connie came up the two girls smiled at each other and Connie said, "How was the movie?" and the girl said, "*You* should know." They rode off with the girl's father, sleepy and pleased, and Connie couldn't help but look at the darkened shopping plaza with its big empty parking lot and its signs that were faded and ghostly now, and over at the drive-in restaurant where cars were still circling tirelessly. She couldn't hear the music at this distance.

Next morning June asked her how the movie was and Connie said, "So-so."

She and that girl and occasionally another girl went out several times a week that way, and the rest of the time Connie spent around the house—it was summer vacation—getting in her mother's way and thinking, dreaming, about the boys she met. But all the boys fell back and dissolved into a single face that was not even a face, but an idea, a feeling, mixed up with the urgent insistent pounding of the music and the humid night air of July. Connie's mother kept dragging her back to the daylight by finding things for her to do or saying suddenly, "What's this about the Pettinger girl?"

And Connie would say nervously, "Oh, her. That dope." She always drew thick clear lines between herself and such girls, and her mother was simple and kindly enough to believe her. Her mother was so simple, Connie thought, that it was maybe cruel to fool her so much. Her mother went scuffling around the house in old bedroom slippers and complained over the telephone to one sister about the other, then the other called up and the two of them complained about the third one. If June's name was mentioned her mother's tone was approving, and if Connie's name was mentioned it was disapproving. This did not really mean she disliked Connie and actually Connie thought that her mother preferred her to June because she was prettier, but the two of them kept up a pretense of exasperation, a sense that they were tugging and struggling over something of little value to either of them. Sometimes, over coffee, they were almost friends, but something would come up—some vexation that was like a fly buzzing suddenly around their heads—and their faces went hard with contempt.

One Sunday Connie got up at eleven—none of them bothered with church—and washed her hair so that it could dry all day long, in the sun. Her parents and sister were going to a barbecue at an aunt's house and Connie said no, she wasn't interested, rolling her eyes, to let her mother know just what she thought of it. "Stay home alone then," her mother said sharply. Connie sat out back in a lawn chair and watched them drive away, her father quiet and bald, hunched around so that he could back the car out, her mother with a look that was still angry and not at all softened through the windshield, and in the back seat poor old June all dressed up as if she didn't know what a barbecue was, with all the running yelling kids and the flies. Connie sat with her eyes closed in the sun, dreaming and dazed with the warmth about her as if this were a kind of love, the caresses of love, and her mind slipped over onto thoughts of the boy she had been with the night before and how nice he had been, how sweet it always was, not the way someone like June would suppose but sweet, gentle, the way it was in movies and promised in songs; and when she opened her eyes she hardly knew where she was, the back yard ran off into weeds and a fenceline of trees and behind it the sky was perfectly blue and still. The asbestos "ranch house" that was now three years old startled her—it looked small. She shook her head as if to get awake.

It was too hot. She went inside the house and turned on the radio to drown out the quiet. She sat on the edge of her bed, barefoot, and listened for an hour and a half to a program called XYZ Sunday Jamboree, record after record of hard, fast, shrieking songs she sang along with, interspersed by exclamations from "Bobby King": "An' look here you girls at Napoleon's—Son and Charley want you to pay real close attention to this song coming up!"

And Connie paid close attention herself, bathed in a glow of slow-pulsed joy that seemed to rise mysteriously out of the music itself and lay languidly about the airless little room, breathed in and breathed out with each gentle rise and fall of her chest.

After a while she heard a car coming up the drive. She sat up at once, startled, because it couldn't be her father so soon. The gravel kept crunching all the way in from the road—the driveway was long—and Connie ran to the window. It was a car she didn't know. It was an open jalopy, painted a bright gold that caught the sun opaquely. Her heart began to pound and her fingers snatched at her hair, checking it, and she whispered "Christ. Christ," wondering how bad she looked. The car came to a stop at the side door and the horn sounded four short taps as if this were a signal Connie knew.

She went into the kitchen and approached the door slowly, then hung out the screen door, her bare toes curling down off the step. There were two boys in the car and now she recognized the driver: he had shaggy, shabby black hair that looked crazy as a wig and he was grinning at her.

"I ain't late, am I?" he said.

"Who the hell do you think you are?" Connie said.

"Toldja I'd be out, didn't I?"

"I don't even know who you are."

She spoke sullenly, careful to show no interest or pleasure, and he spoke in a fast bright monotone. Connie looked past him to the other boy, taking her time. He had fair brown hair, with a lock that fell onto his forehead. His sideburns gave him a fierce, embarrassed look, but so far he hadn't even bothered to glance at her. Both boys wore sunglasses. The driver's glasses were metallic and mirrored everything in miniature.

"You wanta come for a ride?" he said.

Connie smirked and let her hair fall loose over one shoulder.

"Don'tcha like my car? New paint job," he said. "Hey."

"What?"

"You're cute."

She pretended to fidget, chasing flies away from the door.

"Don'tcha believe me, or what?" he said.

"Look, I don't even know who you are," Connie said in disgust.

"Hey, Ellie's got a radio, see. Mine's broke down." He lifted his friend's arm and showed her the little transistor the boy was holding, and now Connie began to hear the music. It was the same program that was playing inside the house.

"Bobby King?" she said.

"I listen to him all the time. I think he's great."

"He's kind of great," Connie said reluctantly.

"Listen, that guy's *great*. He knows where the action is."

Connie blushed a little, because the glasses made it impossible for her to see just what this boy was looking at. She couldn't decide if she liked him or if he was just a jerk, and so she dawdled in the doorway and wouldn't come down or go back inside. She said, "What's all that stuff painted on your car?"

"Can'tcha read it?" He opened the door very carefully, as if he was afraid it might fall off. He slid out just as carefully, planting his feet firmly on the ground, the tiny metallic world in his glasses slowing down like gelatine hardening and in the midst of it Connie's bright green blouse. "This here is my name, to begin with," he said. ARNOLD FRIEND was written in tar-like black letters on the side, with a drawing of a round grinning face that reminded Connie of a pumpkin, except it wore sunglasses. "I wanta introduce myself, I'm Arnold Friend and that's my real name and I'm gonna be your friend, honey, and inside the car's Ellie Oscar, he's kinda shy." Ellie brought his transistor up to his shoulder and balanced it there. "Now these numbers are a secret code, honey," Arnold Friend explained. He read off the numbers 33, 19, 17 and raised his eyebrows at her to see what she thought of that, but she didn't think much of it. The left rear fender had been smashed and around it was written on the gleaming gold background: DONE BY CRAZY WOMAN DRIVER. Connie had to laugh at that. Arnold Friend was pleased at her laughter and looked up at her. "Around the other side's a lot more—you wanta come and see them?"

"No."

"Why not?"

"Why should I?"

"Don'tcha wanta see what's on the car? Don'tcha wanta go for a ride?"

"I don't know."

"Why not?"

"I got things to do."

"Like what?"

"Things."

He laughed as if she had said something funny. He slapped his thighs. He was standing in a strange way, leaning back against the car as if he were balancing himself. He wasn't tall, only an inch or so taller than she would be if she came down to him. Connie liked the way he was dressed, which was the way all of them dressed: tight faded jeans stuffed into black, scuffed boots, a belt that pulled his waist in and showed how lean he was, and a white pullover shirt that was a little soiled and showed the hard small muscles of his arms and shoulders. He looked as if he probably did hard work, lifting and carrying things. Even his neck looked muscular. And his face was a familiar face, somehow: the jaw and chin and cheeks slightly darkened, because he hadn't shaved for a day or two, and the nose long and hawk-like, sniffing as if she were a treat he was going to gobble up and it was all a joke.

"Connie, you ain't telling the truth. This is your day set aside for a ride with me and you know it," he said, still laughing. The way he straightened and recovered from his fit of laughing showed that it had been all fake.

"How do you know what my name is?" she said suspiciously.

"It's Connie."

"Maybe and maybe not."

"I know my Connie," he said, wagging his finger. Now she remembered him even better, back at the restaurant, and her cheeks warmed at the thought of how she sucked in her breath just at the moment she passed him—how she must have looked to him. And he had remembered her. "Ellie and I come out here especially for you," he said. "Ellie can sit in back. How about it?"

"Where?"

"Where what?"

"Where're we going?"

He looked at her. He took off the sunglasses and she saw how pale the skin around his eyes was, like holes that were not in shadow but instead in light. His eyes were like chips of broken glass that catch the light in an amiable way. He smiled. It was as if the idea of going for a ride somewhere, to some place, was a new idea to him.

"Just for a ride, Connie sweetheart."

"I never said my name was Connie," she said.

"But I know what it is. I know your name and all about you, lots of things," Arnold Friend said. He had not moved yet but stood still leaning back against the side of his jalopy. "I took a special interest in you, such a pretty girl, and found out all about you like I know your parents and sister are gone somewheres and I know where and how long they're going to be gone, and I know who you were with last night, and your best friend's name is Betty. Right?"

He spoke in a simple lilting voice, exactly as if he were reciting the words to a song. His smile assured her that everything was fine. In the car Ellie turned up the volume on his radio and did not bother to look around at them.

"Ellie can sit in the back seat," Arnold Friend said. He indicated his friend with a casual jerk of his chin, as if Ellie did not count and she could not bother with him.

"How'd you find out all that stuff?" Connie said.

"Listen: Betty Schultz and Tony Fitch and Jimmy Pettinger and Nancy Pettinger," he said, in a chant. "Raymond Stanley and Bob Hutter—"

"Do you know all those kids?"

"I know everybody."

"Look, you're kidding. You're not from around here."

"Sure."

"But—how come we never saw you before?"

"Sure you saw me before," he said. He looked down at his boots, as if he were a little offended. "You just don't remember."

"I guess I'd remember you," Connie said.

"Yeah?" He looked up at this, beaming. He was pleased. He began to mark time with the music from Ellie's radio, tapping his fists lightly together. Connie looked away from his smile to the car, which was painted so bright it almost hurt her eyes to look at it. She looked at that name, ARNOLD FRIEND. And up at the front fender was an expression that was familiar—MAN THE FLYING SAUCERS. It was an expression kids had used the year before, but didn't use this year. She looked at it for a while as if the words meant something to her that she did not yet know.

"What're you thinking about? Huh?" Arnold Friend demanded. "Not worried about your hair blowing around in the car, are you?"

"No."

"Think I maybe can't drive good?"

"How do I know?"

"You're a hard girl to handle. How come?" he said. "Don't you know I'm your friend? Didn't you see me put my sign in the air when you walked by?"

"What sign?"

"My sign." And he drew an X in the air, leaning out toward her. They were maybe ten feet apart. After his hand fell back to his side the X was still in the air, almost visible. Connie let the screen door close and stood perfectly still inside it, listening to the music from her radio and the boy's blend together. She stared at Arnold Friend. He stood there so stiffly relaxed, pretending to be relaxed, with one hand idly on the door handle as if he were keeping himself up that way and had no intention of ever moving again. She recognized most things about him, the tight jeans that showed his thighs and buttocks and the greasy leather boots and the tight shirt, and even that slippery friendly smile of his, that sleepy dreamy smile that all the boys used to get across ideas they didn't want to put into words. She recognized all this and also the singsong way he talked, slightly mocking, kidding, but serious and a little melancholy, and she recognized the way he tapped one fist against the other in homage to the perpetual music behind him. But all these things did not come together.

She said suddenly, "Hey, how old are you?"

His smile faded. She could see then that he wasn't a kid, he was much older—thirty, maybe more. At this knowledge her heart began to pound faster.

"That's a crazy thing to ask. Can'tcha see I'm your own age?"

"Like hell you are."

"Or maybe a coupla years older, I'm eighteen."

"Eighteen?" she said doubtfully.

He grinned to reassure her and lines appeared at the corners of his mouth. His teeth were big and white. He grinned so broadly his eyes became slits and she saw how thick the lashes were, thick and black as if painted with a black tar-like material. Then he seemed to become embarrassed, abruptly, and looked over his shoulder at Ellie. "*Him*, he's crazy," he said. "Ain't he a riot, he's a nut, a real character." Ellie was still listening to the music. His sunglasses told nothing about what he was thinking. He wore a bright orange shirt unbuttoned halfway to show his chest, which was a pale, bluish chest and not muscular like Arnold Friend's. His shirt collar was turned up all around and the very tips of the collar pointed out past his chin as if they were protecting him. He was pressing the transistor radio up against his ear and sat there in a kind of daze, right in the sun.

"He's kinda strange," Connie said.

"Hey, she says you're kinda strange! Kinda strange!" Arnold Friend cried. He pounded on the car to get Ellie's attention. Ellie turned for the first time and Connie saw with shock that he wasn't a kid either—he had a fair, hairless face, cheeks reddened slightly as if the veins grew too close to the surface of his skin, the face of a forty-year-old baby. Connie felt a wave of dizziness rise in her at this sight and she stared at him as if waiting for something to change the shock of the moment, make it all right again. Ellie's lips kept shaping words, mumbling along with the words blasting his ear.

"Maybe you two better go away," Connie said faintly.

"What? How come?" Arnold Friend cried. "We come out here to take you for a ride. It's Sunday." He had the voice of the man on the radio now. It was the same voice, Connie thought. "Don'tcha know it's Sunday all day and honey, no matter who you were with last night today you're with Arnold Friend and don't you forget it!— Maybe you better step out here," he said, and this last was in a different voice. It was a little flatter, as if the heat was finally getting to him.

"No. I got things to do."

"Hey."

"You two better leave."

"We ain't leaving until you come with us."

"Like hell I am—"

"Connie, don't fool around with me. I mean—I mean, don't fool *around*," he said, shaking his head. He laughed incredulously. He placed his sunglasses on top of his head, carefully, as if he were indeed wearing a wig, and brought the stems down behind his ears. Connie stared at him, another wave of dizziness and fear rising in her so that for a moment he wasn't even in focus but was just a blur, standing there against his gold car, and she had the idea that he had driven up the driveway all right but had come from nowhere before that and belonged nowhere and that everything about him and even the music that was so familiar to her was only half real.

"If my father comes and sees you—"

"He ain't coming. He's at a barbecue."

"How do you know that?"

"Aunt Tillie's. Right now they're—uh—they're drinking. Sitting around," he said vaguely, squinting as if he were staring all the way to town and over to Aunt Tillie's back yard. Then the vision seemed to clear and he nodded energetically. "Yeah. Sitting around. There's your sister in a blue dress, huh? And high heels, the poor sad bitch—nothing like you, sweetheart! And your mother's helping some fat woman with the corn, they're cleaning the corn—husking the corn—"

"What fat woman?" Connie cried.

"How do I know what fat woman. I don't know every goddamn fat woman in the world!" Arnold Friend laughed.

"Oh, that's Mrs. Hornby . . . Who invited her?" Connie said. She felt a little light-headed. Her breath was coming quickly.

"She's too fat. I don't like them fat. I like them the way you are, honey," he said, smiling sleepily at her. They stared at each other for a while, through the screen door. He said softly, "Now what you're going to do is this: you're going to come out that door. You're going to sit up front with me and Ellie's going to sit in the back, the hell with Ellie, right? This isn't Ellie's date. You're my date. I'm your lover, honey."

"What? You're crazy—"

"Yes, I'm your lover. You don't know what that is but you will," he said. "I know that too. I know all about you. But look: it's real nice and you couldn't ask for nobody better than me, or more polite. I always keep my word. I'll tell you how it is, I'm always nice at first, the first time. I'll hold you so tight you won't think you have to try to get away or pretend anything because you'll know you can't. And I'll come inside you where it's all secret and you'll give in to me and you'll love me—"

"Shut up! You're crazy!" Connie said. She backed away from the door. She put her hands against her ears as if she'd heard something terrible, something not meant for her. "People don't talk like that, you're crazy," she muttered. Her heart was almost too big now for her chest and its pumping made sweat break out all over her. She looked out to see Arnold Friend pause and then take a step toward the porch lurching. He almost fell. But, like a clever drunken man, he managed to catch his balance. He wobbled in his high boots and grabbed hold of one of the porch posts.

"Honey?" he said. "You still listening?"

"Get the hell out of here!"

"Be nice, honey. Listen."

"I'm going to call the police—"

He wobbled again and out of the side of his mouth came a fast spat curse, an aside not meant for her to hear. But even this "Christ!" sounded forced. Then he began to smile again. She watched this smile come, awkward as if he were smiling from inside a mask. His whole face was a mask, she thought wildly, tanned down onto his throat but then running out as if he had plastered makeup on his face but had forgotten about his throat.

"Honey—? Listen, here's how it is. I always tell the truth and I promise you this: I ain't coming in that house after you."

"You better not! I'm going to call the police if you—if you don't—"

"Honey," he said, talking right through her voice, "honey, I'm not coming in there but you are coming out here. You know why?"

She was panting. The kitchen looked like a place she had never seen before, some room she had run inside but which wasn't good enough, wasn't going to help her. The kitchen window had never had a curtain, after three years, and there were dishes in the sink for her to do—probably—and if you ran your hand across the table you'd probably feel something sticky there.

"You listening, honey? Hey?"

"—going to call the police—"

"Soon as you touch the phone I don't need to keep my promise and can come inside. You won't want that."

She rushed forward and tried to lock the door. Her fingers were shaking. "But why lock it," Arnold Friend said gently, talking right into her face. "It's just a screen door. It's just nothing." One of his boots was at a strange angle, as if his foot wasn't in it. It pointed out to the left, bent at the ankle. "I mean, anybody can break through a screen door and glass and wood and iron or anything else if he needs to, anybody at all and specially Arnold Friend. If the place got lit up with a fire, honey, you'd come runnin' out into my arms, right into my arms an' safe at home—like you knew I was your lover and'd stopped fooling around, I don't mind a nice shy girl but I don't like no fooling around." Part of those words were spoken with a slight rhythmic lilt, and Connie somehow recognized them—the echo of a song from last year, about a girl rushing into her boy friend's arms and coming home again—

Connie stood barefoot on the linoleum floor, staring at him. "What do you want?" she whispered.

"I want you," he said.

"What?"

"Seen you that night and thought, that's the one, yes sir. I never needed to look any more."

"But my father's coming back. He's coming to get me. I had to wash my hair first—" She spoke in a dry, rapid voice, hardly raising it for him to hear.

"No, your daddy is not coming and yes, you had to wash your hair and you washed it for me. It's nice and shining and all for me. I thank you, sweetheart," he said, with a mock bow, but again he almost lost his balance. He had to bend and adjust his boots. Evidently his feet did not go all the way down; the boots must have been stuffed with something so that he would seem taller. Connie stared out at him and behind him at Ellie in the car, who seemed to be looking off toward Connie's right, into nothing. Then Ellie said, pulling the words out of the air one after another as if he were just discovering them, "You want me to pull out the phone?"

"Shut your mouth and keep it shut," Arnold Friend said, his face red from bending over or maybe from embarrassment because Connie had seen his boots. "This ain't none of your business."

"What—what are you doing? What do you want?" Connie said. "If I call the police they'll get you, they'll arrest you—"

"Promise was not to come in unless you touch that phone, and I'll keep that promise," he said. He resumed his erect position and tried to force his shoulders back. He sounded like a hero in a movie, declaring something important. He spoke too loudly and it was as if he were speaking to someone behind Connie. "I ain't made plans for coming in that house where I don't belong but just for you to come out to me, the way you should. Don't you know who I am?"

"You're crazy," she whispered. She backed away from the door but did not want to go into another part of the house, as if this would give him permission to come through the door. "What do you . . . You're crazy, you . . ."

"Huh? What're you saying, honey?"

Her eyes darted everywhere in the kitchen. She could not remember what it was, this room.

"This is how it is, honey: you come out and we'll drive away, have a nice ride. But if you don't come out we're gonna wait till your people come home and then they're all going to get it."

"You want that telephone pulled out?" Ellie said. He held the radio away from his ear and grimaced, as if without the radio the air was too much for him.

"I toldja shut up, Ellie," Arnold Friend said, "you're deaf, get a hearing aid, right? Fix yourself up. This little girl's no trouble and's gonna be nice to me, so Ellie keep to yourself, this ain't your date—right? Don't hem in on me, don't hog, don't crush, don't bird dog, don't trail me," he said in a rapid, meaningless voice, as if he were running through all the expressions he'd learned but was no longer sure which one of them was in style, then rushing on to new ones, making them up with his eyes closed. "Don't crawl under my fence, don't squeeze in my chipmunk hole, don't sniff my glue, suck my Popsicle, keep your own greasy fingers on yourself!" He shaded his eyes and peered in at Connie, who was backed against the kitchen table. "Don't mind him, honey, he's just a creep. He's a dope. Right? I'm the boy for you and like I said, you come out here nice like a lady and give me your hand, and nobody else gets hurt, I mean, your nice old bald-headed daddy and your mummy and your sister in her high heels. Because listen: why bring them in this?"

"Leave me alone," Connie whispered.

"Hey, you know that old woman down the road, the one with the chickens and stuff—you know her?"

"She's dead!"

"Dead? What? You know her?" Arnold Friend said.

"She's dead—"

"Don't you like her?"

"She's dead—she's—she isn't here anymore—"

"But don't you like her, I mean, you got something against her? Some grudge or something?" Then his voice dipped as if he were conscious of rudeness. He touched the sunglasses on top of his head as if to make sure they were still there. "Now you be a good girl."

"What are you going to do?"

"Just two things, or maybe three," Arnold Friend said. "But I promise it won't last long and you'll like me that way you get to like people you're close to. You will. It's all over for you here, so come on out. You don't want your people in any trouble, do you?"

She turned and bumped against a chair or something, hurting her leg, but she ran into the back room and picked up the telephone. Something roared in her ear, a tiny roaring, and she was so sick with fear that she could do nothing but listen to it—the telephone was clammy and very heavy and her fingers groped down to the dial but were too weak to touch it. She began to scream into the phone, into the roaring. She cried out, she cried for her mother, she felt her breath start jerking back and forth in her lungs as if it were something Arnold Friend was stabbing her with again and again with no tenderness. A noisy sorrowful wailing rose all about her and she was locked inside it the way she was locked inside this house.

After a while she could hear again. She was sitting on the floor, with her wet back against the wall.

Arnold Friend was saying from the door, "That's a good girl. Put the phone back."

She kicked the phone away from her.

"No, honey. Pick it up. Put it back right."

She picked it up and put it back. The dial tone stopped.

"That's a good girl. Now you come outside."

She was hollow with what had been fear but what was now just an emptiness. All that screaming had blasted it out of her. She sat, one leg cramped under her, and deep inside her brain was something like a pinpoint of light that kept going and would not let her relax. She thought, I'm not going to see my mother again. She thought, I'm not going to sleep in my bed again. Her bright green blouse was all wet.

Arnold Friend said, in a gentle-loud voice that was like a stage voice, "The place where you came from ain't there anymore, and where you had in mind to go is cancelled out. This place you are now—inside your daddy's house—is nothing but a cardboard box I can knock down any time. You know that and always did know it. You hear me?"

She thought, I have got to think. I have got to know what to do.

"We'll go out to a nice field, out in the country here where it smells so nice and it's sunny," Arnold Friend said. "I'll have my arms tight around you so you won't need to try to get away and I'll show you what love is like, what it does. The hell with this house! It looks solid all right," he said. He ran a fingernail down the screen and the noise did not make Connie shiver, as it would have the day before. "Now put your hand on your heart, honey. Feel that? That feels solid too but we know better. Be nice to me, be sweet like you can because what else is there for a girl like you but to be sweet and pretty and give in?—and get away before her people get back?"

She felt her pounding heart. Her hand seemed to enclose it. She thought for the first time in her life that it was nothing that was hers, that belonged to her, but just a pounding, living thing inside this body that wasn't really hers either.

"You don't want them to get hurt," Arnold Friend went on. "Now get up, honey. Get up all by yourself."

She stood.

"Now turn this way. That's right. Come over to me—Ellie, put that away, didn't I tell you? You dope. You miserable creepy dope," Arnold Friend said. His words were not angry but only part of an incantation. The incantation was kindly. "Now come out through the kitchen to me honey and let's see a smile, try it, you're a brave sweet little girl and now they're eating corn and hotdogs cooked to bursting over an outdoor fire, and they don't know one thing about you and never did and honey you're better than them because not a one of them would have done this for you."

Connie felt the linoleum under her feet; it was cool. She brushed her hair back out of her eyes. Arnold Friend let go of the post tentatively and opened his arms for her, his elbows pointing in toward each other and his wrists limp, to show that this was an embarrassed embrace and a little mocking, he didn't want to make her self-conscious.

She put out her hand against the screen. She watched herself push the door slowly open as if she were back safe somewhere in the other doorway, watching this body and this head of long hair moving out into the sunlight where Arnold Friend waited.

"My sweet little blue-eyed girl," he said in a half-sung sigh that had nothing to do with her brown eyes but was taken up just the same by the vast sunlit reaches of the land behind him and on all sides of him—so much land that Connie had never seen before and did not recognize except to know that she was going to it.

Reading as a Writer

1. How does Oates define Connie's character?

2. How would you characterize the relationship between Connie and her mother? Is it one-dimensional? Or is there something that keeps it from being flat and overly familiar?

3. How does Oates create tension in the piece? What aspects of the piece are the most suspenseful, and why?

SANDRA CISNEROS

Woman Hollering Creek

THE DAY DON SERAFIN GAVE Juan Pedro Martínez Sánchez permission to take Cleófilas Enriqueta DeLeón Hernández as his bride, across her father's threshold, over several miles of dirt road and several miles of paved, over one border and beyond to a town *en el otro lado*—on the other side—already did he divine the morning his daughter would raise her hand over her eyes, look south and dream of returning to the chores that never ended, six good-for-nothing brothers, and one old man's complaints.

He had said, after all, in the hubbub of parting: I am your father, I will never abandon you. He *had* said that, hadn't he, when he hugged and then let her go. But at the moment Cleófilas was busy looking for Chela, her maid of honor, to fulfill their bouquet conspiracy. She would not remember her father's parting words until later. *I am your father, I will never abandon you.*

Only now as a mother did she remember. Now, when she and Juan Pedrito sat by the creek's edge. How when a man and a woman love each other, sometimes that love sours. But a parent's love for a child, a child's for its parents, is another thing entirely.

This is what Cleófilas thought evenings when Juan Pedro did not come home, and she lay on her side of the bed listening to the hollow roar of the interstate, a distant dog barking, the pecan trees rustling like ladies in stiff petticoats—*shh-shh-shh, shh-shh-shh*—soothing her to sleep.

In the town where she grew up, there isn't very much to do except accompany the aunts and godmothers to the house of one or the other to play cards. Or walk to the cinema to see this week's film again, speckled and with one hair quivering annoyingly on the screen. Or to the center of town to order a milk shake that will appear in a day and a half as a pimple on her backside. Or to the girlfriend's house to watch the latest *telenovela* episode and try to copy the way the women comb their hair, wear their makeup.

But what Cleófilas has been waiting for, has been whispering and sighing and giggling for, has been anticipating since she was old enough to lean against the window displays of gauze and butterflies and lace, is passion. Not the kind on the cover of the

¡Alarma! magazines, mind you, where the lover is photographed with the bloody fork she used to salvage her good name. But passion in its purest crystalline essence. The kind the books and songs and *telenovelas* describe when one finds, finally, the great love of one's life, and does whatever one can, must do, at whatever the cost.

Tú o Nadie. "You or No One." The title of the current favorite *telenovela*. The beautiful Lucía Méndez having to put up with all kinds of hardships of the heart, separation and betrayal, and loving, always loving no matter what, because *that* is the most important thing, and did you see Lucía Méndez on the Bayer aspirin commercials—wasn't she lovely? Does she dye her hair do you think? Cleófilas is going to go to the *farmacía* and buy a hair rinse; her girlfriend Chela will apply it—it's not that difficult at all.

Because you didn't watch last night's episode when Lucía confessed she loved him more than anyone in her life. In her life! And she sings the song "You or No One" in the beginning and end of the show. *Tú o Nadie.* Somehow one ought to live one's life like that, don't you think? You or no one. Because to suffer for love is good. The pain all sweet somehow. In the end.

Seguín. She had liked the sound of it. Far away and lovely. Not like *Monclova Coahuia.* Ugly.

Seguín, Tejas. A nice sterling ring to it. The tinkle of money. She would get to wear outfits like the women on the *tele*, like Lucía Méndez. And have a lovely house, and wouldn't Chela be jealous.

And yes, they will drive all the way to Laredo to get her wedding dress. That's what they say. Because Juan Pedro wants to get married right away, without a long engagement since he can't take off too much time from work. He has a very important position in Seguin with, with . . . a beer company, I think. Or was it tires? Yes, he has to be back. So they will get married in the spring when he can take off work, and then they will drive off in his new pickup—did you see it?—to their new home in Seguin. Well, not exactly new, but they're going to repaint the house. You know newlyweds. New paint and new furniture. Why not? He can afford it. And later on add maybe a room or two for the children. May they be blessed with many.

Well, you'll see. Cleófilas has always been so good with her sewing machine. A little *rrr, rrr, rrr* of the machine and *¡zas!* Miracles. She's always been so clever, that girl. Poor thing. And without even a mama to advise her on things like her wedding night. Well, may God help her. What with a father with a head like a burro, and those six clumsy brothers. Well, what do you think! Yes, I'm going to the wedding. Of course! The dress I want to wear just needs to be altered a teensy bit to bring it up to date. See, I saw a new style last night that I thought would suit me. Did you watch last night's episode of *The Rich Also Cry*? Well, did you notice the dress the mother was wearing?

La Gritona. Such a funny name for such a lovely *arroyo*. But that's what they called the creek that ran behind the house. Though no one could say whether the woman had hollered from anger or pain. The natives only knew the *arroyo* one crossed on the way to San Antonio, and then once again on the way back, was called Woman Hollering, a name no one from these parts questioned, little less understood. *Pues, allá de los indios, quién sabe*—who knows, the townspeople shrugged, because it was of no concern to their lives how this trickle of water received its curious name.

"What do you want to know for?" Trini the laundromat attendant asked in the same gruff Spanish she always used whenever she gave Cleófilas change or yelled at her for something. First for putting too much soap in the machines. Later, for sitting on a washer. And still later, after Juan Pedrito was born, for not understanding that in this country you cannot let your baby walk around with no diaper and his pee-pee hanging out, it wasn't nice, *entiendes? Pues.*

How could Cleófilas explain to a woman like this why the name Woman Hollering fascinated her. Well, there was no sense talking to Trini.

On the other hand there were the neighbor ladies, one on either side of the house they rented near the *arroyo*. The woman Soledad on the left, the woman Dolores on the right.

The neighbor lady Soledad liked to call herself a widow, though how she came to be one was a mystery. Her husband had either died, or run away with an ice-house floozie, or simply gone out for cigarettes one afternoon and never came back. It was hard to say which since Soledad, as a rule, didn't mention him.

In the other house lived *la señora* Dolores, kind and very sweet, but her house smelled too much of incense and candles from the altars that burned continuously in memory of two sons who had died in the last war and one husband who had died shortly after from grief. The neighbor lady Dolores divided her time between the memory of these men and her garden, famous for its sunflowers—so tall they had to be supported with broom handles and old boards; red red cockscombs, fringed and bleeding a thick menstrual color; and, especially, roses whose sad scent reminded Cleófilas of the dead. Each Sunday *la señora* Dolores clipped the most beautiful of these flowers and arranged them on three modest headstones at the Sequin cemetery.

The neighbor ladies, Soledad, Dolores, they might've known once the name of the *arroyo* before it turned English but they did not know now. They were too busy remembering the men who had left through either choice or circumstance and would never come back.

Pain or rage, Cleófilas wondered when she drove over the bridge the first time as a newlywed and Juan Pedro had pointed it out. *La Gritona,* he had said, and she had laughed. Such a funny name for a creek so pretty and full of happily ever after.

The first time she had been so surprised she didn't cry out or try to defend herself. She had always said she would strike back if a man, any man, were to strike her.

But when the moment came, and he slapped her once, and then again, and again, until the lip split and bled an orchid of blood, she didn't fight back, she didn't break into tears, she didn't run away as she imagined she might when she saw such things in the *telenovelas.*

In her own home her parents had never raised a hand to each other or to their children. Although she admitted she may have been brought up a little leniently as an only daughter—*la consentida,* the princess—there were some things she would never tolerate. Ever.

Instead, when it happened the first time, when they were barely man and wife, she had been so stunned, it left her speechless, motionless, numb. She had done nothing but to reach up to the heat on her mouth and stare at the blood on her hand as if even then she didn't understand.

She could think of nothing to say, said nothing. Just stroked the dark curls of the man who wept and would weep like a child, his tears of repentance and shame, this time and each.

The men at the ice house. From what she can tell, from the times during her first year when still a newlywed she is invited and accompanies her husband, sits mute beside their conversation, waits and sips a beer until it grows warm, twists a paper napkin into a knot, then another into a fan, one into a rose, nods her head, smiles, yawns, politely grins, laughs at the appropriate moments, leans against her husband's sleeve, tugs at his elbow, and finally becomes good at predicting where the talk will lead, from this Cleófilas concludes each is nightly trying to find the truth lying at the bottom of the bottle like a gold doubloon on the sea floor.

They want to tell each other what they want to tell themselves. But what is bumping like a helium balloon at the ceiling of the brain never finds its way out. It bubbles and rises, it gurgles in the throat, it rolls across the surface of the tongue, and erupts from the lips—a belch.

If they are lucky, there are tears at the end of the long night. At any given moment, the fists try to speak. They are dogs chasing their own tails before lying down to sleep, trying to find a way, a route, an out, and—finally—get some peace.

In the morning sometimes before he opens his eyes. Or after they have finished loving. Or at times when he is simply across from her at the table putting pieces of food into his mouth and chewing. Cleófilas thinks, This is the man I have waited my whole life for.

Not that he isn't a good man. She has to remind herself why she loves him when she changes the baby's Pampers, or when she mops the bathroom floor, or tries to make the curtains for the doorways without doors, or whiten the linen. Or wonder a little when he kicks the refrigerator and says he hates this shitty house and is going out where he won't be bothered with the baby's howling and her suspicious questions, and her requests to fix this and this and this because if she had any brains in her head she'd realize he's been up before the rooster earning his living to pay for the food in her belly and the roof over her head and would have to wake up again early the next day so why can't you just leave me in peace, woman.

He is not very tall, no, and he doesn't look like the men on the *telenovelas*. His face still scarred from acne. And he has a bit of a belly from all the beer he drinks. Well, he's always been husky.

This man who farts and belches and snores as well as laughs and kisses and holds her. Somehow this husband whose whiskers she finds each morning in the sink, whose shoes she must air each evening on the porch, this husband who cuts his fingernails in public, laughs loudly, curses like a man, and demands each course of din-

ner be served on a separate plate like at his mother's, as soon as he gets home, on time
or late, and who doesn't care at all for music or *telenovelas* or romance or roses or the
moon floating pearly over the *arroyo*, or through the bedroom window for that matter, shut the blinds and go back to sleep, this man, this father, this rival, this keeper,
this lord, this master, this husband till kingdom come.

A doubt. Slender as a hair. A washed cup set back on the shelf wrong-side-up. Her
lipstick, and body talc, and hairbrush all arranged in the bathroom a different way.

No. Her imagination. The house the same as always. Nothing.

Coming home from the hospital with her new son, her husband. Something com-
forting in discovering her house slippers beneath the bed, the faded housecoat where
she left it on the bathroom hook. Her pillow. Their bed.

Sweet sweet homecoming. Sweet as the scent of face powder in the air, jasmine,
sticky liquor.

Smudged fingerprint on the door. Crushed cigarette in a glass. Wrinkle in the
brain crumpling to a crease.

Sometimes she thinks of her father's house. But how could she go back there? What a
disgrace. What would the neighbors say? Coming home like that with one baby on
her hip and one in the oven. Where's your husband?

The town of gossips. The town of dust and despair. Which she has traded from this
town of gossips. This town of dust, despair. Houses farther apart perhaps, though no
more privacy because of it. No leafy *zócalo* on the center of the town, though the
murmur of talk is clear enough all the same. No huddled whispering on the church
steps each Sunday. Because here the whispering begins at sunset at the ice house
instead.

This town with its silly pride for a bronze pecan the size of a baby carriage in front
of the city hall. TV repair shop, drugstore, hardware, dry cleaners, chiropractor's,
liquor store, bail bonds, empty storefront, and nothing, nothing, nothing of interest.
Nothing one could walk to, at any rate. Because the towns here are built so that you
have to depend on husbands. Or you stay home. Or you drive. If you're rich enough
to own, allowed to drive, your own car.

There is no place to go. Unless one counts the neighbor ladies. Soledad on one side,
Dolores on the other. Or the creek.

Don't go out there after dark, *mi'jita*. Stay near the house. *No es bueno para la salud.*
Mala suerte. Bad Luck. *Mal aire.* You'll get sick and the baby too!

You'll catch a fright wandering about in the dark, and then you'll see how right we
were.

The stream sometimes only a muddly puddle in the summer, though now in the
springtime, because of the rains, a good-size alive thing, a thing with a voice all its
own, all day and all night calling in its high, silver voice. Is it La Llorona, the weeping
woman? La Llorona, who drowned her own children. Perhaps La Llorona is the one
they named the creek after, she thinks, remembering all the stories she learned as a
child.

La Llorona calling to her. She is sure of it. Cleófilas sets the baby's Donald Duck blanket on the grass. Listens. The day sky turning to night. The baby pulling up fist-fuls of grass and laughing. La Llorona. Wonders if something as quiet as this drives a woman to the darkness under the trees.

What she needs is . . . and made a gesture as if to yank a woman's buttocks to his groin. Maximiliano, the foul-smelling fool from across the road, said this and set the men laughing, but Cleófilas just muttered, *Grosera,* and went on washing dishes.

She knew he said it not because it was true, but more because it was he who needed to sleep with a woman, instead of drinking each night at the ice house and stumbling home alone.

Maximiliano who was said to have killed his wife in an ice-house brawl when she came at him with a mop. I had to shoot, he had said—she was armed.

Their laughter outside the kitchen window. Her husband's, his friends'. Manolo, Beto, Efraín, el Perico. Maximiliano.

Was Cleófilas just exaggerating as her husband always said? It seemed the news-papers were full of such stories. This woman found on the side of the interstate. This one pushed from a moving car. This one's cadaver, this one unconscious, this one beaten blue. Her ex-husband, her husband, her lover, her father, her brother, her uncle, her friend, her co-worker. Always. The same grisly news in the pages of the dailies. She dunked a glass under the soapy water for a moment—shivered.

He had thrown a book. Hers. From across the room. A hot welt across the cheek. She could forgive that. But what stung more was the fact it was *her* book, a love story by Corín Tellado, what she loved most now that she lived in the U.S., without a televi-sion set, without the *telenovelas.*

Except now and again when her husband was away and she could manage it, the few episodes glimpsed at the neighbor lady Soledad's house because Dolores didn't care for that sort of thing, though Soledad was often kind enough to retell what had happened on what episode of *María de Nadie,* the poor Argentine country girl who had the ill fortune of falling in love with the beautiful son of the Arrocha family, the very family she worked for, whose roof she slept under and whose floors she vacu-umed, while in that same house, with the dust brooms and floor cleaners as wit-nesses, the square-jawed Juan Carlos Arrocha had uttered words of love, I love you, María, listen to me, *mi querida,* but it was she who had to say No, no, we are not of the same class, and remind him it was not his place nor hers to fall in love, while all the while her heart was breaking, can you imagine.

Cleófilas thought her life would have to be like that, like a *telenovela,* only now the episodes got sadder and sadder. And there were no commercials in between for comic relief. And no happy ending in sight. She thought this when she sat with the baby out by the creek behind the house. Cleófilas de . . . ? But somehow she would have to change her name to Topazio, or Yesenia, Cristal, Adriana, Stefania, Andrea, something more poetic than Cleófilas. Everything happened to women with names like jewels. But what happened to a Cleófilas? Nothing. But a crack in the face.

Because the doctor has said so. She has to go. To make sure the new baby is all right, so there won't be any problems when he's born, and the appointment card says next Tuesday. Could he please take her. And that's all.

No, she won't mention it. She promises. If the doctor asks she can say she fell down the front steps or slipped when she was out in the backyard, slipped out back, she could tell him that. She had to go back next Tuesday, Juan Pedro, please, for the new baby. For their child.

She could write to her father and ask maybe for money, just a loan, for the new baby's medical expenses. Well then if he'd rather she didn't. All right, she won't. Please don't anymore. Please don't. She knows it's difficult saving money with all the bills they have, but how else are they going to get out of debt with the truck payments? And after the rent and the food and the electricity and the gas and the water and the who-knows-what, well, there's hardly anything left. But please, at least for the doctor visit. She won't ask for anything else. She has to. Why is she so anxious? Because.

Because she is going to make sure the baby is not turned around backward this time to split her down the center. Yes. Next Tuesday at five-thirty. I'll have Juan Pedrito dressed and ready. But those are the only shoes he has. I'll polish them, and we'll be ready. As soon as you come from work. We won't make you ashamed.

Felice? It's me, Graciela.

No, I can't talk louder. I'm at work.

Look, I need kind of a favor. There's a patient, a lady here who's got a problem.

Well, wait a minute. Are you listening to me or what?

I can't talk real loud 'cause her husband's in the next room.

Well, would you just listen?

I was going to do this sonogram on her—she's pregnant, right?—and she just starts crying on me. *Híjole*, Felice! This poor lady's got black-and-blue marks all over. I'm not kidding.

From her husband. Who else? Another one of those brides from across the border. And her family's all in Mexico.

Shit. You think they're going to help her? Give me a break. This lady doesn't even speak English. She hasn't been allowed to call home or write or nothing. That's why I'm calling you.

She needs a ride.

Not to Mexico, you goof. Just to the Greyhound. In San Anto.

No, just a ride. She's got her own money. All you'd have to do is drop her off in San Antonio on your way home. Come on, Felice. Please? If we don't help her, who will? I'd drive her myself, but she needs to be on that bus before her husband gets home from work. What do you say?

I don't know. Wait.

Right away, tomorrow even.

Well, if tomorrow's no good for you . . .

It's a date, Felice, Thursday. At the Cash N Carry off I-10. Noon. She'll be ready.

Oh, and her name's Cleófilas.

I don't know. One of those Mexican saints, I guess. A martyr or something. Cleófilas. C-L-E-O-F-I-L-A-S. Cle. O. Fi. Las. Write it down.

Thanks, Felice. When her kid's born she'll have to name her after us, right?

Yeah, you got it. A regular soap opera sometimes. *Qué vida, comadre. Bueno* buy.

All morning that flutter of half-fear, half-doubt. At any moment Juan Pedro might appear in the doorway. On the street. At the Cash N Carry. Like in the dreams she dreamed.

There was that to think about, yes, until the woman in the pickup drove up. Then there wasn't time to think about anything but the pickup pointed toward San Antonio. Put your bags in the back and get in.

But when they drove across the *arroyo,* the driver opened her mouth and let out a yell as loud as any mariachi. Which startled not only Cleófilas, but Juan Pedrito as well.

Pues, look how cute. I scared you two, right? Sorry. Should've warned you. Every time I cross that bridge I do that. Because of the name, you know. Woman Hollering. *Pues,* I holler. She said this in a Spanish pocked with English and laughed. Did you ever notice, Felice continued, how nothing around here is named after a woman? Really. Unless she's the Virgin. I guess you're only famous if you're a virgin. She was laughing again.

That's why I like the name of that *arroyo.* Makes you want to holler like Tarzan, right?

Everything about this woman, this Felice, amazed Cleófilas. The fact that she drove a pickup. A pickup, mind you, but when Cleófilas asked if it was her husband's, she said she didn't have a husband. The pickup was hers. She herself had chosen it. She herself was paying for it.

I used to have a Pontiac Sunbird. But those cars are for *viejas.* Pussy cars. Now this here is a *real* car.

What kind of talk was that coming from a woman? Cleófilas thought. But then again, Felice was like no woman she'd ever met. Can you imagine, when we crossed the *arroyo* she just started yelling like a crazy, she would say later to her father and brothers. Just like that. Who would've thought?

Who would've? Pain or rage, perhaps, but not a hoot like the one Felice had just let go. Makes you want to holler like Tarzan, Felice had said.

Then Felice began laughing again, but it wasn't Felice laughing. It was gurgling out of her own throat, a long ribbon of laughter, like water.

Reading as a Writer

1. What methods or techniques does Cisneros use to make the "ordinary" aspects of the protagonist's life—TV, local places, even words—evocative and fresh?

2. How does Cisneros avoid melodrama in her portrayal of the protagonist's situation?

3. What is the central conflict in the story? What does the protagonist want? How is the conflict resolved?

CHAPTER THREE

Details, Details
The Basic Building Blocks

Details are the lifeblood of good writing—and not just any details, but *concrete* details, or details that are grounded in the five senses. By first and foremost relying on what we see, feel, hear, touch, and taste when we render our thoughts and emotions on the page, we are ensuring that we immerse our readers in a concrete sensory world of our own making.

We've all heard the truism that "you can't see the forest for the trees" as a way of warning against paying too much attention to detail—the implication being that you can get lost in the particulars and not see the big picture. Well, in riveting fiction the opposite is true: you won't see the forest unless you see *this* tree and *that* tree and *that* tree—unless you focus on the details with great specificity.

Of course, you have to be selective. That's what being a writer is all about: making choices. You can't show the entire video of your summer vacation; you have to be discriminating—that is, if you want anyone to be interested. Choosing your trees and rendering them precisely are the heart of all good writing.

And among other things, attention to details keeps us honest. As Virginia Woolf wrote, "Let a man get up and say, 'Behold, this is the truth,' and instantly I perceive a sandy cat filching a piece of fish in the background. Look, you have forgotten the cat, I say."

In this chapter we first define what an image is and discover the ways to build effective imagery in our creative work. Then we practice our control of details with exercises designed to address the need for beginning writers to think with specificity. At the end of the chapter, you'll find some masterpieces of fiction to read and learn from.

On Thinking Small

In Chapter 2, we heard about triggering and real subjects: how you often start out in one place when writing only to end up in another place—and only after you've arrived being able (perhaps) to discover what you're really writing about.

Richard Hugo also stresses the need to "think small":

> Often, if the triggering subject is too big (love, death, faith) rather than localized and finite, the mind tends to shrink. Sir Alexander Fleming observed some mold, and a few years later we had a cure for gonorrhea. But what if the British government had told him to find a cure for gonorrhea? He might have worried so much he would not have noticed the mold. Think small. If you have a big mind, that will show itself. If you can't think small, try philosophy or social criticism. —RICHARD HUGO, *The Triggering Town*

In this chapter we advocate starting off your writing career based on smallness and specificity—eschewing grand ideas in favor of thinking particularly. As Flannery O'Connor put it:

> The fact is that the materials of the fiction writer are the humblest. Fiction is about everything human and we are made out of dust, and if you scorn getting yourself dusty, then you shouldn't try to write fiction. It's not a grand enough job for you. —FLANNERY O'CONNOR, *Mystery and Manners*

What both these writers are talking about is the difference between abstraction and specificity, the difference between generalizations and attention to detail. "We are made out of dust" is O'Connor's way of saying that we belong to this sensory world, with its noise and dirt and various tastes and textures; and it's in this sensory world that we have to spend most of our time as writers.

First, some definitions:

SPECIFIC: Limiting or limited. Precise. Peculiar to, or characteristic of, something. Exclusive or special.

CONCRETE: Characterized by things or events that can be perceived by the senses. Real. Actual. Referring to a particular. Specific, not general or abstract. The reproduction, using descriptions embodying the five senses, of a place, person, or thing.

ABSTRACT: Dissociated from any specific instance. Expressing a quality apart from an object. The reverse of a concrete detail: something that is *not* about a particular person, place, or object.

GENERAL: Emphasizing the general character rather than the specific details of something. Vague or indefinite.

One of the problems beginning writers have is that they start out with the abstract, or the general. They want to write about love. Or family life. Or war. Or divorce. They start above the fray, rather than in it. To paraphrase O'Connor, they want to forget that we are made of dust. And things, as a result, never get off the ground.

Let's look at some examples of the difference between the general/abstract and the specific:

GENERAL/ABSTRACT: *She was sad.*

SPECIFIC: *She sat in her favorite rocking chair in her room, knitting a gray scarf and weeping into the unfinished woolen stitches.*

GENERAL/ABSTRACT: *My father hated noise.*
SPECIFIC: *The neighbors became accustomed to my father throwing open the windows of our living room and dumping a bucket of cold water on neighborhood children who were playing too loudly near the front porch.*

GENERAL/ABSTRACT: *She had a drinking problem.*
SPECIFIC: *Three times a week she opened a bottle of white wine, not even chilled, and drank it from a coffee cup until it was dry. She brought the cup into the bathroom and would continue sipping even as she brushed her teeth.*

Notice how, in each of these examples, we've moved from something indefinite to something definite; from something that we can understand in theory, to something we can actually *see* and, one hopes, experience.

Defining "Image" within a Literary Context

When you hear the word "image" you probably think of something visual. *She was the image of her mother.* (She looked just like her mother.) Yet *Merriam-Webster's Collegiate Dictionary* defines "image" as "a reproduction or imitation of the form of a person or thing; *especially* [emphasis mine] an imitation in solid form."

In other words, an image involves more than simply the visual—it includes something in "solid form" that presumably can be touched, heard, tasted, and smelled in addition to being seen.

> Images haunt. There is a whole mythology built on this fact: Cézanne painting till his eyes bled, Wordsworth wandering the Lake Country hills in an impassioned daze. Blake describes it very well, and so did the colleague of Tu Fu who said to him, "It is like being alive twice."   —ROBERT HASS, "Images"

Let's look at some images so we can see how precisely they reproduce the person, place, or thing in question, and also how they represent something more than just the thing itself: how the person, place, or thing has accumulated *meaning* through the rendering.

> I was there when the blind went down, one of those dirty brown roller affairs, throwing a ball for a little white dog as chance would have it. I happened to look up and there it was. All over and done with, at last. I sat on for a few moments with the ball in my hand and the dog yelping and pawing at me. [*Pause.*] Moments. Her moments, my moments. [*Pause.*] The dog's moments. [*Pause.*] In the end I held it out to him and he took it in his mouth, gentle, gentle. A small, old, black hard solid rubber ball. [*Pause.*] I shall feel it, in my hand, until my dying day. [*Pause.*] I might have kept it. [*Pause.*] But I gave it to the dog. [*Pause.*] Ah, well . . .   —SAMUEL BECKETT, "Krapp's Last Tape"

In this play, we experience the moment that a man's mother dies captured in a series of concrete images: the window blind going down, the ball being held in the hand, and the dog yelping for it. The specifics of the blind, the ball, and the dog help us comprehend the reality of the mother's death—and what it means to the narrator.

In the vivid passage below, we see the room in great detail, and the imagery arouses intense emotions—we feel the narrator's longing for the days when he could actually be in this room, his yearning for the past, and what it represents to him now, in the present day.

> The space between the fireplace and the door to the kitchen is filled with shelves and a shallow cupboard. The tea cart is kept under the stairs. Then comes the door to the coat closet, the inside of which is painted a particularly beautiful shade of Chinese red, and the door to the hall. On the sliding door cabinet (we have turned the corner now and are moving toward the windows) there is a pottery lamp with a wide perforated gray paper shade and such a long thin neck that it seems to be trying to turn into a crane. Also a record player that plays only 78s and has to be wound after every record. The oil painting over the couch is of a rock quarry in Maine, and we have discovered that it changes according to the time of day and the color of the sky. It is particularly alive after a snowfall.   —WILLIAM MAXWELL, "The Thistles in Sweden"

Imagery That Works on Two Levels

The notion that imagery works on two levels is a critical one. On the one hand, you want to portray the way things *are* in the world of your story. You want to describe the small town, or the mountains, or the scene in the restaurant in the city, and you want readers to be able to experience it as deeply as if they were there themselves. On the other hand, there is no such thing as a completely objective image: just think of how things look different on a day you are blissfully happy as opposed to a day you are angry or blue.

Imagery is your way *in* to material. It's your way of reaching down into your subconscious and finding out what you really think about a person, place, thing, or event. By describing it honestly and completely, and by not leaving out anything, no matter how seemingly incongruous, you are finally *writing*. This is what writing is all about. It centers around the senses and your ability to create complex, messy images that bring a situation to life—specifically the life *you* re-create through them.

Here's a passage that succinctly lays out the role of imagery in fiction:

> Consider the following as a possible exercise in description: Describe a barn as seen by a man whose son has just been killed in a war. Do not mention the son, or war, or death. Do not mention the man who does the seeing. [. . .] If the writer works hard, and if he has the talent to be a writer, the result of his work should be a powerful and disturbing image, a faithful description of some apparently real barn but one from which the reader gets a sense of the father's emotion; though exactly what that emotion is he may not be able to pin down.
> —JOHN GARDNER, *The Art of Fiction*

A critical part of this passage comes when Gardner stresses that "no amount of intel-lectual study can determine for the writer what he will include." *No amount of intel-lectual study.* We're talking right (intuitive) brain needed here, not left (logical) brain. Gardner continues:

> And one of the things he will discover, inevitably, is that the images of death and loss that come to him are not necessarily those we might expect. The hack mind leaps instantly to images of, for instance, darkness, heaviness, decay. But those may not be at all the kinds of images that drift into the mind that has emptied itself of all but the desire to "tell the truth"; that is, to get the feeling down in concrete details.

What Gardner rather judgmentally calls the "hack mind" we might call the inexpe-rienced writer, who feels that death must necessarily have to do with "darkness, heaviness, decay." But we know from our discussion of sentimentality in Chapter 1 that more surprising images may come out of this exercise; the barn might be bathed in a glorious light, or it might be a dull mud brown under a clouded sky.

And here's a passage by Shakespeare that comments beautifully on the dual nature of images (from *Hamlet*, Act 2, Scene 2):

> HAMLET: I have of late—but wherefore I know not—lost all my mirth, forgone all custom of exercises; and indeed it goes so heavily with my disposition that this goodly frame the earth seems to me a sterile promontory; this most excellent canopy, the air, look you, this brave o'erhanging firmament, this majestical roof fretted with golden fire—why it appeareth nothing to me but a foul and pestilent congregation of vapors.

Hamlet is saying that if not for his bad mood, the world would look a completely dif-ferent place to him—the images themselves would be completely altered, even though he would be looking at the very same world.

Regarding the dual nature of images, let's look at two examples:

> The flashlight beams explored her body, causing its whiteness to gleam. Her breasts were floppy; her nipples looked shriveled. Her belly appeared inflated by gallons of water. For a moment, a beam focused on her mound of pubic hair which was overlapped by the swell of her belly, and then moved almost shyly away down her legs, and the cops all glanced at us—at you, especially—above their lights; and you hugged your blanket closer as if they might confiscate it as evidence or to use as a shroud.   —STUART DYBEK, "We Didn't"

In this passage we get a sense of the fear of sensuality that haunts the story—a fear of what sex, and desiring sex, can do to people. We're immersed in the sensory expe-rience of what is happening, and we feel the emotional undercurrents as well.

> The new boy was Quadberry. He came in, but he was meek, and when he tuned up he put his head almost on the floor, bending over trying to be inconspicuous. The girls in the band had wanted him to be handsome, but

> Quadberry refused and kept himself in such hiding among the sax section that he was neither handsome, ugly, cute or anything. What he was was pretty near invisible, except for the bell of his horn, the all but closed eyes, the Arabian nose, the brown hair with its halo of white ends, the desperate oralness, the giant reed punched into his face, and hazy Quadberry, loving the wound in a private dignified ecstasy.   —BARRY HANNAH, "Testimony of Pilot"

In this passage we get a vivid picture of the sax player that puts us right there in the scene—we can really *see* him—but the image is also imbued with a sense of the player's desperation, his obsession with his instrument, and how this estranges him from his fellow students.

Writers of popular fiction tend to do well on the concrete side of things: they bounce their characters around from New York to London and Paris and in and out of restaurants and beds and whatnot, but somehow it doesn't add up to much emotionally. At the other end of the spectrum are well-meaning beginning writers whose prose is filled with intense emotions and insightful moments of clarity, or epiphanies, but which lack the concrete to make it real. It is only when we marry the two that we get truly compelling fiction.

On Seeing the General in the Particular

The German philosopher Goethe wrote: "There is a great difference, whether the poet seeks the particular for the sake of the general, or sees the general in the particular."

What was he saying? He was talking about symbols and imagery, and he was being a bit cryptic, but let me paraphrase: there is a big difference between whether I say,

> "Living in San Francisco is a great experience, and by way of illustrating it, I'm going to tell you something that happened to me on the way to school today."

or,

> "This thing happened to me on the way to school today. I want to tell you about it. I want to tell you about it in great detail. Do you think this has something to do with living in San Francisco?"

In the first case I am trying to bolster, or prove, a generalization ("living in San Francisco is a great experience") by using a specific example. In the second case I want to see if a general picture can arise from a specific event—but the event comes first, not the generalization. It's the difference between trying to categorize things neatly and trying to observe things the way they really are.

Let's start with a statement that fits neatly within the "box":

> Living in San Francisco is a really great experience.

If we think in terms of this generalization, then we will automatically begin looking for details and experiences that fit neatly within the "box" of this general statement. When approaching writing in this way, we'll try (unconsciously, for the most part) to keep things clean, to keep things simple. If things don't fit, we'll adjust them or leave them out. We do this all the time in real life and are applauded for it: seeking examples to suit a situation, we choose examples that prove whatever point we are trying to make. We've been trained to do that. So when I think about living in San Francisco as a "great experience" I might think of afternoons spent in Golden Gate Park, delicious lunches in Chinatown, shopping expeditions along Union Street. I'm choosing details that fit a preconceived, *general* idea that I have in mind. It might make for a pretty travelogue, but it's not particularly interesting. It certainly doesn't show the teeming life of the city itself.

But what happens if I first seek the *particular*? What happens if I first come up with particular instances of what it's like to live in San Francisco without worrying about some general conclusion first?

- I went to the Gay Pride march, which attracted more than 1,000,000 people. Up and down Market Street, all you could see was an ocean of humanity, bright colors, waving signs.

- There are homeless people on the corner of California and Polk begging for food. Many of them are painfully thin, with sores on their arms and legs.

- Once I saw someone fall off a streetcar. It was in Chinatown, and he didn't seem upset by it, just picked himself up and walked off.

- My next-door neighbor, a lifetime San Francisco resident, shocked me by making a racist remark.

Suddenly, it's a lot harder to put all these particulars in a nice neat box. Things keep jumping out, refusing to be easily categorized. And messy is good, complex is good. Even if you managed to see something general in these particulars (which is something we want people to do—to see the universality in our writing), it would be a *complex* conclusion you would reach. By going from the particular to the general, and not the other way around, you ensure that you will avoid oversimplistic views, and thus sentimentality.

So, by paying attention to what is small, by thinking small, you allow a much more complex and less easily categorized picture to emerge—a messy picture. And rather than being alarmed by this, you should be gratified, because messiness and chaos are hallmarks of something that has the potential to be really interesting and worth exploring further.

All good, even great, writing must do this. If your goal is to make something *true*, that's where the things that don't make sense, don't quite add up, begin to creep in. It's only when you reinvent the experience through the particular—*this* man and *this* woman, or *this* woman and *this* woman, or *this* man and *this* man—and render the specifics and the ambiguities of that *exact* interaction, that you rise above the bane of every writer, which is to not be exact.

Not house, but *this* house: with the broken front-door lock and the tomato bushes with fruit just beginning to ripen and the lone banana peel left on the lawn by a neighborhood child.

Reflecting an apparent contradiction, beginning writing students often only say, "I want the reader to identify with the story by imagining the first car he or she ever owned, so I'm not going to describe this car in detail." No. It's one of the mysteries of writing that in order to evoke a universal reaction or emotion you must use the tools of specificity.

On Crowding Out the Reader

"What you're trying to do when you write is to crowd the reader out of his own space and occupy it with yours, in a good cause. You're trying to take over his sensibility and deliver an experience that moves from mere information," wrote the novelist Robert Stone. Below are two passages that are first written more generally, and then written tighter, smaller. See which ones crowd you most particularly out of your own interpretive space into the space prepared for you by the writer.

> "He's crude," Laura told her sister as they wandered around the place trying to find some eggs. They found some fake ones and then some real ones. The fake ones had cheap jewelry in them; the real ones had either the beginnings or endings of stupid riddles pasted onto them. They also found chocolates in the form of naked women.
>
> "He's crude," Laura told her sister as they wandered around the swimming pool, looking halfheartedly for eggs. The first they'd found was plastic and contained a cheap necklace and pendant: turned one way, Betty Boop smiled under her long lashes; turned the other way, her mouth became an "O" and her dotted dress disappeared. They found hard-boiled eggs with the beginnings of riddles on them ("How many Catholics does it take to change a light bulb?") or with the answers ("Because it was a *hung* jury.") and they found chocolates in the shape of naked women—buxom, foil-wrapped little candies nestled in the tender crocuses.   —ANTONYA NELSON, "Naked Ladies"

The servant came in, she seemed proud of what she was carrying, but it only turned out to be an underdone leg of rather tough mutton and a pile of overcooked vegetables.

Here the girl came in. She wore an air of importance derived apparently from the dish she carried, for it was covered with a great metal cover. She raised the cover with a flourish. There was a leg of mutton underneath. "Let's dine," Sara said. "I'm hungry," he added. They sat down and she took the carving-knife and made a long incision. A thin trickle of red juice ran out; it was underdone. She looked at it. Then she lifted the lids of the vegetable dishes. There was a slabbed-down mass of cabbage in one oozing green water; in the other yellow potatoes that looked hard.   —VIRGINIA WOOLF, *The Years*

You can see, in both these cases, that the second version works much better: the details are sharper, more particular, more apt to crowd you out of your own interpretive space and, instead, to draw you into a specific emotional and physical space prepared for you by the writer.

Don't Lose Any of Your Senses

An interesting exercise, after you've tried to describe something on the page, is to go through it and see what senses you have used to create the image. Chances are, you'll be depending primarily (if not completely) on the sense of sight alone. Yet imagery has to do with all five senses, not just one.

Let's look at an exercise in which we start with a visual image but then add the other four senses. See how much more satisfying and complex the image is when we are through.

> She was tall, thin, and gawky. Her hair fell straight to her waist and her feet were stuck into the oddest shoes. They looked like black boats, and her bony white ankles protruded out of them like pale masts.

Now add the other four senses—smell, touch, sound, and (a difficult one) taste:

> She was tall, thin, and gawky. Her hair smelled of violet, and her feet were stuck into the oddest shoes you've ever seen: they looked like black boats, and her bony white ankles protruded out of them like pale masts. When she walked you heard kallump *kaalumph*. Once I'd inadvertently brushed against her arm, and an electrical shock had buzzed through me, as though she were pulsing with a hidden current. When we kissed, I tasted mint toothpaste.

See how much richer the second passage is than the first one? One of the best exercises on imagery is to imagine yourself blind and to describe the objects of the world around you without the sense of vision. It makes the other senses come alive—it *forces* them to come alive.

Use and Abuse of Metaphor

If you go over the images we've looked at thus far, you might notice something: very few metaphors, or comparisons. For the most part, the passages quoted in this book thus far have largely described things as they *are* rather than what they *are like*. But metaphor, or comparison, can be a very powerful tool to use in our creative work.

Consider Chekhov, to his brother, on the subject of using metaphorical statements (which include similes):

> Evoke a moonlit night by writing that on the mill dam the glass fragments of a broken bottle flashed like a bright little star; and that the black shadow of a dog or a wolf rolled along like a ball.

Let's first define our terms. A *metaphor* is a comparison of two unlike things. A *simile* is a metaphorical statement (or a comparison of two unlike things) using *like* or *as*. The basic difference between a simile and a metaphor is that one is explicit and one is implied.

Here are some examples of similes, where the comparison is explicit:

- My love is *like* a red red rose. (Byron)
- Clouds *like* great gray brains. (Denis Johnson)
- A face *as* broad and *as* innocent *as* a cabbage. (Flannery O'Connor)
- The weather *as* cool and gray *as* wash water. (George Garrett)

In a metaphor, the comparison is implied:

- These are the dog days of summer. (Shakespeare)
- What do the sightless windows see, I wonder, when the sun throws passersby against them? (William Gass)
- . . . and Murphy can feel her shy skeleton waltzing away with him in a fit of ribbons, the bursting bouquets of a Christmas they are going to spend apart . . . (Mark Costello)

Writers use metaphorical statements (both metaphors and similes) to add extra power to a description. We're asking our readers to make a comparison in their mind that evokes a response that deepens their understanding of the person, place, or thing being described.

Look at the metaphorical statements in this poem, which first compares a bunch of tulips to an "awful baby" and then to a "dozen red lead sinkers":

> The tulips are too red in the first place, they hurt me.
> Even through the gift paper I could hear them breathe
> Lightly, through their white swaddlings, like an awful baby,
> Their redness talks to my wound, it corresponds.
> They are subtle: they seem to float, though they weigh me down,
> Upsetting me with their sudden tongues and their color,
> A dozen red lead sinkers round my neck.
> —SYLVIA PLATH, "Tulips"

A good metaphor gives us a little shock: it stretches our imagination by forcing us to see something in a new light, yet it also immediately *convinces* us that it is true.

In addition to the comparisons we've been discussing here, there are other types of metaphorical statements. *Dead metaphors* have been absorbed into the language to the point where we don't even notice them anymore. Dead metaphors enrich our language, making it more colloquial and colorful.

- He ran for office.
- She flew from one task to another.
- The car ran smoothly.
- The dog worried the bone.
- I am open to suggestions.

Clichéd similes and metaphors are on their way to being dead. Once they were good and fresh and riveting. If not, they wouldn't have lasted. But they haven't yet been completely absorbed into our language; there is the imaginative effort required to make that leap from the literal to the metaphorical, without the payoff—the surprise and delight of a fresh comparison that illuminates.

- She cackled like a hen.
- He raved like a lunatic.
- She ran as fast as the wind.
- His heart felt like it would burst.

Clichéd metaphors involving eyes are especially difficult to avoid for beginning writers—you'd be surprised how easy it is for them to creep into your prose. Again, the instinct is good: we do indeed look at people's eyes for expressions, for emotion, for finding things that might not be revealed in other ways: hard eyes, gentle eyes, steely eyes, cold eyes. But eyes aren't literally "hard" or "gentle" or "steely." Those are clichéd metaphors that we must be very careful not to allow into our pieces. If you're depending too much on eye metaphors, it's usually a sign you're taking the easy way out, trying to attribute all sorts of character traits through a character's eyes rather than focusing on other, possibly more relevant, and certainly fresher details.

Conceit is when two very unlike things are brought together in a non-intuitive comparison that requires an explanation to be understood. As an example of conceit, here's the section of the novel *Fifth Business* in which the title is explained:

> Who are you? Where do you fit into poetry and myth? Do you know? You are Fifth Business.
>
> You don't know that that is? Well, in opera in a permanent company of the kind we keep up in Europe you must have a prima donna—always a soprano, always the heroine, often a fool; and a tenor who always plays the lover to her; and then you must have a contralto, who is a rival to the soprano, or a sorceress or something; and a basso, who is the villain or the rival or whatever threatens the tenor.
>
> So far so good, but you cannot make a plot work without another man, and this is usually a baritone, and he is called in the profession Fifth Business, because he is the odd man out, the person who has no opposite of the other sex. And you must have Fifth Business because he is the one who knows the secret of the hero's birth, or comes to the assistance of the heroine when she thinks all is lost, or keeps the hermitess in her cell, or may even be the cause of somebody's death if that is part of the plot. The prima donna and the tenor, the contralto and the basso, get all the best music and do all the spectacular things, but you cannot manage the plot without Fifth Business! It is not spectacular, but it is a good line of work, I can tell you, and those who play it sometimes have a career that outlasts the golden voices.   —ROBERTSON DAVIES, *Fifth Business*

Personification is the attribution of human characteristics to non-human entities. An example of personification can be found in the story "Araby" by James Joyce, when he writes: "The houses, conscious of decent lives within them, gazed at one another with brown imperturbable faces."

When Should You Use Metaphor?

Some beginning writers feel that their imagery isn't truly compelling without metaphor. But the reverse is often true. Gratuitous use of metaphors or similes can clutter up a piece of writing—especially if the metaphors are clichéd or otherwise overly familiar.

That's because sometimes beginning writers are in such a hurry to say what something is like, they fail in saying what it *is*. Metaphors tend to be organic—they must grow out of the story itself. Trying to impose metaphor for its own sake is to force language into something contrived, artificial, not true. And, as we've discussed, truth is what we're ultimately after when we sit down to write.

A good metaphor (or simile) resonates within the story; your readers will immediately see its truth. It should be grasped at once; readers shouldn't have to stop, go back, and reread; they shouldn't have to figure it out, like a puzzle. Readers shouldn't (especially) be struck by your cleverness at devising such a wonderful metaphor.

There is absolutely no way to do a metaphor writing exercise, because that defeats the purpose. If it doesn't come up organically within the creative process of the story, then it isn't worth anything. Its only value is within the context. This doesn't mean you can't come up with some terrific comparisons of unlike objects. But consider metaphor as that one extra suitcase, a very heavy one, that you should always think about before putting it in the car on the way to the airport. Do you really need it? All too often, we resort to metaphor when we don't know what else to do. So the figurative stuff gets piled on, and things bog down, and tension lags.

Sometimes you'll know that a particular sentence or phrase is dying for a comparison, something to illuminate it, and you can feel it hovering but can't quite put your finger on it. Well, okay, work on it. But don't force it; you're better off sticking with a plain image—describing what something *is* by using one or more of the five senses—than putting in a metaphor that is imprecise or strained.

The "S" Word: Avoiding Conscious Symbols

A *symbol* is something specific (an object or event) that stands for something else. That is, it is not a comparison; there is a range of meaning beyond the "thing" itself. The cross stands for the crucifixion of Jesus, as well as all the ideals and beliefs of Christianity. In *Moby-Dick* the whale stands for some complex, God-like knowledge or power that must not be pursued by man.

A symbol must be part of the story (or poem) yet mean more than the story (or poem). It can be a shared symbol—something common to a culture, language, religion, nationality; or it can be created within the work of fiction or poetry.

One frequently hears people say, "X *has become* a symbol" or "Y *is becoming* a symbol." This reflects the fact that a symbol is the result of the *accumulation of experience,* not just a label that can be pasted onto any object.

A word of warning about symbols: a good symbol is not imposed on the story, but evolves from within it. It is not, repeat *not,* something you put in afterward because you think it will "deepen" the meaning of your story. If you haven't managed to create a deep, moving story through characterization and plot and imagery, I'd suggest that trying to beef it up through symbolism is cheating, and your reader will see through you. It's an emotional shorthand for the real work. For example, sticking in a bunch of crosses and references to Judas and last suppers, and hoping the reader "gets it," rather than fully dramatizing the emotional suffering of a deeply religious and moral man who deliberately injures his best friend, would be cheating indeed.

Imagery, in contrast, should be used as often as possible. It's the heart of riveting, dramatic prose. It fulfills many purposes: not just helping the reader see and hear and taste and touch and smell and otherwise perceive the world of the story, but pushing the reader toward deeper understanding and judgment.

It may be that an image is so strong, and so organic within your story, that it gradually gathers strength as the story progresses and ultimately *becomes* a symbol. But let the PhD students discover that later. When writing, we want to think in terms of images and their impact and meaning within the piece; but to think consciously of symbols is to invite heavy-handedness, an over-reliance on symbolism to carry the meaning of a piece rather than having all the parts of the piece working in concert together.

Imagery as Creative Source

We don't just use imagery to render the world of the story (although that is certainly one thing it does). We can also use imagery as the impetus to creating and discovering situation, meaning, possibilities within material. Here is a section of an essay by the author of *The Raj Quartet* that explains this concept:

> A novel is a sequence of images. In sequence these images tell a story. Its purpose is not to *tell* you but to *show* you. The words used to convey the images and the act of juxtaposing the images in a certain way are the mechanics of the novel. *But the images are what matter* [emphasis mine]. They are the novel's raw material. Images are what we are really working with, and they are infinitely complex.
>
> Constructing a novel—telling a tale, for me at any rate—is not a business of thinking of a story, arranging it in a certain order, and then finding images to fit it. The images come first. I may have a general notion of wanting to write a

book about a certain time, or place, *but unless the general notion is given the impetus of an image that seems to be connected, the notion never gets off the ground* [emphasis mine].

Well, there is a problem there, because as writers, our minds teem with images. We have unending stocks of these private little mysteries, and it is all too easy to think of a story, a situation, and come up with an adequate supply of mental pictures to illustrate it. I call that automatic writing. I don't decry it. It can be very effective. But it isn't my way, and in automatic writing of this kind you seldom feel, as a reader, that there is much underneath. The images conveyed are flat, two-dimensional. In fitting an image to a situation, the image lacks density, it has little ability to stand on its own, it has no inner mystery. *The situation, somehow, must be made to rise out of the image* [emphasis mine].

You need, to begin with, a strong central image that yields a strong situation, or series of situations. By strong I don't necessarily mean strongly dramatic. I mean strong in the sense of tenacious, one that won't let you off the hook. Almost every one of your waking hours is spent considering it, exploring it. You can carry on a conversation and still be thinking of it—although you do tend to lose your awareness of the lapse of real time. When in the grip of this kind of image, my wife may say to me over the breakfast table, "Darling, is it raining?" Two seconds later—but actually two minutes—after she has been to the window, looked out and seen for herself that it is, I will probably say, "No, I don't think so." This is called absence of mind. But absent is exactly what the mind is not. At least it isn't absent from the place where its duty is to be—in the embryo book, wallowing through all the sticky, unmapped, unexplored regions of this extraordinary picture that so far has not been fully transformed into a *situation*.   —PAUL SCOTT, "Method: The Mystery and the Mechanics"

In the short short story below, five images make up the story. Let's look at each of the five images and see what they convey.

One day I was listening to the AM radio. I heard a song: "Oh, I Long To See My Mother In The Doorway." By God! I said, I understand that song. I have often longed to see my mother in the doorway. As a matter of fact, she did stand frequently in various doorways looking at me. [1] She stood one day, just so, at the front door, the darkness of the hallway behind her. It was New Year's Day. She said sadly, If you come home at 4 a.m. when you're seventeen, what time will you come home when you're twenty? She asked this question without humor or meanness. She had begun her worried preparations for death. She would not be present, she thought, when I was twenty. So she wondered.

[2] Another time she stood in the doorway of my room. I had just issued a political manifesto attacking the family's position on the Soviet Union. She said, Go to sleep for godsakes, you damn fool, you and your Communist ideas. We saw them already, Papa and me, in 1905. We guessed it all.

[3] At the door of the kitchen she said, You never finish your lunch. You run around senselessly. What will become of you?

Then she died.

Naturally for the rest of my life I longed to see her, not only in doorways, in a great number of places—in the dining room with my aunts, at the window looking up and down the block, in the country garden among zinnias and marigolds, [4] in the living room with my father.

They sat in comfortable leather chairs. They were listening to Mozart. They looked at one another amazed. It seemed to them that they'd just come over on the boat. They'd just learned the first English words. It seemed to them that he had just proudly handed in a 100 percent correct exam to the American anatomy professor. It seemed as though she'd just quit the shop for the kitchen.

[5] I wish I could see her in the doorway of the living room.

She stood there a minute. Then she sat beside him. They owned an expensive record player. They were listening to Bach. She said to him, Talk to me a little. We don't talk so much anymore.

I'm tired, he said. Can't you see? I saw maybe thirty people today. All sick, all talk talk talk talk. Listen to the music, he said. I believe you once had perfect pitch. I'm tired, he said.

Then she died.   —GRACE PALEY, "Mother"

1. In the first image we get the sense of how vividly the narrator sees her mother, how she's standing "just so" as if the narrator is gesturing toward an actual picture that *we* can see. We see the worried mother and the relationship between the two of them.

2. In the second image we sense the impatience but also the affection (however exasperated) the mother has for her daughter, whose only crime is that she is young and passionate. A different slant on their relationship is revealed.

3. In the third image we're back to the worried mother. The fact that this is immediately followed by the words "Then she died" implies that this is the mother that was frozen in the narrator's mind upon death.

4. In the fourth image we see the woman not as a mother, but as a person: an immigrant full of wonder and excitement at having succeeded in America. We also see the father for the first time, and we get a glimpse of the relationship between them and a sense of the marriage that produced the narrator.

5. In the fifth image we get the depiction of a woman who is disappointed, unappreciated, lonely. That this is followed by "Then she died" again shows the narrator's enhanced understanding of her mother as a person (not as a mother) and how she regrets having failed her while she was alive.

EXERCISES

Exercise 1: *Harper's* Index on a Personal Level

GOAL: To show how very specific, even quantifiable, details can add up to a "big picture"—in this case, a self-portrait.

1. First, look at the *Harper's* Index (below), and see how the editors choose facts and details, some of them quite small and seemingly arcane, to add up to a particular view of our society.

2. Now write down ten things about yourself that are *quantifiable* in some way (i.e., can be expressed with numbers). Look at the example for inspiration.

Harper's *Index, May 2006*

Percentage of the 156 provisions of 2001's USA Patriot Act that were permanent in the original law: 88

Number of the sixteen remaining provisions that were made permanent by Congress in March: 14

Years by which the other two were extended: 4

Number of U.S. cities and towns so far that have passed resolutions calling for the impeachment of President Bush: 8

Ratio of the entire U.S. federal budget in 1948, adjusted for inflation, to the amount spent so far on the Iraq war: 1:1

Percentage of U.S. soldiers in Iraq who say the war was a retaliation for Saddam Hussein's role in the 9/11 attacks: 85

Chances that an American believes that the U.S. will suffer a "major terrorist attack" by next March: 2 in 3

Number of beetles that right-wing entomologists have named after Bush Administration officials: 3

Estimated number of animal and plant species known to science: 1,800,000

Estimated number of different official names that have been applied to them: 6,000,000

Rank of "Christian" among one-word descriptions of George W. Bush offered by Americans in February 2005: 15

Rank this March: 5

Number of times that Mary, Jesus's mother, is referenced by name in the Bible and the Koran, respectively: 19, 34

Percentage of U.S. megachurches that "always" or "often" use electric guitar or bass in services: 93

Percentage change last year in the number of CDs sold at Starbucks: +307

Minimum number of shopping carts that went missing from L.A.–area stores last year: 6,220,000

Years that Hillary Clinton sat on Wal-Mart's board of directors: 5

Number of "Wal-ocaust" T-shirts sold by a Georgia man before Wal-Mart ordered him to cease and desist: 1

Ratio, in the U.S., of the number of Wal-Mart employees to the number of high school teachers: 1:1

Percentage change since 1940 in the average iron content of milk: −62

Percentage alcohol content in a 300-year-old whiskey recipe being revived by a Scottish distillery: 90

Months after Hamas's electoral victory that the only Palestinian brewery will release its nonalcoholic beer: 5

Estimated number of Ugandan prisoners who escaped in February while guards celebrated the president's reelection: 400

Maximum number of Africans brought to America in any single year during the trans-Atlantic slave trade: 35,000

Average number of Africans who have legally emigrated to the United States each year since 2000: 55,000

Estimated percentage share of global Gross Domestic Product in 1974 that came from "developed" and "emerging" nations, respectively: 61, 39

Estimated percentage from those nations today: 49, 51

Minimum number of world nations that have at least one legislator from a communist party: 27

Percentage of South Korean youth who say their country should back North Korea in the event of war with the U.S.: 48

Percentage of China's investable assets that are controlled by the richest half-percent of households: 62

Percentage of white-collar Chinese workers who have personal blogs: 52

Chances that an unprotected PC will become infected with a virus within an hour of being on the Internet: 9 in 10

Chance that a British youth reports having been bullied via text message: 1 in 7

Number of billboards with the names and faces of convicted sex offenders that Mississippi will put up this spring: 100

Percentage change last year in the number of stolen cattle recovered in Texas and Oklahoma: +104

Minimum number of ranches in Texas where one can shoot a zebra: 56

Weeks in advance that Al Qaeda operatives must request vacation time, according to seized documents: 10

Number of Harlequin novels published last year that feature love between a Western woman and an Arab sheikh: 15

Number by 2008 that will feature NASCAR races: 22

Below is a "composite" example of how this exercise can be done, taken from numerous student attempts over the years:

Harper's Index for an Individual

Years after I started menstruating that I learned to always keep a box of tampons in the house: 25

Number of sisters I have: 5

Number of sisters who are talking to me at present: 3

Average number of minutes after two of my sisters have a fight that I hear about it: 15

Chances that when my husband goes to the video store he'll return with something with the word "planet" in the title: 100 percent

Number of times I've put on *Beauty and the Beast* by Cocteau and eaten a pint of Chunky Monkey ice cream when I'm feeling blue: 17

Chances that my son will say, "But I'm not tired!" when it's bedtime: 100 percent

Hours after my sister-in-law hears about someone being sick that she also gets sick: 2

Number of unread books by my bedside table: 7

Diet Coke, water, and milk as my No. 1, 2, and 3 favorite beverages

Exercise 2: Render a Tree, Capture the Forest

GOAL: To show how you can render something big—the whole forest—by selectively choosing *this* tree, then *that* tree.

1. Read "Nebraska" by Ron Hansen (pp. 92–95) and see how he captures the entire state of Nebraska through the use of carefully chosen details.

2. By carefully choosing a dozen details—for example, a donut shop, an interaction on a street corner between a husband and wife—attempt to capture an entire place: a town, a state, a city, a county.

The following example was provided by Susan Wood:

Northwestern Illinois had been beautiful once, you could see that. Even now, beyond the edges of our subdivision, there were traces of the rolling prairie, grasses rippling out as far as eye could see, the sun bleaching the sheaves of stalks a honey gold. But the sprawl was approaching from Chicago, 30 miles to the south. Huge bulldozers and cranes moved in, tearing raw holes in the earth, shaving off the rich topsoil and topping it with red clay in which nothing could grow. Huge mountains of dirt appeared from these excavations, bleeding bronzed trickles of water polluted by oil runoffs, discarded soda cans, and cigarette lighters. In between the large rectangular cuts in the ground that would become the basements of houses ran the roads, already finished, pristine black ribbons bordered by fresh cement curbs and punctuated with street lights that already turned on automatically when dusk fell.

Our house was one of the few that had been finished, and the only one in which humans resided. We ran wild all day among the construction sites, stealing bits of lumber to build a playhouse on our grassless yard, throwing mud bombs into the unfinished entry halls and living rooms of the houses that would one day be occupied by our neighbors. At night we'd walk along the ghostly roads, splitting up at corners and walking in different directions only to have the maze-like roads bring us back again to each other within minutes. There was an unearthly silence on those evenings. Not a bird, not a cricket; all of nature had fled as if from a war zone.

READINGS

TIM O'BRIEN

The Things They Carried

FIRST LIEUTENANT JIMMY CROSS carried letters from a girl named Martha, a junior at Mount Sebastian College in New Jersey. They were not love letters, but Lieutenant Cross was hoping, so he kept them folded in plastic at the bottom of his rucksack. In the late afternoon, after a day's march, he would dig his foxhole, wash his hands under a canteen, unwrap the letters, hold them with the tips of his fingers, and spend the last hour of light pretending. He would imagine romantic camping trips into the White Mountains in New Hampshire. He would sometimes taste the envelope flaps, knowing her tongue had been there. More than anything, he wanted Martha to love him as he loved her, but the letters were mostly chatty, elusive on the matter of love. She was a virgin, he was almost sure. She was an English major at Mount Sebastian, and she wrote beautifully about her professors and roommates and midterm exams, about her respect for Chaucer and her great affection for Virginia Woolf. She often quoted lines of poetry; she never mentioned the war, except to say, Jimmy, take care of yourself. The letters weighed ten ounces. They were signed "Love, Martha," but Lieutenant Cross understood that "Love" was only a way of signing and did not mean what he sometimes pretended it meant. At dusk, he would carefully return the letters to his rucksack. Slowly, a bit distracted, he would get up and move among his men, checking the perimeter, then at full dark he would return to his hole and watch the night and wonder if Martha was a virgin.

The things they carried were largely determined by necessity. Among the necessities or near necessities were P-38 can openers, pocket knives, heat tabs, wristwatches, dog tags, mosquito repellent, chewing gum, candy, cigarettes, salt tablets, packets of Kool-Aid, lighters, matches, sewing kits, Military Payment Certificates, C rations, and two or three canteens of water. Together, these items weighed between fifteen and twenty pounds, depending upon a man's habits or rate of metabolism. Henry Dobbins, who was a big man, carried extra rations; he was especially fond of canned peaches in heavy syrup over pound cake. Dave Jensen, who practiced field hygiene, carried a toothbrush, dental floss, and several hotel-size bars of soap he'd stolen on R&R in Sydney, Australia. Ted Lavender, who was scared, carried tranquilizers until he was shot in the head outside the village of Than Khe in mid-April. By necessity, and because it was SOP,[1] they all carried steel helmets that weighed five pounds including the liner and camouflage cover. They carried the standard fatigue jackets and trousers. Very few carried underwear. On their feet they carried jungle boots—2.1 pounds—and Dave Jensen carried three pairs of socks and a can of Dr. Scholl's foot powder as a precaution against trench foot. Until he was shot, Ted Lavender carried six or seven ounces of premium dope, which for him was a necessity. Mitchell

1. Standard operating procedure.

Sanders, the RTO,[2] carried condoms. Norman Bowker carried a diary. Rat Kiley carried comic books. Kiowa, a devout Baptist, carried an illustrated New Testament that had been presented to him by his father, who taught Sunday school in Oklahoma City, Oklahoma. As a hedge against bad times, however, Kiowa also carried his grandmother's distrust of the white man, his grandfather's old hunting hatchet. Necessity dictated. Because the land was mined and booby-trapped, it was SOP for each man to carry a steel-centered, nylon-covered flak jacket, which weighed 6.7 pounds, but which on hot days seemed much heavier. Because you could die so quickly, each man carried at least one large compress bandage, usually in the helmet band for easy access. Because the nights were cold, and because the monsoons were wet, each carried a green plastic poncho that could be used as a raincoat or groundsheet or makeshift tent. With its quilted liner, the poncho weighed almost two pounds, but it was worth every ounce. In April, for instance, when Ted Lavender was shot, they used his poncho to wrap him up, then to carry him across the paddy, then to lift him into the chopper that took him away.

They were called legs or grunts.

To carry something was to "hump" it, as when Lieutenant Jimmy Cross humped his love for Martha up the hills and through the swamps. In its intransitive form, "to hump" meant "to walk," or "to march," but it implied burdens far beyond the intransitive.

Almost everyone humped photographs. In his wallet, Lieutenant Cross carried two photographs of Martha. The first was a Kodachrome snapshot signed "Love," though he knew better. She stood against a brick wall. Her eyes were gray and neutral, her lips slightly open as she stared straight-on at the camera. At night, sometimes, Lieutenant Cross wondered who had taken the picture, because he knew she had boyfriends, because he loved her so much, and because he could see the shadow of the picture taker spreading out against the brick wall. The second photograph had been clipped from the 1968 Mount Sebastian yearbook. It was an action shot—women's volleyball—and Martha was bent horizontal to the floor, reaching, the palms of her hands in sharp focus, the tongue taut, the expression frank and competitive. There was no visible sweat. She wore white gym shorts. Her legs, he thought, were almost certainly the legs of a virgin, dry and without hair, the left knee cocked and carrying her entire weight, which was just over one hundred pounds. Lieutenant Cross remembered touching that left knee. A dark theater, he remembered, and the movie was *Bonnie and Clyde*, and Martha wore a tweed skirt, and during the final scene, when he touched her knee, she turned and looked at him in a sad, sober way that made him pull his hand back, but he would always remember the feel of the tweed skirt and the knee beneath it and the sound of the gunfire that killed Bonnie and Clyde, how embarrassing it was, how slow and oppressive. He remembered kissing her good night at the dorm door. Right then, he thought, he should've done something brave. He should've carried her up the stairs to her room and tied her to the bed

2. Radiotelephone operator.

and touched that left knee all night long. He should've risked it. Whenever he looked at the photographs, he thought of new things he should've done.

What they carried was partly a function of rank, partly of field specialty.

As a first lieutenant and platoon leader, Jimmy Cross carried a compass, maps, code books, binoculars, and a .45-caliber pistol that weighed 2.9 pounds fully loaded. He carried a strobe light and the responsibility for the lives of his men.

As an RTO, Mitchell Sanders carried the PRC-25 radio, a killer, twenty-six pounds with its battery.

As a medic, Rat Kiley carried a canvas satchel filled with morphine and plasma and malaria tablets and surgical tape and comic books and all the things a medic must carry, including M&M's for especially bad wounds, for a total weight of nearly twenty pounds.

As a big man, therefore a machine gunner, Henry Dobbins carried the M-60, which weighed twenty-three pounds unloaded, but which was almost always loaded. In addition, Dobbins carried between ten and fifteen pounds of ammunition draped in belts across his chest and shoulders.

As PFCs or Spec 4s, most of them were common grunts and carried the standard M-16 gas-operated assault rifle. The weapon weighed 7.5 pounds unloaded, 8.2 pounds with its full twenty-round magazine. Depending on numerous factors, such as topography and psychology, the riflemen carried anywhere from twelve to twenty magazines, usually in cloth bandoliers, adding on another 8.4 pounds at minimum, fourteen pounds at maximum. When it was available, they also carried M-16 maintenance gear—rods and steel brushes and swabs and tubes of LSA oil—all of which weighed about a pound. Among the grunts, some carried the M-79 grenade launcher, 5.9 pounds unloaded, a reasonably light weapon except for the ammunition, which was heavy. A single round weighed ten ounces. The typical load was twenty-five rounds. But Ted Lavender, who was scared, carried thirty-four rounds when he was shot and killed outside Than Khe, and he went down under an exceptional burden, more than twenty pounds of ammunition, plus the flak jacket and helmet and rations and waters and toilet paper and tranquilizers and all the rest, plus the unweighed fear. He was dead weight. There was no twitching or flopping. Kiowa, who saw it happen, said it was like watching a rock fall, or a big sandbag or something—just boom, then down—not like the movies where the dead guy rolls around and does fancy spins and goes ass over teakettle—not like that, Kiowa said, the poor bastard just flat-fuck fell. Boom. Down. Nothing else. It was a bright morning in mid-April. Lieutenant Cross felt the pain. He blamed himself. They stripped off Lavender's canteens and ammo, all the heavy things, and Rat Kiley said the obvious, the guy's dead, and Mitchell Sanders used his radio to report one U.S. KIA[3] and to request a chopper. Then they wrapped Lavender in his poncho. They carried him out to a dry paddy, established security, and sat smoking the dead man's dope until the chopper came. Lieutenant Cross kept to himself. He pictured Martha's smooth young face, thinking

3. Killed in action.

he loved her more than anything, more than his men, and now Ted Lavender was dead because he loved her so much and could not stop thinking about her. When the dust-off arrived, they carried Lavender aboard. Afterward they burned Than Khe. They marched until dusk, then dug their holes, and that night Kiowa kept explaining how you had to be there, how fast it was, how the poor guy just dropped like so much concrete. Boom-down, he said. Like cement.

In addition to the three standard weapons—the M-60, M-16, and M-79—they carried whatever presented itself, or whatever seemed appropriate as a means of killing or staying alive. They carried catch-as-catch-can. At various times, in various situations, they carried M-14s and CAR-15s and Swedish Ks and grease guns and captured AK-47s and Chi-Coms and RPGs and Simonov carbines and black-market Uzis and .38-caliber Smith & Wesson handguns and 66 mm LAWs and shotguns and silencers and blackjacks and bayonets and C-4 plastic explosives. Lee Strunk carried a slingshot; a weapon of last resort, he called it. Mitchell Sanders carried brass knuckles. Kiowa carried his grandfather's feathered hatchet. Every third or fourth man carried a Claymore antipersonnel mine—3.5 pounds with its firing device. They all carried fragmentation grenades—fourteen ounces each. They all carried at least one M-18 colored smoke grenade—twenty-four ounces. Some carried CS or teargas grenades. Some carried white-phosphorus grenades. They carried all they could bear, and then some, including a silent awe for the terrible power of the things they carried.

In the first week of April, before Lavender died, Lieutenant Jimmy Cross received a good-luck charm from Martha. It was a simple pebble, an ounce at most. Smooth to the touch, it was a milky-white color with flecks of orange and violet, oval-shaped, like a miniature egg. In the accompanying letter, Martha wrote that she had found the pebble on the Jersey shoreline, precisely where the land touched water at high tide, where things came together but also separated. It was this separate-but-together quality, she wrote, that had inspired her to pick up the pebble and to carry it in her breast pocket for several days, where it seemed weightless, and then to send it through the mail, by air, as a token of her truest feelings for him. Lieutenant Cross found this romantic. But he wondered what her truest feelings were, exactly, and what she meant by separate-but-together. He wondered how the tides and waves had come into play on that afternoon along the Jersey shoreline when Martha saw the pebble and bent down to rescue it from geology. He imagined bare feet. Martha was a poet, with the poet's sensibilities, and her feet would be brown and bare, the toenails unpainted, the eyes chilly and somber like the ocean in March, and though it was painful, he wondered who had been with her that afternoon. He imagined a pair of shadows moving along the strip of sand where things came together but also separated. It was phantom jealousy, he knew, but he couldn't help himself. He loved her so much. On the march, through the hot days of early April, he carried the pebble in his mouth, turning it with his tongue, tasting sea salts and moisture. His mind wandered. He had difficulty keeping his attention on the war. On occasion he would yell at his men to spread out the column, to keep their eyes open, but then he would slip away into daydreams, just pretending, walking barefoot along the Jersey shore, with Martha, carrying nothing. He would feel himself rising. Sun and waves and gentle winds, all love and lightness.

What they carried varied by mission.

When a mission took them to the mountains, they carried mosquito netting, machetes, canvas tarps, and extra bug juice.

If a mission seemed especially hazardous, or if it involved a place they knew to be bad, they carried everything they could. In certain heavily mined AOs,[4] where the land was dense with Toe Poppers and Bouncing Betties, they took turns humping a twenty-eight-pound mine detector. With its headphones and big sensing plate, the equipment was a stress on the lower back and shoulders, awkward to handle, often useless because of the shrapnel in the earth, but they carried it anyway, partly for safety, partly for the illusion of safety.

On ambush, or other night missions, they carried peculiar little odds and ends. Kiowa always took along his New Testament and a pair of moccasins for silence. Dave Jensen carried night-sight vitamins high in carotin. Lee Strunk carried his slingshot; ammo, he claimed, would never be a problem. Rat Kiley carried brandy and M&M's. Until he was shot, Ted Lavender carried the starlight scope, which weighed 6.3 pounds with its aluminum carrying case. Henry Dobbins carried his girlfriend's pantyhose wrapped around his neck as a comforter. They all carried ghosts. When dark came, they would move out single file across the meadows and paddies to their ambush coordinates, where they would quietly set up the Claymores and lie down and spend the night waiting.

Other missions were more complicated and required special equipment. In mid-April, it was their mission to search out and destroy the elaborate tunnel complexes in the Than Khe area south of Chu Lai. To blow the tunnels, they carried one-pound blocks of pentrite high explosives, four blocks to a man, sixty-eight pounds in all. They carried wiring, detonators, and battery-powered clackers. Dave Jensen carried earplugs. Most often, before blowing the tunnels, they were ordered by higher command to search them, which was considered bad news, but by and large they just shrugged and carried out orders. Because he was a big man, Henry Dobbins was excused from tunnel duty. The others would draw numbers. Before Lavender died there were seventeen men in the platoon, and whoever drew the number seventeen would strip off his gear and crawl in head first with a flashlight and Lieutenant Cross's .45-caliber pistol. The rest of them would fan out as security. They would sit down or kneel, not facing the hole, listening to the ground beneath them, imagining cobwebs and ghosts, whatever was down there—the tunnel walls squeezing in—how the flashlight seemed impossibly heavy in the hand and how it was tunnel vision in the very strictest sense, compression in all ways, even time, and how you had to wiggle in—ass and elbows—a swallowed-up feeling—and how you found yourself

4. Areas of operations.

worrying about odd things—will your flashlight go dead? Do rats carry rabies? If you screamed, how far would the sound carry? Would your buddies hear it? Would they have the courage to drag you out? In some respects, though not many, the waiting was worse than the tunnel itself. Imagination was a killer.

On April 16, when Lee Strunk drew the number seventeen, he laughed and muttered something and went down quickly. The morning was hot and very still. Not good, Kiowa said. He looked at the tunnel opening, then out across a dry paddy toward the village of Than Khe. Nothing moved. No clouds or birds or people. As they waited, the men smoked and drank Kool-Aid, not talking much, feeling sympathy for Lee Strunk but also feeling the luck of the draw. You win some, you lose some, said Mitchell Sanders, and sometimes you settle for a raincheck. It was a tired line and no one laughed.

Henry Dobbins ate a tropical chocolate bar. Ted Lavender popped a tranquilizer and went off to pee.

After five minutes, Lieutenant Jimmy Cross moved to the tunnel, leaned down, and examined the darkness. Trouble, he thought—a cave-in maybe. And then suddenly, without willing it, he was thinking about Martha. The stresses and fractures, the quick collapse, the two of them buried alive under all that weight. Dense, crushing love. Kneeling, watching the hole, he tried to concentrate on Lee Strunk and the war, all the dangers, but his love was too much for him, he felt paralyzed, he wanted to sleep inside her lungs and breathe her blood and be smothered. He wanted her to be a virgin and not a virgin, all at once. He wanted to know her. Intimate secrets—why poetry? Why so sad? Why the grayness in her eyes? Why so alone? Not lonely, just alone—riding her bike across campus or sitting off by herself in the cafeteria. Even dancing, she danced alone—and it was the aloneness that filled him with love. He remembered telling her that one evening. How she nodded and looked away. And how, later, when he kissed her, she received the kiss without returning it, her eyes wide open, not afraid, not a virgin's eyes, just flat and uninvolved.

Lieutenant Cross gazed at the tunnel. But he was not there. He was buried with Martha under the white sand at the Jersey shore. They were pressed together, and the pebble in his mouth was her tongue. He was smiling. Vaguely, he was aware of how quiet the day was, the sullen paddies, yet he could not bring himself to worry about matters of security. He was beyond that. He was just a kid at war, in love. He was twenty-two years old. He couldn't help it.

A few moments later Lee Strunk crawled out of the tunnel. He came up grinning, filthy but alive. Lieutenant Cross nodded and closed his eyes while the others clapped Strunk on the back and made jokes about rising from the dead.

Worms, Rat Kiley said. Right out of the grave. Fuckin' zombie.

The men laughed. They all felt great relief.

Spook City, said Mitchell Sanders.

Lee Strunk made a funny ghost sound, a kind of moaning, yet very happy, and right then, when Strunk made that high happy moaning sound, when he went *Ahhooooo*, right then Ted Lavender was shot in the head on his way back from peeing.

He lay with his mouth open. The teeth were broken. There was a swollen black bruise under his left eye. The cheekbone was gone. Oh shit, Rat Kiley said, the guy's dead. The guy's dead, he kept saying, which seemed profound—the guy's dead. I mean really.

The things they carried were determined to some extent by superstition. Lieutenant Cross carried his good-luck pebble. Dave Jensen carried a rabbit's foot. Norman Bowker, otherwise a very gentle person, carried a thumb that had been presented to him as a gift by Mitchell Sanders. The thumb was dark brown, rubbery to the touch, and weighed four ounces at most. It had been cut from a VC[5] corpse, a boy of fifteen or sixteen. They'd found him at the bottom of an irrigation ditch, badly burned, flies in his mouth and eyes. The boy wore black shorts and sandals. At the time of his death he had been carrying a pouch of rice, a rifle, and three magazines of ammunition.

You want my opinion, Mitchell Sanders said, there's a definite moral here.

He put his hand on the dead boy's wrist. He was quiet for a time, as if counting a pulse, then he patted the stomach, almost affectionately, and used Kiowa's hunting hatchet to remove the thumb.

Henry Dobbins asked what the moral was.

Moral?

You know. *Moral.*

Sanders wrapped the thumb in toilet paper and handed it across to Norman Bowker. There was no blood. Smiling, he kicked the boy's head, watched the flies scatter, and said, It's like with that old TV show—Paladin. Have gun, will travel.

Henry Dobbins thought about it.

Yeah, well, he finally said. I don't see no moral.

There it *is*, man.

Fuck off.

They carried USO stationery and pencils and pens. They carried Sterno, safety pins, trip flares, signal flares, spools of wire, razor blades, chewing tobacco, liberated joss sticks and statuettes of the smiling Buddha, candles, grease pencils, *The Stars and Stripes*, fingernail clippers, Psy Ops[6] leaflets, bush hats, bolos, and much more. Twice a week, when the resupply choppers came in, they carried hot chow in green Mermite cans and large canvas bags filled with iced beer and soda pop. They carried plastic water containers, each with a two-gallon capacity. Mitchell Sanders carried a set of starched tiger fatigues for special occasions. Henry Dobbins carried Black Flag insecticide. Dave Jensen carried empty sandbags that could be filled at night for added protection. Lee Strunk carried tanning lotion. Some things they carried in common. Taking turns, they carried the big PRC-77 scrambler radio, which weighed thirty

5. Viet Cong.

6. Psychological operations.

pounds with its battery. They shared the weight of memory. They took up what others could no longer bear. Often, they carried each other, the wounded or weak. They carried infections. They carried chess sets, basketballs, Vietnamese-English dictionaries, insignia of rank, Bronze Stars and Purple Hearts, plastic cards imprinted with the Code of Conduct. They carried diseases, among them malaria and dysentery. They carried lice and ringworm and leeches and paddy algae and various rots and molds. They carried the land itself—Vietnam, the place, the soil—a powdery orange-red dust that covered their boots and fatigues and faces. They carried the sky. The whole atmosphere, they carried it, the humidity, the monsoons, the stink of fungus and decay, all of it, they carried gravity. They moved like mules. By daylight they took sniper fire, at night they were mortared, but it was not battle, it was just the endless march, village to village, without purpose, nothing won or lost. They marched for the sake of the march. They plodded along slowly, dumbly, leaning forward against the heat, unthinking, all blood and bone, simple grunts, soldiering with their legs, toiling up the hills and down into the paddies and across the rivers and up again and down, just humping, one step and then the next and then another, but no volition, no will, because it was automatic, it was anatomy, and the war was entirely a matter of posture and carriage, the hump was everything, a kind of inertia, a kind of emptiness, a dullness of desire and intellect and conscience and hope and human sensibility. Their principles were in their feet. Their calculations were biological. They had no sense of strategy or mission. They searched the villages without knowing what to look for, not caring, kicking over jars of rice, frisking children and old men, blowing tunnels, sometimes setting fires and sometimes not, then forming up and moving on to the next village, then other villages, where it would always be the same. They carried their own lives. The pressures were enormous. In the heat of early afternoon, they would remove their helmets and flak jackets, walking bare, which was dangerous but which helped ease the strain. They would often discard things along the route of march. Purely for comfort, they would throw away rations, blow their Claymores and grenades, no matter, because by nightfall the resupply choppers would arrive with more of the same, then a day or two later still more, fresh watermelons and crates of ammunition and sunglasses and woolen sweaters—the resources were stunning—sparklers for the Fourth of July, colored eggs for Easter. It was the great American war chest—the fruits of science, the smokestacks, the canneries, the arsenals at Hartford, the Minnesota forests, the machine shops, the vast fields of corn and wheat—they carried like freight trains; they carried it on their backs and shoulders—and for all the ambiguities of Vietnam, all the mysteries and unknowns, there was at least the single abiding certainty that they would never be at a loss for things to carry.

After the chopper took Lavender away, Lieutenant Jimmy Cross led his men into the village of Than Khe. They burned everything. They shot chickens and dogs, they trashed the village well, they called in artillery and watched the wreckage, then they marched for several hours through the hot afternoon, and then at dusk, while Kiowa explained how Lavender died, Lieutenant Cross found himself trembling.

He tried not to cry. With his entrenching tool, which weighed five pounds, he began digging a hole in the earth.

He felt shame. He hated himself. He had loved Martha more than his men, and as a consequence Lavender was now dead, and this was something he would have to carry like a stone in his stomach for the rest of the war.

All he could do was dig. He used his entrenching tool like an ax, slashing, feeling both love and hate, and then later, when it was full dark, he sat at the bottom of his foxhole and wept. It went on for a long while. In part, he was grieving for Ted Lavender, but mostly it was for Martha, and for himself, because she belonged to another world, which was not quite real, and because she was a junior at Mount Sebastian College in New Jersey, a poet and a virgin and uninvolved, and because he realized she did not love him and never would.

Like cement, Kiowa whispered in the dark. I swear to God—boom-down. Not a word.

I've heard this, said Norman Bowker.

A pisser, you know? Still zipping himself up. Zapped while zipping.

All right, fine. That's enough.

Yeah, but you had to see it, the guy just—

I *heard*, man. Cement. So why not shut the fuck up?

Kiowa shook his head sadly and glanced over at the hole where Lieutenant Jimmy Cross sat watching the night. The air was thick and wet. A warm, dense fog had settled over the paddies and there was the stillness that precedes rain.

After a time Kiowa sighed.

One thing for sure, he said. The Lieutenant's in some deep hurt. I mean that crying jag—the way he was carrying on—it wasn't fake or anything, it was real heavy-duty hurt. The man cares.

Sure, Norman Bowker said.

Say what you want, the man does care.

We all got problems.

Not Lavender.

No, I guess not, Bowker said. Do me a favor, though.

Shut up?

That's a smart Indian. Shut up.

Shrugging, Kiowa pulled off his boots. He wanted to say more, just to lighten up his sleep, but instead he opened his New Testament and arranged it beneath his head as a pillow. The fog made things seem hollow and unattached. He tried not to think about Ted Lavender, but then he was thinking how fast it was, no drama, down and dead, and how it was hard to feel anything except surprise. It seemed un-Christian. He wished he could find some great sadness, or even anger, but the emotion wasn't there and he couldn't make it happen. Mostly he felt pleased to be alive. He liked the smell of the New Testament under his cheek, the leather and ink and paper and glue, whatever the chemicals were. He liked hearing the sounds of night. Even his fatigue, it felt fine, the stiff muscles and the prickly awareness of his own body, a floating feeling. He enjoyed not being dead. Lying there, Kiowa admired Lieutenant Jimmy Cross's capacity for grief. He wanted to share the man's pain, he wanted to care as Jimmy Cross cared. And yet when he closed his eyes, all he could think was Boom-down, and all he could feel was the pleasure of having his boots off and the fog curling in around him and the damp soil and the Bible smells and the plush comfort of night.

After a moment Norman Bowker sat up in the dark.

What the hell, he said. You want to talk, *talk*. Tell it to me.

Forget it.

No, man, go on. One thing I hate, it's a silent Indian.

For the most part they carried themselves with poise, a kind of dignity. Now and then, however, there were times of panic, when they squealed or wanted to squeal but couldn't, when they twitched and made moaning sounds and covered their heads and said Dear Jesus and flopped around on the earth and fired their weapons blindly and cringed and sobbed and begged for the noise to stop and went wild and made stupid promises to themselves and to God and to their mothers and fathers, hoping not to die. In different ways, it happened to all of them. Afterward, when the firing ended, they would blink and peek up. They would touch their bodies, feeling shame, then quickly hiding it. They would force themselves to stand. As if in slow motion, frame by frame, the world would take on the old logic—absolute silence, then the wind, then sunlight, then voices. It was the burden of being alive. Awkwardly, the men would reassemble themselves, first in private, then in groups, becoming soldiers again. They would repair the leaks in their eyes. They would check for casualties, call in dust-offs, light cigarettes, try to smile, clear their throats and spit and begin cleaning their weapons. After a time someone would shake his head and say, No lie, I almost shit my pants, and someone else would laugh, which meant it was bad, yes, but the guy had obviously not shit his pants, it wasn't that bad, and in any case nobody would ever do such a thing and then go ahead and talk about it. They would squint into the dense, oppressive sunlight. For a few moments, perhaps, they would fall silent, lighting a joint and tracking its passage from man to man, inhaling, holding in the humiliation. Scary stuff, one of them might say. But then someone else would grin or flick his eyebrows and say, Roger-dodger, almost cut me a new asshole, *almost*.

There were numerous such poses. Some carried themselves with a sort of wistful resignation, others with pride or stiff soldierly discipline or good humor or macho zeal. They were afraid of dying but they were even more afraid to show it.

They found jokes to tell.

They used a hard vocabulary to contain the terrible softness. *Greased*, they'd say. *Offed, lit up, zapped while zipping*. It wasn't cruelty, just stage presence. They were actors and the war came at them in 3-D. When someone died, it wasn't quite dying, because in a curious way it seemed scripted, and because they had their lines mostly memorized, irony mixed with tragedy, and because they called it by other names, as if to encyst and destroy the reality of death itself. They kicked corpses. They cut off thumbs. They talked grunt lingo. They told stories about Ted Lavender's supply of tranquilizers, how the poor guy didn't feel a thing, how incredibly tranquil he was.

There's a moral here, said Mitchell Sanders.

They were waiting for Lavender's chopper, smoking the dead man's dope.

The moral's pretty obvious, Sanders said, and winked. Stay away from drugs. No joke, they'll ruin your day every time.

Cute, said Henry Dobbins.

Mind-blower, get it? Talk about wiggy—nothing left, just blood and brains.

They made themselves laugh.

There it is, they'd say, over and over, as if the repetition itself were an act of poise, a balance between crazy and almost crazy, knowing without going. There it is, which meant be cool, let it ride, because oh yeah, man, you can't change what can't be changed, there it is, there it absolutely and positively and fucking well *is*.

They were tough.

They carried all the emotional baggage of men who might die. Grief, terror, love, longing—these were intangibles, but the intangibles had their own mass and specific gravity, they had tangible weight. They carried shameful memories. They carried the common secret of cowardice barely restrained, the instinct to run or freeze or hide, and in many respects this was the heaviest burden of all, for it could never be put down, it required perfect balance and perfect posture. They carried their reputations. They carried the soldier's greatest fear, which was the fear of blushing. Men killed, and died, because they were embarrassed not to. It was what had brought them to the war in the first place, nothing positive, no dreams of glory or honor, just to avoid the blush of dishonor. They died so as not to die of embarrassment. They crawled into tunnels and walked point and advanced under fire. Each morning, despite the unknowns, they made their legs move. They endured. They kept humping. They did not submit to the obvious alternative, which was simply to close the eyes and fall. So easy, really. Go limp and tumble to the ground and let the muscles unwind and not speak and not budge until your buddies picked you up and lifted you into the chopper that would roar and dip its nose and carry you off to the world. A mere matter of falling, yet no one ever fell. It was not courage, exactly; the object was not valor. Rather, they were too frightened to be cowards.

By and large they carried these things inside, maintaining the masks of composure. They sneered at sick call. They spoke bitterly about guys who had found release by shooting off their own toes or fingers. Pussies, they'd say. Candyasses. It was fierce, mocking talk, with only a trace of envy or awe, but even so, the image played itself out behind their eyes.

They imagined the muzzle against flesh. They imagined the quick, sweet pain, then the evacuation to Japan, then a hospital with warm beds and cute geisha nurses.

They dreamed of freedom birds.

At night, on guard, staring into the dark, they were carried away by jumbo jets. They felt the rush of takeoff. *Gone!* they yelled. And then velocity, wings and engines, a smiling stewardess—but it was more than a plane, it was a real bird, a big sleek silver bird with feathers and talons and high screeching. They were flying. The weights fell off, there was nothing to bear. They laughed and held on tight, feeling the cold slap of wind and altitude, soaring, thinking *It's over, I'm gone!*—they were naked, they were light and free—it was all lightness, bright and fast and buoyant, light as light, a helium buzz in the brain, a giddy bubbling in the lungs as they were taken up over the clouds and the war, beyond duty, beyond gravity and mortification and global entanglements—*Sin loi!*[7] they yelled, *I'm sorry, motherfuckers, but I'm out of it, I'm goofed, I'm on a space cruise, I'm gone!*—and it was a restful, disencumbered sensation, just riding the light waves, sailing that big silver freedom bird over the mountains and oceans, over America, over the farms and great sleeping cities and cemeteries and highways and the golden arches of McDonald's. It was flight, a kind of fleeing, a kind of falling, falling higher and higher, spinning off the edge of the earth and beyond the sun and through the vast, silent vacuum where there were no burdens and where everything weighed exactly nothing. *Gone!* they screamed, *I'm sorry but I'm gone!* And so at night, not quite dreaming, they gave themselves over to lightness, they were carried, they were purely borne.

On the morning after Ted Lavender died, First Lieutenant Jimmy Cross crouched at the bottom of his foxhole and burned Martha's letters. Then he burned the two photographs. There was a steady rain falling, which made it difficult, but he used heat tabs and Sterno to build a small fire, screening it with his body, holding the photographs over the tight blue flame with the tips of his fingers.

He realized it was only a gesture. Stupid, he thought. Sentimental, too, but mostly just stupid.

Lavender was dead. You couldn't burn the blame.

Besides, the letters were in his head. And even now, without photographs, Lieutenant Cross could see Martha playing volleyball in her white gym shorts and yellow T-shirt. He could see her moving in the rain.

When the fire died out, Lieutenant Cross pulled his poncho over his shoulders and ate breakfast from a can.

There was no great mystery, he decided.

In those burned letters Martha had never mentioned the war, except to say, Jimmy, take care of yourself. She wasn't involved. She signed the letters "Love," but it wasn't love, and all the fine lines and technicalities did not matter.

The morning came up wet and blurry. Everything seemed part of everything else, the fog and Martha and the deepening rain.

It was a war, after all.

Half smiling, Lieutenant Jimmy Cross took out his maps. He shook his head hard, as if to clear it, then bent forward and began planning the day's march. In ten minutes, or maybe twenty, he would rouse the men and they would pack up and head west, where the maps showed the country to be green and inviting. They would do

7. "Sorry about that!" (Vietnamese).

what they had always done. The rain might add some weight, but otherwise it would be one more day layered upon all the other days.

He was realistic about it. There was that new hardness in his stomach.

No more fantasies, he told himself.

Henceforth, when he thought about Martha, it would be only to think that she belonged elsewhere. He would shut down the daydreams. This was not Mount Sebastian, it was another world, where there were no pretty poems or midterm exams, a place where men died because of carelessness and gross stupidity. Kiowa was right. Boom-down, and you were dead, never partly dead.

Briefly, in the rain, Lieutenant Cross saw Martha's gray eyes gazing back at him.

He understood.

It was very sad, he thought. The things men carried inside. The things men did or felt they had to do.

He almost nodded at her, but didn't.

Instead he went back to his maps. He was now determined to perform his duties firmly and without negligence. It wouldn't help Lavender, he knew that, but from this point on he would comport himself as a soldier. He would dispose of his good-luck pebble. Swallow it, maybe, or use Lee Strunk's slingshot, or just drop it along the trail. On the march he would impose strict field discipline. He would be careful to send out flank security, to prevent straggling or bunching up, to keep his troops moving at the proper pace and at the proper interval. He would insist on clean weapons. He would confiscate the remainder of Lavender's dope. Later in the day, perhaps, he would call the men together and speak to them plainly. He would accept the blame for what had happened to Ted Lavender. He would be a man about it. He would look them in the eyes, keeping his chin level, and he would issue the new SOPs in a calm, impersonal tone of voice, an officer's voice, leaving no room for argument or discussion. Commencing immediately, he'd tell them, they would no longer abandon equipment along the route of march. They would police up their acts. They would get their shit together, and keep it together, and maintain it neatly and in good working order.

He would not tolerate laxity. He would show strength, distancing himself.

Among the men there would be grumbling, of course, and maybe worse, because their days would seem longer and their loads heavier, but Lieutenant Cross reminded himself that his obligation was not to be loved but to lead. He would dispense with love; it was not now a factor. And if anyone quarreled or complained, he would simply tighten his lips and arrange his shoulders in the correct command posture. He might give a curt little nod. Or he might not. He might just shrug and say Carry on, then they would saddle up and form into a column and move out toward the villages of Than Khe.

Reading as a Writer

1. How do the concrete details affect the story? At what point does O'Brien slip in some abstractions to good effect?

2. Why does O'Brien tell us that Lavender is dead so early in the story? How does that impact the suspense? Why do you want to read on if you know that Lavender is dead (i.e., you know the whole story)?

3. Notice that the full story has been told by the end of the third page. Then O'Brien goes back and tells it again, in more detail. Why does he structure the story this way?

4. What is the story ultimately about? What happens at the end when Jimmy Cross burns the letters and decides to be a stricter leader? Is he merely facing reality, or is he substituting one fantasy with another?

RON HANSEN

Nebraska

THE TOWN IS AMERICUS, Covenant, Denmark, Grange, Hooray, Jerusalem, Sweetwater—one of the lesser-known moons of the Platte, conceived in sickness and misery by European pioneers who took the path of least resistance and put down roots in an emptiness like the one they kept secret in their youth. In Swedish and Danish and German and Polish, in anxiety and fury and God's providence, they chopped at the Great Plains with spades, creating green sod houses that crumbled and collapsed in the rain and disappeared in the first persuasive snow and were so low the grown-ups stooped to go inside; and yet were places of ownership and a hard kind of happiness, the places their occupants gravely stood before on those plenary occasions when photographs were taken.

And then the Union Pacific stopped by, just a camp of white campaign tents and a boy playing his Harpoon at night, and then a supply store, a depot, a pine water tank, stockyards, and the mean prosperity of the twentieth century. The trains strolling into town to shed a boxcar in the depot sideyard, or crying past at sixty miles per hour, possibly interrupting a girl in her high-wire act, her arms looping up when she tips to one side, the railtop as slippery as a silver spoon. And then the yellow and red locomotive rises up from the heat shimmer over a mile away, the August noonday warping the sight of it, but cinders tapping away from the spikes and the iron rails already vibrating up inside the girl's shoes. She steps down to the roadbed and then into high weeds as the Union Pacific pulls Wyoming coal and Georgia-Pacific lumber and snowplow blades and aslant Japanese pickup trucks through the open countryside and on to Omaha. And when it passes by, a worker she knows is opposite her, like a pedestrian at a stoplight, the sun not letting up, the plainsong of grasshoppers going on and on between them until the worker says, "Hot."

Twice the Union Pacific tracks cross over the sidewinding Democrat, the water slow as an oxcart, green as silage, croplands to the east, yards and houses to the west, a green ceiling of leaves in some places, whirlpools showing up in it like spinning plates that lose speed and disappear. In winter and a week or more of just above zero, high-school couples walk the gray ice, kicking up snow as quiet words are passed between them, opinions are mildly compromised, sorrows are apportioned. And

Emil Jedlicka unslings his blue-stocked .22 and slogs through high brown weeds and snow, hunting ring-necked pheasant, sidelong rabbits, and—always suddenly— quail, as his little brother Orin sprints across the Democrat in order to slide like an otter.

July in town is a gray highway and a Ford hay truck spraying by, the hay sailing like a yellow ribbon caught in the mouth of a prancing dog, and Billy Awalt up there on the camel's hump, eighteen years old and sweaty and dirty, peppered and dappled with hay dust, a lump of chew like an extra thumb under his lower lip, his blue eyes happening on a Dairy Queen and a pretty girl licking a pale trickle of ice cream from the cone. And Billy slaps his heart and cries, "Oh! I am pierced!"

And late October is orange on the ground and blue overhead and grain silos stacked up like white poker chips, and a high silver water tower belittled one night by the sloppy tattoo of one year's class at George W. Norris High. And below the silos and water tower are stripped treetops, their gray limbs still lifted up in alleluia, their yellow leaves crowding along yard fences and sheeping along the sidewalks and alleys under the shepherding wind.

Or January and a heavy snow partitioning the landscape, whiting out the highways and woods and cattle lots until there are only open spaces and steamed-up windowpanes, and a Nordstrom boy limping pitifully in the hard plaster of his clothes, the snow as deep as his hips when the boy tips over and cannot get up until a little Schumacher girl sitting by the stoop window, a spoon in her mouth, a bowl of Cheerios in her lap, says in plain voice, "There's a boy," and her mother looks out to the sidewalk.

Houses are big and white and two stories high, each a cousin to the next, with pigeon roosts in the attic gables, green storm windows on the upper floor, and a green screened porch, some as pillowed and couched as parlors or made into sleeping rooms for the boy whose next step will be the Navy and days spent on a ship with his hometown's own population, on gray water that rises up and is allayed like a geography of cornfields, sugar beets, soybeans, wheat, that stays there and says, in its own way, "Stay." Houses are turned away from the land and toward whatever is not always, sitting across from each other like dressed-up children at a party in daylight, their parents looking on with hopes and fond expectations. Overgrown elm and sycamore trees poach the sunlight from the lawns and keep petticoats of snow around them into April. In the deep lots out back are wire clotheslines with flapping white sheets pinned to them, property lines are hedged with sour green and purple grapes, or with rabbit wire and gardens of peonies, roses, gladiola, irises, marigolds, pansies. Fruit trees are so closely planted that they cannot sway without knitting. The apples and cherries drop and sweetly decompose until they're only slight brown bumps in the yards, but the pears stay up in the wind, drooping under the pecks of birds, withering down like peppers until their sorrow is justly noticed and they one day disappear.

Aligned against an alley of blue shale rock is a garage whose doors slash weeds and scrape up pebbles as an old man pokily swings them open, teetering with his last weak push. And then Victor Johnson rummages inside, being cautious about his gray sweater and high-topped shoes, looking over paint cans, junked electric motors, grass rakes and garden rakes and a pitchfork and sickles, gray doors and ladders piled overhead in the rafters, and an old windup Victrola and heavy platter records from the twenties, on one of them a soprano singing "I'm a Lonesome Melody." Under a green tarpaulin is a wooden movie projector he painted silver and big cans of tan celluloid, much of it orange and green with age, but one strip of it preserved: of an Army pilot in jodhpurs hopping from one biplane onto another's upper wing. Country people who'd paid to see the movie had been spellbound by the slight dip of the wings at the pilot's jump, the slap of his leather jacket, and how his hair strayed wild and was promptly sleeked back by the wind. But looking at the strip now, pulling a ribbon of it up to a windowpane and letting it unspool to the ground, Victor can make out only twenty frames of the leap, and then snapshot after snapshot of an Army pilot clinging to the biplane's wing. And yet Victor stays with it, as though that scene of one man staying alive were what he'd paid his nickel for.

Main Street is just a block away. Pickup trucks stop in it so their drivers can angle out over their brown left arms and speak about crops or praise the weather or make up sentences whose only real point is their lack of complication. And then a cattle truck comes up and they mosey along with a touch of their cap bills or a slap of the door metal. High-school girls in skintight jeans stay in one place on weekends, and jacked-up cars cruise past, rowdy farmboys overlapping inside, pulling over now and then in order to give the girls cigarettes and sips of pop and grief about their lipstick. And when the cars peel out, the girls say how a particular boy measured up or they swap gossip about Donna Moriarity and the scope she permitted Randy when he came back from boot camp.

Everyone is famous in this town. And everyone is necessary. Townspeople go to the Vaughn Grocery Store for the daily news, and to the Home Restaurant for history class, especially at evensong when the old people eat graveled pot roast and lemon meringue pie and calmly sip coffee from cups they tip to their mouths with both hands. The Kiwanis Club meets here on Tuesday nights, and hopes are made public, petty sins are tidily dispatched, the proceeds from the gumball machines are tallied up and poured into the upkeep of a playground. Yutesler's Hardware has picnic items and kitchen appliances in its one window, in the manner of those prosperous men who would prefer to be known for their hobbies. And there is one crisp, white, Protestant church with a steeple, of the sort pictured on calendars; and the Immaculate Conception Catholic Church, grayly holding the town at bay like a Gothic wolfhound. And there is an insurance agency, a county coroner and justice of the peace, a secondhand shop, a handsome chiropractor named Koch who coaches the Pony League baseball team, a post office approached on unpainted wood steps outside of a cheap mobile home, the Nighthawk tavern where there's Falstaff tap beer, a green pool table, a poster recording the Cornhuskers scores, a crazy man patiently tolerated, a gray-haired woman with an unmoored eye, a boy in spectacles thick as paperweights, a carpenter missing one index finger, a plump waitress whose day job is in a basement beauty shop, an old woman who creeps up to the side door at eight in order to purchase one shot glass of whiskey.

And yet passing by, and paying attention, an outsider is only aware of what isn't, that there's no bookshop, no picture show, no pharmacy or dry cleaners, no cocktail parties, extreme opinions, jewelry or piano stores, motels, hotels, hospital, political headquarters, philosophical theories about Being and the soul.

High importance is only attached to practicalities, and so there is the Batchelor Funeral Home, where a proud old gentleman is on display in a dark brown suit, his yellow fingernails finally clean, his smeared eyeglasses in his coat pocket, a grandchild on tiptoes by the casket, peering at the lips that will not move, the sparrow chest that will not rise. And there's Tommy Seymour's for Sinclair gasoline and mechanical repairs, a green balloon dinosaur bobbing from a string over the cash register, old tires piled beneath the cottonwood, For Sale in the sideyard a Case tractor, a John Deere reaper, a hay mower, a red manure spreader, and a rusty grain conveyor, green weeds overcoming them, standing up inside them, trying slyly and little by little to inherit machinery for the earth.

And beyond that are woods, a slope of pasture, six empty cattle pens, a driveway made of limestone pebbles, and the house where Alice Sorensen pages through a child's World Book Encyclopedia, stopping at the descriptions of California, Capetown, Ceylon, Colorado, Copenhagen, Corpus Christi, Costa Rica, Cyprus.

Widow Dworak has been watering the lawn in an open raincoat and apron, but at nine she walks the green hose around to the spigot and screws down the nozzle so that the spray is a misty crystal bowl softly baptizing the ivy. She says, "How about some camomile tea?" And she says, "Yum. Oh, boy. That hits the spot." And bends to shut the water off.

The Union Pacific night train rolls through town just after ten o'clock when a sixty-year-old man named Adolf Schooley is a boy again in bed, and when the huge weight of forty or fifty cars jostles his upstairs room like a motor he'd put a quarter in. And over the sighing industry of the train, he can hear the train saying *Nebraska, Nebraska, Nebraska, Nebraska.* And he cannot sleep.

Mrs. Antoinette Heft is at the Home Restaurant, placing frozen meat patties on waxed paper, pausing at times to clamp her fingers under her arms and press the sting from them. She stops when the Union Pacific passes, then picks a cigarette out of a pack of Kools and smokes it on the back porch, smelling air as crisp as Oxydol, looking up at stars the Pawnee Indians looked at, hearing the low harmonica of big rigs on the highway, in the town she knows like the palm of her hand, in the country she knows by heart.

Reading as a Writer

1. How does Hansen manage to capture the essence of the entire region using concrete details?

2. What are the some of the images that spring to mind after you've read the piece?

3. What techniques does Hansen use that you could apply to make your own work more vivid and emotionally satisfying?

CHAPTER FOUR

The Short Story
Defining and Shaping

"Bᴜᴛ ɪs ɪᴛ ᴀ sᴛᴏʀʏ?" is one of the main questions that comes up in creative writing workshops. Very frequently, it isn't—yet. Early short story drafts from beginning writers often include mostly rough character sketches, theories about life, abstract ideas, anecdotes, or morality tales that fail to deliver the same emotional satisfaction as a completely rendered piece of short fiction.

So what *is* a short story? It's not an easy question to answer. Indeed, a great deal of debate has taken place on what makes a story a story, and some very learned and intelligent people disagree on a number of key points.

This chapter focuses on the shape of fiction, specifically the short story. It gives you a definition of what makes a short story, and identifies the key narrative conventions that have accrued over the years. The exercises at the end of the chapter give you a chance to practice some of these concepts and will help you get started on writing short fiction.

To better understand the concepts introduced in this chapter, you'll want to do one of the readings ahead of time: Francine Prose's "What Makes a Short Story?" (pp. 109–118).

Some Basic Definitions

Perhaps nothing is as daunting as reading any of the very fine books on writing and then trying to reconcile exactly what a short story *is*. After all, what possible definition can we come up with that includes stories we love by Anton Chekhov, Donald Barthelme, Alice Munro, Jorge Luis Borges, Henry James, Grace Paley, and others?

Here are just a few of the definitions:

> A short piece of prose fiction having few characters and aiming at unity of effect. —*The American Heritage Dictionary*

> A shaft driven straight into the heart of human experience. —Eᴅɪᴛʜ Wʜᴀʀᴛᴏɴ

> An account of a character struggling to reach a goal. —Sᴛᴇᴠᴇɴ Sᴄʜᴏᴇɴ

> What you see when you look out the window. —Mᴀᴠɪs Gᴀʟʟᴀɴᴛ

> A dramatic event that involves a person because he is a person, and a particular person—that is, because he shares in the general human condition and in some specific human situation. —FLANNERY O'CONNOR

Many people base their definition of a story on Aristotle's admonition that it must have a beginning, middle, and end. This is generally assumed to mean that a story follows the three-part shape of conflict, crisis, and resolution. (More on this shortly.)

Other definitions center on Edgar Allan Poe's theory that a story must achieve "a certain unique or single effect" and be readable in one sitting, "a half hour to one or two hours in its perusal." This view of the short story is perhaps best summed up in an introduction to a 1907 anthology of short fiction:

> [T]he short story must do one thing only, and it must do this completely and perfectly; it must not loiter or digress; it must have unity of action, unity of temper, unity of tone, unity of color, unity of effect; and it must vigilantly exclude everything that might interfere with its singleness of intention.
> —BRANDER MATTHEWS, *The Short Story*

Former *Esquire* fiction editor Rust Hills says that "a short story tells of something that happened to someone" but modifies it to say that as a result of that "something" the character is significantly changed, or "moved," to use Hills's term. Indeed, this notion that a change must occur in a character is commonly viewed as "required" by many teachers and students of writing alike.

There is no better commentary on this issue than Francine Prose's essay, "What Makes a Short Story?" Prose debunks most of the common platitudes regarding the short story. "The real problem is that the most obvious answer is the most correct," she writes. "We *know* what a short story is: a work of fiction of a certain length, a length with apparently no minimum."

Joyce Carol Oates agrees in her introduction to *The Oxford Book of American Short Stories*:

> Formal definitions of the short story are commonplace, yet there is none quite democratic enough to accommodate an art that includes so much variety and an art that so readily lends itself to experimentation and idiosyncratic voices. Perhaps length alone should be the sole criterion? Whenever critics try to impose other, more subjective strictures on the genre (as on any genre) too much work is excluded.

Unlike many theorists, neither Prose nor Oates dictates that to be a "real story" a piece must contain easily identifiable components or fulfill any given form. For Prose, there is one basic requirement other than that of length (Prose writes that some literary critics believe Joseph Conrad's "Heart of Darkness" stretches the length of a short story as far as it can go without being considered a novella): a short story cannot be summarized; it contains some irreducible germ at its heart that defies expression. In this, she is echoing the words of Flannery O'Connor and

Goethe: that true literature "resists paraphrase" and "finds the general in the particular."

Oates adds another requirement: that "no matter its mysteries or experimental properties, it achieves closure—meaning that, when it ends, the attentive reader understands why." In other words, a story that is a real story delivers a unit of satisfaction to the reader that cannot be delivered by merely summarizing the events of the story. In some cases, this sense of closure might be very subtle. Joyce Carol Oates's own "Where Are You Going, Where Have You Been?" (pp. 40–53) often frustrates readers because it seems to end before the end, yet a careful reading of the work shows that it has indeed reached closure—and very powerful closure indeed.

And then we have Henry James. In a famous essay he says that the "good health" of an art demands that it be "perfectly free." He was talking about novel writing (rebutting an essay that tried to lay out all the rules a novel must supposedly obey to *be* a novel), but we can extend what he says to the short story as well. James continues:

> [Art] lives upon exercise, and the very meaning of exercise is freedom. The only obligation to which in advance we may hold a novel without incurring the accusation of being arbitrary, is that it be interesting. That general responsibility rests upon it, but it is the only one I can think of.
> —Henry James, "The Art of Fiction"

Let's continue building our definition of what a short story is by borrowing this nugget of wisdom as well: the short story has the obligation to be interesting.

So what do we have as our final, composite definition? A short story is a short work of prose, with no minimum number of words and a maximum length of, say, 20,000 words. And the only three requirements we will put on it ahead of time are that it be interesting, resist paraphrase, and end up providing some unit of satisfaction, or sense of completeness, to the reader.

The Conflict–Crisis–Resolution Model

One of the first things we must address in a section on story is the conflict–crisis–resolution model. It is so predominant that many beginning writers—as well as a good number of experienced teachers—feel that a story is not a real story unless it fits into this model.

According to this definition of a short story, there is always an "arc" to a narrative that looks like the diagram below:

Called the Freitag triangle after the nineteenth-century literary critic who first formulated this theory, the idea is that every story has conflict that gradually intensifies and culminates in a crisis, after which there is a resolution.

We can be even more specific and label no less than five different stages of a short story, according to Freitag: the beginning is called the *exposition*, which provides background on the characters, the setting, the situation, and so on; the next stage is called the *rising action*, during which the character(s) face increasingly intensive conflict; then the *climax*, or culmination of the conflict; after that the *falling action*, or denouement, during which the tension is palpably eased; and, finally, the *resolution*, or ending.

You can find this diagram, or one like it, in just about every book on fiction. (If you paid attention in high school, you might even remember categorizing the three kinds of conflict that are possible: man against man, man against nature, man against himself.) But while this concept might be useful when dissecting a certain type of story, it is certainly not a way of reading *all* stories. A good number of very fine stories—including many included in this book—simply do not fit into the conflict–crisis–resolution model.

Moreover, even though the conflict–crisis–resolution model might fit the majority of stories we read, I am hard-pressed to use it as an example of how to *write* them.

So this is the question: while theories like this probably cover the narrative bases in a neat, abstracted way, in what way do they help us write? How do we take an abstract model like this and make it useful for our purpose—creating art?

Let's first backtrack and look at an example of a story that *does* fit fairly well into the crisis–conflict–resolution model: Flannery O'Connor's "Everything That Rises Must Converge" (pp. 178–189). You'll notice that the conflict in the story would probably be better described as a series of "complications" (another word used in conjunction with the Freitag triangle), but in all other respects it conforms nicely to our needs.

We start with the *exposition:* Julian and his mother are getting ready to leave the house. The mother is going to a "reducing class" that is "designed for working girls over fifty, who weighed from 165 to 200 pounds." We learn that Julian feels obligated to take his mother downtown, although he is clearly unhappy about it. We also learn about a new hat (hideous, in Julian's opinion) that his mother has just bought for herself, and that she rarely indulges herself in that way. Instead, she appears to have come down a bit in the world—at least she thinks so—and despite Julian's sneering at her for holding on to what she considers higher social standards, he secretly likes the fact that he came from grander places than he now occupies.

The *rising action* begins almost immediately as Julian uses every opportunity to fight with his mother and be rude to her. When they reach the bus stop, he deliberately takes off his tie and stuffs it in his pocket to annoy her. On the bus, Julian's mother makes some openly racist remarks, causing Julian to cringe and retreat into himself—and into an interior monologue in which he commends himself on his own intelligence and sensitivity while condemning his mother for her small mind and stifled spirit. When a well-dressed black man boards the bus, Julian, apparently displeased with his mother, indulges in a number of mean-spirited fantasies in which he attempts to humiliate and anger her. The rising action continues to rise as a black woman with a small boy, wearing the exact same hat as Julian's mother, gets on the bus. The two women silently confront each other, but just when Julian begins to believe—quite happily—that his mother is going to get her comeuppance, he realizes with severe disappointment that she is going to be able to laugh the whole incident off.

But then the *crisis* approaches. Julian and his mother and the black woman and her child get off at the same stop. Julian tries to prevent his mother from giving the little boy a penny, but he fails. The black woman then wallops Julian's mother with her purse and knocks her down on the sidewalk. Despite the fact that his mother seems ill and confused, Julian begins berating her; he triumphantly tells her "the old world is gone" before understanding that something is seriously wrong with her (she has apparently had a stroke). At this Julian falls apart. "Darling, sweetheart, wait!" he cries, and finally, with the *falling action,* he runs to get help but understands that his life is changed forever and that he is about to enter a "world of guilt and sorrow."

I've oversimplified (and, by the way, proven that you can't tell a story by summarizing the plot), but you can see how this fits roughly into the Freitag model. A good number of stories can be analyzed thus, and although none follows the formula exactly, you can make the case that this is the form most short stories take.

But now let's look at another famous story included in this book: "The Things They Carried" (pp. 79–92).

There is no exposition: the story starts abruptly with a description of what Lieutenant Jimmy Cross, an officer in Vietnam commanding a platoon, carried (love letters). This is rapidly followed by lists of what the other soldiers in the platoon carried (pocket knives, heat tabs, lighters, matches, C rations, water). We hear about the central event of the story halfway through the second paragraph: one of the men, Lavender, is shot. This would arguably be considered the climax in a traditional story. But rather than building up to it, we are told about it upfront, quite casually. The narrative then circles around and around, revisiting the shooting incident in a number of ways, all the while being periodically interrupted by the lists of the things the men carried, which gradually change from real, physical things to more abstract things, such as fear and anguish and guilt. We're put into the mind of characters other than Jimmy Cross (which complicates the story). Finally, the story ends with Jimmy Cross burning his love letters and determining to repudiate love and human emotion in favor of what he considers the more worthy goal of taking care of his men.

To try to chart this story along the conflict–crisis–resolution model is silly—and I would even venture to say that this story couldn't have been written if O'Brien had been thinking in such simplistic terms.

Linear versus Modular Stories

Madison Smartt Bell makes a distinction between linear and modular story structures. In his view, "linear" stories follow the conflict–crisis–resolution model of the Freitag triangle; "modular" stories are composed as a mosaic, a design made up of component parts:

> If linear design can be understood as somehow subtractive, a process of removing the less essential material so as to reveal the movement of narrative vectors more clearly and cleanly, then modular design is additive. The writer adds and arranges more and more modular units which may be attractive in themselves for all sorts of different reasons, but which also must serve the purpose of clarifying the overall design of the text as a whole. . . .
>
> What modular design can do is liberate the writer from linear logic, those chains of cause and effect, strings of dominoes always falling forward.
>
> —MADISON SMARTT BELL, *Narrative Design*

One of the most famous examples of modular design is the story "In the Heart of the Heart of the Country" by William Gass. Although you might be able to piece together a sort of narrative (English professor has affair with a student that ends, leaving him heartbroken), that's hardly what the story is *about*. (If it were, why include all the other information about geography, local flora and fauna, the town, the weather, the neighbors, etc.) The material is modular; none of it depends for causality on anything else. You could conceivably move the different modules around, although there are doubtless some very specific reasons that the author arranged them as he did.

Even with so-called linear stories, there are a number of reasons why thinking conflict–crisis–resolution might not be helpful. First is the language used: "conflict" and "rising action" bring to mind fistfights and guns and rather melodramatic events. Yet think of stories like Grace Paley's "Mother" (p. 74–75) or Anton Chekhov's "The Lady with the Little Dog" (pp. 208–220); to use the word "conflict" to describe how they capture and hold our attention seems incongruous. These characters desire things, *yearn* for things; they do not fight or otherwise clash in any obvious or simplistic way.

Second, even stories that follow this model seldom have a steady rising action that never falters. Instead, there are ebbs and flows in the story: pockets of tension built up and tension released, all of which contribute to the story's culmination. Indeed, I prefer to use a diagram I call the "earthquake model" to indicate how tension can build, subside, then build again, before arriving at the pivotal moment, or climax.

Third, and finally, abstract theory is simply not where stories tend to come from. They come from some dark, secretive place, and from material that doesn't offer itself easily. Knowing the so-called rules about conflict, crisis, and resolution doesn't help you *write* a good story. It may even impede you, if you feel you have to write by some formula.

Still, knowing about the conflict–crisis–resolution model can be very helpful *after* a story has been written. If the story seems to want to fit into this general form (and most stories written today do fall within this domain), knowing the general shape of stories of this kind can be very useful in editing it.

As Madison Smartt Bell concludes:

> It's easy to get silly with these pictures [the Freitag triangle]. And indeed, most writers can get by very handily without them (or at any rate, without actually chalking them on the board) during the process of writing. The diagrams are no more than crude representations of the shape which the writer's intuition should be giving to the material as the process of composition goes forward. The Freitag triangle is a left brain superimposition over what is for the most part a right brain activity. But if intuition fails or goes astray, the triangle and its variants can be quite useful as diagnostic tools, perhaps even as problem-solving devices.

This is probably the most useful way to think of the Freitag triangle: not as a model to follow, but as a way of going back into a story and seeing how it measures up, structurally, to this conventional view of short fiction. Note my use of "conventional": this works for stories that want to be conventional conflict–crisis–resolution stories, but never, under any circumstances, should it be applied to *all* stories. If you get nothing else out of this chapter, please take this with you: you do not have to write to this conventional model.

To Epiphany or Not to Epiphany?

Another common presumption about short stories is that a piece is not *really* a short story unless it culminates in a revelation, or "epiphany," as James Joyce described it. In an *epiphany*, a character is brought (or forced into) a state of enlightenment, experiencing a moment when he or she realizes something of great importance to his or her life. This is what Aristotle called "recognition" (and which, along with "reversal" and "suffering," made up what he considered the three parts of plot).

We can see the epiphany model at work in many stories. Two famous ones are "Araby" by James Joyce and "A & P" by John Updike. They have very similar plots: a young boy views an (unattainable) object of beauty and wishes to make a gesture, give a gift, to her. The effort fails, in both stories, leaving the Joyce hero to lament, "Gazing up into the darkness I saw myself as a creature driven and derided by vanity; and my eyes burned with anguish and anger," and the Updike protagonist to conclude, "[. . .] my stomach kind of fell as I felt how hard the world was going to be to me hereafter." Both are epiphanies, or moments of insight, that the characters achieve as a result of the specific events that transpire in the story. And many beautiful stories have been written in which an epiphany is prevalent—not the least of which is "The Things They Carried."

But Charles Baxter points out that perhaps epiphanies are being overused:

Suddenly I realized . . .

The language of literary epiphanies naturally has something in common with the rhetoric of religious revelation. The veil of appearances is pulled aside and an inner truth is revealed. A moment of radiant vision brings forth the sensation, if not the content, of meaning.

—CHARLES BAXTER, "Against Epiphanies"

Baxter also comments that "the loss of innocence, and the arrival of knowingness, can become an addiction":

A mode that began with moves of elegant feeling and energy, particularly in stories that have to deal with worlds within worlds of urban or small town or even familial hypocrisy, can get stale. Worse than stale: rotten. The mass production of insight, in fiction or elsewhere, is a dubious phenomenon. But because it is a private experience, it can't be debated or contested. Suddenly, it seems, everyone is having insights. Possibly we have entered the Age of Insight.

Everywhere there is a glut of epiphanies. Radiance rules. But some of the insights have seemed disturbingly untrustworthy. There is a smell about them of recently molded plastic. At the level of discursive rhetoric, it is a bit like the current craze for angels. Perhaps these are not true insights at all. What then?

As Baxter observes, we can name many fine stories that possess literary epiphanies. But to view that as the *only* way to bring a story to fruition is to paint yourself into a very tight creative corner indeed.

The novelist Jim Shepard, also a teacher, noticed the same phenomenon as Baxter in his students' work:

More and more I've been seeing stories in which the protagonists are whooshed along the little conveyor belts of their narratives to that defining moment of insight or clarification that will allow them to see with new eyes the essential emotional or spiritual furniture of their lives. The implication is nearly always that this moment of insight removes one of the last major obstacles on the road to personal fulfillment. . . .

Now, as I understand it, a short story, by definition, does have a responsibility, in its closing gestures, to enlarge *our* understanding, but it seems to be increasingly difficult for writers to resist allowing their hapless *protagonist* a new understanding as well—an understanding that will set him or her on the path to a more actualized life.

—JIM SHEPARD, "I Know Myself Real Well. That's the Problem"

In my own classroom, people seem to feel dissatisfied if this insight has not been provided for the character. They want revelation, they want the possibility of

redemption, they want to *fix* things for the characters involved. All wonderful generous bounty to bestow on characters, but perhaps our job isn't to rescue all the
characters that come under our care. Perhaps our job is simply to *render* what their
predicament is, rather than solving their problems for them?

Is Change Necessary? (The Debate Continues)

The notion that *reversal* (as Aristotle called it), or change, is a requirement of a piece
of fiction is also a prevalent one. That is, a character must not only realize some truth
that was previously obscure to him or her, but also he or she must act upon it. Yet in
life, we are given opportunities for change all the time, and we fail to make those
changes, either out of stupidity, or laziness, or even ignorance—we didn't know the
possibility for change was a possibility.

   The novelist John L'Heureux has a way of describing a certain type of story—he
doesn't believe that all stories must follow this model—that deals with this question
of to-change-or-not-to-change: "Capture a moment after which nothing can ever be
the same again," he advises. This is a wonderfully flexible definition of a short story—
again, for certain types of stories—because it drives home the fact that change is not
necessary. Change can be offered to a character—and that character may decline to
accept the opportunity. The "crisis" of a piece can be of negative, rather than positive, action: something not done, a sin not committed, an act of grace not performed.
But a moment of significance has passed, and things cannot be the same again.

   Consider the following passage, in which two adult women, mourning the death
of their father, refuse to grow up; they have a chance to re-examine their lives, and
perhaps determine to live them differently, but in the end are unable to break
through the years of habit and repression that have smothered them for so long:

> She turned away from the Buddha with one of her vague gestures. She went
> over to where Josephine was standing. She wanted to say something
> to Josephine, something frightfully important, about—about the future and
> what . . .
>   "Don't you think perhaps—" she began.
>   But Josephine interrupted her. "I was wondering if now—" she murmured.
> They stopped; they waited for each other.
>   "Go on, Con," said Josephine.
>   "No, no, Jug, after you," said Constantia.
>   "No, say what you were going to say. You began," said Josephine.
>   "I'd . . . I'd rather hear what you were going to say first," said Constantia.
>   "Don't be absurd, Con."
>   "Really, Jug."
>   "Connie!"
>   "Oh, *Jug*!"
>   A pause. Then Constantia said faintly, "I can't say what I was going to say,
> Jug, because I've forgotten what it was . . . that I was going to say."

Josephine was silent for a moment. She stared at a big cloud where the sun had been. Then she replied shortly, "I've forgotten too."

—KATHERINE MANSFIELD, "Daughters of the Late Colonel"

On Not Becoming Slaves to Theory

"I feel that discussing story-writing in terms of plot, character, and theme is like trying to describe the expression on a face by saying where the eyes, nose, and mouth are," Flannery O'Connor wrote in celebrated essay. She continues:

> You want to know how you can actually write a good story, and further, how you can tell when you've done it; and so you want to know what the form of a short story is, as if the form were something that existed outside of each story and could be applied or imposed on the material. Of course, the more you write, the more you will realize that the form is organic; that it is something that grows out of the material, that the form of each story is unique. [. . .] The only way, I think, to learn to write short stories is to write them, and then to try to discover what you have done. The time to think of technique is when you've actually got the story in front of you.
>
> —FLANNERY O'CONNOR, "Writing Short Stories"

One of the things that distinguishes a creative writer from, say, an accountant or a systems analyst is that the writer's process is shrouded in mystery. Writers use their own sense of not knowing to delve into the heart of some ambiguity of personal interest. From these personal mysteries they generate prose that can then grow and, under the right circumstances, be shaped into a short story or a novel. But very few writers know what they are going to write beforehand. The creative mind usually doesn't work that way, as Donald Barthelme writes:

> Let us suppose that someone is writing a story. From the world of conventional signs he takes an azalea bush, plants it in a pleasant park. He takes a gold pocket watch from the world of conventional signs and places it under the azalea bush. He takes from the same rich source a handsome thief and a chastity belt, places the thief in the chastity belt and lays him tenderly under the azalea, not neglecting to wind the gold pocket watch so that its ticking will, at length, awaken the now-sleeping thief. From the Sarah Lawrence campus he borrows a pair of seniors, Jacqueline and Jemima, and sets them to walking into the vicinity of the azalea bush and the handsome, chaste thief. Jacqueline and Jemima have just failed the Graduate Record Examination and are cursing God in colorful Sarah Lawrence language. What happens next?
>
> Of course, I don't know. *It's appropriate to say that the writer is someone who, confronted with a blank page, does not know anything* [emphasis mine].
>
> —DONALD BARTHELME, "Not Knowing"

Willa Cather, alternatively, makes the distinction between writing as an exercise "as safe and commendable as making soap or breakfast foods" and what happens when we attempt to create art, "which is always a search for something for which there is no market demand, something new and untried, *where the values are intrinsic and have nothing to do with standardized values* [emphasis mine]."

So it's always critical to keep in mind that there are no rules in fiction, only *conventions* that have been built up over the years based on the way that writers have crafted their stories. (A convention is "an established technique, practice, or device," according to *Merriam-Webster's Collegiate Dictionary*.) Conventions can be useful, because they provide successful models we can emulate and learn from, and which help guide us in the reading and writing of fiction. But too many beginning writers translate them into hard-core rules that *must* be followed. Among all the other reasons we've stated why this won't work, it's just plain impossible: as you'll see, many of the so-called rules contradict each other. Try to follow them all (just like trying to follow all the advice given in a writing workshop), and you'll either go mad or end up with a chaotic mess rather than a story or novel.

There's no doubt that writing short fiction would be easier if there were some hard-set rules. Indeed, some writers cling to the conflict–crisis–resolution model or the change model as a way of avoiding the fear and ambiguity of the blank page or the blank computer screen. As we'll say time and time again, any way "in" to a story is a good one, and so if it is helpful for you to think of short fiction in this way, then do it.

But it's wrong-headed to approach the writing of fiction in an overly formulaic way. I was once surprised to hear that a writer giving seminars was handing out this formula, ABCDE:

Action
Backstory
Crisis
Denouement
Ending

While it might be a useful *exercise* (you might even want to try it yourself) to begin a story with an action (begin in the middle), only to backtrack and fill in the blanks (we'll talk about this in Chapter 11), we wouldn't want to structure every story like this. We're in the business of exploring material through writing, not filling out formulas. If you wanted formulas, you'd be reading a mathematics or chemistry textbook, not this one.

Rick DeMarinis makes a heart-warming "confession" about writing short stories in his book on the topic:

> I don't know how to write a short story even though I've written hundreds of them, published five collections of them, sold them to magazines, both literary and commercial. I have also taught the subject for more than twenty years in various university English departments that hired me for that purpose. But

here's the thing: I don't have a set of rules, a formula, a system, that tells me how to set about writing a story of *literary quality*. I don't have a "how." If I had such a system, one that would fit every interesting human situation, I'd write a prizewinner every day of the week. I'd make Chekhov look like a backslider. I'd make Cheever look like he was working out of laundry lists. I'd make Hemingway look punch-drunk. But the hard truth is that there is no system, no set of rules that guarantee able composition or abundant production. There is no magic formula that will make hard work, commitment, inspiration, taste, and good luck unnecessary.

—Rick DeMarinis, *The Art and the Craft of the Short Story*

If in this chapter I seem to be arguing as much against the conventions as explaining them, it's because all too often I see a wonderfully complex beginning of a story either squashed early on by unsubtle uses of "conflict" or killed off in workshop as not fulfilling, in some obvious way, the conflict–crisis–resolution model.

EXERCISES

Trying to assimilate what a short story is has stymied many very smart people. There are enough rigid definitions and so-called rules to make your head spin. The exercises in this section are intended to help you understand the basic concepts of what constitutes a story and to help you see past some of the so-called conventions that may stifle you as you try to write your own story.

Exercise 1: False Epiphanies I Have Had

Goal: To examine your own thoughts and assumptions about epiphanies in fiction, and to understand that sometimes we try to force false epiphanies into our stories in order to fit a preconceived model.

1. Think of a time when you (or a character in a story you're working on) had an epiphany—a moment when you believed, finally and absolutely, that you had the answer to something (yes, this is the woman I want to marry; no, I was never meant to be an architect; yes, it's the right thing to move to Columbus), but it turned out to be wrong. If you want, use the phrase "suddenly I realized" as a way of spurring the epiphany on.

2. Write down the precise events that led up to the epiphany (what you were doing, where you were, who you were with, etc.).

3. Now write "the morning after" by capturing a moment of doubt and uncertainty that followed the false epiphany. As always, ground it in a specific place and time—no abstractions. (And it doesn't have to be the literal morning after—the false epiphany can be proven wrong years after it occurs, as in the example below.)

The following was written by Christie Cochrell:

1. I realized I could love Oliver.

2. His ancient cat, all spine and tail, lays itself against me, its whole length, and I realize how much love Oliver needs, how much I can provide, because this lovely creature, his only companion, is not much longer for this world, clearly. Oliver and I have been in Italy for three weeks, and have just come home from the airport—to his home, his home of five or so years, in which the sofa is still draped with drop cloths, these boxes still to be unpacked. He is so lonely. There is the insignificant but mortal weight of this cat that has come to me immediately, gray and forlorn, there is time ahead to get to be its friend, to get lonely Oliver out of his boxes, trusting in love again.

3. The next morning, saddened at being apart for the first time in three weeks, I impulsively go to find Oliver at his favorite café (remembering his reading the *Herald Tribune* every morning in Rome). He'll be happy to see me, missing me too. I'm daring, taking this chance at love. I find him at the café, after thinking he isn't there after all, go up to the table, happily. He looks startled when I say hi quietly; then taken aback—unhappy to be interrupted in his reading, his solitary routine. After a telling moment of silence he says, politely, that I can sit down. We are as if strangers again. I know I'll never again see his lovely cat. We'll both go on being lonely apart.

Exercise 2: Opportunities Not Taken

GOAL: To examine moments when change was possible, but declined.

1. Think of a time when you (or a character) made a negative decision: chose *not* to do something, *not* to go somewhere, *not* to act in a certain way.

2. Write it down *precisely:* where were you (or your character), what were you wearing, what did you say and do?

The following was written by Steve Marvin:

My mother believes in giving me choices: she's done this since I was a baby, she read it in some book that you give kids choices, not open-ended questions. Not, "What do you want to eat?" but "Do you want to eat pizza or chicken tonight?" She's raised me this way and I guess I've gotten in the habit of thinking in terms of choices too when I've had a hard time deciding what to do about something. What exactly is the choice that I am making? And so the other night, it was late, and Joanne was over of course—her roommate is giving her trouble—and of course as usual I offered her the couch but this time she refused. Now she was upset, she was wearing that coffee-colored short short dress she wears when she wants to look hot even though she's a little too heavy for getting the right effect. She's got her ass-kicking boots on. She wants to go out, she's not ready to go to sleep and I can tell this is going to be one of the difficult nights when she won't take no for an answer. In this case I've made my choice: I want to stay home and get some sleep before class tomorrow, but she is getting madder and madder and I see my choice is between having a friend and not having a friend. In the past I've always gone along and I don't know what it was but at that moment I had an inkling that I had a real choice, because of course it was never a choice, when Joanne wants to do something, you do it, because the choice is unacceptable, which is having Joanne mad at you or having her acting nice to you, and believe me, that is not a choice. So there I am, dressed like a bum, hardly ready to go out and something in me snapped and I said, I'm not going, but she didn't even have to open her mouth, I saw that *look* and of course I went to get dressed.

READINGS

FRANCINE PROSE

What Makes a Short Story?

THERE MUST BE more difficult questions than "What makes a short story?"

What is man, that Thou art mindful of him? What does a woman want? What is love? What walks on four legs at dawn, two legs at noon, three legs in the evening? What can you say about a twenty-five-year-old girl who died? Tell me where is fancy bred, in the heart or in the head?

Yet all of these seemingly impossible questions are, in fact, far easier to address than the deceptively straightforward matter of what constitutes the short story. For all of these classic puzzlers—except for the sphinx's riddle—suggest variant solutions and multiple possibilities, invite expansion and rumination, whereas any attempt to establish the identifying characteristics of the short story seems to require a narrowing, a winnowing, a definition by exclusion. A short story is probably this—but definitely not that.

The real problem is that the most obvious answer is the most correct. We *know* what a short story is: a work of fiction of a certain length, a length with apparently no minimum. An increasing number of anthologies feature stories of no more than a humble page, or a single flashy paragraph, and one of the most powerful stories in all of literature, Isaac Babel's "Crossing Into Poland," less than three pages long, is capacious enough to include a massive and chaotic military campaign, a soldier's night of troubled dreams, and the report of a brutal murder. Similarly, Cynthia Ozick's "The Shawl" is only four pages long.

But, nearing the opposite end of the spectrum, Robert Boswell's "The Darkness of Love" is over forty pages. After a certain point (to be on the safe side, let's say seventy or eighty pages, though one short-story theoretician has argued that Conrad's "Heart of Darkness"—not one word more or less—defines the outer limits of the form) the extended short story begins to impinge on novella territory.

Lacking anything clearer or more definitive than these vague mumblings about size, we imagine that we can begin to define the short story by distinguishing it from other forms of fiction, by explaining why it is not a sketch, a fairy tale, or a myth.

And yet some of our favorite stories seem a lot like the sort of casual anecdote we might hear a friend tell at a dinner party. Somerset Maugham, in what must have been a demented moment, claimed that many of Chekhov's great stories *were* anecdotes and not proper stories at all. ("If you try to tell one of his stories you will find that there is nothing to tell. The anecdote, stripped of its trimmings, is insignificant and often inane. It was grand for people who wanted to write a story and couldn't think of a plot to discover that you could very well manage without one.") And just to confuse things further, many fairy tales—the best of Hans Christian Andersen and the Brothers Grimm—are as carefully constructed, as densely layered, as elaborately crafted as the stories (or are they tales?) of, for example, Hawthorne and Poe.

Why do we feel so certain that a masterpiece such as Tolstoy's "The Three Hermits" is a short story, though it so clearly bears—and takes so little trouble to hide—the stamp of its origins in "an old legend current in the Volga district" and though its structure has more in common with the shaggy-dog story than with the artful, nuanced studies of Henry James, who, in fact, was quite insistent that a short story "must be an idea—it can't be a 'story' in the vulgar sense of the word. It must be a picture; it must illustrate something . . . something of the real essence of the subject."

Just to take on James, always something of a challenge, let's look at "The Three Hermits," which could hardly be more of a "story," in the most fabulously, unashamedly "vulgar sense of the word." The protagonist, if we can call him that—we know nothing about his background or the subtler depths of his character, absolutely nothing, in short, except that he is a Bishop of the Orthodox Church—is traveling on a ship that passes near an island on which, he hears, live three monks who spend their lives in prayer. The Bishop insists on being ferried to the island, where he meets the hermits—again described with a minimum of the sort of physical and psychological description that, we have been taught, is essential for fiction in general and for the short story in particular. One of the monks is tall "with a piece of matting tied round his waist"; the second is shorter, in a "tattered peasant coat"; and the third is "very old, bent with age and wearing an old cassock." To his horror, the Bishop discovers that the hermits have their own way of praying ("Three are ye, three are we, have mercy on us") and have never heard of the Lord's Prayer.

The bulk of the story, the shaggy-dog part, concerns the Bishop's efforts to teach these comically slow learners how to pray correctly—a Herculean task that consumes the entire day and that is completed, more or less, to the visitor's satisfaction. That night, as the Bishop is sailing away from the island, he sees a light skimming toward him across the water. "Was it a seagull, or the little gleaming of some small boat?" No, in fact, the radiance is an aura surrounding the hermits, flying hand in hand over the water, desperately chasing the Bishop's boat because they have forgotten what they learned from the church official, who—educated at last—tells them, "It is not for me to teach you. Pray for us sinners."

Even in summary, this story retains some of its power to astonish and move us, and yet the full effect of reading the work in its entirety is all but lost. Which brings us to one of the few things that *can* be said about the short story: Like all great works of art, it cannot be summarized or reduced without sacrificing the very qualities that do in fact distinguish an amusing dinner-party anecdote from a great work of art— depth, resonance, harmony, plus all the less quantifiable marks of artistic creation. This is especially true of stories in which the plot line is not so clear, so succinct, so distilled to its folkloric essentials, and of writers who achieve their effects almost entirely by the use of tone, by the accretion of minute detail, and by the precise use of language.

What can we possibly—accurately—conclude about Turgenev's "Bezhin Meadow" when we hear that it concerns a few hours that the narrator spends among a group of peasant boys who scare themselves and each other by telling ghost stories? At the end of the story, we learn—in a sort of brief epilogue—that one of the boys was killed a short time after that evening on the meadow. When we hear it summarized, the plot seems sketchy and indistinct—why is this not a vignette or a "mood piece"? But when we read the story itself—a work of art that feels utterly complete and in which every sentence and phrase contributes to the whole—we are certain, beyond any doubt, that it is indeed a story. We cannot imagine anything that needs to be added or omitted.

What remains of the humor and breathtaking originality of Katherine Mansfield's "Daughters of the Late Colonel" when we describe it as a story about two childlike (but ostensibly adult) sisters attempting to get through the days following the death of their father? What survives of the many small gestures and lines of deceptively whimsical dialogue that lead us to understand that the distribution of power between the more "grown-up" sensible Josephine and the fanciful, impulsive, skittish Constantia is the same as it must have been in early childhood? What remains of Josephine's certainty that their dead father is hiding in his chest of drawers, or of his former nurse's—Nurse Andrew's—upsetting, "simply fearful" greed for butter, or of the "white, terrified" blancmange that the cook sets on the table, or of that final, elliptical moment of forgetting in which we intuit the impossible and tragic cost of remembering?

It is hard to *recognize* Chekhov's "The Lady with the Pet Dog" from the following description: A jaded womanizer falls deeply in love despite himself and for the first time, and in the course of that love affair discovers that his whole world—that he himself—has changed. How sentimental and obvious it sounds, how romantic and unconvincing. Yet when we actually read the story, we feel that it is of enormous, immeasurable consequence and resonance, and that it tells us all we need to know about Gurov and Anna's whole lives. We feel that the story's details—the slice of watermelon in the hotel room, the description of Gurov's wife's eyebrows—are as important as its "action," and that if we left out these details, the perfect but somehow fragile architecture of the story would begin to crumble.

Not much remains of the short story, retold in summary—but not *nothing*. For this also can be said, of the short story: If we find a way to describe what the story is *really* about, not its plot but its essence, what small or large part of life it has managed to translate onto the page, there is always *something* there—enough to engage us, and pique our interest.

But isn't the same true of novels? What do we lose when we try to explain what *Mrs. Dalloway* is *about*? Or when we become hopelessly enmired in the tangles—lovers, generations, narrators, stories within stories, frames within frames—of *Wuthering Heights*? Or when we say that we just read the most harrowing novel about a provincial French housewife whose life is ruined by her silly and impractical fantasies of love and romance? The answer's the same: Nearly everything, though some "germ" (to quote James again) stays ineradicably present.

A similarly illusory distinction that is often made between the short story and the novel claims that the short story—unlike its more expansive or discursive older sibling—works more often by implication, by indirection, that it more frequently achieves its results by what has *not* been said or what has been left out. But although it is undeniably true that certain stories function this way—the situation that has caused all the trouble between the lovers in Ernest Hemingway's "Hills Like White Elephants" is never directly mentioned in the course of the lovers' painful conversation—it is also true that in the greatest works of fiction, regardless of their length, every line tells us pages *more* than it appears to communicate on the surface. So even in Proust's *In Search of Lost Time*—hardly the most concise and economical of novels—each seemingly insignificant phrase and incident assumes additional meaning and resonance as the book progresses; every incident, every minor exchange takes on levels of significance that we cannot hope to apprehend until we go back and reread the whole. In fact the most important way to read—the way that teaches us most about what a great writer does, and what *we* should be doing—is to take a story apart (line by line, word by word) the way a mechanic takes apart an automobile engine, and to ask ourselves how each word, each phrase, and each sentence contributes to the entirety.

In their efforts to define the formal qualities of the short story form, critics are often driven back to invoke basic Aristotelian principles (short stories, we hear, have a beginning, a middle, and an end) and to quote the early masters of the genre, writers who must have had, one supposes, a more sharply focused view of the new frontier toward which they were heading. So introductions to anthologies, textbook chapters, and surveys of the latest developments in the academic field of "short story theory" are all fond of invoking Edgar Allan Poe's notion of the "single effect."

> A skillful literary artist has constructed a tale. If wise, he has not fashioned his thoughts to accommodate his incidents; but having conceived, with deliberate care, a certain unique or single *effect* to be wrought out, he then invents such incidents— he then combines such events as may best aid him in establishing this preconceived effect . . . in the whole composition, there should be no word written, of which the tendency, direct or indirect, is not to the one pre-established design. And by such means, with such care and skill, a picture is at length painted which leaves in the mind of he who contemplates it with a kindred art, a sense of the fullest satisfaction.

The idea of the tale has been presented unblemished, because undisturbed, and this is an end unattainable to the novel.

More recent—and also frequently quoted—is V. S. Pritchett's characteristically elegant and incisive formulation:

The novel tends to tell us everything whereas the short story tells us only one thing, and that, intensely. . . . It is, as some have said, a "glimpse through," resembling a painting or even a song which we can take in at once, yet bring the recesses and contours of larger experience to the mind.

And Chekhov—whom some readers (this one, for example) consider the greatest writer of the modern short story—had himself some very definite ideas on the necessity of keeping things simple:

In planning a story one is bound to think first about its framework; from a crowd of leading characters one selects one person only—wife or husband; one puts him on the canvas and paints him alone, making him prominent, while the others one scatters over the canvas like small coins, and the result is something like the vault of heaven: one big moon and a number of very small stars around it. . . . It is not necessary to portray many characters. . . . The center of gravity should be in two persons: him and her. [to A. P. Chekhov, 1886] . . . One must write about simple things: how Peter Semionovich married Maria Ivanovna. That is all.

Certainly this is true of his own "The Lady with the Pet Dog," in which the center of gravity seems to turn—slowly at first, and then more and more intensely—around those all-important "two persons."

No sensible reader could argue with Pritchett or Poe. But then again, few readers could explain exactly what "a single effect" is, or what precisely is the "one thing" that our favorite short story is telling us so intensely. And Chekhov should have known—and *did* know—better, since many of his most successful and beautifully realized stories encompass a good deal more than "him and her" or the nuptial arrangements of Peter Semionovich and Maria Ivanovna.

Indeed, the minute one tries to make any sweeping declarations about the proper limitations or boundaries of the short story, one thinks (as with any "rule" for the writing of fiction) of an example—a masterpiece!—that embodies the very opposite of the law that one has just proposed. So let's take just a few of the many assumptions that the casual reader—or the student hungry for some definitive parameters—might make about the short story.

Perhaps we should begin by addressing Chekhov's statement about that big moon and those very small stars, about that "him and her" whose interaction should form the core of the story. One might assume that for reasons of economy or artistic harmony, the short story should limit itself to depicting the situation of a main protagonist or at least a somewhat restricted—a *manageable*—cast of characters. And many stories do. There are only three major characters—the narrator, his wife, and the blind man—in Raymond Carver's "Cathedral." And only one character, really, in Poe's "The Pit and the Pendulum." In Flannery O'Connor's "Everything That Rises Must

Converge" the "him and her" are the overbearing, heartbreaking mother and her snobbish and long-suffering son Julian. And in James Baldwin's "Sonny's Blues," the narrator and Sonny are the big moon around whom the others—Isabel, the mother and father, the other musicians—revolve.

But who, one might ask, is the "big moon" in Tim O'Brien's "The Things They Carried," or in Chekhov's own "In the Ravine," a story that focuses not on any central character, but on the life of an entire community, Ukleevo, a village that "was never free from fever, and there was boggy mud there even in summer, especially under the fences over which hung old willow-trees that gave deep shade. Here there was always a smell from the factory refuse and the acetic acid which was used in the finishing of the cotton print." In this polluted and horrifically corrupt little hamlet, the most powerful family—a clan of shopkeepers—devotes itself to lying and cheating their neighbors; their dishonesty and general depravity are repaid, eventually, by heartbreak and ruin.

The story does have a villain, the vicious Aksinya (who, as the very worst person in her family, naturally is spared the destruction that befalls the somewhat less culpable others), and a heroine, of sorts, the innocent peasant girl Lipa, who does not appear until quite a few pages into the story. Nonetheless, we feel throughout that Chekhov is less interested in depicting particular destinies than in painting a broader picture; the story is the literary equivalent of a monumental canvas, crowded with figures—Rembrandt's "Night Watch," for one. We never know exactly, we can never answer that question that writing teachers so often ask: Whose story is it?

But even the story that lacks a central character should, presumably, limit itself to a single point of view, a controlling intelligence that guides us through the narrative. Or should it? Once more the answer seems to be: not necessarily. "Sonny's Blues," "Cathedral," and John Updike's "A & P" are examples of short fictions that stay fixedly within the consciousness of their narrators. Kafka's "The Judgment" adheres more or less faithfully to the close-third-person viewpoint through which we observe the tormented last hours of Georg Bendermann.

Yet another of Kafka's stories—"The Metamorphosis"—also begins in the close third person, with the understandable astonishment of Gregor Samsa, who (when we meet him) has just woken in his bed to find that he has been transformed, overnight, into a giant insect. And there the story remains until the narrative must leave the room in which Gregor is imprisoned in order to follow the action in the other parts of the apartment and chart the effects that Gregor's peculiar transformation has had on the members of his family. Finally, after Gregor's death, the story can—for obvious reasons—no longer be told from his point of view, and a more detached omniscience describes the process by which his parents and his sister repair themselves and go on with their lives after the regrettable but unavoidable demise of the unfortunate Gregor.

Still other stories pay even less heed to the somewhat schoolmarmish admonition that they color neatly within the lines of a single perspective. In "The Lady with the Pet Dog," we feel that Chekhov is constantly shifting his—and our—distance from Gurov. Sometimes (for example, in the scene in which he watches the sunset) we feel that we are looking through his eyes, and down into his soul; at other moments (when he first sees Anna and toys with the idea of seducing her) we feel that we are watching him with a somewhat greater and more ironic remove.

Alice Munro's "Friend of My Youth" begins with a dream that the first person narrator has about her mother, and then narrates the rest of the story from the point of view of "my mother" with occasional, stabilizing swings back to that initial "I." Katherine Mansfield's "Prelude" moves seamlessly from one family member to another, exposing the innermost—tormented or fortuitously ignorant—thoughts of an extended family: a mother and father, their children, and the mother's unmarried sister. Tatiana Tolstaya's "Heavenly Flame" behaves as if it has never heard of the whole issue of point of view, and skips around from character to character, alighting from time to time on a sort of group perspective, a "we" representing the minisociety vacationing at a country house near a convalescent home. And though John Cheever's "Goodbye, My Brother" begins in the first person plural—not the royal *we* or the editorial *we* but the family *we*—we readers soon understand that this plural ("We are a family that is very close in spirit") is by its very nature ironic, and functions as a key to the fortress and the prison in which the narrator chooses and is forced to reside. Much of the story, in fact, is about the efforts to break away from that "we" (the Pommeroy family) so that point of view becomes, in an intriguing way, part of the plot—and the problem—of the story.

But even if the short story refuses to fall in line with any of our notions about the number and range of its characters, and the importance of a single perspective, shouldn't it observe the most (one would think) easy to follow of the Aristotelian conventions, the prescriptions concerning the length of time that the action may comfortably span? It's true that "Hills Like White Elephants" nearly restricts itself to the real time of a single conversation, and that Tillie Olsen's "I Stand Here Ironing" takes place entirely during a session at the ironing board.

On the other hand, "Sonny's Blues" moves back and forth through decades of the two main characters' histories, covering the most significant parts of the lifetimes of two men; at the same time, it fits a huge wedge of social history into the confines of a short story. And Lars Gustafsson's "Greatness Strikes Where It Pleases" takes, as its subject, the existence—and especially the inner life—of an unnamed retarded man, who grows up in the country and spends his later years in a home. In the space breaks, the black space between sections, months, days, or years elapse—black spots that, we soon realize, matter far less than we might have supposed, since our hero has been liberated by consciousness from the narrow strictures of time:

> At the end of the '50s, his parents died. Nobody tried to explain it to him, and he didn't know in what order they died or when, but when he hadn't seen them for a few years—his mother would visit him regularly twice a year and always brought him candy and apples, an anxious lot of apples, as if the lack of apples were his problem—he started to miss them, in some vague fashion, about the way you might all of a sudden long for mustard or honey or a certain kind of floury gravy with just a taste of burned pork.

As much as we might like the short story to keep its borders modest, crisp, and neat, the form keeps defying our best efforts to wrap it up and present it in a tidy package. Pick up those helpful, instructional books—Anyone Can Write a Short Story—and you're bound to find one of those diagrams, those EKGs of the "typical plot line," its slow ascent, its peak and valley (or peaks and valleys) meant to indicate the tensing or slackening of dramatic interest.

But any attempt to draw such a chart for a story such as Bruno Schulz's "Sanitarium Under the Sign of the Hour Glass"—with its labyrinthine plot turns and disorienting switchbacks—will look less like that comprehensible medical or seismographic chart than one of those webs spun by those poor spiders whom scientists used to torment with doses of mind-altering drugs. How does one draw up a chart for "The Things They Carried," which is structured like an obsessive, repetitive list of *stuff*—the materials that a group of Vietnam soldiers are humping through the jungle—and contains, hidden inside, a story of life and death.

Some stories have huge amounts of plot—it has been said that Heinrich von Kleist's "The Marquise of O." was used, unedited, as a shooting script for Eric Rohmer's full-length film (of the same name) based on the novella. And some stories—John Updike's "A & P," Raymond Carver's "Cathedral"—have, by comparison, almost no plot at all.

The understandable longing to keep things tidy and nice and neat also leads many critics and teachers to put the "epiphany"—the burst of understanding, self-knowledge, or knowledge about the world that may occur to a character at some crucial point in the story—at the highest peak of that EKG graph, like the cherry on a sundae. Some even insist that this sort of mini-enlightenment is necessary for the short story—is, in fact, a hallmark and sine qua non of the form.

It's my understanding that the word epiphany first came into common currency—in the literary rather than the religious sense—in connection with the fiction of James Joyce, many of whose characters do seem to "get something" by the end of many of his brilliant stories. Sometimes, characters in stories do learn something. By the end of "Sonny's Blues," the narrator has had a vision (however unwelcome and unwilled) of what music means to his brother, and of what sort of musician his brother is. The recognition that her precious new hat is the very same one worn by the black woman on the bus has overwhelming—and tragic—consequences for the mother in "Everything That Rises Must Converge." Gurov learns one startling lesson after another in "The Lady with the Pet Dog," and the story ends with the realization that "the hardest part was still before" the two lovers. But just because Joyce's or Baldwin's or Chekhov's or O'Connor's characters wise up, even for a moment, doesn't mean that anyone else's characters do, or should be expected to.

One could spend pages listing short fictions in which characters come out the other end of the story every bit as benighted as they were in the first sentence. By the end of "Everything That Rises Must Converge," Julian could hardly *not* know that something has happened to change his life. But the story concludes before he—or the reader—has had a chance to intuit what that change is, or what it will mean. It's hard to say what the unnamed narrator learns in Samuel Beckett's thrilling and upsetting story "First Love." To claim that every short story should include a moment of epiphany is like insisting that every talented, marvelous dog jump through the same narrow hoop.

It is simply not true that a character always learns something in the course of a short story. Heaven forbid that someone should *have* to see life or the world in a brighter or darker light, that someone *has* to be changed—or, even worse, improved. How deadly dull it would be if that were the case for all those stories in all those anthologies—all those epistemological light bulbs going on, one right after another.

A story creates its own world, often—though not always—with clear or mysterious correspondences to our own, a world in which we are too involved to keep track of what anyone is learning. While reading the story, we enter that world. We feel that everything in it belongs there, and has not been forced on it by its reckless or capricious creator. In fact, we tend to forget the creator, who has wound the watch of the story and vanished from creation. We may feel this world is something like life and at the same time better than life, since this short-story world—unlike life—has reached some miraculous ecological balance, so that everything in that world has been put there for a reason.

Unlike most novels, great short stories make us marvel at their integrity, their economy. If we went at them with our blue pencils, we might find we had nothing to do. We would discover there was nothing that the story could afford to lose without the whole delicate structure collapsing like a soufflé or meringue. And yet we are left with a feeling of completeness, a conviction that we know exactly as much as we need to know, that all of our questions have been answered—even if we are unable to formulate what exactly those questions and answers *are*.

This sense of the artistic whole, this assurance that nothing has been left out and that nothing extraneous has been included, is part of what distinguishes the short story from other pieces of writing with which it shares certain outward characteristics—what separates it, for example, from the newspaper account, which, like the short story, most often features characters and at least some vestige of a plot. But the newspaper version of "The Lady with the Pet Dog"—MAN'S AFFAIR TURNS SERIOUS—manages to leave out every single thing that makes the story so beautiful, significant, and moving.

Everything in the story resonates at its own unique, coherent, and recognizable pitch, along with everything else in the story, creating an effect that Joyce described—quoting Aquinas, and in another context—as "wholeness, harmony, and radiance." As readers, we may feel that after finishing the story we understand something new, something solid. And we recognize the short story (what a short story *is*) in a visceral, quasi-physiological way; we feel—to paraphrase what Emily Dickinson said about poetry—as if the top of our head had come off. Maybe, that is something like what Poe meant by his unity of effect—the short work of fiction, so beautifully made that it cannot be broken down into components or spare parts. Reading a masterpiece like

Chekhov's "The Lady with the Pet Dog," we cannot think of anything we would add, anything else we need to know; nor is there anything extra or superfluous.

To understand what a short story is requires reading dozens and dozens of them, far more than the examples collected in [an] anthology, more than the additional stories mentioned in this essay. By reading many and varied examples, we develop an almost instinctive sense of what a short story is, so that when we read one we recognize it, just as we recognize our own instincts and emotions. We know what a short story is, just as we know what it is to be afraid, or to fall in love.

To really communicate the entirety of what a short story has given us, of what it has done for us, of what it has helped us understand or see in a new way, would involve repeating the whole story, every one of our favorite stories [. . .] and also the stories I have mentioned above—stories that lovers of the short story should know practically by heart. It would mean quoting all those stories sentence by sentence, line by line, word by word—the only real answer to that most difficult of questions: What makes a short story?

Reading as a Writer

1. Do you agree with Prose's conclusions about the best way to define a short story? Why or why not?

2. Can you think of any short stories that you love (or just like) that transgress all the so-called "rules" of what constitutes a short story?

3. Is there any more specific way to define the "sense of artistic whole" that Prose talks about? Why or why not?

John Edgar Wideman

Fever

To Matthew Carey, Esq., who fled Philadelphia in its
hour of need and upon his return published a libelous
account of the behavior of black nurses and undertakers,
thereby injuring all people of my race and especially
those without whose unselfish, courageous labours the
city could not have survived the late calamity.

*Consider Philadelphia from its centrical situation, the extent
of its commerce, the number of its artificers, manufacturers
and other circumstances, to be to the United States what the
heart is to the human body in circulating the blood.*
                    —*Robert Morris, 1777.*

HE STOOD STARING through a tall window at the last days of November. The trees were barren women starved for love and they'd stripped off all their clothes, but nobody cared. And not one of them gave a fuck about him, sifting among them, weightless and naked, knowing just as well as they did, no hands would come to touch them, warm them, pick leaves off the frozen ground and stick them back in place. Before he'd gone to bed a flutter of insects had stirred in the dark outside his study. Motion worrying the corner of his eye till he turned and focused where light pooled on the deck, a cone in which he could trap slants of snow so they materialized into wet, gray feathers that blotted against the glass, the planks of the deck. If he stood seven hours, dark would come again. At some point his reflection would hang in the glass, a ship from the other side of the world, docked in the ether. Days were shorter now. A whole one spent wondering what goes wrong would fly away, fly in the blink of an eye.

Perhaps, perhaps it may be acceptable to the reader to know how we found the sick affected by the sickness; our opportunities of hearing and seeing them have been very great. They were taken with a chill, a headache, a sick stomach, with pains in their limbs and back, this was the way the sickness in general began, but all were not affected alike, some appeared but slightly affected with some of these symptoms, what confirmed us in the opinion of a person being smitten was the colour of their eyes.

Victims in this low-lying city perished every year, and some years were worse than others, but the worst by far was the long hot dry summer of '93, when the dead and dying wrested control of the city from the living. Most who were able, fled. The rich to their rural retreats, others to relatives and friends in the countryside or neighboring towns. Some simply left, with no fixed destination, the prospect of privation or starvation on the road preferable to cowering in their homes awaiting the fever's fatal scratching at their door. Busy streets deserted, commerce halted, members of families shunning one another, the sick abandoned to suffer and die alone. Fear ruled. From August when the first cases of fever appeared below Water Street, to November when merciful frosts ended the infestation, the city slowly deteriorated, as if it, too, could suffer the terrible progress of the disease: fever, enfeeblement, violent vomiting and diarrhea, helplessness, delirium, settled dejection when patients *concluded they must go (so the phrase for dying was), and therefore in a kind of fixed determined state of mind went off.*

In some it raged more furiously than in others—some have languished for seven and ten days, and appeared to get better the day, or some hours before they died, while others were cut off in one, two or three days, but their complaints were similar. Some lost their reason and raged with all the fury madness could produce, and died in strong convulsions. Others retained their reason to the last, and seemed rather to fall asleep than die.

Yellow fever: an acute infectious disease of subtropical and tropical New World areas, caused by a filterable virus transmitted by a mosquito of the genus *Aëdes* and characterized by jaundice and dark colored vomit resulting from hemorrhages. Also called *yellow jack.*

Dengue: an infectious, virulent tropical and subtropical disease transmitted by mosquitos and characterized by fever, rash and severe pains in the joints. Also called *breakbone fever, dandy.* [Spanish, of African origin, akin to Swahili *kindinga.*]

Curled in the black hold of the ship he wonders why his life on solid green earth had to end, why the gods had chosen this new habitation for him, floating, chained to other captives, no air, no light, the wooden walls shuddering, battered, as if some madman is determined to destroy even this last pitiful refuge where he skids in foul puddles of waste, bumping other bodies, skinning himself on splintery beams and planks, always moving, shaken and spilled like palm nuts in the diviner's fist, and Esu casts his fate, constant motion, tethered to an iron ring.

In the darkness he can't see her, barely feels her light touch on his fevered skin. Sweat thick as oil but she doesn't mind, straddles him, settles down to do her work. She enters him and draws his blood up into her belly. When she's full, she pauses, dreamy, heavy. He could kill her then; she wouldn't care. But he doesn't. Listens to the whine of her wings lifting till the whimper is lost in the roar and crash of waves, creaking wood, prisoners groaning. If she returns tomorrow and carries away another drop of him, and the next day and the next, a drop each day, enough days, he'll be gone. Shrink to nothing, slip out of this iron noose and disappear.

Aëdes aegypti: a mosquito of the family *Culicidae,* genus *Aëdes* in which the female is distinguished by a long proboscis for sucking blood. This winged insect is a vector (or organism that carries pathogens from one host to another) of yellow fever and dengue. [New Latin *Aëdes,* from Greek *aedes,* unpleasant: *a-,* not + *edos,* pleasant . . .]

All things arrive in the waters and waters carry all things away. So there is no beginning or end, only the waters' flow, ebb, flood, trickle, tides emptying and returning, salt seas and rivers and rain and mist and blood, the sun drowning in an ocean of night, wet sheen of dawn washing darkness from our eyes. This city is held in the water's palm. A captive as surely as I am captive. Long fingers of river, Schuylkill, Delaware, the rest of the hand invisible; underground streams and channels feed the soggy flesh of marsh, clay pit, sink, gutter, stagnant pool. What's not seen is heard in the suck of footsteps through spring mud of unpaved streets. Noxious vapors that sting your eyes, cause you to gag, spit and wince are evidence of a presence, the dead hand cupping this city, the positions that circulate through it, the sweat on its rotting flesh.

No one has asked my opinion. No one will. Yet I have seen this fever before, and though I can prescribe no cure, I could tell stories of other visitations, how it came and stayed and left us, the progress of disaster, its several stages, its horrors and mitigations. My words would not save one life, but those mortally affrighted by the fever, by the prospect of universal doom, might find solace in knowing there are limits to the power of this scourge that has befallen us, that some, yea, most will survive, that this condition is temporary, a season, that the fever must disappear with the first deep frosts and its disappearance is as certain as the fact it will come again.

They say the rat's-nest ships from Santo Domingo brought the fever. Frenchmen and their black slaves fleeing black insurrection. Those who've seen Barbados's distemper say our fever is its twin born in the tropical climate of the hellish Indies. I know better. I hear the drum, the forest's heartbeat, pulse of the sea that chains the moon's wandering, the spirit's journey. Its throb is source and promise of all things being connected, a mirror storing everything, forgetting nothing. To explain the fever we need no boatloads of refugees, ragged and wracked with killing fevers, bring death to our shores. We have bred the affliction within our breasts. Each solitary heart contains all the world's tribes, and its precarious dance echoes the drum's thunder. We are our ancestors and our children, neighbors and strangers to ourselves. Fever descends when the waters that connect us are clogged with filth. When our seas are garbage. The waters cannot come and go when we are shut off one from the other, each in his frock coat, wig, bonnet, apron, shop, shoes, skin, behind locks, doors, sealed faces, our blood grows thick and sluggish. Our bodies void infected fluids. Then we are dry and cracked as a desert country, vital parts wither, all dust and dry bones inside. Fever is a drought consuming us from within. Discolored skin caves in upon itself, we burn, expire.

I regret there is so little comfort in this explanation. It takes into account neither climatists nor contagionists, flies in the face of logic and reason, the good doctors of the College of Physicians who would bleed us, purge us, quarantine, plunge us in icy baths, starve us, feed us elixirs of bark and wine, sprinkle us with gunpowder, drown us in vinegar according to the dictates of their various healing sciences. Who, then, is this foolish, old man who receives his wisdom from pagan drums in pagan forests? Are these the delusions of one whose brain the fever has already begun to gnaw? Not quite. True, I have survived other visitations of the fever, but while it prowls this city, I'm in jeopardy again as you are, because I claim no immunity, no magic. The messenger who bears the news of my death will reach me precisely at the stroke determined when it was determined I should tumble from the void and taste air the first time. Nothing is an accident. Fever grows in the secret places of our hearts, planted there when one of us decided to sell one of us to another. The drum must pound ten thousand thousand years to drive that evil away.

Fires burn on street corners. Gunshots explode inside wooden houses. Behind him a carter's breath expelled in low, labored pants warns him to edge closer to housefronts forming one wall of a dark, narrow, twisting lane. Thick wheels furrow the unpaved street. In the fire glow the cart stirs a shimmer of dust, faint as a halo, a breath smear on a mirror. Had the man locked in the traces of the cart cursed him or was it just a wheeze of exertion, a complaint addressed to the unforgiving weight of his burden? Creaking wheels, groaning wood, plodding footsteps, the cough of dust, bulky silhouette blackened as it lurches into brightness at the block's end. All gone in a moment. Sounds, motion, sight extinguished. What remained, as if trapped by a lid clamped over the lane, was the stench of dead bodies. A stench cutting through the ubiquitous pall of vinegar and gunpowder. Two, three, four corpses being hauled to Potter's Field, trailed by the unmistakable wake of decaying flesh. He'd heard they

raced their carts to the burial ground. Two or three entering Potter's Field from different directions would acknowledge one another with challenges, raised fists, gather
their strength for a last dash to the open trenches where they tip their cargoes. Their
brethren would wager, cheer, toast the victor with tots of rum. He could hear the
rumble of coffins crashing into a common grave, see the comical chariots bouncing,
the men's legs pumping, faces contorted by fires that blazed all night at the burial
ground. Shouting and curses would hang in the torpid night air, one more nightmare
troubling the city's sleep.

He knew this warren of streets as well as anyone. Night or day he could negotiate
the twists and turnings, avoid cul-de-sacs, find the river even if his vision was
obscured in tunnel-like alleys. He anticipated when to duck a jutting signpost, new
how to find doorways where he was welcome, wooden steps down to a cobbled ter-
race overlooking the water where his shod foot must never trespass. Once beyond the
grand houses lining one end of Water Street, in this quarter of hovels, beneath these
wooden sheds leaning shoulder to shoulder were cellars and caves dug into the earth,
poorer men's dwellings under these houses of the poor, an invisible region where his
people burrow, pull earth like blanket and quilt round themselves to shut out cold
and dampness, sleeping multitudes to a room, stacked and crosshatched and spoon
fashion, themselves the only fuel, heat of one body passed to others and passed back
from all to one. Can he blame the lucky ones who are strong enough to pull the death
carts, who celebrate and leap and roar all night around the bonfires? Why should
they return here? Where living and dead, sick and well must lie face to face, shivering or sweltering on the same dank floor.

Below Water Street the alleys proliferate. Named and nameless. He knows where
he's going but fever has transformed even the familiar. He'd been waiting in Dr.
Rush's entrance hall. An English mirror, oval framed in scalloped brass, drew him.
He watched himself glide closer, a shadow, a blur, then the shape of his face materialized from silken depths. A mask he did not recognize. He took the thing he saw and
murmured to it. Had he once been in control? Could he tame it again? Like a garden
ruined overnight, pillaged, overgrown, trampled by marauding beasts. He stares at
the chaos until he can recall familiar contours of earth, seasons of planting, harvest-
ing, green shoots, nodding blossoms, scraping, digging, watering. Once upon a time
he'd cultivated this thing, this plot of flesh and blood and bone, but what had it
become? Who owned it now? He'd stepped away. His eyes constructed another face
and set it there, between him and the wizened old man in the glass. He'd aged twenty
years in a glance and the fever possessed the same power to alter suddenly what it
touched. This city had grown ancient and fallen into ruin in two months since early
August, when the first cases of fever appeared. Something in the bricks, mortar,
beams and stones had gone soft, had lost its permanence. When he entered sick-
rooms, walls fluttered, floors buckled. He could feel roofs pressing down. Putrid heat
expanding. In the bodies of victims. In rooms, buildings, streets, neighborhoods.
Members that preserved the integrity of substances and shapes, kept each in its
proper place, were worn thin. He could poke his finger through yellowed skin. A

stone wall. The eggshell of his skull. What should be separated was running together. Threatened to burst. Nothing contained the way it was supposed to be. No clear lines of demarcation. A mongrel city. Traffic where there shouldn't be traffic. An awful void opening around him, preparing itself to hold explosions of bile, vomit, gushing bowels, ooze, sludge, seepage.

Earlier in the summer, on a July afternoon, he'd tried to escape the heat by walking along the Delaware. The water was unnaturally calm, isolated into stagnant pools by outcroppings of wharf and jetty. A shell of rotting matter paralleled the river edge. As if someone had attempted to sweep what was unclean and dead from the water. Bones, skins, entrails, torn carcasses, unrecognizable tatters and remnants broomed into a neat ridge. No sigh of the breeze he'd sought, yet fumes from the rim of garbage battered him in nauseating waves, a palpable medium intimate as wind. Beyond the tidal line of refuse, a pale margin lapped clean by receding waters. Then the iron river itself, flat, dark, speckled by sores of foam that puckered and swirled, worrying the stillness with a life of their own.

Spilled. Spoiled. Those words repeated themselves endlessly as he made his rounds. Dr. Rush had written out his portion, his day's share from the list of dead and dying. He'd purged, bled, comforted and buried victims of the fever. In and out of homes that had become tombs, prisons, charnel houses. Dazed children wandering the streets, searching for their parents. How can he explain to a girl, barely more than an infant, that the father and mother she sobs for are gone from this earth? Departed. Expired. They are resting, child. Asleep forever. In a far, far better place, my sweet, dear, suffering one. In God's bosom. Wrapped in His incorruptible arms. A dead mother with a dead baby at her breast. Piteous cries of the helpless offering all they own for a drink of water. How does he console the delirious boy who pummels him, fastens himself on his leg because he's put the boy's mother in a box and now must nail shut the lid?

Though light-headed from exhaustion, he's determined to spend a few hours here, among his own people. But were these lost ones really his people? The doors of his church were open to them, yet these were the ones who stayed away, wasting their lives in vicious pastimes of the idle, the unsaved, the ignorant. His benighted brethren who'd struggled to reach this city of refuge and then, once inside the gates, had fallen, prisoners again, trapped by chains of dissolute living as they'd formerly been snared in the bonds of slavery. He'd come here and preached to them. Thieves, beggars, loose women, debtors, fugitives, drunkards, gamblers, the weak, crippled and outcast with nowhere else to go. They spurned his church so he'd brought church to them, preaching in gin mills, whoring dens, on street corners. He'd been jeered and hooted, spat upon, clods of unnameable filth had spattered his coat. But a love for them, as deep and unfathomable as his sorrow, his pity, brought him back again and again, exhorting them, setting the gospel before them so they might partake of its bounty, the infinite goodness, blessed sustenance therein. Jesus had toiled among the wretched, the outcast, that flotsam and jetsam deposited like a ledge of filth on the banks of the city. He understood what had brought the dark faces of his brethren north, to the Quaker promise of this town, this cradle and capital of a New World, knew the misery they were fleeing, the bright star in the Gourd's handle that guided them, the joy leaping in their hearts when at last, at last the opportunity to be viewed as men instead of things was theirs. He's dreamed such dreams himself, oh yes, and prayed that the light of hope would never be extinguished. He'd been praying for deliverance, for peace and understanding when God had granted him a vision, hordes of sable bondsmen throwing off their chains, marching, singing, a path opening in the sea, the sea shaking its shaggy shoulders, resplendent with light and power. A radiance sparkling in this walkway through the water, pearls, diamonds, spears o flight. This was the glistening way home. Waters parting, glory blinking and winking. Too intense to stare at, a promise shimmering, a rainbow arching over the end of the path. A hand tapped him. He'd waited for it to blend into the vision, for its meaning to shine forth in the language neither word nor thought, God was speaking in His visitation. Tapping became a grip. Someone was shoving him. He was being pushed off his knees, hauled to his feet. Someone was snatching him from the honeyed dream of salvation. When his eyes popped open he knew the name of each church elder manhandling him. Pale faces above a wall of black cloth belonged to his fellow communicants. He knew without looking the names of the men whose hands touched him gently, steering, coaxing, and those whose hands dug into his flesh, the impatient, imperious, rough hands that shunned any contact with him except as overseer or master.

Allen, Allen. Do you hear me? You and your people must not kneel at the front of the gallery. On your feet. Come. Come. Now. On your feet.

Behind the last row of pews. There ye may fall down on your knees and give praise.

And so we built our African house of worship. But its walls could not imprison the Lord's word. Go forth. Go forth. And he did so. To this sinful quarter. Tunnels, cellars and caves. Where no sunlight penetrates. Where wind off the river cuts like a knife. Chill of icy spray channeled here from the ocean's wintry depths. Where each summer the brackish sea that is mouth and maw and bowel deposits its waste in puddles stinking to high heaven.

Water Street becomes what it's named, rises round his ankles, soaks his boots, threatens to drag him down. Patrolling these murky depths he's predator, scavenger, the prey of some dagger-toothed creature whose shadow closes over him like a net.

When the first settlers arrived here they'd scratched caves into the soft earth of the riverbank. Like ants. Rats. Gradually they'd pushed inland, laying out a geometrical grid of streets, perpendicular, true angled and straight edged, the mirror of their rectitude. Black Quaker coats and dour visages were remembrances of mud, darkness, the place of their lying in, cocooned like worms, propagating dreams of a holy city. The latest comers must always start here, on this dotted line, in this riot of alleys, lanes, tunnels. Wave after wave of immigrants unloaded here, winnowed here, dying in these shanties, grieving in strange languages. But white faces move on, bury their dead, bear their children, negotiate the invisible reef between this broken place and the foursquare town. Learn enough of their new tongue to say to the blacks they've left hind, *thou shalt not pass.*

I watched him bring the scalding liquid to his lips and thought to myself that's where his color comes from. The black brew he drinks every morning. Coloring him, changing him. A hue I had not considered until that instant as other than absence, something nonwhite and therefore its opposite, what light would be if extinguished, sky or sea drained of the color blue when the sun disappears, the blackness of cinders. As he sips, steam rises. I peer into the cup that's become mine, at the moon in its center, waxing, waning. A light burning in another part of the room caught there, as my face would be if I leaned over the cup's hot mouth. But I have no wish to see my face. His is what I study as I stare into my cup and see not absence, but the presence of wood darkly stained, wet plowed earth, a boulder rising from a lake, blackly glistening as it sheds crowns and beards and necklaces of water. His color neither neglect nor abstention, nor mystery, but a swelling tide in his skin of this bitter morning beverage it is my habit to imbibe.

We were losing, clearly losing the fight. One day in mid-September fifty-seven were buried before noon.

He'd begun with no preamble. Our conversation taken up again directly as if the months since our last meeting were no more than a cobweb his first words lightly brush away. I say conversation but a better word would be soliloquy because I was only a listener, a witness learning his story, a story buried so deeply he couldn't recall it, but dreamed pieces, a conversation with himself, a reverie with the power to sink us both into its unreality. So his first words did not begin the story where I remembered him ending it in our last session, but picked up midstream the ceaseless play of voices only he heard, always, summoning him, possessing him, enabling him to speak, to be.

Despair was in my heart. The fiction of our immunity had been exposed for the vicious lie it was, a not so subtle device for wresting us from our homes, our loved ones, the afflicted among us, and sending us to aid strangers. First they blamed us, called the sickness Barbados fever, a contagion from those blood-soaked islands, brought to these shores by refugees from the fighting in Santo Domingo. We were not welcome anywhere. A dark skin was seen not only as a badge of shame for its wearer. Now we were evil incarnate, the mask of long agony and violent death. Black servants were discharged. The draymen, carters, barbers, caterers, oyster sellers, street vendors could find no custom. It mattered not that some of us were born here and spoke no language but the English language, second-, even third-generation African Americans who knew no other country, who laughed at the antics of newly landed immigrants, Dutchmen, Welshmen, Scots, Irish, Frenchmen who had turned our marketplaces into Babel, stomping along in their clodhopper shoes, strange costumes, haughty airs, Lowlander gibberish that sounded like men coughing or dogs barking. My fellow countrymen searching everywhere but in their own hearts, the foulness upon which this city is erected, to lay blame on others for the killing fever, pointed their fingers at foreigners and called it Palastine fever, a pestilence imported from those low countries in Europe where, I have been told, war for control of the sea-lanes, the human cargoes transported thereupon, has raged for a hundred years.

But I am losing the thread, the ironical knot I wished to untangle for you. How the knife was plunged in our hearts, then cruelly twisted. We were proclaimed carriers of the fever and treated as pariahs, but when it became expedient to command our services to nurse the sick and bury the dead, the previous allegations were no longer mentioned. Urged on by desperate counselors, the mayor granted us a blessed immunity. We were ordered to save the city.

I swear to you, and the bills of mortality, published by the otherwise unreliable Mr. Carey, support my contention, that the fever dealt with us severely. Among the city's poor and destitute the fever's ravages were most deadly and we are always the poorest of the poor. If an ordinance forbidding ringing of bells to mourn the dead had not been passed, that awful tolling would have marked our days, the watches of the night in our African American community, as it did in those environs of the city we were forbidden to inhabit. Every morning before I commenced my labors for the sick and dying, I would hear moaning, screams of pain, fearful cries and supplications, a chorus of lamentations scarring daybreak, my people awakening to a nightmare that was devouring their will to live.

The small strength I was able to muster each morning was sorely tried the moment my eyes and ears opened upon the sufferings of my people, the reality that gave the lie to the fiction of our immunity. When my duties among the whites were concluded, how many nights did I return and struggle till dawn with victims here, my friends, parishioners, wandering sons of Africa whose faces I could not look upon without seeing my own. I was commandeered to rise and go forth to the general task of saving the city, forced to leave this neighborhood where my skills were sorely needed. I nursed those who hated me, deserted the ones I loved, who loved me.

I recite the story many, many times to myself, let many voices speak to me till one begins to sound like the sea or rain or my feet those mornings shuffling through thick dust.

We arrived at Bush Hill early. To spare ourselves a long trek in the oppressive heat of day. Yellow haze hung over the city. Plumes of smoke from blazes in Potter's Field, from fires on street corners curled above the rooftops, lending the dismal aspect of a town sacked and burned. I've listened to the Santo Domingans tell of the burning of Cap François. How the capital city was engulfed by fires set in the cane fields by the rebelling slaves. Horizon in flames all night as they huddled offshore in ships, terrified, wondering where next they'd go, if any port would permit them to land, empty-handed slaves, masters whose only wealth now was naked black bodies locked in the hold, wide-eyed witnesses of an empire's downfall, chanting, moaning, uncertain as the sea rocked them, whether or not anything on earth could survive the fearful conflagration consuming the great city of Cap François.

   Dawn breaking on a smoldering landscape, writhing columns of smoke, a general cloud of haze the color of a fever victim's eyes. I turn and stare at it a moment, then fall in again with my brother's footsteps trudging through untended fields girding Bush Hill.

From a prisoner-of-war ship in New York harbor where the British had interned him he'd seen that city shed its grave-clothes of fog. Morning after morning it would paint itself damp and gray, a flat sketch on the canvas of sky, a tentative, shivering screen of housefronts, sheds, sprawling warehouses floating above the river. Then shadows and hollows darkened. A jumble of masts, spars, sails began to sway, little boats plied lanes between ships, tiny figures inched along wharves and docks, doors opened, windows slid up or down, lending an illusion of depth and animation to the portrait. This city infinitely beyond his reach, this charade other men staged to mock him, to mark the distance he could not travel, the shore he'd never reach, the city, so to speak, came to life and with its birth each morning dropped the palpable weight of his despair. His loneliness and exile. Moored in pewter water, on an island that never stopped moving but never arrived anywhere. The city a mirage of light and air, chimera of paint, brush and paper, mattered naught except that it was denied him. It shimmered. Tolled. Unsettled the watery place where he was sentenced to dwell. Conveyed to him each morning the same doleful tidings: *The dead are legion, the living a froth on dark, layered depths. But you are neither, and less than both.* Each night he dreamed it burning, razed the city till nothing remained but a dry, black crust, crackling, crunching under his boots as he strides, king of the nothing he surveys.

We passed holes dug into the earth where the sick are interred. Some died in these shallow pits, awash in their own vomited and voided filth, before a bed in the hospital could be made ready for them. Others believed they were being buried alive, and unable to crawl out, howled till reason or strength deserted them. A few, past caring, slept soundly in these ditches, resisted the attendants sent to rouse them and transport them inside, once they realized they were being resurrected to do battle again with the fever. I'd watched the red-bearded French doctor from Santo Domingo with his charts and assistants inspecting this zone, his *salle d'attente*[1] he called it, greeting and reassuring new arrivals, interrogating them, nodding and bowing, hurrying from pit to pit, peering down at his invisible patients like a gardener tending seeds.

   An introduction to the grave, a way into the hospital that prefigured the way most would leave it. That's what this bizarre rite of admission had seemed at first. But through this and other peculiar strategems, Deveze, with his French practice, had transformed Bush Hill from lazarium to a clinic where victims of the fever, if not too weak upon arrival, stood a chance of surviving.

   The cartman employed by Bush Hill had suddenly fallen sick. Faithful Wilcox had never missed a day, ferrying back and forth from town to hospital, hospital to Potter's Field. Bush Hill had its own cemetery now. Daily rations of dead could be disposed

---

1. Waiting room.

of less conspicuously in a plot on the grounds of the estate, screened from the horror-struck eyes of the city. No one had trusted the hospital. Tales of bloody chaos reigning there had filtered back to the city. Citizens believed it was a place where the doomed were stored until they died. Fever victims would have to be dragged from their beds into Bush Hill's cart. They'd struggle and scream, pitch themselves from the rolling cart, beg for help when the cart passed a rare pedestrian daring or foolish enough to be abroad in the deadly streets.

I wondered for the thousandth time why some were stricken, some not. Dr. Rush and this Deveze dipped their hands into the entrails of corpses, stirred the black, corrupted blood, breathed infected vapors exhaled from mortified remains. I'd observed both men steeped in noxious fluids expelled by their patients, yet neither had fallen prey to the fever. Stolid, dim Wilcox maintained daily concourse with the sick and buried the dead for two months before he was infected. They say a woman, undiscovered until boiling stench drove her neighbors into the street crying for aid, was the cause of Wilcox's downfall. A large woman, bloated into an even more cumbersome package by gases and liquids seething inside her body, had slipped from his grasp as he and another hoisted her up into the cart. Catching against a rail, her body had slammed down and burst, spraying Wilcox like a fountain. Wilcox did not pride himself on being the tidiest of men, nor did his job demand one who was overfastidious, but the reeking stench from that accident was too much even for him and he departed in a huff to change his polluted garments. He never returned. So there I was at Bush Hill, where Rush had assigned me with my brother, to bury the flow of dead that did not ebb just because the Charon who was their familiar could no longer attend them.

The doctors believe they can find the secret of the fever in the victims' dead bodies. They cut, saw, extract, weigh, measure. The dead are carved into smaller and smaller bits and the butchered parts studied but they do not speak. What I know of the fever I've learned from the words of those I've treated, from stories of the living that are ignored by the good doctors. When lancet and fleam bleed the victims, they offer up stories like prayers.

*   *   *

It was a jaunty day. We served our white guests and after they'd eaten, they served us at the long, linen-draped tables. A sumptuous feast in the oak grove prepared by many and willing hands. All the world's eyes seemed to be watching us. The city's leading men, black and white, were in attendance to celebrate laying the cornerstone of St. Thomas Episcopal African Church. In spite of the heat and clouds of mettlesome insects, spirits were high. A gathering of whites and blacks in good Christian fellowship to commemorate the fruit of shared labor. Perhaps a new day was dawning. The picnic occurred in July. In less than a month the fever burst upon us.

When you open the dead, black or white, you find: the dura mater covering the brain is white and fibrous in appearance. The leptomeninges covering the brain are clear and without opacifications. The brain weighs 1450 grams and is formed symmetrically. Cut sections of the cerebral hemispheres reveal normal-appearing gray matter throughout. The white matter of the corpus callosum is intact and bears no lesions. The basal ganglia are in their normal locations and grossly appear to be without lesions. The ventricles are symmetrical and filled with crystal-clear cerebrospinal fluid.

The cerebellum is formed symmetrically. The nuclei of the cerebellum are unremarkable. Multiple sections through the pons, medulla oblongata and upper brain stem reveal normal gross anatomy. The cranial nerves are in their normal locations and unremarkable.

The muscles of the neck are in their normal locations. The cartilages of the larynx and the hyoid bone are intact. The thyroid and parathyroid glands are normal on their external surface. The mucosa of the larynx is shiny, smooth and without lesions. The vocal chords are unremarkable. A small amount of bloody material is present in the upper trachea.

The heart weighs 380 grams. The epicardial surface is smooth, glistening and without lesions. The myocardium of the left ventricle and septum are of a uniform meaty-red, firm appearance. The endocardial surfaces are smooth, glistening and without lesions. The auricular appendages are free from thrombi. The valve leaflets are thin and delicate, and show no evidence of vegetation.

The right lung weighs 400 grams. The left lung 510 grams. The pleural surfaces of the lungs are smooth and glistening.

The esophageal mucosa is glistening, white and folded. The stomach contains a large amount of black, noxious bile. A veriform appendix is present. The ascending, transverse and descending colon reveal hemorrhaging, striations, disturbance of normal mucosa patterns throughout. A small amount of bloody, liquid feces is present in the ano-rectal canal.

The liver weighs 1720 grams. The spleen weighs 150 grams. The right kidney weighs 190 grams. The left kidney weighs 180 grams. The testes show a glistening white tunica albuginea. Sections are unremarkable.

Dr. Rush and his assistants examined as many corpses as possible in spite of the hurry and tumult of never-ending attendance on the sick. Rush hoped to prove his remedy, his analysis of the cause and course of the fever correct. Attacked on all sides by his medical brethren for purging and bleeding patients already in a drastically weakened state, Rush lashed back at his detractors, wrote pamphlets, broadsides, brandished the stinking evidence of his postmortems to demonstrate conclusively how the sick drowned in their own poisoned fluids. The putrefaction, the black excess, he proclaimed, must be drained away, else the victim inevitably succumbs.

Dearest:
   I shall not return home again until this business of the fever is terminated. I fear bringing the dread contagion into our home. My life is in the hands of God and as long as He sees fit to spare me I will persist in my labors on behalf of the sick, dying and dead. We are losing the battle. Eighty-eight were buried this past Thursday. I

tremble for your safety. Wish the lie of immunity were true. Please let me know by way of a note sent to the residence of Dr. Rush that you and our dear Martha are well. I pray every hour that God will preserve you both. As difficult as it is to rise each morning and go with Thomas to perform our duties, the task would be unbearable if I did not hold in my heart a vision of these horrors ending, a blessed shining day when I return to you and drop this weary head upon your sweet bosom.

Allen, Allen, he called to me. Observe how even after death, the body rejects this bloody matter from nose and bowel and mouth. Verily, the patient who had expired at least an hour before, continued to stain the cloth I'd wrapped round him. We'd searched the rooms of a regal mansion, discovering six members of a family, patriarch, son, son's wife and three children, either dead or in the last frightful stages of the disease. Upon the advice of one of Dr. Rush's most outspoken critics, they had refused mercury purges and bleeding until now, when it was too late for any earthly remedy to preserve them. In the rich furnishings of this opulent mansion, attended by one remaining servant whom fear had not driven away, three generations had withered simultaneously, this proud family's link to past and future cut off absolutely, the great circle broken. In the first bedroom we'd entered we'd found William Spurgeon, merchant, son and father, present manager of the family fortune, so weak he could not speak, except with pained blinks of his terrible golden eyes. Did he welcome us? Was he apologizing to good Dr. Rush for doubting his cure? Did he fear the dark faces of my brother and myself? Quick, too quickly, he was gone. Answering no questions. Revealing nothing of his state of mind. A savaged face frozen above the blanket. Ancient beyond years. Jaundiced eyes not fooled by our busy ministrations, but staring through us, fixed on the eternal stillness soon to come. And I believe I learned in that yellow cast of his eyes, the exact hue of the sky, if sky it should be called, hanging over the next world where we abide.

Allen, Allen. He lasted only moments and then I wrapped him in a sheet from the chest at the foot of his canopied bed. We lifted him into a humbler litter, crudely nailed together, the lumber still green. Allen, look. Stench from the coffin cut through the oppressive odors permeating this doomed household. See. Like an infant the master of the house had soiled his swaddling clothes. Seepage formed a dark river and dripped between roughly jointed boards. We found his wife where she'd fallen, naked, yellow above the waist, black below. As always the smell presaged what we'd discover behind a closed door. This woman had possessed closets of finery, slaves who dressed, fed, bathed and painted her, and yet here she lay, no one to cover her modesty, to lift her from the floor. Dr. Rush guessed from the discoloration she'd been dead two days, a guess confirmed by the loyal black maid, sick herself, who'd elected to stay when all others had deserted her masters. The demands of the living too much for her. She'd simply shut the door on her dead mistress. No breath, no heartbeat, Sir. I could not rouse her, Sir. I intended to return, Sir, but I was too weak to move her, too exhausted by my labors, Sir. Tears rolled down her creased black face and I wondered in my heart how this abused and despised old creature in her filthy apron and turban, this frail, worn woman, had survived the general calamity while the strong and pampered toppled round her.

I wanted to demand of her why she did not fly out the door now, finally freed of her burden, her lifelong enslavement to the whims of white people. Yet I asked her nothing. Considered instead myself, a man who'd worked years to purchase his wife's freedom, then his own, a so-called freeman, and here I was following in the train of Rush and his assistants, a functionary, a lackey, insulted daily by those I risked my life to heal.

Why did I not fly? Why was I not dancing in the streets, celebrating God's judgment on this wicked city? Fever made me freer than I'd ever been. Municipal government had collapsed. Anarchy ruled. As long as fever did not strike me I could come and go anywhere I pleased. Fortunes could be amassed in the streets. I could sell myself to the highest bidder, as nurse or undertaker, as surgeon trained by the famous Dr. Rush to apply his lifesaving cure. Anyone who would enter houses where fever was abroad could demand outrageous sums for negligible services. To be spared the fever was a chance for anyone, black or white, to be a king.

So why do you follow him like a loyal puppy, you confounded black fool? He wagged his finger. *You. . . .* His finger a gaunt, swollen-jointed, cracked-bone, chewed thing. Like the nose on his face. The nose I'd thought looked more like finger than nose. *Fool. Fool.* Finger wagging, then the cackle. The barnyard braying. Berserk chickens cackling in his skinny, goiter-knobbed throat. You are a fool, you black son of Ham. You slack-witted, Nubian ape. You progeny of Peeping Toms and orangutans. Who forces you to accompany the madman Rush on his murderous tours? He kills a hundred for every one he helps with his lamebrain, nonsensical, unnatural, Sangrado cures. Why do you tuck your monkey tail between your legs and skip after that butcher? Are you his shadow, a mindless, spineless black puddle of slime with no will of its own?

You are a good man, Allen. You worry about the souls of your people in this soulless wilderness. You love your family and your God. You are a beacon and steadfast. Your fatal flaw is narrowness of vision. You cannot see beyond these shores. The river, that stinking gutter into which the city shovels its shit and extracts its drinking water, that long-suffering string of spittle winds to an ocean. A hundred miles downstream the foamy mouth of the land sucks on the Atlantic's teat, trade winds saunter and a whole wide world awaits the voyager. I know, Allen. I've been everywhere. Buying and selling everywhere.

If you would dare be Moses to your people and lead them out of this land, you'd find fair fields for your talent. Not lapdogging or doggy-trotting behind or fetch doggy or lie doggy or doggy open your legs or doggy stay still while I beat you. Follow the wound that is a river bank to the sea. Be bone, be gone. While there's still time. If there is time, *mon frère.* If the pestilence has not settled in you already, breathed from my foul guts into yours, even as we speak.

Here'a a master for you. A real master, Allen. The fever that's supping on my innards. I am more slave than you've ever been. I do its bidding absolutely. Cough up my lungs. Shit hunks of my bowel. When I die, they say my skin will turn as black as yours, Allen.

Return to your family. Do not leave them again. Whatever the Rushes promise, whatever they threaten.

Once, ten thousand years ago I had a wife and children. I was like you, Allen, proud, innocent, forward looking, well-spoken, well-mannered, a beacon and steadfast. I began to believe the whispered promise that I could have more. More of what, I didn't ask. Didn't know, but I took my eyes off what I loved in order to obtain this more. Left my wife and children and when I returned they were gone. Forever lost to me. The details are not significant. Suffice to say the circumstances of my leaving were much like yours. Very much like yours, Allen. And I lost everything. Became a wanderer among men. Bad news people see coming from miles away. A pariah. A joke. I'm not black like you, Allen. But I will be soon. Sooner than you'll be white. And if you're ever white, you'll be as dead as I'll be when I'm black.

Why do you desert your loved ones? What impels you to do what you find so painful, so unjust? Are you not a man? And free?

Her sleepy eyes, your lips on her warm cheek, each time may be the last meeting on this earth. The circumstances are similar, my brother. My shadow. My dirty face.

The dead are legion, the living a froth on dark, layered depths.

Master Abraham. There's a gentleman to see you, Sir. The golden-haired lad bound to me for seven years was carted across the seas, like you, Allen, in the bowels of a leaky tub. A son to replace my son his fathers had clubbed to death when they razed the ghetto of Antwerp. But I could not tame the inveterate hate, his aversion and contempt for me. From my aerie, at my desk secluded among barrels, bolts, crates and trunks of the shop's attic, I watched him steal, drink, fornicate. I overheard him denounce me to a delegate sent round to collect a tithe during the emergency. 'Tis well know in the old country that Jews bring the fever. Palatine fever that slays whole cities. They carry it under dirty fingernails, in the wimples of lizardy private parts. Pass it on with the evil eye. That's why we hound them from our towns, exterminate them. Beware of Master Abraham's glare. And the black-coated vulture listened intently. I could see him toting up the account in his small brain. Kill the Jew. Gain a shop and sturdy prentice, too. But I survived till fever laid me low and the cart brought me here to Bush Hill. For years he robbed and betrayed me and all my revenge was to treat him better. Allow him to pilfer, lie, embezzle. Let him grow fat and careless as I knew he would. With a father's boundless kindness I destroyed him. The last sorry laugh coming when I learned he died in agony, fever shriven, following by a day his Water Street French whore my indulgence allowed him to keep.

In Amsterdam I sold diamonds, Allen. In Barcelona they plucked hairs from my beard to fashion charms that brought ill fortune to their enemies. There were nights in dungeons when the mantle of my suffering was all I possessed to wrap round me and keep off mortal cold. I cursed God for choosing me, choosing my people to cuckold and slaughter. Have you heard of the Lamed-Vov, the Thirty Just Men set apart to suffer the reality humankind cannot bear? Saviors. But not Gods like your Christ. Not magicians, not sorcerers with bags of tricks, Allen. No divine immunities. Flesh and blood saviors. Men like we are, Allen. If man you are beneath your sable hide. Men who cough and scratch their sores and bleed and stink. Whose teeth rot. Whose wives and children are torn from them. Who wander the earth unable to die, but men always, men till God plucks them up and returns them to His side where they must thaw ten centuries to melt the crust of earthly grief and misery they've taken upon themselves. Ice men. Snowmen. I thought for many years I might be one of them. In my vanity. My self-pity. My foolishness. But no. One lifetime of sorrows enough for me. I'm just another customer. One more in the crowd lined up at his stall to purchase his wares.

You do know, don't you, Allen, that God is a bookseller? He publishes one book— the text of suffering—over and over again. He disguises in between new boards, in different shapes and sizes, prints on varying papers, in many fonts, adds prefaces and postscripts to deceive the buyer, but it's always the same book.

You say you do not return to your family because you don't want to infect them. Perhaps your fear is well-founded. But perhaps it also masks a greater fear. Can you imagine yourself, Allen, as other than you are? A free man with no charlatan Rush to blame. The weight of your life in your hands.

You've told me tales of citizens paralyzed by fear, of slaves on shipboard who turn to stone in their chains, their eyes boiled in the sun. Is it not possible that you suffer the converse of this immobility? You, sir, unable to stop an endless round of duty and obligation. Turning pages as if the next one or the next will let you finish the story and return to your life.

Your life, man. Tell me what sacred destiny, what nigger errand keeps you standing here at my filthy pallet? Fly, fly, fly away home. Your house is on fire, your children burning.

I have lived to see the slaves free. My people frolic in the streets. Black and white. The ones who believe they are either or both or neither. I am too old for dancing. Too old for foolishness. But this full moon makes me wish for two good legs. For three. Straddled a broomstick when I was a boy. Giddy-up, Giddy-up. Galloping m'lord, m'lady, around the yard I should be sweeping. Dust in my wake. Chickens squawking. My eyes everywhere at once so I would not be caught out by mistress or master in the sin of idleness. Of dreaming. Of following a child's inclination. My broom steed snatched away. Become a rod across my back. Ever cautious. Dreaming with one eye open. The eye I am now, old and gimpy limbed, watching while my people celebrate the rumor of Old Pharaoh's capitulation.

I've shed this city like a skin, wiggling out of it tenscore and more years, by miles and els, fretting, twisting. Many days I did not know whether I'd wrenched freer or crawled deeper into the sinuous pit. Somewhere a child stood, someplace green, keeping track, waiting for me. Hoping I'd meet him again, hoping my struggle was not in vain. I search that child's face for clues to my blurred features. Flesh drifted and banked, eroded by wind and water, the landscape of this city fitting me like a skin. Pray for me, child. For my unborn parents I carry in this orphan's potbelly. For this ancient face that slips like water through my fingers.

Night now. Bitter cold night. Fires in the hearths of lucky ones. Many of us still abide in dark cellars, caves dug into the earth below poor men's houses. For we are poorer still, burrow there, pull earth like a blanket and quilt round us to shut out cold, sleep multitudes to a room, stacked and crosshatched and spoon fashion, ourselves the fuel, heat of one body passed to others and passed back from all to one. No wonder then the celebration does not end as a blazing chill sweeps off the Delaware. Those who leap and roar round the bonfires are better off where they are. They have no place else to go.

Given the derivation of the words, you could call the deadly, winged visitors an *unpleasantness from Egypt.*

Putrid stink rattles in his nostrils. He must stoop to enter the cellar. No answer as he shouts his name, his mission of mercy. Earthen floor, ceiling and walls buttressed by occasional beams, slabs of wood. Faint bobbing glow from his lantern. He sees himself looming and shivering on the walls, a shadowy presence with more substance than he feels he possesses at this late hour. After a long day of visits, this hovel his last stop before returning to his brother's house for a few hours of rest. He has learned that exhaustion is a swamp he can wade through and on the far side another region where a thin trembling version of himself toils while he observes, bemused, slipping in and out of sleep, amazed at the likeness, the skill with which that other mounts and sustains him. Mimicry. Puppetry. Whatever controls this other, he allows the impostor to continue, depends upon it to work when he no longer can. After days in the city proper with Rush, he returns to these twisting streets beside the river that are infected veins and arteries he must bleed.

At the rear of the cave, so deep in shadow he stumbles against it before he see it, is a mound of rags. When he leans over it, speaking down into the darkness, he knows instantly this is the source of the terrible smell, that something once alive is rotting under the rags. He thinks of autumn leaves blown into mountainous, crisp heaps, the north wind cleansing itself and the city of summer. He thinks of anything, any image that will rescue him momentarily from the nauseating stench, postpone what he must do next. He screams no, no to himself as he blinks away his wife's face, the face of his daughter. His neighbors had promised to check on them, he hears news almost daily. There is no rhyme or reason in whom the fever takes, whom it spares, but he's in the city every day, exposed to its victims, breathing fetid air, touching corrupted flesh. Surely if someone in his family must die, it will be him. His clothes are drenched in vinegar, he sniffs the nostrum of gunpowder, bark and asafetida in a bag pinned to his coat. He's prepared to purge and bleed himself, he's also ready and quite willing to forgo these precautions and cures if he thought surrendering his life might save theirs. He thinks and unthinks a picture of her hair, soft against his cheek, the wet warmth of his daughter's backside in the crook of his arm as he carries her to her mother's side where she'll be changed and fed. No. Like a choking mist, the smell of decaying flesh stifles him, forces him to turn away, once, twice, before he watches himself bend down into the brunt of it and uncover the sleepers.

Two Santo Domingan refugees, slave or free, no one knew for sure, inhabited this cellar. They had moved in less than a week before, the mother huge with child, man and woman both wracked by fever. No one knows how long the couple's been unattended. There was shame in the eyes and voices of the few from whom he'd gleaned bits and pieces of the Santo Domingans' history. Since no one really knew them and few nearby spoke their language, no one was willing to risk, et cetera. Except for screams one night, no one had seen or heard signs of life. If he'd been told nothing about them, his nose would have led him here.

He winces when he sees the dead man and woman, husband and wife, not entwined as in some ballad of love eternal, but back to back, distance between them, as if the horror were too visible, too great to bear, doubled in the other's eyes. What had they seen before they flung away from each other? If he could, he would rearrange them, spare the undertakers this vision.

Rat feet and rat squeak in the shadows. He'd stomped his feet, shooed them before he entered, hollered as he threw back the covers, but already they were accustomed to his presence, back at work. They'd bit indiscriminately, dead flesh, his flesh. He curses and flails his staff against the rags, strikes the earthen floor to keep the scavengers at bay. Those sounds are what precipitate the high-pitched cries that first frighten him, then shame him, then propel him to a tall packing crate turned on its end, atop which another crate is balanced. Inside the second wicker container, which had imported some item from some distant place into this land, twin brown babies hoot and wail.

We are passing over the Dismal Swamp. On the right is the Appalachian range, some of the oldest mountains on earth. Once there were steep ridges and valleys all through here but erosion off the mountains created landfill several miles deep in places. This accounts for the rich loamy soil of the region. Over the centuries several southern states were formed from this gradual erosion. The cash crops of cotton and tobacco so vital to southern prosperity were ideally suited to the fertile soil.

Yeah, I nurse these old funky motherfuckers, all right. White people, specially old white people, lemme tell you, boy, them peckerwoods stink. Stone dead fishy wet stink. Talking all the time bout niggers got BO. Well, white folks got the stink and gone, man. Don't be putting my hands on them, neither. Never. Huh uh. If I touch them, be wit gloves. They some nasty people, boy. And they don't be paying me enough to take no chances wit my health. Matter of fact they ain't paying me enough to really be expecting me to work. Yeah. Starvation wages. So I ain't hardly touching them. Or doing much else either. Got to smoke a cigarette to get close to some of them. Piss and shit theyselves like babies. They don't need much taking care anyway. Most of them three-quarters dead, already. Ones that ain't is crazy. Nobody don't want them round, that's why they here. Talking to theyselves. Acting like they speaking to a roomful of people and not one soul in the ward paying attention. There's one old black dude, must be a hundred, he be muttering away to hisself non-stop everyday. Pitiful, man. Hope I don't never get that old. Shoot me, bro, if I start to getting old and fucked up in body and mind like them. Don't want no fools like me hanging over me when I can't do nothing no more for my ownself. Shit. They ain't paying me nothing so that's what I do. Nothing. Least I don't punch em or tease em or steal they shit like some of the staff. And I don't pretend I'm God like these so-called professionals and doctors flittin round here drawing down that long bread. Naw. I just mind my own business, do my time. Cop a little TV, sneak me a joint when nobody's around. It ain't all that bad, really. Long as I ain't got no ole lady and crumb crushers. Don't know how the married cats make it on the little bit of chump change they pay us. But me, I'm free. It ain't that bad, really.

By the time his brother brought him the news of their deaths . . .

Almost an afterthought. The worst, he believed, had been overcome. Only a handful of deaths the last weeks of November. The city was recovering. Commerce thriving. Philadelphia must be revictualed, refueled, rebuilt, reconnected to the countryside, to markets foreign and domestic, to products, pleasures and appetites denied during the quarantine months of the fever. A new century would soon be dawning. We must forget the horrors. The Mayor proclaims a new day. Says let's put the past behind us. Of the eleven who died in the fire he said extreme measures were necessary as we cleansed ourselves of disruptive influences. The cost could have been much greater, he said I regret the loss of life, especially the half dozen kids, but I commend all city officials, all volunteers who helped return the city to the arc of glory that is its proper destiny.

When they cut him open, the one who decided to stay, to be a beacon and steadfast, they will find: liver (1720 grams), spleen (150 grams), right kidney (190 grams), left kidney (180 grams), brain (1450 grams), heart (380 grams) and right next to his heart, the miniature hand of a child, frozen in a grasping gesture, fingers like hard tongues of flame, still reaching for the marvel of the beating heart, fascinated still, though the heart is cold, beats not, the hand as curious about this infinite stillness as it was about thump and heat and quickness.

Reading as a Writer

1. What is the structure of this story? If possible, draw a diagram that illustrates this structure.

2. How does the structure deviate from that of a more traditional story? Does the structure make it *easier* or *harder* to understand the story? How so?

3. What might the story have lost if Wideman had chosen a more conventional approach to the material?

JUNOT DÍAZ

Fiesta, 1980

MAMI'S YOUNGEST SISTER—my tía Yrma—finally made it to the United States that year. She and tío Miguel got themselves an apartment in the Bronx, off the Grand Concourse and everybody decided that we should have a party. Actually, my pops decided, but everybody—meaning Mami, tía Yrma, tío Miguel and their neighbors— thought it a dope idea. On the afternoon of the party Papi came back from work around six. Right on time. We were all dressed by then, which was a smart move on our part. If Papi had walked in and caught us lounging around in our underwear, he would have kicked our asses something serious.

He didn't say nothing to nobody, not even my moms. He just pushed past her, held up his hand when she tried to talk to him and headed right into the shower. Rafa gave me the look and I gave it back to him; we both knew Papi had been with that Puerto Rican woman he was seeing and wanted to wash off the evidence quick.

Mami looked really nice that day. The United States had finally put some meat on her; she was no longer the same flaca[1] who had arrived here three years before. She had cut her hair short and was wearing tons of cheap-ass jewelry which on her didn't look too lousy. She smelled like herself, like the wind through a tree. She always waited until the last possible minute to put on her perfume because she said it was a waste to spray it on early and then have to spray it on again once you got to the party.

We—meaning me, my brother, my little sister and Mami—waited for Papi to finish his shower. Mami seemed anxious, in her usual dispassionate way. Her hands adjusted the buckle of her belt over and over again. That morning, when she had gotten us up for school, Mami told us that she wanted to have a good time at the party. I want to dance, she said, but now, with the sun sliding out of the sky like spit off a wall, she seemed ready just to get this over with.

Rafa didn't much want to go to no party either, and me, I never wanted to go anywhere with my family. There was a baseball game in the parking lot outside and we could hear our friends, yelling, Hey, and, Cabrón, to one another. We heard the pop of a ball as it sailed over the cars, the clatter of an aluminum bat dropping to the concrete. Not that me or Rafa loved baseball; we just liked playing with the local kids, thrashing them at anything they were doing. By the sounds of the shouting, we both knew the game was close, either of us could have made a difference. Rafa frowned and when I frowned back, he put up his fist. Don't you mirror me, he said.

1. Skinny girl.

Don't you mirror me, I said.

He punched me—I would have hit him back but Papi marched into the living room with his towel around his waist, looking a lot smaller than he did when he was dressed. He had a few strands of hair around his nipples and a surly closed-mouth expression, like maybe he'd scalded his tongue or something.

Have they eaten? he asked Mami.

She nodded. I made you something.

You didn't let him eat, did you?

Ay, Dios mío, she said, letting her arms fall to her side.

Ay, Dios mío is right, Papi said.

I was never supposed to eat before our car trips, but earlier, when she had put out our dinner of rice, beans and sweet platanos, guess who had been the first one to clean his plate? You couldn't blame Mami really, she had been busy—cooking, getting ready, dressing my sister Madai. I should have reminded her not to feed me but I wasn't that sort of son.

Papi turned to me. Coño, muchacho, why did you eat?

Rafa had already started inching away from me. I'd once told him I considered him a low-down chickenshit for moving out of the way every time Papi was going to smack me.

Collateral damage, Rafa had said. Ever heard of it?

No.

Look it up.

Chickenshit or not, I didn't dare glance at him. Papi was old-fashioned; he expected your undivided attention when you were getting your ass whupped. You wouldn't look him in the eye either—that wasn't allowed. Better to stare at his belly button, which was perfectly round and immaculate. Papi pulled me to my feet by my ear.

If you throw up—

I won't, I cried, tears in my eyes, more out of reflex than pain.

Ya, Ramón, ya. It's not his fault, Mami said.

They've know about this party forever. How did they think we were going to get there? Fly?

He finally let go of my ear and I sat back down. Madai was too scared to open her eyes. Being around Papi all her life had turned her into a major-league wuss. Anytime Papi raised his voice her lip would start trembling, like some specialized tuning fork. Rafa pretended that he had knuckles to crack and when I shoved him, he gave me a *Don't start* look. But even that little bit of recognition made me feel better.

I was the one who was always in trouble with my dad. It was like my God-given duty to piss him off, to do everything the way he hated. Our fights didn't bother me too much. I still wanted him to love me, something that never seemed strange or contradictory until years later, when he was out of our lives.

By the time my ear stopped stinging Papi was dressed and Mami was crossing each one of us, solemnly, like we were heading off to war. We said, in turn, Bendición, Mami, and she poked us in our five cardinal spots while saying, Que Dios te bendiga.

This was how all our trips began, the words that followed me every time I left the house.

None of us spoke until we were inside Papi's Volkswagen van. Brand-new, lime-green and bought to impress. Oh, we were impressed, but me, every time I was in that VW and Papi went above twenty miles an hour, I vomited. I'd never had trouble with cars before—that van was like my curse. Mami suspected it was the upholstery. In her mind, American things—appliances, mouthwash, funny-looking upholstery—all seemed to have an intrinsic badness about them. Papi was careful about taking me anywhere in the VW, but when he had to, I rode up front in Mami's usual seat so I could throw up out a window.

¿Cómo te sientas? Mami asked over my shoulder when Papi pulled onto the turn-pike. She had her hand on the base of my neck. One thing about Mami, her palms never sweated.

I'm OK, I said, keeping my eyes straight ahead. I definitely didn't want to trade glances with Papi. He had this one look, furious and sharp, that always left me feel-ing bruised.

Toma. Mami handed me four mentas. She had thrown three out her window at the beginning of our trip, an offering to Eshú; the rest were for me.

I took one and sucked it slowly, my tongue knocking it up against my teeth. We passed Newark Airport without any incident. If Madai had been awake she would have cried because the planes flew so close to the cars.

How's he feeling? Papi asked.

Fine, I said. I glanced back at Rafa and he pretended like he didn't see me. That was the way he was, at school and at home. When I was in trouble, he didn't know me. Madai was solidly asleep, but even with her face all wrinkled up and drooling she looked cute, her hair all separated into twists.

I turned around and concentrated on the candy. Papi even started to joke that we might not have to scrub the van out tonight. He was beginning to loosen up, not checking his watch too much. Maybe he was thinking about the Puerto Rican woman or maybe he was just happy that we were all together. I could never tell. At the toll, he was feeling positive enough to actually get out of the van and search around under the basket for dropped coins. It was something he had once done to amuse Madai, but now it was habit. Cars behind us honked their horns and I slide down in my seat. Rafa didn't care; he grinned back at the other cars and waved. His actually job was to make sure no cops were coming. Mami shook Madai awake and as soon as she saw Papi stooping for a couple of quarters she let out this screech of delight that almost took off the top of my head.

That was the end of the good times. Just outside the Washington Bridge, I started feeling woozy. The smell of the upholstery got all up inside my head and I found myself with a mouthful of saliva. Mami's hand tensed on my shoulder and when I caught Papi's eye, he was like, No way. Don't do it.

The first time I got sick in the van Papi was taking me to the library. Rafa was with us and he couldn't believe I threw up. I was famous for my steel-lined stomach. A third-world childhood could give you that. Papi was worried enough that just as quick as Rafa could drop off the books we were on our way home. Mami fixed me one of her honey-and-onion concoctions and that made my stomach feel better. A week later we tried the library again and on this go-around I couldn't get the window open in time. When Papi got me home, he went and cleaned out the van himself, an expression of askho on his face. This was a big deal, since Papi almost never cleaned anything himself. He came back inside and found me sitting on the couch feeling like hell.

It's the car, he said to Mami. It's making him sick.

This time the damage was pretty minimal, nothing Papi couldn't wash off the door with a blast of the hose. He was pissed, though; he jammed his finger into my cheek, a nice solid thrust. That was the way he was with his punishments: imaginative. Earlier that year I'd written an essay in school called "My Father the Torturer," but the teacher made me write a new one. She thought I was kidding.

We drove the rest of the way to the Bronx in silence. We only stopped once, so I could brush my teeth. Mami had brought along my toothbrush and a tube of toothpaste and while every car known to man sped by us she stood outside with me so I wouldn't feel alone.

Tío Miguel was about seven feet tall and had his hair combed up and out, into a demifro. He gave me and Rafa big spleen-crushing hugs and then kissed Mami and finally ended up with Madai on his shoulder. The last time I'd seen Tío was at the airport, his first day in the United States. I remembered how he hadn't seemed all that troubled to be in another country.

He looked down at me. Carajo, Yunior, you look horrible!

He threw up, my brother explained.

I pushed Rafa. Thanks a lot, ass-face.

Hey, he said. Tílo asked.

Tío clapped a bricklayer's hand on my shoulder. Everybody gets sick sometimes, he said. You should have seen me on the plane over here. Dios mio! He rolled his Asian-looking eyes for emphasis. I thought we were all going to die.

Everybody could tell he was lying. I smiled like he was making me feel better.

Do you want me to get you a drink? Tío asked. We got beer and rum.

Miguel, Mami said. He's young.

Young? Back in Santo Domingo, he'd be getting laid by now.

Mami thinned her lips, which took some doing.

Well, it's true, Tío said.

So, Mami, I said. when do I get to go visit the D.R.?

That's enough, Yunior.

It's the only pussy you'll ever get, Rafa siad to me in English.

Not counting your girlfriend, of course.

Rafa smiled. He had to give me that one.

Papi came in from parking the van. He and Miguel gave each other the sort of handshakes that would have turned my fingers into Wonder bread.

Coño, compa'i, ¿cómo va todo? they said to each other.

Tía came out then, with an apron on and maybe the longest Lee Press-On Nails I've ever seen in my life. There was this one guru motherfucker in the *Guiness Book of World Records* who had longer nails, but I tell you, it was close. she gave everybody kisses, told me and Rafa how guapo we were—Rafa, of course, believed her—told Madai how bella she was, but when she got to Papi, she froze a little, like maybe she'd seen a wasp on the tip of his nose, but then kissed him all the same.

Mami told us to join the other kids in the living room. Tío said, Wait a minute, I want to show you the apartment. I was glad Tía said, Hold on, because from what I'd seen so far, the place had been furnished in Contemporary Dominican Tacky. The less I saw, the better. I mean, I liked plastic sofa covers but damn, Tío and Tía had taken it to another level. They had a disco ball hanging in the living room and the type of stucco ceilings that looked like stalactite heaven. The sofas all had golden tassels dangling from their edges. Tía came out of the kitchen with some people I didn't know and by the time she got done introducing everybody, only Papi and Mami were given the guided tour of the four-room third-floor apartment. Me and Rafa joined the kids in the living room. They'd already started eating. We were hungry, one of the girls explained, a pastelito in hand. The boy was about three years younger than me but the girl who'd spoken, Leti, was my age. She and another girl were on the sofa together and they were cute as hell.

Leti introduced them: the boy was her brother Wilquins and the other girl was her neighbor Mari. Leti had some serious tetas and I could tell that my brother was going to gun for her. His taste in girls was predictable. He sat down right between Leti and Mari and by the way they were smiling at him I knew he'd do fine. Neither of the girls gave me more than cursory one-two, which didn't bother me. Sure, I liked girls but I was always too terrified to speak to them unless we were arguing or I was calling them stupidos, which was one of my favorite words that year. I turned to Wilquins and asked him what there was to do around here. Mari, who had the lowest voice I'd ever heard, said, He can't speak.

What does that mean?

He's mute.

I looked at Wilquins incredulously. He smiled and nodded, as if he'd won a prize or something.

Does he understand? I asked.

Of course he understands, Rafa said. He's not dumb.

I could tell Rafa had said that just to score points with the girls. Both of them nodded. Low-voice Mari said, He's the best student in his grade.

I thought, Not bad for a mute. I sat next to Wilquins. After about two seconds of TV Wilquins whipped out a bag of dominos and motioned to me. Did I want to play? Sure. Me and him played Rafa and Leti and we whupped their collective asses twice, which put Rafa in a real bad mood. He looked at me like maybe he wanted to take a swing, just one to make him feel better. Leti kept whispering into Rafa's ear, telling him it was OK.

In the kitchen I could hear by parents slipping into their usual modes. Papi's voice was loud and argumentative; you didn't have to be anywhere near him to catch his drift. And Mami, you had to put cups to your ears to hear hers. I went into the kitchen a few times—once so the tíos could show off how much bullshit I'd been able to cram in my head the last few years; another time for a bucket-sized cup of soda. Mami and Tía were frying tostones and the last of the pastelitos. She appeared happier now and the way her hands worked on our dinner you would think she had a life somewhere else making rare and precious things. She nudged Tía every now and then, shit they must have been doing all their lives. As soon as Mami saw me though, she gave me the eye. Don't stay long, that eye said. Don't piss your old man off.

Papi was too busy arguing about Elvis to notice me. Then somebody mentioned María Montez and Papi barked, María Montez? Let me tell *you* about María Montez, compa'i.

Maybe I was used to him. His voice—louder than most adults'—didn't bother me none, though the other kids shifted uneasily in their seats. Wilquins was about to raise the volume on the TV, but Rafa said, I wouldn't do that. Muteboy had balls, though. He did it anyway and then sat down. Wilquins's pop came into the living room a second later, a bottle of Presidente in hand. That dude must have had Spider-senses or something. Did you raise that? he asked Wilquins and Wilquins nodded.

Is this your house? his pops asked. He looked ready to beat Wilquins silly but he lowered the volume instead.

See, Rafa said. You nearly got your ass *kicked.*

I met the Puerto Rican woman right after Papi had gotten the van. He was taking me on short trips, trying to cure me of my vomiting. It wasn't really working but I looked forward to our trips, even though at the end of each one I'd be sick. These were the only times me and Papi did anything together. When we were alone he treated me much better, like maybe I was his son or something.

Before each drive Mami would cross me.

Benedición, Mami, I'd say.

She'd kiss my forehead. Que Dios te bendiga. And then she would give me a handful of mentas because she wanted me to be OK. Mami didn't think these excursions would cure anything, but the one time she had brought it up to Papi he had told her to shut up, what did she know about anything anyway?

Me and Papi didn't talk much. We just drove around our neighborhood. Occasionally he'd ask, How is it?

And I'd nod, no matter how I felt.

One day I was sick outside of Perth Amboy. Instead of taking me home he went the other way on Industrial Avenue, stopping a few minutes later in front of a light blue house I didn't recognize. It reminded me of the Easter eggs we colored at school, the ones we threw out the bus windows at other cars.

The Puerto Rican woman was there and she helped me clean up. She had dry papery hands and when she rubbed the towel on my chest, she did it hard, like I was a bumper she was waxing. She was very thin and had a cloud of brown hair rising above her narrow face and the sharpest black eyes you've ever seen.

He's cute, she said to Papi.

Not when he's throwing up, Papi said.

What's your name? she asked me. Are you Rafa?

I shook my head.

Then it's Yunior, right?

I nodded.

You're the smart one, she said, suddenly happy with herself. Maybe you want to see my books?

They weren't hers. I recognized them as ones my father must have left in her house. Papi was a voracious reader, couldn't even go cheating without a paperback in his pocket.

Why don't you go watch TV? Papi suggested. He was looking at her like she was the last piece of chicken on earth.

We got plenty of channels, she said. Use the remote if you want.

The two of them went upstairs and I was too scared of what was happening to poke around. I just sat there, ashamed, expected something big and fiery to crash down on our heads. I watched a whole hour of the news before Papi came downstairs and said, Let's go.

About two hours later the women laid out the food and like always nobody but the kids thanked them. It must be some Dominican tradition or something. There was everything I liked—chicharrones, fried chicken, tostones, sancocho, rice, fried cheese, yuca, avocado, potato salad, a meteor-sized hunk of pernil, even a tossed salad which I could do without—but when I joined the other kids around the serving table, Papi said, Oh no you don't, and took the paper plate out of my hand. His fingers weren't gentle.

What's wrong now? Tía asked, handing me another plate.

He ain't eating, Papi said. Mami pretended to help Rafa with the pernil.

Why can't he eat?

Because I said so.

The adults who didn't know us made like they hadn't heard a thing and Tío just smiled sheepishly and told everybody to go ahead and eat. All the kids—about ten of them now—trooped back into the living room with their plates a-heaping and all the adults ducked into the kitchen and the dining room, where the radio was playing loud-ass bachatas. I was the only one without a plate. Papi stopped me before I could get away from him. He kept his voice nice and low so nobody else could hear him.

If you eat anything, I'm going to beat you. ¿Entiendes?

I nodded.

And if your brother gives you any food, I'll beat him too. Right here in front of everybody. ¿Entiendes?

I nodded again. I wanted to kill him and he must have sensed it because he gave my head a little shove.

All the kids watched me come in and sit down in front of the TV.

What's wrong with your dad? Leti asked.

He's a dick, I said.

Rafa shook his head. Don't say that shit in front of people.

Easy for you to be nice when you're eating, I said.

Hey, if I was a pukey little baby, I wouldn't get no food either.

I almost said something back but I concentrated on the TV. I wasn't going to start it. No fucking way. So I watched Bruce Lee beat Chuck Norris into the floor of the Colosseum and tried to pretend that there was no food anywhere in the house. It was Tía who finally saved me. She came into the living room and said, Since you ain't eating, Yunior, you can at least help me get some ice.

I didn't want to, but she mistook my reluctance for something else.

I already asked your father.

She held my hand while we walked; Tía didn't have any kids but I could tell she wanted them. She was the sort of relative who always remembered your birthday but who you only went to visit because you had to. We didn't get past the first-floor landing before she opened her pocketbook and handed me the first of three pastelitos she had smuggled out of the apartment.

Go ahead, she said. And as soon as you get inside make sure you brush your teeth.

Thanks a lot, Tía, I said.

Those pastelitos didn't stand a chance.

She sat next to me on the stairs and smoked her cigarette. All the way down on the first floor and we could still hear the music and the adults and the television. Tía looked a tone like Mami; the two of them were both short and light-skinned. Tía smiled a lot and that was what set them apart the most.

How is it at home, Yunior?

What do you mean?

How's it going in the apartment? Are you kids OK?

I knew an interrogation when I heard one, no matter how sugar-coated it was. I didn't say anything. Don't get me wrong, I loved my tía, but something told me to keep my mouth shut. Maybe it was family loyalty, maybe I just wanted to protect Mami or I was afraid that Papi would find out—it could have been anything really.

Is your mom all right?

I shrugged.

Have there been lots of fights?

None, I said. Too many shrugs would have been just as bad as an answer. Papi's at work too much.

Work, Tía said, like it was somebody's name she didn't like.

Me and Rafa, we didn't talk much about the Puerta Rican woman. When we ate dinner at her house, the few times Papi had taken us over there, we still acted like nothing was out of the ordinary. Pass the ketchup, man. No sweat, bro. The affair was like a hole in our living room floor, one we'd gotten so used to circumnavigating that we sometimes forgot it was there.

By midnight all the adults were crazy dancing. I was sitting outside Tía's bedroom—where Madai was sleeping—trying not to attract attention. Rafa had me guarding the door; he and Leti were in there too, with some of the other kids, getting busy no doubt. Wilquins had gone across the hall to bed so I had me and the roaches to mess around with.

Whenever I peered into the main room I saw about twenty moms and dads dancing and drinking beers. Every now and then somebody yelled, Quisqueya! And then everybody else would yell and stomp their feet. From what I could see my parents seemed to be enjoying themselves.

Mami and Tía spent a lot of time side by side, whispering, and I kept expecting something to come of this, a brawl maybe. I'd never once been out with my family when it hadn't turned to shit. We weren't even theatrical or straight crazy like other families. We fought like sixth-graders, without any real dignity. I guess the whole night I'd been waiting for a blowup, something between Papi and Mami. This was how I always figured Papi would be exposed, out in public, where everybody would know.

You're a cheater!

But everything was calmer than usual. And Mami didn't look like she was about to say anything to Papi. The two of them danced every now and then but they never lasted more than a song before Mami joined Tía again in whatever conversation they were having.

I tried to imagine Mami before Papi. Maybe I was tired, or just sad, thinking about the way my family was. Maybe I already knew how it would all end up in a few years, Mami without Papi, and that was why I did it. Picturing her alone wasn't easy. It seemed like Papi had always been with her, even when we were waiting in Santo Domingo for him to send for us.

The only photograph our family had of Mami as a young woman, before she married Papi, was the one that somebody took of her at an election party that I found one day while rummaging for money to go to the arcade. Mami had it tucked into her immigration papers. In the photo, she's surrounded by laughing cousins I will never meet, who are all shiny from dancing, whose clothes are rumpled and loose. You can tell it's night and hot and that the mosquitos have been biting. She sits straight and even in a crowd she stands out, smiling quietly like maybe she's the one everybody's celebrating. You can't see her hands but I imagined they're knotting a straw or a bit of thread. This was the woman my father met a year later on the Malecón, the woman Mami thought she'd always be.

Mami must have caught me studying her because she stopped what she was doing and gave me a smile, maybe her first one of the night. Suddenly I wanted to go over and hug her, for no other reason than I loved her, but there were about eleven fat jiggling bodies between us. So I sat down on the tiled floor and waited.

I must have fallen asleep because the next thing I knew Rafa was kicking me and saying, Let's go. He looked like he'd been hitting those girls off; he was all smiles. I got to my feet in time to kiss Tía and Tío good-bye. Mami was holding the serving dish she had brought with her.

Where's Papi? I asked.

He's downstairs, bringing the van around. Mami leaned down to kiss me.

You were good today, she said.

And then Papi burst in and told us to get the hell downstairs before some pendejo cop gave him a ticket. More kisses, more handshakes and then we were gone.

I don't remember being out of sorts after I met the Puerto Rican woman but I must have been because Mami only asked me questions when she thought something was wrong in my life. It took her about ten passes but finally she cornered me one afternoon when we were alone in the apartment. Our upstairs neighbors were beating the crap out of their kids, and me and her had been listening to it all afternoon. She put her hand on mine and said, Is everything OK, Yunior? Have you been fighting with your brother?

Me and Rafa had already talked. We'd been in the basement, where our parents couldn't hear us. He told me that yeah, he knew about her.

Papi's taken me there twice now, he said.

Why didn't you tell me? I asked.

What the hell was I going to say? *Hey, Yunior, guess what happened yesterday? I met Papi's sucia!*

I didn't say anything to Mami either. She watched me, very very closely. Later I would think, maybe if I had told her, she would have confronted him, would have done something, but who can know these things? I said I'd been having trouble in school and like that everything was back to normal between us. She put her hand on my shoulder and squeezed and that was that.

*   *   *

We were on the turnpike, just past Exit 11, when I started feeling it again. I sat up from leaning against Rafa. His fingers smelled and he'd gone to sleep almost as soon as he got into the van. Madai was out too but at least she wasn't snoring.

In the darkness, I saw that Papi had a hand on Mami's knee and that the two of them were quiet and still. They weren't slumped back or anything; they were both wide awake, bolted into their seats. I couldn't see either of their faces and no matter how hard I tried I could not imagine their expressions. Neither of them moved. Every now and then the van was filled with the bright rush of somebody else's headlights. Finally I said, Mami, and they both looked back, already knowing what was happening.

Reading as a Writer

1. In what ways is this a traditional story with a beginning, middle, and end?

2. In what ways is the story less traditional?

3. Point out several places where you were surprised by what happened in the story, and explain why.

CHAPTER FIVE

Why You Need to Show *and* Tell
Dramatizing and Narrating

"SHOW, NOT TELL." If you've ever taken a creative writing workshop, shown a story or essay to a writer friend who has taken workshops, or read just about any beginning book on creative writing, you will have bumped into this piece of conventional wisdom.

The only problem is, it's wrong.

Well, wrong is perhaps too strong a word. Let's say that it's certainly not always right. And it could be wrong for you. Very wrong. Even if it was right for Ernest Hemingway, or is still right for Richard Ford, or for Tobias Wolff.

This chapter first defines the terms "showing" and "telling." It then looks at writing samples that show the broad range of ways that these two basic writing tools can be used. The exercises give you hands-on practice in incorporating what you've learned into your own writing. Finally, you have a chance to see how some masters of the short story have used their own unique combinations of showing and telling.

Some Basic Definitions

Let's first try to understand the reason this show-not-tell advice is so freely passed out. Quite frankly, it's because even experienced writers—and even university professors—don't always pay attention to the real meanings of the terms they are using. Either that, or they are trying to oversimplify a terribly complex issue in the hope of getting beginners to avoid making some basic (and common) errors. In either case, it makes sense to first define as best as we can what we're talking about.

> SHOWING: *The American Heritage Dictionary* defines "to show" as "to cause or allow to be seen." In literature, "showing" is also referred to as dramatizing. If something is shown, or dramatized, the reader is allowed to be an eyewitness (of sorts) to the events of the story, novel, or essay through the use of dialogue (what characters say) and action (what characters do or have done to them). Another way to think about showing is to think of what can be performed in a *dramatic* genre, such as the stage, television, or movies. Indeed, the definition of "to dramatize" is "to be adaptable to dramatic form."

TELLING: Also referred to as summary or narration, writers *tell* to directly communicate or describe to the reader what is happening in a creative work. That is, as a writer you can describe the setting (*It was a dark and stormy night*); you can describe the characters (*She had a face as broad and as innocent as a cabbage*); and you can even "tell" the plot by summarizing what happens at a particular point in the story (*She told him she'd had enough and that she was leaving for Peoria on the morning train*).

Let's be even more precise. When a story is dramatized, or shown, the reader is presented with concrete evidence of what's happening. What does this include? Think of anything you could witness in the real world (a couple fighting at a restaurant), or on a stage (a revival of *Cat on a Hot Tin Roof*), or in a movie (*Casablanca*):

- Words spoken, or dialogue between characters. (*"Why did you order that? You know I'm a vegetarian!"*)

- Actions and reactions among characters. (*She picks up the fork and stabs the tablecloth twice.*)

- Basic *objective* descriptions of objects or settings that a reader would naturally see if the situation were videotaped or photographed. (*It was dark outside the restaurant. There were twelve tables in the room, only four of which were occupied.*)

Everything other than these things is narration, or telling. This includes the following:

- History, or background information that supplements our knowledge of what's currently happening in the story.

- Explanations or definitions that clarify whatever things are currently happening in the story.

- Specific thoughts or emotions of the characters involved.

- Any analysis of or commentary on what is happening in the story.

- Fiddling with the "clock" of the ongoing piece, by transporting the reader backward or forward in time without showing the interim events.

Showing and telling. That pretty much covers everything creative writers do with words. You can show, or you can tell. Understanding the difference between these two tools, and figuring out how you can best use them given your own voice and material, is a critical aspect of your development as a writer.

Why "Show, Not Tell" Is Such Common Advice

Now let's look at an example of why "showing" is generally considered more effective than "telling." Read through the following two versions of sample text. It's a section from "Helping," a superb short story by Robert Stone, presented in two deliberately different ways. (Grateful thanks and credit for this way of explaining showing versus telling goes to novelist John L'Heureux of Stanford University.) The only thing you need to know about the situation is that the main character (named Elliot), a Vietnam vet, has recently fallen off the wagon and has spent the night in heavy drinking and fighting with his wife. At this point in the story, Elliot, still somewhat drunk and very angry and confused, has taken his shotgun outside his house.

Example 1

Elliot took his shotgun and went out into the fields behind his house. There he met his neighbor, a professor at a local college. The professor didn't seem to understand the state that Elliot was in. He taunted him about not shooting in a bird sanctuary. Elliot took the safety latch off his shotgun. He imagined filling the professor's mouth with deer shot. The professor finally seemed to grasp the idea that he was in danger. He stopped smiling. Elliot felt his anger dissipate.

You can see right away why this version isn't very good. It's a clumsy, hackneyed telling of what has happened. Everything is summarized too quickly. We don't hear any words spoken or see any gestures or other movement by the characters. The writer has not really done a good job—readers are forced to do all the imaginative work themselves.

When beginning writers churn out this kind of prose, it is probably a good thing to instruct them to tell less and show more. So a diligent student will try again and will usually come up with something much better—much less "told"—without too much difficulty once thus directed.

Example 2

Elliot took his shotgun and went out into the field. There he met his neighbor, a professor at a local college. The shotgun Elliot was carrying seemed to grow heavier when he saw his neighbor. He yawned and shook his head, trying unsuccessfully to clear it. The sight of Anderson's eyes gave him a little thrill.

"What are you after?" the professor asked.

"Whatever there is," Elliot said.

Anderson took a quick look at the pasture behind him. Elliot could see his teeth through the mask. The mouth hole of the professor's mask filled with teeth. The professor made a joke about how a neighbor's cows were safe because they were locked up.

This infuriated Elliot. He turned the gun's safety latch to Off.

In his mind, Elliot fired a load of deer shot into the teeth.

Finally, the professor realized what danger he was in. Elliot was relieved to see that he stopped smiling.

Elliot told the professor that he'd hardly slept.

The professor finally understood he was perhaps in danger. Elliot felt his anger dissipate.

You can see how much better this version is. We're beginning to actually witness what's happening in that field. It's coming to life. It's shown, or dramatized. Yes, it's still a bit sketchy, still incomplete; the reader is still forced to create most of the images in his or her own mind in order to fully visualize what's happening. But it's vastly improved. This example seems to indicate that showing is better than telling.

Or is it? Consider the following passage:

> Lolita, light of my life, fire of my loins. My sin, my soul. Lo-lee-ta: the tip of the tongue taking a trip of three steps down the palate to tap, at three, on the teeth. Lo. Lee. Ta.
>
> She was Lo, plain Lo, in the morning, standing four feet ten in one sock. She was Lola in slacks. She was Dolly at school. She was Dolores on the dotted line. But in my arms she was always Lolita.
>
> Did she have a precursor? She did, indeed she did. In point of fact, there might have been no Lolita at all had I not loved, one summer, a certain initial girl-child. In a princedom by the sea. Oh when? About as many years before Lolita was born as my age was that summer. You can always count on a murderer for a fancy prose style.
>
> Ladies and gentlemen of the jury, exhibit number one is what the seraphs, the misinformed, simple, noble-winged seraphs, envied. Look at this tangle of thorns.   —VLADIMIR NABOKOV, *Lolita*

This is the opening passage of the novel. Would you tell Nabokov that he's "telling" too much? Because he is—telling, that is. The first five pages or so of this acknowledged masterpiece of twentieth-century literature are completely told. There's no dramatization, no "showing," in sight. And we wouldn't have it any other way. The narration is so strong and evocative, the voice so compelling, that we wouldn't mind being told many more things in this manner.

The Show-and-Tell Balancing Act

There are many other examples of terrific telling—read the openings of classic literary works and see for yourself—so as writing advice goes, "show not tell" is perhaps not always good advice. After all, *The American Heritage Dictionary* definition of "tell" is "To give a detailed account of; narrate: *tell what happened; told us a story*" [emphasis mine], which is the essence of what we are trying to do with creative writing.

Let's look at Stone's actual text and deconstruct it enough to see that it's not completely shown. In fact, there's quite a lot of telling involved. (In the section below, the "telling" is in boldface.)

Example 3: Stone's Actual Text

He stood in the middle of the field **and listened to the crows. Fear, anger, and sleep were the three primary conditions of life. He had learned that over there. Once he had thought fear the worst, but he had learned that the worst was anger. Nothing could fix it; neither alcohol nor medicine. It was a worm. It left him no peace. Sleep was the best.**

He opened his eyes **and pushed on until he came to the brow that overlooked the swamp. Just below, gliding along among the frozen cattails and bare scrub maple, was a man on skis.** Elliot stopped **to watch the man approach.**

The skier's face **was concealed by** a red-and-blue ski mask. He wore snow goggles, a blue jumpsuit, and a red **woolen Norwegian hat. As he came, he leaned into the turns of the trail, moving silently and gracefully along.** At the foot of the slope on which Elliot stood, the man looked up, saw him, and slid to a halt. The man stood staring at him for a moment and then began to herringbone up the slope. In no time at all the skier stood no more than ten feet away, removing his goggles, **and inside the woolen mask Elliot recognized the clear blue eyes of his neighbor, Professor Loyall Anderson. The shotgun Elliot was carrying seemed to grow heavier. He yawned and shook his head, trying unsuccessfully to clear it. The sight of Anderson's eyes gave him a little thrill of revulsion.**

"What are you after?" the young professor asked him, nodding toward the shotgun Elliot was cradling.

"Whatever there is," Elliot said.

Anderson took a quick look at the distant pasture behind him and then turned back to Elliot. **The mouth hole of the professor's mask filled with teeth. Elliot thought that Anderson's teeth were quite as he had imagined them earlier.** "Well, Polonski's cows are locked up," the professor said. "So they at least are safe."

Elliot realized that the professor had made a joke and was smiling. "Yes," he agreed.

Professor Anderson and his wife had been the moving force behind an initiative to outlaw the discharge of firearms within the boundaries of East Ilford Township. The initiative had been defeated, because East Ilford was not that kind of town.

"I think I'll go over by the river." Elliot said. **He said it only to have something to say, to fill the silence before Anderson spoke again. He was afraid of what Anderson might say to him and of what might happen.**

"You know," Anderson said, "that's all bird sanctuary over there now."

"Sure," Elliot agreed.

Outfitted as he was, the professor attracted Elliot's anger in an elemental manner. The mask made him appear a kind of doll, a kachina figure or a marionette. His eyes and mouth, all on their own, were disagreeable.

Elliot began to wonder if Anderson could smell the whiskey on his breath. He pushed the little red bull's-eye safety button on his gun to Off.

"Seriously," Anderson said. "I'm always having to run hunters out of there. Some people don't understand the word 'posted.'"

"I would never do that," Elliot said, "I would be afraid."

Anderson nodded his head. He seemed to be laughing. "Would you?" he asked Elliot merrily.

In imagination, Elliot rested the tip of his shotgun barrel against Anderson's smiling teeth. If he fired a load of deer shot into them, he thought, they

might make a noise like broken china. "Yes," Elliot said. "I wouldn't know who they were or where they'd been. They might resent my being alive. Telling them where they could shoot and where not."

Anderson's teeth remained in place. "That's pretty strange," he said. "I mean, to talk about resenting someone for being alive."

"It's all relative," Elliot said. "They might think, 'Why should he be alive when some brother of mine isn't?' Or they might think, 'Why should he be alive when I'm not?'"

"Oh," Anderson said.

"You see?" Elliot said. Facing Anderson, he took a long step backward. "All relative."

"Yes," Anderson said.

"That's so often true, isn't it?" Elliot asked. "Values are often relative."

"Yes," Anderson said. **Elliot was relieved to see that he had stopped smiling.**

"I've hardly slept, you know," Elliot told Professor Anderson. "Hardly at all. All night. I've been drinking."

"Oh," Anderson said. He licked his lips in the mouth of the mask. "You should get some rest."

"You're right," Elliot said.

"Well," Anderson said, "got to go now."

Elliot thought he sounded a little thick in the tongue. A little slow in the jaw.

"It's a nice day," Elliot said, **wanting now to be agreeable.**

"It's great," Anderson said, shuffling on his skis.

"Have a nice day," Elliot said.

"Yes," Anderson said, and pushed off.

How do you determine what is showing and what is telling? There are two basic questions you can ask when determining if any one section of a text is narration or scene:

How objective is the "information" being presented? Is it something you could witness for yourself without any help from the author? Then it's showing. Is the information being filtered or interpreted in order to push you toward a conclusion or emotional reaction that otherwise you might not have? That's telling. This is why, in the Stone text, "watched the man approach" and "concealed" are boldfaced as telling. This is information we wouldn't necessarily pick up for ourselves if the events were being played out on a movie screen. We might use different phrases, like "the man skied toward him" and "hidden," depending on our personal feelings toward the movie or situation. The fact that these specific words were chosen makes the information subjective, not objective. Likewise, we would only see a hat, not know that it was woolen or Norwegian unless told. "Elliot recognized the clear blue eyes of his neighbor, Professor Loyall Anderson" is also telling for two reasons. "Recognized" is a state we can't observe objectively, although there are a number of gestures that imply recognition, such as a start or double take. And using "clear" to describe Anderson's eyes reveals Elliot's state of mind—his envy of his neighbor's placid state—rather than an objective show- ing of the facts.

Has the "clock" of the story or novel been stopped for any reason? Another aspect of narration, or telling, is that it usually involves stopping or starting the "clock" of the piece. It's the equivalent of the aside used in theatre or the time out in a sports event: the action needs to cease temporarily in order for other information to be presented. In the case of "Helping," Robert Stone used telling to manipulate the narration clock in the following instances:

1. Stop the clock—you need to know that this character is imagining filling his neighbor's teeth with deershot.

2. Stop the clock—you should probably know that Elliot is relieved to see that his neighbor has stopped smiling.

Now that your eyes are open, you will become aware of how much "telling" is done by past and contemporary masters of fiction. Indeed, the precise mix of scene and narration that a writer chooses to use is one of the most defining elements of his or her particular voice, or style.

Traditional Uses of Narration (Telling)

How do you choose when to show, and when to tell?

Traditionally, it's been assumed that you want to show the important stuff: important behaviors, important interactions, important speeches, conversations. The convention has been that anything that changes the situation of the story in a significant way should happen in "eyewitness" mode. After all, readers have a nat- ural desire to be present when the drama heats up—they tend not to be satisfied by having key scenes summarized for them.

Narration has been used, *traditionally*, to supplement what is being shown, or dramatized. It has traditionally been understood that showing is the cornerstone for constructing creative work and that narration, although important, plays second fid- dle. As an example, we will look at the opening of Hemingway's "Hills Like White Elephants" (pp. 269–272), which limits the use of narration to the most basic level:

> The hills across the valley of the Ebro were long and white. On this side there was no shade and no trees and the station was between two lines of rails in the sun. Close against the side of the station there was a warm shadow of the build- ing and a curtain, made of strings of bamboo beads, hung across the open door into the bar, to keep out flies. The American and the girl with him sat at a table in the shade, outside the building. It was very hot and the express from

Barcelona would come in forty minutes. It stopped at this junction for two minutes and went on to Madrid.

1. Narration is used to "set the scene" or prepare the reader for what will shortly be shown. ("The hills across the valley of the Ebro were long and white.")

2. Narration is used to provide important information that would be difficult or awkward to dramatize in the existing context. (The train from Barcelona was due in forty minutes.) This can include background, history, facts, or thoughts or emotions that a character would not be able to express using the spoken word.

3. Narration is used to manipulate the interior "clock" of the story in order to either insert or omit certain information.

Why Narration Is Such an Important Tool

Let's now look at a piece that proves how much we'd lose without the use of this very important tool. The following sample texts are excerpts from, respectively, *Peter Pan* the novella, written by J. M. Barrie, and *Peter Pan* the stage play, also written by Barrie.

Playwrights can't use narration. It's not in their box of artistic tools. Of course, they have other, extremely valuable tools that prose writers don't have access to— such as actors who can bring characters to life; real physical objects, not just descriptions; and physical gestures and actions. But playwrights can't *tell* us anything, not without resorting to artificial devices, such as asides to the audience, or commentary by an observing chorus or narrator.

So let's see how Barrie compensated for the fact that he was not able to utilize narration in the stage play. (Barrie wrote the play first, the novella second.)

And first you must forget all other versions of *Peter Pan*—especially the Disney version. This is the original, and it is enchanting.

From Peter Pan: The Novella

[Wendy's mother] was a lovely lady, with a romantic mind and such a sweet mocking mouth. Her romantic mind was like the tiny boxes, one within the other, that come from the puzzling East, however many you discover there is always one more; and her sweet mocking mouth had one kiss on it that Wendy could never get, though there it was, perfectly conspicuous in the right-hand corner.

The way Mr. Darling won her was this: the many gentlemen who had been boys when she was a girl discovered simultaneously that they loved her, and they all ran to her house to propose to her except Mr. Darling, who took a cab and nipped in first, and so he got her. He got all of her, except the innermost box and the kiss. He never knew about the box, and in time he gave up trying for the kiss. Wendy thought Napoleon could have got it, but I can picture him trying, and then going off in a passion, slamming the door.

Mr. Darling used to boast to Wendy that her mother not only loved him but respected him. He was one of those deep ones who know about stocks and shares. Of course, no one really knows, but he quite seemed to know, and he often said stocks were up and shares were down in a way that would have made any woman respect him.

From Peter Pan: The Play

MICHAEL *(obstreperous)*: I won't go to bed, I won't, I won't. Nana it isn't six o'clock yet. Two minutes more, please one minute more?

(Here the bathroom door closes on them, and Mrs. Darling, who has perhaps heard his cry, enters the nursery. She is the loveliest lady in Bloomsbury, with a sweet mocking mouth, and as she is going out to dinner tonight she is already wearing her evening gown because she knows her children like to see her in it. It is a delicious confection made by herself out of nothing and other people's mistakes. She does not often go out to dinner, preferring when the children are in bed to sit beside them tidying up their minds, just as if they were drawers. If Wendy and the boys could keep awake they might see her repacking into their proper places the many articles of the mind that have strayed during the day, lingering humorously over some of their contents, wondering where on earth they picked this thing up, making discoveries sweet and not so sweet, pressing this to her cheek and hurriedly stowing that out of sight. When they wake in the morning the naughtinesses with which they went to bed are not, alas, blown away, but they are placed at the bottom of the drawer; and on the top, beautifully aired, are their prettier thoughts ready for the new day. As she enters the room she is startled to see a strange little face outside the window and a hand groping as if it wanted to come in.)

MRS. DARLING: Who are you? *(The unknown disappears; she hurries to the window)* No one there. And yet I feel sure I saw a face. My children!

(She throws open the bathroom door and Michael's head appears gaily over the bath. He splashes; she throws kisses to him and closes the door) Wendy, John! *(she cries, and gets reassuring answers from the day nursery. She sits down, relieved, on Wendy's bed; and Wendy and John come in, looking their smallest size, as children tend to do to a mother suddenly in fear for them)*

JOHN *(histrionically)*: We are doing an act; we are playing at being you and father. *(He imitates the only father who has come under his special notice)* A little less noise there.

WENDY: Now let us pretend we have a baby.

JOHN *(good-naturedly)*: I am happy to inform you, Mrs. Darling, that you are now a mother. *(Wendy gives way to ecstasy)* You have missed the chief thing; you haven't asked, boy or girl?

WENDY: I am so glad to have one at all, I don't care which it is.

Writing students always laugh when they compare these two versions. Yes, it's clear that Barrie the novelist is having trouble showing and not telling when he puts on his dramatist hat. So he crams all the lovely narration into the stage directions. The actors get this information, but the audience doesn't—not directly, at least, although Barrie can hope that these subtle, funny observations are absorbed by the actors and somehow influence their performances.

How Showing and Telling Complement Each Other

Ideally, these two elements of writing are organically intertwined. That is, what we tell doesn't just echo or repeat what we show. We use the two together to achieve whatever effect we want. When a section of "telling" can be eliminated without taking away from a creative work's meaning, then by all means cut it, and allow the showing to carry the piece. But the opposite is also true: often we can *tell* something more efficiently, elegantly, beautifully, or subtly than we could hope to do if dramatizing it. In such cases, we should eliminate the dramatization, or scene, in favor of the narration.

Good Intentions, Bad Advice

So why do so many well-meaning—and competent!—creative writing instructors use "show, not tell" as their mantra?

Because good telling is difficult to do.

It goes back to the need to be concrete, the need for specificity. It's a relatively straightforward thing to be concrete when showing, or dramatizing, something; after all, the characters are either there, or they aren't. They are sitting on chairs, or they are standing on the deck of a boat. They are speaking words, or they are silent; they are polishing their eyeglasses, or they are throwing coffee cups at walls.

Telling, however, is where the temptation to generalize or go abstract is strongest. It's my guess that when creative writing professors urge their classes to show and not to tell, they are really trying to urge students to be more concrete and specific. They see student writing that is too general or abstract, and they make the mistake of blaming the technique—narration—for the poor writing that results.

What about this version of the opening of *Lolita* (my apologies to Nabokov)?

> Lolita. Oh, she was something. Really sexy. Really hot. I loved saying her name, over and over. Lolita, Lolita, Lolita. I liked the way she looked in her school uniform. She was pretty damn cute. Oh yes.

We know, having read the original (p. 150), that the problem isn't that this is narration, but that it's not very good narration—certainly not comparable to the real thing that Nabokov wrote. We wouldn't necessarily want Nabokov to open his novel with a dramatized scene of Humbert Humbert acting out his passion for Lolita. But we do want to hear his narration here. A better way to think about it, perhaps, is that we want Nabokov to use his artistic judgment about where to show and where to tell, and that telling, in his expert hands, is sublime.

This is critical, because most creative writing classes today use the workshop technique in one form or another. In order for students to provide helpful advice to each other, they need to be able to correctly diagnose the problems found in the stories they review. There's a big difference between a creative piece that is truly crying out for more scenes and a piece in which the narration is technically weak. In the first case, we want to urge the writer to show more. In the latter case, we want the writer to practice his or her narration techniques in order to employ narration more successfully.

The Showing-Telling Continuum

It can be very helpful to think about showing and telling as representing the two extreme ends of the same continuum. In this section we look at how various stories fall along this line.

Let's start at the "pure showing" end. It's rare (off-stage) to find creative work that is purely shown, or dramatized. The following is from a Pulitzer Prize–winning novel. The boldfaced parts are the narration—what is being told. Everything else is shown—the reader is an eyewitness to what occurs. The telling is kept to a minimum:

> **We stopped by our place first, where I took off my hat and changed my dress and Ty put on work clothes—there would be plenty to do after dinner. When I got to my dad's, the only person in the house was Jess Clark. He was making coffee and everyone else was out in the fields, looking things over. Ty took the pickup and went to find them.** Jess poured me a cup of coffee and said, "Things are moving pretty quick, huh?" He sat down across the table.
>
> "Well, I've never thought of my father as a creature of impulse before. Today I'm thinking I should be more optimistic. Anyway, I don't think much will change, really."
>
> "New buildings? Expanded hog operation? A plantation of black walnuts? Ten acres of gladiolus? Those are changes."
>
> "Ten acres of gladiolus?"
>
> "Oh, your brother-in-law Pete was talking about that before you came. Eighty thousand bulbs an acre."
>
> "Eight hundred thousand gladiolus?"
>
> "He says he can sell them at five for a dollar in Minneapolis. That's a hundred and sixty thousand bucks."
>
> "Oh, Pete."
>
> "I was impressed. I talked to him for fifteen minutes and he must have come up with five or six well-thought-out ideas. Over at our place, Loren and my father don't have any ideas at all. Just corn and beans, beans and corn. When I was a kid, at least there were some hogs and cattle, and those sheep Loren raised for 4-H. And my mom's garden, too. She was always trying new varieties, or buying a few okra seeds to see if she could get them to grow this far north. Now even hogs would seem radical to them."

"The markets are different these days. Anyway, I'm tired of talking about farming. That's all anyone around here ever talks about. Tell me what sorts of things you did in Seattle."

"Delving into my secret life, huh?" He looked at me **until I felt myself blushing** then he smiled and said, "I'll tell you."   —JANE SMILEY, *A Thousand Acres*

Now let's move a little bit further along the sliding scale toward more telling. Is the passage below less competent because it depends more heavily on narration? I don't think so, but let's take a look at it:

There was a hole in the station wagon's floor and through it spurted occasional geysers of dirty rainwater. Quoyle thought enviously of the aunt's pickup. He couldn't afford a new truck. Frightening how fast the insurance money was going. He didn't know where the aunt got it. She'd paid for all the house repairs, put in her share for groceries. He'd paid for the road, the new dock. For the girls' beds, clothes, the motel bill, gas for the station wagon. And the new transmission.

"Wish I'd worn me logans," shouted Billy Pretty. "Didn't know the bottom half of your car was missin'."

Quoyle slowed not to splash the **graceful, straight-backed** woman in the green slicker. **God, did it rain every day?** The child was with her. Her eyes **straight** to Quoyle. His to her.

"Who is that? Seems like I see her walking along the road every time I come out."

"That's Wavey. Wavey Prowse. She's takin' her boy back from the special class at the school. There's a bunch of them goes. She got it started, the special class. He's not right. It was grief that caused the boy to be like he is. Wavey was carrying him when Sevenseas Hector went over. Lost her husband. We should of give her a ride, boy."

"She was going the other way."

"Wouldn't take a minute to turn round. Rain coming down like stair rods," said Billy.

Quoyle pulled in at the cemetery entrance, turned, drove back. As the woman and child got in Billy said their names. Wavey Prowse. Herry. **The woman apologized for their wetness, sat silent the rest of the way to a small house half a mile beyond the *Gammy Bird*. Didn't look at Quoyle. The yard beyond the small house held a phantasmagoria of painted wooden figures, galloping horses, dogs balanced on wheels, a row of chrome hubcaps on sticks. A zoo of the mind.**

"That's some yard," said Quoyle.

"Dad's stuff," said Wavey Prowse and slammed the door.

Back along the flooding road again toward Killick-Claw.

"You ought to see the chair he made out of moose antlers," said Billy. "You set in it, it's comfortable enough, but to the others it looks like you sprouted golden wings."

"She has very good posture," said Quoyle. **Tried to cancel the stupid remark.** "What I mean is, she has a good stride. I mean, tall. She seems tall."

Man Sounds Like Fatuous Fool. In a way he could not explain she seized his attention; because she seemed sprung from wet stones, the stench of fish and tide.

"Maybe she's the tall and quiet woman, boy."

"What does that mean?"

"A thing me old dad used to say."   —E. Annie Proulx, *The Shipping News*

And here's the opening of Flannery O'Connor's masterpiece "Everything That Rises Must Converge" (pp. 178–189). You can see that she uses telling even more generously than either Smiley or Proulx:

Her doctor had told Julian's mother that she must lose twenty pounds on account of her pressure, so on Wednesday nights Julian had to take her downtown on the bus for a reducing class at the Y. The reducing class was designed for working girls over fifty, who weighed from 165 to 200 pounds. His mother was one of the slimmer ones, but she said ladies did not tell their age or weight. She would not ride the buses by herself at night since they had been integrated, and because the reducing class was one of her few pleasures, necessary for her health, and *free*, she said Julian could at least put himself out to take her, considering all she did for him. Julian did not like to consider all she did for him, but every Wednesday night he braced himself and took her.

She was **almost ready to go,** standing before the hall mirror, putting on her hat, while he, his hands behind him, **appeared pinned to the door frame, waiting like Saint Sebastian for the arrows to begin piercing him. The hat was new and had cost her seven dollars and a half.** She kept saying, "Maybe I should have paid that for it. No, I shouldn't have. I'll take it off and return it tomorrow. I shouldn't have bought it."

Julian raised his eyes **to heaven.** "Yes, you should have bought it," he said. "Put it on and let's go." **It was a hat.** A purple velvet flap came down on one side of it and stood up on the other; the rest of it was green **and looked like a cushion with the stuffing out. He decided it was less comical than jaunty and pathetic. Everything that gave her pleasure was small and depressed him.**

Although the entire story takes place on a single evening and could have been dramatized, like Hemingway's "Hills Like White Elephants" (pp. 269–272), using dialogue and gesture, O'Connor makes the deliberate choice to tell us many things: that Julian considered himself a martyr for what he was doing for his mother; that it was a hideous hat; and finally, and most importantly, O'Connor reaches into Julian's mind and comes out with that lovely line of narration "Everything that gave her pleasure was small and depressed him." Just think what the passage would have been like without those things.

Finally, the following is a complete short story (this kind of piece is sometimes called a "short short"). It is pure narration—what we often call a "voice" story, because it really sounds like a character talking without interruption by other characters or events. There's no dramatization whatsoever, but since the voice is so compelling, the piece succeeds. (Because it's all narration, it's all in boldface.)

How many threads have I broken with my teeth. How many times have I looked at the stars and felt ill. Time here is divided into before and since your shuttering in 1978. I remember hanging onto the hood of the big-fendered Olds with a mess of money in my purse. Call that romance. Some memory precedes you: when I wanted lederhosen because I'd read *Heidi*. And how I wanted my folks to build a fallout shelter so I could arrange the cans. And coveting mother's muskrat. I remember college. And being in Vista; I asked the librarian in Banks, the state's tomato capital, if she had any black literature and she said they used to have *Lil Black Sambo* but the white children tore out pages and wrote ugly words inside. Someone said if I didn't like Banks I should go to Moscow. I said, Come on, let's go outside and shoot the hoop. I've got a jones to beat your butt. I haven't changed. Now if I think of the earth's origins, I get vertigo. When I think of its death, I fall, I've picked up a few things, I know if you want songbirds, plant berry trees. If you don't want birds, buy a rubber snake. I remember that town with the Alcoa plant I toured. The manager kept referring to the workers as Alcoans, I thought of hundreds of flexible metal beings bent over assemblages. They sparked. What would I do in Moscow. I have these dreams—relatives loom over my bed. We should put her to sleep Lonnie says, Go home old girl, go home, my aunt says. Why should I go home before her I want to say. But I am bereft. So how is Life in The Other World. Do you get the news. Are you allowed a pet. But I wanted to show you how I've grown, what I know: I keep my bees far from the stable, they can't stand how horses smell. And I know sooner or later an old house will need a new roof. And more than six years have whistled by since you blew your heart out like the porch light. Reason and meaning don't step into another lit spot like a well-meaning stranger with a hat. And mother's mother who has lived in the same house ten times six years, told me. We didn't know we had termites until they swarmed. Then we had to pull up the whole floor. "Too late, no more . . ." you know the poem. But you, you bastard. You picked up a gun in winter as if it were a hat and you were leaving a restaurant; full, weary, and thankful to be spending the evening with no one.   —C. D. WRIGHT, "Scratch Music"

Here's the continuum with the stories mapped out according to their use of scene and narration:

Pure Showing				Pure Telling
"Hills Like White Elephants"	*A Thousand Acres*	*The Shipping News*	"Everything That Rises Must Converge"	"Scratch Music"

Let's be very clear: it's not that it's important to clinically dissect all showing and telling. In fact, sometimes it's very difficult to do so. The point is to recognize that *both* are important, both make up what we call creative writing, and to universally declare that "more of one is good and less of the other is better" is to impose rigid thinking on our own creative process as well as that of others.

EXERCISES

Since determining the particular mix of showing and telling that is right for you is a major part of finding your voice as a writer, the following exercises provide you with ways to experiment and see what feels comfortable.

Exercise 1: Tell Me a Story

GOAL: To practice the techniques of showing and telling, and to understand the artistic as well as technical differences between scene and narration.

1. If possible, find an audience and begin with oral story-telling: talk (briefly) about something you witnessed in the past week or month. (You could have been an uninvolved bystander or involved in the event.)

2. Next, take fifteen minutes to write a pure narration (telling) version of the event in question.

3. Next, do a pure scene version.

4. Finally, write a version that is a combination of both scene and narration.

5. If possible, do this in a group, and read each version out loud (the sharing of these exercises is critical for enabling you to learn from your colleagues).

Here's an example of scene versus narration done by Paul Wood:

Pure Narration

My mother and I were having an argument. Like all our arguments, it was purportedly about something very specific—in this case, who was the winner of the 1986 World Series—yet it seemed to indicate something of the larger issues facing us. We tended to mystify each other, my mother and me, and we got closest to one another in our arguments, when we could crystallize or at least point to something concrete between us that we didn't agree on. Most of the time we existed in a floating state of nebulous bewilderment. She said the Yankees had won. I said the Orioles. That was basically all there was to our argument: each stating the position over and over again, each stating for evidence such things like our personal emotions about the outcome. She said she knew it was the Yankees because she had visited New York that year (she hated New York) and had come back with a Yankees T-shirt for me and my father. I said I knew it was the Orioles because the fact that they were *birds* had impressed itself upon my teenaged mind. I remembered thinking, I told her, how strange it was that birds were the national baseball champions.

Pure Scene

"Yankees," my mother said. "The Yankees won that year."

   "No," I told her. "In 1986, it was the Orioles. I'm sure it was."

   "The Yankees," she repeated.

"The Orioles," I said.

"Are we just going to keep this up all night?" she asked.

"We may," I said. "We just may. Unless you have some hard-core evidence to the contrary . . . ?"

"I remember it was the Yankees, because I'd just come back from a visit to that godforsaken place," she said.

"You mean New York?" I asked.

"Shush. Yes. New York. I had just come back, and I brought home two Yankee T-shirts: one for you and one for your father. Later, I remembered thinking how remarkably far-sighted that had been of me."

"Well, I have a memory of my own regarding the World Series from that year," I told her. "I remember thinking how wimpy it was that the champions were *birds*. Birds, for Christsakes."

"Don't swear," she said.

"I'm just saying, it struck me as ironic that the birds had beaten any number of fiercer animals," I said. "It was irony that would not have escaped anyone's notice who was in a noticing mood."

Scene and Narration

"Yankees," my mother said. "The Yankees won that year."

"No," I told her. "In 1986 it was the Orioles. I'm sure it was." To which my mother had nothing to say except to repeat her earlier assertion. No, she was sure it was the Yankees. I was equally sure it was the Orioles. We both repeated our positions a number of times without gaining an inch in the other's viewpoint. We tended to mystify each other, my mother and me, and we got closest to one another in our arguments, when we could crystallize or at least point to something concrete between us that we didn't agree on. Most of the time we existed in a floating state of nebulous bewilderment. She asked me if we were going to keep it up all night.

"We may," I said. "We just may. Unless you have some hard-core evidence to the contrary . . . ?"

"I remember it was the Yankees, because I'd just come back from a visit to that godforsaken place," she said.

"You mean New York?" I asked.

"Shush. Yes. New York. I had just come back, and I brought home two Yankee T-shirts: one for you and one for your father. Later, I remembered thinking how remarkably far-sighted that had been of me." I said I knew it was the Orioles because the fact that they were *birds* had impressed itself upon my teenaged mind. I remembered thinking, I told her, how strange it was that birds were the national baseball champions.

"That proves nothing," she said.

Exercise 2: What Everyone Knows / What I Know

GOAL: To practice using narration to move from public knowledge to private knowledge.

1. Think of a place, person, or event (something that happened) that you are intimately familiar with (if possible, something that you have intimate knowledge of that no one else does).

2. Next, do a freewrite using the first sentence, "What everyone knows about X is . . ." where X is the person, place, or event.

3. After this step has been concluded, write a second piece beginning with the sentence, "But what *I* know about X is . . ." where you reveal your special private knowledge or unique perspective.

The following was written by Jenna Philpott:

What everyone knows about her is that she buys expensive shoes and wears them. Tod's. Gucci. Choo. Her boss and her underlings all know her quip, "The pain of a beautiful three-hour shoe can keep you awake for a twelve-hour day!" She calls her nanny at 10 a.m. and 4 p.m. and rubs her sore feet during those calls. She gives a generous bonus to her household help each Christmas and summer vacation. "I'm not cheap." Cocktail hour has returned after the birth of her child, "Weekends at four if you can make it!" Everyone knows they haven't really been invited and won't ever go.

What *I* know is that her daughter is deaf and blind. No pictures of the girl beside the woman and her husband. A grin for Aspen! Two grins for Tahiti! A kiss for Iceland! Her daughter lies on her back on the floor surrounded by toys she can neither see nor hear. The infant starts to squirm when the cleaning lady vacuums an arc around her. The vibrations stir something in her brain, "Others are near!" I also know that the woman's vacation days are her daughter's surgery days. This Friday her daughter's right eye will be removed, its pressure too great for a brain to develop. If the child recovers well, heart surgery is on the docket the day before Thanksgiving.

READINGS

ZZ Packer

Brownies

BY THE END OF OUR FIRST DAY at Camp Crescendo, the girls in my Brownie troop had decided to kick the asses of each and every girl in Brownie Troop 909. Troop 909 was doomed from the first day of camp; they were white girls, their complexions like a blend of ice cream: strawberry, vanilla. They turtled out from their bus in pairs, their rolled-up sleeping bags chromatized with Disney characters—Sleeping Beauty, Snow White, Mickey Mouse—or the generic ones cheap parents bought—washed-out rainbows, unicorns, curly-eyelashed frogs. Some clutched Igloo coolers and still others held onto stuffed toys like pacifiers, looking all around them like tourists determined to be dazzled.

Our troop wended its way past their bus, past the ranger station, past the colorful trail guide drawn like a treasure map, locked behind glass.

"Man, did you smell them?" Arnetta said, giving the girls a slow once-over. "They smell like Chihuahuas. *Wet* Chihuahuas." Although we had passed their troop by yards, Arnetta raised her nose in the air and grimaced.

Arnetta said this from the very rear of the line, far away from Mrs. Margolin, who strung our troop behind her like a brood of obedient ducklings. Mrs. Margolin even looked like a mother duck—she had hair cropped close to a small ball of a head, almost no neck, and huge, miraculous breasts. She wore enormous belts that looked like the kind weight lifters wear, except hers were cheap metallic gold or rabbit fur or covered with gigantic fake sunflowers. Often these belts would become nature lessons in and of themselves. "See," Mrs. Margolin once said to us, pointing to her belt. "This one's made entirely from the feathers of baby pigeons."

The belt layered with feathers was uncanny enough, but I was more disturbed by the realization that I had never actually *seen* a baby pigeon. I searched for weeks for one, in vain—scampering after pigeons whenever I was downtown with my father.

But nature lessons were not Mrs. Margolin's top priority. She saw the position of troop leader as an evangelical post. Back at the AME church where our Brownie meetings were held, she was especially fond of imparting religious aphorisms by means of acrostics—Satan was the "Serpent Always Tempting And Noisome"; she'd refer to the Bible as "Basic Instructions Before Leaving Earth." Whenever she occasionally quizzed us on these at the beginning of the Brownie meeting, expecting to hear the acrostics parroted back to her, only Arnetta's correct replies soared over our vague mumblings. "Jesus?" Mrs. Margolin might ask expectantly, and Arnetta alone would dutifully answer, "Jehovah's Example, Saving Us Sinners."

Arnetta made a point of listening to Mrs. Margolin's religious talk and giving her what she wanted to hear. Because of this, Arnetta could have blared through a megaphone that the white girls of Troop 909 were "wet Chihuahuas" without arousing so much as a blink from Mrs. Margolin. Once Arnetta killed the troop goldfish by feeding it a French fry covered in ketchup, and when Mrs. Margolin demanded an explanation, Arnetta claimed that the goldfish had been eyeing her meal for *hours*, until—giving in to temptation—it had leapt up and snatched the whole golden fry from her fingertips.

"*Serious* Chihuahua," Octavia added—though neither Arnetta nor Octavia could *spell* "Chihuahua" or had ever *seen* a Chihuahua. Trisyllabic words had gained a sort of exoticism within our fourth-grade set at Woodrow Wilson Elementary. Arnetta and Octavia, compelled to outdo each other, would flip through the dictionary, determined to work the vulgar-sounding ones like "Djibouti" and "asinine" into conversation.

"*Caucasian* Chihuahuas," Arnetta said.

That did it. Drema and Elise doubled up on each other like inextricably entwined kites; Octavia slapped the skin of her belly; Janice jumped straight up in the air, then did it again, just as hard, as if to slam-dunk her own head. No one had laughed so hard since a boy named Martez had stuck his pencil in the electric socket and spent the whole day with a strange grin on his face.

"Girls, girls," said our parent helper, Mrs. Hedy. Mrs. Hedy was Octavia's mother. She wagged her index finger perfunctorily, like a windshield wiper. "Stop it now. Be

good." She said this loudly enough to be heard, but lazily, nasally, bereft of any feeling or indication that she meant to be obeyed, as though she would say these words
again at the exact same pitch if a button somewhere on her were pressed.

But the girls didn't stop laughing; they only laughed louder. It was the word
"Caucasian" that had got them all going. One day at school, about a month before the
Brownie camping trip, Arnetta had turned to a boy wearing impossibly high-ankled
floodwater jeans, and said "What are *you? Caucasian?*" The word took off from there,
and soon everything was Caucasian. If you ate too fast, you ate like a Caucasian; if
you ate too slow, you ate like a Caucasian. The biggest feat anyone at Woodrow Wilson could do was to jump off the swing in midair, at the highest point in its arc, and
if you fell (like I had, more than once) instead of landing on your feet, knees bent
Olympic-gymnast-style, Arnetta and Octavia were prepared to comment. They'd
look at each other with the silence of passengers who'd narrowly escaped an accident, then nod their heads, and whisper with solemn horror and haughtiness,
"*Caucasian.*"

Even the only white kid in our school, Dennis, got in on the Caucasian act. That
time when Martez stuck the pencil in the socket, Dennis had pointed, and yelled,
"That was *so* Caucasian!"

Living in the south suburbs of Atlanta, it was easy to forget about whites. Whites
were like those baby pigeons: real and existing, but rarely thought about. Everyone
had been to Rich's to go clothes shopping, everyone had seen white girls and their
mothers coo-cooing over dresses; everyone had gone to the downtown library and
seen white businessmen swish by importantly, wrists flexed in front of them to check
the time on their watches as though they would change from Clark Kent into Superman any second. But those images were as fleeting as cards shuffled in a deck,
whereas the ten white girls behind us—*invaders,* Arnetta would later call them—were
instantly real and memorable, with their long shampoo-commercial hair, as straight
as spaghetti from the box. This alone was reason for envy and hatred. The only black
girl most of us had ever seen with hair that long was Octavia, whose hair hung past
her butt like a Hawaiian hula dancer's. The sight of Octavia's mane prompted other
girls to listen to her reverentially, as though whatever she had to say would somehow
activate their own follicles. For example, when, on the first day of camp, Octavia
made as if to speak, a silence began. "Nobody," Octavia said, "calls us niggers."

At the end of that first day, when half of our troop made its way back to the cabin
after tag-team restroom visits, Arnetta said she'd heard one of the girls in Troop 909
call Daphne a nigger. The other half of the girls and I were helping Mrs. Margolin
clean up the pots and pans from the ravioli dinner. When we made our way to the
restrooms to wash up and brush our teeth, we met up with Arnetta midway.

"Man, I completely heard the girl," Arnetta reported. "Right, Daphne?"

Daphne hardly ever spoke, but when she did her voice was petite and tinkly, the
voice one might expect from a shiny new earring. She'd written a poem once, for
Langston Hughes Day, a poem brimming with all the teacher-winning ingredients—
trees and oceans, sunsets and moons—but what cinched the poem for the grown-ups,

snatching the win from Octavia's musical ode to Grandmaster Flash and the Furious Five, were Daphne's last lines:

> You are my father, the veteran
> When you cry in the dark
> It rains and rains and rains in my heart

She'd worn clean, though faded, jumpers and dresses when Chic jeans were the fashion, but when she went up to the dais to receive her prize journal, pages trimmed in gold, she wore a new dress with a velveteen bodice and a taffeta skirt as wide as an umbrella. All the kids clapped, though none of them understood the poem. I'd read encyclopedias the way others read comics, and I didn't get it. But those last lines pricked me, they were so eerie, and as my father and I ate cereal, I'd whisper over my Froot Loops, like a mantra, *"You are my father, the veteran. You are my father, the veteran, the veteran, the veteran,"* until my father, who acted in plays as Caliban and Othello and was not a veteran, marched me up to my teacher one morning, and said, "Can you tell me what the hell's wrong with this kid?"

I had thought Daphne and I might become friends, but she seemed to grow spooked by me whispering those lines to her, begging her to tell me what they meant, and I had soon understood that two quiet people like us were better off quiet alone.

"Daphne? Didn't you hear them call you a nigger?" Arnetta asked, giving Daphne a nudge.

The sun was setting through the trees, and their leafy tops formed a canopy of black lace for the flame of the sun to pass through. Daphne shrugged her shoulders at first, then slowly nodded her head when Arnetta gave her a hard look.

Twenty minutes later, when my restroom group returned to the cabin, Arnetta was still talking about Troop 909. My restroom group had passed by some of the 909 girls. For the most part, they had deferred to us, waving us into the restrooms, letting us go even though they'd gotten there first.

We'd seen them, but from afar, never within their orbit enough to see whether their faces were the way all white girls appeared on TV—ponytailed and full of energy, bubbling over with love and money. All I could see was that some rapidly fanned their faces with their hands, though the heat of the day had long passed. A few seemed to be lolling their heads in slow circles, half-purposefully, as if exercising the muscles of their necks, half-ecstatically, rolling their heads about like Stevie Wonder.

"We can't let them get away with that," Arnetta said, dropping her voice to a laryngitic whisper. "We can't let them get away with calling us niggers. I say we teach them a lesson." She sat down cross-legged on a sleeping bag, an embittered Buddha, eyes glimmering acrylic black. "We can't go telling Mrs. Margolin, either. Mrs. Margolin'll say something about doing unto others and the path of righteousness and all. Forget that shit." She let her eyes flutter irreverently till they half closed, as though ignoring an insult not worth returning. We could all hear Mrs. Margolin outside, gathering the last of the metal campware.

Nobody said anything for a while. Arnetta's tone had an upholstered confidence that was somehow both regal and vulgar at once. It demanded a few moments of silence in its wake, like the ringing of a church bell or the playing of taps. Sometimes Octavia would ditto or dissent whatever Arnetta had said, and this was the signal that others could speak. But this time Octavia just swirled a long cord of hair into pretzel shapes.

"Well?" Arnetta said. She looked as if she had discerned the hidden severity of the situation and was waiting for the rest of us to catch up. Everyone looked from Arnetta to Daphne. It was, after all, Daphne who had supposedly been called the name, but Daphne sat on the bare cabin floor, flipping through the pages of the Girl Scout handbook, eyebrows arched in mock wonder, as if the handbook were a catalogue full of bright and startling foreign costumes. Janice broke the silence. She clapped her hands to broach her idea of a plan.

"They gone be sleeping," she whispered conspiratorially, "then we gone sneak into they cabin, then we gone put daddy longlegs in they sleeping bags. Then they'll wake up. Then we gone beat 'em up till they flat as frying pans!" She jammed her fist into the palm of her hand, then made a sizzling sound.

Janice's country accent was laughable, her looks homely, her jumpy acrobatics embarrassing to behold. Arnetta and Octavia volleyed amused, arrogant smiles whenever Janice opened her mouth, but Janice never caught the hint, spoke whenever she wanted, fluttered around Arnetta and Octavia futilely offering her opinions to their departing backs. Whenever Arnetta and Octavia shooed her away, Janice loitered until the two would finally sigh, "What *is* it, Miss Caucasoid? What do you want?"

"Oh shut up, Janice," Octavia said, letting a fingered loop of hair fall to her waist as though just the sound of Janice's voice had ruined the fun of her hair twisting.

"All right," Arnetta said, standing up. "We're going to have a secret meeting and talk about what we're going to do."

The word "secret" had a built-in importance. Everyone gravely nodded her head. The modifier form of the word had more clout than the noun. A secret meant nothing; it was like gossip: just a bit of unpleasant knowledge about someone who happened to be someone other than yourself. A secret *meeting*, or a secret *club*, was entirely different.

That was when Arnetta turned to me, as though she knew doing so was both a compliment and a charity.

"Snot, you're not going to be a bitch and tell Mrs. Margolin, are you?"

I had been called "Snot" ever since first grade, when I'd sneezed in class and two long ropes of mucus had splattered a nearby girl.

"Hey," I said. "Maybe you didn't hear them right—I mean—"

"Are you gonna tell on us or not?" was all Arnetta wanted to know, and by the time the question was asked, the rest of our Brownie troop looked at me as though they'd already decided their course of action, me being the only impediment. As though it were all a simple matter of patriotism.

Camp Crescendo used to double as a high school band and field hockey camp until an arching field hockey ball landed on the clasp of a girl's metal barrette, knifing a skull nerve, paralyzing the right side of her body. The camp closed down for a few years, and the girl's teammates built a memorial, filling the spot on which the girl fell with hockey balls, upon which they had painted—all in nail polish—get-well tidings, flowers, and hearts. The balls were still stacked there, like a shrine of ostrich eggs embedded in the ground.

On the second day of camp, Troop 909 was dancing around the mound of nail polish–decorated hockey balls, their limbs jangling awkwardly, their cries like the constant summer squeal of an amusement park. There was a stream that bordered the field hockey lawn, and the girls from my troop settled next to it, scarfing down the last of lunch: sandwiches made from salami and slices of tomato that had gotten waterlogged from the melting ice in the cooler. From the stream bank, Arnetta eyed the Troop 909 girls, scrutinizing their movements to glean inspiration for battle.

"Man," Arnetta said, "we could bum-rush them right now if that damn lady would *leave*."

The 909 troop leader was a white woman with the severe pageboy hairdo of an ancient Egyptian. She lay sprawled on a picnic blanket, sphinxlike, eating a banana, sometimes holding it out in front of her like a microphone. Beside her sat a girl slowly flapping one hand like a bird with a broken wing. Occasionally, the leader would call out the names of girls who'd attempted leapfrogs and flips, or of girls who yelled too loudly or strayed far from the circle.

"I'm just glad Big Fat Mama's not following us here," Octavia said. "At least we don't have to worry about her." Mrs. Margolin, Octavia assured us, was having her Afternoon Devotional, shrouded in mosquito netting, in a clearing she'd found. Mrs. Hedy was cleaning mud from her espadrilles in the cabin.

"I handled them." Arnetta sucked on her teeth and proudly grinned. "I told her we was going to gather leaves."

"Gather leaves," Octavia said, nodding respectfully. "That's a good one. They're so mad-crazy about this camping thing." She looked from ground to sky, sky to ground. Her hair hung down her back in two braids like a squaw's. "I mean, I really don't know why it's even called *camping*—all we ever do with Nature is find some twigs and say something like, 'Wow, this fell from a tree.'" She then studied her sandwich. With two disdainful fingers, she picked out a slice of dripping tomato, the sections congealed with red slime. She pitched it into the stream embrowned with dead leaves and the murky effigies of other dead things, but in the opaque water a group of small silver-brown fish appeared. They surrounded the tomato and nibbled.

"Look!" Janice cried. "Fishes! Fishes!" As she scrambled to the edge of the stream to watch, a covey of insects threw up tantrums from the wheatgrass and nettle, a throng of tiny electric machines, all going at once. Octavia snuck up behind Janice as if to push her in. Daphne and I exchanged terrified looks. It seemed as though only we knew that Octavia was close enough—and bold enough—to actually push Janice into the stream. Janice turned around quickly, but Octavia was already staring serenely into the still water as though she were gathering some sort of courage from it. "What's so funny?" Janice said, eyeing them all suspiciously.

Elise began humming the tune to "Karma Chameleon," all the girls joining in, their hums light and facile. Janice began to hum, against everyone else, the high-octane opening chords of "Beat It."

"I love me some Michael Jackson," Janice said when she'd finished humming, smacking her lips as though Michael Jackson were a favorite meal. "I will marry Michael Jackson."

Before anyone had a chance to impress upon Janice the impossibility of this, Arnetta suddenly rose, made a sun visor of her hand, and watched Troop 909 leave the field hockey lawn.

"Dammit!" she said. "We've got to get them *alone.*"

"They won't ever be alone," I said. All the rest of the girls looked at me. If I spoke even a word, I could count on someone calling me Snot, but everyone seemed to think that we could beat up these girls; no one entertained the thought that they might fight *back.* "The only time they'll be unsupervised is in the bathroom."

"Oh shut up, Snot," Octavia said.

But Arnetta slowly nodded her head. "The bathroom," she said. "The bathroom," she said, again and again. "The bathroom! The bathroom!" She cheered so blissfully that I thought for a moment she was joking.

According to Octavia's watch, it took us five minutes to hike to the restrooms, which were midway between our cabin and Troop 909's. Inside, the mirrors above the sinks returned only the vaguest of reflections, as though someone had taken a scouring pad to their surfaces to obscure the shine. Pine needles, leaves, and dirty flattened wads of chewing gum covered the floor like a mosaic. Webs of hair matted the drain in the middle of the floor. Above the sinks and below the mirrors, stacks of folded white paper towels lay on a long metal counter. Shaggy white balls of paper towels sat on the sink tops in a line like corsages on display. A thread of floss snaked from a wad of tissues dotted with the faint red-pink of blood. One of those white girls, I thought, had just lost a tooth.

The restroom looked almost the same as it had the night before, but it somehow seemed stranger now. We had never noticed the wooden rafters before, coming together in great V's. We were, it seemed, inside a whale, viewing the ribs of the roof of its mouth.

"Wow. It's a mess," Elise said.

"You can say that again."

Arnetta leaned against the doorjamb of a restroom stall. "This is where they'll be again," she said. Just seeing the place, just having a plan, seemed to satisfy her. "We'll go in and talk to them. You know, 'How you doing? How long will you be here?' that sort of thing. Then Octavia and I are gonna tell them what happens when they call any one of us a nigger."

"I'm going to say something, too," Janice said.

Arnetta considered this. "Sure," she said. "Of course. Whatever you want."

Janice pointed her finger like a gun at Octavia and rehearsed the line she'd thought up, "'We're gonna teach you a *lesson*.' That's what I'm going to say." She narrowed her eyes like a TV mobster. "'We're gonna teach you little girls a lesson!'"

With the back of her hand, Octavia brushed Janice's finger away. "You couldn't teach me to shit in a toilet."

"But," I said, "what if they say, 'We didn't say that. We didn't call anyone a N-I-G-G-E-R'?"

"Snot," Arnetta sighed. "Don't think. Just fight. If you even know how."

Everyone laughed while Daphne stood there. Arnetta gently laid her hand on Daphne's shoulder. "Daphne. You don't have to fight. We're doing this for you."

Daphne walked to the counter, took a clean paper towel, and carefully unfolded it like a map. With this, she began to pick up the trash all around. Everyone watched.

"C'mon," Arnetta said to everyone. "Let's beat it." We all ambled toward the restroom doorway, where the sunshine made one large white rectangle of light. We were immediately blinded and shielded our eyes with our hands, our forearms.

"Daphne?" Arnetta asked. "Are you coming?"

We all looked back at the girl, who was bending, the thin of her back hunched like a maid caught in stage limelight. Stray strands of her hair were lit nearly transparent, thin fiber-optic threads. She did not nod yes to the question, nor did she shake her head no. She abided, bent. Then she began again, picking up leaves, wads of paper, the cotton fluff innards from a torn stuffed toy. She did it so methodically, so exquisitely, so humbly, she must have been trained. I thought of those dresses she wore, faded and old, yet so pressed and clean; I then saw the poverty in them, I then could imagine her mother, cleaning the houses of others, returning home, weary.

"I guess she's not coming."

We left her, heading back to our cabin, over pine needles and leaves, taking the path full of shade.

"What about our secret meeting?" Elise asked.

Arnetta enunciated in a way that defied contradiction: "We just had it."

Just as we caught sight of our cabin, Arnetta violently swerved away from Octavia. "You farted," she said.

Octavia began to sashay, as if on a catwalk, then proclaimed, in a Hollywood-starlet voice, "My farts smell like perfume."

It was nearing our bedtime, but in the lengthening days of spring, the sun had not yet set.

"Hey, your mama's coming," Arnetta said to Octavia when she saw Mrs. Hedy walk toward the cabin, sniffling. When Octavia's mother wasn't giving bored, parochial orders, she sniffled continuously, mourning an imminent divorce from her husband. She might begin a sentence, "I don't know what Robert will do when Octavia and I are gone. Who'll buy him cigarettes?" and Octavia would hotly whisper *"Mama"* in a way that meant: Please don't talk about our problems in front of everyone. Please shut up.

But when Mrs. Hedy began talking about her husband, thinking about her husband, seeing clouds shaped like the head of her husband, she couldn't be quiet, and no one could ever dislodge her from the comfort of her own woe. Only one thing could perk her up—Brownie songs. If the rest of the girls were quiet, and Mrs. Hedy was in her dopey sorrowful mood, she would say, "Y'all know I like those songs, girls. Why don't you sing one?" Everyone would groan except me and Daphne. I, for one, liked some of the songs.

"C'mon, everybody," Octavia said drearily. "She likes 'The Brownie Song' best."

We sang, loud enough to reach Mrs. Hedy:

> I've something in my pocket;
> It belongs across my face.
> And I keep it very close at hand in a most convenient place.
> I'm sure you couldn't guess it
> If you guessed a long, long while.
> So I'll take it out and put it on—
> It's a great big Brownie Smile!

"The Brownie Song" was supposed to be sung as though we were elves in a workshop, singing as we merrily cobbled shoes, but everyone except me hated the song and sang it like a maudlin record, played at the most sluggish of rpms.

"That was good," Mrs. Hedy said, closing the cabin door behind her. "Wasn't that nice, Linda?"

"Praise God," Mrs. Margolin answered without raising her head from the chore of counting out Popsicle sticks for the next day's session of crafts.

"Sing another one," Mrs. Hedy said, with a sort of joyful aggression, like a drunk I'd once seen who'd refused to leave a Korean grocery.

"God, Mama, get over it," Octavia whispered in a voice meant only for Arnetta, but Mrs. Hedy heard it and started to leave the cabin.

"Don't go," Arnetta said. She ran after Mrs. Hedy and held her by the arm. "We haven't finished singing." She nudged us with a single look. "Let's sing 'The Friends Song.' For Mrs. Hedy."

Although I liked some of the songs, I hated this one:

> Make new friends
> But keep the o-old,
> One is silver
> And the other gold.

If most of the girls in my troop could be any type of metal, they'd be bunched-up wads of tinfoil maybe, or rusty iron nails you had to get tetanus shots for.

"No, no, no," Mrs. Margolin said before anyone could start in on "The Friends Song." "An uplifting song. Something to lift her up and take her mind off all these earthly burdens."

Arnetta and Octavia rolled their eyes. Everyone knew what song Mrs. Margolin was talking about, and no one, no one, wanted to sing it.

"Please, no," a voice called out. "Not 'The Doughnut Song.'"

"Please not 'The Doughnut Song,'" Octavia pleaded.

"I'll brush my teeth twice if I don't have to sing 'The Doughnut—'"

"Sing!" Mrs. Margolin demanded.

We sang:

> Life without Jesus is like a do-ough-nut!
> Like a do-ooough-nut!
> Like a do-ooough-nut!
> Life without Jesus is like a do-ough-nut!
> There's a hole in the middle of my soul!

There were other verses, involving other pastries, but we stopped after the first one and cast glances toward Mrs. Margolin to see if we could gain a reprieve. Mrs. Margolin's eyes fluttered blissfully, half-asleep.

"Awww," Mrs. Hedy said, as though giant Mrs. Margolin were a cute baby. "Mrs. Margolin's had a long day."

"Yes indeed," Mrs. Margolin answered. "If you don't mind, I might just go to the lodge where the beds are. I haven't been the same since the operation."

I had not heard of this operation, or when it had occurred, since Mrs. Margolin had never missed the once-a-week Brownie meetings, but I could see from Daphne's face that she was concerned, and I could see that the other girls had decided that Mrs. Margolin's operation must have happened long ago in some remote time unconnected to our own. Nevertheless, they put on sad faces. We had all been taught that adulthood was full of sorrow and pain, taxes and bills, dreaded work and dealings with whites, sickness, and death.

"Go right ahead, Linda," Mrs. Hedy said. "I'll watch the girls." Mrs. Hedy seemed to forget about divorce for a moment; she looked at us with dewy eyes, as if we were mysterious, furry creatures. Meanwhile, Mrs. Margolin walked through the maze of sleeping bags until she found her own. She gathered a neat stack of clothes and pajamas slowly, as though doing so were almost painful. She took her toothbrush, her toothpaste, her pillow. "All right!" Mrs. Margolin said, addressing us all from the threshold of the cabin. "Be in bed by nine." She said it with a twinkle in her voice, as though she were letting us know she was allowing us to be naughty and stay up till nine-fifteen.

"C'mon, everybody," Arnetta said after Mrs. Margolin left. "Time for us to wash up."

Everyone watched Mrs. Hedy closely, wondering whether she would insist on coming with us since it was night, making a fight with Troop 909 nearly impossible. Troop 909 would soon be in the bathroom, washing their faces, brushing their teeth—completely unsuspecting of our ambush.

"We won't be long," Arnetta said. "We're old enough to go to the restroom by ourselves."

Mrs. Hedy pursed her lips at this dilemma. "Well, I guess you Brownies are almost Girl Scouts, right?"

"Right!"

"Just one more badge," Drema said.

"And about," Octavia droned, "a million more cookies to sell." Octavia looked at all of us. *Now's our chance,* her face seemed to say, but our chance to do *what* I didn't exactly know.

Finally, Mrs. Hedy walked to the doorway where Octavia stood, dutifully waiting to say good-bye and looking bored doing it. Mrs. Hedy held Octavia's chin. "You'll be good?"

"Yes, Mama."

"And remember to pray for me and your father? If I'm asleep when you get back?"

"Yes, Mama."

When the other girls had finished getting their toothbrushes and washcloths and flashlights for the group restroom trip, I was drawing pictures of tiny birds with too many feathers. Daphne was sitting on her sleeping bag, reading.

"You're not going to come?" Octavia asked.

Daphne shook her head.

"I'm also gonna stay, too," I said. "I'll go to the restroom when Daphne and Mrs. Hedy go."

Arnetta leaned down toward me and whispered so that Mrs. Hedy, who had taken over Mrs. Margolin's task of counting Popsicle sticks, couldn't hear. "No, Snot. If we get in trouble, you're going to get in trouble with the rest of us."

We made our way through the darkness by flashlight. The tree branches that had shaded us just hours earlier, along the same path, now looked like arms sprouting menacing hands. The stars sprinkled the sky like spilled salt. They seemed fastened to the darkness, high up and holy, their places fixed and definite as we stirred beneath them.

Some, like me, were quiet because we were afraid of the dark; others were talking like crazy for the same reason.

"Wow," Drema said, looking up. "Why are all the stars out here? I never see stars back on Oneida Street."

"It's a camping trip, that's why," Octavia said. 'You're supposed to see stars on camping trips."

Janice said, "This place smells like the air freshener my mother uses."

"These woods are *pine*," Elise said. "Your mother probably uses pine air freshener."

Janice mouthed an exaggerated "Oh," nodding her head as though she just then understood one of the world's great secrets.

No one talked about fighting. Everyone was afraid enough just walking through the infinite deep of the woods. Even without seeing anyone's face, I could tell this wasn't about Daphne being called a nigger. The word that had started it all seemed melted now into some deeper, unnameable feeling. Even though I didn't want to fight, was afraid of fighting, I felt as though I were part of the rest of the troop, as though I were defending something. We trudged against the slight incline of the path, Arnetta leading the way. I wondered, looking at her back, what she could be thinking.

"You know," I said, "their leader will be there. Or they won't even be there. It's dark already. Last night the sun was still in the sky. I'm sure they're already finished."

"Whose flashlight is this?" Arnetta said, shaking the weakening beam of the light she was holding. "It's out of batteries.' "

Octavia handed Arnetta her flashlight. And that's when I saw it. The bathroom was just ahead.

But the girls were there. We could hear them before we could see them.

"Octavia and I will go in first so they'll think there's just two of us. Then wait till I say, 'We're gonna teach you a lesson,' " Arnetta said. "Then bust in. That'll surprise them."

"That's what I was supposed to say," Janice said.

Arnetta went inside, Octavia next to her. Janice followed, and the rest of us waited outside.

They were in there for what seemed like whole minutes, but something was wrong. Arnetta hadn't given the signal yet. I was with the girls outside when I heard one of the Troop 909 girls say, "NO. That did NOT happen!"

That was to be expected, that they'd deny the whole thing. What I hadn't expected was *the voice* in which the denial was said. The girl sounded as though her tongue were caught in her mouth. "That's a BAD word!" the girl continued. "We don't say BAD words!"

"Let's go in," Elise said.

"No," Drema said. "I don't want to. What if we get beat up?"

"Snot?" Elise turned to me, her flashlight blinding. It was the first time anyone had asked my opinion, though I knew they were just asking because they were afraid.

"I say we go inside, just to see what's going on."

"But Arnetta didn't give us the signal," Drema said. "She's supposed to say, 'We're going to teach you a lesson,' and I didn't hear her say it."

"C'mon," I said. "Let's just go in."

We went inside. There we found the white girls, but about five girls were huddled up next to one big girl. I instantly knew she was the owner of the voice we'd heard. Arnetta and Octavia inched toward us as soon as we entered.

"Where's Janice?" Elise asked, then we heard a flush. "Oh."

"I think," Octavia said, whispering to Elise, "they're retarded."

"We ARE NOT retarded!" the big girl said, though it was obvious that she was. That they all were. The girls around her began to whimper.

"They're just pretending," Arnetta said, trying to convince herself. "I know they are."

Octavia turned to Arnetta. "Arnetta. Let's just leave."

Janice came out of a stall, happy and relieved, then she suddenly remembered her line, pointed to the big girl, and said, "We're gonna teach you a lesson."

"Shut up, Janice," Octavia said, but her heart was not in it. Arnetta's face was set in a lost, deep scowl. Octavia turned to the big girl, and said loudly, slowly, as if they were all deaf, "We're going to leave. It was nice meeting you, okay? You don't have to tell anyone that we were here. Okay?"

"Why not?" said the big girl, like a taunt. When she spoke, her lips did not meet, her mouth did not close. Her tongue grazed the roof of her mouth, like a little pink fish. "You'll get in trouble. I know. I know."

Arnetta got back her old cunning. "If you said anything, then you'd be a tattletale."

The girl looked sad for a moment, then perked up quickly. A flash of genius crossed her face: "I *like* tattletale."

"It's all right, girls. It's gonna be all right!" the 909 troop leader said. It was as though someone had instructed all of Troop 909 to cry at once. The troop leader had girls under her arm, and all the rest of the girls crowded about her. It reminded me of a hog I'd seen on a field trip, where all the little hogs would gather about the mother at feeding time, latching on to her teats. The 909 troop leader had come into the bathroom shortly after the big girl threatened to tell. Then the ranger came, then, once the ranger had radioed the station, Mrs. Margolin arrived with Daphne in tow.

The ranger had left the restroom area, but everyone else was huddled just outside, swatting mosquitoes.

"Oh. They *will* apologize," Mrs. Margolin said to the 909 troop leader, but Mrs. Margolin said this so angrily, I knew she was speaking more to us than to the other troop leader. "When their parents find out, every one a them will be on punishment."

"It's all right. It's all right," the 909 troop leader reassured Mrs. Margolin. Her voice lilted in the same way it had when addressing the girls. She smiled the whole time she talked. She was like one of those TV cooking show women who talk and dice onions and smile all at the same time.

"See. It could have happened. I'm not calling your girls fibbers or anything." She shook her head ferociously from side to side, her Egyptian-style pageboy flapping against her cheeks like heavy drapes. "It *could* have happened, see. Our girls are *not* retarded. They are *delayed* learners." She said this in a syrupy instructional voice, as though our troop might be delayed learners as well. "We're from the Decatur Children's Academy. Many of them just have special needs."

"Now we won't be able to walk to the bathroom by ourselves!" the big girl said.

"Yes you will," the troop leader said, "but maybe we'll wait till we get back to Decatur—"

"I don't want to wait!" the girl said. "I want my Independence patch!"

The girls in my troop were entirely speechless. Arnetta looked as though she were soon to be tortured but was determined not to appear weak. Mrs. Margolin pursed her lips solemnly and said, "Bless them, Lord. Bless them."

In contrast, the Troop 909 leader was full of words and energy. "Some of our girls are echolalic—" She smiled and happily presented one of the girls hanging on to her, but the girl widened her eyes in horror and violently withdrew herself from the center of attention, as though she sensed she were being sacrificed for the village sins.

"Echolalic," the troop leader continued. "That means they will say whatever they hear, like an echo—that's where the word comes from. It comes from 'echo.'" She ducked her head apologetically. "I mean, not all of them have the most *progressive* of parents, so if they heard a bad word they might have repeated it. But I guarantee it would not have been *intentional*."

Arnetta spoke. "I saw her say the word. I heard her." She pointed to a small girl, smaller than any of us, wearing an oversized T-shirt that read: EAT BERTHA'S MUSSELS.

The troop leader shook her head and smiled. "That's impossible. She doesn't speak. She can, but she doesn't."

Arnetta furrowed her brow. "No. It wasn't her. That's right. It was *her*."

The girl Arnetta pointed to grinned as though she'd been paid a compliment. She was the only one from either troop actually wearing a full uniform: the mocha-colored A-line shift, the orange ascot, the sash covered with patches, though all the same one—the Try-It patch. She took a few steps toward Arnetta and made a grand sweeping gesture toward the sash. "See," she said, full of self-importance, "I'm a Brownie." I had a hard time imagining this girl calling anyone a "nigger"; the girl looked perpetually delighted, as though she would have cuddled up with a grizzly if someone had let her.

*   *   *

On the fourth morning, we boarded the bus to go home.

The previous day had been spent building miniature churches from Popsicle sticks. We hardly left the cabin. Mrs. Margolin and Mrs. Hedy guarded us so closely, almost no one talked for the entire day.

Even on the day of departure from Camp Crescendo, all was serious and silent. The bus ride began quietly enough. Arnetta had to sit beside Mrs. Margolin, Octavia had to sit beside her mother. I sat beside Daphne, who gave me her prize journal without a word of explanation.

"You don't want it?"

She shook her head no. It was empty.

Then Mrs. Hedy began to weep. "Octavia," Mrs. Hedy said to her daughter without looking at her, "I'm going to sit with Mrs. Margolin. All right?"

Arnetta exchanged seats with Mrs. Hedy. With the two women up front, Elise felt it safe to speak. "Hey," she said, then she set her face into a placid vacant stare, trying to imitate that of a Troop 909 girl. Emboldened, Arnetta made a gesture of mock pride toward an imaginary sash, the way the girl in full uniform had done. Then they all made a game of it, trying to do the most exaggerated imitations of the Troop 909 girls, all without speaking, all without laughing loud enough to catch the women's attention.

Daphne looked at her shoes, white with sneaker polish. I opened the journal she'd given me. I looked out the window, trying to decide what to write, searching for lines, but nothing could compare with the lines Daphne had written, *"My father, the veteran,"* my favorite line of all time. The line replayed itself in my head, and I gave up trying to write.

By then, it seemed as though the rest of the troop had given up making fun of the 909 girls. They were now quietly gossiping about who had passed notes to whom in school. For a moment the gossiping fell off, and all I heard was the hum of the bus as we sped down the road and the muffled sounds of Mrs. Hedy and Mrs. Margolin talking about serious things.

"You know," Octavia whispered, "why did *we* have to be stuck at a camp with retarded girls? You know?"

"*You* know why," Arnetta answered. She narrowed her eyes like a cat. "My mama and I were in the mall in Buckhead, and this white lady just kept looking at us. I mean, like we were foreign or something. Like we were from China."

"What did the woman say?" Elise asked.

"Nothing," Arnetta said. "She didn't say nothing."

A few girls quietly nodded their heads.

"There was this time," I said, "when my father and I were in the mall and—"

"Oh, shut up, Snot," Octavia said.

I stared at Octavia, then rolled my eyes from her to the window. As I watched the trees blur, I wanted nothing more than to be through with it all: the bus ride, the troop, school—all of it. But we were going home. I'd see the same girls in school the next day. We were on a bus, and there was nowhere else to go.

"Go on, Laurel," Daphne said to me. It was the first time she'd spoken the whole trip, and she'd said my name. I turned to her and smiled weakly so as not to cry, hoping she'd remember when I'd tried to be her friend, thinking maybe that her gift of the journal was an invitation of friendship. But she didn't smile back. All she said was, "What happened?"

I studied the girls, waiting for Octavia to tell me to "shut up" again before I even had a chance to utter another word, but everyone was amazed that Daphne had spoken. I gathered my voice. "Well," I said. "My father and I were in this mall, but *I* was the one doing the staring." I stopped and glanced from face to face. I continued. "There were these white people dressed like Puritans or something, but they weren't Puritans. They were Mennonites. They're these people who, if you ask them to do a favor, like paint your porch or something, they have to do it. It's in their rules."

"That sucks," someone said.

"C'mon," Arnetta said. "You're lying."

"I am not."

"How do you know that's not just some story someone made up?" Elise asked, her head cocked, full of daring. "I mean, who's gonna do whatever you ask?"

"It's not made up. I know because when I was looking at them, my father said, 'See those people. If you ask them to do something, they'll do it. Anything you want.'"

No one would call anyone's father a liar. Then they'd have to fight the person, but Drema parsed her words carefully. "How does your *father* know that's not just some story? Huh?"

"Because," I said, "he went up to the man and asked him would he paint our porch, and the man said, 'Yes.' It's their religion."

"Man, I'm glad I'm a Baptist," Elise said, shaking her head in sympathy for the Mennonites.

"So did the guy do it?" Drema asked, scooting closer to hear if the story got juicy.

"Yeah," I said. "His whole family was with him. My dad drove them to our house. They all painted our porch. The woman and girl were in bonnets and long, long skirts with buttons up to their necks. The guy wore this weird hat and these huge suspenders."

"Why," Arnetta asked archly, as though she didn't believe a word, "would someone pick a *porch*? If they'll do anything, why not make them paint the whole *house*? Why not ask for a hundred bucks?"

I thought about it, and I remembered the words my father had said about them painting our porch, though I had never seemed to think about his words after he'd said them.

"He said," I began, only then understanding the words as they uncoiled from my mouth, "it was the only time he'd have a white man on his knees doing something for a black man for free."

I remembered the Mennonites bending like Daphne had bent, cleaning the restroom. I remembered the dark blue of their bonnets, the black of their shoes. They painted the porch as though scrubbing a floor. I was already trembling before Daphne asked quietly, "Did he thank them?"

I looked out the window. I could not tell which were the thoughts and which were the trees. "No," I said, and suddenly knew there was something mean in the world that I could not stop.

Arnetta laughed. "If I asked them to take off their long skirts and bonnets and put on some jeans, they would do it?"

And Daphne's voice—quiet, steady: "Maybe they would. Just to be nice."

Reading as a Writer

1. What is the balance of showing and telling in this story? How important are the scenes (as opposed to the narration)?

2. Can you pick three instances of "telling" that would be difficult, if not impossible, to show?

3. Can you point to any instances of "showing" that seem absolutely necessary to the story?

FLANNERY O'CONNOR

Everything That Rises Must Converge

HER DOCTOR had told Julian's mother that she must lose twenty pounds on account of her blood pressure, so on Wednesday nights Julian had to take her downtown on the bus for a reducing class at the Y. The reducing class was designed for working girls over fifty, who weighed from 165 to 200 pounds. His mother was one of the slimmer ones, but she said ladies did not tell their age or weight. She would not ride the buses by herself at night since they had been integrated, and because the reducing class was one of her few pleasures, necessary for her health, and *free*, she said Julian could at least put himself out to take her, considering all she did for him. Julian did not like to consider all she did for him, but every Wednesday night he braced himself and took her.

She was almost ready to go, standing before the hall mirror, putting on her hat, while he, his hands behind him, appeared pinned to the door frame, waiting like Saint Sebastian for the arrows to begin piercing him. The hat was new and had cost her seven dollars and a half. She kept saying, "Maybe I shouldn't have paid that for it. No, I shouldn't have. I'll take it off and return it tomorrow. I shouldn't have bought it."

Julian raised his eyes to heaven. "Yes, you should have bought it," he said. "Put it on and let's go." It was a hideous hat. A purple velvet flap came down on one side of it and stood up on the other; the rest of it was green and looked like a cushion with the stuffing out. He decided it was less comical than jaunty and pathetic. Everything that gave her pleasure was small and depressed him.

She lifted the hat one more time and set it down slowly on top of her head. Two wings of gray hair protruded on either side of her florid face, but her eyes, sky-blue, were as innocent and untouched by experience as they must have been when she was ten. Were it not that she was a widow who had struggled fiercely to feed and clothe and put him through school and who was supporting him still, "until he got on his feet," she might have been a little girl that he had to take to town.

"It's all right, it's all right," he said. "Let's go." He opened the door himself and started down the walk to get her going. The sky was a dying violet and the houses stood out darkly against it, bulbous liver-colored monstrosities of a uniform ugliness though no two were alike. Since this had been a fashionable neighborhood forty years ago, his mother persisted in thinking they did well to have an apartment in it. Each house had a narrow collar of dirt around it in which sat, usually, a grubby child. Julian walked with his hands in his pockets, his head down and thrust forward, and his eyes glazed with the determination to make himself completely numb during the time he would be sacrificed to her pleasure.

The door closed and he turned to find the dumpy figure, surmounted by the atrocious hat, coming toward him. "Well," she said, "you only live once and paying a little more for it, I at least won't meet myself coming and going."

"Some day I'll start making money," Julian said gloomily—he knew he never would—"and you can have one of those jokes whenever you take the fit." But first they would move. He visualized a place where the nearest neighbor would be three miles away on either side.

"I think you're doing fine," she said, drawing on her gloves. "You've only been out of school a year. Rome wasn't built in a day."

She was one of the few members of the Y reducing class who arrived in hat and gloves and who had a son who had been to college. "It takes time," she said, "and the world is in such a mess. This hat looked better on me than any of the others, though when she brought it out I said, 'Take that thing back. I wouldn't have it on my head,' and she said, 'Now wait till you see it on,' and when she put it on me, I said, 'We-ull,' and she said, 'If you ask me, that hat does something for you and you do something for the hat, and besides,' she said, 'with that hat, you won't meet yourself coming and going.'"

Julian thought he could have stood his lot better if she had been selfish, if she had been an old hag who drank and screamed at him. He walked along, saturated in depression, as if in the midst of his martyrdom he had lost his faith. Catching sight of his long, hopeless, irritated face, she stopped suddenly with a grief-stricken look, and pulled back on his arm. `Wait on me," she said. "I'm going back to the house and take this thing off and tomorrow I'm going to return it. I was out of my head. I can pay the gas bill with the seven-fifty."

He caught her arm in a vicious grip. "You are not going to take it back," he said. "I like it."

"Well," she said, "I don't think I ought . . ."

"Shut up and enjoy it," he muttered, more depressed than ever.

"With the world in the mess it's in," she said, "it's a wonder we can enjoy anything. I tell you, the bottom rail is on the top."

Julian sighed.

"Of course," she said, "if you know who you are, you can go anywhere." She said this every time he took her to the reducing class. "Most of them in it are not our kind of people," she said, "but I can be gracious to anybody. I know who I am."

"They don't give a damn for your graciousness," Julian said savagely. "Knowing who you are is good for one generation only. You haven't the foggiest idea where you stand now or who you are."

She stopped and allowed her eyes to flash at him. "I most certainly do know who I am," she said, "and if you don't know who you are, I'm ashamed of you."

"Oh hell," Julian said.

"Your great-grandfather was a former governor of this state," she said. "Your grandfather was a prosperous landowner. Your grandmother was a Godhigh."

"Will you look around you," he said tensely, "and see where you are now?" and he swept his arm jerkily out to indicate the neighborhood, which the growing darkness at least made less dingy.

"You remain what you are," she said. "Your great-grandfather had a plantation and two hundred slaves."

"There are no more slaves," he said irritably.

"They were better off when they were," she said. He groaned to see that she was off on that topic. She rolled onto it every few days like a train on an open track. He knew every stop, every junction, every swamp along the way, and knew the exact point at which her conclusion would roll majestically into the station: "It's ridiculous. It's simply not realistic. They should rise, yes, but on their own side of the fence."

"Let's skip it," Julian said.

"The ones I feel sorry for," she said, "are the ones that are half white. They're tragic."

"Will you skip it?"

"Suppose we were half white. We would certainly have mixed feelings."

"I have mixed feelings now," he groaned.

"Well let's talk about something pleasant," she said. "I remember going to Grandpa's when I was a little girl. Then the house had double stairways that went up to what was really the second floor—all the cooking was done on the first. I used to like to stay down in the kitchen on account of the way the walls smelled. I would sit with my nose pressed against the plaster and take deep breaths. Actually the place belonged to the Godhighs but your grandfather Chestny paid the mortgage and saved it for them. They were in reduced circumstances," she said, "but reduced or not, they never forgot who they were."

"Doubtless that decayed mansion reminded them," Julian muttered. He never spoke of it without contempt or thought of it without longing. He had seen it once when he was a child before it had been sold. The double stairways had rotted and had been torn down. Negroes were living in it. But it remained in his mind as his mother had known it. It appeared in his dreams regularly. He would stand on the wide porch, listening to the rustle of oak leaves, then wander through the high-ceilinged hall into the parlor that opened onto it and gaze at the worn rags and faded draperies. It occurred to him that it was he, not she, who could have appreciated it. He preferred its threadbare elegance to anything he could name and it was because of it that all the neighborhoods they had lived in had been a torment to him—whereas she had hardly known the difference. She called her insensitivity "being adjustable."

"And I remember the old darky who was my nurse, Caroline. There was no better person in the world. I've always had a great respect for my colored friends," she said. "I'd do anything in the world for them and they'd . . ."

"Will you for God's sake get off that subject?" Julian said. When he got on a bus by himself, he made it a point to sit down beside a Negro, in reparation as it were for his mother's sins.

"You're mighty touchy tonight," she said. "Do you feel all right?"

"Yes I feel all right," he said. "Now lay off."

She pursed her lips. "Well, you certainly are in a vile humor," she observed. "I just won't speak to you at all."

They had reached the bus stop. There was no bus in sight and Julian, his hands still jammed in his pockets and his head thrust forward, scowled down the empty street. The frustration of having to wait on the bus as well as ride on it began to creep up his neck like a hot hand. The presence of his mother was borne in upon him as she gave a pained sigh. He looked at her bleakly. She was holding herself very erect under the preposterous hat, wearing it like a banner of her imaginary dignity. There was in him an evil urge to break her spirit. He suddenly unloosened his tie and pulled it off and put it in his pocket.

She stiffened. "Why must you look like *that* when you take me to town?" she said. "Why must you deliberately embarrass me?"

"If you'll never learn where you are," he said, "you can at least learn where I am."

"You look like a—thug," she said.

"Then I must be one," he murmured.

"I'll just go home," she said. "I will not bother you. If you can't do a little thing like that for me . . ."

Rolling his eyes upward, he put his tie back on. "Restored to my class," he muttered. He thrust his face toward her and hissed, "True culture is in the mind, the *mind*," he said, and tapped his head, "the mind."

"It's in the heart," she said, "and in how you do things and how you do things is because of who you *are*."

"Nobody in the damn bus cares who you are."

"I care who I am," she said icily.

The lighted bus appeared on top of the next hill and as it approached, they moved out into the street to meet it. He put his hand under her elbow and hoisted her up on the creaking step. She entered with a little smile, as if she were going into a drawing room where everyone had been waiting for her. While he put in the tokens, she sat down on one of the broad front seats for three which faced the aisle. A thin woman with protruding teeth and long yellow hair was sitting on the end of it. His mother moved up beside her and left room for Julian beside herself. He sat down and looked at the floor across the aisle where a pair of thin feet in red and white canvas sandals were planted.

His mother immediately began a general conversation meant to attract anyone who felt like talking. "Can it get any hotter?" she said and removed from her purse a folding fan, black with a Japanese scene on it, which she began to flutter before her.

"I reckon it might could," the woman with the protruding teeth said, "but I know for a fact my apartment couldn't get no hotter."

"It must get the afternoon sun," his mother said. She sat forward and looked up and down the bus. It was half filled. Everybody was white. "I see we have the bus to ourselves," she said. Julian cringed.

"For a change," said the woman across the aisle, the owner of the red and white canvas sandals. "I come on one the other day and they were thick as fleas—up front and all through."

"The world is in a mess everywhere," his mother said. "I don't know how we've let it get in this fix."

"What gets my goat is all those boys from good families stealing automobile tires," the woman with the protruding teeth said. "I told my boy, I said you may not be rich but you been raised right and if I ever catch you in any such mess, they can send you on to the reformatory. Be exactly where you belong."

"Training tells," his mother said. "Is your boy in high school?"

"Ninth grade," the woman said.

"My son just finished college last year. He wants to write but he's selling typewriters until he gets started," his mother said.

The woman leaned forward and peered at Julian. He threw her such a malevolent look that she subsided against the seat. On the floor across the aisle there was an abandoned newspaper. He got up and got it and opened it out in front of him. His mother discreetly continued the conversation in a lower tone but the woman across the aisle said in a loud voice, "Well that's nice. Selling typewriters is close to writing. He can go right from one to the other."

"I tell him," his mother said, "that Rome wasn't built in a day."

Behind the newspaper Julian was withdrawing into the inner compartment of his mind where he spent most of his time. This was a kind of mental bubble in which he established himself when he could not bear to be part of what was going on around him. From it he could see out and judge but in it he was safe from any kind of penetration from without. It was the only place where he felt free of the general idiocy of his fellows. His mother had never entered it but from it he could see her with absolute clarity.

The old lady was clever enough and he thought that if she had started from any of the right premises, more might have been expected of her. She lived according to the laws of her own fantasy world, outside of which had never seen her set foot. The law of it was to sacrifice herself for him after she had first created the necessity to do so by making a mess of things. If he had permitted her sacrifices, it was only because her lack of foresight had made them necessary. All of her life had been a struggle to act like a Chestny without the Chestny goods, and to give him everything she thought a Chestny ought to have; but since, said she, it was fun to struggle, why complain? And when you had won, as she had won, what fun to look back on the hard times! He could not forgive her that she had enjoyed the struggle and that she thought *she* had won.

What she meant when she said she had won was that she had brought him up successfully and had sent him to college and that he had turned out so well—good looking (her teeth had gone unfilled, so that his could be straightened), intelligent (he realized he was too intelligent to be a success), and with a future ahead of him (there was of course no future ahead of him). She excused his gloominess on the grounds that he was still growing up and his radical ideas on his lack of practical experience. She said he didn't yet know a thing about "life," that he hadn't even entered the real world—when already he was as disenchanted with it as a man of fifty.

The further irony of all this was that in spite of her, he had turned out so well. In spite of going to only a third-rate college, he had, on his own initiative, come out with a first-rate education; in spite of growing up dominated by a small mind, he had ended up with a large one; in spite of all her foolish views, he was free of prejudice and unafraid to face facts. Most miraculous of all, instead of being blinded by love for her as she was for him, he had cut himself emotionally free of her and could see her with complete objectivity. He was not dominated by his mother.

The bus stopped with a sudden jerk and shook him from his meditation. A woman from the back lurched forward with little steps and barely escaped falling in his newspaper as she righted herself. She got off and a large Negro got on. Julian kept his paper lowered to watch. It gave him a certain satisfaction to see injustice in daily operation. It confirmed his view that with a few exceptions there was no one worth knowing within a radius of three hundred miles. The Negro was well dressed and carried a briefcase. He looked round and then sat down on the other end of the seat where the woman with the red and white canvas sandals was sitting. He immediately unfolded a newspaper and obscured himself behind it. Julian's mother's elbow at once prodded insistently into his ribs. "Now you see why I won't ride on these buses by myself," she whispered.

The woman with the red and white canvas sandals had risen at the same time the Negro sat down and had gone further back in the bus and taken the seat of the woman who had got off. His mother leaned forward and cast her an approving look.

Julian rose, crossed the aisle, and sat down in the place of the woman with the canvas sandals. From this position, he looked serenely across at his mother. Her face had turned an angry red. He stared at her, making his eyes the eyes of a stranger. He felt his tension suddenly lift as if he had openly declared war on her.

He would have liked to get in conversation with the Negro and to talk with him about art or politics or any subject that would be above the comprehension of those around them, but the man remained entrenched behind his paper. He was either ignoring the change of seating or had never noticed it. There was no way for Julian to convey his sympathy.

His mother kept her eyes fixed reproachfully on his face. The woman with the protruding teeth was looking at him avidly as if he were a type of monster new to her.

"Do you have a light?" he asked the Negro.

Without looking away from his paper, the man reached in his pocket and handed him a packet of matches.

"Thanks," Julian said. For a moment he held the matches foolishly. A NO SMOKING sign looked down upon him from over the door. This alone would not have deterred him; he had no cigarettes. He had quit smoking some months before because he could not afford it. "Sorry," he muttered and handed back the matches. The Negro lowered the paper and gave him an annoyed look. He took the matches and raised the paper again.

His mother continued to gaze at him but she did not take the advantage of his momentary discomfort. Her eyes retained their battered look. Her face seemed to be unnaturally red, as if her blood pressure had risen. Julian allowed no glimmer of sympathy to show on his face. Having got the advantage, he wanted desperately to keep it and carry it through. He would have liked to teach her a lesson that would last her a while; but there seemed no way to continue the point. The Negro refused to come out from behind his paper.

Julian folded his arms and looked stolidly before him, facing her but as if he did not see her, as if he had ceased to recognize her existence. He visualized a scene in which, the bus having reached their stop, he would remain in his seat and when she said, "Aren't you going to get off?" he would look at her as a stranger who had rashly addressed him. The corner they got off on was usually deserted, but it was well lighted and it would not hurt her to walk by herself the four blocks to the Y. He decided to wait until the time came and then decide whether or not he would let her get off by herself. He would have to be at the Y at ten to bring her back, but he could leave her wondering if he was going to show up. There was no reason for her to think she could always depend on him.

He retired again into the high-ceilinged room sparsely settled with large pieces of antique furniture. His soul expanded momentarily but then he became aware of his mother across from him and the vision shriveled. He studied her coldly. Her feet in little pumps dangled like a child's and did not quite reach the floor. She was training on him an exaggerated look of reproach. He felt completely detached from her. At that moment he could with pleasure have slapped her as he would have slapped a particularly obnoxious child in his charge.

He began to imagine various unlikely ways by which he could teach her a lesson. He might make friends with some distinguished Negro professor or lawyer and bring him home to spend the evening. He would be entirely justified but her blood pressure would rise to 300. He could not push her to the extent of making her have a stroke, and moreover, he had never been successful at making any Negro friends. He had tried to strike up an acquaintance on the bus with some of the better types, with ones that looked like professors or ministers or lawyers. One morning he had sat down next to a distinguished-looking dark brown man who had answered his questions with a sonorous solemnity but who had turned out to be an undertaker. Another day he had sat down beside a cigar-smoking Negro with a diamond ring on his finger, but after a few stilted pleasantries, the Negro had rung the buzzer and risen, slipping two lottery tickets into Julian's hand as he climbed over him to leave.

He imagined his mother lying desperately ill and his being able to secure only a Negro doctor for her. He toyed with that idea for a few minutes and then dropped it for a momentary vision of himself participating as a sympathizer in a sit-in demonstration. This was possible but he did not linger with it. Instead, he approached the ultimate horror. He brought home a beautiful suspiciously Negroid woman. Prepare yourself, he said. There is nothing you can do about it. This is the woman I've chosen. She's intelligent, dignified, even good, and she's suffered and she hasn't thought it *fun*. Now persecute us, go ahead and persecute us. Drive her out of here, but remember, you're driving me too. His eyes were narrowed and through the indignation he had generated, he saw his mother across the aisle, purplefaced, shrunken to the dwarf-like proportions of her moral nature, sitting like a mummy beneath the ridiculous banner of her hat.

He was tilted out of his fantasy again as the bus stopped. The door opened with a sucking hiss and out of the dark a large, gaily dressed, sullen-looking colored woman got on with a little boy. The child, who might have been four, had on a short plaid suit and a Tyrolean hat with a blue feather in it. Julian hoped that he would sit down beside him and that the woman would push in beside his mother. He could think of no better arrangement.

As she waited for her tokens, the woman was surveying the seating possibilities—he hoped with the idea of sitting where she was least wanted. There was something familiar-looking about her but Julian could not place what it was. She was a giant of a woman. Her face was set not only to meet opposition but to seek it out. The downward tilt of her large lower lip was like a warning sign: DON'T TAMPER WITH ME. Her bulging figure was encased in a green crepe dress and her feet overflowed in red shoes. She had on a hideous hat. A purple velvet flap came down on one side of it and stood up on the other; the rest of it was green and looked like a cushion with the stuffing out. She carried a mammoth red pocketbook that bulged throughout as if it were stuffed with rocks.

To Julian's disappointment, the little boy climbed up on the empty seat beside his mother. His mother lumped all children, black and white, into the common category, "cute," and she thought little Negroes were on the whole cuter than little white children. She smiled at the little boy as he climbed on the seat.

Meanwhile the woman was bearing down upon the empty seat beside Julian. To his annoyance, she squeezed herself into it. He saw his mother's face change as the woman settled herself next to him and he realized with satisfaction that this was more objectionable to her than it was to him. Her face seemed almost gray and there was a look of dull recognition in her eyes, as if suddenly she had sickened at some awful confrontation. Julian saw that it was because she and the woman had, in a sense, swapped sons. Though his mother would not realize the symbolic significance of this, she would feel it. His amusement showed plainly on his face.

The woman next to him muttered something unintelligible to herself. He was conscious of a kind of bristling next to him, muted growling like that of an angry cat. He could not see anything but the red pocketbook upright on the bulging green thighs. He visualized the woman as she had stood waiting for her tokens—the ponderous figure, rising from the red shoes upward over the solid hips, the mammoth bosom, the haughty face, to the green and purple hat.

His eyes widened.

The vision of the two hats, identical, broke upon him with the radiance of a brilliant sunrise. His face was suddenly lit with Joy. He could not believe that Fate had thrust upon his mother such a lesson. He gave a loud chuckle so that she would look at him and see that he saw. She turned her eyes on him slowly. The blue in them seemed to have turned a bruised purple. For a moment he had an uncomfortable sense of her innocence, but it lasted only a second before principle rescued him. Justice entitled him to laugh. His grin hardened until it said to her as plainly as if he were saving aloud: Your punishment exactly fits your pettiness. This should teach you a permanent lesson.

Her eyes shifted to the woman. She seemed unable to bear looking at him and to find the woman preferable. He became conscious again of the bristling presence at his side. The woman was rumbling like a volcano about to become active. His mother's mouth began to twitch slightly at one corner. With a sinking heart, he saw incipient signs of recovery on her face and realized that this was going to strike her suddenly as funny and was going to be no lesson at all. She kept her eyes on the woman and an amused smile came over her face as if the woman were a monkey that had stolen her hat. The little Negro was looking up at her with large fascinated eyes. He had been trying to attract her attention for some time.

"Carver," the woman said suddenly. "Come heah!"

When he saw that the spotlight was on him at last, Carver drew his feet up and turned himself toward Julian's mother and giggled.

"Carver!" the woman said. "You heah me? Come Heah!"

Carver slid down from the seat but remained squatting with his back against the base of it, his head turned slowly around toward Julian's mother who was smiling at him. The woman reached a hand across the aisle and snatched him to her. He righted himself and hung backwards on her knees, grinning at Julian's mother. "Isn't he cute?" Julian's mother said to the woman with the protruding teeth.

"I reckon he is," the woman said without conviction.

The Negress yanked him upright but he eased out of her grip and shot across the aisle and scrambled, giggling wildly, onto the seat beside his love.

"I think he likes me," Julian's mother said, and smiled at the woman. It was the smile she used when she was being particularly gracious to an inferior. Julian saw everything lost. The lesson had rolled off her like rain on a roof.

The woman stood up and yanked the little boy off the seat as if she were snatching him from contagion. Julian could feel the rage in her at having no weapon like his mother's smile. She gave the child a sharp slap across his leg. He howled once and then thrust his head into her stomach and kicked his feet against her shins. "Behave," she said vehemently.

The bus stopped and the Negro who had been reading the newspaper got off. The woman moved over and set the little boy down with a thump between herself and Julian. She held him firmly by the knee. In a moment he put his hands in front of his face and peeped at Julian's mother through his fingers.

"I see yoooooooo!" she said and put her hand in front of her face and peeped at him.

The woman slapped his hand down. "Quit yo' foolishness," she said, "before I knock the living Jesus out of you!"

Julian was thankful that the next stop was theirs. He reached up and pulled the cord. The woman reached up and pulled it at the same time. Oh my God, he thought. He had the terrible intuition that when they got off the bus together, his mother would open her purse and give the little boy a nickel. The gesture would be as natural to her as breathing. The bus stopped and the woman got up and lunged to the front, dragging the child, who wished to stay on, after her. Julian and his mother got up and followed. As they neared the door, Julian tried to relieve her of her pocketbook.

"No," she murmured, "I want to give the little boy a nickel."

"No!" Julian hissed. "No!"

She smiled down at the child and opened her bag. The bus door opened and the woman picked him up by the arm and descended with him, hanging at her hip. Once in the street she set him down and shook him.

Julian's mother had to close her purse while she got down the bus step but as soon as her feet were on the ground, she opened it again and began to rummage inside. "I can't find but a penny," she whispered, "but it looks like a new one."

"Don't do it!" Julian said fiercely between his teeth. There was a streetlight on the corner and she hurried to get under it so that she could better see into her pocketbook. The woman was heading off rapidly down the street with the child still hanging backward on her hand.

"Oh little boy!" Julian's mother called and took a few quick steps and caught up with them just beyond the lamppost. "Here's a bright new penny for you," and she held out the coin, which shone bronze in the dim light.

The huge woman turned and for a moment stood, her shoulders lifted and her face frozen with frustrated rage, and stared at Julian's mother. Then all at once she seemed to explode like a piece of machinery that had been given one ounce of pressure too much. Julian saw the black fist swing out with the red pocketbook. He shut his eyes and cringed as he heard the woman shout, "He don't take nobody's pennies!" When he opened his eyes, the woman was disappearing down the street with the little boy staring wide-eyed over her shoulder. Julian's mother was sitting on the sidewalk.

"I told you not to do that," Julian said angrily. "I told you not to do that!"

He stood over her for a minute, gritting his teeth. Her legs were stretched out in front of her and her hat was on her lap. He squatted down and looked her in the face. It was totally expressionless. "You got exactly what you deserved," he said. "Now get up."

He picked up her pocketbook and put what had fallen out back in it. He picked the hat up off her lap. The penny caught his eye on the sidewalk and he picked that up and let it drop before her eyes into the purse. Then he stood up and leaned over and held his hands out to pull her up. She remained immobile. He sighed. Rising above them on either side were black apartment buildings, marked with irregular rectangles of light. At the end of the block a man came out of a door and walked off in the opposite direction. "All right," he said, "suppose somebody happens by and wants to know why you're sitting on the sidewalk?"

She took the hand and, breathing hard, pulled heavily up on it and then stood for a moment, swaying slightly as if the spots of light in the darkness were circling around her. Her eyes, shadowed and confused, finally settled on his face. He did not try to conceal his irritation. "I hope this teaches you a lesson," he said. She leaned forward and her eyes raked his face. She seemed trying to determine his identity. Then, as if she found nothing familiar about him, she started off with a headlong movement in the wrong direction.

"Aren't you going to the Y?" he asked.

"Home," she muttered.

"Well, are we walking?"

For answer she kept going. Julian followed along, his hands behind him. He saw no reason to let the lesson she had had go without backing it up with an explanation of its meaning. She might as well be made to understand what had happened to her. "Don't think that was just an uppity Negro woman," he said. "That was the whole colored race which will no longer take your condescending pennies. That was your black double. She can wear the same hat as you, and to be sure," he added gratuitously (because he thought it was funny), "it looked better on her than it did on you. What all this means," he said, "is that the old world is gone. The old manners are obsolete and your graciousness is not worth a damn." He thought bitterly of the house that had been lost for him. "You aren't who you think you are," he said.

She continued to plow ahead, paying no attention to him. Her hair had come undone on one side. She dropped her pocketbook and took no notice. He stopped and picked it up and handed it to her but she did not take it.

"You needn't act as if the world had come to an end," he said, "because it hasn't. From now on you've got to live in a new world and face a few realities for a change. Buck up," he said, "it won't kill you."

She was breathing fast.

"Let's wait on the bus," he said.

"Home," she said thickly.

"I hate to see you behave like this," he said. "Just like a child. I should be able to expect more of you." He decided to stop where he was and make her stop and wait for a bus. "I'm not going any farther," he said, stopping. "We're going on the bus."

She continued to go on as if she had not heard him. He took a few steps and caught her arm and stopped her. He looked into her face and caught his breath. He was looking into a face he had never seen before. "Tell Grandpa to come get me," she said.

He stared, stricken.

"Tell Caroline to come get me," she said.

Stunned, he let her go and she lurched forward again, walking as if one leg were shorter than the other. A tide of darkness seemed to be sweeping her from him. "Mother!" he cried. "Darling, sweetheart, wait!" Crumpling, she fell to the pavement. He dashed forward and fell at her side, crying, "Mamma, Mamma." He turned her over. Her face was fiercely distorted. One eye, large and staring, moved slightly to the left as if it had become unmoored. The other remained fixed on him, raked his face again, found nothing, and closed.

"Wait here, wait here!" he cried and jumped up and began to run for help toward a cluster of lights he saw in the distance ahead of him. "Help, help!" he shouted, but his voice was thin, scarcely a thread of sound. The lights drifted farther away the faster he ran and his feet moved numbly as if they carried him nowhere. The tide of darkness seemed to sweep him back to her, postponing from moment to moment his entry into the world of guilt and sorrow.

Reading as a Writer

1. Does the balance of scene versus narration remain more or less the same throughout this story?

2. Does the story feel as if it is being "told" too much? Can you find any places in the story that would have been more effective if they'd been "shown" instead of "told"?

3. How would this be a different story if the narration had been minimized and the story rendered primarily through scene?

CHAPTER SIX

Who's Telling This Story?
Point of View

Sometimes you'll want to tell your readers things directly—to narrate things, as we discussed in Chapter 5. And even if you like to keep narrative to a bare minimum, it's almost a given that you'll have *some* telling to do. You might want to set the scene ("the prairie was hot and dry, and the ground shimmered in the heat"), or start or stop the clock of the story ("later that same day," or "ten years passed without incident"). All this requires telling.

To do this telling, or narration, you must have a *narrator*. After all, someone must be telling those parts of the story that can't be witnessed first-hand in scenes. This is called *point of view,* and the point of view is one of the key things you must decide when you sit down and try to get your story onto paper.

This chapter first defines "narrator" and then talks about the different narrative choices you have when settling on a point of view. Next some exercises—complete with student examples—will allow you to practice the different kinds of point of view. Finally, two readings illustrate the different points of view you can choose when writing a story.

Some Basic Definitions

First, let's define "narrator." It's important to understand that only in fiction, a narrator is different from the author. The author is writing the words, but the narrator is the *intelligence* that is *telling the story.* In fiction, the author controls the narrator but is not synonymous with the narrator.

A brief warning: when you read about fiction writing and point of view in many textbooks, the word "narrator" is used in various ways. It's more than a little confusing. Some texts might even tell you that the only stories that have narrators are those with first person narrators (an "I" who is telling the story). For the purposes of this textbook, however, *every* made-up story has a narrator. Even if the story is being told by an invisible and bodiless intelligence that never personally enters the story as a character, and that appears to be godlike in its scope of knowledge, we will refer to that as the narrator. Some people assume and/or insist that it is the author, that we're getting the author's perception of the world. That might be true sometimes. But it's untrue enough of the time in fiction for us never to assume that.

Think of it this way: it's like the relationship between a puppeteer and a puppet. They might sometimes raise their right hands at the same time or move to the left simultaneously, but they are not the same. The author controls the narrator but is not synonymous with him or her.

So what are our choices of narrators? Just three: *first person, second person,* and *third person.* Let's define these terms and look at some examples.

First Person

First person point of view is possibly the most popular point of view for beginning writers. With it, the narrative is being told by an actual character within the piece, an "I." This character is made up, not real. In fiction, we never assume that it's the author, even if the narrator tells you, "I am writing this down for you. I am the author."

There are actually two kinds of first person narrators. First, there's a narrator who is *directly* involved in the story, someone who is intimately and obviously affected by what is happening. Second, there's a first person "observer," a character that is standing back, saying, "I have a story to tell you, about something I witnessed, but I was not directly involved."

It's a fine distinction, but let's look at examples of both.

> "Tell me things I won't mind forgetting," she said. "Make it useless stuff or skip it."
>
> I began. I told her insects fly through rain, missing every drop, never getting wet. I told her no one in America owned a tape recorder before Bing Crosby did. I told her the shape of the moon is like a banana—you see it looking full, you're seeing it end-on.
>
> The camera made me self-conscious and I stopped. It was trained on us from a ceiling mount—the kind of camera banks use to photograph robbers. It played our image to the nurses down the hall in Intensive Care. "Go on, girl," she said. "you get used to it."
>
> I had my audience. I went on.
>
> —AMY HEMPEL, "In the Cemetery Where Al Jolson Is Buried"

This is first person of the involved kind. The narrator, a character in Hempel's story (pp. 529–535), is telling a story that directly involves her. We know, in a story of this kind, to look at the narrator as key to what the story's about; it's "her" story, because all the events and emotions are filtered through her point of view. We're interested, ultimately, in the impact of the events of the story on the narrator, because that's where our attention is focused. It's pretty unambiguous in that regard.

Now a famous example of a detached first person narrator:

> In my younger and more vulnerable years my father gave me some advice that I've been turning over in my mind ever since.

"Whenever you feel like criticizing any one," he told me, "just remember that all the people in this world haven't had the advantages that you've had."

He didn't say any more, but we've always been unusually communicative in a reserved way, and I understood that he meant a great deal more than that. In consequence, I'm inclined to reserve all judgments, a habit that has opened up many curious natures to me, and also made me the victim of not a few veteran bores. The abnormal mind is quick to detect and attach itself to this quality when it appears in a normal person, and so it came about that in college I was unjustly accused of being a politician, because I was privy to the secret griefs of wild, unknown men. Most of the confidences were unsought—frequently, I have feigned sleep, preoccupation, or a hostile levity when I realized by some unmistakable sign that an intimate revelation was quivering on the horizon; for the intimate revelations of young men, or at least the terms in which they express them, are usually plagiaristic and marred by obvious suppressions. Reserving judgments is a matter of infinite hope. I am still a little afraid of missing something if I forget that, as my father snobbishly suggested, and I snobbishly repeat, a sense of the fundamental decencies is parceled out unequally at birth.

And, after boasting this way of my tolerance, I come to the admission that it has a limit. Conduct may be founded on the hard rock or the wet marshes, but after a certain point I don't care what it's founded on. When I came back from the East last autumn I felt that I wanted the world to be in uniform and at a sort of moral attention forever; I wanted no more riotous excursions with privileged glimpses into the human heart.   —F. SCOTT FITZGERALD, *The Great Gatsby*

Probably every American, at one point or another, has read *The Great Gatsby*—most of us for the first time in high school. We tend to remember it as the story of the doomed love affair between the mysterious, flamboyant Gatsby and the beautiful (and married) Daisy, and we sometimes forget it's told by a first person narrator, Nick, a distant cousin of Daisy who is a transplant from the Midwest and who witnesses the entire riotous affair. It's a terrific example of a *detached* first person narrator.

Whose Story Is It?

Now here's the important part. Whose story is it when we have a first person narrator? This is an important question, and one that invariably comes up when we analyze a story.

What do we mean when we ask that question? We're asking, who are we primarily focused upon, who does the piece end up being *about*? The answer with an involved first person narrator is easy: the narrator. It's about him or her. But what about first person observer, you might ask? And the answer one comes back to, almost inevitably, even with the most detached first person narrators, is that the piece is ultimately about that narrator. Nick in *The Great Gatsby* is detached. In the opening section shown above, as we saw, he goes to great lengths to talk about his propensity to be told the stories of "wild, unknown men" and boasts about his tolerance for being an observer of all sorts of humanity. You might say he pats himself on the back a little bit about his abilities as a detached, non-judgmental listener (even as he makes judgments all over the place—to the point of saying that some of his confidants have "abnormal minds"). A little later in the book he says, "Everyone suspects himself of at least one of the cardinal virtues, and this is mine: I am one of the few honest people that I have ever known."

As it turns out, the book really revolves around Nick. Despite all his disclaimers that he's just an innocent bystander, it's about Nick's involvement in the events of the summer and his propensity to fool himself by calling himself honest. By the end of the book, it's the impact of the events on *Nick* that matters—on his moral fiber, on his ability to think honestly about himself.

This is one of the conventions of modern creative writing, and I cannot think of many exceptions. When you have a first person narrator, when you have a character telling a story—no matter how detached or impartial he or she seems to be—it's *that* person's story. Somehow, it's the effect on that narrator that is the important thing—even when the events being observed are as dramatic as in *The Great Gatsby*. Otherwise, why filter it, unless there's a point to having it filtered? Why not just tell it from a straight third person point of view?

Here's another first person narrator from a short story by Richard Shelton in which the narrator starts out being very present but ends up dropping out of the story altogether:

> I love to go out on summer nights and watch the stones grow. I think they grow better here in the desert, where it is warm and dry, than almost anywhere else. Or perhaps it is only that the young ones are more active here.
>
> Young stones tend to move about more than their elders consider good for them. Most young stones have a secret desire which their parents had before them but have forgotten ages ago. And because this desire involves water, it is never mentioned. The older stones disapprove of water and say, "Water is a gadfly who never stays in one place long enough to learn anything." But the young stones try to work themselves into a position, slowly and without their elders noticing it, in which a sizable stream of water during a summer storm might catch them broadside and unknowing, so to speak, and push them along over a slope or down an arroyo. In spite of the danger this involves, they want to travel and see something of the world and settle in a new place, far from home, where they can raise their own dynasties away from the domination of their parents.
>
> And although family ties are very strong among stones, many of the more daring ones have succeeded, and they carry scars to prove to their children that they once went on a journey, helter-skelter and high water, and traveled perhaps fifteen feet, an incredible distance. As they grow older, they cease to brag about such clandestine adventures.
>
> It is true that old stones get to be very conservative. They consider all movement either dangerous or downright sinful. They remain comfortable where they are and often get fat. Fatness, as a matter of fact, is a mark of distinction.

> And on summer nights, after the young stones are asleep, the elders turn to a serious and frightening subject—the moon, which is always spoken of in whispers. "See how it glows and whips across the sky, always changing its shape," one says. And another says, "Feel how it pulls at us, urging us to follow." And a third whispers, "It is a stone gone mad."
>
> —Richard Shelton, "The Stones"

Why did Shelton make the narrator first person? Why not tell this straight third person ("Stones grow better in the desert, where it is warm and dry, than almost anywhere else")? Because this story is, ultimately, about the narrator's experience of the stones, about his or her (we never know the sex of the narrator) own thoughts and fantasies about what stones believe and feel and act like. The story has meaning because of what is *projected* onto the stones by the first person narrator.

Here's an interesting variation on first person narration: *plural* first person (i.e., there's a group of people telling the story). *"We did this, we saw that."* This is relatively rare, but here are two examples:

> Whenever we saw Mrs. Lisbon we looked in vain for some sign of the beauty that must have once been hers. But the plump arms, the brutally cut steel-wool hair, and the librarian's glasses foiled us every time. We saw her only rarely, in the morning, fully dressed though the sun hadn't come up, stepping out to snatch up the dewy milk cartons, or on Sundays when the family drove in their paneled station wagon.   —Jeffrey Eugenides, *The Virgin Suicides*

> When Miss Emily Grierson died, our whole town went to her funeral: the men through a sort of respectful affection for a fallen monument, the women mostly out of curiosity to see the inside of her house, which no one save an old manservant—a combined gardener and cook—had seen in at least ten years.
>
> —William Faulkner, "A Rose for Emily"

As always, our eye is on the first person narrator when figuring out what the story is about. Just because in these examples it's a *group* of people (in the first case, a group of young men who have worshipped a family of girls from afar; in the second, an entire town that has been interested in an eccentric old woman for decades) doesn't alter that basic rule: it's the narrators' story, ultimately. This is one of the strongest conventions of fiction writing: when in doubt, in a first person story, look at the narrator for clues as to what the story is really about.

Second Person

Second person is one of the more complex points of view, and it is much less common. In second person, the narrator speaks via a "you," who can be one of four types of characters:

1. The "you" is actually an *inverted* form of first person. That is, it is a first person narrator referring to himself or herself as "you"—usually in an effort to disassoci-

ate himself or herself from distasteful thoughts, actions, or memories. For example, "You really don't like yourself very much when you act like this."

2. The "you" refers to a specific character, so that the piece, in effect, becomes a monologue addressed to a person or persons. For example, "David, you didn't realize how much damage you could cause; you obviously weren't thinking when you stole that letter from my desk."

3. The "you" is a direct address to the reader: "And you people, you who are reading this book . . ."

4. The "you" can also, occasionally, be an attempt to turn the reader into an active character in the story. "You walk into the room. You are aware that something is wrong. You can't figure out what it is."

Let's look at each of these second person narrators in turn.

The *inverted first person* is, in fact, the most frequent use of this type of point of view:

> You're not the kind of guy who would be at a place like this at this time of the morning. But here you are, and you cannot say that the terrain is entirely unfamiliar, although the details are fuzzy. You are at a nightclub talking to a girl with a shaved head. The club is either Heartbreak or the Lizard Lounge. All might come clear if you could just slip into the bathroom and do a little more Bolivian Marching Powder. Then again, it might not. A small voice inside you insists that this epidemic lack of clarity is a result of too much of that already. The night has already turned on that imperceptible pivot where 2 a.m. changes to 6 a.m. You know this moment has come and gone, but you are not yet willing to concede that you have crossed the line beyond which all is gratuitous damage and the palsy of unraveled nerve endings.
>
> —Jay McInerney, *Bright Lights, Big City*

This famous example of second person has a narrator who is so distanced from himself, so psychologically removed from his actions (and wanting so much not to take responsibility for them), that he refers to himself as "you."

The next use of second person, that of *direct address to a specific character* or characters, is used in stories that are written as either oral monologues or letters. Here is an example:

> You must be aware, first, that because Susan is my girlfriend pretty much everything she discusses with you she also discusses with me. She tells me what she said and what you said. We have been seeing each other for about six months now and I am pretty familiar with her story, or stories. Similarly, with your responses, at least the general pattern. I know, for example, that my habit of referring to you as "the sandman" annoys you but let me assure you that I mean nothing unpleasant by it. It is simply a nickname. The reference is to the old rhyme: "Sea-sand does the sandman bring / Sleep to end the day / He dusts the children's eyes with sand / And steals their dreams away."
>
> —Donald Barthelme, "The Sandman"

Notice that here, too, there's a first person narrator involved in this form of second person. Even if the first person narrator is hidden behind the "you"—even if the words "I" or "me" never appear—he or she is there, close by. In this very funny story, the first person narrator is a man who is writing a letter to his girlfriend's psychiatrist.

The third example of second person is also usually a first person narrator who has slipped temporarily into second person; nineteenth-century novelists, for example, were fond of occasionally *addressing the reader directly*. But this is usually not sustained beyond a sentence or two. For example: "Dear reader, you might be wondering what happened; yes, I married him!"

The fourth type of second person—in which *you, the reader, become a character in the story*—is very rare in fiction, although it is seen quite frequently in nonfiction, particularly in feature journalism as published in daily papers and monthly magazines. Here's an example:

> You are always in danger in the forest, where no people are. Step between the portals of the great pines where the shaggy branches tangle about you, trapping the unwary traveler in nets as if the vegetation itself were in plot with the wolves who live there, as though the wicked trees go fishing on behalf of their friends—step between the gateposts of the forest with the great trepidation and infinite precautions, for if you stray from the path for one instant, the wolves will eat you. They are grey as famine, they are as unkind as plague.
> —ANGELA CARTER, "The Company of Wolves"

In the example above, you are being instructed to step through the forest and warned, directly, of the dangers if you should do so.

Second person point of view is not widely used. It can work, but it's a little gimmicky and runs the danger of getting tiresome except in shorter pieces. Still, you can experiment with it, and see what you think for yourself.

Third Person

Third person point of view is the most complex point of view. In it, the narrator is a disembodied intelligence who does *not* appear directly in the piece as a character. Rather, he or she exists above the story, observing it from outside.

Third person point of view is actually a continuum of possible narrators, based on how much the third person narrator *knows*. Let's look at this continuum of knowledge as it pertains to point of view:

```
                    ┌─────────── Limited Third Person ───────────┐
                    │                                            │
Omniscient          └────────────────────────────────────────────┘         Direct Observer

Godlike                                                                     Fly on Wall
```

At one end is unlimited knowledge, an omniscient narrator. He or she sees all, knows all: knows what characters are thinking, what they are feeling, what happened in the past, what will happen in the future. This is a godlike being with unlimited powers of observation and knowledge of the world of the story.

Anything to the right of this is a *limited third person* narrator, someone whose knowledge has been limited in some way. A limited third person narrator might only be able to see what one character is thinking or feeling; or may only know what characters are thinking, not what they are feeling; or may only have knowledge of the past, but no knowledge of the future. There are many ways that a narrator's knowledge can be limited.

At the far right side of the continuum is the most *limited* knowledge. Called a "direct observer," this kind of third person narrator is like a fly on the wall—he or she can see and hear what is going on, but that's it: no power to read into characters' hearts or minds, no power to interpret thoughts or explain emotions, no power to explain history or predict the future.

Exactly where on this continuum your third person narrator resides—if you choose this point of view—is completely up to you. And as you'll see, this opens up a lot of potential choices.

Let's look at some examples of these different kinds of third person narrators.

> Elizabeth listened in silence, but was not convinced; their behavior at the assembly had not been calculated to please in general; and with more quickness of observation and less pliancy of temper than her sister, and with a judgment too unassailed by any attention to herself, she was very little disposed to approve them.
>
> They were in fact very fine ladies, not deficient in good humour when they were pleased, not in the power of being agreeable when they chose it, but proud and conceited. They were rather handsome, had been educated in one of the first private seminaries in town, had a fortune of twenty thousand pounds, were in the habit of spending more than they ought, and of associating with people of rank, and were therefore in every respect entitled to think well of themselves, and meanly of others. They were of a respectable family in the north of England; a circumstance more deeply impressed on their memories than that their brother's fortune and their own had been acquired by trade.
>
> Mr. Bingley inherited property to the amount of nearly a hundred thousand pounds from his father, who had intended to purchase an estate, but did not live to do it. Mr. Bingley intended it likewise, and sometimes made choice of his county; but as he was now provided with a good house and the liberty of a manor, it was doubtful to many of those who best knew the easiness of his temper, whether he might not spend the remainder of his days at Netherfield, and leave the next generation to purchase.
>
> His sisters were very anxious for his having an estate of his own; but, though he was now established only as a tenant, Miss Bingley was by no means unwill-

ing to preside at his table—nor was Mrs. Hurst, who had married a man of more fashion than fortune, less disposed to consider his house as her home when it suited her.   —JANE AUSTEN, *Pride and Prejudice*

Pride and Prejudice is a wonderful example of omniscient third person point of view: we see into the minds and lives of a broad range of characters. There seems to be no limit to the powers of this narrator.

At the other end of the continuum is the "direct observer." Let's look again at "Hills Like White Elephants":

> The hills across the valley of the Ebro were long and white. On this side there was no shade and no trees and the station was between two lines of rails in the sun. Close against the side of the station there was the warm shadow of the building and a curtain, made of strings of bamboo beads, hung across the open door into the bar, to keep out flies. The American and the girl with him sat at a table in the shade, outside the building. It was very hot and the express from Barcelona would come in forty minutes. It stopped at this junction for two minutes and went on to Madrid.
>
> —ERNEST HEMINGWAY, "Hills Like White Elephants"

It is unusual to have narrators this limited. Most narrators, especially in short fiction, are closer to the middle of the continuum.

But here is another case where many of the books about writing don't serve you very well: as we explained above, there are many variations of limited third person narrators. Yet in most writing books, limited third person is said to be the case when the knowledge of the narrator is limited to the heart and mind of a single character. But there are many ways that a narrator's knowledge can be less than that possessed by an omniscient narrator. Here are just a few:

1. It can be limited to just the *thoughts* of a character, but not the emotions.

2. It can see beyond those thoughts and actually perceive the *emotions*.

3. It can peek into the *subconscious*—things that the character(s) are not aware of— but not have any powers to relate past events.

Or any variation thereof. All limited third person means is that the writer has chosen to limit the knowledge of the narrator in some way.

Let's look at some examples of limited third person narrators.

> Now is the time for drastic action. He contemplates taking Wayne's hand, then checks himself. He has never done anything in her presence to indicate that the sexuality he confessed to five years ago was a reality and not an invention. Even now, he and Wayne might as well be friends, college roommates. Then Wayne, his savior, with a single, sweeping gesture, reaches for his hand, and clasps it, in the midst of a joke he is telling about Saudi Arabians. By the time he is laughing, their hands are joined. Neil's throat contracts; his heart begins to beat violently. He notices his mother's eyes flicker, glance downward; she

never breaks the stride of her sentence. The dinner goes on and every taboo nurtured since childhood falls quietly away.   —DAVID LEAVITT, "Territory"

Here we're limited to the heart and mind of a single character—the other characters are opaque to us; we cannot see through the surface of their external behavior. This is the most common type of limited third person narrator.

Below is another example of a third person limited narrator. In this one the character that the narrator is limited to observing changes as the story progresses; the narrative insight into thoughts and emotions is passed from one character to another. See how it starts out third person omniscient, then turns into third person limited for one character after another:

> None of them knew the color of the sky. Their eyes glanced level, and were fastened upon the waves that swept toward them. These waves were of the hue of slate, save for the tops, which were of foaming white, and all of the men knew the colors of the sea. The horizon narrowed and widened and dipped and rose, and at all times its edge was jagged with waves that seemed thrust up in points like rocks.
>
> Many a man ought to have a bath-tub larger than the boat which here rode upon the sea. These waves were most wrongfully and barbarously abrupt and tall, and each froth-top was a problem in small boat navigation.
>
> The cook squatted in the bottom and looked with both eyes at the six inches of gunwale which separated him from the ocean. His sleeves were rolled over his fat forearms, and the two flaps of his unbuttoned vest dangled as he bent to bail out the boat. Often he said: "Gawd! That was a narrow clip." As he remarked it he invariably gazed eastward over the broken sea.
>
> The oiler, steering with one of the two oars in the board, sometimes raised himself suddenly to keep clear of water that swirled in over the stern. It was a thin little boat and it seemed often ready to snap.
>
> The correspondent, pulling at the other oar, watched the waves and wondered why he was there.
>
> The injured captain, lying in the bow, was at this time buried in that profound dejection and indifference which comes, temporarily, at least, to even the bravest and most enduring when, willy nilly, the firm fails, the army loses, the ship goes down.   —STEPHEN CRANE, "The Open Boat"

You can see how the narrator "travels" from one character to another, giving us information about each one in equal parts. There's another interesting limitation that the author has chosen: the third person narrator cannot give us any information about the world of the story other than what is happening on the boat. This is not a narrator who can tell us, "Not far away, on shore, a group of men was preparing a rescue mission." No, this narrator is physically rooted in a particular place and time, and so our knowledge of the world of the story is limited in that way.

Here's another way to think about this whole idea of knowledge as it pertains to third person narrators: think of it as standing in a house that borders a big open field.

With an omniscient narrator, you are standing in front of a large clear window that allows you to view a scene that stretches for miles in every direction. With limited third person narrator, you have a smaller window that gives you access to a smaller view of the world of the story. The more limited your narrator, the smaller your window, and the less you can see (and hear, feel, etc.).

A Word about Attitude

It's important to understand that a third person narrator doesn't have to be a middle-of-the-road, "objective" reporter of what goes on. He or she can have *attitude,* judgment; this narrator can comment editorially on what is happening, approve or disapprove of what characters are like. "She was a rubbishy little creature and she knew it" is a wonderful line of third person narrative from E. M. Forster's *Howards End.* Likewise, "he, his hands behind him, appeared pinned to the door frame, waiting like Saint Sebastian for the arrows to begin piercing him," is a very funny observation of a character by one of Flannery O'Connor's third person narrators. And we are given judgments of nearly all of Jane Austin's characters by a decidely non-impartial ominiscient narrator. Indeed, your omniscient narrator doesn't need to be unbiased and neutral. He or she can have opinions and express them freely—even to the point of liking or disdaining individual characters or the actions they engage in.

So give your third person narrators *personality:* a Texas accent; opinions about the world, about politics. Whatever you choose is fair game.

Distance and Point of View

It's important to understand that it's not just knowledge that affects your point of view. Distance is also a factor. In other words, a narrator, in addition to knowing more or less about the world of the story, can be at greater or lesser distance from it.

A very popular point of view these days, especially in short stories, is *close* third person point of view. (It's also referred to as *third person intimate.*) This occurs when the narrator is so close to the action that the narration can be indistinguishable from first person.

Let's first look at some examples of close third person narrators. Note that the relative closeness of a narrator is independent of the *knowledge* that narrator possesses. You can have a very limited third person narrator who is far from the story, or an omniscient narrator who is very close to the action of the story. Let's examine the examples below in terms of both knowledge and distance.

> Although Bertha Young was thirty she still had moments like this when she wanted to run instead of walk, to take dancing steps on and off the pavement, to bowl a hoop, to throw something up in the air and catch it again, or to stand still and laugh at—nothing—at nothing, simply.
>
> What can you do if you are thirty and, turning the corner of your own street you are overcome, suddenly, by a feeling of bliss—absolute bliss!—as though

you'd suddenly swallowed a bright piece of that late afternoon sun and it burned in your bosom, sending out a little shower of sparks into every particle, into every finger and toe . . . ?

Oh, is there no way you can express it without being "drunk and disorderly"? How idiotic civilization is! Why be given a body if you have to keep it shut up in a case like a rare, rare fiddle?   —KATHERINE MANSFIELD, "Bliss"

This story has a close limited third person narrator—a narrator who happens to be limited (in knowledge) to the thoughts and feelings of just one character, but who is very, very close to that character—so close as to be practically identical to first person at certain times in the text. The last paragraph, for example, has no "she thought" attached to the text, yet these are clearly the thoughts of the character; that shows how deeply embedded we are in this character's mind.

Here's another example:

The dream was set in Shady Hill—she dreamed that she woke in her own bed. Donald was always gone. She was at once aware of the fact that the bomb had exploded. Mattress stuffing and a trickle of brown water were coming through a big hole in the ceiling. The sky was gray—lightless—although there were in the west a few threads of red light, like those charming vapor trails we see in the air after the sun has set. She didn't know if these were vapor trails or some part of that force that would destroy the marrow in her bones. The gray air seemed final. The sky would never shine with light again. From her window she could see a river, and now, as she watched, boats began to come upstream. At first, there were only two or three. Then there were tens, and then there were hundreds. There were outboards, excursion boats, yachts, schooners with auxiliary motors; there were even rowboats. The number of boats grew until the water was covered with them, and the noise of motors rose to a loud din. The jockeying for position in this retreat up the river became aggressive, then savage.   —JOHN CHEEVER, "The Wrysons"

This happens to be an omniscient narrator (you can't tell from this passage, but the narrator can see into the hearts and minds of all the characters in the story) who is also very, very close: so close that we melt into the reality of Irene Wryson's dream just as if it were reality.

Now what about this example?

Christina Goering's father was an American industrialist of German parentage and her mother was a New York lady of a very distinguished family. Christina spent the first half of her life in a very beautiful house (not more than an hour from the city) which she had inherited from her mother. It was in this house that she had been brought up as a child with her sister Sophie.

As a child Christina had been very much disliked by other children. She had never suffered particularly because of this, having led, even at a very early age, an active inner life that curtailed her observation of whatever went on around her, to such a degree that she never picked up the mannerisms then in vogue, and at the age of ten was called old-fashioned by other little girls. Even then she wore the look of certain fanatics who think of themselves as leaders without once having gained the respect of a single human being.

Christina was troubled horribly by ideas which never would have occurred to her companions, and at the same time took for granted a position in society which any other child would have found unbearable. Every now and then a schoolmate would take pity on her and try to spend some time with her, but far from being grateful for this, Christina would instead try her best to convert her new friend to the cult of whatever she believed in at the time. [. . .] She was in the habit of going through many mental struggles—generally of a religious nature—and she preferred to be with other people and organize games. These games, as a rule, were very moral, and often involved god. However, no one else enjoyed them and she was obliged to spend a great part of the day alone.

—JANE BOWLES, *Two Serious Ladies*

This is a very distant third person omniscient: the narrator sees all, knows all, and is able to make value judgments about the characters. But the tone is very distant despite this omniscience.

To see an example of a very distant, very limited third person narrator, go to page 269 and look at "Hills Like White Elephants." In that piece, not only are we working with the most limited third person narrator possible, but the narrator is also very far removed from the characters.

Shifts in Narrative Distance

The previous section might imply that you have to pick a distance and stick to it throughout a story. Nothing could be further from the truth. In good fiction, shifts in distance are common. They must also be carefully controlled. Often, at the beginning of a story, we find the narrative distance fairly large. Often, distance will decrease—sometimes collapsing to the point of nonexistence—in order to allow the author to more thoroughly investigate the heart or mind of a character. A skillful writer will know how to pan in and pan out, just like a skilled camera operator on a movie set. Consider the following passage:

It was too hot. She went inside the house and turned on the radio to drown out the quiet. She sat on the edge of her bed, barefoot, and listened for an hour and a half to a program called XYZ Sunday Jamboree, record after record of hard, fast, shrieking songs she sang along with, interspersed by exclamations from "Bobby King": "An' look here you girls at Napoleon's—Son and Charley want you to pay real close attention to this song coming up!"

And Connie paid close attention herself, bathed in a glow of slow-pulsed joy that seemed to rise mysteriously out of the music itself and lay languidly about the airless little room, breathed in and breathed out with each gentle rise and fall of her chest.

—JOYCE CAROL OATES, "Where Are You Going, Where Have You Been?"

In this scene from "Where Are You Going, Where Have You Been?" (pp. 40–53), the distance starts out very close ("It was too hot" puts us directly in Connie's mind) but then lengthens, and we pull back a bit to get information about Connie going inside the house and listening to the radio. Then the distance closes in again, putting us right in the heart of Connie, what she's thinking and feeling. This is one of the advantages of third person intimate: you can have all the advantages of first person (being intimate) and still pull back and get more perspective on the larger world.

But it's important to note that sudden shifts in distance can be disconcerting for your readers. If you've been referring to the character as "Doris" and she suddenly becomes "Mrs. Mannerling," that is an obvious sudden shift that will jolt the reader. John Gardner calls this sudden change a problem in "psychic distance":

> Careless shifts in psychic distance can also be distracting. By psychic distance we mean the distance the reader feels between himself and the events in the story. Compare the following examples, the first meant to establish great psychic distance, the next meant to establish slightly less, and so on until in the last example, psychic distance, theoretically at least, is nil.
>
> 1. It was winter of the year 1853. A large man stepped out of a doorway.
> 2. Henry J. Warburton had never much cared for snowstorms.
> 3. Henry hated snowstorms.
> 4. God how he hated these damn snowstorms.
> 5. Snow. Under your collar, down inside your shoes, freezing and plugging up your miserable soul . . .
>
> —JOHN GARDNER, *The Art of Fiction*

The point isn't that narrative distance needs to stay constant, but that shifts in distance need to be carefully managed so as not to jolt the reader out of what Gardner calls "the dream of the story."

Choosing a Point of View

What point of view do you choose? You might hope there is some objective, quantifiable way of choosing, but unfortunately it doesn't work that way. Often, the choice of a point of view is a completely intuitive one; the writer may not know why he or she chose first person, or third person limited, only that the choice is the right one for a particular story.

Still, there are some conventionally accepted pros and cons for each kind of point of view. Let's look at some of them.

First person point of view: The conventionally stated advantage of this is that it provides immediacy, involves the reader, pulls him or her in, is helpful in getting sympathy for the main character (who happens to be the narrator).

The disadvantage of this point of view is its very limited scope. Everything is filtered through only the eyes, ears, and brains of one character.

Another disadvantage: Is it possible to be *too* close to a story? We're going to be talking about unreliable narrators in Chapter 7, but I want to point out that especially when writing about a very emotionally charged situation, putting it in first person can work against you: you can risk losing your reader. Victim stories fall into this category. Sometimes, if you are trying to garner sympathy or understanding for a character, the last thing you want to do is put it in first person. The narrator can be seen as self-serving, or self-pitying. You risk it becoming maudlin. Nothing will eliminate sympathy faster than having to listen to a character whine—even if he or she has been victimized in some horrifying way.

With an *omniscient narrator,* the advantages are that you have the "big window" onto the terrain of the story: your readers can see all, do all, go back to the beginning of time, take time out to give a lecture on nautical knots (*The Shipping News*) or the correct way to skin a whale (*Moby-Dick*) or whatever else you choose.

The conventionally accepted disadvantage of an omniscient narrator is that it can be too much, can give too much information, can distract the reader from what really matters in the story.

Limited third is a very popular choice, especially in the last few decades. The conventional wisdom is that it focuses the reader's attention on what matters, narrows down the scope of the story to make it manageable. And, of course, by using shifts in narrative distance you can easily get into the heart and mind of a character, just like first person, yet you have the advantage of pulling back (panning the camera, if you will) to show readers more of the world of the story.

Again, keep in mind that the amount of knowledge you give the narrator (either unlimited, as in omniscient, or very limited, as in direct observer or first person) is separate from the distance that narrator can invoke in the tone. Just because very close third person narrators are generally linked to those that are limited in knowledge doesn't mean that you have to follow that route. You can choose a limited third person narrator who is distant from the events of the story, or an omniscient narrator who is extremely close to the events. It's up to you.

Interestingly enough, an oft-heard piece of advice in creative writing workshops is to "change the point of view," as if changing the point of view is a panacea for all sorts of problems. Sometimes this advice has to do with the narrative *distance:* readers feel uncomfortable with the distance that the narrator has from the events in the story (either too close or too distant) and think that changing the point of view will fix that. But distance is independent of knowledge. Even first person point of view can be distant if the character is alienated from himself or herself. Here's an example to prove this point:

> I sat down in the waiting area across the hall. In forty-five minutes the nurse came out and said to me, "Michelle is comfortable now."
> "Is she dead?"
> "Of course not."
> "I kind of wish she was."

She looked frightened. "I don't know what you mean."

I went in through the curtain to see Michelle. She smelled bad.

"How are you feeling?"

"I feel fine."

"What did they stick up you?"

"What?" she said. "*What?*"

The nurse said, "Hey. Out of here. Out of here."

She went through the curtain and came back with a big black guy wearing a starched white shirt and one of those phony gold badges. "I don't think this man needs to be in the building," she said to him, and then she said to me, "Would you like to wait outside, sir?"

"Yeah yeah yeah," I said, and all the way down the big stairs and out the front I said "Yeah yeah yeah yeah yeah yeah yeah."

It was raining outdoors and most of the Catholics were squashed up under an awning next door with their signs held overhead against the weather. They splashed holy water on my cheek and on the back of my neck, and I didn't feel a thing. Not for many years.   —DENIS JOHNSON, "Dirty Wedding"

In this passage we have a first person narrator who is so distanced from his own thoughts and emotions that he's put up a shield against allowing any feelings to seep into his consciousness. We're kept at a distance because he keeps himself at a distance.

Common Point of View Problems

One of the most common ways to break with point of view conventions is to tell a story from one point of view and then suddenly shift to another. For instance, if we're following the action of a story from the point of view of one of the characters and suddenly find out what one of the other characters is thinking or feeling, that can be very disconcerting. In general, once you establish your narrative point of view, you should stick with it. The point isn't to follow some esoteric rule, but to avoid jolting your readers out of the story. Of course, you can find stories—good stories—in which the point of view shifts, say from one kind of limited third person to another kind of limited third person. In such cases, we assume that the author felt it important enough to risk jolting the reader to get some additional information into the text. Does it work? Does the author get away with it? Only the reader can say.

Here's an example of a shift in point of view that might be considered an error:

Claire sat on the bus, wringing her hands and trying not to cry. This was going to be her first time away from home, and she was already homesick. Already the lure of camp from reading those brochures was fading. She moved slightly in her seat to allow room for a young man about her own age who was carrying what looked to be a heavy satchel. He looked at Claire and felt pity, so he took out of his pocket a piece of chocolate and offered it to her.

Do you see how we suddenly shift from a third person point of view limited to Claire to one that includes insight into what the young man is feeling? Whether this is an error or something that adds to the story is only something that readers of the complete story can decide. The "point of view police" will always decry this sort of shift, but the fact remains that many fine stories embody shifts of this kind. It's entirely about what you can get away with.

Of course, if you have a first person narrator and suddenly give information, or access to a conversation or a letter or a phone call that your narrator has no way of knowing about, that's a pretty obvious error. You must either cut it or figure out some way of getting that information filtered through your narrator. For example, she might overhear a telephone conversation; or he might be told about an argument; or she might read someone else's letter.

In terms of more subtle errors, all of a sudden the narrator might make a value judgment or a leap of logic that is markedly different from what he or she was capable of before, *for no plausible reason. Caution:* I'm not saying a character has to be consistent, that's something else altogether. Your character can act in different ways at different times for myriad reasons. Your character can grow, change, regress. But if there's an *implausible* leap of knowledge or insight or wisdom by a character with a previously limited point of view, that could be a point of view problem.

Keep in mind that this is just an introduction to point of view, which is a marvelously complex topic. We'll continue on in Chapter 7 when we talk about point of view and *reliability*.

EXERCISES

Choosing the point of view is one of the most important things you will do when writing a story. You have many choices—although sometimes it won't feel like a choice. Sometimes you'll just make a leap of faith when it comes to the point of view. Other times, you'll need to question it, explore, and experiment.

Exercise 1: Changing Point of View: Experiments in Narration

GOAL: To show you how changing the point of view dramatically affects how the material reads. (It's not just a case of doing a universal search and replace of "I" for "he" or "she." Different things enter or come out of the material depending on the point of view that you use.)

1. Pick an incident that happened to you in the past month or so—something that has stuck in your mind, although for what reason you're not quite sure.

2. Tell about the event in three different ways: first person point of view, second person point of view, and third person *omniscient* point of view.

The following passage was written by Steven Marvin:

I was sitting at the bus station waiting for a bus downtown. My wife was with me, we were going to a department store to buy stuff for our child, who was to be born in about six weeks. I still hadn't gotten used to the sight of my wife's swollen belly, and the fact that *I* had done that to her—sometimes I felt like I was going to get into trouble, that I had done something really, really wrong—when I felt a sharp pain in my stomach. Really sharp, like a knife pushing in from the outside. I doubled over in pain. My wife, of course, was very concerned, and actually knelt down in front of me, her great belly brushing against the dirty floor of the station.

You are sitting in a bus station. You are with your wife. She is heavy with your child. You've done enough reading to know that bad things lie ahead for her. And you're getting off scot free. Today is what you've come in your mind to call "D-Day. You've agreed to buy the diapers, and the underwear, and the clothes, and all the other things you'll need to bring the baby home from the hospital. You've already been given a ton of stuff by friends and family. Then suddenly there is a pain in your stomach. Is this what giving birth is like, you wonder briefly, but not for long; the pain is too intense. Your immensely pregnant wife is kneeling on the dirty linoleum floor in front of you. You can hardly breathe. What is happening?

The young couple was sitting quietly together in the bus terminal. You would have thought they'd been married for decades, the way they leaned against each other calmly, no passion or excitement, just calm support. The woman was very pregnant. She looked happy, but a little worried; her hands clasped her backpack hard and occasionally she swallowed hard. It was hard to guess at what the young man was thinking. He wore a zipped-up black sweatshirt with the hood up over his head, making him look a little like a pointy-headed elf. He was carrying a shopping bag that seemed to be filled with papers. Occasionally, he reached out with his right hand and brushed his knuckles against the cheekbone of his wife. Then, suddenly, he bent over, grabbing his stomach. The woman panicked, first standing up, letting her backpack slide to the floor, then bending down over her husband, and finally kneeling before him in a supplicating manner.

Exercise 2: Using Point of View as a Way "In" to Difficult Material

GOAL: To play with point of view as a way to gain access to material that has previously been difficult to write about.

1. Pick an incident or event that you've tried to write about, or that you've hesitated to write about because it is so personal or difficult.

2. First, write it in the first person point of view. Just write it straight out, no matter how difficult (or how poor a job you might think you're doing).

3. Now write it in third person omniscient point of view, meaning that there is a narrator who knows all and sees all and who is commenting on what is happen-

ing according to the "truth" of the incident. Don't be shy about making judgments or otherwise commenting on the thoughts or actions of your characters; a third person omniscient narrator, after all, sees all and knows all.

Here's a passage from John Garcia:

I've been trying to write about the stroke my father had about a month ago. It wasn't a severe one; he's getting all his faculties back, his slowed speech is just temporary, the doctors say, but it was still scary and it was a wake-up call. He's seventy-four, but I'd been used to thinking of him as immortal. The bastard. The same bastard who'd made my life miserable growing up. Things have calmed down a lot lately, of course. We no longer fight—what's there to fight about? My tattoos are there, they're not going anywhere; I no longer use all the piercings in my body, just my right ear, and of course I have a good job. The fact that I still lead what he considered a rootless existence is a sticking point, but when I drop by to visit he actually seems glad to see me. I think he's bored in his retirement. Terribly bored. He was always so full of energy, but now he just naps on the couch and flips through the channels of his satellite TV.

John's first view of his father after the stroke was a terrifying one: his father, the strong, the mighty, the invincible, lying quiet and still in the hospital room. Asleep. He was drooling out of the right side of his mouth. His left arm was thrown up against his chest, as though he was warding off some attack. John's heart throbbed with pity and anger. The old bastard. He sat down. His mother was holding his father's hand. She had stopped crying, but she was far from calm. What would she do if he died? She didn't even know where the checkbook was. She didn't know their credit card companies—he took care of all that. John felt a sudden sharp stab of fear and loss as he began to comprehend what this could mean for his mother—and for him.

READINGS

Anton Chekhov

The Lady with the Little Dog

Translated by Richard Pevear and Larissa Volokhonsky

I

THE TALK was that a new face had appeared on the embankment: a lady with a little dog. Dmitri Dmitrich Gurov, who had already spent two weeks in Yalta and was used to it, also began to take an interest in new faces. Sitting in a pavilion at Vernet's, he saw a young woman, not very tall, blond, in a beret, walking along the embankment; behind her ran a white spitz.

And after that he met her several times a day in the town garden or in the square. She went strolling alone, in the same beret, with the white spitz; nobody knew who she was, and they called her simply "the lady with the little dog."

"If she's here with no husband or friends," Gurov reflected, "it wouldn't be a bad idea to make her acquaintance."

He was not yet forty, but he had a twelve-year-old daughter and two sons in school. He had married young, while still a second-year student, and now his wife seemed half again his age. She was a tall woman with dark eyebrows, erect, impos- ing, dignified, and a thinking person, as she called herself. She read a great deal, used the new orthography, called her husband not Dmitri but Dimitri, but he secretly con- sidered her none too bright, narrow-minded, graceless, was afraid of her, and dis- liked being at home. He had begun to be unfaithful to her long ago, was unfaithful often, and, probably for that reason, almost always spoke ill of women, and when they were discussed in his presence, he would say of them:

"An inferior race!"

It seemed to him that he had been taught enough by bitter experience to call them anything he liked, and yet he could not have lived without the "inferior race" even for two days. In the company of men he was bored, ill at ease, with them he was tac- iturn and cold, but when he was among women, he felt himself free and knew what to talk about with them and how to behave; and he was at ease even being silent with them. In his appearance, in his character, in his whole nature there was something attractive and elusive that disposed women towards him and enticed them; he knew that, and he himself was attracted to them by some force.

Repeated experience, and bitter experience indeed, had long since taught him that every intimacy, which in the beginning lends life such pleasant diversity and presents itself as a nice and light adventure, inevitably, with decent people—especially irres- olute Muscovites, who are slow starters—grows into a major task, extremely compli- cated, and the situation finally becomes burdensome. But at every new meeting with an interesting woman, this experience somehow slipped from his memory, and he wanted to live, and everything seemed quite simple and amusing.

And so one time, towards evening, he was having dinner in the garden, and the lady in the beret came over unhurriedly to take the table next to his. Her expression, her walk, her dress, her hair told him that she belonged to decent society, was mar- ried, in Yalta for the first time, and alone, and that she was bored here. . . In the sto- ries about the impurity of local morals there was much untruth, he despised them and knew that these stories were mostly invented by people who would eagerly have sinned themselves had they known how; but when the lady sat down at the next table, three steps away from him, he remembered those stories of easy conquests, of trips to the mountains, and the tempting thought of a quick, fleeting liaison, a romance with an unknown woman, of whose very name you are ignorant, suddenly took possession of him.

He gently called the spitz, and when the dog came over, he shook his finger at it. The spitz growled. Gurov shook his finger again.

The lady glanced at him and immediately lowered her eyes.

"He doesn't bite," she said and blushed.

"May I give him a bone?" and, when she nodded in the affirmative, he asked affably: "Have you been in Yalta long?"

"About five days."

"And I'm already dragging through my second week here."

They were silent for a while.

"The time passes quickly, and yet it's so boring here!" she said without looking at him.

"It's merely the accepted thing to say it's boring here. The ordinary man lives somewhere in his Belevo or Zhizdra and isn't bored, then he comes here: 'Ah, how boring! Ah, how dusty!' You'd think he came from Granada."

She laughed. Then they went on eating in silence, like strangers; but after dinner they walked off together—and a light, bantering conversation began, of free, contented people, who do not care where they go or what they talk about. They strolled and talked of how strange the light was on the sea; the water was of a lilac color, so soft and warm, and over it the moon cast a golden strip. They talked of how sultry it was after the hot day. Gurov told her he was a Muscovite, a philologist by education, but worked in a bank; had once been preparing to sing in an opera company, but had dropped it, owned two houses in Moscow . . . And from her he learned that she grew up in Petersburg, but was married in S., where she had now been living for two years, that she would be staying in Yalta for about a month, and that her husband might come to fetch her, because he also wanted to get some rest. She was quite unable to explain where her husband served—in the provincial administration or the zemstvo[1] council—and she herself found that funny. And Gurov also learned that her name was Anna Sergeevna.

Afterwards, in his hotel room, he thought about her, that tomorrow she would probably meet him again. It had to be so. Going to bed, he recalled that still quite recently she had been a schoolgirl, had studied just as his daughter was studying now, recalled how much timorousness and angularity there was in her laughter, her conversation with a stranger—it must have been the first time in her life that she was alone in such a situation, when she was followed, looked at, and spoken to with only one secret purpose, which she could not fail to guess. He recalled her slender, weak neck, her beautiful gray eyes.

"There's something pathetic in her all the same," he thought and began to fall asleep.

II

A week had passed since they became acquainted. It was Sunday. Inside it was stuffy, but outside the dust flew in whirls, hats blew off. They felt thirsty all day, and Gurov often stopped at the pavilion, offering Anna Sergeevna now a soft drink, now ice cream. There was no escape.

1. County council.

In the evening when it relented a little, they went to the jetty to watch the steamer come in. There were many strollers on the pier; they had come to meet people, they were holding bouquets. And here two particularities of the smartly dressed Yalta crowd distinctly struck one's eye: the elderly ladies were dressed like young ones, and there were many generals.

Owing to the roughness of the sea, the steamer arrived late, when the sun had already gone down, and it was a long time turning before it tied up. Anna Sergeevna looked at the ship and the passengers through her lorgnette, as if searching for acquaintances, and when she turned to Gurov, her eyes shone. She talked a lot, and her questions were abrupt, and she herself immediately forgot what she had asked; then she lost her lorgnette in the crowd.

The smartly dressed crowd was dispersing, the faces could no longer be seen, the wind had died down completely, and Gurov and Anna Sergeevna stood as if they were expecting someone else to get off the steamer. Anna Sergeevna was silent now and smelled the flowers, not looking at Gurov.

"The weather's improved towards evening," he said. "Where shall we go now? Shall we take a drive somewhere?"

She made no answer.

Then he looked at her intently and suddenly embraced her and kissed her on the lips, and he was showered with the fragrance and moisture of the flowers, and at once looked around timorously—had anyone seen them?

"Let's go to your place . . ." he said softly.

And they both walked quickly.

Her hotel room was stuffy and smelled of the perfumes she had bought in a Japanese shop. Gurov, looking at her now, thought: "What meetings there are in life!" From the past he had kept the memory of carefree, good-natured women, cheerful with love, grateful to him for their happiness, however brief; and of women—his wife, for example—who loved without sincerity, with superfluous talk, affectedly, with hysteria, with an expression as if it were not love, not passion, but something more significant; and of those two or three very beautiful, cold ones, in whose faces a predatory expression would suddenly flash, a stubborn wish to take, to snatch from life more than it could give, and these were women not in their first youth, capricious, unreasonable, domineering, unintelligent, and when Gurov cooled towards them, their beauty aroused hatred in him, and the lace of their underwear seemed to him like scales.

But here was all the timorousness and angularly of inexperienced youth, a feeling of awkwardness, and an impression of bewilderment, as if someone had suddenly knocked at the door. Anna Sergeevna, the "lady with the little dog," somehow took a special, very serious attitude towards what had happened, as if it were her fall—so it seemed, and that was strange and inopportune. Her features drooped and faded, and her long hair hung down sadly on both sides of her face, she sat pondering in a dejected pose, like the sinful woman in an old painting.

"It's not good," she said. "You'll be the first not to respect me now."

There was a watermelon on the table in the hotel room. Gurov cut himself a slice and unhurriedly began to eat it. At least half an hour passed in silence.

Anna Sergeevna was touching, she had about her a breath of the purity of a proper, naive, little-experienced woman; the solitary candle burning on the table barely lit up her face, but it was clear that her heart was uneasy.

"Why should I stop respecting you?" asked Gurov. "You don't know what you're saying yourself."

"God forgive me!" she said, and her eyes filled with tears. "This is terrible."

"It's like you're justifying yourself."

"How can I justify myself? I'm a bad, low woman, I despise myself and am not even thinking of any justification. It's not my husband I've deceived, but my own self! And not only now, I've been deceiving myself for a long time. My husband may be an honest and good man, but he's a lackey! I don't know what he does there, how he serves, I only know that he's a lackey. I married him when I was twenty, I was tormented by curiosity, I wanted something better. I told myself there must be a different life. I wanted to live! To live and live . . . I was burning with curiosity . . . you won't understand it, but I swear to God that I couldn't control myself any longer, something was happening to me, I couldn't restrain myself, I told my husband I was ill and came here . . . And here I go about as if in a daze, as if I'm out of my mind . . . and now I've become a trite, trashy woman, whom anyone can despise."

Gurov was bored listening, he was annoyed by the naive tone, by this repentance, so unexpected and out of place; had it not been for the tears in her eyes, one might have thought she was joking or playing a role.

"I don't understand," he said softly, "what is it you want?"

She hid her face on his chest and pressed herself to him.

"Believe me, believe me, I beg you . . ." she said. "I love an honest, pure life, sin is vile to me, I myself don't know what I'm doing. Simple people say, 'The unclean one beguiled me.' And now I can say of myself that the unclean one has beguiled me."

"Enough, enough . . ." he muttered.

He looked into her fixed, frightened eyes, kissed her, spoke softly and tenderly, and she gradually calmed down, and her gaiety returned. They both began to laugh.

Later, when they went out, there was not a soul on the embankment, the town with its cypresses looked completely dead, but the sea still beat noisily against the shore; one barge was rocking on the waves, and the lantern on it glimmered sleepily.

They found a cab and drove to Oreanda.

"I just learned your last name downstairs in the lobby: it was written on the board—von Dideritz," said Gurov. "Is your husband German?"

"No, his grandfather was German, I think, but he himself is Orthodox."

In Oreanda they sat on a bench not far from the church, looked down on the sea, and were silent. Yalta was barely visible through the morning mist, white clouds stood motionless on the mountaintops. The leaves of the trees did not stir, cicadas called, and the monotonous, dull noise of the sea, coming from below, spoke of the peace, of the eternal sleep that awaits us. So it had sounded below when neither Yalta nor Oreanda were there, so it sounded now and would go on sounding with the same dull indifference when we are no longer here. And in this constancy, in this utter indifference to the life and death of each of us, there perhaps lies hidden the pledge of our eternal salvation, the unceasing movement of life on earth, of unceasing perfection. Sitting beside the young woman, who looked so beautiful in the dawn, appeased and enchanted by the view of this magical décor—sea, mountains, clouds, the open sky—Gurov reflected that, essentially, if you thought of it, everything was beautiful in this world, everything except for what we ourselves think and do when we forget the higher goals of being and our human dignity.

Some man came up—it must have been a watchman—looked at them, and went away. And this detail seemed such a mysterious thing, and also beautiful. The steamer from Feodosia could be seen approaching in the glow of the early dawn, its lights out.

"There's dew on the grass," said Anna Sergeevna after a silence.

"Yes. It's time to go home."

They went back to town.

After that they met on the embankment every noon, had lunch together, dined, strolled, admired the sea. She complained that she slept poorly and that her heart beat anxiously, kept asking the same questions, troubled now by jealousy, now by fear that he did not respect her enough. And often on the square or in the garden, when there was no one near them, he would suddenly draw her to him and kiss her passionately. Their complete idleness, those kisses in broad daylight, with a furtive look around and the fear that someone might see them, the heat, the smell of the sea, and the constant flashing before their eyes of idle, smartly dressed, well-fed people, seemed to transform him; he repeatedly told Anna Sergeevna how beautiful she was, and how seductive, was impatiently passionate, never left her side, while she often brooded and kept asking him to admit that he did not respect her, did not love her at all, and saw in her only a trite woman. Late almost every evening they went somewhere out of town, to Oreanda or the cascade; these outings were successful, their impressions each time were beautiful, majestic.

They were expecting her husband to arrive. But a letter came from him in which he said that his eyes hurt and begged his wife to come home quickly. Anna Sergeevna began to hurry.

"It's good that I'm leaving," she said to Gurov. "It's fate itself."

She went by carriage, and he accompanied her. They drove for a whole day. When she had taken her seat in the express train and the second bell had rung, she said:

"Let me have one more look at you . . . One more look. There."

She did not cry, but was sad, as if ill, and her face trembled.

"I'll think of you . . . remember you," she said. "God be with you. Don't think ill of me. We're saying good-bye forever, it must be so, because we should never have met. Well, God be with you."

The train left quickly, its lights soon disappeared, and a moment later the noise could no longer be heard, as if everything were conspiring on purpose to put a speedy end to this sweet oblivion, this madness. And, left alone on the platform and gazing into the dark distance, Gurov listened to the chirring of the grasshoppers and the hum of the telegraph wires with a feeling as if he had just woken up. And he thought that now there was one more affair or adventure in his life, and it, too, was now over, and all that was left was the memory . . . He was touched, saddened, and felt some slight remorse; this young woman whom he was never to see again had not been happy with him; he had been affectionate with her, and sincere, but all the same, in his treatment of her, in his tone and caresses, there had been a slight shade of mockery, the somewhat coarse arrogance of a happy man, who was, moreover, almost twice her age. She had all the while called him kind, extraordinary, lofty; obviously, he had appeared to her not as he was in reality, and therefore he had involuntarily deceived her . . .

Here at the station there was already a breath of autumn, the wind was cool.

"It's time I headed north, too," thought Gurov, leaving the platform. "High time!"

III

At home in Moscow everything was already wintry, the stoves were heated, and in the morning, when the children were getting ready for school and drinking their tea, it was dark, and the nanny would light a lamp for a short time. The frosts had already set in. When the first snow falls, on the first day of riding in sleighs, it is pleasant to see the white ground, the white roofs; one's breath feels soft and pleasant, and in those moments one remembers one's youth. The old lindens and birches, white with hoarfrost, have a good-natured look, they are nearer one's heart than cypresses and palms, and near them one no longer wants to think of mountains and the sea.

Gurov was a Muscovite. He returned to Moscow on a fine, frosty day, and when he put on his fur coat and warm gloves and strolled down Petrovka, and when on Saturday evening he heard the bells ringing, his recent trip and the places he had visited lost all their charm for him. He gradually became immersed in Moscow life, now greedily read three newspapers a day and said that he never read the Moscow newspapers on principle. He was drawn to restaurants, clubs, to dinner parties, celebrations, and felt flattered that he had famous lawyers and actors among his clients, and that at the Doctors' Club he played cards with a professor. He could eat a whole portion of selyanka[2] from the pan . . .

A month would pass and Anna Sergeevna, as it seemed to him, would be covered by mist in his memory and would only appear to him in dreams with a touching smile, as other women did. But more than a month passed, deep winter came, and yet everything was as clear in his memory as if he had parted with Anna Sergeevna only the day before. And the memories burned brighter and brighter. Whether from the voices of his children doing their homework, which reached him in his study in the evening quiet, or from hearing a romance, or an organ in a restaurant, or the blizzard howling in the chimney, everything would suddenly rise up in his memory: what had happened on the jetty, and the early morning with mist on the mountains, and the steamer from Feodosia, and the kisses. He would pace the room for a long time, and remember, and smile, and then his memories would turn to reveries, and in his imagination the past would mingle with what was still to be. Anna Sergeevna was not a dream, she followed him everywhere like a shadow and watched him. Closing

2. Meat stewed with pickled cabbage and served in a pan.

his eyes, he saw her as if alive, and she seemed younger, more beautiful, more tender than she was; and he also seemed better to himself than he had been then, in Yalta. In the evenings she gazed at him from the bookcase, the fireplace, the corner, he could hear her breathing, the gentle rustle of her skirts. In the street he followed women with his eyes, looking for one who resembled her . . .

And he was tormented now by a strong desire to tell someone his memories. But at home it was impossible to talk of his love, and away from home there was no one to talk with. Certainly not among his tenants nor at the bank. And what was there to say? Had he been in love then? Was there anything beautiful, poetic, or instructive, or merely interesting, in his relations with Anna Sergeevna? And he found himself speaking vaguely of love, of women, and no one could guess what it was about, and only his wife raised her dark eyebrows and said:

"You know, Dimitri, the role of fop doesn't suit you at all."

One night, as he was leaving the Doctors' Club together with his partner, an official, he could not help himself and said:

"If you only knew what a charming woman I met in Yalta!"

The official got into a sleigh and drove off, but suddenly turned around and called out:

"Dimitri Dmitrich!"

"What?"

"You were right earlier: the sturgeon was a bit off!"

Those words, so very ordinary, for some reason suddenly made Gurov indignant, struck him as humiliating, impure. Such savage manners, such faces! These senseless nights, and such uninteresting, unremarkable days! Frenzied card-playing, gluttony, drunkenness, constant talk about the same thing. Useless matters and conversations about the same thing took for their share the best part of one's time, the best of one's powers, and what was left in the end was some sort of curtailed, wingless life, some sort of nonsense, and it was impossible to get away or flee, as if you were sitting in a madhouse or a prison camp!

Gurov did not sleep all night and felt indignant, and as a result had a headache all the next day. And the following nights he slept poorly, sitting up in bed all the time and thinking, or pacing up and down. He was sick of the children, sick of the bank, did not want to go anywhere or talk about anything.

In December, during the holidays, he got ready to travel and told his wife he was leaving for Petersburg to solicit for a certain young man—and went to S. Why? He did not know very well himself. He wanted to see Anna Sergeevna and talk with her, to arrange a meeting, if he could.

He arrived at S. in the morning and took the best room in the hotel, where the whole floor was covered with gray army flannel and there was an inkstand on the table, gray with dust, with a horseback rider, who held his hat in his raised hand, but whose head was broken off. The hall porter gave him the necessary information: von Dideritz lives in his own house on Staro-Goncharnaya Street, not far from the hotel; he has a good life, is wealthy, keeps his own horses, everybody in town knows him. The porter pronounced it "Dridiritz."

Gurov walked unhurriedly to Staro-Goncharnaya Street, found the house. Just opposite the house stretched a fence, long, gray, with spikes.

"You could flee from such a fence," thought Gurov, looking now at the windows, now at the fence.

He reflected: today was not a workday, and the husband was probably at home. And anyhow it would be tactless to go in and cause embarrassment. If he sent a message, it might fall into the husband's hands, and that would ruin everything. It would be best to trust to chance. And he kept pacing up and down the street and near the fence and waited for his chance. He saw a beggar go in the gates and saw the dogs attack him, then, an hour later, he heard someone playing a piano, and the sounds reached him faintly, indistinctly. It must have been Anna Sergeevna playing. The front door suddenly opened and some old woman came out, the familiar white spitz running after her. Gurov wanted to call the dog, but his heart suddenly throbbed, and in his excitement he was unable to remember the spitz's name.

He paced up and down, and hated the gray fence more and more, and now he thought with vexation that Anna Sergeevna had forgotten him, and was perhaps amusing herself with another man, and that that was so natural in the situation of a young woman who had to look at this cursed fence from morning till evening. He went back to his hotel room and sat on the sofa for a long time, not knowing what to do, then had dinner, then took a long nap.

"How stupid and upsetting this all is," he thought, when he woke up and looked at the dark windows: it was already evening. "So I've had my sleep. Now what am I to do for the night?"

He sat on the bed, which was covered with a cheap, gray, hospital-like blanket, and taunted himself in vexation:

"Here's the lady with the little dog for you . . . Here's an adventure for you . . . Yes, here you sit."

That morning, at the train station, a poster with very big lettering had caught his eye: it was the opening night of *The Geisha*. He remembered it and went to the theater.

"It's very likely that she goes to opening nights," he thought.

The theater was full. And here, too, as in all provincial theaters generally, a haze hung over the chandeliers, the gallery stirred noisily; the local dandies stood in the front row before the performance started, their hands behind their backs; and here, too, in the governor's box, the governor's daughter sat in front, wearing a boa, while the governor himself modestly hid behind the portière, and only his hands could be seen; the curtain swayed, the orchestra spent a long time tuning up. All the while the public came in and took their seats, Gurov kept searching greedily with his eyes.

Anna Sergeevna came in. She sat in the third row, and when Gurov looked at her, his heart was wrung, and he realized clearly that there was now no person closer, dearer, or more important for him in the whole world; this small woman, lost in the provincial crowd, not remarkable for anything, with a vulgar lorgnette in her hand, now filled his whole life, was his grief, his joy, the only happiness he now wished for himself; and to the sounds of the bad orchestra, with its trashy local violins, he thought how beautiful she was. He thought and dreamed.

A man came in with Anna Sergeevna and sat down next to her, a young man with little side-whiskers, very tall, stooping; he nodded his head at every step, and it seemed he was perpetually bowing. This was probably her husband, whom she, in an outburst of bitter feeling that time in Yalta, had called a lackey. And indeed, in his long figure, his side-whiskers, his little bald spot, there was something of lackeyish modesty; he had a sweet smile, and the badge of some learned society gleamed in his buttonhole, like the badge of a lackey.

During the first intermission the husband went to smoke; she remained in her seat. Gurov, who was also sitting in the stalls, went up to her and said in a trembling voice and with a forced smile:

"How do you do?"

She looked at him and paled, then looked again in horror, not believing her eyes, and tightly clutched her fan and lorgnette in her hand, obviously struggling with herself to keep from fainting. Both were silent. She sat, he stood, alarmed at her confusion, not venturing to sit down next to her. The tuning-up violins and flutes sang out, it suddenly became frightening, it seemed that people were gazing at them from all the boxes. But then she got up and quickly walked to the exit, he followed her, and they both went confusedly through corridors and stairways, going up, then down, and the uniforms of the courts, the schools, and the imperial estates flashed before them, all with badges; ladies flashed by, fur coats on hangers, a drafty wind blew, drenching them with the smell of cigar stubs. And Gurov, whose heart was pounding, thought: "Oh, Lord! Why these people, this orchestra . . ."

And just then he suddenly recalled how, at the station in the evening after he had seen Anna Sergeevna off, he had said to himself that everything was over and they would never see each other again. But how far it still was from being over!

On a narrow, dark stairway with the sign "To the Amphitheater," she stopped.

"How you frightened me!" she said, breathing heavily, still pale, stunned. "Oh, how you frightened me! I'm barely alive. Why did you come? Why?"

"But understand, Anna, understand . . ." he said in a low voice, hurrying. "I beg you to understand . . ."

She looked at him with fear, with entreaty, with love, looked at him intently, the better to keep his features in her memory.

"I've been suffering so!" she went on, not listening to him. "I think only of you all the time, I've lived by my thoughts of you. And I've tried to forget, to forget, but why, why did you come?"

Further up, on the landing, two high-school boys were smoking and looking down, but Gurov did not care, he drew Anna Sergeevna to him and began kissing her face, her cheeks, her hands.

"What are you doing, what are you doing!" she repeated in horror, pushing him away from her. "We've both lost our minds. Leave today, leave at once . . . I adjure you by all that's holy, I implore you . . . Somebody's coming!"

Someone was climbing the stairs.

"You must leave . . ." Anna Sergeevna went on in a whisper. "Do you hear, Dmitri Dmitrich? I'll come to you in Moscow. I've never been happy, I'm unhappy now, and

I'll never, never be happy, never! Don't make me suffer still more! I swear I'll come to Moscow. But we must part now! My dear one, my good one, my darling, we must part!"

She pressed his hand and quickly began going downstairs, turning back to look at him, and it was clear from her eyes that she was indeed not happy . . . Gurov stood for a little while, listened, then, when everything was quiet, found his coat and left the theater.

IV

And Anna Sergeevna began coming to see him in Moscow. Once every two or three months she left S., and told her husband she was going to consult a professor about her female disorder—and her husband did and did not believe her. Arriving in Moscow, she stayed at the Slavyansky Bazaar and at once sent a man in a red hat to Gurov. Gurov came to see her, and nobody in Moscow knew of it.

Once he was going to see her in that way on a winter morning (the messenger had come the previous evening but had not found him in). With him was his daughter, whom he wanted to see off to school, which was on the way. Big, wet snow was falling.

"It's now three degrees above freezing, and yet it's snowing," Gurov said to his daughter. "But it's warm only near the surface of the earth, while in the upper layers of the atmosphere the temperature is quite different."

"And why is there no thunder in winter, papa?"

He explained that, too. He spoke and thought that here he was going to a rendezvous, and not a single soul knew of it or probably would ever know. He had two lives: an apparent one, seen and known by all who needed it, filled with conventional truth and conventional deceit, which perfectly resembled the lives of his acquaintances and friends, and another that went on in secret. And by some strange coincidence, perhaps an accidental one, everything that he found important, interesting, necessary, in which he was sincere and did not deceive himself, which constituted the core of his life, occurred in secret from others, while everything that made up his lie, his shell, in which he hid in order to conceal the truth—for instance, his work at the bank, his arguments at the club, his "inferior race," his attending official celebrations with his wife—all this was in full view. And he judged others by himself, did not believe what he saw, and always supposed that every man led his own real and very interesting life under the cover of secrecy, as under the cover of night. Every personal existence was upheld by a secret, and it was perhaps partly for that reason that every cultivated man took such anxious care that his personal secret should be respected.

After taking his daughter to school, Gurov went to the Slavyansky Bazaar. He took his fur coat off downstairs, went up, and knocked softly at the door. Anna Sergeevna, wearing his favorite gray dress, tired from the trip and the expectation, had been waiting for him since the previous evening; she was pale, looked at him and did not smile, and he had barely come in when she was already leaning on his chest. Their kiss was long, lingering, as if they had not seen each other for two years.

"Well, how is your life there?" he asked. "What's new?"

"Wait, I'll tell you . . . I can't."

She could not speak because she was crying. She turned away from him and pressed a handkerchief to her eyes.

"Well, let her cry a little, and meanwhile I'll sit down," he thought, and sat down in an armchair.

Then he rang and ordered tea; and then, while he drank tea, she went on standing with her face turned to the window . . . She was crying from anxiety, from a sorrowful awareness that their life had turned out so sadly; they only saw each other in secret, they hid from people like thieves! Was their life not broken?

"Well, stop now," he said.

For him it was obvious that this love of theirs would not end soon, that there was no knowing when. Anna Sergeevna's attachment to him grew ever stronger, she adored him, and it would have been unthinkable to tell her that it all really had to end at some point; and she would not have believed it.

He went up to her and took her by the shoulders to caress her, to make a joke, and at that moment he saw himself in the mirror.

His head was beginning to turn gray. And it seemed strange to him that he had aged so much in those last years, had lost so much of his good looks. The shoulders on which his hands lay were warm and trembled. He felt compassion for this life, still so warm and beautiful, but probably already near the point where it would begin to fade and wither, like his own life. Why did she love him so? Women had always taken him to be other than he was, and they had loved in him, not himself, but a man their imagination had created, whom they had greedily sought all their lives; and then, when they had noticed their mistake, they had still loved him. And not one of them had been happy with him. Time passed, he met women, became intimate, parted, but not once did he love; there was anything else, but not love.

And only now, when his head was gray, had he really fallen in love as one ought to—for the first time in his life.

He and Anna Sergeevna loved each other like very close, dear people, like husband and wife, like tender friends; it seemed to them that fate itself had destined them for each other, and they could not understand why he had a wife and she a husband; and it was as if they were two birds of passage, a male and a female, who had been caught and forced to live in separate cages. They had forgiven each other the things they were ashamed of in the past, they forgave everything in the present, and they felt that this love of theirs had changed them both.

Formerly, in sad moments, he had calmed himself with all sorts of arguments, whatever had come into his head, but now he did not care about any arguments, he felt deep compassion, he wanted to be sincere, tender . . .

"Stop, my good one," he said, "you've had your cry—and enough . . . Let's talk now, we'll think up something."

Then they had a long discussion, talked about how to rid themselves of the need for hiding, for deception, for living in different towns and not seeing each other for long periods. How could they free themselves from these unbearable bonds?

"How? How?" he asked, clutching his head. "How?"

And it seemed that, just a little more—and the solution would be found, and then a new, beautiful life would begin; and it was clear to both of them that the end was still far, far off, and that the most complicated and difficult part was just beginning.

Reading as a Writer

1. What kind of narrator does this story have? How much does he or she know? What is his or her distance from the events of the story?

2. What are the pivotal moments of the story? At what points in the story does the character Gurov experience an epiphany, or realize some truth about his situation?

3. What is the "resolution" of the story? What do you make of resolutions like this (where nothing is really resolved)?

Dan Chaon

The Bees

GENE'S SON FRANKIE wakes up screaming. It has become frequent, two or three times a week, at random times: midnight—three a.m.—five in the morning. Here is a high, empty wail that severs Gene from his unconsciousness like sharp teeth. It is the worst sound that Gene can imagine, the sound of a young child dying violently— falling from a building, or caught in some machinery that is tearing an arm off, or being mauled by a predatory animal. No matter how many times he hears it he jolts up with such images playing in his mind, and he always runs, thumping into the child's bedroom to find Frankie sitting up in bed, his eyes closed, his mouth open in an oval like a Christmas caroler. Frankie appears to be in a kind of peaceful trance, and if someone took a picture of him he would look like he was waiting to receive a spoonful of ice cream rather than emitting that horrific sound.

"Frankie!" Gene will shout, and claps his hands hard in the child's face. The clapping works well. At this, the scream always stops abruptly, and Frankie opens his eyes, blinking at Gene with vague awareness before settling back down into his pillow, nuzzling a little before growing still. He is sound asleep, he is always sound asleep, though even after months Gene can't help leaning down and pressing his ear to the child's chest, to make sure he's still breathing, his heart is still going. It always is.

There is no explanation that they can find. In the morning the child doesn't remember anything, and on the few occasions that they have managed to wake him in the midst of one of his screaming attacks, he is merely sleepy and irritable. Once, Gene's wife, Karen, shook him and shook him, until finally he opened his eyes, groggily. "Honey?" she said. "Honey? Did you have a bad dream?" But Frankie only moaned a little. "No," he said, puzzled and unhappy at being awakened, but nothing more.

They can find no pattern to it. It can happen any day of the week, any time of the night. It doesn't seem to be associated with diet, or with his activities during the day, and it doesn't stem, as far as they can tell, from any sort of psychological unease. During the day he seems perfectly normal and happy.

They have taken him several times to the pediatrician, but the doctor seems to have little of use to say. There is nothing wrong with the child physically, Dr. Banerjee says. She advises that such things are not uncommon for children of Frankie's age group—he is five—and that more often than not, the disturbance simply passes away.

"He hasn't experienced any kind of emotional trauma, has he?" the doctor says. "Nothing out of the ordinary at home?"

"No, no," they both murmur, together. They shake their heads, and Dr. Banerjee shrugs.

"Parents," she says. "It's probably nothing to worry about." She gives them a brief smile. "As difficult as it is, I'd say that you may just have to weather this out."

But the doctor has never heard those screams. In the mornings after the "nightmares," as Karen calls them, Gene feels unnerved, edgy. He works as a driver for the United Parcel Service, and as he moves through the day after a screaming attack, there is a barely perceptible hum at the edge of his hearing, an intent, deliberate static sliding along behind him as he wanders through streets and streets in his van. He stops along the side of the road and listens. The shadows of summer leaves tremble murmurously against the windshield, and cars are accelerating on a nearby road. In the tree-tops, a cicada makes its trembly, pressure-cooker hiss.

Something bad has been looking for him for a long time, he thinks, and now, at last, it is growing near.

When he comes home at night everything is normal. They live in an old house in the suburbs of Cleveland, and sometimes after dinner they work together in the small patch of garden out in back of the house—tomatoes, zucchini, string beans, cucumbers—while Frankie plays with Legos in the dirt. Or they take walks around the neighborhood, Frankie riding his bike in front of them, his training wheels recently removed. They gather on the couch and watch cartoons together, or play board games, or draw pictures with crayons. After Frankie is asleep, Karen will sit at the kitchen table and study—she is in nursing school—and Gene will sit outside on the porch, flipping through a newsmagazine or a novel, smoking the cigarettes that he has promised Karen he will give up when he turns thirty-five. He is thirty-four now, and Karen is twenty-seven, and he is aware, more and more frequently, that this is not the life he deserves. He has been incredibly lucky, he thinks. Blessed, as Gene's favorite cashier at the supermarket always says. "Have a blessed day," she says when Gene pays the money and she hands him his receipt, and he feels as if she has sprinkled him with her ordinary, gentle beatitude. It reminds him of long ago, when an old nurse held his hand in the hospital and said that she was praying for him.

Sitting out in his lawn chair, drawing smoke out of his cigarette, he thinks about that nurse, even though he doesn't want to. He thinks of the way she leaned over him and brushed his hair as he stared at her, imprisoned in a full body cast, sweating his way through withdrawal and DTs.[1]

He had been a different person, back then. A drunk, a monster. At nineteen, he'd married the girl he'd gotten pregnant, and then had set about slowly, steadily, ruining all their lives. When he'd abandoned them, his wife and son, back in Nebraska, he had been twenty-four, a danger to himself and others. He'd done them a favor by leaving, he thought, though he still felt guilty when he remembered it. Years later, when he was sober, he'd even tried to contact them. He wanted to own up to his behavior, to pay the back child support, to apologize. But they were nowhere to be found. Mandy was no longer living in the small Nebraska town where they'd met and married, and there was no forwarding address. Her parents were dead. No one seemed to know where she'd gone.

Karen didn't know the full story. She had been, to his relief, uncurious about his previous life, though she knew he had some drinking days, some bad times. She knew that he'd been married before, too, though she didn't know the extent of it, didn't know that he had another son, for example, didn't know that he had left them one night, without even packing a bag, just driving off in the car, a flask tucked between his legs, driving east as far as he could go. She didn't know about the car crash, the wreck he should have died in. She didn't know what a bad person he'd been.

She was a nice lady, Karen. Maybe a little sheltered. And truth to tell, he was ashamed—and even scared—to imagine how she would react to the truth about his past. He didn't know if she would have ever really trusted him if she'd known the full story, and the longer they knew one another, the less inclined he was to reveal it. He'd escaped his old self, he thought, and when Karen got pregnant, shortly before they were married, he told himself that now he had a chance to do things over, to do it better. They had purchased the house together, he and Karen, and now Frankie will be in kindergarten in the fall. He has come full circle, has come exactly to the point when his former life with Mandy and his son DJ had completely fallen apart. He looks up as Karen comes to the back door and speaks to him through the screen. "I think it's time for bed, sweetheart," she says softly, and he shudders off these thoughts, these memories. He smiles.

He's been in a strange frame of mind lately. The months of regular awakenings have been getting to him, and he has a hard time getting back to sleep after an episode with Frankie. When Karen wakes him in the morning, he often feels muffled, sluggish—as if he's hung over. He doesn't hear the alarm clock. When he stumbles out of bed, he finds he has a hard time keeping his moodiness in check. He can feel his temper coiling up inside him.

He isn't that type of person anymore, and hasn't been for a long while. Still, he can't help but worry. They say that there is a second stretch of craving, which sets in

---

1. Delirium tremens, a severe form of alcohol withdrawal.

after several years of smooth sailing; five or seven years will pass, and then it will come back without warning. He has been thinking of going to AA meetings again, though he hasn't in some time—not since he met Karen.

It's not as if he gets trembly every time he passes a liquor store, or even as if he has a problem when he goes out with buddies and spends the evening drinking soda and nonalcoholic beer. No. The trouble comes at night, when he's asleep.

He has begun to dream of his first son. DJ. Perhaps it is related to his worries about Frankie, but for several nights in a row the image of DJ—aged about five—has appeared to him. In the dream, Gene is drunk, and playing hide-and-seek with DJ in the yard behind the Cleveland house where he is now living. There is the thick weeping willow out there, and Gene watches the child appear from behind it and run across the grass, happily, unafraid, the way Frankie would. DJ turns to look over his shoulder and laughs, and Gene stumbles after him, at least a six-pack's worth of good mood, a goofy, drunken dad. It's so real that when he wakes, he still feels intoxicated. It takes him a few minutes to shake it.

One morning after a particularly vivid version of this dream, Frankie wakes and complains of a funny feeling—"right here," he says, and points to his forehead. It isn't a headache, he says. "It's like bees!" he says. "Buzzing bees!" He rubs his hand against his brow. "Inside my head." He considers for a moment. "You know how the bees bump against the window when they get in the house and want to get out?" This description pleases him, and he taps his forehead lightly with his fingers, humming, zzzzzzz, to demonstrate.

"Does it hurt?" Karen says.

"No," Frankie says. "It tickles."

Karen gives Gene a concerned look. She makes Frankie lie down on the couch and tells him to close his eyes for a while. After a few minutes he rises up, smiling, and says that the feeling has gone.

"Honey, are you sure?" Karen says. She pushes her hair back and slides her palm across his forehead. "He's not hot," she says, and Frankie sits up impatiently, suddenly more interested in finding a matchbox car he dropped under a chair.

Karen gets out one of her nursing books, and Gene watches her face tighten with concern as she flips slowly through the pages. She is looking at Chapter Three: Neurological System, and Gene observes as she pauses here and there, skimming down a list of symptoms. "We should probably take him back to Dr. Banerjee again," she says. Gene nods, recalling what the doctor said about "emotional trauma."

"Are you scared of bees?" he asks Frankie. "Is that something that's bothering you?"

"No," Frankie says. "Not really."

When Frankie was three, a bee stung him above his left eyebrow. They had been out hiking together, and they hadn't yet learned that Frankie was "moderately allergic" to bee stings. Within minutes of the sting, Frankie's face had begun to distort, to puff up, his eye swelling shut. He looked deformed. Gene didn't know if he'd ever been more frightened in his entire life, running down the trail with Frankie's head pressed against his heart, trying to get to the car and drive him to the doctor, terrified that the child was dying. Frankie himself was calm.

Gene clears his throat. He knows the feeling that Frankie is talking about—he has felt it himself, that odd, feathery vibration inside his head. And in fact feels it again, now. He presses the pads of his fingertips against his brow. Emotional trauma, his mind murmurs, but he is thinking of DJ, not Frankie.

"What are you scared of?" Gene asks Frankie after a moment. "Anything?"

"You know what the scariest thing is?" Frankie says, and widens his eyes, miming a frightened look. "There's a lady with no head, and she went walking through the woods, looking for it. "Give . . . me . . . back . . . my . . . head . . ."

"Where on earth did you hear a story like that!" Karen says.

"Daddy told me," Frankie says. "When we were camping."

Gene blushes, even before Karen gives him a sharp look. "Oh, great," she says. "Wonderful."

He doesn't meet her eyes. "We were just telling ghost stories," he says softly. "I thought he would think the story was funny."

"My God, Gene," she says. "With him having nightmares like this? What were you thinking?"

It's a bad flashback, the kind of thing he's usually able to avoid. He thinks abruptly of Mandy, his former wife. He sees in Karen's face that look Mandy would give him when he screwed up. "What are you, some kind of idiot?" Mandy used to say. "Are you crazy?" Back then, Gene couldn't do anything right, it seemed, and when Mandy yelled at him it made his stomach clench with shame and inarticulate rage. I was trying, he would think, I was trying, damn it, and it was as if no matter what he did, it wouldn't turn out right. That feeling would sit heavily in his chest, and eventually, when things got worse, he hit her once. "Why do you want me to feel like shit," he had said through clenched teeth. "I'm not an asshole," he said, and when she rolled her eyes at him, he slapped her hard enough to knock her out of her chair.

That was the time he'd taken DJ to the carnival. It was a Saturday, and he'd been drinking a little so Mandy didn't like it, but after all—he thought—DJ was his son too, he had a right to spend some time with his own son. Mandy wasn't his boss even if she might think she was. She liked to make him hate himself.

What she was mad about was that he'd taken DJ on the Velocerator. It was a mistake, he'd realized afterward. But DJ himself had begged to go on. He was just recently four years old, and Gene had just turned twenty-three, which made him feel inexplicably old. He wanted to have a little fun.

Besides, nobody told him he couldn't take DJ on the thing. When he led DJ through the gate, the ticket-taker even smiled, as if to say, "Here is a young guy showing his kid a good time." Gene winked at DJ and grinned, taking a nip from a flask of peppermint schnapps. He felt like a good dad. He wished his own father had taken him on rides at the carnival!

The door to the Velocerator opened like a hatch in a big silver flying saucer. Disco music was blaring from the entrance and became louder as they went inside. It was a circular room with soft padded walls, and one of the workers had Gene and DJ stand with their backs to the wall, strapping them in side by side. Gene felt warm and expansive from the schnapps. He took DJ's hand, and he almost felt as if he were glowing with love. "Get ready, kiddo," Gene whispered. "This is going to be wild."

The hatch door of the Velocerator sealed closed with a pressurized sigh. And then, slowly, the walls they were strapped to began to turn. Gene tightened on DJ's hand as they began to rotate, gathering speed. After a moment the wall pads they were strapped to slid up, and the force of velocity pushed them back, held to the surface of the spinning wall like iron to a magnet. Gene's cheeks and lips seemed to pull back, and the sensation of helplessness made him laugh.

At that moment, DJ began to scream. "No! No! Stop! Make it stop!" They were terrible shrieks, and Gene grabbed the child's hand tightly. "It's all right," he yelled jovially over the thump of the music. "It's okay! I'm right here!" But the child's wailing only got louder in response. The scream seemed to whip past Gene in a circle, tumbling around and around the circumference of the ride like a spirit, trailing echoes as it flew. When the machine finally stopped, DJ was heaving with sobs, and the man at the control panel glared. Gene could feel the other passengers staring grimly and judgmentally at him.

Gene felt horrible. He had been so happy—thinking that they were finally having themselves a memorable father-and-son moment—and he could feel his heart plunging into darkness. DJ kept on weeping, even as they left the ride and walked along the midway, even as Gene tried to distract him with promises of cotton candy and stuffed animals. "I want to go home," DJ cried, and "I want my mom! I want my mom!" And it had wounded Gene to hear that. He gritted his teeth.

"Fine!" he hissed. "Let's go home to your mommy, you little crybaby. I swear to God, I'm never taking you with me anywhere again." And he gave DJ a little shake. "Jesus, what's wrong with you? Lookit, people are laughing at you. See? They're saying, 'Look at that big boy, bawling like a girl.'"

This memory comes to him out of the blue. He had forgotten all about it, but now it comes to him over and over. Those screams were not unlike the sounds Frankie makes in the middle of the night, and they pass repeatedly through the membrane of his thoughts, without warning. The next day he finds himself recalling it again, the memory of the scream impressing his mind with such force that he actually has to pull his UPS truck off to the side of the road and put his face in his hands: awful! awful! He must have seemed like a monster to the child.

Sitting there in his van, he wishes he could find a way to contact them—Mandy and DJ. He wishes that he could tell them how sorry he is, and send them money. He puts his fingertips against his forehead, as cars drive past on the street, as an old man parts the curtains and peers out of the house Gene is parked in front of, hopeful that Gene might have a package for him.

Where are they? Gene wonders. He tries to picture a town, a house, but there is only a blank. Surely, Mandy being Mandy, she would have hunted him down by now to demand child support. She would have relished treating him like a deadbeat dad, she would have hired some company who would garnish his wages.

Now, sitting at the roadside, it occurs to him suddenly that they are dead. He recalls the car wreck that he was in, just outside Des Moines, and if he had been killed they would never have known. He recalls waking up in the hospital, and the elderly nurse who said, "You're very lucky, young man. You should be dead."

Maybe they are dead, he thinks. Mandy and DJ. The idea strikes him a glancing blow, because of course it would make sense. The reason they'd never contacted him. Of course.

He doesn't know what to do with such premonitions. They are ridiculous, they are self-pitying, they are paranoid, but especially now, with their concerns about Frankie, he is at the mercy of his anxieties. He comes home from work and Karen stares at him heavily.

"What's the matter?" she says, and he shrugs. "You look terrible," she says.

"It's nothing," he says, but she continues to look at him skeptically. She shakes her head.

"I took Frankie to the doctor again today," she says after a moment, and Gene sits down at the table with her, where she is spread out with her textbooks and notepaper.

"I suppose you'll think I'm being a neurotic mom," she says. "I think I'm too immersed in disease, that's the problem."

Gene shakes his head. "No, no," he says. His throat feels dry. "You're right. Better safe than sorry."

"Mmm," she says thoughtfully. "I think Dr. Banerjee is starting to hate me."

"Naw," Gene says. "No one could hate you." With effort, he smiles gently. A good husband, he kisses her palm, her wrist. "Try not to worry," he says, though his own nerves are fluttering. He can hear Frankie in the back yard, shouting orders to someone.

"Who's he talking to?" Gene says, and Karen doesn't look up.

"Oh," she says. "It's probably just Bubba." Bubba is Frankie's imaginary playmate.

Gene nods. He goes to the window and looks out. Frankie is pretending to shoot at something, his thumb and forefinger cocked into a gun. "Get him! Get him!" Frankie shouts, and Gene stares out as Frankie dodges behind a tree. Frankie looks nothing like DJ, but when he pokes his head from behind the hanging foliage of the willow, Gene feels a little shudder—a flicker—something. He clenches his jaw.

"This class is really driving me crazy," Karen says. "Every time I read about a worst-case scenario, I start to worry. It's strange. The more you know, the less sure you are of anything."

"What did the doctor say this time?" Gene says. He shifts uncomfortably, still staring out at Frankie, and it seems as if dark specks circle and bob at the corner of the yard. "He seems okay?"

Karen shrugs. "As far as they can tell." She looks down at her textbook, shaking her head. "He seems healthy." He puts his hand gently on the back of her neck, and she lolls her head back and forth against his fingers. "I've never believed that anything really terrible could happen to me," she had once told him, early in their marriage, and it had scared him. "Don't say that," he'd whispered, and she'd laughed.

"You're superstitious," she said. "That's cute."

He can't sleep. The strange presentiment that Mandy and DJ are dead has lodged heavily in his mind, and he rubs his feet together underneath the covers, trying to find a comfortable posture. He can hear the soft ticks of the old electric typewriter as Karen finishes her paper for school, words rattling out in bursts that remind him of some sort of insect language. He closes his eyes, pretending to be asleep when Karen finally comes to bed, but his mind is ticking with small, scuttling images: his former wife and son, flashes of the photographs he didn't own, hadn't kept. They're dead, a firm voice in his mind says, very distinctly. They were in a fire. And they burned up. It is not quite his own voice that speaks to him, and abruptly he can picture the burning house. It's a trailer, somewhere on the outskirts of a small town, and the black smoke is pouring out of the open door. The plastic window frames have warped and begun to melt, and the smoke billows from the trailer into the sky in a way that reminds him of an old locomotive. He can't see inside, except for crackling bursts of deep orange flames, but he's aware that they're inside. For a second he can see DJ's face, flickering, peering steadily from the window of the burning trailer, his mouth open in an unnatural circle, as if he's singing.

He opens his eyes. Karen's breathing has steadied, she's sound asleep, and he carefully gets out of bed, padding restlessly through the house in his pajamas. They're not dead, he tries to tell himself, and stands in front of the refrigerator, pouring milk from the carton into his mouth. It's an old comfort, from back in the days when he was drying out, when the thick taste of milk would slightly calm his craving for a drink. But it doesn't help him now. The dream, the vision, has frightened him badly, and he sits on the couch with an afghan over his shoulders, staring at some science program on television. On the program, a lady scientist is examining a mummy. A child. The thing is bald—almost a skull but not quite. A membrane of ancient skin is pulled taut over the eye sockets. The lips are stretched back, and there are small, chipped, rodentlike teeth. Looking at the thing, he can't help but think of DJ again, and he looks over his shoulder, quickly, the way he used to.

The last year that he was together with Mandy, there were times when DJ would actually give him the creeps—spook him. DJ had been an unusually skinny child, with a head like a baby bird and long, bony feet with toes that seemed strangely extended, as if they were meant for gripping. He can remember the way the child would slip barefoot through rooms, slinking, sneaking, watching, Gene had thought, always watching him.

It is a memory that he has almost, for years, succeeded in forgetting, a memory he hates and mistrusts. He was drinking heavily at the time, and he knows now that alcohol grotesquely distorted his perceptions. But now that it has been dislodged, that old feeling moves through him like a breath of smoke. Back then, it had seemed to him that Mandy had turned DJ against him, that DJ had in some strange way almost physically transformed into something that wasn't Gene's real son. Gene can remember how sometimes he would be sitting on the couch, watching TV, and he'd get a funny feeling. He'd turn his head and DJ would be at the edge of the room, with his bony spine hunched and his long neck craned, staring with those strangely over-sized eyes. Other times, Gene and Mandy would be arguing and DJ would suddenly slide into the room, creeping up to Mandy and resting his head on her chest, right in the middle of some important talk. "I'm thirsty," he would say, in imitation baby-talk. Though he was five years old, he would play-act this little toddler voice. "Mama," he would say. "I is firsty." And DJ's eyes would rest on Gene for a moment, cold and full of calculating hatred.

Of course, Gene knows now that this was not the reality of it. He knows: he was a drunk, and DJ was just a sad, scared little kid, trying to deal with a rotten situation. Later, when he was in detox, these memories of his son made him actually shudder with shame, and it was not something he could bring himself to talk about even when he was deep into his twelve steps. How could he say how repulsed he'd been by the child, how actually frightened he was? Jesus Christ, DJ was a poor wretched five-year-old kid! But in Gene's memory there was something malevolent about him, rest-ing his head pettishly on his mother's chest, talking in that sing-song, lisping voice, staring hard and unblinking at Gene with a little smile. Gene remembers catching DJ by the back of the neck. "If you're going to talk, talk normal," Gene had whispered through his teeth, tightening his fingers on the child's neck. "You're not a baby. You're not fooling anybody." And DJ had actually bared his teeth, making a thin, hissing whine.

He wakes and he can't breathe. There is a swimming, suffocating sensation of being stared at, being watched by something that hates him, and he gasps, choking for air. A lady is bending over him, and for a moment he expects her to say, "You're very lucky, young man. You should be dead."

But it's Karen, "What are you doing?" she says. It's morning, and he struggles to orient himself—he's on the living room floor, and the television is still going.

"Jesus," he says, and coughs. "Oh, Jesus." He is sweating, his face feels hot, but he tries to calm himself in the face of Karen's horrified stare. "A bad dream," he says, trying to control his panting breaths. "Jesus," he says, and shakes his head, trying to smile reassuringly for her. "I got up last night and I couldn't sleep. I must have passed out while I was watching TV."

But Karen just gazes at him, her expression frightened and uncertain, as if some-thing about him is transforming, "Gene," she says. "Are you all right?"

"Sure," he says hoarsely, and a shudder passes over him involuntarily. "Of course." And then he realizes that he is naked. He sits up, covering his crotch self-consciously with his hands, and glances around. He doesn't see his underwear or his pajama bottoms anywhere nearby. He doesn't even see the afghan, which he had draped over him on the couch while he was watching the mummies on TV. He starts to stand up, awkwardly, and he notices that Frankie is standing there in the archway between the kitchen and the living room, watching him, his arms at his sides like a cowboy who is ready to draw his holstered guns.

"Mom?" Frankie says. "I'm thirsty."

He drives through his deliveries in a daze. The bees, he thinks. He remembers what Frankie had said a few mornings before, about bees inside his head, buzzing and bumping against the inside of his forehead like a windowpane they were tapping against. That's the feeling he has now. All the things that he doesn't quite remember are circling and alighting, vibrating their cellophane wings insistently. He sees himself striking Mandy across the face with the flat of his hand, knocking her off her chair; he sees his grip tightening around the back of DJ's thin, five-year-old neck, shaking him as he grimaced and wept; and he is aware that there are other things, perhaps even worse, if he thought about it hard enough. All the things that he'd prayed that Karen would never know about him.

He was very drunk on the day that he left them, so drunk that he can barely remember. It was hard to believe that he'd made it all the way to Des Moines on the interstate before he went off the road, tumbling end over end into darkness. He was laughing, he thought, as the car crumpled around him, and he has to pull his van over to the side of the road, out of fear, as the tickling in his head intensifies. There is an image of Mandy sitting on the couch as he stormed out, with DJ cradled in her arms, one of DJ's eyes swollen shut and puffy. There is an image of him in the kitchen, throwing glasses and beer bottles onto the floor, listening to them shatter.

And whether they are dead or not, he knows that they don't wish him well. They would not want him to be happy—in love with his wife and child. His normal, undeserved life.

When he gets home that night, he feels exhausted. He doesn't want to think anymore, and for a moment it seems that he will be allowed a small reprieve. Frankie is in the yard, playing contentedly. Karen is in the kitchen, making hamburgers and corn on the cob, and everything seems okay. But when he sits down to take off his boots, she gives him an angry look.

"Don't do that in the kitchen," she says icily. "Please. I've asked you before."
He looks down at his feet: one shoe unlaced, half off. "Oh," he says. "Sorry."

But when he retreats to the living room, to his recliner, she follows him. She leans against the doorframe, her arms folded, watching as he releases his tired feet from the boots and rubs his hand over the bottom of his socks. She frowns heavily.

"What?" he says, and tries on an uncertain smile.

She sighs. "We need to talk about last night," she says. "I need to know what's going on."

"Nothing," he says, but the stern way she examines him activates his anxieties all over again. "I couldn't sleep, so I went out to the living room to watch TV. That's all."

She stares at him. "Gene," she says after a moment. "People don't usually wake up naked on their living room floor and not know how they got there. That's just weird, don't you think?"

Oh, please, he thinks. He lifts his hands, shrugging—a posture of innocence and exasperation, though his insides are trembling. "I know," he says. "It was weird to me too. I was having nightmares. I really don't know what happened."

She gazes at him for a long time, her eyes heavy. "I see," she says, and he can feel the emanation of her disappointment like waves of heat. "Gene," she says. "All I'm asking is for you to be honest with me. If you're having problems, if you're drinking again, or thinking about it. I want to help. We can work it out. But you have to be honest with me."

"I'm not drinking," Gene says firmly. He holds her eyes earnestly. "I'm not thinking about it. I told you when we met, I'm through with it. Really." But he is aware again of an observant, unfriendly presence, hidden, moving along the edge of the room. "I don't understand," he says. "What is it? Why would you think I'd lie to you?"

She shifts, still trying to read something in his face, still, he can tell, doubting him. "Listen," she says at last, and he can tell she is trying not to cry. "Some guy called you today. A drunk guy. And he said to tell you that he had a good time hanging out with you last night, and that he was looking forward to seeing you again soon." She frowns hard, staring at him as if this last bit of damning information will show him for the liar he is. A tear slips out of the corner of her eye and along the bridge of her nose. Gene feels his chest tighten.

"That's crazy," he says. He tries to sound outraged, but he is in fact suddenly very frightened. "Who was it?"

She shakes her head sorrowfully. "I don't know," she says. "Something with a *B*. He was slurring so badly I could hardly understand him. BB or BJ or . . ."

Gene can feel the small hairs on his back prickling. "Was it DJ?" he says softly.

And Karen shrugs, lifting a now teary face to him. "I don't know!" she says hoarsely. "I don't know. Maybe." And Gene puts his palms across his face. He is aware of that strange, buzzing, tickling feeling behind his forehead.

"Who is DJ?" Karen says. "Gene, you have to tell me what's going on."

But he can't. He can't tell her, even now. Especially now, he thinks, when to admit that he'd been lying to her ever since they met would confirm all the fears and suspicions she'd been nursing for—what? Days? Weeks?

"He's someone I used to know a long time ago," Gene tells her. "Not a good person. He's the kind of guy who might . . . call up, and get a kick out of upsetting you."

They sit at the kitchen table, silently watching as Frankie eats his hamburger and corn on the cob. Gene can't quite get his mind around it. DJ, he thinks as he presses his finger against his hamburger bun but doesn't pick it up. DJ. He would be fifteen by now. Could he, perhaps, have found them? Maybe stalking them? Watching the house? Gene tries to fathom how DJ might have been causing Frankie's screaming episodes. How he might have caused what happened last night—snuck up on Gene while he was sitting there watching TV and drugged him or something. It seems far-fetched.

"Maybe it was just some random drunk," he says at last, to Karen. "Accidentally calling the house. He didn't ask for me by name, did he?"

"I don't remember," Karen says softly. "Gene . . ."

And he can't stand the doubtfulness, the lack of trust in her expression. He strikes his fist hard against the table, and his plate clatters in a circling echo. "I did not go out with anybody last night!" he says. "I did not get drunk! You can either believe me, or you can . . ."

They are both staring at him. Frankie's eyes are wide, and he puts down the corn-cob he was about to bite into, as if he doesn't like it anymore. Karen's mouth is pinched.

"Or I can what?" she says.

"Nothing," Gene breathes.

There isn't a fight, but a chill spreads through the house, a silence. She knows that he isn't telling her the truth. She knows that there's more to it. But what can he say? He stands at the sink, gently washing the dishes as Karen bathes Frankie and puts him to bed. He waits, listening to the small sounds of the house at night. Outside, in the yard, there is the swing set, and the willow tree—silver-gray and stark in the security light that hangs above the garage. He waits for a while longer, watching, half expecting to see DJ emerge from behind the tree as he'd done in Gene's dream, creeping along, his bony hunched back, the skin pulled tight against the skull of his oversized head. There is that smothering, airless feeling of being watched, and Gene's hands are trembling as he rinses a plate under the tap.

When he goes upstairs at last, Karen is already in her nightgown, in bed, reading a book.

"Karen," he says, and she flips a page, deliberately.

"I don't want to talk to you until you're ready to tell me the truth," she says. She doesn't look at him. "You can sleep on the couch, if you don't mind."

"Just tell me," Gene says. "Did he leave a number? To call him back?"

"No," Karen says. She doesn't look at him. "He just said he'd see you soon."

He thinks that he will stay up all night. He doesn't even wash up, or brush his teeth, or get into his bedtime clothes. He just sits there on the couch, in his uniform and stocking feet, watching television with the sound turned low, listening. Midnight. One a.m.

He goes upstairs to check on Frankie, but everything is okay. Frankie is asleep with his mouth open, the covers thrown off. Gene stands in the doorway, alert for movement, but everything seems to be in place. Frankie's turtle sits motionless on its rock, the books are lined up in neat rows, the toys put away. Frankie's face tightens and untightens as he dreams.

Two a.m. Back on the couch, Gene startles, half asleep as an ambulance passes in the distance, and then there is only the sound of crickets and cicadas. Awake for a moment, he blinks heavily at a rerun of *Bewitched*, and flips through channels. Here is some jewelry for sale. Here is someone performing an autopsy.

In the dream, DJ is older. He looks to be nineteen or twenty, and he walks into a bar where Gene is hunched on a stool, sipping a glass of beer. Gene recognizes him right away—his posture, those thin shoulders, those large eyes. But now DJ's arms are long and muscular, tattooed. There is a hooded, unpleasant look on his face as he ambles up to the bar, pressing in next to Gene. DJ orders a shot of Jim Beam—Gene's old favorite.

"I've been thinking about you a lot, ever since I died," DJ murmurs. He doesn't look at Gene as he says this, but Gene knows who he is talking to, and his hands are shaky as he takes a sip of beer.

"I've been looking for you for a long time," DJ says softly, and the air is hot and thick. Gene puts a trembly cigarette to his mouth and breathes on it, choking on the taste. He wants to say, I'm sorry. Forgive me.

But he can't breathe. DJ shows his small, crooked teeth, staring at Gene as he gulps for air.

"I know how to hurt you," DJ whispers.

Gene opens his eyes, and the room is full of smoke. He sits up, disoriented: for a second he is still in the bar with DJ before he realizes that he's in his own house.

There is a fire somewhere: he can hear it. People say that fire "crackles," but in fact it seems like the amplified sound of tiny creatures eating, little wet mandibles, thousands and thousands of them, and then a heavy, whispered *whoof* as the fire finds another pocket of oxygen.

He can hear this even as he chokes blindly in the smoky air. The living room has a filmy haze over it, as if it is atomizing, fading away, and when he tries to stand up it disappears completely. There is a thick membrane of smoke above him, and he drops again to his hands and knees, gagging and coughing, a thin line of vomit trickling onto the rug in front of the still chattering television.

He has the presence of mind to keep low, crawling on his knees and elbows underneath the thick, billowing fumes. "Karen!" he calls. "Frankie!" But his voice is swallowed into the white noise of diligently licking flame. "Ach," he chokes, meaning to utter their names.

When he reaches the edge of the stairs he sees only flames and darkness above him. He puts his hands and knees on the bottom steps, but the heat pushes him back. He feels one of Frankie's action figures underneath his palm, the melting plastic adhering to his skin, and he shakes it away as another bright burst of flame reaches out of Frankie's bedroom for a moment. At the top of the stairs, through the curling fog, he can see the figure of a child watching him grimly, hunched there, its face lit and flickering. Gene cries out, lunging into the heat, crawling his way up the stairs to where the bedrooms are. He tries to call to them again, but instead he vomits.

There is another burst that covers the image that he thinks is a child. He can feel his hair and eyebrows shrinking and sizzling against his skin as the upstairs breathes out a concussion of sparks. He is aware that there are hot, floating bits of substance in the air, glowing orange and then winking out, turning to ash. The air is thick with angry buzzing, and that is all he can hear as he slips, turning end over end down the stairs, the humming and his own voice, a long vowel wheeling and echoing as the house spins into a blur.

And then he is lying on the grass. Red lights tick across his opened eyes in a steady, circling rhythm, and a woman, a paramedic, lifts her lips up from his. He draws in a long, desperate breath.

"Shhhhh," she says softly, and passes her hand along his eyes. "Don't look," she says.

But he does. He sees, off to the side, the long black plastic sleeping bag, with a strand of Karen's blond hair hanging out from the top. He sees the blackened, shriveled body of a child, curled into a fetal position. They place the corpse into the spread, zippered plastic opening of the body bag, and he can see the mouth, frozen, calcified, into an oval. A scream.

Reading as a Writer

1. What kind of narrator did Chaon choose for his story? What do you think of his choice?

2. What is the narrator's distance from the events of the story? Does it vary as the narrative progresses? In what sections is it closer and in what sections is it more distant?

3. Is this a traditional conflict–crisis–resolution story? Why or why not? What keeps you reading—where is the tension in the piece?

CHAPTER SEVEN

How Reliable Is This Narrator?
How Point of View Affects Our Understanding

Now that you understand the different point of view choices and how they can vary according to knowledge and distance, you come to the issue of *reliability*. "Okay, this narrator is telling me a story. How trustworthy is he or she? How much of this story do I believe?"

In this chapter we look at issues of reliability, particularly as related to first and third person narrators. Then there are some exercises to practice what you've read about. Finally, we present two stories with narrators who may or may not be unreliable.

How We Judge the Integrity of Stories

Whether you realize it or not, every time someone tells you something, you are evaluating the integrity of the information. In life, we size up the people around us and have pretty strong judgments about their biases, the limits of their knowledge, their ability to understand complex or abstract thought. We factor all that into our willingness to "buy" what someone tells us.

It's the same with what we read. We constantly question the reliability of the teller of the story. We allow our interpretation of reliability to affect our digestion of the work.

There are different issues of reliability based on the point of view options. We'll examine them individually.

First Person Point of View and Reliability

If you choose a first person narrator, you're going to run into the issue of reliability. Even the most reliable, the most honest, the most straightforward, intelligent, and moral first person narrator is going to have limitations.

What are some of these limitations? Unless you are writing science fiction or some other kind of nonrealistic prose, the following limitations generally apply:

- Geographic: The narrator, who is a character in the story, can only be in one place at a time.
- Temporal: The narrator can only exist at one time period.

- Physical: The narrator is limited by his or her (human or otherwise) body, and the abilities of that body.

- Intellectual: The narrator's intellect almost certainly has limitations, even if he or she is highly intelligent.

- Experiential: The narrator can only have so much knowledge of the world, only so much personal experience.

- Moral/spiritual: The narrator can be quite intelligent and experienced but morally deficient.

- Emotional: What we frequently refer to today as "emotional intelligence" can figure into a character's abilities and limitations.

Okay, so limitations are going to exist for any first person narrator. In fiction, you need to know what those limitations are and how they affect your story.

It's important to note that the more you decide to limit your narrator's honesty, intelligence, moral judgment, and so on, the more it will distort your story. Not only will you have a distorted story, but also you will need some way of showing the reader that you, *the author,* are aware of the limitations of the narrator and how they distort the piece. You must give readers clues as to how to compare what the narrator says with what the reality of your story truly is.

Let's look at some examples.

Through the fence, between the curling flower spaces, I could see them hitting. They were coming toward where the flag was and I went along the fence. Luster was hunting in the grass by the flower tree. They took the flag out, and they were hitting. Then they put the flag back and they went to the table, and he hit and the other hit. Then they went on, and I went along the fence. Luster came away from the flower tree and we went along the fence and they stopped and we stopped and I looked through the fence while Luster was hunting in the grass.

"Here, caddie." He hit. They went away across the pasture. I held to the fence and watched them going away.

"Listen at you, now," Luster said. "Aint you something, thirty-three years old, going on that way. After I done went all the way to town to buy you that cake. Hush up that moaning. Aint you going to help me find that quarter so I can go to the show tonight."

They were hitting little, across the pasture. I went along the fence to where the flag was. It flapped on the bright grass and the trees.

"Come on," Luster said. "We done looked there. They aint no more coming right now. Lets go down to the branch and find that quarter before them niggers finds it."

It was red, flapping on the pasture. Then there was a bird slanting and tilting on it. Luster threw. The flag flapped on the bright grass and the trees. I held onto the fence.

"Shut up that moaning," Luster said. "I cant make them come if they aint coming, can I. If you dont hush up, mammy aint going to have no birthday for you. If you dont hush, you know what I going to do. I going to eat that cake all up. Eat them candles, too. Eat all them thirty-three candles. Come on, lets go down to the branch. I got to find my quarter. Maybe you can find one of they balls. Here. Here they is. Way over yonder. See." He came to the fence and pointed his arm. "See them. They aint coming back here no more. Come on."

We went along the fence and came to the garden fence where our shadows were. My shadow was higher than Luster's on the fence.

—WILLIAM FAULKNER, *The Sound and the Fury*

The title of this book comes from Shakespeare: "Life is a tale told by an idiot, full of sound and fury, signifying nothing." It's told by a whole series of unreliable narrators, of whom Benjy, a retarded man, is just one. None are quite as dramatically unreliable (in one sense, anyway) as Benjy. But if you read through the excerpt again, carefully, you'll see that although we are getting physical things described without a context that easily allows us to make sense of it, the physical descriptions seem to be accurate (if you haven't figured it out yet, Benjy is watching a game of golf being played). We're also getting dialogue that seems to be reliable—it gives us clues about what is going on. Gradually, a picture of what is happening arises, based on the descriptions of what is happening and the dialogue. (Benjy is watching a game of golf, he's crying and making a fuss, and his keeper, Luster, is trying to quiet him down. It happens to be Benjy's birthday; he is thirty-three years old today.)

Always, with an unreliable narrator, we are asking ourselves (whether we know it or not): What information are we getting that we can trust? What can't we trust? In this case, Benjy is telling us the truth, to the best of his ability. He's very honest, observant, intuitive. He just doesn't have the ability to assimilate and analyze and explain things. But he reports things honestly and accurately, and his judgment in many ways is more trustworthy than that of any of the other more "normal" characters in the book.

And now, a convention alert: Generally, even when the narrator is unreliable, the aspects of scene—the showing—tend to be reliable, trustworthy. That is, when a scene consists of dialogue and action, the convention is that we are seeing things the way they actually happened. We're hearing what was actually said. It's the *telling*, or narrative, that is potentially unreliable.

What is the reason for this? Because if we don't get some hard-core evidence of reality somewhere in a story, some way of knowing what is actually going on, we are going to be dreadfully confused. Thus scenes have traditionally acted as a "reality check" with unreliable narrators.

Now, interpreting what is said, or how people looked, or how they said something has always been fair game for distortion. But generally speaking, if a physical action is described, or words in quotation marks are provided in a scene—even by a very unreliable first person narrator—we are supposed to believe them.

Here's another example of an unreliable narrator. Can you tell what can be believed from this passage?

> They're out there.
>
> Black boys in white suits up before me to commit sex acts in the hall and get it mopped up before I can catch them.
>
> They're mopping when I come out the dorm, all three of them sulky and hating everything, the time of day, the place they're at here, the people they got to work around. When they hate like this, better if they don't see me. I creep along the wall quiet as dust in my canvas shoes, but they got special sensitive equipment detects my fear and they all look up, all three at once, eyes glittering out of the black faces like the hard glitter of radio tubes out of the back of an old radio.
>
> "Here's the Chief. The *soo*-pah Chief, fellas. Ol' Chief Broom. Here you go, Chief Broom . . ."
>
> Stick a mop in my hand and motion to the spot they aim for me to clean today, and I go. One swats the backs of my legs with a broom handle to hurry me past.
>
> "Haw, you look at 'im shag it? Big enough to eat apples off my head an' he mind me like a baby."
>
> They laugh and I hear them mumbling behind me, heads close together. Hum of black machinery, humming hate and death and other hospital secrets. They don't bother not talking out loud about their hate secrets when I'm nearby because they think I'm deaf and dumb. Everybody thinks so. I'm cagey enough to fool them that much. If my being half Indian ever helped me in any way in this dirty life, it helped me being cagey, helped me all these years.
>
> I'm mopping near the ward door when a key hits it from the other side and I know it's the Big Nurse by the way the lockworks cleave to the key, soft and swift and familiar she been around locks so long. She slides through the door with a gust of cold and locks the door behind her and I see her fingers trail across the polished steel—tip of each finger the same color as her lips. Funny orange. Like the tip of a soldering iron. Color so hot or so cold if she touches you with it, you can't tell which.
>
> She's carrying her woven wicker bag like the ones the Umpqua tribe sells out along the hot August highway, a bag shape of a tool box with a hemp handle. She's had it all the years I been here. It's a loose weave and I can see inside it; there's no compact or lipstick or woman stuff, she's got that bag full of a thousand parts she aims to use in her duties today—wheels and gears, cogs polished to a hard glitter, tiny pills that gleam like porcelain, needles, forceps, watchmakers' pliers, rolls of copper wire.
>
> —KEN KESEY, *One Flew over the Cuckoo's Nest*

The opening of Kesey's novel shows us we are in the hands of a very unreliable first person narrator indeed. Special sensitive equipment? A thousand parts—including wheels and gears, cogs, needles, forceps—in a nurse's personal handbag? Unlikely. Yet *some* of it seems plausible: the men mopping the hallway, the woman sweeping into the hospital, full of confidence and bringing with her a cold fear. These seem to ring true. And in fact we can glean from this very unreliable narrator a sense of what is happening, a lot of it from the dialogue, which we know, by convention, to trust, but also from a sense of the emotional truth inherent in the observations.

Which leads us to one of the key reasons that you might choose to employ an unreliable narrator: sometimes-unreliable narrators can be used to get at deeper truths. Much of what they tell us is obviously not true and obviously distorted. But in a case like this, where clearly we're not supposed to take what he says literally, in some way an unreliable narrator can get at more important information. In this case, Chief Broom has a clearer view of what is going on in the mental hospital than anyone else. He sees the danger posed by the often malicious staff to the inmates—especially those inmates who rock the boat. It's exaggerated and paranoid, but it's very real. In this case, the facts are less important than the truth that emerges from the narrative.

Third Person Point of View and Reliability

Now here's an important piece of information: when a third person narrator tells us something about a story, it is, *by convention,* always true. Take a moment to think about this. Remember, it's not a character with flaws (human or otherwise), like with a first person narrator. No, this is an outsider who is not involved in the story; not a human character but a disembodied intelligence telling us about the events of the story. And when the third person narrator speaks, according to convention, it is always the truth, always reliable.

If that is the case, what do you make of this opening to a very famous story?

> When Gregor Samsa woke up one morning from unsettling dreams, he found himself changed in his bed into a monstrous vermin. He was lying on his back as hard as armor plate, and when he lifted his head a little, he saw his vaulted brown belly, sectioned by arch-shaped ribs, to whose dome the cover, about to slide off completely, could barely cling. His many legs, pitifully thin compared with the size of the rest of him, were waving helplessly before his eyes.
>
> "What's happened to me?" he thought. It was no dream.
>
> —FRANZ KAFKA, "The Metamorphosis"

What's going on here? People don't turn into cockroaches overnight. We know this. Yet it's a third person narrator. How are we to make sense of a story that begins like this?

Well, we have four options to consider when we're told something that doesn't make sense (given that we know that a third person narrator is, by definition, always reliable):

1. Perhaps we're in a world in which this implausible, improbable, unbelievable thing is real. We're being asked, according to Coleridge's famous phrase, to make

a "willing suspension of disbelief." This is perfectly valid. As creators of our fictional worlds, we can make the sky pink and pigs fly—anything we want. In this particular case, we have to consider the possibility that this is a world in which people *can* turn into cockroaches.

2. Perhaps we're in a character's mind, accomplished through the use of very close third person point of view. In other words, we're seeing the world from an unreliable character's perspective even though we're in third person. In effect, our third person narrator has been "possessed" by a character in the story and can only tell us what that character sees and believes. Stories of unpleasant or implausible events that end with a character waking up and realizing "it was all a dream" fall into this category. So do stories in which we find out, at some point, that the character is insane.

3. Perhaps we've entered the realm of metafiction: mocking the conventions, turning the conventions on their heads. This kind of writing attempts to draw attention to the writing itself, or to the ridiculous nature of conventions or of tradition, in order to say something about art, the creative process, the artificiality of fictional form, and so on. The characters aren't what is important—or not what's primarily important. The author is deliberately playing with the conventions for reasons of his or her own.

4. Finally, perhaps the author simply made a mistake. (Oops, people can't turn into cockroaches.) This is a bad thing. The last thing we want is for the *author* to lose credibility with the readers.

In the case of "The Metamorphosis" our choice is between the first and second options above: either this is a world in which young men can inexplicably turn into cockroaches, or we're in the mind of an unreliable (mad or dreaming) character. As it turns out, reading into the story further, we can eliminate the second possibility; Gregor has indeed been turned into a giant insect, and his life is terribly plagued as a result.

Let's examine the second possibility a little closer: What happens when distance has collapsed and we're in the mind of a character through third person intimate point of view?

The kettle is about to boil, and the telephone rings. He dries his hands slowly and goes to answer it, expecting Mandy Navarrete's fourth child. Christmas Day, a long silent day, will end now with a long unpleasant night. There was a time when deliveries excited him; during the gene-pool study he looked forward to those infant eyes, and setting up his camera and lights. But there is nothing to study now. Mandy Navarrete is all muscles and resistance, a woman who delivers in her own time. Her grandmother Concepcion Navarrete was his first grade teacher. She was similarly muscular, and disapproved of his family.

He lifts the receiver slowly on the fourth or fifth ring. The voice speaks in hurried Spanish but he answers in English because he knows they can understand. He hasn't spoken Spanish since the day he married Alice. "There is plenty of time," he says. "I know this process. We don't need to be in a panic."

He hears silence, static, several different voices and questions and then the same voice again, emphatically repeating its word. *Secuestrada*. Kidnapped.

"Who is this?"

He listens. The voice is very distant and often breaks. It is a woman, a friend of his daughter. He tries to understand which daughter they mean. *Secuestrada*. Codi has been away for a few days, but this voice is saying, "Hollie." Someone is keeping her. She was in the field alone, with her horse, when they came to blow up the building. He understands none of this.

Hollie, the woman insists, as if trying to wake him from sleep. Are you the father? We are very much afraid.   —BARBARA KINGSOLVER, *Animal Dreams*

You can see, in this excerpt, how the third person narration leads us to believe one thing (that the doctor is waiting to deliver a child), when actually we are in the mind of an unreliable narrator through the use of close third person point of view. The character in question is elderly, senile, and terribly unreliable. He believes he is still a practicing doctor although he has not delivered a baby in decades. Eventually the third person narrator pulls back and lets us see how we have been fooled by the close narrative distance.

Sometimes we can spend quite a bit of time wondering whether we are in a strange world, with its own rules, or whether we have entered into the mind of one character or another. Let's look at another example:

Riding up the winding road of Saint Agnes Cemetery in the back of the rattling old truck, Francis Phelan became aware that the dead, even more than the living, settled down in neighborhoods. The truck was suddenly surrounded by fields of monuments and cenotaphs of kindred design and striking size, all guarding the privileged dead. But the truck moved on and the limits of mere privilege became visible, for here now came the acres of truly prestigious death: illustrious men and women, captains of life without their diamonds, furs, carriages, and limousines, but buried in pomp and glory, vaulted in great tombs built like heavenly safe deposit boxes, or parts of the Acropolis. And ah yes, here too, inevitably, came the flowing masses, row upon row of them under simple headstones and simpler crosses. Here was the neighborhood of the Phelans.

Francis's mother twitched nervously in her grave as the truck carried him nearer to her; and Francis's father lit his pipe, smiled at his wife's discomfort, and looked out from his own bit of sod to catch a glimpse of how much his son had changed since the train accident.

Francis's father smoked roots of grass that died in the periodic droughts afflicting the cemetery. He stored the root essence in his pockets until it was brittle to the touch, then pulverized it between his fingers and packed his pipe. Francis's mother wove crosses from the dead dandelions and other deep-rooted weeds; careful to preserve their fullest length, she wove them while they were still in the green stage of death, then ate them with an insatiable revulsion.

> "Look at that tomb," Francis said to his companion. "Ain't that somethin'? That's Arthur T. Grogan. I saw him around Albany when I was a kid. He owned all the electricity in town."
> "He ain't got much of it now," Rudy said.
> "Don't bet on it," Francis said. "Them kind of guys hang onto a good thing."
> —WILLIAM KENNEDY, *Ironweed*

Kennedy's Pulitzer Prize–winning novel puts us in the mind of Francis Phelan, and we see the world from his point of view through the use of close, limited third person point of view. These ghosts are Francis's ghosts: only he can see them and interact with them, and they appear to him throughout the book. Are they for real? Or are we seeing the world through an unreliable character's point of view? You should read the book yourself to find out what you think, but I think we're supposed to believe in the ghosts. They're so authoritative, know so much about the history of Albany, about Francis's family—they know things that Francis doesn't know, which makes them infinitely credible. So this is a world in which a character gets visits from ghosts from his past, who inform him of things, or accuse him, or otherwise interact with him. He is not dreaming, and he is not insane. The ghosts are real (even though no one else can see or hear them).

Again, the rules of narration are yours to set. You are the one making a contract with your reader, and the only stipulation is that you make the terms of the contract clear and that you don't break the contract. Be consistent. Let there be logic. That logic can be complex—it can be, like in James Joyce's work, so convoluted that it keeps scholars guessing for decades as to who is narrating any particular section, and what he or she knows. But it has to be there.

EXERCISES

Determining the reliability of your narrator is one of the critical aspects of working with both first and third person points of view. It's important for first person point of view because any character, no matter how intelligent or morally upright or experienced, is going to have limitations; it's important for third person because if you decide to play with reliability by manipulating the narrative distance, you need to have a way of showing what the truth is.

Exercise 1: The Way I See It

GOAL: To show how different characters' perceptions of an event can differ based on their individual biases.

1. Choose two characters who are in a situation in which one confronts the other as having done something wrong or broken the rules in some way.

2. Tell about the incident from both perspectives, using first person point of view (POV) each time. Show how each character distorts things in his or her favor.

Here's an example by Perry Stuart:

POV 1

I was walking down the street when suddenly, out of nowhere, came a car, going way over the speed limit (which is 35 on residential streets, but 25 on our street because we have a school here). A cat happened to be crossing the road at the same time, and whoosh! Suddenly there was a screech and the car had stopped, but no cat in sight. I was sure that the cat was dead, I was sure I had heard the thump, it wouldn't have surprised me if the cat had dragged itself off bleeding to die on its own, only no blood, no sign of the cat. The driver was unrepentant. "Stupid animal," he said, thinking I was sympathetic to him. "You'd think they'd learn to stay out of the way of traffic." Well, I certainly told him off! I was enraged! I told him that I would take his license plate and report him to the police. He was unmoved by my anger, just put his foot on the gas and zoomed on.

POV 2

It was one of those streets that you're not supposed to go down unless you actually live there. "Closed to local traffic" is what the sign said. There used to be speed bumps, but they took them out, too many complaints. But it was the fastest way to the freeway and I was late (of course) and this job really mattered to me, but I wasn't going that fast, perhaps 40 miles an hour, which I think is below the speed limit on these streets, when a black and white cat suddenly streaked out into the road in front of me. Holy cow! Of course, I slammed on the brakes, and waited for that sickening thud (I hate that part of it). There was a guy standing there, who'd witnessed the whole thing. I could tell he was just as shocked as I was. "Stupid animal," I told him, and he agreed. He added, quite mildly, that perhaps I was going a little over the speed limit, and I told him that the speed limit was too slow on these streets, which were wide enough to go at least 10 miles an hour faster. He didn't say anything, but I could tell he agreed. I said goodbye and powered myself out of there. Still no sign of the cat, but who cares? The little bastards have nine lives, after all.

Exercise 2: See What I See, Hear What I Hear

GOAL: To focus on the concrete details that are solid evidence of the reality of a particular creative world.

1. Place your character in a situation that should be familiar but isn't (e.g., imagine that your character has temporary amnesia and is doubting his or her grasp of reality, and is looking for clues as to what reality is).

2. Write about the situation using concrete sensory details to show your reader what reality is.

Here are two passages by Carl Czyzewski:

I was aware of a few things right away. That I was inside a room, a room in a house by the looks of it. There was a sofa, a yellow tapestry-like covering to it, I could feel the rough texture of the material with my fingers. When I sat down, it held my weight firmly, with bounce. At my feet, a luxurious oriental carpet on top of a hardwood floor, polished to a high gleam. A man sitting across from me, he seemed to be talking, but the meaning of the words escaped me. Just meaningless syllables.

There was a bench. That was a reality. He could feel its cold, hard surface. Droplets of something damp on top. Dew? Someone's tears? He shuddered at the thought. A slight movement out of the corner of his eye. No. Concentrate on facts. There was the bench. And over here. A tree. There was the coolness of standing under its branches, out of the hot sun. The sun. The brightness. The ground he was walking on, the newspaper he held in his hand. "I am going for a walk," he said out loud, as if to verify that he existed.

READINGS

ROBERT OLEN BUTLER

A Good Scent from a Strange Mountain

HO CHI MINH CAME TO ME again last night, his hands covered with confectioner's sugar. This was something of a surprise to me, the first time I saw him beside my bed, in the dim light from the open shade. My oldest daughter leaves my shades open, I think so that I will not forget that the sun has risen again in the morning. I am a very old man. She seems to expect that one morning I will simply forget to keep living. This is very foolish. I will one night rise up from my bed and slip into her room and open the shade there. Let *her* see the sun in the morning. She is sixty-four years old and she should worry for herself. I could never die from forgetting.

But the light from the street was enough to let me recognize Ho when I woke, and he said to me, "Dao, my old friend, I have heard it is time to visit you." Already on that first night there was a sweet smell about him, very strong in the dark, even before I could see his hands. I said nothing, but I stretched to the nightstand beside me and I turned on the light to see if he would go away. And he did not. He stood there beside the bed—I could even see him reflected in the window—and I knew it was real because he did not appear as he was when I'd known him but as he was when he'd died. This was Uncle Ho before me, the thin old man with the dewlap beard wearing the dark clothes of a peasant and the rubber sandals, just like in the news pictures I studied with such a strange feeling for all those years. Strange because when I knew him, he was not yet Ho Chi Minh. It was 1917 and he was Nguyen Ai Quoc and we were both young men with clean-shaven faces, the best of friends, and we worked at the Carlton Hotel in London, where I was a dishwasher and he was a pastry cook under the great Escoffier. We were the best of friends and we saw snow for the first time together. This was before we began to work at the hotel. We shoveled snow and Ho would stop for a moment and blow his breath out before him and it would make him smile, to see what was inside him, as if it was the casting of bones to tell the future.

On that first night when he came to me in my house in New Orleans, I finally saw what it was that smelled so sweet and I said to him, "Your hands are covered with sugar."

He looked at them with a kind of sadness.

I have received that look myself in the past week. It is time now for me to see my family, and the friends I have made who are still alive. This is our custom from Vietnam. When you are very old, you put aside a week or two to receive the people of your life so that you can tell one another your feelings, or try at last to understand one another, or simply say good-bye. It is a formal leave-taking, and with good luck you can do this before you have your final illness. I have lived almost a century and perhaps I should have called them all to me sooner, but at last I felt a deep weariness and I said to my oldest daughter that it was time.

They look at me with sadness, some of them. Usually the dull-witted ones, or the insincere ones. But Ho's look was, of course, not dull-witted or insincere. He considered his hands and said, "The glaze. Maestro's glaze."

There was the soft edge of yearning in his voice and I had the thought that perhaps he had come to me for some sort of help. I said to him, "I don't remember. I only washed dishes." As soon as the words were out of my mouth, I decided it was foolish for me to think he had come to ask me about the glaze.

But Ho did not treat me as foolish. He looked at me and shook his head. "It's all right," he said. "I remember the temperature now. Two hundred and thirty degrees, when the sugar is between the large thread stage and the small orb stage. The Maestro was very clear about that and I remember." I knew from his eyes, however, that there was much more that still eluded him. His eyes did not seem to move at all from my face, but there was some little shifting of them, a restlessness that perhaps only I could see, since I was his close friend from the days when the world did not know him.

I am nearly one hundred years old, but I can still read a man's face. Perhaps better than I ever have. I sit in the overstuffed chair in my living room and I receive my visitors and I want these people, even the dull-witted and insincere ones—please excuse an old man's ill temper for calling them that—I want them all to be good with one another. A Vietnamese family is extended as far as the bloodline strings us together, like so many paper lanterns around a village square. And we all give off light together. That's the way it has always been in our culture. But these people who come to visit me have been in America for a long time and there are very strange things going on that I can see in their faces.

None stranger than this morning. I was in my overstuffed chair and with me there were four of the many members of my family: my son-in-law, Thang, a former colonel in the Army of the Republic of Vietnam and one of the insincere ones, sitting on my Castro convertible couch; his youngest son, Loi, who had come in late, just a few minutes earlier, and had thrown himself down on the couch as well, youngest but a man old enough to have served as a lieutenant under his father as our country fell to the communists more than a decade ago; my daughter Lam, who is Thang's wife, hovering behind the both of them and refusing all invitations to sit down; and my oldest daughter leaning against the door frame, having no doubt just returned from my room, where she had opened the shade that I had closed when I awoke.

It was Thang who gave me the sad look I have grown accustomed to, and perhaps seemed to him at that moment a little weak, a little distant. I had stopped listening to the small talk of these people and I had let my eyes half close, though I could still see them clearly and I was very alert. Thang has a steady face and the quick eyes of a man who is ready to come under fire, but I have always read much more there, in spite of his efforts to show nothing. So after he thought I'd faded from the room, it was with slow eyes, not quick, that he moved to his son and began to speak of the killing.

You should understand that Mr. Nguyen Bich Le had been shot dead in our community here in New Orleans just last week. There are many of us Vietnamese living in New Orleans and one man, Mr. Le, published a little newspaper for all of us. He had recently made the fatal error—though it should not be that in America—of writing that it was time to accept the reality of the communist government in Vietnam and begin to talk with them. We had to work now with those who controlled our country. He said that he remained a patriot to the Republic of Vietnam, and I believed him. If anyone had asked an old man's opinion on this whole matter, I would not have been afraid to say that Mr. Le was right.

But he was shot dead last week. He was forty-five years old and he had a wife and three children and he was shot as he sat behind the wheel of his Chevrolet pickup truck. I find a detail like that especially moving, that this man was killed in his Chevrolet, which I understand is a strongly American thing. We knew this in Saigon. In Saigon it was very American to own a Chevrolet, just as it was French to own a Citroën.

And Mr. Le had taken one more step in his trusting embrace of this new culture. He had bought not only a Chevrolet but a Chevrolet pickup truck, which made him not only American but also a man of Louisiana, where there are many pickup trucks. He did not, however, also purchase a gun rack for the back window, another sign of this place. Perhaps it would have been well if he had, for it was through the back window that the bullet was fired. Someone had hidden in the bed of his truck and had killed him from behind in his Chevrolet and the reason for this act was made very clear in a phone call to the newspaper office by a nameless representative of the Vietnamese Party for the Annihilation of Communism and for the National Restoration.

And Thang, my son-in-law, said to his youngest son, Loi, "There is no murder weapon." What I saw was a faint lift of his eyebrows as he said this, like he was inviting his son to listen beneath his words. Then he said it again, more slowly, like it was code. "There is *no weapon*." My grandson nodded his head once, a crisp little snap. Then my daughter Lam said in a very loud voice, with her eyes on me, "That was a terrible thing, the death of Mr. Le." She nudged her husband and son, and both men turned their faces sharply to me and they looked at me squarely and said, also in very loud voices, "Yes, it was terrible."

I am not deaf, and I closed my eyes further, having seen enough and wanting them to think that their loud talk had not only failed to awake me but had put me more completely to sleep. I did not like to deceive them, however, even though I have already spoken critically of these members of my family. I am a Hao Buddhist and I believe in harmony among all living things, especially the members of a Vietnamese family.

After Ho had reassured me, on that first visit, about the temperature needed to heat Maestro Escoffier's glaze, he said, "Dao, my old friend, do you still follow the path you chose in Paris?"

He meant by this my religion. It was in Paris that I embraced the Buddha and disappointed Ho. We went to France in early 1918, with the war still on, and we lived in the poorest street of the poorest part of the Seventeenth Arrondissement. Number nine, Impasse Compoint, a blind alley with a few crumbling houses, all but ours rented out for storage. The cobblestones were littered with fallen roof tiles and Quoc and I each had a tiny single room with only an iron bedstead and a crate to sit on. I could see my friend Quoc in the light of the tallow candle and he was dressed in a dark suit and a bowler hat and he looked very foolish. I did not say so, but he knew it himself and he kept seating and reseating the hat and shaking his head very slowly, with a loudly silent anger. This was near the end of our time together, for I was visiting daily with a Buddhist monk and he was drawing me back to the religion of my father. I had run from my father, gone to sea, and that was where I had met Nguyen Ai Quoc and we had gone to London and to Paris and now my father was calling me back, through a Vietnamese monk I met in the Tuileries.

Quoc, on the other hand, was being called not from his past but from his future. He had rented the dark suit and bowler and he would spend the following weeks in Versailles, walking up and down the mirrored corridors of the Palace trying to gain an audience with Woodrow Wilson. Quoc had eight requests for the Western world concerning Indochina. Simple things. Equal rights, freedom of assembly, freedom of the press. The essential things that he knew Wilson would understand, based as they were on Wilson's own Fourteen Points. And Quoc did not even intend to ask for independence. He wanted Vietnamese representatives in the French Parliament. That was all he would ask. But his bowler made him angry. He wrenched out of the puddle of candlelight, both his hands clutching the bowler, and I heard him muttering in the darkness and I felt that this was a bad sign already, even before he had set foot in Versailles. And as it turned out, he never saw Wilson, or Lloyd George either, or even Clemenceau. But somehow his frustration with his hat was what made me sad, even now, and I reached out from my bedside and said, "Uncle Ho, it's all right."

He was still beside me. This was not an awakening, as you might expect; this was not a dream ending with the bowler in Paris and I awaking to find that Ho was never there. He was still beside my bed, though he was just beyond my outstretched hand and he did not move to me. He smiled on one side of his mouth, a smile full of irony, as if he, too, was thinking about night he'd tried on his rented clothes. He said, "Do you remember how I worked in Paris?"

I thought about this and I did remember, with the words of his advertisement in the newspaper "La Vie Ouvrière": "If you would like a lifelong memento of your family, have your photos retouched at Nguyen Ai Quoc's." This was his work in Paris; he retouched photos with a very delicate hand, the same fine hand that Monsieur Escoffier had admired in London. I said, "Yes, I remember."

Ho nodded gravely. "I painted the blush into the cheeks of Frenchmen."

I said, "A lovely portrait in a lovely frame for forty francs," another phrase from his advertisement.

"Forty-five," Ho said.

I thought now of his question that I had not answered. I motioned to the far corner of the room where the prayer table stood. "I still follow the path."

He looked and said, "At least you became a Hoa Hao."

He could tell this from the simplicity of the table. There was only a red cloth upon it and four Chinese characters: Bao Son Ky Huong. This is the saying of the Hoa Haos. We follow the teachings of a monk who broke away from the fancy rituals of the other Buddhists. We do not need elaborate pagodas or rituals. The Hoa Hao believes that the maintenance of our spirits is very simple, and the mystery of joy is simple, too. The four characters mean "A good scent from a strange mountain."

I had always admired the sense of humor of my friend Quoc, so I said, "You never did stop painting the blush into the faces of Westerners."

Ho looked back to me but he did not smile. I was surprised at this but more surprised at my little joke seeming to remind him of his hands. He raised them and studied them and said, "After the heating, what was the surface for the glaze?"

"My old friend," I said, "you worry me now."

But Ho did not seem to hear. He turned away and crossed the room and I knew he was real because he did not vanish from my sight but opened the door and went out and closed the door behind him with a loud click.

I rang for my daughter. She had given me a porcelain bell, and after allowing Ho enough time to go down the stairs and out the front door, if that was where he was headed, I rang the bell, and my daughter, who is a very light sleeper, soon appeared.

"What is it, Father?" she asked with great patience in her voice. She is a good girl. She understands about Vietnamese families and she is a smart girl. "Please feel the door knob," I said.

She did so without the slightest hesitation and this was a lovely gesture on her part, a thing that made me wish to rise up and embrace her, though I was very tired and did not move.

"Yes?" she asked after touching the knob.

"Is it sticky?"

She touched it again. "Ever so slightly," she said. "Would you like me to clean it?"

"In the morning," I said.

She smiled and crossed the room and kissed me on the forehead. She smelled of lavender and fresh bedclothes and there are so many who have gone on before me into the world of spirits and I yearn for them all, yearn to find them all together in a village square, my wife there smelling of lavender and our own sweat, like on a night in Saigon soon after the terrible fighting in 1968 when we finally opened the windows onto the night and there were sounds of bombs falling on the horizon and there was no breeze at all, just the heavy stillness of the time between the dry season and the wet, and Saigon smelled of tar and motorcycle exhaust and cordite but when I opened the window and turned to my wife, the room was full of a wonderful scent, a sweet smell that made her sit up, for she sensed it, too. This was a smell that had nothing to do with flowers but instead reminded us that flowers were always ready to fall into dust, while this smell was as if a gemstone had begun to give off a scent, as if a mountain of emerald had found its own scent. I crossed the room to my wife and we were already old, we had already buried children and grandchildren that we prayed waited for us in that village square at the foot of the strange mountain, but when I came near the bed, she lifted her silk gown and threw it aside and I pressed close to her and our own sweat smelled sweet on that night. I want to be with her in that square and with the rest of those we'd buried, the tiny limbs and the sullen eyes and the gray faces of the puzzled children and the surprised adults and the weary old people who have gone before us, who know the secrets now. And the sweet smell of the glaze on Ho's hands reminds me of others that I would want in the square, the people from the ship, too, the Vietnamese boy from a village near my own who died of a fever in the Indian Ocean and the natives in Dakar who were forced by colonial officials to swim out to our ship in shark-infested waters to secure the moorings and two were killed before our eyes without a French regret. Ho was very moved by this, and I want those men in our square and I want the Frenchman, too, who called Ho "monsieur" for the first time. A man on the dock in Marseilles. Ho spoke of him twice more during our year together and I want that Frenchman there. And, of course, Ho. Was he in the village square even now, waiting? Heating his glaze fondant? My daughter smoothing my covers around me and the smell of lavender on her was still strong.

"He was in this room," I said to her to explain the sticky doorknob.

"Who was?"

But I was very sleepy and I could say no more, though perhaps she would not have understood anyway, in spite of being the smart girl that she is.

The next night I left my light on to watch for Ho's arrival, but I dozed off and he had to wake me. He was sitting in a chair that he'd brought from across the room. He said to me, "Dao. Wake up, my old friend."

I must have awakened when he pulled the chair near to me, for I heard each of these words. "I am awake," I said. "I was thinking of the poor men who had to swim out to our ship."

"They are already among those I have served," Ho said. "Before I forgot." And he raised his hands and they were still covered with sugar.

I said, "Wasn't it a marble slab?" I had a memory, strangely clear after these many years, as strange as my memory of Ho's Paris business card.

"A marble slab," Ho repeated, puzzled.

"That you poured the heated sugar on."

"Yes." Ho's sweet-smelling hands came forward but they did not quite touch me. I thought to reach out from beneath the covers and take them in my own hands, but Ho leaped up and paced about the room. "The marble slab, moderately oiled. Of course. I am to let the sugar half cool and then use the spatula to move it about in all directions, every bit of it, so that it doesn't harden and form lumps."

I asked, "Have you seen my wife?"

Ho had wandered to the far side of the room, but he turned and crossed back to me at this. "I'm sorry, my friend. I never knew her."

I must have shown some disappointment in my face, for Ho sat down and brought his own face near mine. "I'm sorry," he said. "There are many other people that I must find here."

"Are you very disappointed in me?" I asked. "For not having traveled the road with you?"

"It's very complicated," Ho said softly. "You felt that you'd taken action. I am no longer in a position to question another soul's choice."

"Are you at peace, where you are?" I asked this knowing of his worry over the recipe for the glaze, but I hoped that this was only a minor difficulty in the afterlife, like the natural anticipation of the good cook expecting guests when everything always turns out fine in the end.

But Ho said, "I am not at peace."

"Is Monsieur Escoffier over there?"

"I have not seen him. This has nothing to do with him, directly."

"What is it about?"

"I don't know."

"You won the country. You know that, don't you?"

Ho shrugged. "There are no countries here."

I should have remembered Ho's shrug when I began to see things in the eyes of my son-in-law and grandson this morning. But something quickened in me, a suspicion. I kept my eyes shut and laid my head to the side, as if I was asleep, encouraging them to talk more.

My daughter said, "This is not the place to speak."

But the men did not regard her. "How?" Loi asked his father, referring to the missing murder weapon.

"It's best not to know too much," Thang said.

Then there was a silence. For all the quickness I'd felt at the first suspicion, I was very slow now. In fact, I did think of Ho from that second night. Not his shrug. He had fallen silent for a long time and I had dosed my eyes, for the light seemed very bright. I listened to his silence just as I listened to the silence of these two conspirators before me.

And then Ho said, "They were fools, but I can't bring myself to grow angry anymore."

I opened my eyes in the bedroom and the light was off. Ho had turned it off, knowing that it was bothering me. "Who were fools?" I asked.

"We had fought together to throw out the Japanese. I had very good friends among them. I smoked their lovely Salem cigarettes. They had been repressed by colonialists themselves. Did they not know their own history?"

"Do you mean the Americans?"

"There are a million souls here with me, the young men of our country, and they are all dressed in black suits and bowler hats. In the mirrors they are made ten million, a hundred million."

"I chose my path, my dear friend Quoc, so that there might be harmony."

And even with that yearning for harmony I could not overlook what my mind made of what my ears had heard this morning. Thang was telling Loi that the murder weapon had been disposed of Thang and Loi both knew the killers, were in sympathy with them, perhaps were part of the killing. The father and son had been airborne rangers and I had several times heard them talk bitterly of the exile of our people. We were fools for trusting the Americans all along, they said. We should have taken matters forward and disposed of the infinitely corrupt Thieu and done what needed to be done. Whenever they spoke like this in front of me, there was soon a quick exchange of side-ways glances at me and then a turn and an apology. "We're sorry Grandfather. Old times often bring old anger. We are happy our family is living a new life."

I would wave my hand at this, glad to have the peace of the family restored. Glad to turn my face and smell the dogwood tree or even smell the coffee plant across the highway. These things had come to be the new smells of our family. But then a weakness often came upon me. The others would drift away, the men, and perhaps one of my daughters would come to me and stroke my head and not say a word and none of them ever would ask why I was weeping. I would smell the rich blood smells of the afterbirth and I would hold our first son, still slippery in my arms, and there was the smell of dust from the square and the smell of the South China Sea just over the rise of the hill and there was the smell of the blood and of the inner flesh from my wife as my son's own private sea flowed from this woman that I loved, flowed and carried him into the life that would disappear from him so soon. In the afterlife would he stand before me on unsteady child's legs? Would I have to bend low to greet him or would he be a man now?

My grandson said, after the silence had nearly carried me into real sleep, troubled sleep, my grandson Loi said to his father, "I would be a coward not to know."

Thang laughed and said, "You have proved yourself no coward."

And I wished then to sleep, I wished to fall asleep and let go of life somewhere in my dreams and seek my village square. I have lived too long, I thought. My daughter was saying, "Are you both mad?" And then she changed her voice, making the words very precise. "Let Grandfather sleep."

So when Ho came tonight for the third time, I wanted to ask his advice. His hands were still covered with sugar and his mind was, as it had been for the past two nights, very much distracted. "There's something still wrong with the glaze," he said to me in the dark, and I pulled back the covers and swung my legs around to get up. He did not try to stop me, but he did draw back quietly into the shadows.

"I want to pace the room with you," I said. "As we did in Paris, those tiny rooms of ours. We would talk about Marx and about Buddha and I must pace with you now."

"Very well," he said. "Perhaps it will help me remember."

I slipped on my sandals and I stood up and Ho's shadow moved past me, through the spill of streetlight and into the dark near the door. I followed him, smelling the sugar on his hands, first before me and then moving past me as I went on into the darkness he'd just left. I stopped as I turned and I could see Ho outlined before the window and I said, "I believe my son-in-law and grandson are involved in the killing of a man. A political killing."

Ho stayed where he was, a dark shape against the light, and he said nothing and I could not smell his hands from across the room and I smelled only the sourness of Loi as he laid his head on my shoulder. He was a baby and my daughter Lam retreated to our balcony window after handing him to me and the boy turned his head and I turned mine to him and I could smell his mother's milk, sour on his breath, he had a sour smell and there was incense burning in the room, jasmine, the smoke of souls, and the boy sighed on my shoulder, and I turned my face away from the smell of him. Thang was across the room and his eyes were quick to find his wife and he was waiting for her to take the child from me.

"You have never done the political thing," Ho said.

"Is this true?"

"Of course."

I asked, "Are there politics where you are now, my friend?"

I did not see him moving toward me, but the smell of the sugar on his hands grew stronger, very strong, and I felt Ho Chi Minh very close to me, though I could not see him. He was very close and the smell was strong and sweet and it was filling my lungs as if from the inside, as if Ho was passing through my very body, and I heard the door open behind me and then close softly shut.

I moved across the room to the bed. I turned to sit down but I was facing the window, the scattering of a streetlamp on the window like a nova in some far part of the universe. I stepped to the window and touched the reflected light there, wondering if there was a great smell when a star explodes, a great burning smell of gas and dust. Then I closed the shade and slipped into bed, quite gracefully, I felt, I was quite wonderfully graceful, and I lie here now waiting for sleep. Ho is right, of course. I will never say a word about my grandson. And perhaps I will be as restless as Ho when I join him. But that will be all right. He and I will be together again and perhaps we can help each other. I know now what it is that he has forgotten. He has used confectioners' sugar for his glaze fondant and he should be using granulated sugar. I was only a washer of dishes but I did listen carefully when Monsieur Escoffier spoke. I wanted to understand everything. His kitchen was full of such smells that you knew you had to understand everything or you would be incomplete forever.

Reading as a Writer

1. This is a story about someone facing death. How does Butler avoid melodrama in his portrayal of the situation?

2. How reliable is this narrator? Are we supposed to believe the things he tells us that he experiences? Why or why not?

3. What is the central conflict in the story? How is that conflict resolved? What, ultimately, is the story about?

GABRIEL GARCÍA MÁRQUEZ

A Very Old Man with Enormous Wings

Translated by Gregory Rabassa

ON THE THIRD DAY OF RAIN they had killed so many crabs inside the house that Pelayo had to cross his drenched courtyard and throw them into the sea, because the newborn child had a temperature all night and they thought it was due to the stench. The world had been sad since Tuesday. Sea and sky were a single ash-gray thing and the sands of the beach, which on March nights glimmered like powdered light, had become a stew of mud and rotten shellfish. The light was so weak at noon that when Pelayo was coming back to the house after throwing away the crabs, it was hard for him to see what it was that was moving and groaning in the rear of the courtyard. He had to go very close to see that it was an old man, a very old man, lying face down in the mud, who, in spite of his tremendous efforts, couldn't get up, impeded by his enormous wings.

Frightened by that nightmare, Pelayo ran to get Elisenda, his wife, who was putting compresses on the sick child, and he took her to the rear of the courtyard. They both looked at the fallen body with mute stupor. He was dressed like a ragpicker. There were only a few faded hairs left on his bald skull and very few teeth in his mouth, and his pitiful condition of a drenched great-grandfather had taken away any sense of grandeur he might have had. His huge buzzard wings, dirty and half-plucked, were forever entangled in the mud. They looked at him so long and so closely that Pelayo and Elisenda very soon overcame their surprise and in the end found him familiar. Then they dared speak to him, and he answered in an incomprehensible dialect with a strong sailor's voice. That was how they skipped over the inconvenience of the wings and quite intelligently concluded that he was a lonely castaway from some foreign ship wrecked by the storm. And yet, they called in a neighbor woman who knew everything about life and death to see him, and all she needed was one look to show them their mistake.

"He's an angel," she told them. "He must have been coming for the child, but the poor fellow is so old that the rain knocked him down."

On the following day everyone knew that a flesh-and-blood angel was held captive in Pelayo's house. Against the judgment of the wise neighbor woman, for whom angels in those times were the fugitive survivors of a celestial conspiracy, they did not have the heart to club him to death. Pelayo watched over him all afternoon from the kitchen, armed with his bailiff's club, and before going to bed he dragged him out of the mud and locked him up with the hens in the wire chicken coop. In the middle of the night, when the rain stopped, Pelayo and Elisenda were still killing crabs. A short time afterward the child woke up without a fever and with a desire to eat. Then they felt magnanimous and decided to put the angel on a raft with fresh water and provisions for three days and leave him to his fate on the high seas. But when they went out into the courtyard with the first light of dawn, they found the whole neighborhood in front of the chicken coop having fun with the angel, without the slightest reverence, tossing him things to eat through the openings in the wire as if he weren't a supernatural creature but a circus animal.

Father Gonzaga arrived before seven o'clock, alarmed at the strange news. By that time onlookers less frivolous than those at dawn had already arrived and they were making all kinds of conjectures concerning the captive's future. The simplest among them thought that he should be named mayor of the world. Others of sterner mind felt that he should be promoted to the rank of five-star general in order to win all wars. Some visionaries hoped that he could be put to stud in order to implant on earth a race of winged wise men who could take charge of the universe. But Father Gonzaga, before becoming a priest, had been a robust woodcutter. Standing by the wire, he reviewed his catechism in an instant and asked them to open the door so that he could take a close look at that pitiful man who looked more like a huge decrepit hen among the fascinated chickens. He was lying in a corner drying his open wings in the sunlight among the fruit peels and breakfast leftovers that the early risers had thrown him. Alien to the impertinences of the world, he only lifted his antiquarian eyes and murmured something in his dialect when Father Gonzaga went into the chicken coop and said good morning to him in Latin. The parish priest had his first suspicion of an impostor when he saw that he did not understand the language of God or know how to greet His ministers. Then he noticed that seen close up he was much too human: he had an unbearable smell of the outdoors, the back side of his wings was strewn with parasites and his main feathers had been mistreated by terrestrial winds, and nothing about him measured up to the proud dignity of angels. Then he came out of the chicken coop and in a brief sermon warned the curious against the risks of being ingenuous. He reminded them that the devil had the bad habit of making use of carnival tricks in order to confuse the unwary. He argued that if wings were not the essential element in determining the difference between a hawk and an airplane, they were even less so in the recognition of angels. Nevertheless, he promised to write a letter to his bishop so that the latter would write to his primate so that the latter would write to the Supreme Pontiff in order to get the final verdict from the highest courts.

His prudence fell on sterile hearts. The news of the captive angel spread with such rapidity that after a few hours the courtyard had the bustle of a marketplace and they had to call in troops with fixed bayonets to disperse the mob that was about to knock the house down. Elisenda, her spine all twisted from sweeping up so much marketplace trash, then got the idea of fencing in the yard and charging five cents admission to see the angel.

The curious came from far away. A traveling carnival arrived with a flying acrobat who buzzed over the crowd several times, but no one paid any attention to him because his wings were not those of an angel but, rather, those of a sidereal bat. The most unfortunate invalids on earth came in search of health: a poor woman who since childhood had been counting her heartbeats and had run out of numbers; a Portuguese man who couldn't sleep because the noise of the stars disturbed him; a sleepwalker who got up at night to undo the things he had done while awake; and many others with less serious ailments. In the midst of that shipwreck disorder that made the earth tremble, Pelayo and Elisenda were happy with fatigue, for in less than a week they had crammed their rooms with money and the line of pilgrims waiting their turn to enter still reached beyond the horizon.

The angel was the only one who took no part in his own act. He spent his time trying to get comfortable in his borrowed nest, befuddled by the hellish heat of the oil lamps and sacramental candles that had been placed along the wire. At first they tried to make him eat some mothballs, which, according to the wisdom of the wise neighbor woman, were the food prescribed for angels. But he turned them down, just as he turned down the papal lunches that the penitents brought him, and they never found out whether it was because he was an angel or because he was an old man that in the end he ate nothing but eggplant mush. His only supernatural virtue seemed to be patience. Especially during the first days, when the hens pecked at him, searching for the stellar parasites that proliferated in his wings, and the cripples pulled out feathers to touch their defective parts with, and even the most merciful threw stones at him, trying to get him to rise so they could see him standing. The only time they succeeded in arousing him was when they burned his side with an iron for branding steers, for he had been motionless for so many hours that they thought he was dead. He awoke with a start, ranting in his hermetic language and with tears in his eyes, and he flapped his wings a couple of times, which brought on a whirlwind of chicken dung and lunar dust and a gale of panic that did not seem to be of this world. Although many thought that his reaction had been one not of rage but of pain, from then on they were careful not to annoy him, because the majority understood that his passivity was not that of a hero taking his ease but that of a cataclysm in repose.

Father Gonzaga held back the crowd's frivolity with formulas of maidservant inspiration while awaiting the arrival of a final judgment on the nature of the captive. But the mail from Rome showed no sense of urgency. They spent their time finding out if the prisoner had a navel, if his dialect had any connection with Aramaic, how many times he could fit on the head of a pin, or whether he wasn't just a Norwegian with wings. Those meager letters might have come and gone until the end of time if a providential event had not put an end to the priest's tribulations.

It so happened that during those days, among so many other carnival attractions, there arrived in town the traveling show of the woman who had been changed into a spider for having disobeyed her parents. The admission to see her was not only less than the admission to see the angel, but people were permitted to ask her all manner of questions about her absurd state and to examine her up and down so that no one would ever doubt the truth of her horror. She was a frightful tarantula the size of a ram and with the head of a sad maiden. What was most heart-rending, however, was not her outlandish shape but the sincere affliction with which she recounted the details of her misfortune. While still practically a child she had sneaked out of her parents' house to go to a dance, and while she was coming back through the woods after having danced all night without permission, a fearful thunderclap rent the sky in two and through the crack came the lightning bolt of brimstone that changed her into a spider. Her only nourishment came from the meatballs that charitable souls chose to toss into her mouth. A spectacle like that, full of so much human truth and with such a fearful lesson, was bound to defeat without even trying that of a haughty angel who scarcely deigned to look at mortals. Besides, the few miracles attributed to the angel showed a certain mental disorder, like the blind man who didn't recover his sight but grew three new teeth, or the paralytic who didn't get to walk but almost won the lottery, and the leper whose sores sprouted sunflowers. Those consolation miracles, which were more like mocking fun, had already ruined the angel's reputation when the woman who had been changed into a spider finally crushed him completely. That was how Father Gonzaga was cured forever of his insomnia and Pelayo's courtyard went back to being as empty as during the time it had rained for three days and crabs walked through the bedrooms.

The owners of the house had no reason to lament. With the money they saved they built a two-story mansion with balconies and gardens and high netting so that crabs wouldn't get in during the winter, and with iron bars on the windows so that angels wouldn't get in. Pelayo also set up a rabbit warren close to town and gave up his job as bailiff for good, and Elisenda bought some satin pumps with high heels and many dresses of iridescent silk, the kind worn on Sunday by the most desirable women in those times. The chicken coop was the only thing that didn't receive any attention. If they washed it down with creolin and burned tears of myrrh inside it every so often, it was not in homage to the angel but to drive away the dungheap stench that still hung everywhere like a ghost and was turning the new house into an old one. At first, when the child learned to walk, they were careful that he not get too close to the chicken coop. But then they began to lose their fears and got used to the smell, and before the child got his second teeth he'd gone inside the chicken coop to play, where the wires were falling apart. The angel was no less standoffish with him than with other mortals, but he tolerated the most ingenious infamies with the patience of a dog who had no illusions. They both came down with chicken pox at the same time. The doctor who took care of the child couldn't resist the temptation to listen to the angel's heart, and he found so much whistling in the heart and so many sounds in his kidneys that it seemed impossible for him to be alive. What surprised him most, however, was the logic of his wings. They seemed so natural on that completely human organism that he couldn't understand why other men didn't have them too.

When the child began school it had been some time since the sun and rain had caused the collapse of the chicken coop. The angel went dragging himself about here and there like a stray dying man. They would drive him out of the bedroom with a broom and a moment later find him in the kitchen. He seemed to be in so many places at the same time that they grew to think that he'd been duplicated, that he was reproducing himself all through the house, and the exasperated and unhinged Elisenda shouted that it was awful living in that hell full of angels. He could scarcely eat and his antiquarian eyes had also become so foggy that he went about bumping into posts. All he had left were the bare cannulae of his last feathers. Pelayo threw a blanket over him and extended him the charity of letting him sleep in the shed, and only then did they notice that he had a temperature at night, and was delirious with the tongue twisters of an old Norwegian. That was one of the few times they became alarmed, for they thought he was going to die and not even the wise neighbor woman had been able to tell them what to do with dead angels.

And yet he not only survived his worst winter, but seemed improved with the first sunny days. He remained motionless for several days in the farthest corner of the courtyard, where no one would see him, and at the beginning of December some large, stiff feathers began to grow on his wings, the feathers of a scarecrow, which looked more like another misfortune of decrepitude. But he must have known the reason for those changes, for he was quite careful that no one should notice them, that no one should hear the sea chanteys that he sometimes sang under the stars. One morning Elisenda was cutting some bunches of onions for lunch when a wind that seemed to come from the high seas blew into the kitchen. Then she went to the window and caught the angel in his first attempts at flight. They were so clumsy that his fingernails opened a furrow in the vegetable patch and he was on the point of knocking the shed down with the ungainly flapping that slipped on the light and couldn't get a grip on the air. But he did manage to gain altitude. Elisenda let out a sigh of relief, for herself and for him, when she saw him pass over the last houses, holding himself up in some way with the risky flapping of a senile vulture. She kept watching him even when she was through cutting the onions and she kept on watching until it was no longer possible for her to see him, because then he was no longer an annoyance in her life but an imaginary dot on the horizon of the sea.

Reading as a Writer

1. What kind of narrator does this story have?

2. How are we supposed to interpret some of the more incredible things that happen in the story? Are we supposed to believe they really happened? Point to places in the story that support your answer.

3. How does Márquez convince us of the integrity of the narration?

CHAPTER EIGHT

He Said, She Said
Crafting Effective Dialogue

Oᴘᴇɴ ᴊᴜsᴛ ᴀʙᴏᴜᴛ ᴀɴʏ ʙᴏᴏᴋ—fiction or nonfiction—and chances are you'll find dialogue in it. Some of this dialogue will be short and terse; some, expansive and lyrical. You'll find different characters using different idioms, syntax, grammar, vocabulary. You'll find dialogue that sounds like what you'd hear at the local coffee shop, and dialogue that no one on earth has ever spoken yet that somehow works within the context.

Learning to craft good dialogue is one of the most critical aspects of learning to write good fiction. Without understanding how to render on the page a realistic approximation of the way real people talk to (and at) each other, you will fail to develop one of the key tools you have for generating truly compelling creative work.

In this chapter we will first examine what good dialogue should accomplish. We will look at a number of examples—from fiction as well as from dramatic works written for theater (we can learn a lot from theater, since in drama, words *are* action). Then you have a chance to practice what we've discussed in exercises. Finally, the readings for this chapter provide examples of good dialogue.

What Dialogue Is Good For

Dialogue isn't just the words your characters speak to each other. Good dialogue works on a number of different levels. Here are the main things you want to accomplish with it:

1. Add to the reader's knowledge of the situation. (Knowledge is different from facts.)

2. Keep the piece moving forward.

3. Reveal things about the speaker. (What is *not* being said is called the subtext—read on.)

4. Show relationships between characters who are engaged in a conversation.

Keep in mind that good dialogue is not necessarily realistic dialogue. You do not want to copy what you heard on the street. You want to make it *sound* natural, but that doesn't mean it *is* natural. It takes careful editing to create natural-sounding dialogue. Generally, that means paying attention to the rhythm of sentences, varying the length of sentences, making a conscious effort to be non-grammatical (people seldom speak in full sentences). More on this later in the chapter.

Dialogue also needs to be extremely specific. We're leery of characters who talk in generalities or abstractions. "I think I'm in love with you, darling," is always suspect. "Oh my God, so *that's* the way you brush your teeth!" is a wonderful piece of dialogue that I've borrowed from a friend of mine who is writing a story about the beginning of a love affair.

Every character should speak differently. Each should have a distinct way of phrasing, of opinion, of subject matter. Extremely clever dialogue that bounces back and forth effortlessly between characters is no good if one or more of the characters is saying things they wouldn't or couldn't say.

Also, dialogue for a particular character can change depending on:

1. Who he or she is talking to (if the character is talking to more than one person, the matter gets even more complicated).

2. Whether the characters are in a private or a public place.

3. The mood of the speaker (angry: might say things harsher than usual; frightened: might try to placate the listener).

For example, we talk differently to our friends than to our mothers. Likewise, our words vary depending on whether we are annoyed, or impatient, or saddened by something. All the things that affect character will affect dialogue. (More on this in Chapter 10, on characterization.)

What Dialogue Is Not

In many ways, it's easier to define dialogue by saying what it *isn't*, rather than what it *is*. As coauthors Robie MacAuley and George Lanning say:

> Dialogue should never be an exchange of commonplaces designed to feed the reader information. It is seldom suitable for describing persons or places; it is no substitute for direct narrative, and individual speech is useless as a vehicle for the philosophical brooding of the hero or heroine.
> —ROBIE MACAULEY AND GEORGE LANNING, *Technique in Fiction*

Let's go over MacAuley's points one by one (paraphrasing a bit):

Dialogue is not an important source of facts about a piece.
So not:

> "You've missed your 8:34 train to San Francisco, and if you think I'm going to drive you 34 miles to your job at the law firm of Harris and Sullivan, for the fifth time since we were mistakenly married at your parents' summer house in the Hamptons three years ago, you're mistaken."

Instead:

"You missed it again."
"Oh, no. Can't be!"
"Just look at the time."
"It's the damn clock. I told you not to buy one with a snooze button."
"Yes, my fault. As always."

Dialogue is not good for describing people, places, or objects in detail.
So not:

"My, you look stunning in your gold lamé gown with beads around the collar that shimmers when you walk sexily around the room."

Instead:

"Wow."
"What?"
"That dress, what's it made of? It kind of glows. Wow."

Dialogue absolutely should not be used in cases when direct narrative would work better. If you have basic facts to supply to the reader, if in doubt, put it in narrative.

For example, make sure you don't have "empty" scenes, like the following, that could be replaced with a few sentences of narrative:

"Hello, may I speak to Amy?"
   "This is Amy."
   "Hi, Amy, how are you? I know you're my sister, but I haven't seen you in three weeks."
   "I know, Gail. I feel bad about that. I was afraid you were still mad about the fact that I ripped your favorite sweater. How about meeting for coffee this afternoon?"
   "Fine. Café Verona, at noon?"
   "Sounds great. See you there."
   "Bye."

Instead:

Gail hadn't seen her sister Amy in three weeks, not since Amy had borrowed Gail's vintage red beaded sweater only to let her cat unravel one of the sleeves. They decided to meet on neutral ground: Café Verona at noon.

Dialogue especially should not be used for extended "philosophical brooding" by a character.

"I can't help wondering, why were we put on this planet? We are specks of humanity, drowning in our despair, with no joy, no hope, nothing to bring us salvation in our pathetic, small lives."

No. If in doubt, always put it in narrative. *Tell* us ("Arnold went on a rant of philo-sophical brooding that all the others mostly tuned out") rather than waste our time in an empty scene.

A Word about Attribution

We need to know who is talking when words are spoken in a piece. Most of the time, you should use the word "said." If you can, drop it. But don't worry about it being repetitive, as it is so much a part of fiction that it is virtually invisible. Do not—repeat, do not—feel you need to use substitutes such as "hissed," "threatened," "exploded," "smirked," "sneered," "chuckled," "growled," and so on. Take them out. Use "said" or occasionally (as appropriate) "shouted" or "yelled" or "whispered."

Also, most of the time, using adverbs to describe how something was said is unnecessary. It can even weaken the effect of the dialogue ("she said angrily," "he said hopefully," "I said happily"). Word choices and carefully chosen gestures can be much more effective than mere adverbs can be.

So not:

"What are you talking about," he asked angrily.

Instead:

"What the hell are you talking about?" he asked, slamming the Bible down onto the table so that the glasses tinkled.

Five Important Things to Remember about Dialogue

To write better dialogue, keep the following five things in mind:

1. Gesture is a part of dialogue.
2. Dialogue is what characters *do* to one another.
3. Silence is a part of dialogue.
4. Dialogue is not necessarily grammatically correct.
5. Make the world part of your dialogue.

Let's now go over each of these points in detail:

Gesture is a part of dialogue. Using gesture to show *how* something is said can be one of the most effective means of writing dialogue. Consider the following excerpt from "Hills Like White Elephants" (pp. 269–272). The gestures are boldfaced.

> The woman brought two glasses of beer and two felt pads. **She put the felt pads and the beer glasses on the table** and looked at the man and the girl. The girl was looking off at the line of hills. They were white in the sun and the country was brown and dry.

"They look like white elephants," she said.

"I've never seen one," **the man drank his beer.**

"No, you wouldn't have."

"I might have," the man said. "Just because you say I wouldn't have doesn't prove anything."

The girl looked at the bead curtain. "They've painted something on it," she said. "What does it say?"

Notice how the gestures inform the way the dialogue is spoken. When the man drinks his beer after saying, "I've never seen one," he is dismissing what the girl says. When the girl looks at the bead curtain, she is trying to change the subject to defuse the tension between them. In both cases, the gestures inform the words spoken to such an extent that they can be considered extensions of the dialogue.

In general, having your characters *do* something while they're speaking adds verisimilitude to the exchange; we rarely just sit there, frozen, as we speak to one another. We're either fidgeting—with our rings, our watches—or we're in the middle of another activity, like kneading bread or fixing a car. In such cases, it is natural for gestures and actions that are part of the scene to enter into the dialogue itself.

Dialogue is what characters do to one another. Think in terms of verbal sparring. In our stories, characters rarely, if ever, come to actual blows. But they do come to words. If you think of dialogue as a *physical* exchange between characters, you'll fare much better at crafting effective prose speech. In the example below, we see how the jargon spouted by the therapist is met with contempt and hostility by the family members seeking therapy for Rose. They are definitely "doing things" to the therapist in exchange for what they perceive as his insincerity.

Mr. Walker said, "I wonder why it is that everyone is so entertained by Rose behaving inappropriately."

Rose burped and then we all laughed. This was the seventh family therapist we had seen, and none of them had lasted very long. Mr. Walker, unfortunately, was determined to do right by us.

"What do you think of Rose's behavior, Violet?" They did this sometimes. In their manual it must say, If you think the parents are too weird, try talking to the sister.

"I don't know. Maybe she's trying to get you to stop talking about her in the third person."

"Nicely put," my mother said.

"Indeed," my father said.

"Fuckin' A," Rose said.

"Well, this is something that the whole family agrees upon," Mr. Walker said, trying to act as if he understood or even liked us.

"This was not a successful intervention, Ferret Face," Rose said.

—AMY BLOOM, "Silver Water"

Silence is a part of dialogue. When a character refuses to answer a remark or question, or looks off into the distance, or even pauses just slightly, that is part of a verbal communication. Indeed, silence can be one of the most powerful tools you have when constructing effective dialogue. In the passage that follows, silence works to indicate how the character is listening and responding to the person on the other end of the phone.

> ALBERT: Hello? *(brief pause as he listens)* Where *are* you? *(brief pause after each phrase as he listens)*
>
> Albert.
>
> Albert *Litko.*
>
> *(As ALBERT talks we see the Museum lights being extinguished, one by one until he is sitting in the dark.)*
>
> At the Museum.
>
> Waiting for *you.*
>
> Well, we *did.*
>
> We certainly *did.*
>
> Well, *I* thought we did.
>
> I'm sorry, too.
>
> At the Museum, I told you.
>
> *(SILENCE)*
>
> It's okay. *(pause)* Well, what are you doing *tonight?*
>
> Oh. *(long pause)*
>
> What are you doing *tomorrow* night?
>
> Oh.
>
> No. I'm not. I'm not.
>
> No. Don't be silly.
>
> No. Okay.
>
> —DAVID MAMET, "The Museum of Science and Industry Story"

So, how do you write silence into your dialogue? Sometimes you might want to simply put in a line of narrative—"There was quiet for a moment"—but sometimes you might want to be more subtle than that. Here are some other ways of infusing silence or pauses into dialogue:

- Insert some sensory clues to what is happening during the silence. "The clock ticked away" is a cliché, as is "A dog barked in the distance." But these are examples of the kind of sensory clues you can provide (in narrative) that creates a pause, or brief silence:

  "Are you sure about this, Anne?" he asked. "Really sure?"

  They could hear the wind rustling through the trees outside. An ant crawled along the counter between them.

  "Yes," she said, finally. "I'm sure."

- Provide a descriptive passage of the setting (place) where the scene is occurring:

    "I'm sure I could make you h-h-h-happy," he said, stuttering a bit. "I'm a very hard w-w-w-worker."

    The sky over his head was a deep, deep blue; there were cows in the fields and the few houses that could be seen seemed to blend into the grayish-brown landscape.

    "I know, I just can't quite *see* it," she said. "It eludes me."

- Provide the character with an (unspoken) thought that is a reaction to the dialogue at hand:

    "I've got a sixth sense for these things," she said. "I know how to make money. It's in my blood."

    Right, he thought as he looked at her sullen face. I'm really going to give you my life's savings.

    "And what would you do first?" he asked.

- Provide a character with an association, like a memory (flashback) related to the dialogue at hand:

    "You must have been a pretty cute kid," he said.

    After he spoke, she had a sudden image of herself at age seven, standing on the threshold of the house, holding on to her dog's leash and pulling back, not gently, in order to keep the dog inside.

    "Not particularly," she said.

Dialogue is not necessarily grammatically correct. People generally don't speak in complete sentences with perfect grammar. Plus, there's often a rhythm or cadence to the language that defies conventional syntax. Instead of worrying about getting the grammar right, you might try focusing on varying sentence length (interposing shortened sentences among longer ones is very effective) and on the *music* of the words. In the passage that follows, even though the language is foreign to us (Burgess made up his own language for this piece, a combination of cockney and Russian) we can hear the music and rhythm of the sentences, and how they flow:

> "We got worried," said Georgie. "There we were, awaiting and peeting away at the old knify moloko, and you had not turned up. So then Pete here thought how you might have been like offended by some veshch or other, so round we come to your abode. That's right, Pete, right?"
>
> "Oh, yes, right," said Pete.
>
> "Apy polly loggies," I said, careful. "I had something of a pain in the gulliver so had to sleep. I was not wakened when I gave orders for wakening. Still, here we all are, ready for what the old nochy offers, yes?" I seemed to have picked up that yes? from P. R. Deltoid, my Post-Corrective Adviser. Very strange.
>
> "Sorry about the pain," said Georgie, like very concerned. "Using the gulliver too much like, maybe. Giving orders and discipline and such, perhaps. Sure the pain is going? Sure you'll not be happier going back to the bed?" And they all had a bit of a malenky grin.   —ANTHONY BURGESS, *A Clockwork Orange*

Dialogue never takes place in a vacuum. Just as we learned in talking about silence, above, you can indicate pauses or silence by involving the sensory world of the story in your dialogue. In a general way, however, it's a good idea to interject sensory cues from the "real" world into the words spoken. After all, there are always things going on around the speakers: sounds and sights and smells and other sensory details that can be incorporated into the dialogue in order to provide for a more immersive experience:

> "I'm ready. I've been ready for ten minutes. What's taking you so long?" she asked. She was standing in the hallway of their small apartment, wrapping a scarf around her neck as she watched him pull on his shirt.
>
> "Give me a break, I only woke up thirty minutes ago," he said. He threw first one tie, then another, onto the disheveled bed, before finding the one he wanted from the overstuffed closet.
>
> "Whose fault is that?" she asked. She was finished with her scarf and was now waiting, her hand on the front brass doorknob, polished to a sheen by frequent use.
>
> "Yes, of course, of course, it is my fault, always my fault," he said as he put on his jacket in front of the bathroom mirror. It had a crack running up the left side that distorted his face a little. He grimaced and then strode out to meet his wife.

On Subtext

Dialogue also reveals much by what *isn't* being said. Characters conceal things. They partially conceal things. They outright lie. They exaggerate. They rephrase.

When it's at its best, dialogue must exist on two levels: what is actually being said, which must pertain to the plot or general events of the piece; and what is being implied or revealed, which is the subtext, or emotional undercurrent. In the best creative works, the two go hand in hand.

Here's an example of subtext in action, followed by a humorous "translation":

Listen now, carefully, to the conversation of this mother and daughter. Madeleine and Hilary talk in riddles, as families do, even families as small and circumscribed as this one, using the everyday objects of their lives as symbols of their discontent:

1. HILARY: Mum, I can't find my shoes again.
2. MADELEINE (*looking*): They'll be where you took them off. (*finding*) Here they are.
3. HILARY: Not those old brown things. My new red ones.
4. MADELEINE: You can't possibly wear these to school. They're ridiculous. They'll cripple your feet.
5. HILARY: No they won't. Everyone wears platforms!
6. MADELEINE: In that case, everyone will be going around in plaster casts, and serve them right.
7. HILARY: You only don't like them because Lily [her father's new wife] bought them for me.

8. MADELEINE: I don't like them because they are ugly and ridiculous.

9. HILARY: I can't find the other ones. And anyway, I'm late. Please, Mum? They're my feet.

Which, being translated, is:

1. HILARY: Why is this place always such a mess?

2. MADELEINE: Why are you such a baby?

3. HILARY: You know nothing about me.

4. MADELEINE: I know everything about you.

5. HILARY: I want to be like other people.

6. MADELEINE: Other people aren't worth being like.

7. HILARY: I know all about you, don't think I don't.

8. MADELEINE: You force me to tell the truth. Our whole situation is ugly and ridiculous and I despair of it.

9. HILARY: Then let me find my own way out of it, please.

So Hilary defeats her mother, as the children of guilty mothers do, and goes off to school wearing the red shoes with platform heels.

—FAY WELDON, *Remember Me*

A Word about Dialect

Sometimes you'll want to do something to the dialogue to indicate that a character is speaking less than perfect English. He or she might have an accent, for example, or an imperfect command of grammar. It's out of fashion right now to spell out phonetically such deviations in speech. Typically, today, writers prefer to *suggest* that a character has an unusual speech pattern (foreign accent, lisp, etc.) through word choice, syntax (word placement within the sentence), content (reflecting a foreign way of viewing the world), or narrative. The reason: writing in dialect (or misspelling words in order to indicate pronunciation) can be more distracting than illuminating.

For example, rather than writing:

"He'th a velly thilly perthon, Jameth ith," she lisped.

Instead write:

Doris had trouble articulating the letters "r" and "s," something that James found oddly attractive. When he overheard Doris say to her mother, "He's a very silly person, James is," and heard his own name pronounced "Jameth," he shuddered with pleasure. That night, he lay awake in bed repeating, "Jameth, Jameth, Jameth." It seemed to him that Doris had caused him to be both reborn as well as renamed, and that Jameth was a better, kinder man than James ever could hope to be.

Here's an example of some very realistic dialogue that uses syntax and word choice and a few deliberately phonetically spelled words to indicate that the characters are speaking other than what one might consider to be proper English:

And the big dark woman saying, *Boy, is you all right, what's wrong?* In a husky voiced contralto. And me saying, *I'm all right, just weak,* and trying to stand, and her saying, *Why don't y'all stand back and let the man breathe? Stand back there y'all,* and now echoed by an official tone, *Keep moving, break it up.* And she on one side and a man on the other, helping me to stand and the policeman saying, *Are you all right?* And me answering, *Yes, I just felt weak, must have fainted but all right now,* and him ordering the crowd to move on and the others moving on except the man and woman and him saying, *You sure you okay, daddy,* and me nodding yes, and her saying, *Where you live son, somewhere around here?* And me telling her Men's House and her looking at me shaking her head saying, *Men's House, Men's House, shucks that ain't no place for nobody in your condition what's weak and needs a woman to keep an eye on you awhile* and me saying, *But I'll be all right now,* and her, *Maybe you will and maybe you won't. I live just up the street and round the corner, you better come on round and rest till you feel stronger. I'll phone Men's House and tell em where you at.* And me too tired to resist and already she had one arm and was instructing the fellow to take the other and we went, me between them, inwardly rejecting and yet accepting her bossing, hearing, *You take it easy, I'll take care of you like I done a heap of others, my name's Mary Rambo, everybody knows me round this part of Harlem, you heard of me, ain't you?*

—Ralph Ellison, *Invisible Man*

However, one should never say never in fiction, which is why some very fine writers choose to write in dialect. Here's a passage from a novel by Peter Matthiessen written entirely in dialect (and with no attribution—you have to figure out not only what the characters are saying, but who is saying it):

Domn good thing it was de land of opportunity, cause Desmond took every last centavo dat dey had fore he let'm off of de boat.

I remember one time—Copm Bennie, I b'lieve it was—he wanted to lease dat old shark scow dat Desmond had, and Desmond demanded three hundred pounds for ten days. I told Bennie, I say, Mon, if dat vessel worth thirty pounds a day after all de crewin paid, why in de hell ain't Desmond out dere fishin sharks three hundred and sixty-five days in de year?

Well, dere is one thing Desmond know and dat is sharks.

I told you why—cause he a shark his*self.*

(quietly) Hear dat? Come to Desmond Eden, Raib can hear you in a goddom hurricane.

(louder) You been in dat sharkskin game dere, ain't you Copm? On de Sponnish shore? I heard you was running guns dere, bringing back sharkskin.

—Peter Matthiessen, *Far Tortuga*

Using Placeholders

Sometimes it can be difficult to come up with compelling, believable dialogue with pulsing subtext, that does all the things dialogue should do. A technique that works well for my students is, when in doubt, to write out what needs to be communicated.

Use what I call a *placeholder,* or "serviceable" dialogue, with the understanding that you will go back later and change it.

Say you want to write some dialogue that features an argument between a mother and daughter over the daughter staying out too late the previous night. You might start with serviceable dialogue that communicates the basic information, only later swapping it for better, more concise and spontaneous-sounding words.

Placeholder text:

> "You can't just defy my orders and do whatever you please," Susan told her daughter.
> "Why not?" her daughter said.
> "You are always defying me," Susan said. "I won't have it. You shouldn't have stayed out so late last night. I was worried about you. And what will the neighbors think?"
> "You are so self-centered that you think this is all about you. All you care about is what other people think."
> "What am I to do with you? You really frustrate me. You make me feel like a failure as a mother."

Notice how this lays out the general things that need to be said between the mother and daughter, but how it's not particularly spontaneous-sounding. It's also a little too direct; it would make more sense to have the characters talk by way of something else, more indirectly.

Real dialogue (substituted later):

> "You can't do this to me," Susan told her daughter.
> "To you? This is about you?" her daughter asked.
> "Of course not. No. What I meant was, I was very clear: you were not to stay out past midnight."
> "You were clear all right. But clarity isn't everything."
> "What do you mean?"
> "I mean, credibility counts. And you have none. None whatsoever."
> "I'm the mother here."
> "Maybe you shouldn't be," her daughter said.

This sounds more like a mother and daughter sparring. It conveys all the necessary information and emotion, but in a much more spontaneous and believable way.

EXERCISES

Exercise 1: Nonverbal Communication

GOAL: To practice incorporating gesture and silence (non-responses) into dialogue, as responses.

1. Think of a situation involving two characters, one who is trying to convince the other of something that he or she doesn't agree with.

2. Write the scene, using gesture and silence to indicate reluctance to comply or outright disagreement. *Hint:* Silence can be implied in many ways (as you can see from the sample writing below) as well as stated directly, using narrative.

The following passage was written by Cybele Unger:

"I'm telling you, Carol, this is a cinch. Easy as pie. A sure-fire investment," he said.

Carol hesitated for a moment before answering. "Sure-fire," she said.

"Yes! Absolutely certain!"

Carol picked up her fork and twirled it absently in her right hand. "But the stock market isn't doing so well these days," she said, eventually. "Everyone knows that. How can you be so sure this will work?"

"I'm telling you, it's unbeatable. Larry says so."

There was silence for a moment before Carol replied, flatly. "Larry says so."

"Will you stop repeating what I say? It's driving me nuts. Yes, Larry says so. And he knows."

The kitchen clock ticked away ten, twenty seconds.

"Carol? Did you hear what I said?"

"I heard you."

"Well, how about it?"

Carol sighed, and continued playing with her fork. "I guess so," she said finally.

Exercise 2: Them's Fighting Words

GOAL: To understand dialogue as part of the action of a scene.

1. Think of a situation in which one character is angry with another character for breaking the rules in some way.

2. Write out the scene in the form of dialogue in which the characters "fight" each other with words.

Daniel Tsui wrote the following passage:

"That's *it*. You're gonna get it."

"No, I'm not. It's no big deal. Mom never used that dish anyway. She'll never notice."

"She'll notice if I tell her."

"You wouldn't."

"Just watch me."

"I'll watch you, and then you can watch me tell her about the five dollars that disappeared from her purse last week."

"You have no proof."

"Who needs proof? It'll be enough to plant the seed of suspicion. She'll wonder. That'll be enough."

"She won't be able to punish me. Let her wonder."

"And then, next time you want something from her, watch her hesitate. Like that ski trip coming up in two weeks. I'm gonna enjoy watching you beg."

"You bastard."

"You started it."

READINGS

ERNEST HEMINGWAY

Hills Like White Elephants

THE HILLS ACROSS THE VALLEY of the Ebro were long and white. On this side there was no shade and no trees and the station was between two lines of rails in the sun. Close against the side of the station there was the warm shadow of the building and a curtain, made of strings of bamboo beads, hung across the open door into the bar, to keep out flies. The American and the girl with him sat at a table in the shade, outside the building. It was very hot and the express from Barcelona would come in forty minutes. It stopped at this junction for two minutes and went on to Madrid.

"What should we drink?" the girl asked. She had taken off her hat and put it on the table.

"It's pretty hot," the man said.

"Let's drink beer."

"*Dos cervezas*," the man said into the curtain.

"Big ones?" a woman asked from the doorway.

"Yes. Two big ones."

The woman brought two glasses of beer and two felt pads. She put the felt pads and the beer glasses on the table and looked at the man and the girl. The girl was looking off at the line of hills. They were white in the sun and the country was brown and dry.

"They look like white elephants," she said.

"I've never seen one," the man drank his beer.

"No, you wouldn't have."

"I might have," the man said. "Just because you say I wouldn't have doesn't prove anything."

The girl looked at the bead curtain. "They've painted something on it," she said. "What does it say?"

"Anis del Toro. It's a drink."

"Could we try it?"

The man called "Listen" through the curtain. The woman came out from the bar.

"Four reales."

"We want two Anis del Toro."

"With water?"

"Do you want it with water?"

"I don't know," the girl said. "Is it good with water?"

"It's all right."

"You want them with water?" asked the woman.

"Yes, with water."

"It tastes like licorice," the girl said and put the glass down.

"That's the way with everything."

"Yes," said the girl. "Everything tastes of licorice. Especially all the things you've waited so long for, like absinthe."

"Oh, cut it out."

"You started it," the girl said. "I was being amused. I was having a fine time."

"Well, let's try and have a fine time."

"All right. I was trying. I said the mountains looked like white elephants. Wasn't that bright?"

"That was bright."

"I wanted to try this new drink: That's all we do, isn't it—look at things and try new drinks?"

"I guess so."

The girl looked across at the hills.

"They're lovely hills," she said. "They don't really look like white elephants. I just meant the coloring of their skin through the trees."

"Should we have another drink?"

"All right."

The warm wind blew the bead curtain against the table.

"The beer's nice and cool," the man said.

"It's lovely," the girl said.

"It's really an awfully simple operation, Jig," the man said. "It's not really an operation at all."

The girl looked at the ground the table legs rested on.

"I know you wouldn't mind it, Jig. It's really not anything. It's just to let the air in."

The girl did not say anything.

"I'll go with you and I'll stay with you all the time. They just let the air in and then it's all perfectly natural."

"Then what will we do afterward?"

"We'll be fine afterward. Just like we were before."

"What makes you think so?"

"That's the only thing that bothers us. It's the only thing that's made us unhappy."

The girl looked at the bead curtain, put her hand out, and took hold of two of the strings of beads.

"And you think then we'll be all right and be happy."

"I know we will. You don't have to be afraid. I've known lots of people that have done it."

"So have I," said the girl. "And afterward they were all so happy."

"Well," the man said, "if you don't want to you don't have to. I wouldn't have you do it if you didn't want to. But I know it's perfectly simple."

"And you really want to?"

"I think it's the best thing to do. But I don't want you to do it if you don't really want to."

"And if I do it you'll be happy and things will be like they were and you'll love me?"

"I love you now. You know I love you."

"I know. But if I do it, then it will be nice again if I say things are like white elephants, and you'll like it?"

"I'll love it. I love it now but I just can't think about it. You know how I get when I worry."

"If I do it you won't ever worry?"

"I won't worry about that because it's perfectly simple."

"Then I'll do it. Because I don't care about me."

"What do you mean?"

"I don't care about me."

"Well, I care about you."

"Oh, yes. But I don't care about me. And I'll do it and then everything will be fine."

"I don't want you to do it if you feel that way."

The girl stood up and walked to the end of the station. Across, on the other side, were fields of grain and trees along the banks of the Ebro. Far away, beyond the river, were mountains. The shadow of a cloud moved across the field of grain and she saw the river through the trees.

"And we could have all this," she said. "And we could have everything and every day we make it more impossible."

"What did you say?"

"I said we could have everything."

"We can have everything."

"No, we can't."

"We can have the whole world."

"No, we can't."

"We can go everywhere."

"No, we can't. It isn't ours anymore."

"It's ours."

"No, it isn't. And once they take it away, you never get it back."

"But they haven't taken it away."

"We'll wait and see."

"Come on back in the shade," he said. "You mustn't feel that way."

"I don't feel any way," the girl said. "I just know things."

"I don't want you to do anything that you don't want to do—"

"Nor that isn't good for me," she said. "I know. Could we have another beer?"

"All right. But you've got to realize—"

"I realize," the girl said. "Can't we maybe stop talking?"

They sat down at the table and the girl looked across at the hills on the dry side of the valley and the man looked at her and at the table.

"You've got to realize," he said, "that I don't want you to do it if you don't want to. I'm perfectly willing to go through with it if it means anything to you."

"Doesn't it mean anything to you? We could get along."

"Of course it does. But I don't want anybody but you. I don't want any one else. And I know it's perfectly simple."

"Yes, you know it's perfectly simple."

"It's all right for you to say that, but I do know it."

"Would you do something for me now?"

"I'd do anything for you."

"Would you please please please please please please please stop talking?"

He did not say anything but looked at the bags against the wall of the station. There were labels on them from all the hotels where they had spent nights.

"But I don't want you to," he said, "I don't care anything about it."

"I'll scream," the girl said.

The woman came out through the curtains with two glasses of beer and put them down on the damp felt pads. "The train comes in five minutes," she said.

"What did she say?" asked the girl.

"That the train is coming in five minutes."

The girl smiled brightly at the woman, to thank her.

"I'd better take the bags over to the other side of the station," the man said. She smiled at him.

"All right. Then come back and we'll finish the beer."

He picked up the two heavy bags and carried them around the station to the other tracks. He looked up the tracks but could not see the train. Coming back, he walked through the barroom, where people waiting for the train were drinking. He drank an Anis at the bar and looked at the people. They were all waiting reasonably for the train. He went out through the bead curtain. She was sitting at the table and smiled at him.

"Do you feel better?" he asked.

"I feel fine," she said. "There's nothing wrong with me. I feel fine."

Reading as a Writer

1. Point out places where word choice, syntax, and gesture help us understand *how* something is said.

2. Point out places where the adage "dialogue is what characters do to one another" rings true.

3. Point out places where the dialogue is deliberately non-grammatical in order to sound spontaneous and reveal emotion.

Toni Cade Bambara

My Man Bovanne

BLIND PEOPLE GOT A HUMMIN JONES if you notice. Which is understandable completely once you been around one and notice what no eyes will force you into to see people, and you get past the first time, which seems to come out of nowhere, and it's like you in church again with fat-chest ladies and old gents gruntin a hum low in the throat to whatever the preacher be saying. Shakey Bee bottom lip all swole up with Sweet Peach and me explainin how come the sweet-potato bread was a dollar-quarter this time stead of dollar regular and he say uh hunh he understand, then he break into this *thizzin* kind of hum which is quiet, but fiercesome just the same, if you ain't ready for it. Which I wasn't. But I got used to it and the onliest time I had to say somethin bout it was when he was playin checkers on the stoop one time and he commenst to hummin quite churchy seem to me. So I says, "Look here Shakey Bee, I can't beat you and Jesus too." He stop.

So that's how come I asked My Man Bovanne to dance. He ain't my man mind you, just a nice ole gent from the block that we all know cause he fixes things and the kids like him. Or used to fore Black Power got hold their minds and mess em around till they can't be civil to ole folks. So we at this benefit for my niece's cousin who's runnin for somethin with this Black party somethin or other behind her. And I press up close to dance with Bovanne who blind and I'm hummin and he hummin, chest to chest like talkin. Not jammin my breasts into the man. Wasn't bout tits. Was bout vibrations. And he dug it and asked me what color dress I had on and how my hair was fixed and how I was doin without a man, not nosy but nice-like, and who was at this affair and was the canapés dainty-stingy or healthy enough to get hold of proper. Comfy and cheery is what I'm tryin to get across. Touch talkin like the heel of the hand on the tambourine or on a drum.

But right away Joe Lee come up on us and frown for dancin so close to the man. My own son who knows what kind of warm I am about; and don't grown men call me long distance and in the middle of the night for a little Mama comfort? But he frown. Which ain't right since Bovanne can't see and defend himself. Just a nice old man who fixes toasters and busted irons and bicycles and things and changes the lock on my door when my men friends get messy. Nice man. Which is not why they invited him. Grass roots you see. Me and Sister Taylor and the woman who does heads at Mamies and the man from the barber shop, we all there on account of we grass roots. And I ain't never been souther than Brooklyn Battery and no more country than the window box on my fire escape. And just yesterday my kids tellin me to take them countrified rags off my head and be cool. And now can't get Black enough to suit em. So everybody passin sayin My Man Bovanne. Big deal, keep steppin and don't even stop a minute to get the man a drink or one of them cute sandwiches or tell him what's goin on. And him standin there with a smile ready case someone do speak he want to be ready. So that's how come I pull him on the dance floor and we dance squeezin past the tables and chairs and all them coats and people standin round up in each other face talkin bout this and that but got no use for this blind man who mostly fixed skates and skooters for all these folks when they was just kids. So I'm pressed up close and we touch talkin with the hum. And here come my daughter cuttin her eye at me like she do when she tell me about my "apolitical" self like I got hoof and mouf disease and there ain't no hope at all. And I don't pay her no mind and just look up in Bovanne shadow face and tell him his stomach like a drum and he laugh. Laugh real loud. And here come my youngest, Task, with a tap on my elbow like he the third grade monitor and I'm cuttin up on the line to assembly.

"I was just talkin on the drums," I explained when they hauled me into the kitchen. I figured drums was my best defense. They can get ready for drums what with all this heritage business. And Bovanne stomach just like that drum Task give me when he come back from Africa. You just touch it and it hum thizzm, thizzm. So I stuck to the drum story. "Just drummin that's all."

"Mama, what are you talkin about?"

"She had too much to drink," say Elo to Task cause she don't hardly say nuthin to me direct no more since that ugly argument about my wigs.

"Look here Mama," say Task, the gentle one. "We just tryin to pull your coat. You were makin a spectacle of yourself out there dancing like that."

"Dancin like what?"

Task run a hand over his left ear like his father for the world and his father before that.

"Like a bitch in heat," say Elo.

"Well uhh, I was goin to say like one of them sex-starved ladies gettin on in years and not too discriminating. Know what I mean?"

I don't answer cause I'll cry. Terrible thing when your own children talk to you like that. Pullin me out the party and hustlin me into some stranger's kitchen in the back of a bar just like the damn police. And ain't like I'm old old. I can still wear me some sleeveless dresses without the meat hangin off my arm. And I keep up with some thangs through my kids. Who ain't kids no more. To hear them tell it. So I don't say nuthin.

"Dancin with that tom," say Elo to Joe Lee, who leanin on the folks' freezer. "His feet can smell a cracker a mile away and go into their shuffle number post haste. And them eyes. He could be a little considerate and put on some shades. Who wants to look into them blown-out fuses that—"

"Is this what they call the generation gap?" I say.

"Generation gap," spits Elo, like I suggested castor oil and fricassee possum in the milk-shakes or somethin. "That's a white concept for a white phenomenon. There's no generation gap among Black people. We are a col—"

"Yeh, well never mind," says Joe Lee. "The point is Mama . . . well, it's pride. You embarrass yourself and us too dancin like that."

"I wasn't shame." Then nobody say nuthin. Them standin there in they pretty clothes with drinks in they hands and gangin up on me, and me in the third-degree chair and nary a olive to my name. Felt just like the police got hold to me.

"First of all," Task say, holdin up his hand and tickin off the offenses, "the dress. Now that dress is too short, Mama, and too low-cut for a woman your age. And Tamu's going to make a speech tonight to kick off the campaign and will be introducin you and expecting you to organize the council of elders—"

"Me? Didn nobody ask me nuthin. You mean Nisi? She change her name?"

"Well, Norton was supposed to tell you about it. Nisi wants to introduce you and then encourage the older folks to form a Council of the Elders to act as an advisory—"

"And you going to be standing there with your boobs out and that wig on your head and that hem up to your ass. And people'll say, 'Ain't that the horny bitch that was-grindin with the blind dude?'"

"Elo, be cool a minute," say Task, gettin to the next finger."And then there's the drinkin. Mama, you know you can't drink cause next thing you know you be laughin loud and carryin on," and he grab another finger for the loudness. "And then there's the dancin. You been tattooed on the man for four records straight and slow draggin even on the fast numbers. How you think that look for a woman your age?"

"What's my age?"

"What?"

"I'm axin you all a simple question. You keep talkin bout what's proper for a woman my age. How old am I anyhow?" And Joe Lee slams his eyes shut and squinches up his face to figure. And Task run a hand over his ear and stare into his glass like the ice cubes goin calculate for him. And Elo just starin at the top of my head like she goin rip the wig off any minute now.

"Is your hair braided up under that thing? If so, why don't you take it off? You always did do a neat cornroll."

"Uh huh," cause I'm thinkin how she couldn't undo her hair fast enough talking bout cornroll so countrified. None of which was the subject. "How old, I say?"

"Sixtee-one or —"

"You a damn lie Joe Lee Peoples."

"And that's another thing," say Task on the fingers.

"You know what you all can kiss," I say, gettin up and brushin the wrinkles out my lap.

"Oh, Mama," Elo say, puttin a hand on my shoulder like she hasn't done since she left home and the hand landin light and not sure it supposed to be there. Which hurt me to my heart. Cause this was the child in our happiness fore Mr. Peoples die. And I carried that child strapped to my chest till she was nearly two. We was close is what I'm tryin to tell you. Cause it was more me in the child than the others. And even after Task it was the girlchild I covered in the night and wept over for no reason at all less it was she was a chub-chub like me and not very pretty, but a warm child. And how did things get to this, that she can't put a sure hand on me and say Mama we love you and care about you and you entitled to enjoy yourself cause you a good woman?

"And then there's Reverend Trent," say Task, glancin from left to right like they hatchin a plot and just now lettin me in on it. "You were suppose to be talking with him tonight, Mama, about giving us his basement for campaign headquarters and —"

"Didn nobody tell me nuthin. If grass roots mean you kept in the dark I can't use it. I really can't. And Reven Trent a fool anyway the way he tore into the widow man up there on Edgecomb cause he wouldn't take in three of them foster children and the woman not even comfy in the ground yet and the man's mind messed up and—"

"Look here," say Task. "What we need is a family conference so we can get all this stuff cleared up and laid out on the table. In the meantime I think we better get back into the other room and tend to business. And in the meantime, Mama, see if you can't get to Reverend Trent and—"

"You want me to belly rub with the Reven, that it?"

"Oh damn," Elo say and go through the swingin door.

"We'll talk about all this at dinner. How's tomorrow night, Joe Lee?" While Joe Lee being self-important I'm wonderin who's doin the cookin and how come no body ax me if I'm free and do I get a corsage and things like that. Then Joe nod that it's O.K. and he go through the swingin door and just a little hubbub come through from the other room. Then Task smile his smile, lookin just like his daddy and he leave. And it just me in this stranger's kitchen, which was a mess I wouldn't never let my kitchen look like. Poison you just to look at the pots. Then the door swing the other way and it's My Man Bovanne standin there savin Miss Hazel but lookin at the deep fry and then at the steam table, and most surprised when I come up on him from the other direction and take him on out of there. Pass the folks pushin up towards the stage where Nisi and some other people settin and ready to talk, and folks gettin to the last of the sandwiches and the booze fore they settle down in one spot and listen serious. And I'm thinkin bout tellin Bovanne what a lovely long dress Nisi got on and the earrings and her hair piled up in a cone and the people bout to hear how we all gettin screwed and gotta form our own party and everybody there listenin and lookin. But instead I just haul the man on out of there, and Joe Lee and his wife look at me like I'm terrible, but they ain't said boo to the man yet. Cause he blind and old and don't nobody there need him since they grown up and don't need they skates fixed no more.

"Where we goin, Miss Hazel?" Him knowin all the time.

"First we gonna buy you some dark sunglasses. Then you comin with me to the supermarket so I can pick up tomorrow's dinner, which is goin to be a grand thing proper and you invited. Then we goin to my house."

"That be fine. I surely would like to rest my feet." Bein cute, but you got to let men play out they little show, blind or not. So he chat on bout how tired he is and how he appreciate me takin him in hand this way. And I'm thinkin I'll have him change the lock on my door first thing. Then I'll give the man a nice warm bath with jasmine leaves in the water and a little Epsom salt on the sponge to do his back. And then a good rubdown with rose water and olive oil. Then a cup of lemon tea with a taste in it. And a little talcum, some of that fancy stuff Nisi mother sent over last Christmas. And then a massage, a good face massage round the forehead which is the worryin part. Cause you gots to take care of the older folks. And let them know they still needed to run the mimeo machine and keep the spark plugs clean and fix the mail-boxes for folks who might help us get the breakfast program goin, and the school for the little kids and the campaign and all. Cause old folks is the nation. That what Nisi was sayin and I mean to do my part.

"I imagine you are a very pretty woman, Miss Hazel."

"I surely am," I say just like the hussy my daughter always say I was.

Reading as a Writer

1. What are some of the techniques Bambara uses to forge dialogue that sounds sponta-neous and genuine? In what ways does the dialogue work on two levels? Choose a section of dialogue and identify the underlying subtext.

2. What other techniques and devices does Bambara use to define her characters? What information about the characters does Bambara reveal through dialogue?

3. What is the plot of this piece? Specifically, what are the "plot points" that drive the story from beginning to end? Is it a traditional conflict–crisis–resolution plot? Why or why not?

CHAPTER NINE

What Happens Next?
Figuring The Plot

"WHAT IS PLOT?" the short story writer Grace Paley once asked rhetorically, before promptly answering herself: "first one thing happens, then another thing, then another . . ." And of course, although she is right, there is more we can say that will be helpful as you work on your short story or novel.

We'll start, as before, with some basic definitions. Then we'll look at a number of different plotting techniques. Then we'll go over some exercises to help you plot your own short story or novel. Finally, two readings that are strong in plot illustrate some of the points of this chapter.

Story versus Plot: Some Basic Definitions

Let's start by going back to the basics. What are we trying to do when we write our story? The most-quoted source on this topic is E. M. Forster:

> Let us listen to three voices. If you ask one type of man, "What does a novel do?" he will reply placidly: "Well—I don't know—it seems a funny sort of question to ask—a novel's a novel—well, I don't know—I suppose it kind of tells a story, so to speak." He is quite good-tempered and vague, and probably driving a motor-bus at the same time and paying no more attention to literature than it merits. Another man, whom I visualize as on a golf-course, will be aggressive and brisk. He will reply: "What does a novel do? Why, tell a story of course, and I've no use for it if it didn't. I like a story. Very bad taste on my part, no doubt, but I like a story. You can take your art, you can take your literature, you can take your music, but give me a good story. And I like a story to be a story, mind, and my wife's the same." And a third man he says in a sort of drooping regretful voice, "Yes—oh dear, yes—the novel tells a story." I respect and admire the first speaker. I detest and fear the second. And the third is myself. Yes—oh dear, yes—the novel tells a story. That is the fundamental aspect without which it could not exist. That is the highest factor common to all novels, and I wish that it was not so, that it could be something different—melody, or perception of the truth, not this low atavistic form.
>
> —E. M. FORSTER, *Aspects of the Novel*

Later, he elaborates on the difference between story and plot:

> Let us define a plot. We have defined a story as a narrative of events arranged in their time-sequence. A plot is also a narrative of events, the emphasis falling on causality. "The king died and then the queen died" is a story. "The king died, and then the queen died of grief" is a plot. The time-sequence is preserved, but the sense of causality overshadows it. [. . .] If it is in a story we say, "and then?" If it is in a plot we ask "why?" That is the fundamental difference.

So, what is Forster saying? First of all, let's be clear: he's using the word "story" in a different way than we have been. He says that the story is a set of events in chronological order—the events that keep readers asking, "and then?"—while plot is something more sophisticated, something that delves into the interior mystery of the piece. To put it another way (a way that mirrors the way we've been talking about creative writing in this book), the story part of a piece can be easily summarized (first this happened, then that happened, then *that* happened), while the plot is part of that aspect of the short story or novel that *resists paraphrase*.

Other critics who have tried to define plot focus more closely on the idea of *causality* that Forster raises. Everything must happen for a reason, and everything that happens must have consequences, and those consequences lead to other consequences until (frequently) the whole thing snowballs and culminates in a crisis. For short fiction, this is where Poe's definition of a short story as having unity of purpose usually kicks in. A novel can have many threads, so this theory goes; a short story has only one.

But although these things might be true in many, or even most, cases, they are not true in all, as Francine Prose reminds us in, "What Makes a Short Story?" (pp. 109–118). But I think we can agree that the events that take place in a novel or short story have to add up to some *effect* or, as we put it in Chapter 4, *unit of satisfaction* (in the case of a novel it might be a very large unit, or even a multifaceted unit).

So *plot*, as we will define it, is that series of events, arranged in a particular order, that brings about the desired final effect of a short story or novel. True, this is a very bare-bones definition. But that is critical. Just as our definition of a short story was delicately wrought lest we exclude any of the fine stories that have been written over the years, let us do the same with plot. And we're going to go out on a limb here and say that even in so-called plotless stories this definition of plot is fulfilled. Because even in plotless stories *things happen*—they must, or they wouldn't be stories, they'd be abstract ruminations.

A Word about Causality

Why did I leave out the word "causality" when formulating a definition of plot? It seems as though that would be a prime determinant of the plot points chosen. And it is—but I'd rather imply it (after all, I do say that the series of events *brings about* the desired effect) than build it more directly into the definition.

To put too much stress on the fact that every plot point *must* have its own particular consequence is to undermine the subtlety of many stories and novels. The problem with thinking too simplistically in terms of causality is that it can cause us to think in direct, linear terms (*John had a poor childhood and therefore he thrived on accumulating riches of all kinds, which led to his downfall as a materialistic narcissist*) whereas we know that life (along with most short stories and novels) is subtler than that. All too often, in a workshop, someone begins criticism with the dreadful phrase "I want to know why . . ."—demanding that sort of simplistic linear movement. Yet we know that human nature—and most short stories and novels, at least the ones we're concentrating on in this book, are about human nature—is more complicated. Mere straws *can* break elephants' backs.

Moreover, most writers work more by intuition rather than by carefully plotting out cause and effect (although as a plotting exercise, that can be very useful). And although it is true that in many beginning stories, certain events might not make a contribution to the plot, in which case they may have to be tweaked or rethought; sometimes a writer will have no more than an urgent sense that *this* has to happen *here,* and the causality works itself out subconsciously.

But there are many reasons why beginning writers might want to avoid elucidating too explicitly that *this* happened directly *because* of that.

Why did the boy beat his dog? the workshop asks. So the writer puts in an unhappy childhood. There. Causality. Or, *why did the girl break off the engagement?* the workshop wants to know. She seemed happy enough with her fiancé, after all. So why? These are valid questions to ask—but never, ever make yourself invent some linear, simplistic "reason" for what can be very complexly motivated behaviors.

Render *How*–Don't Try to Answer *Why*

Remember that our job isn't to solve the mysteries around us, but to render them precisely. So instead of dramatizing the *why* down to the last possible causal factor (*the girl's father had blue eyes, her fiancé had brown ones, the match was therefore incompatible in her mind*) to the point of oversimplifying via pop psychology the complex bundles of thoughts and emotions that are human beings, we depict *how* they acted. Don't try to explain *why* the engagement disintegrated, demonstrate *how* it fell apart. If your story is convincing, we'll have a sense of why, without the oversimplification that often accompanies so much beginning fiction.

In the excerpt below, we see a young girl falling in love with a cad. Although we see *how* it happens, we're not told *why* she's susceptible; it's played out in front of us. Yet the causality is there: something about the original, horrifying encounter that makes her susceptible to this dubious young man the second time she meets him.

> One August evening—she was eighteen at the time—they took her off to the fete at Colleville. From the start she was dazed and bewildered by the noise of

the fiddles, the lamps in the trees, the medley of gaily colored dresses, the gold crosses and lace, and the throng of people jigging up and down. She was standing shyly on one side when a smart young fellow, who had been leaning on the shaft of a cart, smoking his pipe, came up and asked her to dance. He treated her to cider, coffee, griddle-cake, and a silk neckerchief, and imagining that she knew what he was after, offered to see her home. At the edge of a field of oats, he pushed her roughly to the ground. Thoroughly frightened, she started screaming for help. He took to his heels.

Another night, on the road to Beaumont, she tried to get past a big, slow-moving wagon loaded with hay, and as she was squeezing by she recognized Theodore.

He greeted her quite calmly, saying that she must forgive him for the way he had behaved to her, as "it was the drink that did it."

She did not know what to say in reply and felt like running off.

Straight away he began talking about the crops and the notabilities of the commune, saying that his father had left Colleville for the farm at Les Ecots, so that they were now neighbors.

"Ah!" she said.

He added that his family wanted to see him settle but that he was in no hurry and was waiting to find a wife to suit his fancy. She lowered her head. Then he asked her if she was thinking of getting married. She answered with a smile that it was mean of him to make fun of her.

"But I'm not making fun of you!" he said. "I swear I'm not!"

He put his left arm round her waist and she walked on supported by his embrace. Soon they slowed down. There was a gentle breeze blowing, the stars were shining, the huge load of hay was swaying about in front of them, and the four horses were raising clouds of dust as they shambled along. Then without being told, they turned off to the right. He kissed her once more and she disappeared into the darkness.   —GUSTAVE FLAUBERT, "A Simple Heart"

On Metafiction

It's difficult to talk about plot in any meaningful context without talking about character as well. But before we can talk about character and plot, we must first acknowledge a type of fiction that can frequently avoid character altogether: metafiction.

By definition, *metafiction* is fiction about fiction: rather than trying to illuminate the human condition, as the vast majority of stories and novels attempt to do, metafiction is about examining the creative act, or about questioning the conventions of fiction. Writers of metafiction include John Barth, Donald Barthelme, Italo Calvino, and Jorge Luis Borges.

For the purposes of this chapter, however, we will skip metafiction in favor of discussing *character-based fiction*—that is, fiction that attempts to say something about characters, or the human condition.

Character–Based Plotting

If we're focused on character-based fiction, then plot is the specific series of events that befalls a character or a set of characters. And so, if plot is what happens to characters, and if we want those things that happen to have significance, it stands to reason that somehow plot reflects character, and vice versa. If characters take action (or refuse to take an action), if they put themselves in positions of danger or refuse to put themselves in positions of danger, that is the plot. We'll talk more about characterization in Chapter 10. Let's just assume for now that if your character does something, then she or he is capable of doing that; likewise, if that character fails to do something, then it is *possible* (not necessarily determined, but possible) for him or her to fail to do that particular thing.

Along these lines, the writer John Gardner provides one of the most elegant definitions of plot and character ever formulated:

> In the place of the classical writer's clear distinction between the outside world and the inside world—"situation" on one hand and "character" on the other—modern writers see outer reality and inner reality as interpenetrating: The world is whatever we feel it to be, so that the situation character must deal with is partly character.   —JOHN GARDNER, *The Art of Fiction*

Let's look at an example of a story in which "the situation character must deal with is partly character."

In Denis Johnson's "Emergency" (pp. 13–21), the character has placed himself in an emergency room in a hospital; he works there, he has *chosen* to be there. He has also taken drugs and has chosen to make a friend of a rather dubious character named George. These choices he made (as a result of the character he is) naturally lead to his joyride to the county fair and to the adventure with the bunnies. And the bunnies would not have been squashed if he were not the type of person who would forget that they were there and let them roll around to the back of his shirt and be squashed. Throughout this story, we see plot unfolding as a result of choices (actions or reactions, conscious and unconscious) that this character makes.

How can you use this idea that character and plot are intertwined when you write? By asking yourself a simple question: What can I do to my character to unsettle or move or stress or stretch him or her in some way? Sometimes that involves being mean to your characters; sometimes extraordinarily nice. In either case, plot is what we, as authors, *do* to our characters in order to elicit particular responses.

On Conflict

You cannot read about plot without running into that central word, "conflict." A story or a novel must have *conflict*, we're told, or it doesn't (can't) hold the reader's interest. And this is true: a story or novel without conflict is a story or novel without much of anything interesting happening in it.

The problem comes in the nature of the word "conflict." It has connotations that are too violent, too direct; and although doubtless there are writers who sit down and wonder, "What conflict can I put in my story?" there are many others who work in a subtler vein. Philip Roth writes about placing a character in a "situation," for example. Others talk about plot being the intersection between "character and circumstance." One definition that I use to help writers who are working along the conventional conflict–crisis–resolution model is to say that plot is "that series of events that causes your character to crack open in some way." (Change is not necessary; change can be declined, but to bring a character to that potential opening-up point can be a very interesting thing to do.)

Let's look at some of the opening "conflicts" of stories and see how ill-suited they are to being described using that conventional term:

- "Girl" by Jamaica Kincaid: A mother tells her daughter to wash the white clothes on Monday and the colored clothes on Tuesday.
- "Follow the Eagle" by William Kotzwinkle: Two men, half-drunk and exuberant, ride their motorcycles toward the Colorado River one bright sunshine-filled morning.
- "Souvenir" by Jayne Anne Phillips: A woman forgets to send a Valentine's Day card to her mother.
- "Pet Milk" by Stuart Dybek: A man sits drinking his coffee and thinking about his grandmother, long dead.

As E. M. Forster points out, plot isn't as easy as just coming up with a "conflict":

The plot, instead of finding human beings more or less cut to its requirements, as they are in the drama, finds them enormous, shadowy and intractable, and three-quarters hidden like an iceberg. In vain it points out to these unwieldy creatures the advantages of the triple process of complication, crisis, and solution so persuasively expounded by Aristotle. A few of them rise and comply, and a novel which ought to have been a play is the result. But there is no general response. They want to sit apart and brood or something, and the plot (whom I here visualize as a sort of higher government official) is concerned at their lack of public spirit.   —E. M. FORSTER, *Aspects of the Novel*

And as Charles Baxter wrote:

Anyone who writes stories or novels or poems with some kind of narrative structure often imagines a central character, then gives that character a desire or a fear or perhaps some kind of goal and sets another character in a collision course with that person. The protagonist collides with an antagonist. All right: we know where we are. We often talk about this sort of dramatic conflict as if it were all unitary, all of one kind: One person wants something, another person wants something else, and conflict results. But this is not, I think, the way most stories actually work. Not everything is a contest. We are not always fighting our brothers for our share of the worldly goods. Many good stories have no antagonist at all. My friends on the lawn don't tell their stories that way. Actual conflict can be a fairly minor element in most stories, written or told. A more appropriate question might be, "What's emerging here?" or "What's showing up?"   —CHARLES BAXTER, "On Defamiliarization"

Other writers are even more dismissive of formal plots, as evident from this interview published in the *Paris Review*:

I don't work with plots. I work with intuition, apprehension, dreams, concepts. Characters and events come simultaneously to me. Plot implies narrative and a lot of crap. It is a calculated attempt to hold the reader's interest at the sacrifice of moral conviction. Of course, one doesn't want to be boring . . . one needs an element of suspense. But a good narrative is a rudimentary structure, rather like a kidney.   —JOHN CHEEVER

So, think in terms of conflict (man against man, man against nature, man against himself) if that is helpful to you. If not, try one of these other "ways in" to your story:

- Your character wants or desires something that she or he is not getting.
- You want to capture a moment after which nothing can ever be the same.
- You want to find the right events, in the right order, to cause your character(s) to crack open in some way.
- Your character finds himself or herself intersecting with circumstances that are too much for him or her.
- You want to place your character in a "situation."

Analyzing Plot Points

In workshop, we frequently talk about *plot points*—which are, in the most basic terms, the things that happen (again, for the most part to characters, human or otherwise). If you look at some of the finest work of fiction (both short fiction and novels), you'll notice that if the writers were thinking only in simplistic terms of conflict–crisis–resolution, these are hardly the plot points they'd come up with.

Let's look at the plot points of "Sonny's Blues" by James Baldwin (pp. 290–312). We'll see that there's a basic "story" (to use the term the way E. M. Forster uses it) that differs from the basic plot in that the plot of the story is told out of sequence, to wring the greatest impact from the events depicted.

First, here are the plot points as Baldwin renders them:

1. Protagonist reads about the arrest of his brother Sonny in the newspaper.
2. Class lets out, and the laughter of children who "aren't really children" reaches his ears.
3. Someone from the block, Sonny's friend, comes by to talk about Sonny.

4. Protagonist receives letter from Sonny.

5. Protagonist meets Sonny when he comes back to New York after being released from jail.

6. They take a cab ride home, going through the park.

7. Flashback to father, a drunk who nevertheless loved his family.

8. Flashback to the last time the protagonist saw his mother alive, when he hears story (from his mother) about his father losing a brother when young.

9. Flashback: After mother's funeral (still in past), protagonist talks to Sonny about his desire to be a musician.

10. Flashback: Later, away at the army, protagonist hears news of Sonny from his fiancée, Isabel.

11. Flashback: Sonny joins the Navy.

12. Flashback: Protagonist has an "awful fight" with Sonny, and they don't speak for months.

13. Memory of the time that little Gracie died.

14. Back to present (right after what happens in #6 above); now Sonny is living with protagonist and his family. Protagonist talks to Sonny about music, drugs.

15. Protagonist goes to nightclub with Sonny and sees his brother for what he really is.

Now here are the events in chronological order (the "story," if you will). See how they are placed out of order according to the *plot:*

7. Father was a self-destructive drunk who nevertheless loved his family, especially Sonny.

8. Last time protagonist saw his mother alive, they had a conversation about the family, Sonny, the father—specifically, that the father had once lost a brother.

10. Later, in the army, protagonist hears news about Sonny from his fiancée, Isabel.

9. After mother's funeral, protagonist talks to Sonny about his desire to be a musician.

11. Sonny joins the Navy.

12. Protagonist has an "awful fight" with Sonny, and they don't speak for months.

1. Protagonist reads about Sonny's arrest in the newspaper.

2. Class lets out, and the laughter of children who "aren't really children" reaches his ears.

3. Someone from the block, Sonny's friend, comes by to talk about Sonny.

13. Little Gracie dies.

4. Protagonist receives letter from Sonny, who is in prison.

5. Protagonist meets Sonny when he comes back to New York after being released from jail.

6. They take a cab ride home, going through the park.

14. The brothers have a discussion about drugs, music.

15. Protagonist goes to nightclub with Sonny.

Notice that the opening plot point, where the protagonist reads about Sonny in the paper, actually happens very late in the "story" when viewed as a simple chronology. And yes, there is causality: there is a reason for arranging the sequence as Baldwin does. As readers, we end up asking *why* and *how,* which is what we do with a plot, rather than *and then?,* which we tend to do with a simple story (as Forster defines it). We want to know what happens next, and we are sophisticated enough to know that "what happens next" might be something that happened ten years ago. Memory, in the form of flashbacks, is an important aspect of plot.

Joyce Carol Oates's story "Where Are You Going, Where Have You Been?" (pp. 40–53) almost always puzzles young readers when they read it for the first time. "Where's the ending?" they ask, because they haven't realized that the story is effectively over: we're not sure what is going to happen to Connie (we're pretty sure it won't be a good thing), but the author has wrapped up what, for her, was the interesting part, which is that Connie acquiesced and was easily led to her doom. She makes a generous gesture: to spare her family, she goes quietly, like a lamb to what we assume is the slaughter.

The plot points of "Where Are You Going, Where Have You Been?" are relatively simple:

1. Connie spars with her mother, her sister; she rebels in usual teenage ways.

2. Connie goes to the shopping plaza with her best girlfriend.

3. One night in midsummer they lie about going to the movies, instead going to the drive-in restaurant where the older kids hang out.

4. A boy named Eddie comes in to talk to them.

5. A boy with shaggy black hair and a convertible jalopy painted gold grins at her and says, "Gonna get you, baby."

6. Connie spends three hours with Eric, eating and then parking and making out in an alley.

7. The summer continues the same way, with Connie spending evenings with various boys.

8. Connie has a conversation with her mother regarding the Pettinger girl and some more conflict with her.

9. One Sunday Connie gets up late and refuses to go to a family barbecue. She lies around the house, listening to the music on the radio.

10. A car comes up the drive, it's the guy with the dark shaggy hair; they talk for a while before he turns threatening.

11. Connie prepares to leave the house to go with him.

This is done in strict chronological order, but notice that although there are certainly plot points that could be labeled "conflict" (#3, #5, and #8, for example), most of the plot points are more subtle than that. But all are putting pressure on the character, all leading up to the final moment when Connie goes with Arnold Friend to her (apparent) doom.

Avoiding *Scènes à Faire*: Recognizing Clichéd Plot Twists

We talk about clichés in several places: overly familiar language we simply called clichés, and in the next chapter we discuss overly familiar characters, which we call stereotypes. We also have overly familiar plots, which we will call *scènes à faire*.

Scènes à faire is French for "scenes to make," and it is a filmmakers' term as well as (increasingly) a legal one. In recent years, every hit movie has had lawsuits filed against its makers for "stealing" the plot from someone else's book or screenplay. The courts have decided that copyright protection cannot be extended for *scènes à faire*. Legally, as the U.S. District Court for the Southern District of New York defined them in *Alexander v. Haley*, a 1978 copyright case against the miniseries of Alex Haley's *Roots, scènes à faire* are "incidents, characters or settings which are as a practical matter indispensable, or at least standard, in the treatment of a given topic." As Tad Friend explained in a *New Yorker* piece:

> Thus the court suggested that when one is writing about slavery one would almost perforce include, among other things, "attempted escapes, flights through the woods pursued by baying dogs, the sorrowful or happy singing of slaves." Another court held that a realistic portrait of cops in the South Bronx would necessarily contain "drunks, prostitutes, vermin, and derelict cars." [. . .]
>
> The notion of *scènes à faire* is capacious enough to include the manner in which a reasonable person might develop an idea even if another reasonable person had earlier developed the same idea in the same way. For instance, if dinosaurs were reanimated, they obviously have to be kept far away from the nearest nursery school. So a writer who claimed that he had banished his velociraptors to a remote island before Michael Crichton did the same in *Jurassic Park* got nowhere in court: the judge ruled that "placing dinosaurs on a prehistoric island far from the mainland amounts to no more than a *scène à faire* in a dinosaur adventure story."
>
> The well-known Hollywood lawyer Bert Fields, who is defending Fox Searchlight Pictures in a copyright suit against *The Full Monty*, breezily explains the film's similarities to a play called *Ladies Night* by offering a similar argu-

ment. "Once you've got the idea of male strippers," he says, "it's all *scènes à faire;* you've got the inevitable scene when they first put on a G-string, the inevitable scene when someone's naked body is shown as rather unattractive. You've got to have a problem for each of the six guys, so one guy having impotence just goes with the territory."   —TAD FRIEND, "Copy Cats"

Obviously, the last thing you ever want to write is a *scène à faire,* or piece of boilerplate! In fact, if you find yourself thinking that you "must" have a particular scene because the type of story demands it, question that instinct. Must you have the breakup scene in a relationship? You might want to, but anything that feels obligatory might just be considered a *scène à faire,* and maybe you should try to substitute something else. Whatever you do, it must not be what would be used in any other story or novel. In plot, as in every other aspect of creative writing, we aim to *surprise,* to confound expectations.

EXERCISES

Exercise 1: What's Behind the Door of Room 101?

GOAL: To figure out a character's particular vulnerabilities and play on them in a scene-building exercise.

1. First, read the following excerpt from *1984* by George Orwell:

    "You asked me once," said O'Brien, "what was in Room 101. I told you that you know the answer already. Everyone knows it. The thing that is in Room 101 is the worst thing in the world.

    "The worst thing in the world varies from individual to individual. It may be burial alive, or death by fire, or by drowning, or by impalement, or fifty other deaths. *There are cases where it is some quite trivial thing, not fatal."* [emphasis mine]

2. Imagine what is behind the door of Room 101 for your character. It cannot be an abstraction: it must be something real, something physical that can happen to your character (though not necessarily realistic; it can be fantastical or improbable). So not fear, or even fear of heights, but an example of how that might manifest itself in a real *thing,* such as standing on the edge of a 100-story building. (Try to be subtle, and come up with a fear that *defines.* That is, not a "standard" fear that anyone might have, like a fear of walking down dark alleys, or a fear of strangers carrying guns, but one that is irrational and somewhat unique to your character in that not everyone would understand or sympathize.)

3. Write a scene (or have a narrator describe a situation) in which your character faces something that *reminds* him or her of the worst thing in the world. Not the thing itself, but a tangential "trigger" that brings on an exceedingly anxious reaction. Do not mention the "worst thing" itself. Just describe the physical thing or event that sets off your character, and how he or she reacts.

Here's an example of what you might write:

What's behind the door of Room 101: Being crushed by a heavy object.

Her kids were watching one of those colorfully violent Saturday cartoon shows, one where oddly shaped animals chased each other using a variety of improbable vehicles. Periodically, one of the characters would fall off a cliff, or get run over by a steamroller, or get put through a mechanical wringer. Her kids, especially her small daughter, howled with laughter as pancake-thin dogs and cats attempted to regain their proper shapes. But Marilyn felt her chest constrict. Her fingers began to tingle. One of the flat cats put a finger in its mouth and blew, puffing itself up into its proper shape again. A dog stretched out one paw, then another, and watched them spring back into shape. Marilyn found it hard to breathe. She walked over to the television set, and, over the outraged howls of her children, snapped it off.

Exercise 2: "By the Time You Read This . . ."

GOAL: To focus on the *small* things that can happen, plot-wise, and to open up your mind to possibilities.

1. Fix your mind on your main character (or one of your main characters) in a story you are writing.

2. Have the character sit down to write a letter to someone he or she is intimate with, who happens to be not close by at the moment. (It can be an email, if that helps you work, but make it be an email that won't be read for at least twenty-four hours, as an immediate reading of the email would destroy the point of the exercise.)

3. Begin the letter with "By the time you read this," and make a detailed list of all the things that will have happened by the time the intended recipient of the letter actually reads it.

Here's a composite example (written by a number of students over the years) on how this exercise might be completed:

By the time you read this . . .

- The chicken will be roasted, the garlic and rosemary scent spread throughout the house, the new potatoes baked until their skins are crisp.
- The baby will have been bathed, and smell sourly of her grandfather's Old Spice shaving cologne that she insists must be rubbed on her back before she allows herself to be dressed.
- At least three more moths will have found a way into the house, and will be circling around the face of Dan Rather on the TV, reporting the latest agonies suffered in the final moments in the lives of the ValueJet crash victims.
- The cat will have insisted on having her belly scratched, and will have shown her appreciation by gently biting the hand that strokes her.

- The bottle of Merlot will be half empty.
- The phone will have rung twice, and not answered either time. No message will have been left.
- 2,000 miles away, a seventy-four-year-old woman will have been given an injection of morphine, will have nibbled on a Graham Wheat Thin, will have spit it up, will have crushed angrily the stem of a tulip from the bouquet of flowers delivered to her room that day, will have cursed her doctor, and turned her back upon the senile roommate who will croak like a frog throughout the night ahead.

READINGS

James Baldwin

Sonny's Blues

I READ ABOUT IT in the paper, in the subway, on my way to work. I read it, and I couldn't believe it, and I read it again. Then perhaps I just stared at it, at the newsprint spelling out his name, spelling out the story. I stared at it in the swinging lights of the subway car, and in the faces and bodies of the people, and in my own face, trapped in the darkness which roared outside.

It was not to be believed and I kept telling myself that, as I walked from the subway station to the high school. And at the same time I couldn't doubt it. I was scared, scared for Sonny. He became real to me again. A great block of ice got settled in my belly and kept melting there slowly all day long, while I taught my classes algebra. It was a special kind of ice. It kept melting, sending trickles of ice water all up and down my veins, but it never got less. Sometimes it hardened and seemed to expand until I felt my guts were going to come spilling out or that I was going to choke or scream. This would always be at a moment when I was remembering some specific thing Sonny had once said or done.

When he was about as old as the boys in my classes his face had been bright and open, there was a lot of copper in it; and he'd had wonderfully direct brown eyes, and great gentleness and privacy. I wondered what he looked like now. He had been picked up, the evening before, in a raid on an apartment downtown, for peddling and using heroin.

I couldn't believe it: but what I mean by that is that I couldn't find any room for it anywhere inside me. I had kept it outside me for a long time. I hadn't wanted to know. I had had suspicions, but I didn't name them, I kept putting them away. I told myself that Sonny was wild, but he wasn't crazy. And he'd always been a good boy, he hadn't ever turned hard or evil or disrespectful, the way kids can, so quick, so quick, especially in Harlem. I didn't want to believe that I'd ever see my brother going down, coming to nothing, all that light in his face gone out, in the condition I'd already seen so many others. Yet it had happened and here I was, talking about algebra to a lot of boys who might, every one of them for all I knew, be popping off nee- dles every time they went to the head. Maybe it did more for them than algebra could.

I was sure that the first time Sonny had ever had horse, he couldn't have been much older than these boys were now. These boys, now, were living as we'd been liv- ing then, they were growing up with a rush and their heads bumped abruptly against the low ceiling of their actual possibilities. They were filled with rage. All they really knew were two darknesses, the darkness of their lives, which was now closing in on them, and the darkness of the movies, which had blinded them to that other dark- ness, and in which they now, vindictively, dreamed, at once more together than they were at any other time, and more alone.

When the last bell rang, the last class ended, I let out my breath. It seemed I'd been holding it for all that time. My clothes were wet—I may have looked as though I'd been sitting in a steam bath, all dressed up, all afternoon. I sat alone in the classroom a long time. I listened to the boys outside, downstairs, shouting and cursing and laughing. Their laughter struck me for perhaps the first time. It was not the joyous laughter which—God knows why—one associates with children. It was mocking and insular, its intent to denigrate. It was disenchanted, and in this, also, lay the authority of their curses. Perhaps I was listening to them because I was thinking about my brother and in them I heard my brother. And myself.

One boy was whistling a tune, at once very complicated and very simple, it seemed to be pouring out of him as though he were a bird, and it sounded very cool and moving through all that harsh, bright air, only just holding its own through all those other sounds.

I stood up and walked over to the window and looked down into the courtyard. It was the beginning of the spring and the sap was rising in the boys. A teacher passed through them every now and again, quickly, as though he or she couldn't wait to get out of that courtyard, to get those boys out of their sight and off their minds. I started collecting my stuff. I thought I'd better get home and talk to Isabel.

The courtyard was almost deserted by the time I got downstairs. I saw this boy standing in the shadow of a doorway, looking just like Sonny. I almost called his name. Then I saw that it wasn't Sonny, but somebody we used to know, a boy from around our block. He'd been Sonny's friend. He'd never been mine, having been too young for me, and, anyway, I'd never liked him. And now, even though he was a grown-up man, he still hung around that block, still spent hours on the street corners, was always high and raggy. I used to run into him from time to time and he'd often work around to asking me for a quarter or fifty cents. He always had some real good excuse, too, and I always gave it to him, I don't know why.

But now, abruptly, I hated him. I couldn't stand the way he looked at me, partly like a dog, partly like a cunning child. I wanted to ask him what the hell he was doing in the school courtyard.

He sort of shuffled over to me, and he said, "I see you got the papers. So you already know about it."

"You mean about Sonny? Yes, I already know about it. How come they didn't get you?"

He grinned. It made him repulsive and it also brought to mind what he'd looked like as a kid. "I wasn't there. I stay away from them people."

"Good for you." I offered him a cigarette and I watched him through the smoke. "You come all the way down here just to tell me about Sonny?"

"That's right." He was sort of shaking his head and his eyes looked strange, as though they were about to cross. The bright sun deadened his damp dark brown skin and it made his eyes look yellow and showed up the dirt in his kinked hair. He smelled funky. I moved a little away from him and I said, "Well, thanks. But I already know about it and I got to get home."

"I'll walk you a little ways," he said. We started walking. There were a couple of kids still loitering in the courtyard and one of them said goodnight to me and looked strangely at the boy beside me.

"What're you going to do?" he asked me. "I mean, about Sonny?"

"Look. I haven't seen Sonny for over a year. I'm not sure I'm going to do anything. Anyway, what the hell *can* I do?"

"That's right," he said quickly, "ain't nothing you can do. Can't much help old Sonny no more, I guess."

It was what I was thinking and so it seemed to me he had no right to say it.

"I'm surprised at Sonny, though," he went on—he had a funny way of talking, he looked straight ahead as though he were talking to himself—"I thought Sonny was a smart boy, I thought he was too smart to get hung."

"I guess he thought so too," I said sharply, "and that's how he got hung. And how about you? You're pretty goddamn smart, I bet."

Then he looked directly at me, just for a minute. "I ain't smart," he said. "If I was smart, I'd have reached for a pistol a long time ago."

"Look. Don't tell *me* your sad story, if it was up to me, I'd give you one." Then I felt guilty—guilty, probably, for never having supposed that the poor bastard *had* a story of his own, much less a sad one, and I asked, quickly, "What's going to happen to him now?"

He didn't answer this. He was off by himself some place. "Funny thing," he said, and from his tone we might have been discussing the quickest way to get to Brooklyn, "when I saw the papers this morning, the first thing I asked myself was if I had anything to do with it. I felt sort of responsible."

I began to listen more carefully. The subway station was on the corner, just before us, and I stopped. He stopped, too. We were in front of a bar and he ducked slightly, peering in, but whoever he was looking for didn't seem to be there. The juke box was blasting away with something black and bouncy and I half watched the barmaid as she danced her way from the juke box to her place behind the bar. And I watched her face as she laughingly responded to something someone said to her, still keeping time to the music. When she smiled one saw the little girl, one sensed the doomed, still-struggling woman beneath the battered face of the semi-whore.

"I never *give* Sonny nothing," the boy said finally, "but a long time ago I come to school high and Sonny asked me how it felt." He paused, I couldn't bear to watch him, I watched the barmaid, and I listened to the music which seemed to be causing the pavement to shake. "I told him it felt great." The music stopped, the barmaid paused and watched the juke box until the music began again. "It did."

All this was carrying me some place I didn't want to go. I certainly didn't want to know how it felt. It filled everything, the people, the houses, the music, the dark, quicksilver barmaid, with menace; and this menace was their reality.

"What's going to happen to him now?" I asked again.

"They'll send him away some place and they'll try to cure him." He shook his head. "Maybe he'll even think he's kicked the habit. Then they'll let him loose"—he gestured, throwing his cigarette into the gutter. "That's all."

"What do you mean, that's *all?*"

But I knew what he meant.

"I *mean,* that's *all.*" He turned his head and looked at me, pulling down the corners of his mouth. "Don't you know what I mean?" he asked, softly.

"How the hell *would* I know what you mean?" I almost whispered it, I don't know why.

"That's right," he said to the air, "how would *he* know what I mean?" He turned toward me again, patient and calm, and yet I somehow felt him shaking, shaking as though he were going to fall apart. I felt that ice in my guts again, the dread I'd felt all afternoon; and again I watched the barmaid, moving about the bar, washing glasses, and singing. "Listen. They'll let him out and then it'll just start all over again. That's what I mean."

"You mean—they'll let him out. And then he'll just start working his way back in again. You mean he'll never kick the habit. Is that what you mean?"

"That's right," he said, cheerfully. "*You* see what I mean."

"Tell me," I said at last, "why does he want to die? He must want to die, he's killing himself, why does he want to die?"

He looked at me in surprise. He licked his lips. "He don't want to die. He wants to live. Don't nobody want to die, ever."

Then I wanted to ask him—too many things. He could not have answered, or if he had, I could not have borne the answers. I started walking. "Well, I guess it's none of my business."

"It's going to be rough on old Sonny," he said. We reached the subway station. "This is your station?" he asked. I nodded. I took one step down. "Damn!" he said, suddenly. I looked up at him. He grinned again. "Damn it if I didn't leave all my money home. You ain't got a dollar on you, have you? Just for a couple of days, is all."

All at once something inside gave and threatened to come pouring out of me. I didn't hate him any more. I felt that in another moment I'd start crying like a child.

"Sure," I said. "Don't sweat." I looked in my wallet and didn't have a dollar, I only had a five. "Here," I said. "That hold you?"

He didn't look at it—he didn't want to look at it. A terrible closed look came over his face, as though he were keeping the number on the bill a secret from him and me. "Thanks," he said, and now he was dying to see me go. "Don't worry about Sonny. Maybe I'll write him or something."

"Sure," I said. "You do that. So long."

"Be seeing you," he said. I went on down the steps.

And I didn't write Sonny or send him anything for a long time. When I finally did, it was just after my little girl died, he wrote me back a letter which made me feel like a bastard.

Here's what he said:

Dear brother,

You don't know how much I needed to hear from you. I wanted to write you many a time but I dug how much I must have hurt you and so I didn't write. But now I feel like a man who's been trying to climb up out of some deep, real deep and funky hole and just saw the sun up there, outside. I got to get outside.

I can't tell you much about how I got here. I mean I don't know how to tell you. I guess I was afraid of something or I was trying to escape from something and you know I have never been very strong in the head (smile). I'm glad Mama and Daddy are dead and can't see what's happened to their son and I swear if I'd known what I was doing I would never have hurt you so, you and a lot of other fine people who were nice to me and who believed in me.

I don't want you to think it had anything to do with me being a musician. It's more than that. Or maybe less than that. I can't get anything straight in my head down here and I try not to think about what's going to happen to me when I get out-side again. Sometime I think I'm going to flip and *never* get outside and sometime I think I'll come straight back. I tell you one thing, though, I'd rather blow my brains out than go through this again. But that's what they all say, so they tell me. If I tell you when I'm coming to New York and if you could meet me, I sure would appre-ciate it. Give my love to Isabel and the kids and I was sure sorry to hear about little Gracie. I wish I could be like Mama and say the Lord's will be done, but I don't know it seems to me that trouble is the one thing that never does get stopped and I don't know what good it does to blame it on the Lord. But maybe it does some good if you believe it.

Your brother,
Sonny

Then I kept in constant touch with him and I sent him whatever I could and I went to meet him when he came back to New York. When I saw him many things I thought I had forgotten came flooding back to me. This was because I had begun, finally, to wonder about Sonny, about the life that Sonny lived inside. This life, whatever it was, had made him older and thinner and it had deepened the distant stillness in which he had always moved. He looked very unlike my baby brother. Yet, when he smiled, when we shook hands, the baby brother I'd never known looked out from the depths of his private life, like an animal waiting to be coaxed into the light.

"How you been keeping?" he asked me.

"All right. And you?"

"Just fine." He was smiling all over his face. "It's good to see you again."

"It's good to see you."

The seven years' difference in our ages lay between us like a chasm: I wondered if these years would ever operate between us as a bridge. I was remembering, and it made it hard to catch my breath, that I had been there when he was born; and I had heard the first words he had ever spoken. When he started to walk, he walked from our mother straight to me. I caught him just before he fell when he took the first steps he ever took in this world.

"How's Isabel?"

"Just fine. She's dying to see you."

"And the boys?"

"They're fine, too. They're anxious to see their uncle."

"Oh, come on. You know they don't remember me."

"Are you kidding? Of course they remember you."

He grinned again. We got into a taxi. We had a lot to say to each other, far too much to know how to begin.

As the taxi began to move, I asked, "You still want to go to India?"

He laughed. "You still remember that. Hell, no. This place is Indian enough for me."

"It used to belong to them," I said.

And he laughed again. "They damn sure knew what they were doing when they got rid of it."

Years ago, when he was around fourteen, he'd been all hipped on the idea of going to India. He read books about people sitting on rocks, naked, in all kinds of weather, but mostly bad, naturally, and walking barefoot through hot coals and arriving at wisdom. I used to say that it sounded to me as though they were getting away from wisdom as fast as they could. I think he sort of looked down on me for that.

"Do you mind," he asked, "if we have the driver drive alongside the park? On the west side—I haven't seen the city in so long."

"Of course not," I said. I was afraid that I might sound as though I were humoring him, but I hoped he wouldn't take it that way.

So we drove along, between the green of the park and the stony, lifeless elegance of hotels and apartment buildings, toward the vivid, killing streets of our childhood. These streets hadn't changed, though housing projects jutted up out of them now like rocks in the middle of a boiling sea. Most of the houses in which we had grown up had vanished, as had the stores from which we had stolen, the basements in which we had first tried sex, the rooftops from which we had hurled tin cans and bricks. But houses exactly like the houses of our past yet dominated the landscape, boys exactly like the boys we once had been found themselves smothering in these houses, came down into the streets for light and air and found themselves encircled by disaster. Some escaped the trap, most didn't. Those who got out always left something of themselves behind, as some animals amputate a leg and leave it in the trap. It might be said, perhaps, that I had escaped, after all, I was a school teacher; or that Sonny had, he hadn't lived in Harlem for years. Yet, as the cab moved uptown through streets which seemed, with a rush, to darken with dark people, and as I covertly studied Sonny's face, it came to me that what we both were seeking through our separate cab windows was that part of ourselves which had been left behind. It's always at the hour of trouble and confrontation that the missing member aches.

We hit 110th Street and started rolling up Lenox Avenue. And I'd known this avenue all my life, but it seemed to me again, as it had seemed on the day I'd first heard about Sonny's trouble, filled with a hidden menace which was its very breath of life.

"We almost there," said Sonny.

"Almost." We were both too nervous to say anything more.

We live in a housing project. It hasn't been up long. A few days after it was up it seemed uninhabitably new, now, of course, it's already rundown. It looks like a parody of the good, clean, faceless life—God knows the people who live in it do their best to make it a parody. The beat-looking grass lying around isn't enough to make their lives green, the hedges will never hold out the streets, and they know it. The big windows fool no one, they aren't big enough to make space out of no space. They don't bother with the windows, they watch the TV screen instead. The playground is most popular with the children who don't play at jacks, or skip rope, or roller skate, or swing, and they can be found in it after dark. We moved in partly because it's not too far from where I teach, and partly for the kids; but it's really just like the houses in which Sonny and I grew up. The same things happen, they'll have the same things to remember. The moment Sonny and I started into the house I had the feeling that I was simply bringing him back into the danger he had almost died trying to escape.

Sonny has never been talkative. So I don't know why I was sure he'd be dying to talk to me when supper was over the first night. Everything went fine, the oldest boy remembered him, and the youngest boy liked him, and Sonny had remembered to bring something for each of them; and Isabel, who is really much nicer than I am, more open and giving, had gone to a lot of trouble about dinner and was genuinely glad to see him. And she's always been able to tease Sonny in a way that I haven't. It was nice to see her face so vivid again and to hear her laugh and watch her make Sonny laugh. She wasn't, or, anyway, she didn't seem to be, at all uneasy or embarrassed. She chatted as though there were no subject which had to be avoided and she got Sonny past his first, faint stiffness. And thank God she was there, for I was filled with that icy dread again. Everything I did seemed awkward to me, and everything I said sounded freighted with hidden meaning. I was trying to remember everything I'd heard about dope addiction and I couldn't help watching Sonny for signs. I wasn't doing it out of malice. I was trying to find out something about my brother. I was dying to hear him tell me he was safe.

"Safe!" my father grunted, whenever Mama suggested trying to move to a neighborhood which might be safer for children. "Safe, hell! Ain't no place safe for kids, nor nobody."

He always went on like this, but he wasn't, ever, really as bad as he sounded, not even on weekends, when he got drunk. As a matter of fact, he was always on the lookout for "something a little better," but he died before he found it. He died suddenly, during a drunken weekend in the middle of the war, when Sonny was fifteen. He and Sonny hadn't ever got on too well. And this was partly because Sonny was the apple of his father's eye. It was because he loved Sonny so much and was frightened for him, that he was always fighting with him. It doesn't do any good to fight with Sonny. Sonny just moves back, inside himself, where he can't be reached. But the principal reason that they never hit it off is that they were so much alike. Daddy was big and rough and loud-talking, just the opposite of Sonny, but they both had—that same privacy.

Mama tried to tell me something about this, just after Daddy died. I was home on leave from the army.

This was the last time I ever saw my mother alive. Just the same, this picture gets all mixed up in my mind with pictures I had of her when she was younger. The way I always see her is the way she used to be on a Sunday afternoon, say, when the old folks were talking after the big Sunday dinner. I always see her wearing pale blue. She'd be sitting on the sofa. And my father would be sitting in the easy chair, not far from her. And the living room would be full of church folks and relatives. There they sit, in chairs all around the living room, and the night is creeping up outside, but nobody knows it yet. You can see the darkness growing against the windowpanes and you hear the street noises every now and again, or maybe the jangling beat of a tambourine from one of the churches close by, but it's real quiet in the room. For a moment nobody's talking, but every face looks darkening, like the sky outside. And my mother rocks a little from the waist, and my father's eyes are closed. Everyone is looking at something a child can't see. For a minute they've forgotten the children. Maybe a kid is lying on the rug, half asleep. Maybe somebody's got a kid in his lap and is absent-mindedly stroking the kid's head. Maybe there's a kid, quiet and big-eyed, curled up in a big chair in the corner. The silence, the darkness coming, and the darkness in the faces frightens the child obscurely. He hopes that the hand which strokes his forehead will never stop—will never die. He hopes that there will never come a time when the old folks won't be sitting around the living room, talking about where they've come from, and what they've seen, and what's happened to them and their kinfolk.

But something deep and watchful in the child knows that this is bound to end, is already ending. In a moment someone will get up and turn on the light. Then the old folks will remember the children and they won't talk any more that day. And when light fills the room, the child is filled with darkness. He knows that every time this happens he's moved just a little closer to that darkness outside. The darkness outside is what the old folks have been talking about. It's what they've come from. It's what they endure. The child knows that they won't talk any more because if he knows too much about what's happened to *them*, he'll know too much too soon, about what's going to happen to *him*.

The last time I talked to my mother, I remember I was restless. I wanted to get out and see Isabel. We weren't married then and we had a lot to straighten out between us.

There Mama sat, in black, by the window. She was humming an old church song, *Lord, you brought me from a long ways off.* Sonny was out somewhere. Mama kept watching the streets.

"I don't know," she said, "if I'll ever see you again, after you go off from here. But I hope you'll remember the things I tried to teach you."

"Don't talk like that," I said, and smiled. "You'll be here a long time yet."

She smiled, too, but she said nothing. She was quiet for a long time. And I said, "Mama, don't you worry about nothing. I'll be writing all the time, and you be getting the checks. . . ."

"I want to talk to you about your brother," she said, suddenly. "If anything happens to me he ain't going to have nobody to look out for him."

"Mama," I said, "ain't nothing going to happen to you *or* Sonny. Sonny's all right. He's a good boy and he's got good sense."

"It ain't a question of his being a good boy," Mama said, "nor of his having good sense. It ain't only the bad ones, nor yet the dumb ones that gets sucked under." She stopped, looking at me. "Your Daddy once had a brother," she said, and she smiled in a way that made me feel she was in pain. "You didn't never know that, did you?"

"No," I said, "I never knew that," and I watched her face.

"Oh, yes," she said, "your Daddy had a brother." She looked out of the window again. "I know you never saw your Daddy cry. But *I* did—many a time, through all these years."

I asked her, "What happened to his brother? How come nobody's ever talked about him?"

This was the first time I ever saw my mother look old.

"His brother got killed," she said, "when he was just a little younger than you are now. I knew him. He was a fine boy. He was maybe a little full of the devil, but he didn't mean nobody no harm."

Then she stopped and the room was silent, exactly as it had sometimes been on those Sunday afternoons. Mama kept looking out into the streets.

"He used to have a job in the mill," she said, "and, like all young folks, he just liked to perform on Saturday nights. Saturday nights, him and your father would drift around to different places, go to dances and things like that, or just sit around with people they knew, and your father's brother would sing, he had a fine voice, and play along with himself on his guitar. Well, this particular Saturday night, him and your father was coming home from some place, and they were both a little drunk and there was a moon that night, it was bright like day. Your father's brother was feeling kind of good, and he was whistling to himself, and he had his guitar slung over his shoulder. They was coming down a hill and beneath them was a road that turned off from the highway. Well, your father's brother, being always kind of frisky, decided to run down this hill, and he did, with that guitar banging and clanging behind him, and he ran across the road, and he was making water behind a tree. And your father was sort of amused at him and he was still coming down the hill, kind of slow. Then he heard a car motor and that same minute his brother stepped from behind the tree, into the road, in the moonlight. And he started to cross the road. And your father started to run down the hill, he says he don't know why. This car was full of white men. They was all drunk, and when they seen your father's brother they let out a great whoop and holler and they aimed the car straight at him. They was having fun, they just wanted to scare him, the way they do sometimes, you know. But they was drunk. And I guess the boy, being drunk, too, and scared, kind of lost his head. By the time he jumped it was too late. Your father says he heard his brother scream when the car rolled over him, and he heard the wood of that guitar when it give, and he heard them strings go flying, and he heard them white men shouting, and the car kept on a-going and it ain't stopped till this day. And, time your father got down the hill, his brother weren't nothing but blood and pulp."

Tears were gleaming on my mother's face. There wasn't anything I could say.

"He never mentioned it," she said, "because I never let him mention it before you children. Your Daddy was like a crazy man that night and for many a night there-after. He says he never in his life seen anything as dark as that road after the lights of that car had gone away. Weren't nothing, weren't nobody on that road, just your Daddy and his brother and that busted guitar. Oh, yes. Your Daddy never did really get right again. Till the day he died he weren't sure but that every white man he saw was the man that killed his brother."

She stopped and took out her handkerchief and dried her eyes and looked at me.

"I ain't telling you all this," she said, "to make you scared or bitter or to make you hate nobody. I'm telling you this because you got a brother. And the world ain't changed."

I guess I didn't want to believe this. I guess she saw this in my face. She turned away from me, toward the window again, searching those streets.

"But I praise my Redeemer," she said at last, "that He called your Daddy home before me. I ain't saying it to throw no flowers at myself, but, I declare, it keeps me from feeling too cast down to know I helped your father get safely through this world. Your father always acted like he was the roughest, strongest man on earth. And every-body took him to be like that. But if he hadn't had *me* there—to see his tears!"

She was crying again. Still, I couldn't move. I said, "Lord, Lord, Mama, I didn't know it was like that."

"Oh, honey," she said, "there's a lot that you don't know. But you are going to find it out." She stood up from the window and came over to me. "You got to hold on to your brother," she said, "and don't let him fall, no matter what it looks like is happen-ing to him and no matter how evil you gets with him. You going to be evil with him many a time. But don't you forget what I told you, you hear?"

"I won't forget," I said. "Don't you worry, I won't forget. I won't let nothing hap-pen to Sonny."

My mother smiled as though she were amused at something she saw in my face. Then, "You may not be able to stop nothing from happening. But you got to let him know you's *there*."

*   *   *

Two days later I was married, and then I was gone. And I had a lot of things on my mind and I pretty well forgot my promise to Mama until I got shipped home on a spe-cial furlough for her funeral.

And, after the funeral, with just Sonny and me alone in the empty kitchen, I tried to find out something about him.

"What do you want to do?" I asked him.

"I'm going to be a musician," he said.

For he had graduated, in the time I had been away, from dancing to the juke box to finding out who was playing what, and what they were doing with it, and he had bought himself a set of drums.

"You mean, you want to be a drummer?" I somehow had the feeling that being a drummer might be all right for other people but not for my brother Sonny.

"I don't think," he said, looking at me very gravely, "that I'll ever be a good drummer. But I think I can play a piano."

I frowned. I'd never played the role of the older brother quite so seriously before, had scarcely ever, in fact, *asked* Sonny a damn thing. I sensed myself in the presence of something I didn't really know how to handle, didn't understand. So I made my frown a little deeper as I asked: "What kind of musician do you want to be?"

He grinned. "How many kinds do you think there are?"

"Be *serious*," I said.

He laughed, throwing his head back, and then looked at me. "I am serious."

"Well, then, for Christ's sake, stop kidding around and answer a serious question. I mean, do you want to be a concert pianist, you want to play classical music and all that, or—or what?" Long before I finished he was laughing again. "For Christ's *sake*, Sonny!"

He sobered, but with difficulty. "I'm sorry. But you sound so—*scared!*" and he was off again.

"Well, you may think it's funny now, baby, but it's not going to be so funny when you have to make your living at it, let me tell you *that*." I was furious because I knew he was laughing at me and I didn't know why.

"No," he said, very sober now, and afraid, perhaps, that he'd hurt me, "I don't want to be a classical pianist. That isn't what interests me. I mean"—he paused, looking hard at me, as though his eyes would help me to understand, and then gestured helplessly, as though perhaps his hand would help—"I mean, I'll have a lot of studying to do, and I'll have to study *everything*, but, I mean, I want to play *with*—jazz musicians." He stopped. "I want to play jazz," he said.

Well, the word had never before sounded as heavy, as real, as it sounded that afternoon in Sonny's mouth. I just looked at him and I was probably frowning a real frown by this time. I simply couldn't see why on earth he'd want to spend his time hanging around nightclubs, clowning around on bandstands, while people pushed each other around a dance floor. It seemed—beneath him, somehow. I had never thought about it before, had never been forced to, but I suppose I had always put jazz musicians in a class with what Daddy called "good-time people."

"Are you *serious*?"

"Hell, *yes*, I'm serious."

He looked more helpless than ever, and annoyed, and deeply hurt.

I suggested, helpfully: "You mean—like Louis Armstrong?"

His face closed as though I'd struck him. "No. I'm not talking about none of that old-time, down home crap."

"Well, look, Sonny, I'm sorry, don't get mad. I just don't altogether get it, that's all. Name somebody—you know, a jazz musician you admire."

"Bird."

"Who?"

"Bird! Charlie Parker! Don't they teach you nothing in the goddamn army?"

I lit a cigarette. I was surprised and then a little amused to discover that I was trembling. "I've been out of touch," I said. "You'll have to be patient with me. Now. Who's this Parker character?"

"He's just one of the greatest jazz musicians alive," said Sonny, sullenly, his hands in his pockets, his back to me. "Maybe *the* greatest," he added, bitterly, "that's probably why *you* never heard of him."

"All right," I said, "I'm ignorant. I'm sorry. I'll go out and buy all the cat's records right away, all right?"

"It don't," said Sonny, with dignity, "make any difference to me. I don't care what you listen to. Don't do me no favors."

I was beginning to realize that I'd never seen him so upset before. With another part of my mind I was thinking that this would probably turn out to be one of those things kids go through and that I shouldn't make it seem important by pushing it too hard. Still, I didn't think it would do any harm to ask: "Doesn't all this take a lot of time? Can you make a living at it?"

He turned back to me and half leaned, half sat, on the kitchen table. "Everything takes time," he said, "and—well, yes, sure, I can make a living at it. But what I don't seem to be able to make you understand is that it's the only thing I want to do."

"Well, Sonny," I said, gently, "you know people can't always do exactly what they *want* to do—"

"*No*, I don't know that," said Sonny, surprising me. "I think people *ought* to do what they want to do, what else are they alive for?"

"You getting to be a big boy," I said desperately, "it's time you started thinking about your future."

"I'm thinking about my future," said Sonny, grimly. "I think about it all the time."

I gave up. I decided, if he didn't change his mind, that we could always talk about it later. "In the meantime," I said, "you got to finish school." We had already decided that he'd have to move in with Isabel and her folks. I knew this wasn't the ideal arrangement because Isabel's folks are inclined to be dicty and they hadn't especially wanted Isabel to marry me. But I didn't know what else to do. "And we have to get you fixed up at Isabel's."

There was a long silence. He moved from the kitchen table to the window. "That's a terrible idea. You know it yourself."

"Do you have a *better* idea?"

He just walked up and down the kitchen for a minute. He was as tall as I was. He had started to shave. I suddenly had the feeling that I didn't know him at all.

He stopped at the kitchen table and picked up my cigarettes. Looking at me with a kind of mocking, amused defiance, he put one between his lips. "You mind?"

"You smoking already?"

He lit the cigarette and nodded, watching me through the smoke. "I just wanted to see if I'd have the courage to smoke in front of you." He grinned and blew a great cloud of smoke to the ceiling. "It was easy." He looked at my face. "Come on, now. I bet you was smoking at my age, tell the truth."

I didn't say anything but the truth was on my face, and he laughed. But now there was something very strained in his laugh. "Sure. And I bet that ain't all you was doing."

He was frightening me a little. "Cut the crap," I said. "We already decided that you was going to go and live at Isabel's. Now what's got into you all of a sudden?"

"*You* decided it," he pointed out. "*I* didn't decide nothing." He stopped in front of me, leaning against the stove, arms loosely folded. "Look, brother. I don't want to stay in Harlem no more, I really don't." He was very earnest. He looked at me, then over toward the kitchen window. There was something in his eyes I'd never seen before, some thoughtfulness, some worry all his own. He rubbed the muscle of one arm. "It's time I was getting out of here."

"Where do you want to *go*, Sonny?"

"I want to join the army. Or the navy, I don't care. If I say I'm old enough, they'll believe me."

Then I got mad. It was because I was so scared. "You must be crazy. You goddamn fool, what the hell do you want to go and join the *army* for?"

"I just told you. To get out of Harlem."

"Sonny, you haven't even finished *school*. And if you really want to be a musician, how do you expect to study if you're in the *army*?"

He looked at me, trapped, and in anguish. "There's ways. I might be able to work out some kind of deal. Anyway, I'll have the G.I. Bill when I come out."

"*If* you come out." We stared at each other. "Sonny, please. Be reasonable. I know the setup is far from perfect. But we got to do the best we can."

"I ain't learning nothing in school," he said. "Even when I go." He turned away from me and opened the window and threw his cigarette out into the narrow alley. I watched his back. "At least, I ain't learning nothing you'd want me to learn." He slammed the window so hard I thought the glass would fly out, and turned back to me. "And I'm sick of the stink of these garbage cans!"

"Sonny," I said, "I know how you feel. But if you don't finish school now, you're going to be sorry later that you didn't." I grabbed him by the shoulders. "And you only got another year. It ain't so bad. And I'll come back and I swear I'll help you do *whatever* you want to do. Just try to put up with it till I come back. Will you please do that? For me?"

He didn't answer and he wouldn't look at me.

"Sonny. You hear me?"

He pulled away. "I hear you. But you never hear anything *I* say."

I didn't know what to say to that. He looked out of the window and then back at me. "OK," he said, and sighed. "I'll try."

Then I said, trying to cheer him up a little, "They got a piano at Isabel's. You can practice on it."

And as a matter of fact, it did cheer him up for a minute. "That's right," he said to himself. "I forgot that." His face relaxed a little. But the worry, the thoughtfulness, played on it still, the way shadows play on a face which is staring into the fire.

But I thought I'd never hear the end of that piano. At first, Isabel would write me, saying how nice it was that Sonny was so serious about his music and how, as soon as he came in from school, or wherever he had been when he was supposed to be at school, he went straight to that piano and stayed there until suppertime. And, after supper, he went back to that piano and stayed there until everybody went to bed. He was at the piano all day Saturday and all day Sunday. Then he bought a record player and started playing records. He'd play one record over and over again, all day long sometimes, and he'd improvise along with it on the piano. Or he'd play one section of the record, one chord, one change, one progression, then he'd do it on the piano. Then back to the record. Then back to the piano.

Well, I really don't know how they stood it. Isabel finally confessed that it wasn't like living with a person at all, it was like living with sound. And the sound didn't make any sense to her, didn't make any sense to any of them—naturally. They began, in a way, to be afflicted by this presence that was living in their home. It was as though Sonny were some sort of god, or monster. He moved in an atmosphere which wasn't like theirs at all. They fed him and he ate, he washed himself, he walked in and out of their door; he certainly wasn't nasty or unpleasant or rude, Sonny isn't any of those things; but it was as though he were all wrapped up in some cloud, some fire, some vision all his own; and there wasn't any way to reach him.

At the same time, he wasn't really a man yet, he was still a child, and they had to watch out for him in all kinds of ways. They certainly couldn't throw him out. Neither did they dare to make a great scene about that piano because even they dimly sensed, as I sensed, from so many thousands of miles away, that Sonny was at that piano playing for his life.

But he hadn't been going to school. One day a letter came from the school board and Isabel's mother got it—there had, apparently, been other letters but Sonny had torn them up. This day, when Sonny came in, Isabel's mother showed him the letter and asked where he'd been spending his time. And she finally got it out of him that he'd been down in Greenwich Village, with musicians and other characters, in a white girl's apartment. And this scared her and she started to scream at him and what came up, once she began—though she denies it to this day—was what sacrifices they were making to give Sonny a decent home and how little he appreciated it.

Sonny didn't play the piano that day. By evening, Isabel's mother had calmed down but then there was the old man to deal with, and Isabel herself. Isabel says she did her best to be calm but she broke down and started crying. She says she just watched Sonny's face. She could tell, by watching him, what was happening with him. And what was happening was that they penetrated his cloud, they had reached him. Even if their fingers had been a thousand times more gentle than human fingers ever are, he could hardly help feeling that they had stripped him naked and were spitting on that nakedness. For he also had to see that his presence, that music, which was life or death to him, had been torture for them and that they had endured it, not at all for his sake, but only for mine. And Sonny couldn't take that. He can take it a little better today than he could then but he's still not very good at it and, frankly, I don't know anybody who is.

The silence of the next few days must have been louder than the sound of all the music ever played since time began. One morning, before she went to work, Isabel was in his room for something and she suddenly realized that all of his records were gone. And she knew for certain that he was gone. And he was. He went as far as the navy would carry him. He finally sent me a postcard from some place in Greece and that was the first I knew that Sonny was still alive. I didn't see him any more until we were both back in New York and the war had long been over.

He was a man by then, of course, but I wasn't willing to see it. He came by the house from time to time, but we fought almost every time we met. I didn't like the way he carried himself, loose and dreamlike all the time, and I didn't like his friends, and his music seemed to be merely an excuse for the life he led. It sounded just that weird and disordered.

Then we had a fight, a pretty awful fight, and I didn't see him for months. By and by I looked him up, where he was living, in a furnished room in the Village, and I tried to make it up. But there were lots of people in the room and Sonny just lay on his bed, and he wouldn't come downstairs with me, and he treated these other people as though they were his family and I weren't. So I got mad and then he got mad, and then I told him that he might just as well be dead as live the way he was living. Then he stood up and he told me not to worry about him any more in life, that he *was* dead as far as I was concerned. Then he pushed me to the door and the other people looked on as though nothing were happening, and he slammed the door behind me. I stood in the hallway, staring at the door. I heard somebody laugh in the room and then the tears came to my eyes. I started down the steps, whistling to keep from crying, I kept whistling to myself, *You going to need me, baby, one of these cold, rainy days.*

I read about Sonny's trouble in the spring. Little Grace died in the fall. She was a beautiful little girl. But she only lived a little over two years. She died of polio and she suffered. She had a slight fever for a couple of days, but it didn't seem like anything and we just kept her in bed. And we would certainly have called the doctor, but the fever dropped, she seemed to be all right. So we thought it had just been a cold. Then, one day, she was up, playing, Isabel was in the kitchen fixing lunch for the two boys when they'd come in from school, and she heard Grace fall down in the living room. When you have a lot of children you don't always start running when one of them falls, unless they start screaming or something. And, this time, Grace was quiet. Yet, Isabel says that when she heard that *thump* and then that silence, something happened in her to make her afraid. And she ran to the living room and there was little Grace on the floor, all twisted up, and the reason she hadn't screamed was that she couldn't get her breath. And when she did scream, it was the worst sound, Isabel says, that she'd ever heard in all her life, and she still hears it sometimes in her dreams. Isabel will sometimes wake me up with a low, moaning, strangled sound and I have to be quick to awaken her and hold her to me and where Isabel is weeping against me seems a mortal wound.

I think I may have written Sonny the very day that little Grace was buried. I was sitting in the living room in the dark, by myself, and I suddenly thought of Sonny. My trouble made his real.

One Saturday afternoon, when Sonny had been living with us, or, anyway, been in our house, for nearly two weeks, I found myself wandering aimlessly about the living room, drinking from a can of beer, and trying to work up the courage to search Sonny's room. He was out, he was usually out whenever I was home, and Isabel had taken the children to see their grandparents. Suddenly I was standing still in front of the living room window, watching Seventh Avenue. The idea of searching Sonny's room made me still. I scarcely dared to admit to myself what I'd be searching for. I didn't know what I'd do if I found it. Or if I didn't.

On the sidewalk across from me, near the entrance to a barbecue joint, some people were holding an old-fashioned revival meeting. The barbecue cook, wearing a dirty white apron, his conked hair reddish and metallic in the pale sun, and a cigarette between his lips, stood in the doorway, watching them. Kids and older people paused in their errands and stood there, along with some older men and a couple of very tough-looking women who watched everything that happened on the avenue, as though they owned it, or were maybe owned by it. Well, they were watching this, too. The revival was being carried on by three sisters in black, and a brother. All they had were their voices and their Bibles and a tambourine. The brother was testifying and while he testified two of the sisters stood together, seeming to say, amen, and the third sister walked around with the tambourine outstretched and a couple of people dropped coins into it. Then the brother's testimony ended and the sister who had been taking up the collection dumped the coins into her palm and transferred them to the pocket of her long black robe. Then she raised both hands, striking the tambourine against the air, and then against one hand, and she started to sing. And the two other sisters and the brother joined in.

It was strange, suddenly, to watch, though I had been seeing these street meetings all my life. So, of course, had everybody else down there. Yet, they paused and watched and listened and I stood still at the window. *"Tis the old ship of Zion,"* they sang, and the sister with the tambourine kept a steady, jangling beat, *"it has rescued many a thousand!"* Not a soul under the sound of their voices was hearing this song for the first time, not one of them had been rescued. Nor had they seen much in the way of rescue work being done around them. Neither did they especially believe in the holiness of the three sisters and the brother, they knew too much about them, knew where they lived, and how. The woman with the tambourine, whose voice dominated the air, whose face was bright with joy, was divided by very little from the woman who stood watching her, a cigarette between her heavy, chapped lips, her hair a cuckoo's nest, her face scarred and swollen from many beatings, and her black eyes glittering like coal. Perhaps they both knew this, which was why, when, as rarely, they addressed each other, they addressed each other as Sister. As the singing filled the air the watching, listening faces underwent a change, the eyes focusing on something within; the music seemed to soothe a poison out of them; and time seemed, nearly, to fall away from the sullen, belligerent, battered faces, as though they were fleeing back to their first condition, while dreaming of their last. The barbecue cook half shook his head and smiled, and dropped his cigarette and disappeared into his joint. A man fumbled in his pockets for change and stood holding it in his hand impatiently, as though he had just remembered a pressing appointment further up the avenue. He looked furious. Then I saw Sonny, standing on the edge of the crowd. He was carrying a wide, flat notebook with a green cover, and it made him look, from where I was standing, almost like a schoolboy. The coppery sun brought out the copper in his skin, he was very faintly smiling, standing very still. Then the singing stopped, the tambourine turned into a collection plate again. The furious man dropped in his coins and vanished, so did a couple of the women, and Sonny dropped some change in the plate, looking directly at the woman with a little smile. He started across the avenue, toward the house. He has a slow, loping walk, something like the way Harlem hipsters walk, only he's imposed on this his own half-beat. I had never really noticed it before.

I stayed at the window, both relieved and apprehensive. As Sonny disappeared from my sight, they began singing again. And they were still singing when his key turned in the lock.

"Hey," he said.

"Hey, yourself. You want some beer?"

"No. Well, maybe." But he came up to the window and stood beside me, looking out. "What a warm voice," he said.

They were singing *If I could only hear my mother pray again!*

"Yes," I said, "and she can sure beat that tambourine."

"But what a terrible song," he said, and laughed. He dropped his notebook on the sofa and disappeared into the kitchen. "Where's Isabel and the kids?"

"I think they went to see their grandparents. You hungry?"

"No." He came back into the living room with his can of beer. "You want to come some place with me tonight?"

I sensed, I don't know how, that I couldn't possibly say no. "Sure. Where?"

He sat down on the sofa and picked up his notebook and started leafing through it. "I'm going to sit in with some fellows in a joint in the Village."

"You mean, you're going to play, tonight?"

"That's right." He took a swallow of his beer and moved back to the window. He gave me a sidelong look. "If you can stand it."

"I'll try," I said.

He smiled to himself and we both watched as the meeting across the way broke up. The three sisters and the brother, heads bowed, were singing *God be with you till we meet again.* The faces around them were very quiet. Then the song ended. The small crowd dispersed. We watched the three women and the lone man walk slowly up the avenue.

"When she was singing before," said Sonny, abruptly, "her voice reminded me for a minute of what heroin feels like sometimes—when it's in your veins. It makes you feel sort of warm and cool at the same time. And distant. And—and sure." He sipped his beer, very deliberately not looking at me. I watched his face. "It makes you feel—in control. Sometimes you've got to have that feeling."

"Do you?" I sat down slowly in the easy chair.

"Sometimes." He went to the sofa and picked up his notebook again. "Some people do."

"In order," I asked, "to play?" And my voice was very ugly, full of contempt and anger.

"Well"—he looked at me with great, troubled eyes, as though, in fact, he hoped his eyes would tell me things he could never otherwise say—"they *think* so. And *if* they think so—!"

"And what do *you* think?" I asked.

He sat on the sofa and put his can of beer on the floor. "I don't know," he said, and I couldn't be sure if he were answering my question or pursuing his thoughts. His face didn't tell me. "It's not so much to *play*. It's to *stand* it, to be able to make it at all. On any level." He frowned and smiled: "In order to keep from shaking to pieces."

"But these friends of yours," I said, "they seem to shake themselves to pieces pretty goddamn fast."

"Maybe." He played with the notebook. And something told me that I should curb my tongue, that Sonny was doing his best to talk, that I should listen. "But of course you only know the ones that've gone to pieces. Some don't—or at least they haven't *yet* and that's just about all *any* of us can say." He paused. "And then there are some who just live, really, in hell, and they know it and they see what's happening and they go right on. I don't know." He sighed, dropped the notebook, folded his arms. "Some guys, you can tell from the way they play, they on something *all* the time. And you can see that, well, it makes something real for them. But of course," he picked up his beer from the floor and sipped it and put the can down again, "they *want* to, too, you've got to see that. Even some of them that say they don't—*some,* not all."

"And what about you?" I asked—I couldn't help it. "What about you? Do *you* want to?"

He stood up and walked to the window and remained silent for a long time. Then he sighed. "Me," he said. Then: "While I was downstairs before, on my way here, listening to that woman sing, it struck me all of a sudden how much suffering she must have had to go through—to sing like that. It's *repulsive* to think you have to suffer that much."

I said: "But there's no way not to suffer—is there, Sonny?"

"I believe not," he said and smiled, "but that's never stopped anyone from trying." He looked at me. "Has it?" I realized, with this mocking look, that there stood between us, forever, beyond the power of time or forgiveness, the fact that I had held silence—so long!—when he had needed human speech to help him. He turned back to the window. "No, there's no way not to suffer. But you try all kinds of ways to keep from drowning in it, to keep on top of it, and to make it seem—well, like *you.* Like you did something, all right, and now you're suffering for it. You know?" I said nothing. "Well you know," he said, impatiently, "why *do* people suffer? Maybe it's better to do something to give it a reason, *any* reason."

"But we just agreed," I said, "that there's no way not to suffer. Isn't it better, then, just to—take it?"

"But nobody just takes it," Sonny cried, "that's what I'm telling you! *Everybody* tries not to. You're just hung up on the *way* some people try—it's not *your* way!"

The hair on my face began to itch, my face felt wet. "That's not true," I said, "that's not true. I don't give a damn what other people do, I don't even care how they suffer. I just care how *you* suffer." And he looked at me. "Please believe me," I said, "I don't want to see you—die—trying not to suffer."

"I won't," he said, flatly, "die trying not to suffer. At least, not any faster than anybody else."

"But there's no need," I said, trying to laugh, "is there? in killing yourself."

I wanted to say more, but I couldn't. I wanted to talk about will power and how life could be—well, beautiful. I wanted to say that it was all within; but was it? or, rather, wasn't that exactly the trouble? And I wanted to promise that I would never fail him again. But it would all have sounded—empty words and lies.

So I made the promise to myself and prayed that I would keep it.

"It's terrible sometimes, inside," he said, "that's what's the trouble. You walk these streets, black and funky and cold, and there's not really a living ass to talk to, and there's nothing shaking, and there's no way of getting it out—that storm inside. You can't talk it and you can't make love with it, and when you finally try to get with it and play it, you realize *nobody's* listening. So *you've* got to listen. You got to find a way to listen."

And then he walked away from the window and sat on the sofa again, as though all the wind had suddenly been knocked out of him. "Sometimes you'll do *anything* to play, even cut your mother's throat." He laughed and looked at me. "Or your brother's." Then he sobered. "Or your own." Then: "Don't worry. I'm all right now and I think I'll *be* all right. But I can't forget—where I've been. I don't mean just the physical place I've been, I mean where I've *been*. And *what* I've been."

"What have you been, Sonny?" I asked.

He smiled—but sat sideways on the sofa, his elbow resting on the back, his fingers playing with his mouth and chin, not looking at me. "I've been something I didn't recognize, didn't know I could be. Didn't know anybody could be." He stopped, looking inward, looking helplessly young, looking old. "I'm not talking about it now because I feel *guilty* or anything like that—maybe it would be better if I did, I don't know. Anyway, I can't really talk about it. Not to you, not to anybody," and now he turned and faced me. "Sometimes, you know, and it was actually when I was most *out* of the world, I felt that I was in it, that I was *with* it, really, and I could play or I didn't really have to *play*, it just came out of me, it was there. And I don't know how I played, thinking about it now, but I know I did awful things, those times, sometimes, to people. Or it wasn't that I *did* anything to them—it was that they weren't real." He picked up the beer can; it was empty; he rolled it between his palms: "And other times—well, I needed a fix, I needed to find a place to lean, I needed to clear a space to *listen*—and I couldn't find it, and I—went crazy, I did terrible things to *me*, I was terrible *for* me." He began pressing the beer can between his hands, I watched the metal begin to give. It glittered, as he played with it, like a knife, and I was afraid he would cut himself, but I said nothing. "Oh well. I can never tell you. I was all by myself at the bottom of something, stinking and sweating and crying and shaking, and I smelled it, you know? *my* stink, and I thought I'd die if I couldn't get away from it and yet, all the same, I knew that everything I was doing was just locking me in with it. And I didn't know," he paused, still flattening the beer can, "I didn't know, I still *don't* know, something kept telling me that maybe it was good to smell your own stink, but I didn't think that *that* was what I'd been trying to do—and—who can stand it?" and he abruptly dropped the ruined beer can, looking at me with a small, still smile, and then rose, walking to the window as though it were the lodestone rock. I watched his face, he watched the avenue. "I couldn't tell you when Mama died—but the reason I wanted to leave Harlem so bad was to get away from drugs. And then, when I ran away, that's what I was running from—really. When I came back, nothing had changed, *I* hadn't changed, I was just—older." And he stopped, drumming with his fingers on the windowpane. The sun had vanished, soon darkness would fall. I watched his face. "It can come again," he said, almost as though speaking to himself. Then he turned to me. "It can come again," he repeated. "I just want you to know that."

"All right," I said, at last. "So it can come again. All right."

He smiled, but the smile was sorrowful. "I had to try to tell you," he said.

"Yes," I said. "I understand that."

"You're my brother," he said, looking straight at me, and not smiling at all.

"Yes," I repeated, "yes. I understand that."

He turned back to the window, looking out. "All that hatred down there," he said, "all that hatred and misery and love. It's a wonder it doesn't blow the avenue apart."

We went to the only nightclub on a short, dark street, downtown. We squeezed through the narrow, chattering, jam-packed bar to the entrance of the big room, where the bandstand was. And we stood there for a moment, for the lights were very dim in this room and we couldn't see. Then, "Hello, boy," said a voice and an enormous black man, much older than Sonny or myself, erupted out of all that atmospheric lighting and put an arm around Sonny's shoulder. "I been sitting right here," he said, "waiting for you."

He had a big voice, too, and heads in the darkness turned toward us.

Sonny grinned and pulled a little away, and said, "Creole, this is my brother. I told you about him."

Creole shook my hand. "I'm glad to meet you, son," he said, and it was clear that he was glad to meet me *there*, for Sonny's sake. And he smiled, "You got a real musician in *your* family," and he took his arm from Sonny's shoulder and slapped him, lightly, affectionately, with the back of his hand.

"Well. Now I've heard it all," said a voice behind us. This was another musician, and a friend of Sonny's, a coal-black, cheerful-looking man, built close to the ground. He immediately began confiding to me, at the top of his lungs, the most terrible things about Sonny, his teeth gleaming like a lighthouse and his laugh coming up out of him like the beginning of an earthquake. And it turned out that everyone at the bar knew Sonny, or almost everyone; some were musicians, working there, or nearby, or not working, some were simply hangers-on, and some were there to hear Sonny play. I was introduced to all of them and they were all very polite to me. Yet, it was clear that, for them, I was only Sonny's brother. Here, I was in Sonny's world. Or, rather: his kingdom. Here, it was not even a question that his veins bore royal blood.

They were going to play soon and Creole installed me, by myself, at a table in a dark corner. Then I watched them, Creole, and the little black man, and Sonny, and the others, while they horsed around, standing just below the bandstand. The light from the bandstand spilled just a little short of them and, watching them laughing and gesturing and moving about, I had the feeling that they, nevertheless, were being most careful not to step into that circle of light too suddenly: that if they moved into the light too suddenly, without thinking, they would perish in flame. Then, while I watched, one of them, the small, black man, moved into the light and crossed the bandstand and started fooling around with his drums. Then—being funny and being, also, extremely ceremonious—Creole took Sonny by the arm and led him to the piano. A woman's voice called Sonny's name and a few hands started clapping. And Sonny, also being funny and being ceremonious, and so touched, I think, that he could have cried, but neither hiding it nor showing it, riding it like a man, grinned, and put both hands to his heart and bowed from the waist.

Creole then went to the bass fiddle and a lean, very bright-skinned brown man jumped up on the bandstand and picked up his horn. So there they were, and the atmosphere on the bandstand and in the room began to change and tighten. Someone stepped up to the microphone and announced them. Then there were all kinds of murmurs. Some people at the bar shushed others. The waitress ran around, frantically getting in the last orders, guys and chicks got closer to each other, and the lights on the bandstand, on the quartet, turned to a kind of indigo. Then they all looked different there. Creole looked about him for the last time, as though he were making certain that all his chickens were in the coop, and then he—jumped and struck the fiddle. And there they were.

All I know about music is that not many people ever really hear it. And even then, on the rare occasions when something opens within, and the music enters, what we mainly hear, or hear corroborated, are personal, private, vanishing evocations. But the man who creates the music is hearing something else, is dealing with the roar rising from the void and imposing order on it as it hits the air. What is evoked in him, then, is of another order, more terrible because it has no words, and triumphant, too, for that same reason. And his triumph, when he triumphs, is ours. I just watched Sonny's face. His face was troubled, he was working hard, but he wasn't with it. And I had the feeling that, in a way, everyone on the bandstand was waiting for him, both waiting for him and pushing him along. But as I began to watch Creole, I realized that it was Creole who held them all back. He had them on a short rein. Up there, keeping the beat with his whole body, wailing on the fiddle, with his eyes half closed, he was listening to everything, but he was listening to Sonny. He was having a dialogue with Sonny. He wanted Sonny to leave the shoreline and strike out for the deep water. He was Sonny's witness that deep water and drowning were not the same thing—he had been there, and he knew. And he wanted Sonny to know. He was waiting for Sonny to do the things on the keys which would let Creole know that Sonny was in the water.

And, while Creole listened, Sonny moved, deep within, exactly like someone in torment. I had never before thought of how awful the relationship must be between the musician and his instrument. He has to fill it, this instrument, with the breath of life, his own. He has to make it do what he wants it to do. And a piano is just a piano. It's made out of so much wood and wires and little hammers and big ones, and ivory. While there's only so much you can do with it, the only way to find this out is to try; to try and make it do everything.

And Sonny hadn't been near a piano for over a year. And he wasn't on much better terms with his life, not the life that stretched before him now. He and the piano stammered, started one way, got scared, stopped; started another way, panicked, marked time, started again; then seemed to have found a direction, panicked again, got stuck. And the face I saw on Sonny I'd never seen before. Everything had been burned out of it, and, at the same time, things usually hidden were being burned in, by the fire and fury of the battle which was occurring in him up there.

Yet, watching Creole's face as they neared the end of the first set, I had the feeling that something had happened, something I hadn't heard. Then they finished, there was scattered applause, and then, without an instant's warning, Creole started into something else, it was almost sardonic, it was "Am I Blue." And, as though he commanded, Sonny began to play. Something began to happen. And Creole let out the reins. The dry, low, black man said something awful on the drums, Creole answered, and the drums talked back. Then the horn insisted, sweet and high, slightly detached perhaps, and Creole listened, commenting now and then, dry, and driving, beautiful and calm and old. Then they all came together again, and Sonny was part of the family again. I could tell this from his face. He seemed to have found, right there beneath his fingers, a damn brand-new piano. It seemed that he couldn't get over it. Then, for awhile, just being happy with Sonny, they seemed to be agreeing with him that brand-new pianos certainly were a gas.

Then Creole stepped forward to remind them that what they were playing the blues. He hit something in all of them, he hit something in me, myself, and the music tightened and deepened, apprehension began to beat the air. Creole began to tell us what the blues were all about. They were not about anything very new. He and his boys up there were keeping it new, at the risk of ruin, destruction, madness, and death, in order to find new ways to make us listen. For, while the tale of how we suffer, and how we are delighted, and how we may triumph is never new, it always must be heard. There isn't any other tale to tell, it's the only light we've got in all this darkness.

And this tale, according to that face, that body, those strong hands on those strings, has another aspect in every country, and a new depth in every generation. Listen, Creole seemed to be saying, listen. Now these are Sonny's blues. He made the little black man on the drums know it, and the bright, brown man on the horn. Creole wasn't trying any longer to get Sonny in the water. He was wishing him Godspeed. Then he stepped back, very slowly, filling the air with the immense suggestion that Sonny speak for himself.

Then they all gathered around Sonny and Sonny played. Every now and again one of them seemed to say, amen. Sonny's fingers filled the air with life, his life. But that life contained so many others. And Sonny went all the way back, he really began with the spare, flat statement of the opening phrase of the song. Then he began to make it his. It was very beautiful because it wasn't hurried and it was no longer a lament. I seemed to hear with what burning he had made it his, with what burning we had yet to make it ours, how we could cease lamenting. Freedom lurked around us and I understood, at last, that he could help us to be free if we would listen, that he would never be free until we did. Yet, there was no battle in his face now. I heard what he had gone through, and would continue to go through until he came to rest in earth. He had made it his: that long line, of which we knew only Mama and Daddy. And he was giving it back, as everything must be given back, so that, passing through death, it can live forever. I saw my mother's face again, and felt, for the first time, how the stones of the road she had walked on must have bruised her feet. I saw the moonlit road where my father's brother died. And it brought something else back to me, and carried me past it. I saw my little girl again and felt Isabel's tears again, and I felt my own tears begin to rise. And I was yet aware that this was only a moment, that the world waited outside, as hungry as a tiger, and that trouble stretched above us, longer than the sky.

Then it was over. Creole and Sonny let out their breath, both soaking wet, and grinning. There was a lot of applause and some of it was real. In the dark, the girl came by and I asked her to take drinks to the bandstand. There was a long pause, while they talked up there in the indigo light and after awhile I saw the girl put a Scotch and milk on top of the piano for Sonny. He didn't seem to notice it, but just before they started playing again, he sipped from it and looked toward me, and nodded. Then he put it back on top of the piano. For me, then, as they began to play again, it glowed and shook above my brother's head like the very cup of trembling.

Reading as a Writer

1. What effect is created by telling certain aspects of the story "out of sequence"? How would this be a different story if the events were simply told in chronological order?

2. Is there an epiphany in this story? Do any of the characters change in any way? If so, explain how.

MICHAEL CUNNINGHAM

White Angel

WE LIVED THEN IN CLEVELAND, in the middle of everything. It was the sixties—our radios sang out love all day long. This of course is history. It happened before the city of Cleveland went broke, before its river caught fire. We were four. My mother and father, Carlton, and me. Carlton turned sixteen the year I turned nine. Between us were several brothers and sisters, weak flames quenched in our mother's womb. We are not a fruitful or many-branched line. Our family name is Morrow.

Our father was a high school music teacher. Our mother taught children called "exceptional," which meant that some could name the day Christmas would fall in the year 2000 but couldn't remember to drop their pants when they peed. We lived in a tract called Woodlawn—neat one- and two-story houses painted optimistic colors. Our tract bordered a cemetery. Behind our backyard was a gully choked with brush, and beyond that, the field of smooth polished stones. I grew up with the cemetery, and didn't mind it. It could be beautiful. A single stone angel, small-breasted and determined, rose amid the more conservative markers close to our house. Farther away, in a richer section, miniature mosques and Parthenons spoke directly to Cleveland of man's enduring accomplishments. Carlton and I played in the cemetery as children and, with a little more age, smoked joints and drank Southern Comfort there. I was, thanks to Carlton, the most criminally advanced nine-year-old in my fourth-grade class. I was going places. I made no move without his counsel.

Here is Carlton several months before his death, in an hour so alive with snow that earth and sky are identically white. He labors among the markers and I run after, stung by snow, following the light of his red knitted cap. Carlton's hair is pulled back into a ponytail, neat and economical, a perfect pinecone of hair. He is thrifty, in his way.

We have taken hits of acid with our breakfast juice. Or rather, Carlton has taken a hit and I, considering my youth, have been allowed half. This acid is called windowpane. It is for clarity of vision, as Vicks is for decongestion of the nose. Our parents are at work, earning the daily bread. We have come out into the cold so that the house, when we reenter it, will shock us with its warmth and righteousness. Carlton believes in shocks.

"I think I'm coming on to it," I call out. Carlton has on his buckskin jacket, which is worn down to the shine. On the back, across his shoulder blades, his girlfriend has stitched an electric-blue eye. As we walk I speak into the eye. "I think I feel something," I say.

"Too soon," Carlton calls back. "Stay loose, Frisco. You'll know when the time comes."

I am excited and terrified. We are into serious stuff. Carlton has done acid half a dozen times before, but I am new at it. We slipped the tabs into our mouths at breakfast, while our mother paused over the bacon. Carlton likes taking risks.

Snow collects in the engraved letters on the headstones. I lean into the wind, try-ing to decide whether everything around me seems strange because of the drug, or just because everything truly is strange. Three weeks earlier, a family across town had been sitting at home, watching television, when a single-engine plane fell on them. Snow swirls around us, seeming to fall up as well as down.

Carlton leads the way to our spot, the pillared entrance to a society tomb. This tomb is a palace. Stone cupids cluster on the peaked roof, with stunted frozen wings and matrons' faces. Under the roof is a veranda, backed by cast-iron doors that lead to the house of the dead proper. In summer this veranda is cool. In winter it blocks the wind. We keep a bottle of Southern Comfort there.

Carlton finds the bottle, unscrews the cap, and takes a good, long draw. He is studded with snowflakes. He hands me the bottle and I take a more conservative drink. Even in winter, the tomb smells mossy as a well. Dead leaves and a yellow M & M's wrapper, worried by the wind, scrape on the marble floor.

"Are you scared?" Carlton asks me.

I nod. I never think of lying to him.

"Don't be, man," he says. "Fear will screw you right up. Drugs can't hurt you if you feel no fear."

I nod. We stand sheltered, passing the bottle. I lean into Carlton's certainty as if it gave off heat.

"We can do acid all the time at Woodstock," I say.

"Right on. Woodstock Nation. Yow."

"Do people really *live* there?" I ask.

"Man, you've got to stop asking that. The concert's over, but people are still there. It's the new nation. Have faith."

I nod again, satisfied. There is a different country for us to live in. I am already a new person, renamed Frisco. My old name was Robert.

"We'll do acid all the time," I say.

"You better believe we will." Carlton's face, surrounded by snow and marble, is lit. His eyes are bright as neon. Something in them tells me he can see the future, a ghost that hovers over everybody's head. In Carlton's future we all get released from our jobs and schooling. Awaiting us all, and soon, is a bright, perfect simplicity. A life among the trees by the river.

"How are you feeling, man?" he asks me.

"Great," I tell him, and it is purely the truth. Doves clatter up out of a bare tree and turn at the same instant, transforming themselves from steel to silver in the snow-blown light. I know at that moment that the drug is working. Everything before me has become suddenly, radiantly itself. How could Carlton have known this was about to happen? "Oh," I whisper. His hand settles on my shoulder.

"Stay loose, Frisco," he says. "There's not a thing in this pretty world to be afraid of. I'm here."

I am not afraid. I am astonished. I had not realized until this moment how real everything is. A twig lies on the marble at my feet, bearing a cluster of hard brown berries. The broken-off end is raw, white, fleshly. Trees are alive.

"I'm here," Carlton says again, and he is.

Hours later, we are sprawled on the sofa in front of the television, ordinary as Wally and the Beav. Our mother makes dinner in the kitchen. A pot lid bangs. We are undercover agents. I am trying to conceal my amazement.

Our father is building a grandfather clock from a kit. He wants to have something to leave us, something for us to pass along. We can hear him in the basement, sawing and pounding. I know what is laid out on his sawhorses—a long raw wooden box, onto which he glues fancy moldings. A single pearl of sweat meanders down his forehead as he works. Tonight I have discovered my ability to see every room of the house at once, to know every single thing that goes on. A mouse nibbles inside the wall. Electrical wires curl behind the plaster, hidden and patient as snakes.

"Shhh," I say to Carlton, who has not said anything. He is watching television through his splayed fingers. Gunshots ping. Bullets raise chalk dust on a concrete wall. I have no idea what we are watching.

"Boys?" our mother calls from the kitchen. I can, with my new ears, hear her slap hamburger into patties. "Set the table like good citizens," she calls.

"Okay Ma," Carlton replies, in a gorgeous imitation of normality. Our father hammers in the basement. I can feel Carlton's heart ticking. He pats my hand, to assure me that everything's perfect.

We set the table, spoon fork knife, paper napkins triangled to one side. We know the moves cold. After we are done I pause to notice the dining-room wallpaper: a golden farm, backed by mountains. Cows graze, autumn trees cast golden shade. This scene repeats itself three times, on three walls.

"Zap," Carlton whispers. "Zzzzzoom."

"Did we do it right?" I ask him.

"We did everything perfect, little son. How are you doing in there, anyway?" He raps lightly on my head.

"Perfect, I guess." I am staring at the wallpaper as if I were thinking of stepping into it.

"You guess. You guess? You and I are going to other planets, man. Come over here."

"Where?"

"Here. Come here." He leads me to the window. Outside the snow skitters, nervous and silver, under streetlamps. Ranch-style houses hoard their warmth, bleed light into the gathering snow. It is a street in Cleveland. It is our street.

"You and I are going to fly, man," Carlton whispers, close to my ear. He opens the window. Snow blows in, sparking on the carpet. "Fly," he says, and we do. For a moment we strain up and out, the black night wind blowing in our faces—we raise ourselves up off the cocoa-colored deep-pile wool-and-polyester carpet by a sliver of an inch. Sweet glory The secret of flight is this—you have to do it immediately, before your body realizes it is defying the laws. I swear it to this day.

We both know we have taken momentary leave of the earth. It does not strike either of us as remarkable, any more than does the fact that airplanes sometimes fall from the sky, or that we have always lived in these rooms and will soon leave them. We settle back down. Carlton touches my shoulder.

"You wait, Frisco," he says. "Miracles are happening. Fucking miracles."

I nod. He pulls down the window, which reseals itself with a sucking sound. Our own faces look back at us from the cold, dark glass. Behind us, our mother drops the hamburgers sizzling into the skillet. Our father bends to his work under a hooded lightbulb, preparing the long box into which he will lay clockworks, pendulum, a face. A plane drones by overhead, invisible in the clouds. I glance nervously at Carlton. He smiles his assurance and squeezes the back of my neck.

March. After the thaw. I am walking through the cemetery, thinking about my endless life. One of the beauties of living in Cleveland is that any direction feels like progress. I've memorized the map. We are by my calculations three hundred and fifty miles shy of Woodstock, New York. On this raw new day I am walking east, to the place where Carlton and I keep our bottle. I am going to have an early nip, to celebrate my bright future.

When I get to our spot I hear low moans coming from behind the tomb. I freeze, considering my choices. The sound is a long drawn-out agony with a whip at the end, a final high C, something like "ooooooOw." A wolf's cry run backward. What decides me on investigation rather than flight is the need to make a story. In the stories my brother likes best, people always do the foolish, risky thing. I find I can reach decisions this way, by thinking of myself as a character in a story told by Carlton.

I creep around the side of the monument, cautious as a badger, pressed up close to the marble. I peer over a cherub's girlish shoulder. What I find is Carlton on the ground with his girlfriend, in an uncertain jumble of clothes and bare flesh. Carlton's jacket, the one with the embroidered eye, is draped over a stone, keeping watch.

I hunch behind the statue. I can see the girl's naked arms, and the familiar bones of Carlton's spine. The two of them moan together in the dry winter grass. Though I can't make out the girl's expression, Carlton's face is twisted and grimacing, the cords of his neck pulled tight. I had never thought the experience might be painful. I watch, trying to learn. I hold on to the cherub's cold wings.

It isn't long before Carlton catches sight of me. His eyes rove briefly, ecstatically skyward, and what do they light on but his brother's small head, sticking up next to a cherub's. We lock eyes and spend a moment in mutual decision. The girl keeps on clutching at Carlton's skinny back. He decides to smile at me. He decides to wink.

I am out of there so fast I tear up divots. I dodge among the stones, jump the gully, clear the fence into the swing-set-and-picnic-table sanctity of the backyard. Something about that wink. My heart beats fast as a sparrow's.

I go into the kitchen and find our mother washing fruit. She asks what's going on. I tell her nothing is. Nothing at all.

She sighs over an apple's imperfection. The curtains sport blue teapots. Our mother works the apple with a scrub brush. She believes they come coated with poison.

"Where's Carlton?" she asks.

"Don't know," I tell her.

"Bobby?"

"Huh?"

"What exactly is going on?"

"Nothing," I say. My heart works itself up to a hummingbird's rate, more buzz than beat.

"I think something is. Will you answer a question?"

"Okay."

"Is your brother taking drugs?"

I relax a bit. It is only drugs. I know why she's asking. Lately police cars have been browsing our house like sharks. They pause, take note, glide on. Some neighborhood crackdown. Carlton is famous in these parts.

"No," I tell her.

She faces me with the brush in one hand, an apple in the other. "You wouldn't lie to me, would you?" She knows something is up. Her nerves run through this house. She can feel dust settling on the tabletops, milk starting to turn in the refrigerator.

"No," I say.

"Something's going on," she sighs. She is a small, efficient woman who looks at things as if they give off a painful light. She grew up on a farm in Wisconsin and spent her girlhood tying up bean rows, worrying over the sun and rain. She is still trying to overcome her habit of modest expectations.

I leave the kitchen, pretending sudden interest in the cat. Our mother follows, holding her brush. She means to scrub the truth out of me. I follow the cat, his erect black tail and pink anus.

"Don't walk away when I'm talking to you," our mother says.

I keep walking, to see how far I'll get, calling, "Kittykittykitty." In the front hall, our father's homemade clock chimes the half hour. I make for the clock. I get as far as the rubber plant before she collars me.

"I told you not to walk away," she says, and cuffs me a good one with the brush. She catches me on the ear and sets it ringing. The cat is out of there quick as a quarter note.

I stand for a minute, to let her know I've received the message. Then I resume walking. She hits me again, this time on the back of the head, hard enough to make me see colors. "Will you *stop*?" she screams. Still, I keep walking. Our house runs west to east. With every step I get closer to Yasgur's farm.

*   *   *

Carlton comes home whistling. Our mother treats him like a guest who's overstayed. He doesn't care. He is lost in optimism. He pats her cheek and calls her "Professor." He treats her as if she were harmless, and so she is.

She never hits Carlton. She suffers him the way farm girls suffer a thieving crow, with a grudge so old and endless it borders on reverence. She gives him a scrubbed apple, and tells him what she'll do if he tracks mud on the carpet.

I am waiting in our room. He brings the smell of the cemetery with him, its old snow and wet pine needles. He rolls his eyes at me, takes a crunch of his apple. "What's happening, Frisco?" he says.

I have arranged myself loosely on my bed, trying to pull a Dylan riff out of my harmonica. I have always figured I can bluff my way into wisdom. I offer Carlton a dignified nod.

He drops onto his own bed. l can see a crushed crocus, the first of the year, stuck to the black rubber sole of his boot.

"Well, Frisco," he says. "Today you are a man."

I nod again. Is that all there is to it?

"*You*," Carlton says. He laughs, pleased with himself and the world. "That was so perfect."

I pick out what I can of "Blowin' in the Wind."

Carlton says, "Man, when I saw you out there spying on us I thought to myself, *yes*. Now *I'm* really here. You know what I'm saying?" He waves his apple core.

"'Uh-huh," I say.

"Frisco, that was the first time her and I ever did it. I mean, we'd talked. But when we finally got down to it, there you were. My brother. Like you *knew*."

I nod, and this time for real. What happened was an adventure we had together. All right. The story is beginning to make sense.

"Aw, Frisco," Carlton says. "I'm gonna find you a girl, too. You're nine. You been a virgin too long."

"Really?" I say.

"*Man*. We'll find you a woman from the sixth grade, somebody with a little experience. We'll get stoned and all make out under the trees in the boneyard. I want to be present at your deflowering, man. You're gonna need a brother there."

I am about to ask, as casually as I can manage, about the relationship between love and bodily pain, when our mother's voice cuts into the room. "You did it," she screams. "You tracked mud all over the rug."

A family entanglement follows. Our mother brings our father, who comes and stands in the doorway with her, taking in evidence. He is a formerly handsome man. His face has been worn down by too much patience. He has lately taken up some sporty touches—a goatee, a pair of calfskin boots.

Our mother points out the trail of muddy half-moons that lead from the door to Carlton's bed. Dangling over the foot of the bed are the culprits themselves, voluptuously muddy, with Carlton's criminal feet still in them.

"You see?" she says. "You see what he thinks of me?"

Our father, a reasonable man, suggests that Carlton clean it up. Our mother finds that too small a gesture. She wants Carlton not to have done it in the first place. "I don't ask for much," she says. "I don't ask where he goes. I don't ask why the police are suddenly so interested in our house. I ask that he not track mud all over the floor. That's all." She squints in the glare of her own outrage.

"Better clean it right up," our father says to Carlton.

"And that's it?" our mother says. "He cleans up the mess, and all's forgiven?"

"Well, what do you want him to do? Lick it up?"

"I want some consideration," she says, turning helplessly to me. "That's what I want."

I shrug, at a loss. I sympathize with our mother, but am not on her team.

"All right," she says. "I just won't bother cleaning the house anymore. I'll let you men handle it. I'll sit and watch television and throw my candy wrappers on the floor."

She starts out, cutting the air like a blade. On her way she picks up a jar of pencils, looks at it and tosses the pencils on the floor. They fall like fortune-telling sticks, in pairs and crisscrosses.

Our father goes after her, calling her name. Her name is Isabel. We can hear them making their way across the house, our father calling, "Isabel, Isabel, Isabel," while our mother, pleased with the way the pencils had looked, dumps more things onto the floor.

"I hope she doesn't break the TV," I say.

"She'll do what she needs to do," Carlton tells me.

"I hate her," I say. I am not certain about that. I want to test the sound of it, to see if it's true.

"She's got more balls than any of us, Frisco," he says. "Better watch what you say about her."

I keep quiet. Soon I get up and start gathering pencils, because I prefer that to lying around trying to follow the shifting lines of allegiance. Carlton goes for a sponge and starts in on the mud.

"You get shit on the carpet, you clean it up," he says. "Simple."

The time for all my questions about love has passed, and I am not so unhip as to force a subject. I know it will come up again. I make a neat bouquet of pencils. Our mother rages through the house.

Later, after she has thrown enough and we three have picked it all up, I lie on my bed thinking things over. Carlton is on the phone to his girlfriend, talking low. Our mother, becalmed but still dangerous, cooks dinner. She sings as she cooks, some slow forties number that must have been all over the jukes when her first husband's plane went down in the Pacific. Our father plays his clarinet in the basement. That is where he goes to practice, down among his woodworking tools, the neatly hung hammers and awls that throw oversized shadows in the light of the single bulb. If I put my ear to the floor I can hear him, pulling a long low tomcat moan out of that horn. There is some strange comfort in pressing my ear to the carpet and hearing our father's music leaking up through the floorboards. Lying down, with my ear to the floor, I join in on my harmonica.

That spring our parents have a party to celebrate the sun's return. It has been a long, bitter winter and now the first wild daisies are poking up on the lawns and among the graves.

Our parents' parties are mannerly affairs. Their friends, schoolteachers all, bring wine jugs and guitars. They are Ohio hip. Though they hold jobs and meet mortgages, they think of themselves as independent spirits on a spying mission. They have agreed to impersonate teachers until they write their novels, finish their dissertations, or just save up enough money to set themselves free.

Carlton and I are the lackeys. We take coats, fetch drinks. We have done this at every party since we were small, trading on our precocity, doing a brother act. We know the moves. A big, lipsticked woman who has devoted her maidenhood to ninth-grade math calls me Mr. Right. An assistant vice principal in a Russian fur hat asks us both whether we expect to vote Democratic or Socialist. By sneaking sips I manage to get myself semi-crocked.

The reliability of the evening is derailed halfway through, however, by a half dozen of Carlton's friends. They rap on the door and I go for it, anxious as a carnival sharp to see who will step up next and swallow the illusion that I'm a kindly, sober nine-year-old child. I'm expecting callow adults and who do I find but a pack of young outlaws, big-booted and wild-haired. Carlton's girlfriend stands in front, in an outfit made up almost entirely of fringe.

"Hi, Bobby," she says confidently. She comes from New York, and is more than just locally smart.

"Hi," I say. I let them all in despite a retrograde urge to lock the door and phone the police. Three are girls, four boys. They pass me in a cloud of dope smoke and sly-eyed greeting.

What they do is invade the party. Carlton is standing on the far side of the rumpus room, picking the next album, and his girl cuts straight through the crowd to his side. She has the bones and the loose, liquid moves some people consider beautiful. She walks through that room as if she'd been sent to teach the whole party a lesson.

Carlton's face tips me off that this was planned. Our mother demands to know what's going on here. She is wearing a long dark-red dress that doesn't interfere with her shoulders. When she dresses up you can see what it is about her, or what it was. She is responsible for Carlton's beauty. I have our father's face.

Carlton does some quick talking. Though it's against our mother's better judgment, the invaders are suffered to stay. One of them, an Eddie Haskell for all his leather and hair, tells her she is looking good. She is willing to hear it.

So the outlaws, house-sanctioned, start to mingle. I work my way over to Carlton's side, the side unoccupied by his girlfriend. I would like to say something ironic and wised-up, something that will band Carlton and me against every other person in the room. I can feel the shape of the comment I have in mind but, being a tipsy nine-year-old, can't get my mouth around it. What I say is, "Shit, man."

Carlton's girl laughs at me. She considers it amusing that a little boy says "shit." I would like to tell her what I have figured out about her, but I am nine, and three-quarters gone on Tom Collinses. Even sober, I can only imagine a sharp-tongued wit.

"Hang on, Frisco," Carlton tells me. "This could turn into a real party."

I can see by the light in his eyes what is going down. He has arranged a blind date between our parents' friends and his own. It's a Woodstock move—he is plotting a future in which young and old have business together. I agree to hang on, and go to the kitchen, hoping to sneak a few knocks of gin.

There I find our father leaning up against the refrigerator. A line of butterfly-shaped magnets hovers around his head. "Are you enjoying this party?" he asks, touching his goatee. He is still getting used to being a man with a beard.

"Uh-huh."

"I am, too," he says sadly. He never meant to be a high school music teacher. The money question caught up with him.

"What do you think of this music?" he asks. Carlton has put the Stones on the turntable. Mick Jagger sings "19th Nervous Breakdown." Our father gestures in an openhanded way that takes in the room, the party, the whole house—everything the music touches.

"l like it," I say.

"So do I." He stirs his drink with his finger, and sucks on the finger.

"I *love* it," I say, too loud. Something about our father leads me to raise my voice. I want to grab handfuls of music out of the air and stuff them into my mouth.

"I'm not sure I could say l love it," he says. "I'm not sure if I could say that, no. I would say I'm friendly to its intentions. I would say that if this is the direction music is going in, I won't stand in its way."

"Uh-huh," I say. I am already anxious to get back to the party, but don't want to hurt his feelings. If he senses he's being avoided he can fall into fits of apology more terrifying than our mother's rages.

"I think I may have been too rigid with my students," our father says. "Maybe over the summer you boys could teach me a few things about the music people are listening to these days."

"Sure," I say, loudly. We spend a minute waiting for the next thing to say.

"You boys are happy, aren't you?" he asks. "Are you enjoying this parry?"

"We're having a great time," I say.

"I thought you were. I am, too."

I have by this time gotten myself to within jumping distance of the door. I call out, "Well, goodbye," and dive back into the party.

Something has happened in my small absence. The party has started to roll. Call it an accident of history and the weather. Carlton's friends are on decent behavior, and our parents' friends have decided to give up some of their wine-and-folk-song propriety to see what they can learn. Carlton is dancing with a vice principal's wife. Carlton's friend Frank, with his ancient-child face and IQ in the low sixties, dances with our mother. I see that our father has followed me out of the kitchen. He positions himself at the party's edge; I jump into its center. I invite the fuchsia-lipped math teacher to dance. She is only too happy. She is big and graceful as a parade float, and I steer her effortlessly out into the middle of everything. My mother, who is known around school for Sicilian discipline, dances freely, which is news to everybody. There is no getting around her beauty.

The night rises higher and higher. A wildness sets in. Carlton throws new music on the turntable—Janis Joplin, the Doors, the Dead. The future shines for everyone, rich with the possibility of more nights exactly like this. Even our father is pressed into dancing, which he does like a flightless bird, all flapping arms and potbelly. Still, he dances. Our mother has a kiss for him.

Finally I nod out on the sofa, blissful under the drinks. I am dreaming of flight when our mother comes and touches my shoulder. I smile up into her flushed, smiling face.

"It's hours past your bedtime," she says, all velvet motherliness. I nod. I can't dispute the fact.

She keeps on nudging my shoulder. I am a moment or two apprehending the fact that she actually wants me to leave the party and go to bed. "No," I tell her.

"Yes," she smiles.

"No," I say cordially, experimentally. This new mother can dance, and flirt. Who knows what else she might allow?

"Yes." The velvet motherliness leaves her voice. She means business, business of the usual kind. I get myself out of there and no excuses this time. I am exactly nine and running from my bedtime as I'd run from death.

I run to Carlton for protection. He is laughing with his girl, a sweaty question mark of hair plastered to his forehead. I plow into him so hard he nearly goes over.

"Whoa, Frisco," he says. He takes me up under the arms and swings me a half-turn. Our mother plucks me out of his hands and sets me down, with a good farm-style hold on the back of my neck.

"Say good night, Bobby," she says. She adds, for the benefit of Carlton's girl, "He should have been in bed before this party started."

"*No*," I holler. I try to twist loose, but our mother has a grip that could crack walnuts.

Carlton's girl tosses her hair and says, "Good night, baby." She smiles a victor's smile. She smooths the stray hair off Carlton's forehead.

"*No*," I scream again. Something about the way she touches his hair. Our mother calls our father, who comes and scoops me up and starts out of the room with me, holding me like the live bomb I am. Before I go I lock eyes with Carlton. He shrugs and says, "Night, man." Our father hustles me out. I do not take it bravely. I leave flailing, too furious to cry, dribbling a slimy thread of horrible-child's spittle.

Later I lie alone on my narrow bed, feeling the music hum in the coiled springs. Life is cracking open right there in our house. People are changing. By tomorrow, no one will be quite the same. How can they let me miss it? I dream up revenge against our parents, and worse for Carlton. He is the one who could have saved me. He could have banded with me against them. What I can't forgive is his shrug, his mild-eyed "Night, man." He has joined the adults. He has made himself bigger, and taken size from me. As the Doors thump "Strange Days," I hope something awful happens to him. I say so to myself.

Around midnight, dim-witted Frank announces he has seen a flying saucer hovering over the back yard. I can hear his deep, excited voice all the way in my room. He says it's like a blinking, luminous cloud. I hear half the party struggling out through the sliding glass door in a disorganized, whooping knot. By that time everyone is so delirious a flying saucer would be just what was expected. That much celebration would logically attract an answering happiness from across the stars.

I get out of bed and sneak down the hall. I will not miss alien visitors for anyone, not even at the cost of our mother's wrath or our father's disappointment. I stop at the end of the hallway, though, embarrassed to be in pajamas. If there really are aliens, they will think I'm the lowest member of the house. While I hesitate over whether to go back to my room to change, people start coming back inside, talking about a trick of the mist and an airplane. People resume their dancing.

Carlton must have jumped the back fence. He must have wanted to be there alone, singular, in case they decided to take somebody with them. A few nights later I will go out and stand where he would have been standing. On the far side of the gully, now a river swollen with melted snow, the cemetery will gleam like a lost city. The moon will be full. I will hang around just as Carlton must have, hypnotized by the silver light on the stones, the white angel raising her arms up across the river.

According to our parents the mystery is why he ran back to the house full tilt. Something in the graveyard may have scared him, he may have needed to break its spell, but I think it's more likely that when he came back to himself he just couldn't wait to get back to the music and the people, the noisy disorder of continuing life.

Somebody has shut the sliding glass door. Carlton's girlfriend looks lazily out, touching base with her own reflection. I look, too. Carlton is running toward the house. I hesitate. Then I figure he can bump his nose. It will be a good joke on him. I let him keep coming. His girlfriend sees him through her own reflection, starts to scream a warning just as Carlton hits the glass.

It is an explosion. Triangles of glass fly brightly through the room. I think for him it must be more surprising than painful, like hitting water from a great height. He stands blinking for a moment. The whole party stops, stares, getting its bearings. Bob Dylan sings "Just Like a Woman." Carlton reaches up curiously to take out the shard of glass that is stuck in his neck, and that is when the blood starts. It shoots out of him. Our mother screams. Carlton steps forward into his girlfriend's arms and the two of them fall together. Our mother throws herself down on top of him and the girl. People shout their accident wisdom. Don't lift him. Call an ambulance. I watch from the hallway. Carlton's blood spurts, soaking into the carpet, spattering people's clothes. Our mother and father both try to plug the wound with their hands, but the blood just shoots between their fingers. Carlton looks more puzzled than anything, as if he can't quite follow this turn of events. "It's all right," our father tells him, trying to stop the blood. "It's all right, just don't move, it's all right." Carlton nods, and holds our father's hand. His eyes take on an astonished light. Our mother screams, "Is anybody *doing* anything?" What comes out of Carlton grows darker, almost black. I watch. Our father tries to get a hold on Carlton's neck while Carlton keeps trying to take his hand. Our mother's hair is matted with blood. It runs down her face. Carlton's girl holds him to her breasts, touches his hair, whispers in his ear.

He is gone by the time the ambulance gets there. You can see the life drain out of him. When his face goes slack our mother wails. A part of her flies wailing through the house, where it will wail and rage forever. I feel our mother pass through me on her way out. She covers Carlton's body with her own.

He is buried in the cemetery out back. Years have passed—we are living in the future, and it's turned out differently from what we'd planned. Our mother has established

her life of separateness behind the guest-room door. Our father mutters his greetings
to the door as he passes.

One April night, almost a year to the day after Carlton's accident, I hear cautious
footsteps shuffling across the living-room floor after midnight. I run out eagerly,
thinking of ghosts, but find only our father in moth-colored pajamas. He looks
unsteadily at the dark air in front of him.

"Hi, Dad," I say from the doorway.

He looks in my direction. "Yes?"

"It's me. Bobby."

"Oh, Bobby," he says. "What are you doing up, young man?"

"Nothing," I tell him. "Dad?"

"Yes, son."

"Maybe you better come back to bed. Okay?"

"Maybe I had," he says. "I just came out here for a drink of water, but I seem to
have gotten turned around in the darkness. Yes, maybe I better had." I take his hand
and lead him down the hall to his room. The grandfather clock chimes the quarter
hour.

"Sorry" our father says.

I get him into bed. "There," I say. "Okay?"

"Perfect. Could not be better."

"Okay. Good night."

"Good night. Bobby?"

"Uh-huh?"

"Why don't you stay a minute?" he says. "We could have ourselves a talk, you and
me. How would that be?"

"Okay," I say. I sit on the edge of his mattress. His bedside clock ticks off the
minutes.

I can hear the low rasp of his breathing. Around our house, the Ohio night chirps
and buzzes. The small gray finger of Carlton's stone pokes up among the others,
within sight of the angel's blank white eyes. Above us, airplanes and satellites
sparkle. People are flying even now toward New York or California, to take up lives
of risk and invention.

I stay until our father has worked his way into a muttering sleep.

Carlton's girlfriend moved to Denver with her family a month before. I never
learned what it was she'd whispered to him. Though she'd kept her head admirably
during the accident, she lost her head afterward. She cried so hard at the funeral that
she had to be taken away by her mother—an older, redder-haired version of her. She
started seeing a psychiatrist three times a week. Everyone, including my parents,
talked about how hard it was for her, to have held a dying boy in her arms at that age.
I'm grateful to her for holding my brother while he died, but I never once heard her
mention the fact that though she had been through something terrible, at least she
was still alive and going places. At least she had protected herself by trying to warn
him. I can appreciate the intricacies of her pain. But as long as she was in Cleveland,

I could never look her straight in the face. I couldn't talk about the wounds she suffered. I can't even write her name.

Reading as a Writer

1. How is this story structured? Is there a conflict–crisis–resolution?
2. How does Cunningham build up surprising yet convincing characters throughout this story?
3. Is the story emotionally satisfying? Why or why not?

CHAPTER TEN

Recognizable People
Crafting Characters

WHEN WE WRITE CHARACTER-BASED FICTION—creative work that says something about the human condition, the type of writing this book generally focuses on—characters are central to what we do every time we put pen to paper or begin typing on the keyboard. We want to create real people: characters that live and breathe and act in believable ways—and, most important, characters whom our readers will find worth caring about.

Given that characters are so critical, how do we render compelling and believable characters on the page? This chapter is about just that: tips and techniques for creating characters that fulfill the dual requirement of being both surprising *and* convincing.

Character is so important to the kind of writing we're aspiring to accomplish that *everything* is ultimately about character: showing and telling, dialogue, plot, concrete details—everything we've been discussing thus far in this book. This chapter provides an overview of characterization that is backed up by every other chapter in the book.

We will start out by defining what a character is, then we will look at ways in which character is revealed, both directly and indirectly. You'll have a chance to do some exercises that help you define and reveal character. Finally, you'll get to read two pieces in which the characterization is particularly vivid and compelling.

Flat versus Round Characters

When we read a book of fiction, one of the things we're most focused on (whether we realize it or not) is character. Yes, plot is important, and so are scene and narration, and point of view, and all the other things we've been discussing in this book, but whether the characters are compelling or not is really the bottom line. Consciously or subconsciously, we have our radar switched on to detect signs of life. After all, characters are supposed to be human beings (mostly—we'll leave writing about animals and science fiction out for now). They are people with physical features (red hair, size nine shoes), mental talents (good at math, terrible at French), and complex emotional attributes. They have histories, pasts, memories, hopes, and dreams. Even if all of this isn't made explicit in the piece itself, readers can *feel* the presence of a real, live, breathing character on the page. Nowhere else is Hemingway's famous iceberg theory more appropriate: with characters, only 10 percent of what the author knows about the character actually appears in the story—but if he or she doesn't know the other 90 percent, then that will be apparent to the reader: the character will appear lifeless, not believable, *flat* in some way.

The first thing we need to define is the difference between flat and round characters. Flat characters are also called stereotypes, and the hallmark of flat characters is that they are incapable of surprising us; they act in a prescribed way and are utterly consistent, without complexity. Thus the loving mother, the evil stepfather, the cruel boss, the happy prostitute—these are all examples of flat characters that lack the complexity and emotional depth of the real people we know.

A round character is the opposite of this: he or she is capable of *surprising* us—with unexpected fits of anger, or an uplifting sense of humor, or a snide remark about a presumed friend. But a round character also *convinces* us. As E. M. Forster says, if a character never surprises us, then he or she is flat; if characters surprise but do not convince us, they are only flat pretending to be round.

An example of a fully rounded character is Gurov in Chekhov's "The Lady with the Little Dog" (pp. 208–220). Gurov surprises us because he is capable of falling in love with Anna; he tries, but finds he cannot just treat her as another run-of-the-mill affair. In this passage, Gurov realizes he has actually fallen in love with the woman with whom he thought he was just going to have a brief vacation dalliance:

> Anna Sergeevna came in. She sat in the third row, and when Gurov looked at her, his heart was wrung, and he realized clearly that there was now no person closer, dearer, or more important for him in the whole world; this small woman, lost in the provincial crowd, not remarkable for anything, with a vulgar lorgnette in her hand, now filled his whole life, was his grief, his joy, the only happiness he now wished for himself; and to the sounds of the bad orchestra, with its trashy local violins, he thought how beautiful she was. He thought and dreamed.

Likewise, Connie, from "Where Are You Going, Where Have You Been?" (pp. 40–53), is a round character because she is capable—as selfish and ambivalent about her family as she is—of making a sacrifice on their behalf and going with Arnold Friend so he won't carry out his threat of hurting them. Here's the passage where she makes this sacrifice:

> She put out her hand against the screen. She watched herself push the door slowly open as if she were back safe somewhere in the other doorway, watching this body and this head of long hair moving out into the sunlight where Arnold Friend waited.

It sounds like having a flat character in your piece would be a bad thing, and indeed a piece of creative work would be dull and ultimately fail to succeed if all the

characters were flat. To be accused of having flat characters is to be accused of having dull and predictable work—something no one wants to hear. Yet not all the
characters—especially in a longer piece—need to be fully rounded. Sometimes the
waiter needs to just bring the food to the table, not surprise us with his private
joys and sorrows. Usually, however, we want our stories to be populated by round
characters.

Eschewing the General in Favor of the Particular

With characters as well as other aspects of creative writing, we always reject general
statements in favor of ones that are particular and precise. Real people don't act in
"general" ways. Although "in general" people attending funerals act sad or
bereaved, and people attending weddings or christenings are "generally" happy,
these things are not necessarily true of the *particular*. As Gustave Flaubert, writing to
Guy de Maupassant, said:

> When you pass a grocer seated at his shop door, a tailor smoking his pipe, a
> stand of hackney coaches, show me that grocer and that tailor, their attitude,
> their whole physical appearance, including also by a skillful description their
> whole moral nature, so that I cannot confound them with any other grocer or
> any other janitor; make me see, in one word, that a certain cab horse does not
> resemble the fifty others that follow or preceded it . . . there are not in the whole
> world two grains of sand, two specks, two hands, or two noses exactly alike.
>
> —GUSTAVE FLAUBERT

Let's look at some examples of times that characters act in ways that are unique,
and much more particular than what we'd expect if we thought of a "general" reaction to the prompting situations.

> Milo heaved himself up from the sofa, ready for the drive back to New York. It
> is the same way he used to get off the sofa that last year he lived here. He would
> get up, dress for work, and not even go into the kitchen for breakfast—just sit,
> sometimes in his coat as he was sitting just now, and at the last minute he
> would push himself up and go out to the driveway, usually without a good-
> bye, and get in the car and drive off either very fast or very slowly. I liked it bet-
> ter when he made the tires spin in the gravel when he took off.
>
> —ANN BEATTIE, "The Cinderella Waltz"

In this story we see the particular way that a man acts when his marriage is ending—
and the very particular reaction of the narrator, the soon-to-be ex-wife (who would
prefer that he show anger rather than this resigned, passive sadness). Contrast that
with a story in which a man tries to keep the memories of his ex-wife and children
alive in the house as long as possible:

> There were no clothes or cosmetics, but potted plants endured my neglectful
> care as long as they could, and slowly died; I did not kill them on purpose, to

exorcise the house of her, but I could not remember to water them. For weeks, because I did not use it much, the house was as neat as she had kept it, though dust layered the order she had made. The kitchen went first: I got the dishes in and out of the dishwasher and wiped the top of the stove, but did not return cooking spoons and pot holders to their hooks on the wall, and soon the burners and oven were caked with spillings, the refrigerator had more space and was spotted with juices. The living room and my bedroom went next; I did not go into the children's rooms except on bad nights when I went from room to room and looked and touched and smelled, so they did not lose their order until a year later when the kids came for six weeks.

—ANDRE DUBUS, "A Father's Story"

In each of these cases, we don't see general or "expected" behavior in the situation in question; we see highly specific actions and thoughts that individualize these particular characters.

Consistent Characters?

Once we understand about flat and round characters, it follows that one of the first things we have to say about characters is that *consistency* is not necessarily a virtue. True, we won't believe in a character whose behavior is all over the map, yet any character who fails to surprise us *at all* will also fail the test of being a believable, round character. Both are equally flawed in terms of characterization.

What we are striving for, after all, is *complexity*. Human beings are indefinitely multifaceted and behave in ways that are seemingly contradictory. A man may love his family very much, yet act in ways that put them in danger—or even harm them himself. A woman may value her job, yet continually put it in jeopardy by seemingly senseless self-destructive behaviors.

Often in a workshop there comes the phrase "not acting in character." The speaker of this phrase usually means it critically, as a bad thing, yet I've found that it can mean one of two things: either that the character is surprising us by something he or she is doing (which is good), or that the character is surprising us but not convincing us by that surprise (which is indeed a problem). If, for example, a seemingly hard-boiled, cynical man is suddenly capable of true love, we will be surprised; whether we are convinced that this change is possible is up to the skill of the writer. A less sophisticated reader (and critic) will be troubled by the surprising behavior; a more thoughtful reader will take a moment to judge whether that surprising behavior has been convincingly rendered.

Ways of Defining Character

As with all other aspects of writing compelling fiction, you can create characterizations by either showing or telling, or (what is more likely) using some combination of the two. Neither is "correct"; effective characterization can be created either way.

Here are the various ways that characters can be defined and revealed: as you'll see, some of these involve straight "telling" by narrators; others can be shown, or dramatized, in scenes; and others use a combination of both showing and telling.

What the character looks like. This is one of the most basic ways of introducing and defining character: through description of his or her physical characteristics via straight narrative. It is rare, although not unheard of, to create compelling characterization without *some* degree of narrative description of this type. This type of characterization method can also include descriptions of a character's *environment* as well as *possessions*.

> The doctor was a handsome, big-shouldered man with a tanned face. He wore a three-piece blue suit, a striped tie, and ivory cufflinks. His gray hair was combed along the sides of his head, and he looked as if he had just come from a concert.   —RAYMOND CARVER, "A Small, Good Thing"

Here we have a direct "telling" description of a doctor: not only what he looks like and what he is wearing, but also the aura about him; "he looked as if he had just come from a concert" is as revealing a phrase as the concrete details used to render his person on the page.

> Aged and frail, Granny is three-quarters succumbed to the mortality the ache in her bones promises her and almost ready to give in entirely. A boy came out from the village to build up her hearth for the night an hour ago and the kitchen crackles with busy firelight. She has her Bible for company, she is a pious old woman. She is propped up on several pillows in the bed set into the wall peasant-fashion, wrapped up in the patchwork quilt she made before she was married, more years ago than she cares to remember. Two china spaniels with liver-colored blotches on their coats and black noses sit on either side of the fireplace. There is a bright rug of woven rags on the pantiles. The grandfather clock ticks away her eroding time.   —ANGELA CARTER, "The Company of Wolves"

Here we get a portrait of a character (the granny in the traditional "Little Red Riding Hood" story) that is based more on her possessions than on a physical description of the woman herself, yet it is highly effective; we can see her in her bed, we know things about her from the objects she has surrounded herself with, and she becomes a living, breathing person by the end of this brief paragraph.

> A rarity for another reason—a librarian who did not look like one, who wore a Borsalino fedora, his a classic of thirty years, a Bogart raincoat, English boots John Major would covet, a black silk shirt, a vintage tie.
> Never as dashing as he wished to appear, however. Slight, short, and for several years now the bronze-color curls gone gray and the romantically drooping eyelids of his youth now faded flags at half mast.
>   —GINA BERRIAULT, "Who Is It Can Tell Me Who I Am?"

In this story we get another physical description, but with added complexity because the narrator tells us that the character is aging—unhappily—and the imagery mirrors this mournful reality.

What the character says. The words that come out of a character's mouth, in dialogue, are a very powerful means of characterization. Not only *what* a character says
(the content), but also the *manner* in which he or she says it, is critical. This includes
the vocabulary, syntax, use or misuse of words, and general diction as well as any
gesture or emotionally charged way in which a character delivers a line of dialogue.
The use of subtext—what *isn't* being said, or what is being avoided—is also a rich
mining ground for characterization. We discussed these options in Chapter 8, but
here are some further examples:

> "I always wondered what a gold mine would look like when I saw it," Edna
> said, still laughing, wiping a tear from her eye.
>   "Me too," I said. "I was always curious about it."
>   "We're a couple of fools, aren't we, Earl?" she said, unable to quit laughing
> completely. "We're two of a kind."
>   "It might be a good sign, though," I said.
>   "How could it be? It's not our gold mine. There aren't any drive-up win-
> dows." She was still laughing.
>   "We've seen it," I said, pointing. "That's it right there. It may mean we're get-
> ting closer. Some people never see it at all."
>   "In a pig's eye, Earl," she said. "You and me see it in a pig's eye."
>   And she turned and got in the cab to go.   —RICHARD FORD, "Rock Springs"

In this story we learn about the characters not only through what they say, but also
through how they say it. The use of gesture and particular speech syntax poignantly
dramatizes the easy camaraderie that this doomed relationship possesses right
before the end, and it shows how the different ways they view their misfortune
define them as individual characters.

What the character does (how she or he acts). "Actions speak louder than
words," goes the old adage, and this can be true in characterization as well as real
life. How a character behaves, both alone and in response to actions from other
characters, is a critical aspect of characterization. Let's look at some examples.

> Wing Biddlebaum talked much with his hands. The slender expressive fin-
> gers, forever active, forever striving to conceal themselves in his pockets,
> behind his back, came forth and became the piston rods of his machinery of
> expression.
>   The story of Wing Biddlebaum is a story of hands. Their restless activity, like
> unto the beating of the wings of an imprisoned bird, had given him his name.
> Some obscure poet of the town had thought of it. The hands alarmed their
> owner. He wanted to keep them hidden away and looked with amazement at
> the quiet inexpressive hands of other men who worked beside him in the fields,
> or passed, driving sleepy teams on country roads.
>   —SHERWOOD ANDERSON, "Hands"

Here we get a sense of this man not only from the way he moves his hands, but also
from his reaction to the response his hands get from neighbors and townspeople.

In the following passage we see how the tenderness and responsibility a man feels as he takes care of a baby paint a moving picture of a rich, compelling character:

> Jones has the baby on his lap and he is feeding her. The evening meal is lengthy and complex. First he must give her vitamins, then, because she has a cold, a dropper of liquid aspirin. This is followed by a bottle of milk, eight ounces, and a portion of strained vegetables. He gives her a rest now so that the food can settle. On his hip, she rides through the rooms of the huge house as Jones turns lights off and on. He comes back to the table and gives her a little more milk, a half jar of strained chicken and a few spoonfuls of dessert, usually cobbler, buckle, or pudding. The baby enjoys all equally. She is good. She eats rapidly and neatly. Sometimes she grasps the spoon, turns it around and thrusts the wrong end into her mouth. Of course there is nothing that cannot be done incorrectly. Jones adores the baby.   —JOY WILLIAMS, "Taking Care"

What the character thinks or feels. Depending on the point of view, you may be able to convey what your character thinks or feels directly on the page (as opposed to indirectly, through implication, by what he or she says or does). This can also be a very powerful tool for characterization, especially if a character speaks or acts in a way that is different from what he or she is really thinking or feeling.

In the following piece the character's worries define her, and her thoughts betray her real feelings about her husband and family life:

> How was she going to get everything fed?—that was her problem. The dogs had to be fed. There wasn't enough hay in the barn for the horses and the cow. If she didn't feed the chickens how could they lay eggs? Without eggs to sell how could she get things in town, things she had to have to keep the life of the farm going? Thank heaven, she did not have to feed her husband—in a certain way. That hadn't lasted long after their marriage and after the babies came. Where he went on his long trips she did not know. Sometimes he was gone from home for weeks, and after the boy grew up they went off together.
> —SHERWOOD ANDERSON, "Death in the Woods"

In the following passage we get a woman's thoughts about a blind date she is about to go on, and the association of her ideas as they follow one upon the other is what matters. We get a sense of who she is from observing the way she looks, to recalling that she is not pretty but "does her best," to memories of being an undergraduate in a strange world that didn't understand her culture:

> On Sunday she is ready by four-thirty. She doesn't know what the afternoon holds; there are surely no places for "high tea"—a colonial tradition—in Cedar Falls, Iowa. If he takes her back to his place, it will mean he has invited other guests. From his voice she can tell Dr. Chatterji likes to do things correctly. She has dressed herself in a peach-colored nylon georgette sari, jade drop-earrings, and a necklace. The color is good on dark skin. She is not pretty, but she does

her best. Working at it is a part of self-respect. In the mid-seventies, when American women felt rather strongly about such things, Maya had been in trouble with her women's group at Duke. She was too feminine. She had tried to explain the world she came out of. Her grandmother had been married off at the age of five in a village now in Bangladesh. Her great-aunt had been burned to death over a dowry problem. She herself had been trained to speak softly, arrange flowers, sing, be pliant. If she were to seduce Ted Suminski, she thinks as she waits in the front yard for Dr. Chatterji, it would be minor heroism. She has broken with the past. But. —BHARATI MUKHERJEE, "The Tenant"

Character and Plot

As we discussed in Chapter 9, plot is simply those things that happen in order to bring about a certain effect, or final outcome. Character is a big part of plot, because things that happen are usually happening to characters. There are a number of ways that characters and plot intersect.

Character can take action (create a plot point by acting). This is the most obvious way that character and plot relate to each other: a character does something, and the story is one step closer to completion.

In the passage below we see how the narrator's obsession with his girlfriend—and his obsessive personality generally—drive the plot forward:

> I won't bore you with the details. The begging, the crawling over glass, the crying. Let's just say that after two weeks of this, of my driving out to her house, sending her letters, and calling her at all hours of the night, we put it back together. Didn't mean I ever ate with her family again or that her girl-friends were celebrating. Those *cabronas*, they were like, *No, jamas*, never. Even Magda wasn't too hot on the rapprochement at first, but I had the momentum of the past on my side. When she asked me, "Why don't you leave me alone?" I told her the truth: "It's because I love you, *mami*." I know this sounds like a load of doo-doo, but it's true: Magda's my heart. I didn't want her to leave me; I wasn't about to start looking for a girlfriend because I'd fucked up one lousy time. —JUNOT DÍAZ, "The Sun, the Moon, the Stars"

Character can be acted upon (by others, by God, by nature, etc.) and create further plot points by *reacting*. If characters can act, they can also be acted upon: things can happen to them independently of their own actions—and their reactions to those things can cause the plot to unfold even more.

In the following extract the plot unfolds through a character's reaction to a romantic overture by a fellow student:

> That night there was a knock on my door. I was in my nightgown already, doing our assignment, a love poem in the form of a sonnet. I'd been reading it out loud pretty dramatically, trying to get the accents right, so I felt embar-rassed to be caught. I asked who it was. I didn't recognize the name. Rudy?

"The guy who borrowed your pencil," the voice said through the closed door. Strange, I thought, ten-thirty at night. I hadn't yet caught on to some of the strategies. "Did I wake you up?" he wanted to know when I opened the door. "No, no," I said, laughing apologetically. This guy I had sworn never to talk to after he had embarrassed me in class, but my politeness training ran on automatic. I excused myself for not asking him in. "I'm doing my homework." That wasn't an excuse in the circles he ran in. We stood at the door for a long moment, he looking over my shoulder into my room for an invitation. "I just came to return your pencil." He held it out, a small red stub in his palm. "Just to return that?" I said, calling his bluff. He grinned, dimples making parentheses at the corners of his lips as if his smile were a secret between us. "Yeah," he said, and again he had that intent look in his eye, and again he looked over my shoulder. I picked the pencil out of his palm and was glad it had been sharpened to a stub so he couldn't see my name in gold letters inscribed on the side. "Thank you," I said, shifting my weight on my feet and touching the doorknob, little moves, polite preliminaries to closing the door.

—JULIA ALVAREZ, "The Rudy Elmenhurst Story"

Character can remember things (flashbacks). One very rich source of characterization-driven plotting can be found in flashbacks, giving the reader information about what is traditionally called *"backstory,"* or the past of the story. Flashbacks are very important to plot—which, you may remember, is those events *arranged in the proper order the writer thinks best,* not necessarily chronological order. In the following passage from a novel, this character has a flashback while driving that leads to him taking significant action later in the plot:

> Driving home, thinking of his mother and him when he was little more than a baby, a photo. First only his mother for a moment. Doesn't know where the thought came from or why the picture popped in. But suddenly—forgets what he was thinking of just before her, probably nothing much of anything—there was her face and neck and open-collar top of the summer dress she was wearing in the photo and then the whole photo, backdrop and concrete ground and crossed knees included, her shoes and his bare feet, even the white border or frame or outline with the notched or jagged edges or whatever one calls them when they're by design kind of frayed, the style for years then, which he knows has a name because he recently read it in an article on photography but forgets or never recorded it in his head. Something he saw on the road set off the thought?   —STEPHEN DIXON, *Interstate*

Character can imagine things. An often unremarked-upon aspect of plot is that plot points can be created by a character's imagining of things: a fantasy, a daydream, a dream, or a projection.

In following passage a son's fantasies boil his thoughts into a cauldron of ill will that causes him to treat his mother even worse than he had been doing previously—and also prepare him (and the reader) for what is coming at the end of the story.

He began to imagine various unlikely ways by which he could teach her a lesson. He might make friends with some distinguished Negro professor or lawyer and bring him home to spend the evening. He would be entirely justified but her blood pressure would rise to 300. [. . .] He imagined his mother lying desperately ill and his being able to secure only a Negro doctor for her. He toyed with that idea for a few minutes and then dropped it for a momentary vision of himself participating as a sympathizer in a sit-in demonstration. This was possible but he did not linger with it. Instead he approached the ultimate horror. He brought home a beautiful suspiciously Negroid woman. Prepare yourself, he said. There is nothing you can do about it. This is the woman I've chosen. She's intelligent, dignified, even good, and she's suffered and she hasn't thought it *fun*. No persecute us, go ahead and persecute us. Drive her out of here, but remember you're driving me too. His eyes were narrowed and through the indignation he had generated, he saw his mother across the aisle, purple-faced, shrunken to the dwarf-like proportions of her moral nature, sitting like a mummy beneath the ridiculous banner of her hat.

—FLANNERY O'CONNOR, "Everything That Rises Must Converge"

Wants and Needs

Everyone needs things: food, water, shelter. And everyone wants things: love, money, friendship, material possessions. Many writers believe that a key determinant of a good characterization is the depiction of what the character wants and needs (two different things). Indeed, you could say that this is the basis of all characterization: what a character desires is what drives him or her to act (or react, or not act), and therefore what determines the heart of a story.

Here are some examples of characters who urgently *desire* something. In the first passage it's as simple as a young girl desperately wanting a good present from a grab bag:

Having watched the older children opening their gifts, I already knew that the big gifts were not necessarily the nicest ones. One girl my age got a large coloring book of biblical characters, while a less greedy girl who selected a smaller box received a glass vial of lavender toilet water. The sound of the box was also important. A ten-year-old boy had chosen a box that jangled when he shook it. It was a tin globe of the world with a slit for inserting money. He must have thought it was full of dimes and nickels, because when he saw that it had just ten pennies, his face fell with such undisguised disappointment that his mother slapped the side of his head and led him out of the hall, apologizing to the crowd for her son who had such bad manners he couldn't appreciate such a fine gift.

As I peered into the sack, I quickly fingered the remaining presents, testing their weight, imagining what they contained. I chose a heavy compact one that was wrapped in shiny silver foil and a red satin ribbon. It was a twelve-pack of Life Savers and I spent the rest of the party arranging and rearranging the candy tubes in the order of my favorites.   —AMY TAN, *The Joy Luck Club*

In the following story the main character is so frightened by what is happening aboard an aircraft that all she wants is to reach safe ground again. This need for safety drives her actions for the rest of the story:

> She was so frightened that she could only nod, her head filled with the sucking dull hiss of the air jets and the static of the speakers. The man leaned across her and squinted through the gray aperture of the window to the wing beyond. "Fuck, that's all we need. There's no way I'm going to make my connection now."
>
> She didn't understand. Connection? Didn't he realize they were going to die?
>
> She braced herself and murmured a prayer. Voices rose in alarm. Her eyes felt as if they were going to implode in their sockets. But then the flames flickered and dimmed, and she felt the plane lifted up as if in the palm of some celestial hand, and for all the panic, the dimly remembered prayers, the cries and shouts, and the sudden potent reek of urine, the crisis was over almost as soon as it had begun. "I hate to do this to you, folks," the captain drawled, "but it looks like we're going to have to turn around and take her back to LAX."
>
> —T. CORAGHESSAN BOYLE, "Friendly Skies"

Finally, in this famous story we have Gregor, who has mysteriously turned into a giant cockroach, wanting above all things not to be a burden to his family. His obsequiousness prevails throughout the story:

> It was late at night when the light finally went out in the living room, and now it was easy for Gregor to tell that his parents and his sister had stayed up so long, since, as he could distinctly hear, all three were now retiring on tiptoes. Certainly no one would come in to Gregor until the morning; and so he had ample time to consider undisturbed how best to rearrange his life. But the empty high-ceilinged room in which he was forced to lie flat on the floor made him nervous, without his being able to tell why—since it was, after all, the room in which he had lived for the past five years—and turning half unconsciously and not without a slight feeling of shame, he scuttled under the couch where, although his back was a little crushed and he could not raise his head any more, he immediately felt very comfortable and was only sorry that his body was too wide to go completely under the couch.
>
> There he stayed the whole night, which he spent partly in a sleepy trance, from which hunger pangs kept waking him with a start, partly in worries and vague hopes, all of which, however, led to the conclusion that for the time being he would have to lie low and, by being patient and showing his family every possible consideration, help them bear the inconvenience which he simply had to cause them in his present condition.
>
> —FRANZ KAFKA, "The Metamorphosis"

Characters in Relationships

How characters behave and think and feel when in a relationship with other characters is a key point of characterization. Often, a character will think, act, and speak differently depending on who else is around. Think of the way you behave when you're around your friends versus your parents, or your teacher (if you're in school). You talk differently, you act differently, you may even think and feel differently (a reprimand from a social peer feels different from one from a boss, for example).

Here are some examples of character revealed through interaction with others.

> His heart, that bloody motor, is equally old and will not do certain jobs anymore. It still floods his head with brainy light. But it won't let his legs carry the weight of his body around the house. Despite my metaphors, this muscle failure is not due to his old heart, he says, but to a potassium shortage. Sitting on one pillow, leaning on three, he offers last-minute advice and makes a request.
>
> —GRACE PALEY, "A Conversation with My Father"

We feel the affection between the father and daughter (the daughter is describing the father in this first person story), as well as his need to be medically precise about things that the narrator (a writer) uses language to describe.

> Anna was not in lilac, as Kitty had so urgently wished, but in a black, low-cut velvet gown, showing her full throat and shoulders, that looked as though they were carved in old ivory, and her rounded arms, with tiny, slender wrists. The whole gown was trimmed with Venetian guipure. On her head, among her black hair—her own, with no false additions—was a little wreath of pansies, and a bouquet of the same in the black ribbon of her sash among white lace. Her coiffure was not striking. All that was noticeable was the little willful tendrils of her curly hair that would always break free about her neck and temples.
>
> Kitty had been seeing Anna every day; she adored her, and had pictured her invariably in lilac. But now seeing her in black, she felt she had not fully seen Anna's charm. She saw her now as someone quite new and surprising, now she understood that Anna could not have been in lilac.
>
> Anna turned with a soft smile of protection toward Kitty. With a flying glance, and a movement of her head, hardly perceptible, but understood by Kitty, she signified approval of Kitty's dress and looks. "You came into the room dancing," Anna said.   —LEO TOLSTOY, *Anna Karenina*

In the above excerpt we see the protective nature of the relationship that the older woman feels for the younger, and the admiration bordering on adoration that the younger woman feels for the older.

> When he had to get up to go to the bathroom he moved like a ninety-year-old. He couldn't stand straight, but was all bent out of shape, and shuffled. I helped him put on clean clothes. When he lay down on the bed again, a sound of pain came out of him, like tearing thick paper. I went around the room putting things away. He asked me to come sit by him and said I was going to drown him if I went on crying. "You'll submerge the entire North American continent," he said. I can't remember what he said, but he made me laugh finally. It is hard to remember things Simon says, and hard not to laugh when he says them. This is not merely the partiality of affection: He makes everybody laugh.

I doubt that he intends to. It is just that a mathematician's mind works differently from other people's. Then when they laugh, that pleases him.

—URSULA K. LE GUIN, "The New Atlantis"

Here we get a sense of the affection that the well man has for the sick man, how deeply he is pained by the illness, and his sense of impending loss.

EXERCISES

Characters are the lifeblood of your work. Depicting living, breathing people on the page is one of the most important things you can do as a writer.

Exercise 1: Emptying Pockets

GOAL: To learn about your character by writing down all the things that can be found on his or her person.

1. Choose a character, and fix him or her in your mind.

2. Write a list of the things that can be found in his or her pockets, purse, or backpack (you choose).

3. Make sure there is at least one surprising but convincing item found. *Note:* No clichés like guns, drugs, or condoms, please.

Here are some examples of how you might complete this exercise:

Character A

- Walgreen's brand "Naturally Neutral" lipstick, half gone
- Solar calculator
- Mini screwdriver, Phillips head on one end, slot-edged on the other
- Crumpled shopping list containing the words "eggs," "nonfat milk," "Superglue"
- Three ATM slips, each showing $20 cash withdrawals, three consecutive days
- Roll of Fresh Mint Certs, unopened
- Fortune from Chinese fortune cookie that reads "Keep those dangerous plans secret for now"

Character B

- Torn stub from movie theater ticket to *Die Hard VII*
- Reporter's notebook, half-filled with notes on data warehouse design using Oracle 7.0
- Pilot pen, extra fine, black ink, tightly capped
- A dozen keys attached to industrial chain with metal hook

- Half a package of sinus medicine tablets
- $2 in quarters, taped together
- Receipt for 20 gallons of Chevron Supreme, paid with American Express Platinum card
- Mickey Mouse Pez dispenser

Character C

- Expensive sunglasses
- Book: *Seven Habits of Highly Effective People*
- Fine-tipped pen
- Cell phone
- Discount coupon for Jiffy Lube
- Torn half of a movie ticket for a porno movie
- Program for an art gallery opening

Exercise 2: Sins of Commission, Sins of Omission

GOAL: To learn more about your character by (a) finding out what "sins" he or she has committed, while simultaneously (b) discovering what he or she thinks is a sin.

1. Choose a character, and fix him or her in your mind.

2. Write down two lists: one of the sins of omission (the things the character didn't do) and one of the sins of commission (what the character *did* do) that are on his or her conscience.

The following passage was written by James Hanafee:

Sins of Omission

- Didn't acknowledge distress in sister's voice when I called her last Sunday. Pretended the dog was peeing on the carpet and that I needed to hang up when it seemed as though she was about to say something serious.
- Didn't smile at my son when he showed me the family portrait he'd drawn because my bald spot was so prominently displayed.
- Didn't thank wife for making dinner even though it was my turn to cook because no one else has a "meal schedule" posted on their refrigerator.
- Didn't cancel the brunch reservations for twelve people at Emilio's, even though we had decided not to go a week previously.
- Didn't clean the dead insects out of the kids' pool before daughter swam.

Sins of Commission

- Left the Sunday *New York Times* in disarray even though my husband hadn't read it yet.

- Speeded up and refused to let elderly man merge into my lane on 101, even though he was signaling correctly.
- Put together the broken TV remote control in such a way that the next person who picked it up would think they broke it.
- Threw away neighbor's mail that was put in our mailbox by accident.
- Ate a handful of red flame seedless grapes while shopping at Whole Foods without paying for them.
- Made sarcastic comments throughout the broadcast of the season finale of *Star Trek Voyager*, even though it was the highlight of retired father's week.

Exercise 3: Seven or Eight Things I Know about Him/Her

GOAL: To "slant" at a character by coming up with small, odd details from his or her life.

1. Read "7 or 8 Things I Know about Her" by Michael Ondaatje (below).

2. Fix a character in your mind.

3. Write seven or eight brief "facts" about that character, his or her family, his or her surroundings—but try to avoid the sorts of things that you would include in a traditional biography. You can parallel the headings found in the original prose poem, if you like.

MICHAEL ONDAATJE

7 or 8 Things I Know about Her—A Stolen Biography

The Father's Guns

After her father died they found nine guns in the house. Two in his clothing drawers, one under the bed, one in the glove compartment of the car, etc. Her brother took their mother out onto the prairie with a revolver and taught her to shoot.

The Bird

For a while in Topeka parrots were very popular. Her father was given one in lieu of a payment and kept it with him at all times because it was the fashion. It swung above him in the law office and drove back with him in the car at night. At parties friends would bring their parrots and make them perform what they had been taught: the first line from *Twelfth Night*, a bit of Italian opera, cowboy songs, or a surprisingly good rendition of Russ Colombo singing "Prisoner of Love." Her father's parrot could only imitate the office typewriter, along with the *ching* at the end of each line. Later it broke its neck crashing into a bookcase.

The Bread

Four miles out of Topeka on the highway—the largest electric billboard in the state of Kansas. The envy of all Missouri. It advertised bread and the electrical image of a knife cut slice after slice. These curled off endlessly. "Meet you at the bread," "See you at the loaf," were common phrases. Aroused couples would park there under the stars on the open night prairie. Virtue was lost, "kissed all over by every boy in Wichita." Poets, the inevitable visiting writers, were taken to see it, and it hummed over the seductions in cars, over the nightmares of girls in bed. Slice after slice fell towards the earth. A feeding of the multitude in this parched land on the way to Dorrance, Kansas.

First Criticism

She is two weeks old, her mother takes her for a drive. At the gas station the mechanic is cleaning the windshield and watches them through the glass. Wiping his hands he puts his head in the side window and says, "Excuse me for saying this but I know what I'm talking about—that child has a heart condition."

Listening In

Overhear her in the bathroom, talking to a bug: "I don't want you on me, honey." 8 a.m.

Self-Criticism

"For a while there was something about me that had a dubious quality. Dogs would not take meat out of my hand. The town bully kept handcuffing me to trees."

Fantasies

Always one fantasy. To be traveling down the street and a man in a clean white suit (the detail of "clean" impresses me) leaps into her path holding flowers and sings to her while an invisible orchestra accompanies his solo. All her life she has waited for this, and it never happens.

Reprise

In 1956 the electric billboard in Kansas caught fire and smoke plumed into a wild sunset. Bread on fire, broken glass. Birds flew towards it above the cars that circled round to watch. And last night, past midnight, her excited phone call. Her hometown is having a marathon to benefit the symphony. She pays $4 to participate. A tuxedoed gentleman begins the race with a clash of cymbals and she takes off. Along the route at frequent intervals are quartets who play for her. When they stop for water a violinist performs a solo. So here she comes. And there I go, stepping forward in my white suit, with a song in my heart.

The following was written by Jenna Philpott:

Her Mother's Cans

After she died, they found, in the basement of her mother's house, thousands of cans, carefully stripped of their paper labels and washed and dried, stacked neatly in shining towers up to six feet high.

The Cat

Since all the other members of her family were extremely allergic to animal fur, the only pet she could have as a child was a turtle. The turtles kept dying but since they all looked alike her parents secretly replaced them in the middle of the night so she had a single, long-aged turtle from the age of seven to seventeen, when she left for school.

The Bridge

There was a bridge that led over a small inlet of the Bay, and a coming-of-age ritual for all graduating seniors in high school was to jump off the bridge en masse the day before graduation day. It was a town event; the bridge was unofficially closed off (strangers who came by were politely asked to wait or go around the peninsula) and everyone stood on the banks of the inlet to cheer them on. She was horribly frightened, and if someone hadn't pushed her off she would not have had the nerve to do it.

First Criticism

Her father, watching her playing with a small stuffed rabbit, holding it up to her face and rubbing it against it and laughing, said, "That child is going to be terribly lonely."

Listening In

"Are you nuts, you?" overheard in the car as she looked at herself in the rearview mirror.

Self-Criticism

"When I was young I didn't know how to dance. All the other children loved to jump up and down to the music, but I didn't know how, so I always hid behind my parents until the music stopped. I learned to hate music early and associate it with humiliation."

Fantasies

Just one fantasy: To walk into a classroom on the day of an examination and to sit down calmly, and in control and know that she will excel.

READINGS

Akhil Sharma

Surrounded by Sleep

ONE AUGUST AFTERNOON, when Ajay was ten years old, his elder brother, Aman, dove into a pool and struck his head on the cement bottom. For three minutes, he lay there unconscious. Two boys continued to swim, kicking and splashing, until finally

Aman was spotted below them. Water had entered through his nose and mouth. It had filled his stomach. His lungs collapsed. By the time he was pulled out, he could no longer think, talk, chew, or roll over in his sleep.

Ajay's family had moved from India to Queens, New York, two years earlier. The accident occurred during the boys' summer vacation, on a visit with their aunt and uncle in Arlington, Virginia. After the accident, Ajay's mother came to Arlington, where she waited to see if Aman would recover. At the hospital, she told the doctors and nurses that her son had been accepted into the Bronx High School of Science, in the hope that by highlighting his intelligence she would move them to make a greater effort on his behalf. Within a few weeks of the accident, the insurance company said that Aman should be transferred to a less expensive care facility, a long-term one. But only a few of these were any good, and those were full, and Ajay's mother refused to move Aman until a space opened in one of them. So she remained in Arlington, and Ajay stayed too, and his father visited from Queens on the weekends when he wasn't working. Ajay was enrolled at the local public school and in September he started fifth grade.

Before the accident, Ajay had never prayed much. In India, he and his brother used to go with their mother to the temple every Tuesday night, but that was mostly because there was a good *dosa* restaurant nearby. In America, his family went to a temple only on important holy days and birthdays. But shortly after Ajay's mother came to Arlington, she moved into the room that he and his brother had shared during the summer and made an altar in a corner. She threw an old flowered sheet over a cardboard box that had once held a television. On top she put a clay lamp, an incense-stick holder, and postcards depicting various gods. There was also a postcard of Mahatma Gandhi. She explained to Ajay that God could take any form; the picture of Mahatma Gandhi was there because he had appeared to her in a dream after the accident and told her that Aman would recover and become a surgeon. Now she and Ajay prayed for at least half an hour before the altar every morning and night.

At first she prayed with absolute humility. "Whatever you do will be good because you are doing it," she murmured to the postcards of Ram and Shivaji, daubing their lips with water and rice. Mahatma Gandhi got only water, because he did not like to eat. As weeks passed and Aman did not recover in time to return to the Bronx High School of Science for the first day of classes, his mother began doing things that called attention to her piety. She sometimes held the prayer lamp until it blistered her palms. Instead of kneeling before the altar, she lay face down. She fasted twice a week. Her attempts to sway God were not so different from Ajay's performing somersaults to amuse his aunt, and they made God seem human to Ajay.

One morning as Ajay knelt before the altar, he traced an Om, a crucifix, and a Star of David into the pile of the carpet. Beneath these he traced an *S*, for Superman, inside an upside-down triangle. His mother came up beside him.

"What are you praying for?" she asked. She had her hat on, a thick gray knitted one that a man might wear. The tracings went against the weave of the carpet and

were darker than the surrounding nap. Pretending to examine them, Ajay leaned forward and put his hand over the *S*. His mother did not mind the Christian and Jewish
symbols—they were for commonly recognized gods, after all—but she could not tolerate his praying to Superman. She'd caught him doing so once several weeks earlier
and had become very angry, as if Ajay's faith in Superman made her faith in Ram
ridiculous. "Right in front of God," she had said several times.

Ajay, in his nervousness, spoke the truth. "I'm asking God to give me a hundred
percent on the math test."

His mother was silent for a moment. "What if God says you can have the math
grade but then Aman will have to be sick a little while longer?" she asked.

Ajay kept quiet. He could hear cars on the road outside. He knew that his mother
wanted to bewail her misfortune before God so that God would feel guilty. He looked
at the postcard of Mahatma Gandhi. It was a black-and-white photo of him walking
down a city street with an enormous crowd trailing behind him. Ajay thought of how,
before the accident, Aman had been so modest that he would not leave the bathroom
until he was fully dressed. Now he had rashes on his penis from the catheter that
drew his urine into a translucent bag hanging from the guardrail of his bed.

His mother asked again, "Would you say, 'Let him be sick a little while longer'?"

"Are you going to tell me the story about Uncle Naveen again?" he asked.

"Why shouldn't I? When I was sick, as a girl, your uncle walked seven times
around the temple and asked God to let him fail his exams just as long as I got better."

"If I failed the math test and told you that story, you'd slap me and ask what one
has to do with the other."

His mother turned to the altar. "What sort of sons did you give me, God?" she
asked. "One you drown, the other is this selfish fool."

"I will fast today so that God puts some sense in me," Ajay said, glancing away
from the altar and up at his mother. He liked the drama of fasting.

"No, you are a growing boy." His mother knelt down beside him and said to the
altar, "He is stupid, but he has a good heart."

Prayer, Ajay thought, should appeal with humility and an open heart to some greater
force. But the praying that he and his mother did felt sly and confused. By treating
God as someone to bargain with, it seemed to him, they prayed as if they were casting a spell.

This meant that it was possible to do away with the presence of God entirely. For
example, Ajay's mother had recently asked a relative in India to drive a nail into a
holy tree and tie a saffron thread to the nail on Aman's behalf. Ajay invented his own
ritual. On his way to school each morning, he passed a thick tree rooted half on the
sidewalk and half on the road. One day Ajay got the idea that if he circled the tree
seven times, touching the north side every other time, he would have a lucky day.
From then on he did it every morning, although he felt embarrassed and always
looked around beforehand to make sure no one was watching.

One night Ajay asked God whether he minded being prayed to only in need.

"You think of your toe only when you stub it," God replied. God looked like Clark Kent. He wore a gray cardigan, slacks, and thick glasses, and had a forelock that curled just as Ajay's did.

God and Ajay had begun talking occasionally after Aman drowned. Now they talked most nights while Ajay lay in bed and waited for sleep. God sat at the foot of Ajay's mattress. His mother's mattress lay parallel to his, a few feet away. Originally God had appeared to Ajay as Krishna, but Ajay had felt foolish discussing brain damage with a blue god who held a flute and wore a dhoti.

"You're not angry with me for touching the tree and all that?"

"No. I'm flexible."

"I respect you. The tree is just a way of praying to you," Ajay assured God.

God laughed. "I am not too caught up in formalities."

Ajay was quiet. He was convinced that he had been marked as special by Aman's accident. The beginnings of all heroes are distinguished by misfortune. Superman and Batman were both orphans. Krishna was separated from his parents at birth. The god Ram had to spend fourteen years in a forest. Ajay waited to speak until it would not appear improper to begin talking about himself.

"How famous will I be?" he asked finally.

"I can't tell you the future," God answered.

Ajay asked, "Why not?"

"Even if I told you something, later I might change my mind."

"But it might be harder to change your mind after you have said something will happen."

God laughed again. "You'll be so famous that fame will be a problem."

Ajay sighed. His mother snorted and rolled over.

"I want Aman's drowning to lead to something," he said to God.

"He won't be forgotten."

"I can't just be famous, though. I need to be rich too, to take care of Mummy and Daddy and pay Aman's hospital bills."

"You are always practical." God had a soulful and pitying voice, and God's sympathy made Ajay imagine himself as a truly tragic figure, like Amitabh Bachchan in the movie *Trishul*.

"I have responsibilities," Ajay said. He was so excited at the thought of his possible greatness that he knew he would have difficulty sleeping. Perhaps he would have to go read in the bathroom.

"You can hardly imagine the life ahead," God said.

Even though God's tone promised greatness, the idea of the future frightened Ajay. He opened his eyes. There was light coming from the street. The room was cold and had a smell of must and incense. His aunt and uncle's house was a narrow two-story home next to a four-lane road. The apartment building with the pool where Aman had drowned was a few blocks up the road, one in a cluster of tall brick buildings with stucco fronts. Ajay pulled the blanket tighter around him. In India, he could not have imagined the reality of his life in America: the thick smell of meat in the school cafeteria, the many television channels. And, of course, he could not have imagined Aman's accident, or the hospital where he spent so much time.

The hospital was boring. Vinod, Ajay's cousin, picked him up after school and dropped him off there almost every day. Vinod was twenty-two. In addition to attending county college and studying computer programming, he worked at a 7-Eleven near Ajay's school. He often brought Ajay hot chocolate and a comic from the store, which had to be returned, so Ajay was not allowed to open it until he had wiped his hands.

Vinod usually asked him a riddle on the way to the hospital "Why are manhole covers round?" It took Ajay half the ride to admit that he did not know. He was having difficulty talking. He didn't know why. The only time he could talk easily was when he was with God. The explanation he gave himself for this was that just as he couldn't chew when there was too much in his mouth he couldn't talk when there were too many thoughts in his head.

When Ajay got to Aman's room, he greeted him as if he were all right. "Hello, lazy. How much longer are you going to sleep?" His mother was always there. She got up and hugged Ajay. She asked how school had been, and he didn't know what to say. In music class, the teacher sang a song about a sailor who had bared his breast before jumping into the sea. This had caused the other students to giggle. But Ajay could not say the word *breast* to his mother without blushing. He had also cried. He'd been thinking of how Aman's accident had made his own life mysterious and confused. What would happen next? Would Aman die or would he go on as he was? Where would they live? Usually when Ajay cried in school, he was told to go outside. But it had been raining, and the teacher had sent him into the hallway. He sat on the floor and wept. Any mention of this would upset his mother. And so he said nothing had happened that day.

Sometimes when Ajay arrived his mother was on the phone, telling his father that she missed him and was expecting to see him on Friday. His father took a Greyhound bus most Fridays from Queens to Arlington, returning on Sunday night in time to work the next day. He was a bookkeeper for a department store. Before the accident, Ajay had thought of his parents as the same person: MummyDaddy. Now, when he saw his father praying stiffly or when his father failed to say hello to Aman in his hospital bed, Ajay sensed that his mother and father were quite different people. After his mother got off the phone, she always went to the cafeteria to get coffee for herself and Jell-O or cookies for him. He knew that if she took her coat with her, it meant that she was especially sad. Instead of going directly to the cafeteria, she was going to go outside and walk around the hospital parking lot.

That day, while she was gone, Ajay stood beside the hospital bed and balanced a comic book on Aman's chest. He read to him very slowly. Before turning each page, he said, "Okay, Aman?"

Aman was fourteen. He was thin and had curly hair. Immediately after the accident, there had been so many machines around his bed that only one person could stand beside him at a time. Now there was just a single waxy yellow tube. One end of this went into his abdomen; the other, blocked by a green bullet-shaped plug, was what his Isocal milk was poured through. When not being used, the tube was rolled up and bound by a rubber band and tucked beneath Aman's hospital gown. But even with the tube hidden, it was obvious that there was something wrong with Aman. It was in his stillness and his open eyes. Once, in their house in Queens, Ajay had left a plastic bowl on a radiator overnight and the sides had drooped and sagged so that the bowl looked a little like an eye. Aman reminded Ajay of that bowl.

Ajay had not gone with his brother to the swimming pool on the day of the accident, because he had been reading a book and wanted to finish it. But he heard the ambulance siren from his aunt and uncle's house. The pool was only a few minutes away, and when he got there a crowd had gathered around the ambulance. Ajay saw his uncle first, in shorts and an undershirt, talking to a man inside the ambulance. His aunt was standing beside him. Then Ajay saw Aman on a stretcher, in blue shorts with a plastic mask over his nose and mouth. His aunt hurried over to take Ajay home. He cried as they walked, although he had been certain that Aman would be fine in a few days: in a Spider-Man comic he had just read, Aunt May had fallen into a coma and she had woken up perfectly fine. Ajay had cried simply because he felt crying was called for by the seriousness of the occasion. Perhaps this moment would mark the beginning of his future greatness. From that day on, Ajay found it hard to cry in front of his family. Whenever tears started coming, he felt like a liar. If he loved his brother, he knew, he would not have thought about himself as the ambulance had pulled away, nor would he talk with God at night about becoming famous.

When Ajay's mother returned to Aman's room with coffee and cookies, she sometimes talked to Ajay about Aman. She told him that when Aman was six he had seen a children's television show that had a character named Chunu, which was Aman's nickname, and he had thought the show was based on his own life. But most days Ajay went into the lounge to read. There was a TV in the corner and a lamp near a window that looked out over a parking lot. It was the perfect place to read. Ajay liked fantasy novels where the hero, who was preferably under the age of twenty-five, had an undiscovered talent that made him famous when it was revealed. He could read for hours without interruption, and sometimes when Vinod came to drive Ajay and his mother home from the hospital it was hard for him to remember the details of the real day that had passed.

One evening when he was in the lounge, he saw a rock star being interviewed on *Entertainment Tonight*. The musician, dressed in a sleeveless undershirt that revealed a swarm of tattoos on his arms and shoulders, had begun to shout at the audience, over his interviewer, "Don't watch me! Live your life! I'm not you!" Filled with a sudden desire to do something, Ajay hurried out of the television lounge and stood on the sidewalk in front of the hospital entrance. But he did not know what to do. It was cold and dark and there was an enormous moon. Cars leaving the parking lot stopped one by one at the edge of the road. Ajay watched as they waited for an opening in the traffic, their brake lights glowing.

"Are things getting worse?" Ajay asked God. The weekend before had been Thanksgiving. Christmas soon would come, and a new year would start, a year during which Aman would not have talked or walked. Suddenly Ajay understood hopelessness. Hopelessness felt very much like fear. It involved a clutching in the stomach and a numbness in the arms and legs.

"What do you think?" God answered.

"They seem to be."

"At least Aman's hospital hasn't forced him out."

"At least Aman isn't dead. At least Daddy's Greyhound bus has never skidded off a bridge." Lately Ajay had begun talking much more quickly to God than he used to. Before, when he had talked to God, Ajay would think of what God would say in response before he said anything. Now Ajay spoke without knowing how God might respond.

"You shouldn't be angry at me." God sighed. God was wearing his usual cardigan. "You can't understand why I do what I do."

"You should explain better, then."

"Christ was my son. I loved Job. How long did Ram have to live in a forest?"

"What does that have to do with me?" This was usually the cue for discussing Ajay's prospects. But hopelessness made the future feel even more frightening than the present.

"I can't tell you what the connection is, but you'll be proud of yourself."

They were silent for a while.

"Do you love me truly?" Ajay asked.

"Yes."

"Will you make Aman normal?" As soon as Ajay asked the question, God ceased to be real. Ajay knew then that he was alone, lying under his blankets, his face exposed to the cold dark.

"I can't tell you the future," God said softly. These were words that Ajay already knew.

"Just get rid of the minutes when Aman lay on the bottom of the pool. What are three minutes to you?"

"Presidents die in less time than that. Planes crash in less time than that."

Ajay opened his eyes. His mother was on her side and she had a blanket pulled up to her neck. She looked like an ordinary woman. It surprised him that you couldn't tell, looking at her, that she had a son who was brain-dead.

In fact, things were getting worse. Putting away his mother's mattress and his own in a closet in the morning, getting up very early so he could use the bathroom before his aunt or uncle did, spending so many hours in the hospital—all this had given Ajay the reassuring sense that real life was in abeyance, and that what was happening was unreal. He and his mother and brother were just waiting to make a long-delayed bus trip. The bus would come eventually to carry them to Queens, where he would return to school at P.S. 20 and to Sunday afternoons spent at the Hindi movie theater under the trestle for the 7 train. But now Ajay was starting to understand that the world was always real, whether you were reading a book or sleeping, and that it eroded you every day.

He saw the evidence of this erosion in his mother, who had grown severe and unforgiving. Usually when Vinod brought her and Ajay home from the hospital, she had dinner with the rest of the family. After his mother helped his aunt wash the dishes, the two women watched theological action movies. One night, in spite of a headache that had made her sit with her eyes closed all afternoon, she ate dinner, washed dishes, sat down in front of the TV. As soon as the movie was over, she went upstairs, vomited, and lay on her mattress with a wet towel over her forehead. She asked Ajay to massage her neck and shoulders. As he did so, Ajay noticed that she was crying. The tears frightened Ajay and made him angry, "You shouldn't have watched TV," he said accusingly.

"I have to," she said. "People will cry with you once, and they will cry with you a second time. But if you cry a third time, people will say you are boring and always crying."

Ajay did not want to believe what she had said, but her cynicism made him think that she must have had conversations with his aunt and uncle that he did not know about. "That's not true," he told her, massaging her scalp. "Uncle is kind. Auntie Aruna is always kind."

"What do you know?" She shook her head, freeing herself from Ajay's fingers. She stared at him. Upside down, her face looked unfamiliar and terrifying. "If God lets Aman live long enough, you will become a stranger too. You will say, 'I have been unhappy for so long because of Aman, now I don't want to talk about him or look at him.' Don't think I don't know you," she said.

Suddenly Ajay hated himself. To hate himself was to see himself as the opposite of everything he wanted to be: short instead of tall, fat instead of thin. When he brushed his teeth that night, he looked at his face: his chin was round and fat as a heel. His nose was so broad that he had once been able to fit a small rock in one nostril.

His father was also being eroded. Before the accident, Ajay's father loved jokes— he could do perfect imitations—and Ajay had felt lucky to have him as a father. (Once, Ajay's father had convinced his own mother that he was possessed by the ghost of a British man.) And even after the accident, his father had impressed Ajay with the patient loyalty of his weekly bus journeys. But now his father was different.

One Saturday afternoon, as Ajay and his father were returning from the hospital, his father slowed the car without warning and turned into the dirt parking lot of a bar that looked as though it had originally been a small house. It had a pitched roof with a black tarp. At the edge of the lot stood a tall neon sign of an orange hand lifting a mug of sudsy golden beer. Ajay had never seen anybody drink except in the movies. He wondered whether his father was going to ask for directions to somewhere, and if so, to where.

His father said, "One minute," and they climbed out of the car.

They went up wooden steps into the bar. Inside, it was dark and smelled of cigarette smoke and something stale and sweet. The floor was linoleum like the kitchen at his aunt and uncle's. There was a bar with stools around it, and a basketball game played on a television bolted against the ceiling, like the one in Aman's hospital room.

His father stood by the bar waiting for the bartender to notice him. His father had a round face and was wearing a white shirt and dark dress pants, as he often did on the weekend, since it was more economical to have the same clothes for the office and home.

The bartender came over. "How much for a Budweiser?" his father asked.

It was a dollar fifty. "Can I buy a single cigarette?" He did not have to buy; the bartender would just give him one. His father helped Ajay up onto a stool and sat down himself. Ajay looked around and wondered what would happen if somebody started a knife fight. When his father had drunk half his beer, he carefully lit the cigarette. The bartender was standing at the end of the bar. There were only two other men in the place. Ajay was disappointed that there were no women wearing dresses slit all the way up their thighs. Perhaps they came in the evenings.

His father asked him if he had ever watched a basketball game all the way through.

"I've seen the Harlem Globetrotters."

His father smiled and took a sip. "I've heard they don't play other teams, because they can defeat everyone else so easily."

"They only play against each other, unless there is an emergency—like in the cartoon, when they play against the aliens to save the Earth," Ajay said.

"Aliens?"

Ajay blushed as he realized his father was teasing him.

When they left, the light outside felt too bright. As his father opened the car door for Ajay, he said, "I'm sorry." That's when Ajay first felt that his father might have done something wrong. The thought made him worry. Once they were on the road, his father said gently, "Don't tell your mother."

Fear made Ajay feel cruel. He asked his father, "What do you think about when you think of Aman?"

Instead of becoming sad, Ajay's father smiled. "I am surprised by how strong he is. It's not easy for him to keep living. But even before, he was strong. When he was interviewing for high school scholarships, one interviewer asked him, 'Are you a thinker or a doer?' He laughed and said, 'That's like asking, "Are you an idiot or a moron?"'"

From then on they often stopped at the bar on the way back from the hospital. Ajay's father always asked the bartender for a cigarette before he sat down, and during the ride home he always reminded Ajay not to tell his mother.

Ajay found that he himself was changing. His superstitions were becoming extreme. Now when he walked around the good-luck tree he punched it, every other time, hard, so that his knuckles hurt. Afterward, he would hold his breath for a moment longer than he thought he could bear, and ask God to give the unused breaths to Aman.

In December, a place opened in one of the good long-term care facilities. It was in New Jersey. This meant that Ajay and his mother could move back to New York and live with his father again. This was the news Ajay's father brought when he arrived for a two-week holiday at Christmas.

Ajay felt the clarity of panic. Life would be the same as before the accident but also unimaginably different. He would return to P.S. 20, while Aman continued to be fed through a tube in his abdomen. Life would be Aman's getting older and growing taller than their parents but having less consciousness than even a dog, which can become excited or afraid.

Ajay decided to use his devotion to shame God into fixing Aman. The fact that two religions regarded the coming December days as holy ones suggested to Ajay that prayers during this time would be especially potent. So he prayed whenever he thought of it—at his locker, even in the middle of a quiz. His mother wouldn't let him fast, but he started throwing away the lunch he took to school. And when his mother prayed in the morning, Ajay watched to make sure that she bowed at least once toward each of the postcards of deities. If she did not, he bowed three times to the possibly offended god on the postcard. He had noticed that his father finished his prayers in less time than it took to brush his teeth. And so now, when his father began praying in the morning, Ajay immediately crouched down beside him, because he knew his father would be embarrassed to get up first. But Ajay found it harder and harder to drift into the rhythm of sung prayers or into his nightly conversations with God. How could chanting and burning incense undo three minutes of a sunny August afternoon? It was like trying to move a sheet of blank paper from one end of a table to the other by blinking so fast that you started a breeze.

On Christmas Eve his mother asked the hospital chaplain to come to Aman's room and pray with them. The family knelt together beside Aman's bed. Afterward the chaplain asked her whether she would be attending Christmas services. "Of course, Father," she said.

"I'm also coming," Ajay said.

The chaplain turned toward Ajay's father, who was sitting in a wheelchair because there was nowhere else to sit.

"I'll wait for God at home," he said.

That night, Ajay watched *It's a Wonderful Life* on television. To him, the movie meant that happiness arrived late, if ever. Later, when he got in bed and closed his eyes, God appeared. There was little to say.

"Will Aman be better in the morning?"

"No."

"Why not?"

"When you prayed for the math exam, you could have asked for Aman to get better, and instead of your getting an A, Aman would have woken."

This was so ridiculous that Ajay opened his eyes. His father was sleeping nearby on folded-up blankets. Ajay felt disappointed at not feeling guilt. Guilt might have contained some hope that God existed.

When Ajay arrived at the hospital with his father and mother the next morning, Aman was asleep, breathing through his mouth while a nurse poured a can of Isocal into his stomach through the yellow tube. Ajay had not expected that Aman would have recovered; nevertheless, seeing him that way put a weight in Ajay's chest.

The Christmas prayers were held in a large, mostly empty room: people in chairs sat next to people in wheelchairs. His father walked out in the middle of the service.

Later, Ajay sat in a corner of Aman's room and watched his parents. His mother was reading a Hindi women's magazine to Aman while she shelled peanuts into her lap. His father was reading a thick red book in preparation for a civil service exam. The day wore on. The sky outside grew dark. At some point Ajay began to cry. He tried to be quiet. He did not want his parents to notice his tears and think that he was crying for Aman, because in reality he was crying for how difficult his own life was.

His father noticed first. "What's the matter, hero?"

His mother shouted, "What happened?" and she sounded so alarmed it was as if Ajay were bleeding.

"I didn't get any Christmas presents. I need a Christmas present," Ajay shouted. "You didn't buy me a Christmas present." And then, because he had revealed his own selfishness, Ajay let himself sob. "You have to give me something. I should get something for all this." Ajay clenched his hands and wiped his face with his fists. "Each time I come here I should get something."

His mother pulled him up and pressed him into her stomach. His father came and stood beside them. "What do you want?" his father asked.

Ajay had no prepared answer for this.

"What do you want?" his mother repeated.

The only thing he could think was "I want to eat pizza and I want candy."

His mother stroked his hair and called him her little baby. She kept wiping his face with a fold of her sari. When at last he stopped crying, they decided that Ajay's father should take him back to his aunt and uncle's. On the way, they stopped at a mini-mall. It was a little after five, and the streetlights were on. Ajay and his father did not take off their winter coats as they ate, in a pizzeria staffed by Chinese people. While he chewed, Ajay closed his eyes and tried to imagine God looking like Clark Kent, wearing a cardigan and eyeglasses, but he could not. Afterward, Ajay and his father went next door to a magazine shop and Ajay got a bag of Three Musketeers bars and a bag of Reese's peanut butter cups, and then he was tired and ready for home.

He held the candy in his lap while his father drove in silence. Even through the plastic, he could smell the sugar and chocolate. Some of the houses outside were dark, and others were outlined in Christmas lights.

After a while Ajay rolled down the window slightly. The car filled with wind. They passed the building where Aman's accident had occurred. Ajay had not walked past it since the accident. When they drove by, he usually looked away. Now he tried to spot the fenced swimming pool at the building's side. He wondered whether the pool that had pressed itself into Aman's mouth and lungs and stomach had been drained, so that nobody would be touched by its unlucky waters. Probably it had not been emptied until fall. All summer long, people must have swum in the pool and sat on its sides, splashing their feet in the water, and not known that his brother had lain for three minutes on its concrete bottom one August afternoon.

Reading as a Writer

1. How does Sharma characterize Ajay, the main character?

2. What techniques does he use to define the relationships between the characters? How does he make those relationships both surprising and convincing?

3. What picture emerges of the culture of these characters?

BHARATI MUKHERJEE

The Management of Grief

A WOMAN I DON'T KNOW is boiling tea the Indian way in my kitchen. There are a lot of women I don't know in my kitchen, whispering, and moving tactfully. They open doors, rummage through the pantry, and try not to ask me where things are kept. They remind me of when my sons were small, on Mothers' Day or when Vikram and I were tired, and they would make big, sloppy omelettes. I would lie in bed pretending I didn't hear them.

Dr. Sharma, the treasurer of the Indo-Canada Society, pulls me into the hallway. He wants to know if I am worried about money. His wife, who has just come up from the basement with a tray of empty cups and glasses, scolds him. "Don't bother Mrs. Bhave with mundane details." She looks so monstrously pregnant her baby must be days overdue. I tell her she shouldn't be carrying heavy things. "Shaila," she says, smiling, "this is the fifth." Then she grabs a teenager by his shirt-tails. He slips his Walkman off his head. He has to be one of her four children, they have the same domed and dented foreheads. "What's the official word now?" she demands. The boy slips the headphones back on. "They're acting evasive, Ma. They're saying it could be an accident or a terrorist bomb."

All morning, the boys have been muttering, Sikh Bomb, Sikh Bomb. The men, not using the word, bow their heads in agreement. Mrs. Sharma touches her forehead at such a word. At least they've stopped talking about space debris and Russian lasers.

Two radios are going in the dining room. They are tuned to different stations. Someone must have brought the radios down from my boys' bedrooms. I haven't gone into their rooms since Kusum came running across the front lawn in her bathrobe. She looked so funny. I was laughing when I opened the door.

The big TV in the den is being whizzed through American networks and cable channels.

"Damn!" some man swears bitterly. "How can these preachers carry on like nothing's happened?" I want to tell him we're not that important. You look at the audience, and at the preacher in his blue robe with his beautiful white hair, the potted palm trees under a blue sky, and you know they care about nothing.

The phone rings and rings. Dr. Sharma's taken charge. "We're with her," he keeps saying. "Yes, yes, the doctor has given calming pills. Yes, yes, pills are having necessary effect." I wonder if pills alone explain this calm. Not peace, just a deadening quiet. I was always controlled, but never repressed. Sound can reach me, but my body is tensed, ready to scream. I hear their voices all around me. I hear my boys and Vikram cry, "Mommy, Shaila!" and their screams insulate me, like headphones.

The woman boiling water tells her story again and again. "I got the news first. My cousin called from Halifax before six a.m., can you imagine? He'd gotten up for prayers and his son was studying for medical exams and he heard on a rock channel that something had happened to a plane. They said first it had disappeared from the radar, like a giant eraser just reached out. His father called me, so I said to him, what do you mean, 'something bad'? You mean a hijacking? And he said, *behn*,[1] there is no confirmation of anything yet, but check with your neighbors because a lot of them must be on that plane. So I called poor Kusum straightaway. I knew Kusum's husband and daughter were booked to go yesterday.

Kusum lives across the street from me. She and Satish had moved in less than a month ago. They said they needed a bigger place. All these people, the Sharmas and friends from the Indo-Canada Society had been there for the housewarming. Satish and Kusum made homemade tandoori on their big gas grill and even the white neighbors piled their plates high with that luridly red, charred, juicy chicken. Their younger daughter had danced, and even our boys had broken away from the Stanley Cup telecast to put in a reluctant appearance. Everyone took pictures for their albums and for the community newspapers—another of our families had made it big in Toronto—and now I wonder how many of those happy faces are gone. "Why does God give us so much if all along He intends to take it away?" Kusum asks me.

I nod. We sit on carpeted stairs, holding hands like children. "I never once told him that I loved him," I say. I was too much the well brought up woman. I was so well brought up I never felt comfortable calling my husband by his first name.

"It's all right," Kusum says. "He knew. My husband knew. They felt it. Modern young girls have to say it because what they feel is fake."

Kusum's daughter, Pam, runs in with an overnight case. Pam's in her McDonald's uniform. "Mummy! You have to get dressed!" Panic makes her cranky. "A reporter's on his way here."

"Why?"

"You want to talk to him in your bathrobe?" She starts to brush her mother's long hair. She's the daughter who's always in trouble. She dates Canadian boys and hangs out in the mall, shopping for tight sweaters. The younger one, the goody-goody one according to Pam, the one with a voice so sweet that when she sang *bhajans*[2] for Ethiopian relief even a frugal man like my husband wrote out a hundred dollar check, *she* was on that plane. *She* was going to spend July and August with grandparents because Pam wouldn't go. Pam said she'd rather waitress at McDonald's. "If it's a choice between Bombay and Wonderland I'm picking Wonderland," she'd said.

"Leave me alone." Kusum yells. "You know what I want to do? If I didn't have to look after you now, I'd hang myself."

1. No.
2. Hindu devotional song.

Pam's young face goes blotchy with pain. "Thanks," she says, "don't let me stop you."

"Hush," pregnant Mrs. Sharma scolds Pam. "Leave your mother alone. Mr. Sharma will tackle the reporters and fill out the forms. He'll say what has to be said"

Pam stands her ground. "You think I don't know what Mummy's thinking? *Why ever?* that's what. That's sick! Mummy wishes my little sister were alive and I were dead."

Kusum's hand in mine is trembly hot. We continue to sit on the stairs.

She calls before she arrives, wondering if there's anything I need. Her name is Judith Templeton and she's an appointee of the provincial government "Multiculturalism?" I ask, and she says, "partially," but that her mandate is bigger. "I've been told you knew many of the people on the flight," she says. "Perhaps if you'd agree to help us reach the others. . . ?"

She gives me time at least to put on tea water and pick up the mess in the front room. I have a few *samosas*[3] from Kusum's housewarming that I could fry up, but then I think, why prolong this visit?

Judith Templeton is much younger than she sounded. She wears a blue suit with a white blouse and a polka dot tie. Her blond hair is cut short, her only jewelry is pearl drop earrings. Her briefcase is new and expensive looking, a gleaming cordovan leather. She sits with it across her lap. When she looks out the front windows onto the street, her contact lenses seem to float in front of her light blue eyes.

"What sort of help do you want from me?" I ask. She has refused the tea, out of politeness, but I insist, along with some slightly stale biscuits.

"I have no experience," she admits. 'That is, I have an MSW and I've worked in liaison with accident victims, but I mean I have no experience with a tragedy of this scale—"

"Who could?" I ask.

"—and with the complications of culture, language, and customs. Someone mentioned that Mrs. Bhave is a pillar—because you've taken it more calmly."

At this, perhaps, I frown, for she reaches forward, almost to take my hand. "I hope you understand my meaning, Mrs. Bhave. There are hundreds of people in Metro directly affected, like you, and some of them speak no English. There are some widows who've never handled money or gone on a bus, and there are old parents who still haven't eaten or gone outside their bedrooms. Some houses and apartments have been looted. Some wives are still hysterical. Some husbands are in shock and profound depression. We want to help, but our hands are tied in so many ways. We have to distribute money to some people, and there are legal documents—these things can be done. We have interpreters, but we don't always have the human touch, or maybe the right human touch. We don't want to make mistakes, Mrs. Bhave, and that's why we'd like to ask to help us."

"More mistakes, you mean," I say.

3. Fried pastries with meat or vegetable filling.

Police matters are not in my hands," she answers.

"Nothing I can do will make any difference," I say. "We must all grieve in our own way."

"But you are coping very well. All the people said, Mrs. Bhave is the strongest person of all. Perhaps if the others could see you, talk with you, it would help them."

"By the standards of the people you call hysterical, I am behaving very oddly and very badly, Miss Templeton." I want to say to her, *I wish I could scream, starve, walk into Lake Ontario, jump from a bridge.* "They would not see me as a model. I do not see myself as a model."

I am a freak. No one who has ever known me would think of me reacting this way. This terrible calm will not go away.

She asks me if she may call again, after I get back from a long trip that we must make. "Of course," I say. "Feel free to call, anytime.

Four days later, I find Kusum squatting on a rock overlooking a bay in Ireland. It isn't a big rock, but it juts sharply out over water. This is as close as we'll ever get to them. June breezes balloon out her sari and unpin her knee length hair. She has the bewildered look of a sea creature whom the tides have stranded.

It's been one hundred hours since Kusum came stumbling and screaming across my lawn. Waiting around the hospital, we've heard many stories. The police, the diplomats, they tell us things thinking that we're strong, that knowledge is helpful to the grieving, and maybe it is. Some, I know, prefer ignorance, or their own versions. The plane broke into two, they say. Unconsciousness was instantaneous. No one suffered. My boys must have just finished their breakfasts. They loved eating on planes, they loved the smallness of plates, knives, and forks. Last year they saved the airline salt and pepper shakers. Half an hour more and they would have made it to Heathrow.

Kusum says that we can't escape our fate. She says that all those people—our husbands, my boys, her girl with the nightingale voice, all those Hindus, Christians, Sikhs, Muslims, Parsis, and atheists on that plane—were fated to die together off this beautiful bay. She learned this from a swami in Toronto.

I have my Valium.

Six of us "relatives"—two widows and four widowers—choose to spend the day today by the waters instead of sitting in a hospital room and scanning photographs of the dead. That's what they call us now: relatives. I've looked through twenty-seven photos in two days. They're very kind to us, the Irish are very understanding. Sometimes understanding means freeing a tourist bus on this trip to the bay, so we can pretend to spy our loved ones through the glassiness of waves or in sunspeckled cloud shapes.

I could die here, too, and be content.

"What is that, out there?" She's standing and flapping her hands and for a moment I see a head shape bobbing in the waves. She's standing in the water, I, on the boulder. The tide is low, and a round, black, headsized rock has just risen from the waves. She returns, her sari end dripping and ruined and her face is a twisted remnant of hope, the way mine was a hundred hours ago, still laughing but inwardly knowing that nothing but the ultimate tragedy could bring two women together at six o'clock on a Sunday morning. I watch her face sag into blankness.

"That water felt warm. Shaila," she says at length.

"You can't." I say. "Íive have to wait for our turn to come."

I haven't eaten in four days, haven't brushed my teeth.

"I know," she says. "I tell myself I have no right to grieve. They are in a better place than we are. My swami says I should be thrilled for them. My swami says depression is a sign of our selfishness."

Maybe I'm selfish. Selfishly I break away from Kusum and run, sandals slapping against stones, to the water's edge. What if my boys aren't lying pinned under the debris? What if they aren't stuck a mile below that innocent blue chop? What if, given the strong currents. . . .

Now I've ruined my sari, one of my best. Kusum has joined me, knee-deep in water that feels to me like a swimming pool. I could settle in the water, and my husband would take my land and the boys would slap water in my face just to see me scream.

"Do you remember what good swimmers my boys were, Kusum?"

"I saw the medals." she says.

One of the widowers, Dr. Ranganathan from Montreal, walks out to us carrying his shoes in one hand. He's an electrical engineer. Someone at the hotel mentioned his work is famous around the world, something about the place where physics and electricity come together. He has lost a huge family, something indescribable. "With some luck," Dr. Ranganathan suggests to me, "a good swimmer could make it safely to some island. It is quite possible that there may be many, many microscopic islets scattered around."

"You're not just saying that?" I tell Dr. Ranganathan about Vinod, my eldest son. Last year he took diving as well.

"It's a parent's duty to hope," he says. "It is foolish to rule out possibilities that have not been tested. I myself have not surrendered hope."

Kusum is sobbing once again. "Dear lady," he says, laying his free hand on her arm, and she calms down.

"Vinod is how old?" he asks me. He's very careful, as we all are. *Is*, not was.

"Fourteen. Yesterday he was fourteen. His father and uncle were going to take him down to the Taj and give him a big birthday party. I couldn't go with them because I couldn't get two weeks off from my stupid job in June." I process bills for a travel agent. June is a big travel month.

Dr. Ranganathan whips the pockets of his suit jacked inside out. Squashed roses, in darkening shades of pink, float on the water. He tore the roses off creepers in somebody's garden. He didn't ask anyone if he could pluck the roses, but now there's been an article about it in the local papers. When you see an Indian person, it says, please give him or her flowers.

"A strong youth of fourteen," he says, "can very likely pull to safety younger one."

My sons, though four years apart, were very close. Vinod wouldn't let Mithun drown. *Electrical engineering*, I think, foolishly perhaps: this man knows important secrets of the universe, things closed to me. Relief spins me lightheaded. No wonder my boys' photographs haven't turned up in the gallery of photos of the recovered dead. "Such pretty roses," I say.

"My wife loved pink roses. Every Friday I had to bring a bunch home. I used to say, why? After twenty odd years of marriage you're still needing proof positive of my love?" He has identified his wife and three of his children. Then others from Montreal, the lucky ones, intact families with no survivors. He chuckles as he wades back to shore. Then he swings around to ask me a question. "Mrs. Bhave, you are wanting to throw in some roses for your loved ones? I have two big ones left."

But I have other things to float: Vinod's pocket calculator; a half-painted model B-52 for my Mithun. They'd want them on their island. And for my husband? For him let fall into the calm, glassy waters a poem I wrote in the hospital yesterday. Finally he'll know my feelings for him.

"Don't tumble, the rocks are slippery," Dr. Ranganathan cautions. He holds out a hand for me to grab.

Then it's time to get back on the bus, time to rush back to our waiting posts on hospital benches.

Kusum is one of the lucky ones. The lucky ones flew here, identified in multiplicate their loved ones, then will fly to India with the bodies for proper ceremonies. Satish is one of the few males who surfaced. The photos of faces we saw on the walls in an office at Heathrow and here in the hospital are mostly of women. Women have more body fat, a nun said to me matter-of-factly. They float better.

Today I was stopped by a young sailor on the street. He had loaded bodies, he'd gone into the water when—he checks my face for signs of strength—when the sharks were first spotted. I don't blush, and he breaks down. "It's all right," I say. "Thank you." I had heard about the sharks from Dr. Ranganathan. In his orderly mind, science brings understanding, it holds no terror. It is the shark's duty. For every deer there is a hunter, for every fish a fisherman.

The Irish are not shy; they rush to me and give me hugs and some are crying. I cannot imagine reactions like that on the streets of Toronto. Just strangers, and I am touched. Some carry flowers with them and give them to any Indian they see.

After lunch, a policeman I have gotten to know quite well catches hold of me. He says he thinks he has a match for Vinod. I explain what a good swimmer Vinod is.

"You want me with you when you look at photos?" Dr. Ranganathan walks ahead of me into the picture gallery. In these matters, he is a scientist, and I am grateful. It is a new perspective. "They have performed miracles," he says. "We are indebted to them."

The first day or two the policemen showed us relatives only one picture at a time; now they're in a hurry, they're eager to lay out the possibles, and even the probables.

The face on the photo is of a boy much like Vinod; the same intelligent eyes, the same thick brows dipping into a V. But this boy's features, even his cheeks, are puffier, wider, mushier.

"No." My gaze is pulled by other pictures. There are five other boys who look like Vinod.

The nun assigned to console me rubs the first picture with a fingertip. "When they've been in the water for a while, love, they look a little heavier. The bones under the skin are broken, they said on the first day—try to adjust your memories. It's important."

"It's not him. I'm his mother. I'd know."

"I know this one!" Dr. Ranganathan cries out suddenly from the back of the gallery. "And this one!" I think he senses that I don't want to find my boys. "They are the Kuthy brothers. They were also from Montreal." I don't mean to be crying. On the contrary, I am ecstatic. My suitcase in the hotel is packed heavy with dry clothes for my boys.

The policeman starts to cry. "I am so sorry, I am so sorry, ma'am. I really thought we had a match."

With the nun ahead of us and the policeman behind, we, the unlucky ones without our children's bodies, file out of the makeshift gallery.

From Ireland most of us go on to India. Kusum and I take the same direct flight to Bombay, so I can help her clear customs quickly. But we have to argue with a man in uniform. He has large boils on his face. The boils swell and glow with sweat as we argue with him. He wants Kusum to wait in line and he refuses to take authority because his boss is on a tea break. But Kusum won't let her coffins out of sight, and I shan't desert her though I know that my parents elderly and diabetic, must be waiting in a stuffy car in a scorching lot.

"You bastard!" I scream at the man with the popping boils. Other passengers press closer. "You think we're smuggling contraband in those coffins!"

Once upon a time we were well brought up women; we were dutiful wives who kept our heads veiled, our voices shy and sweet.

In India, I become, once again, an only child of rich, ailing parents. Old friends of the family come to pay their respects. Some are Sikh, and inwardly, involuntarily, I cringe. My parents are progressive people; they do not blame communities for a few individuals.

In Canada it is a different story now.

"Stay longer," my mother pleads. "Canada is a cold place. Why would you want to be all by yourself?" I stay.

Three months pass. Then another.

"Vikram wouldn't have wanted you to give up things!" they protest. They call my husband by the name he was born with. In Toronto he'd changed to Vik so the men he worked with at his office would find his name as easy as Rod or Chris. "You know, the dead aren't cut off from us!"

My grandmother, the spoiled daughter of a rich *zamindar*,[4] shaved her head with rusty razor blades when she was widowed at sixteen. My grandfather died of childhood diabetes when he was nineteen, and she saw herself as the harbinger of bad luck. My mother grew up without parents, raised indifferently by an uncle, while her true mother slept in a hut behind the main estate house and took her food with the servants. She grew up a rationalist. My parents abhor mindless mortification.

The zamindar's daughter kept stubborn faith in Vedic rituals; my parents rebelled. I am trapped between two modes of knowledge. At thirty-six, I am too old to start over and too young to give up. Like my husband's spirit, I flutter between worlds.

Courting aphasia, we travel. We travel with our phalanx of servants and poor relatives. To hill stations and to beach resorts. We play contract bridge in dusty gymkhana clubs. We ride stubby ponies up crumbly mountain trails. At tea dances, we let ourselves be twirled twice round the ballroom. We hit the holy spots we hadn't made time for before. In Varanasi, Kalighat, Rishikesh, Hardwar, astrologers and palmists seek me out and for a fee offer me cosmic consolations.

Already the widowers among us are being shown new bride candidates. They cannot resist the call of custom, the authority of their parents and older brothers. They must marry; it is the duty of a man to look after a wife. The new wives will be young widows with children, destitute but of good family. They will make loving wives, but the men will shun them. I've had calls from the men over crackling Indian telephone lines. "Save me," they say, these substantial, educated, successful men of forty. "My parents are arranging a marriage for me." In a month they will have buried one family and returned to Canada with a new bride and partial family.

I am comparatively lucks. No one here thinks of arranging a husband for an unlucky widow.

Then. on the third day of the sixth month into this odyssey, in an abandoned temple in a tiny Himalayan village, as I make my offering of flowers and sweetmeats to the god of a tribe of animists, my husband descends to me. He is squatting next to a scrawny *sadhu*[5] in moth-eaten robes. Vikram wears the vanilla suit he wore the last time I hugged him. The *sadhu* tosses petals on a butter-fed flame, reciting Sanskrit mantras and sweeps his face of flies. My husband takes my hands in his.

You're beautiful, he starts. Then, *What are you doing here?*

Shall I stay? I ask. he only smiles, but already the image is fading. *You must finish alone what we started together.* No seaweed wreathes his mouth. He speaks too fast just as he used to when we were an envied family in our pink split-level. He is one.

In the windowless altar room, smoky with joss sticks and clarified butter lamps, a sweaty hand gropes for my blouse. I do not shriek. The *sadhu* arranges his robe. The lamps hiss and sputter out.

When we come out of the temple, my mother says, "Did you feel something weird in there?"

4. Landowner.
5. An ascetic or practioner of yoga.

My mother has no patience with ghosts, prophetic dreams, holy men, and cults. "No," I lie. "Nothing."

But she knows that she's lost me. She knows that in days I shall be leaving.

Kusum's put her house up for sale. She wants to live in an ashram in Hardwar. Moving to Hardwar was her swami's idea. Her swami runs two ashrams, the one in Hardwar and another here in Toronto.

"Don't run away," I tell her.

"I'm not running away," she says. "I'm pursuing inner peace. You think you or that Ranganathan fellow are better off?"

Pam's left for California. She wants to do some modelling, she says. She says when she comes into her share of the insurance money she'll open a yoga-cum-aerobics studio in Hollywood. She sends me postcards so naughty I daren't leave them on the coffee table. Her mother has withdrawn from her and the world.

The rest of us don't lose touch, that's the point. Talk is all we have, says Dr. Ranganathan, who has also resisted his relatives and returned to Montreal and to his job, alone. He says, whom better to talk with than other relatives? We've been melted down and recast as a new tribe.

He calls me twice a week from Montreal. Every Wednesday night and every Saturday afternoon. He is changing jobs, going to Ottawa. But Ottawa is over a hundred miles away, and he is forced to drive two hundred and twenty miles a day. He can't bring himself to sell his house. The house is a temple, he says, the king-sized bed in the master bedroom is a shrine. He sleeps on a folding cot. A devotee.

There are still some hysterical relatives. Judith Templeton's list of those needing help and those who've "accepted" is in nearly perfect balance. Acceptance means you speak of your family in the past tense and you make active plans for moving ahead with your life. There are courses at Seneca and Ryersonn we could be taking. Her gleaming leather briefcase is full of college catalogues and lists of cultural societies that need our help. She has done impressive work, I tell her.

"In the textbooks on grief management," she replies—I am her confidante, I realize, one of the few whose grief has not sprung bizarre obsessions—"there are stages to pass through: rejection, depression, acceptance, reconstruction." She has compiled a chart and finds that six months after the tragedy, none of us still reject reality, but only a handful are reconstructing. "Depressed Acceptance" is the plateau we've reached. Remarriage is a major step in reconstruction (though she's a little surprised, even shocked, over *how* quickly some of the men have taken on new families). Selling one's house and changing jobs and cities is healthy.

How do I tell Judith Templeton that my family surrounds me, and that like creatures in epics, they've changed shapes? She sees me as calm and accepting but worries that I have no job, no career. My closest friends are worse off than I. I cannot tell her my days, even my nights, are thrilling.

She asks me to help with families she can't reach at all. An elderly couple in Agincourt whose sons were killed just weeks after they had brought their parents over from a village in Punjab. From their names, I know they are Sikh. Judith Templeton and a translator have visited them twice with offers of money for air fare to Ireland, with bank forms, power-of-attorney forms, but they have refused to sign, or to leave their tiny apartment. Their sons' money is frozen in the bank. Their son's investment apartments have been trashed by tenants, the furnishings sold off. The parents fear that anything they sign or any money they receive will end the company's or the country's obligations to them. They fear they are selling their sons for two airline tickets to a place they've never seen.

The high-rise apartment is a tower of Indians and West Indians, with a sprinkling of Orientals. The nearest bus stop kiosk is lined with women in saris. Boys practice cricket in the parking lot. Inside the building, even I wince a bit from the ferocity of onion fumes, the distinctive and immediate Indianness of frying *ghee*,[6] but Judith Templeton maintains a steady flow of information. These poor old people are in imminent danger of losing their place and all their services.

I say to her, "They are Sikh. They will not open up to a Hindu woman." And what I want to add is, as much as I try not to, I stiffen now at the sight of beards and turbans. I remember a time when we all trusted each other in this new country, it was only the new country we worried about.

The two rooms are dark and stuffy. The lights are off, and an oil lamp sputters on the coffee table. The bent old lady has let us in, and her husband is wrapping a white turban over his oiled, hip-length hair. She immediately goes to the kitchen, and I hear the most familiar sound of an Indian home, tap water hitting and filling a teapot.

They have not paid their utility bills, out of fear and the inability to write a check. The telephone is gone; electricity and gas and water are soon to follow. They have told Judith their sons will provide. They are good boys, and they have always earned and looked after their parents.

We converse a bit in Hindi. They do not ask about the crash and I wonder if I should bring it up. If they think I am here merely as a translator, then they may feel insulted. There are thousands of Punjabi-speakers, Sikhs, in Toronto to do a better job. And so I say to the old lady, "I too have lost my sons, and my husband, in the crash."

Her eyes immediately fill with tears. The man mutters a few words which sound like a blessing. "God provides and God takes away," he say.

I want to say, but only men destroy and give back nothing. "My boys and my husband are not coming back," I say. "We have to understand that."

Now the old woman responds. "But who is to say? Man alone does not decide these things." To this her husband adds his agreement.

Judith asks about the bank papers, the release forms. With a stroke of the pen, they will have a provincial trustee to pay their bills, invest their money, and send them a monthly pension.

"Do you know this woman?" I ask them.

6. Clarified butter.

The man raises his hand from the table, turns it over and seems to regard each finger separately before he answers. "This young lady is always coming here, we make tea for her and she leaves papers for us to sign." His eyes scan a pile of papers in the corner of the room. "Soon we will be out of tea, then will she go away?"

The old lady adds, "I have asked my neighbors and no one else gets *angrezi*[7] visitors. What have we done?"

"It's her job," l try to explain. "The government is worried. Soon you will have no place to stay, no lights, no gas, no water."

"Government will get its money. Tell her not to worry, we are honorable people."

I try to explain the government wishes to give money, not take. He raises his hand. "Let them take," he says. "We are accustomed to that. That is no problem."

"We are strong people," says the wife. "Tell her that."

"Who needs all this machinery?" demands the husband. "It is unhealthy, the bright lights, the cold air on a hot day, the cold food, the four gas rings. God will provide, not government."

"When our boys return," the mother says. Her husband sucks his teeth. "Enough talk," he says.

Judith breaks in. "Have you convinced them?" The snaps on her cordovan briefcase go off like firecrackers in that quiet apartment. She lays the sheaf of legal papers on the coffee table. "If they can't write their names, an X will do—I've told them that.

Now the old lady has shuffled to the kitchen and soon emerges with a pot of tea and two cups. "I think my bladder will go first on a job like this," Judith says to me, smiling. "If only there was someway of reaching them. Please thank her for the tea. Tell her she's very kind."

I nod in Judith's direction and tell them in Hindi, "She thanks you for the tea. She thinks you are being very hospitable but she doesn't have the slightest idea what it means."

I want to say, humor her. I want to say, my boys and my husband are with me too, more than ever. I look in the old man's eyes and I can read his stubborn, peasant's message: *I have protected this woman as best I can. She is the only person I have left. Give to me or take from me what you will, but I will not sign for it. I will not pretend that I accept.*

In the car, Judith says, "You see what I'm up against? I'm sure they're lovely people, but their stubbornness and ignorance are driving me crazy. They think signing a paper is signing their sons' death warrants, don't they?"

I am looking out the window. I want to say, *In our culture, it is a parent's way to hope.*"

"Now Shaila, this next woman is a real mess. She cries day and night, and she refuses all medical help. We may have to—"

"—Let me out at the subway," I say.

"I beg your pardon?" I can feel those blue eyes staring at me.

It would not be like her to disobey. She merely disapproves, and slows at a corner to let me out. Her voice is plaintive. "Is there anything I said? Anything I did?"

7. English, Anglo.

I could answer her suddenly in a dozen ways, but I choose not to. "Shaila? Let's talk about it," I hear, then slam the door.

A wife and mother begins her new life in a new country, and that life is cut short. Yet her husband tells her: Complete what we have started. We, who stayed out of politics and came halfway around the world to avoid religious and political feuding have been the first in the New World to die from it. I no longer know what we started, nor how to complete it. I write letters to the editors of local papers and to members of Parliament. Now at least they admit it was a bomb. One MP answers back, with sympathy, but with a challenge. You want to make a difference? Work on a campaign. Work on mine. Politicize the Indian voter.

My husband's old lawyer helps me set up a trust. Vikram was a saver and a careful investor. He had saved the boys' boarding school and college fees. I sell the pink house at four times what we paid for it and take a small apartment downtown. I am looking for a charity to support.

We are deep in the Toronto winter, gray sides, icy pavements. I stay indoors, watching television. I have tried to assess my situation, how best to live my life, to complete what we began so many years ago. Kusum has written me from Hardwar that her life is now serene. She has seen Satish and has heard her daughter sing again. Kusum was on a pilgrimage, passing through a village when she heard a young girl's voice, singing one of her daughter's favorite *bhajans*. She followed the music through the squalor of a Himalayan village, to a hut here a young girl, an exact replica of her daughter, was fanning coals under the kitchen fire. When she appeared, the girl cried out, "Ma!" and ran away. What did I think of that?

I think I can only envy her.

Pam didn't make it to California, but writes me from Vancouver. She works in a department store, giving make-up hints to Indian and Oriental girls. Dr. Ranganathan has given up his commute, given up his house and job, and accepted an academic position in Texas where no one knows his story and he has vowed not to tell it. He calls me now once a week.

I wait, I listen, and I pray, but Vikram has not returned to me. The voices and the shapes and the nights filled with visions ended abruptly several weeks ago.

I take it as a sign.

One rare, beautiful, sunny day last week, returning from a small errand on Yonge Street, I was walking through the park from the subway to my apartment. I live equidistant from the Ontario Houses of Parliament and the University of Toronto. The day was not cold, but something in the bare trees caught my attention. I looked up from the gravel, into the branches and the clear blue sky beyond. I thought I heard the rustling of larger forms, and I waited a moment for voices. Nothing.

"What?" I asked.

Then as I stood in the path looking north to Queen's Park and west to the university, I heard the voices of my family one last time. *Your time has come,* they said. *Go, be brave.*

I do not know where this voyage I have begun will end. I do not know which direction I will take. I dropped the package on a park bench and started walking.

Reading as a Writer

1. What techniques does Mukherjee use to define the main character? How effective are these techniques?

2. How are the characters further defined by their relationships to one another? Point out passages in which character is revealed through interactions.

3. The main character has a number of desires that exist on multiple levels. Try to identify several of these desires.

CHAPTER ELEVEN

Raising the Curtain
Beginning Your Story

"A BAD BEGINNING MAKES FOR A BAD ENDING," wrote Euripides, and indeed few things are as critical as knowing when to raise the curtain on your story. If you start too early, you might bore your readers with a lot of unnecessary history or back-story; if you start too late, you might rob your readers of valuable context.

In this chapter we will first talk about what a good opening must accomplish; we'll talk about your "contract" with your reader and how to make sure that any promises you make (implicit or explicit) are delivered upon. We'll read a number of openings of pieces and talk about what makes them praiseworthy. And we'll look at some time-honored techniques for opening a piece that you can learn from. You'll get a chance to practice the ideas we talk about, and, finally, read two stories that have especially riveting openings.

Your Contract with the Reader

One of the most critical things to understand about openings is that they are promises: they make pledges about everything from the subject matter (what the story or novel is going to be about), to the tone (serious or humorous or ironic), to the fabric, or "world," in which the piece is placed. They also provide some sense of what's at stake. Perhaps most important, a good opening has to convince a reader to keep on reading. That is the lowest common denominator and the highest determinant of success. Will the reader turn the page? If yes, that's a good starting point; if no, nothing else matters.

Now a promise, or contract, doesn't mean there are no surprises. Indeed, fiction should be full of surprises and delights: that's why we read on—to see what happens next. If we know what happens next, we stop reading. It's as simple as that.

But unless you are entering the realm of metafiction (the point of which is to examine the writing of fiction, or the artificiality of the form) you are promising the reader some things within the context of a *particular creative world*. That is, you are making a promise about what will be delivered—and in what form and in what context. To break this promise is to disappoint or frustrate your reader.

This is a tricky subject, because it can lead beginning writers to think that if, say, they start out in a realistic mode and gradually work in magic, the contract has been broken. Yet the contract can be a subtle one: it can leave open the *opportunity* for certain things or the implication that some things might be possible.

Above all, there should be no tricks in an opening. "A shot rang out" is only a good opening under very specific circumstances. Likewise, any mystery that turns out to be extraneous to the story. "A writer has to discriminate wisely between the attention-getting device that soon becomes fairly irrelevant to the story and the beginning that genuinely gathers the reader into the arms of the story," said Robie Macauley and George Lanning, coauthors of *Technique in Fiction*. Raymond Carver talks about the need to avoid unnecessary mystery and tricks in his book *Fires:*

> I overheard the writer Geoffrey Wolff say "No cheap tricks" to a group of writing students. That should go on a three-by-five card. I'd amend it a little. "No tricks." Period. I hate tricks. At the first sign of a trick or a gimmick in a piece of fiction, a cheap trick or even an elaborate trick, I tend to look for cover. Tricks are ultimately boring, and I get bored easily. Extremely clever chi-chi writing or just plain tomfoolery writing puts me to sleep. Writers don't need tricks or gimmicks or even necessarily need to be the smartest fellows on the block. At the risk of appearing foolish, a writer sometimes needs to be able to just stand and gape at this or that thing—a sunset or an old shoe—in absolute and simple amazement . . .

Characteristics of a Good Opening

What are the characteristics of a good opening?

It keeps the reader wondering, "What happens next?" This is the most basic requirement of any piece of creative work, and it is particularly relevant in the opening. As E. M. Forster wrote:

> Neanderthal man listened to stories, if one may judge by the shape of his skull. The primitive audience was an audience of shock-heads, gaping round the campfire, fatigued with contending against the mammoth or the woolly rhinoceros, and only kept awake by suspense. What would happen next? The novelist droned on, and as soon as his audience guessed what happened next, they either fell asleep or killed him. We can estimate the dangers incurred when we think of the career of Scheherazade in somewhat later times. Scheherazade avoided her fate because she knew how to wield the weapon of suspense—the only literary tool that has any effect upon tyrants and savages. Great writer though she was—exquisite in her descriptions, tolerant in her judgments, ingenious in her incidents, advanced in her morality, vivid in her delineations of character, expert in her knowledge of three Oriental capitals—it was yet on none of these gifts that she relied when trying to save her life from her intolerable

husband. They were but incidental. She only survived because she managed to keep the king wondering what would happen next.

—E. M. FORSTER, *Aspects of the Novel*

So: Does your reader want to know what happens next? That's the most basic question you need to ask yourself as you establish the opening of your piece.

It establishes the tone of the piece. Is it fantastical? Realistic? Ironic? Humorous? Whatever the tone of the piece, every word must be saturated with it from the very beginning. A common problem one sees in beginning work is that a story will start out in one vein—say, serious and realistic—and then turn to slapstick comedy, or science fiction, or some other kind of tone. Whatever *feeling* you want your readers to get from the piece should be apparent from the very first sentence.

It immerses the reader in the physical world of the piece. "First sentences are doors to worlds," wrote Ursula Le Guin, reminding us that every piece has a place in the concrete world of sensory perception. Where does the piece take place? At what point in time? What's the physical terrain: A house? A boat on the open sea? Mountains? Suburbia? Whatever the physical setting of the piece, it should be apparent from the very first word.

It introduces characters and situations. Finally, a good opening introduces characters. Who will we be finding out about (or journeying with) on this narrative path? What is their situation; what exactly is *happening* that should cause us to be interested?

Unbalancing Acts

One good way to think about openings is to think in terms of *balance*. Either things are out of kilter, or they will soon be; there's an imbalance or a missing link, some mystery about what is happening that draws us into the story. It can be subtle, as shown below, but it has to be there. Let's look at some examples of what keeps us enough off balance to want to read more and regain our equilibrium.

> I saw her but four times, though I remember them vividly; she made her impression on me. I thought her very pretty and very interesting—a touching specimen of a type with which I had had other and perhaps less charming associations. I'm sorry to hear of her death, and yet when I think of it why *should* I be? The last time I saw her she was certainly not . . . ! But it will be of interest to take our meetings in order.   —HENRY JAMES, "Four Meetings"

In this story what keeps us off balance—and therefore interested—is the narrator's apparently ambiguous feelings toward the character he is going to relate a tale about. And for another intriguing fact, she's dead—death is always interesting: we want to know how, and when, and in what way it matters to the narrator—and then there's that unfinished line, "The last time I saw her she was certainly not . . . !" There's a sense of mystery that propels us into the story.

Now another example of an opening rich with possibilities:

> The woman in front of him was eating roasted peanuts that smelled so good that he could barely contain his hunger. He could not even sleep and wished they'd hurry and begin the bingo game. There, on his right, two fellows were drinking wine out of a bottle wrapped in a paper bag, and he could hear soft gurgling in the dark. His stomach gave a low, gnawing growl. "If this was down South," he thought, "all I'd have to do is lean over and say, 'Lady, gimme a few of those peanuts, please ma'am,' and she'd pass me the bag and never think nothing of it." Or he could ask the fellows for a drink in the same way. Folks down South stuck together that way; they didn't even have to know you. But up here it was different. —RALPH ELLISON, "King of the Bingo Game"

Here we get a sense of someone out of his realm, unhappy and a misfit. He's hungry for more than food; he wants companionship and a kind word, but he's not getting any of what he wants (and remember, having a character want something is a very compelling way to push your story forward).

And what about this?

> You had to know Travis Houpart not to like him, that was the thing. When people first encountered him, women especially, they thought they'd met a man worth meeting. The mustache was so trim, that reassuring dark brown, then the Christlike eyes, clear as scorched butter. The whole of him was so regular-featured and even-toned that the voice was no surprise, warm and crisp as a newscaster's, telling mild jokes and deflecting any question you might ask.
> He bought me a drink on a night I needed one, a night I was down.
> —LOUISE ERDRICH, "Mauser"

In this piece, we're kept off balance in all sorts of ways. We're first warned about this character, Travis Houpart; there's the tension that arises because of the difference between the way he looks (interesting and decent) and his apparent unsavoriness. Then there is also the suggestion that he preyed on the narrator at a point when she was vulnerable, all of which whets the appetite and keeps us reading on.

Starting in the Middle

"Begin in the middle of things," advised Horace: *in medias res*. Chekhov advised young writers to tear up the first three pages of what they'd written, which amounts to the same thing. Beginning in the middle means that the piece already has a sense of momentum, of things in motion. Let's look at some examples.

> "Hey, look at that? You know what that is?" the Wizard says. "That's a goddamn red-winged blackbird. Miss Watts saw four of 'em last week at her feeder. You know what that means?"
> Rensselaer blinks and checks his jockstrap, where he has stuffed two small brown packages. He is an unbelievably skinny twelve-year-old with a dreamy smile and a fine, caramel-colored face. It makes the older boy's face look almost blue.

"'Spring,' asshole."

"Where is the old witch?" Rensselaer asks mildly. They are in Miss Watts's backyard, but she isn't around and he can't feel her little beady eyes creeping out at them from a window.

"She's at Boston City Hospital right this goddamn minute. She's got a dropped bladder and they're tying the whole thing up," the Wizard says.

—C. S. GODSHALK, "The Wizard"

In this story, we join the two main characters in the middle of an adventure. We're told just enough to be interested, and we have lots of questions. What are the two small brown packages? Who is Miss Watts, and why are the boys in her backyard? We haven't gotten a lengthy exposition that lays out clearly what is happening, but we're engaged; we're *there* and that's what counts.

And what about this opening?

Gasping for air, his legs weak from the climb up the stairs, Ernest stopped outside the room surprised to find the door wide open, almost sorry he had made it before the police. An upsurge of nausea, a wave of suffocation forced him to suck violently for breath as he stepped into Gordon's room—his *own* two decades before.

Tinted psychedelic emerald, the room looked like a hippie pad posing for a photograph in *Life,* but the monotonous electronic frenzy he heard was the seventeen-year locusts, chewing spring leaves outside. He wondered whether the sedative had so dazed him that he had stumbled into the wrong room. No, now, as every time in his own college years when he had entered this room, what struck him first was the light falling through the leaded, green-stained windowglass. As the light steeped him in the ambience of the early forties, it simultaneously illuminated the artifacts of the present. Though groggy from the sedative, he experienced intermittent moments of startling clarity when he saw each object separately.

Empty beer can pyramids.

James Dean, stark poster photograph.

Records leaning on orange crate.

Life-sized redheaded girl, banjo blocking her vagina, lurid color.

Rolltop desk, swivel chair, typewriter.

Poster photograph of a teenage hero he didn't recognize.

Large CORN FLAKES carton.

—DAVID MADDEN, "No Trace"

Here we've jumped into the middle of a story where something important has already happened—after all, this character wanted to get to the room before the police did—although we don't know what, and the narrator is already in the middle of some sort of emotional crisis (we know this because of the sedative he's taken). And as with the other stories that begin in the middle, we're caught, hooked, and already being swept along in the stream of events.

Beginning with Action

In Chapter 4, I spoke about being surprised by a formula for writing stories prescribed by a workshop leader who said stories should follow the ABCDE pattern:
Action, Backstory, Conflict, Denouement, Ending. But although it shouldn't be done
all the time, and certainly not in a formulaic manner, sometimes you *will* want to try
to open with an action. "Plays and short stories are similar in that both start when all
but the action is finished," the playwright August Wilson said, so let's look at some
examples of what he meant by this.

> Murphy's drunk on the bright verge of still another Christmas and a car door
> slams. Then he's out in the headlights and in bed waking up the next afternoon
> with Annie kissing his crucified right fist. It's blue and swollen, and when he
> tries to move it, it tingles, it pains and Annie says, How did you hurt your
> hand? Did you hit somebody?
>   Murphy waits while that question fades on her mouth, then the room glitters
> and he sniffs the old fractured acid of remorse asking: Was I sick?
>   Yes.
>   Where?
>   On the floor. And you fell out of bed twice. It was so terrible I don't think I
> could stand it if it happened again promise me you won't get drunk anymore,
> Glover had to teach both of your classes this morning you frighten me when
> you're this way and you've lost so much weight you should have seen yourself
> last night lying naked on the floor like something from a concentration camp in
> your own vomit you were so white you were blue
>   Is the color of Annie's eyes as Murphy sinks into the stars and splinters of the
> sheets with her, making love to her and begging her forgiveness which she
> gives and gives until Murphy can feel her shy skeleton waltzing away with his
> in a fit of ribbons, the bursting bouquets of a Christmas they are going to spend
> apart.   —MARK COSTELLO, "Murphy's Xmas"

This story begins with action—the title character is drunk, even to the point of black-
ing out—and the pace of the story never flags as it moves forward (indeed, unlike the
ABCDE formula mentioned above, it never goes back for any backstory but just
moves relentlessly ahead).

> When Martha Hale opened the storm door and got a cut of the north wind, she
> ran back for her big woolen scarf. As she hurriedly wound that round her head,
> her eye made a scandalized sweep of her kitchen. It was no ordinary thing that
> called her away—it was probably farther from ordinary than anything that had
> ever happened in Dickson County. But what her eye took in was that her
> kitchen was in no shape for leaving: her bread all ready for mixing, half the
> flour sifted and half unsifted.   —SUSAN GLASPELL, "A Jury of Her Peers"

This story starts with a deceptively simple action, the opening of a storm door, and
the feel of wind, which provides a nice launching pad for what follows; the language

is fresh and alive, and we move ahead from the action, wondering what this non ordinary thing is that could have happened. Like the previous example, in this story there's no going back for backstory: the story merely unfolds from this point on.

Beginning with Inaction

But action isn't always the best way to start. Let's take a look at some examples that begin with lengthy expositions or narrative. They're just as compelling, due to the fresh and specific nature of the details.

> This blind man, an old friend of my wife's, he was on his way to spend the night. His wife had died. So he was visiting the dead wife's relatives in Connecticut. He called my wife from his in-laws'. Arrangements were made. He would come by train, a five-hour trip, and my wife would meet him at the station. She hadn't seen him since she worked for him one summer in Seattle ten years ago. But she and the blind man had kept in touch. They made tapes and mailed them back and forth. I wasn't enthusiastic about his visit. He was no one I knew. And his being blind bothered me. My idea of blindness came from the movies, in the movies, the blind moved slowly and never laughed. Sometimes they were led by seeing-eye dogs. A blind man in my house was not something I looked forward to.   —RAYMOND CARVER, "Cathedral"

Instead of getting action in this opening, we get an explanation of the situation, with the narrator's feelings bluntly "told" to us. There's no dramatization, just a setting of the physical and emotional scene. But it works as an opening because of the sense of curiosity we have about this curmudgeonly man (the narrator) and about how the unwelcome visit will turn out for him and his wife.

And how about this one?

> Flo said to watch for White Slavers. She said this was how they operated: an old woman, a motherly or grandmotherly sort, made friends while riding beside you on a bus or train. She offered you candy, which was drugged. Pretty soon you began to droop and mumble, were in no condition to speak for yourself. Oh, help, the woman said, my daughter (granddaughter) is sick, please somebody help me get her off so that she can recover in the fresh air. Up stepped a polite gentleman, pretending to be a stranger, offering assistance. Together, at the next stop, they hustled you off the train or bus, and that was the last the ordinary world ever saw of you. They kept you a prisoner in the White Slave place (to which you had been transported drugged and bound so you wouldn't even know where you were), until such time as you were thoroughly degraded and in despair, your insides torn up by drunken men and invested with vile disease, your mind destroyed by drugs, your hair and teeth fallen out. It took about three years for you to get to this state. You wouldn't want to go home, then, maybe couldn't remember home, or find your way if you did. So they let you out on the streets.

> Flo took ten dollars and put it in a little cloth bag, which she sewed to the
> strap of Rose's slip. Another thing likely to happen was that Rose would get her
> purse stolen.   —ALICE MUNRO, "Wild Swans"

Here we also begin with inaction: with a lengthy lecture by the character Flo as to the
dangers of traveling alone, and what would happen to a young girl taken by the so-
called White Slavers. The action doesn't begin until the very end of the passage, but
the narrative is odd enough, and compelling enough, to keep us reading.

On the Nature of Suspense

What is *suspense? Merriam-Webster's Collegiate Dictionary* defines it as "mental
uncertainty" or "pleasant excitement as to a decision or outcome." And isn't this
what we've been talking about in this chapter? The need, in an opening, to keep
readers in a state of "pleasant excitement" so that they'll read on?

It's important to understand precisely what creates literary suspense: a reader's
partial (or imperfect) awareness that something of dramatic significance is about to
occur. John Gardner wrote the following:

> [Suspense must be achieved] in a piece of fiction just *before* the discovery of a
> body. You might perhaps describe the character's approach to the body he will
> find, or the location, or both. The purpose of the exercise is to develop the tech-
> nique of at once *attracting the reader toward the paragraph to follow—making him
> want to skip ahead, and holding him on this paragraph by virtue of its interest* [empha-
> sis mine]. Without the ability to write such foreplay paragraphs, one can never
> achieve real suspense.   —JOHN GARDNER, *The Art of Fiction*

Let's look at some examples of openings that have this attribute of "partial
knowledge" built into them.

> Every night that winter he said aloud into the dark of the pillow: Half past four!
> Half-past four! Till he felt his brain had gripped the words and held them fast.
> Then he fell asleep at once, as if a shutter had fallen; and lay with his face
> turned to the clock so that he could see it first thing when he woke.
>   —DORIS LESSING, "A Sunrise on the Veld"

This opening makes us wonder what "half past four" is all about. We're intrigued by
our partial knowledge of the situation, and we want to read on.

> A woman I don't know is boiling tea the Indian way in my kitchen. There are a
> lot of women I don't know in my kitchen, whispering and moving tactfully.
> They open doors, rummage through the pantry, and try not to ask me where
> things are kept. They remind me of when my sons were small, on Mother's Day
> or when Vikram and I were tired, and they would make big, sloppy omelets. I
> would lie in bed pretending I didn't hear them.
>   —BHARATI MUKHERJEE, "The Management of Grief"

Something has clearly happened that makes people want to help the narrator and treat her as if she were particularly delicate or vulnerable. The fact that we don't know what has happened—yet—whets our appetite to hear more.

EXERCISES

A good beginning is critical to your story. Without a compelling opening, your readers might lose interest—and you will lose them. Getting the reader to turn the page is just one thing that a good opening will do. The other things discussed in this chapter—introducing the characters, establishing a tone and sense of place and sense of what the story is about—are equally important.

Exercise 1: Give It Your Best Shot

GOAL: To see what happens when you begin a story with your best material rather than "saving it up."

1. Take a piece you've been working on.

2. Take the best, most exciting material from the piece.

3. Begin the piece with this material.

Here's an example written by Susan Jamison:

Original opening

My brothers, as far as I remember, never spoke to each other. They marched silently through the house, spaced regularly. They could have been clones of one another. They took the same courses, went out for the same sports, read the same books, watched the same television shows. My father took great pride in this; he thought it showed the strength of the breeding. "No environmental factors, here," he said. "Genetics all the way." My brothers, as far as I could see, ignored him. But it is true that they had the same tastes. When older, they bought gray or beige Honda compact cars, married blond women or women who dyed their hair blond, worked in number-intensive jobs like accounting or finance.

Revision

When my oldest brother was arrested, it came as a complete shock. Matthew! He of the gentle face and the hobby of breeding cockatiels—not to sell, but for the pleasure of hand-feeding the babies and giving them as gifts. It turned out he'd been selling drugs to schoolchildren out of his garage. We were all in shock. If Matthew could go bad, anything was possible.

Exercise 2: Start in the Middle

GOAL: To see what happens if you follow the ancient poet Horace's advice and start something in the middle.

1. Take a piece you've been working on, and choose an event that occurs in the middle of the piece.

2. Write a new opening based on this "middle."

Here's an example contributed by Mary O'Connor:

Original opening

When we first moved to the house on Walnut Avenue, there was no grass, no trees, nothing: just our house, surrounded by a sea of dirt. The other houses weren't built yet; there were just the bare cement foundations that would eventually grow up to be the houses of our neighbors and playmates. The roads had been laid, however, and the streetlights installed, so one got the sense of this immense expanse of roadways and streaming lights, cutting through the mud and dirt as far as the eye could see in any direction.

Revision

It was the third day that my little sister Ruby got bit by the black widow spider. She couldn't talk yet, so we weren't sure what happened, but she was crying, and there was a huge red welt on her arm growing larger by the second. My mother first did the "now don't make a fuss" thing before we managed to convince her something was really wrong. Ruby had stopped crying but she was having trouble breathing and she was holding her arm out as though it was a slab of rancid meat she'd picked up off the floor.

Exercise 3: Make Them Squirm

GOAL: To practice wielding the weapon of suspense to keep your readers reading.

1. Choose a piece you are working on.

2. Write a few first paragraphs that leave the reader in doubt of something important that is going on.

This passage was written by Thomas Kilhearn:

What could I say? It wasn't the first time I had done it, just the first time I had been caught. And the shame was pushing down on me so I could hardly swallow, but that was nothing new; I had felt this deep crushing shame when I had gotten off scot-free, without any witnesses to my transgressions, in the past. And this wasn't really that bad, was it? I sometimes have trouble keeping perspective on things, my mother tells me.

This passage was written by Jane Towson:

The night he left, I had fallen asleep as he began putting all our books in alphabetical order. Several times he woke me up to ask me questions. "In biography, do you want the books to be listed under the person being written about, or the person writing?" he asked. After the books he started on the records, then on the food in the pantry. At some point I fell asleep. When I awoke, every piece of electronic equipment we owned was gone. So was my husband. There was no note. When I opened the refrigerator, I found the food there alphabetized, too. An avocado stared me in the face.

READINGS

MADISON SMARTT BELL

Customs of the Country

I DON'T KNOW HOW MUCH I REMEMBER about that place anymore. It was nothing but somewhere I came to put in some pretty bad time, though that was not what I had planned on when I went there. I had it in mind to improve things, but I don't think you could fairly claim that's what I did. So that's one reason I might just as soon forget about it. And I didn't stay there all that long, not more than nine months or so, about the same time, come to think, that the child I'd come to try and get back had lived inside my body.

It was a cluster-housing thing called Spring Valley, I wouldn't know why, just over the Botetourt County line on the highway going north out of Roanoke. I suppose it must have been there ten or fifteen years, long enough to lose that raw look they have when they're new built, but not too rundown yet, so long as you didn't look close. There were five or six long two-story buildings running in rows back up the hillside. You got to the upstairs apartments by an outside balcony, like you would in a motel. The one I rented was in the lowest building down the hill, upstairs on the northwest corner. There was a patch of grass out front beyond the gravel of the parking lot, but the manager didn't take much trouble over it. He kept it cut, but it was weedy, and a few yards past the buildings it began to go to brush. By my corner there was a young apple tree that never made anything but small sour-green apples, knotted up like little fists. Apart from that there was nothing nearby that the eye would care to dwell on. But upstairs, out my front windows, I could look way out beyond the interstate to where the mountains were.

You got there driving about two miles up a bumpy two-lane from the state road. It was mostly wooded land along the way, with a couple of pastures spotted in, and one little store. About halfway you crossed the railroad cut, and from the apartment I could hear the trains pulling north out of town, though it wasn't near enough I could see them. I listened to them often enough, though, nights I couldn't sleep, and bad times I might pull a chair out on the concrete slab of balcony so I could hear them better.

The apartment was nothing more than the least I needed, some place that would look all right and yet cost little enough to leave me something to give the lawyer. Two rooms and a bath and a fair-sized kitchen. It would have been better if there'd been one more room for Davey but I couldn't stretch my money far enough to cover that.

It did have fresh paint on the walls and the trim in the kitchen and bathroom was in good enough shape. And it was real quiet mostly, except that the man next door would beat up his wife about two or three times a week. The place was close enough to soundproof I couldn't usually hear talk but I could hear yelling plain as day, and when he got going good he would slam her bang into our common wall. If she hit in just the right spot it would send all my pots and pans flying off the pegboard where I'd hung them there above the stove.

Not that it mattered to me that the pots fell down, except for the noise and the time it took to pick them up again. Living alone like I was I didn't have heart to do much cooking, and if I did fix myself something I mostly used a plain old iron skillet that hung there on the same wall. The rest was a set of Revereware my family give me when Patrick and I got married. They had copper bottoms, and when I first moved in that apartment I polished them to where it practically hurt to look at them head on, but it was all for show.

The whole apartment was done about the same way, made into something I kept spotless and didn't much care to use. A piece of dirt never got a fair chance to settle there, that much was for sure. I wore down the kitchen counters scrubbing out the old stains, I went at the grout between the bathroom tiles with a toothbrush, I did all that kind of thing. Spring Valley was the kind of place where people would sometimes leave too fast to take their furniture along, so I was able to get most everything I needed from the manager, who saved it up to try selling it to whatever new people moved in. Then I bought fabric and sewed covers to where everything matched, and I sewed curtains and got posters to put up on the walls, but I can't say I ever felt at home there. It was an act, and I wasn't putting it on for me or Davey, but for those other people who would come to see it and judge it. And however good I could get it looking, it never felt quite right.

I'd step into the place with the same cross feeling I had when I got in my car, an old Malibu I'd bought a body and paint job for, instead of the new clutch and brakes it really needed. But one way or another I could run the thing, and six days a week I would climb in it and go back down to the state road, turn north and drive up to the interstate crossing. There was a Truck Stops of America up there, and that was where my job was at. I worked the three snake bends of the counter and it was enough to keep me run off my feet most days. Or nights, since I was on a swing shift that rolled over every ten days. I wouldn't have ate the food myself but the place was usually busy and the tips were fair. I'd have made a lot more money working in a bar somewhere, being a cocktail waitress or what have you, but that would have been another case of it not looking the way it was supposed to.

The supervisor out there was a man named Tim that used to know Patrick a little, back from before we split. He was how I got the job, and he was good about letting me have time off when I needed it for the lawyer or something, and he let me take my calls there too. By and large he was an easy enough man to work for except that about once a week he would have a tantrum over something or other and try to scream the walls down for a while. Still, it never went anywhere beyond yelling, and he always acted sorry once he got through.

The other waitress on my shift was about old enough to be my mother, I would guess. Her name was Priscilla but she wanted you to call her Prissy, though it didn't suit her a bit. She was kind of dumpy and she had to wear support hose and she had the worst dye job on her hair I just about ever saw, some kind of home brew that turned her hair the color of French's mustard. But she was good-natured, really a kindly person, and we got along good and helped each other out whenever one of us looked like getting behind.

Well, I was tired all the time with the shifts changing the way they did. The six-to-two I hated the worst because it would have me getting back to my apartment building around three in the morning, which was not the time the place looked its best. It was a pretty sorry lot of people living there, I hadn't quite realized when I moved in, a lot of small-time criminals, dope dealers and thieves, and none of them too good at whatever crime they did. So when I came in off that graveyard shift there was a fair chance I'd find the sheriff's car out there looking for somebody. I suppose they felt like if they came at that time of night they would stand a better chance of catching whoever they were after asleep.

I didn't get to know the neighbors any too well, it didn't seem like a good idea. The man downstairs was a drunk and a check forger. Sometimes he would break into the other apartments looking for whiskey, but he never managed to get into mine. I didn't keep whiskey anyhow, maybe he had some sense for that. The manager liked to make passes at whatever women were home in the day. He even got around to trying me, though not but the one time.

The man next door, the one that beat up his wife, didn't do crimes or work either that I ever could tell. He just seemed to lay around the place, maybe drawing some kind of welfare. There wasn't a whole lot to him, he was just a stringy little fellow, hair and mustache a dishwater brown, cheap-green tattoos running up his arms. Maybe he was stronger than he looked, but I did wonder how come his wife would take it from him, since she was about a head taller and must have outweighed him an easy ten pounds. I might have thought she was whipping on *him*—stranger things have been known to go on—but she was the one that seemed like she might break out crying if you looked at her crooked. She was a big fine-looking girl with a lovely shape, and long brown hair real smooth and straight and shiny. I guess she was too hammered down most of the time to pay much attention to the way she dressed, but she still had pretty brown eyes, big and long-lashed and soft, kind of like a cow's eyes are, except I never saw a cow that looked that miserable.

At first I thought maybe I might make a friend of her, she was about the only one around there I felt like I might want to. Our paths crossed pretty frequent, either around the apartment buildings or in the Quik-Sak back toward town, where I'd find her running the register some days. But she was shy of me—shy of anybody, I suppose. She would flinch if you did so much as say hello. So after a while, I quit trying. She'd get hers about twice a week, maybe other times I wasn't around to hear it happen. It's a wonder all the things you can learn to ignore, and after a month or so I was so accustomed I barely noticed when they would start in. I would just wait till I thought they were good and through, and then get up and hang those pans back on the wall where they were supposed to go.

What with the way the shifts kept rolling over out there at the TOA, I had a lot of trouble sleeping. I never did learn to sleep in the daytime worth a damn. I would just lie down when I got back till some of the ache drained out of me, and then get up and try to think of some way to pass the time. There wasn't a whole lot to do around that apartment. I didn't have any TV, only a radio, and that didn't work too well itself. After the first few weeks I sent off to one of those places that say they'll pay you to stuff envelopes at your own house. My thought was it would be some extra money, but it never amounted to anything much of that. It just killed me some time and gave me something to do with my hands, in between smoking cigarettes. Something to do with myself while I was worrying, and I used to worry a good deal in those days.

The place where Davey had been fostered out was not all that far away, just about ten or twelve miles on up the road, out there in the farm country. The people were named Baker, I never got to first names with them, just called them Mr. and Mrs. They were some older than me, just into their forties, and they didn't have children of their own. The place was just a small farm but Mr. Baker grew tobacco on the most of it and I'm told he made it a paying thing. Mrs. Baker kept a milk cow or two and she grew a garden and canned. Thrifty people, in the old-time way. They were real sweet to Davey and he seemed to like being with them pretty well. It was a place a little boy would expect to enjoy, except there weren't any neighbors too near. And he had been staying there almost the whole two years, which was lucky too, since most children usually got moved around a whole lot more than that.

But that was the trouble, like the lawyer explained to me, it was just too good. Davey was doing too well out there. He'd made out better in the first grade too than anybody would have thought. So nobody really felt like he needed to be moved. The worst of it was the Bakers had got to like him well enough they were saying they wanted to adopt him if they could, and that was what plagued my mind the most. If I thought about that while I was doing those envelopes, it would start me giving myself paper cuts.

Even though he was so close, I didn't go out to see Davey near as much as I would have liked to. The lawyer kept on telling me it wasn't a good idea to look like I was pressing too hard. Better take it easy till all the evaluations came in and we had our court date and all. Still, I would call and go on out there maybe a little more than once a month, most usually on the weekends since that seemed to suit the Bakers better. They never acted like it was any trouble, and they were always pleasant to me, or polite might be the better word. They wanted what I wanted, so I never expected us to turn out good friends. The way it sometimes seemed they didn't trust me, that bothered me a little more. I would have liked to take him out to the movies a time or two, but I could see plain enough the Bakers wouldn't have been easy about me having him off their place.

Still, I can't remember us having a bad time, not any of those times I went. He was always happy to see me, though he'd be quiet when we were in the house, with

Mrs. Baker hovering. So I would get us outside quick as ever I could, and once we were out, we would just play like both of us were children. There was an open pasture, a creek with a patch of woods, and a hay barn where we would play hide-and-go-seek. I don't know what all else we did—silly things, mostly. That was how I could get near him the easiest, he didn't get a whole lot of playing in way out there. The Bakers weren't what you would call playful and there weren't any other children living near. So that was the thing I could give him that was all mine to give. When the weather was good we would stay outside together most all the day and he would just wear me out. After it turned cold we couldn't stay outside so long, though one of our best days of all was when I showed him how to make a snowman. But over the winter those visits seemed to get shorter and shorter, like the days.

Davey called me Momma still, but I suppose he had come to think your mother was something more like a big sister or just some kind of a friend. Mrs. Baker was the one doing for him all the time. I don't know just what he remembered from before, or if he remembered any of the bad part. He would always mind me but he never acted scared around me, and if anybody says he did, they lie. But I never really did get to know what he had going on in the back of his mind about the past. At first I worried the Bakers might have been talking against me, but after I had seen a little more of them I knew they wouldn't have done anything like that, wouldn't have thought it right. So I expect whatever Davey knew about that other time he remembered all on his own. He never mentioned Patrick hardly and I think he really had forgotten about him. Thinking back, I guess he never really saw that much of Patrick even where we all were living together. But Davey had Patrick's mark all over him, the same eyes and the same red hair.

Patrick had thick wavy hair the shade of an Irish setter's and a big rolling mustache the same color. Maybe that was his best feature, but he was a good-looking man altogether—still is, I suppose, though the prison haircut don't suit him. If he ever had much of a thought in his head, I suspect he had knocked it clean out with dope, yet he was always fun to be around. I wasn't but seventeen when I married him and I didn't have any better sense myself. Right through to the end I never thought anything much was the matter, his vices looked so small to me. He was good-tempered almost all the time, and good with Davey when he did notice him. Never one time did he raise his hand to either one of us. In little ways he was unreliable—late, not showing up at all, gone out of the house for days together sometimes. Hindsight shows me he ran with other women, but I managed not to know anything about that at the time. He had not quite finished high school and the best job he could hold was being an orderly down at the hospital, but he made a good deal of extra money stealing pills out of there and selling them on the street.

That was something else I didn't allow myself to think on much back then. Patrick never told me a lot about it anyhow, always acted real mysterious about whatever he was up to in that line. He would disappear on one of his trips and come back with a whole mess of money, and I would spend up my share and be glad I had it too. Never thought much about where it was coming from, the money or the pills, either one. He used to keep all manner of pills around the house, Valium and ludes and a lot of different kinds of speed, and we both took what we felt like whenever we felt in the mood. But what Patrick made the most on was Dilaudid. I used to take that without ever knowing what it really was, but once everything fell in on us I found out it was a bad thing, bad as heroin they said, and not much different, and that was what they gave Patrick most of his time for.

I truly was surprised to find out that was the strongest dope we had, because I never really felt like it made me all that high. It sure didn't have anything like the punch the speed did. Yet you could fall into the habit of taking a good bit of it, never noticing how much. You would just take one and kick back on a long slow stroke and whatever trouble you might have, it would not be able to find you. It came on like nothing but it was the hardest habit to lose, and I was a long time shaking it. I might be thinking about it yet if I would let myself, and there were times, all through the winter I spent in that apartment, I'd catch myself remembering the feeling.

I had come just before the leaves started turning, and then I believed it was all going to happen quick. I thought to have Davey back with me inside of a month or six weeks. But pretty soon the lawyer was singing me a different tune, delaying it all for this reason or that. He had a whole lot of different schemes in his mind, having to do with which judge, which social worker, which doctor might help us out the most. I got excited over everything he told me, in the beginning I did at least, but then nothing ever seemed to come of it at all. It turned off cold, the leaves came down, that poor little apple tree underneath my window was bare as a stick, and still nothing had happened.

You couldn't call it a real bad winter, there wasn't much snow or anything, but I was cold just about all the time, except when I was at work. The TOA was hot as a steam bath, especially back around the kitchen, and when I was there I'd sweat until I smelled. In the apartment, though, all I had was some electric baseboard heaters, and they cost too much for me to leave them running very long at a stretch. I'd keep it just warm enough I couldn't see my breath, and spend my time in a hot bathtub or under a big pile of blankets on the bed. Or else I would just be cold.

Outside wasn't all that much colder than in, and I spent a lot of time sitting there on that balcony, looking way out yonder toward the mountains. I got a pair of those gloves with the fingers out so I could keep on stuffing my envelopes while I was sitting out there. Day or night, it didn't matter, I was so familiar with it I could do it in the dark. I'd sit there sometimes for hours on end, counting the time by the trains that went by. Sound seemed to carry better in the cold, and I felt like I could hear every clack of the rails when a train was coming, and when they let the horn off it rang that whole valley like a bell.

But inside the apartment it was mostly dead quiet. I might hear the pipes moaning now and again and that was all. If the phone rang it would make me jump. Didn't seem like there was any TV or radio next door. The only sound coming out of there was Susan getting beat up once in a while. That was her name, a sweet name, I think. I found it out from hearing him say it, which he used to do almost every time before he started in on her. "Susan," he'd call out, loud enough I could just hear him through the wall. He'd do it a time or two, he might have been calling her to him, I don't

know. After that would come a bad silence that reminded you of a snake being somewhere around. Then a few minutes' worth of hitting sounds and then the big slam as
she hit the wall and the clatter of my pots falling down on the floor. He'd throw her
at the wall maybe once or twice, usually when he was about to get through. By the
time the pots had quit spinning on the floor it would be real quiet over there again,
and the next time I saw Susan she'd be walking in that ginger way people have when
they're hiding a hurt, and if I said hello to her she'd give a little jump and look away.

After a while I quit paying it much mind, it didn't feel any different to me than
hearing the news. All their carrying on was not any more than one wall of the rut I
had worked myself into, going back and forth from the job, cleaning that apartment
till it hurt, calling up the lawyer about once a week to find out about the next post-
ponement. I made a lot of those calls from the TOA, and Tim and Prissy got pretty
interested in the whole business. I would tell them all about it, too. Sometimes, when
our shift was done, Prissy and I would pour coffee and sit in a booth for as much as a
couple of hours, just chewing that subject over and over, with Tim passing by now
and again to chip in his opinion of what was going to happen. But nothing much ever
did happen, and after a while I got to where I didn't want to discuss it anymore. I kept
ahead making those calls but every one of them just wore down my hope a little
more, like a drip of water wearing down a stone. And little by little I got in the habit
of thinking that nothing really was going to change.

It was spring already by the time things finally did begin to move. That sad little
apple tree was beginning to try and put out some leaves, and the weather was getting
warmer every day, and I was starting to feel it inside me too, the way you do. That
was when the lawyer called *me*, for a change, and told me he had some people lined
up to see me at last.

Well, I was all ready for them to come visit, come see how I'd fixed up my house
and all the rest of my business to get set for having Davey back with me again. But as
it turned out, nobody seemed to feel like they were called on to make that trip. "I
don't think that will be necessary" was what one of them said, I don't recall which.
They both talked about the same, in voices that sounded like filling out forms.

So all I had to do was drive downtown a couple of times and see them in their
offices. The child psychologist was the first and I doubt he kept me more than half an
hour. I couldn't even tell the point of most of the questions he asked. My second trip
I saw the social worker, who turned out to be a black lady once I got down there,
though I never could have told it over the phone. Her voice sounded like it was coming out of the TV. She looked me in the eye while she was asking her questions, but I
couldn't make out a thing about what she thought. It wasn't till afterward, when I
was back in the apartment, that I understood she must have already had her mind
made up.

That came to me in a sort of flash, while I was standing in the kitchen washing out
a cup. Soon as I walked back in the door I'd seen my coffee mug left over from breakfast, and kicked myself for letting it sit out. I was giving it a hard scrub with a scouring pad when I realized it didn't matter anymore. I might just as well have dropped
it on the floor and got what kick I could out of watching it smash, because it wasn't

going to make any difference to anybody now. But all the same I rinsed it and set it in the drainer, careful as if it might have been an eggshell. Then I stepped backward out of the kitchen and took a long look around that cold shabby place and thought it might be for the best that nobody was coming. How could I have expected it to fool anybody else when it wasn't even good enough to fool me? A lonesomeness came over me, I felt like I was floating all alone in the middle of the cold air, and then I began to remember some things I would just as soon have not.

No, I never did like to think about this part, but I have had to think about it time and again, with never a break for a long, long time, because I needed to get to understand it at least well enough to believe it never would ever happen anymore. And I had come to believe that, in the end. If I hadn't I never would have come back at all. I had found a way to trust myself again, though it took me a full two years to do it, and though of course it still didn't mean that anybody else would trust me.

What had happened was that Patrick went off on one of his mystery trips and stayed gone a deal longer than usual. Two nights away, I was used to that, but on the third I did start to wonder. He normally would have called, at least, if he meant to be gone that long of a stretch. But I didn't hear a peep until about halfway through the fourth day. And it wasn't Patrick himself that called, but one of those public assistance lawyers from downtown.

Seemed like the night before Patrick had got himself stopped on the interstate loop down there. The troopers said he was driving like a blind man, and he was messed up on whiskey and ludes I suppose he must have been pretty near blind. Well, maybe he would have just lost his license or something like that, only that the back seat of the car was loaded up with all he had lately stole out of the hospital.

So it was bad. It was so bad my mind just could not contain it, and every hour it seemed to get worse. I spent the next couple of days running back and forth between the jail and that lawyer, and I had to haul Davey along with me wherever I went. He was too little for school and I couldn't find anybody to take him right then, though all that running around made him awful cranky. Patrick was just grim, he would barely speak. He already knew for pretty well sure he'd be going to prison. The lawyer had told him there wasn't no use in getting a bondsman, he might just as well sit in there and start pulling his time. I don't know how much he really saved himself that way, though, since what they ended up giving him was twenty-five years.

That was when all my troubles found me, quick. The second day after Patrick got arrested, I came down real sick with something. I thought at first it was a bad cold or the flu. My nose kept running and I felt so wore out I couldn't hardly get up off the bed and yet at the same time I felt real restless, like all my nerves had been scraped raw. Well, I didn't really connect it up to the fact that I'd popped the last pill in the house about two days before. What was really the matter was me coming off that Dilaudid, but I didn't have any notion of that at the time.

I was laying there in the bed not able to get up, and about ready to jump right out of my skin at the same time, when Davey got the drawer underneath the stove open. Of course he was getting restless himself with everything that had been going on, and me not able to pay him much attention. All our pots and pans were down in that drawer then, and he began to take them out one at a time and throw them on the floor. It made a hell of a racket, and the shape I was in I started feeling like he must be doing it on purpose, to devil me. I called out to him and asked him to quit. Nice at first: "You stop that now, Davey. Momma don't feel good." But he kept right ahead. All he wanted was a little noticing, I know, but my mind wasn't working like it should. I knew I should get up and just go lead him away from there, but I couldn't seem to get myself to move. I had a picture of myself doing what I ought to do, but I just wasn't doing it. I was still laying there calling for him to quit and he was still banging those pots around, and before long I was screaming at him outright, and starting to cry at the same time. But he never stopped a minute. I guess I had scared him some already and he was just locked into doing it, or maybe he wanted to drown me out. Every time he flung a pot it felt like I was getting shot at. And the next thing I knew, I had got myself in the kitchen somehow and was snatching him up off the floor.

To this day I don't remember doing it, though I have tried and tried. I thought if I could call it back, then maybe I could root it out of myself and be rid of it for good. But all I ever knew was, one minute I was grabbing hold of him and the next he was laying on the far side of the room with his right leg folded up funny where it was broke, not even crying, just looking surprised. And I knew it had to be me that threw him over there because sure as hell is real, there was nobody else around that could have done it.

I drove him to the hospital myself. I laid him out straight on the front seat beside me and drove with one hand all the way so I could hold on to him with the other. He was real quiet and real brave the whole time, never cried the least bit, just kept a tight hold of my hand with his. I was crying a river myself, couldn't hardly see the road. It's a wonder we didn't crash, I suppose. Well, we got there and they ran him off somewhere to get his leg set and pretty soon this doctor came back out and asked me how it had happened.

It was the same hospital where Patrick had worked and I even knew that doctor a little bit. Not that being connected to Patrick would have done me a whole lot of good around there at that time. Still, I've often thought since that things might have come out better for me and Davey if I only could have lied to that man, but I was not up to telling a lie that anybody would be apt to believe. All I could do was start to scream and jabber like a crazy person, and it ended up I stayed in that hospital a good few days myself. They took me for a junkie and I guess I really was one too, though that was the first time I'd known it. And I never saw Davey again for a whole two years, not till the first time they let me go out to the Bakers'.

Sometimes you don't get but one mistake, if the one you pick is bad enough. Do as much as step in the road the wrong time without looking, and your life could be over with then and there. But during those two years I taught myself to believe that this mistake of mine could be wiped out, that if I struggled hard enough with myself and the world I could make it like it never had been.

Three weeks went by after I went to see that social worker, and I didn't have any idea what was happening, or if anything was. Didn't call anybody, I expect I was afraid to. Then one day the phone rang for me out there at the TOA. It was that lawyer and I could tell right off from the sound of his voice that I wasn't going to care for his news. Well, he told me all the evaluations had come in now, sure enough, and they weren't running in our favor. They weren't against *me*—he made sure to say that—it was more like they were *for* the Bakers. And his judgment was, it wouldn't pay me anything if we went on to court. It looked like the Bakers would get Davey for good, and they were likely to be easier about visitation if there wasn't any big tussle. But if I drug them into court, then we would have to start going back over that whole case history—

That was the word he used, *case history*, and it was around about there that I hung up. I went walking stiff-legged back across to the counter and just let myself sort of drop on a stool. Prissy had been covering the counter while I was on the phone and she came right over to me then.

"What is it?" she said. I guess she could tell it was something by the look on my face.

"I lost him," I said.

"Oh, hon, you know I'm so sorry," she said. She reached out for my hand but I snatched it back. I know she meant well but I was just not in the mood to be touched.

"There's no forgiveness," I said. I felt bitter about it. It had been a hard road for me to come as near forgiving myself as ever I could. And Davey forgave me, I really knew that, I could tell it in the way he behaved when we were together. And if us two could do it, I didn't feel like it ought to be anybody's business but ours. Tim walked up then and Prissy whispered something to him, and then he took a step nearer to me.

"I'm sorry" he told me.

"Not like I am," I said.

"Go ahead and take off the rest of your shift if you feel like it," he said. "I'll wait on these tables myself, need be."

"I don't know it would make any difference," I said.

"Better take it easy on yourself," he said. "No use in taking it so hard. You're just going to have to get used to it."

"Is that a fact," I said. And I lit myself a cigarette and turned my face away. We had been pretty busy, it was lunchtime, and the people were getting restless seeing us all bunched up there and not doing a whole lot about bringing them their food. Somebody called out something to Tim, I didn't hear too well what it was, but it set off one of his temper fits.

"Go on and get out of here if that's how you feel," he said. "You think you're the most important thing to us in here? Well, you're wrong." He was getting red in the face and waving his arms at the whole restaurant, including them all in what he was saying. "Go on and clear out of here, every last one of you, and we don't care if you never come back. We don't need your kind in here and never did. There's not a one of you couldn't stand to miss a meal anyhow. Take a look at yourselves, you're all fat as hogs. . . ."

And he kept on, looked like he meant to go for the record. He had already said I could leave, so I hung up my apron and got my purse and I left. It was the first time he ever blew up at the customers that way, it had always been me or Prissy or one of the cooks. I never did find out what came of it all because I never went back to that place again.

I drove home in a poison mood. The brakes on the car were so bad by that I time I had to pump like crazy to get the thing stopped, but I didn't really care all that much if I got killed or not. I kept thinking about what Tim had said about having to get used to it. It came to me that I was used to it already, I hadn't really been all that surprised. That's what I'd really been doing all those months, just gradually getting used to losing my child forever.

When I got back to the apartment I just fell in a chair and sat there staring across at the kitchen wall. It was in my mind to pack my traps and leave that place, but I hadn't yet figured out what place I would go to. I sat there a good while, I guess. The door was ajar from me not paying attention, it wasn't cold enough out to make any difference. If I turned my head that way I could see a slice of the parking lot. I saw Susan drive up and come limping toward the building with an armload of groceries. Because of the angle I couldn't see her go into their apartment but I heard the door open and shut, and after that it was quiet as the tomb. I kept on sitting there thinking about how used to everything I had got. There must have been God's plenty of other people too, I thought, who had got themselves accustomed to all kinds of things. Some were used to taking the pain and the rest were used to serving it up. About half the world was screaming in misery, and it wasn't anything but a habit.

When I started to hear the hitting sounds come through the wall, a smile came on my face like it was cut there with a knife. I'd been expecting it, you see, and the mood I was in I felt satisfied to see what I expected was going to happen. So I listened a little more carefully than I'd been inclined to do before. It was *hit hit hit* going along together with a groan and a hiss of the wind being knocked out of her. I had to strain pretty hard to hear that breathing part, and I could hear him grunt, too, when he got in a good one. There was about three minutes of that with some little breaks, and then a longer pause. When she hit that wall it was the hardest she had yet, I think. It brought all my pots down at one time, including that big iron skillet that was the only one I ever used.

It was the first time they'd ever managed to knock that skillet down, and I was so impressed I went over and stood looking down at it like I needed to make sure it was a real thing. I stared at that skillet so long it went out of focus and started looking more like a big black hole in the floor. That's when it dawned on me that this was one thing I didn't really have to keep on being used to.

It took three or four knocks before he came to the door, but that didn't worry me at all. I had faith, 1 knew he was going to come. I meant to stay right there until he did. When he came, he opened the door wide and stood there with his arms folded and his face all stiff with his secrets. It was fairly dark behind him, they had all the curtains drawn. I had that skillet held out in front of me in both my hands, like maybe I had come over to borrow a little hot grease or something. It was so heavy it kept wanting to dip down toward the floor like a water witch's rod. When I saw he wasn't expecting anything, I twisted the skillet back over my shoulder like baseball players do their bats, and I hit him bang across the face as hard as I knew how. He went down and out at the same time and fetched up on his back clear in the middle of the room. Then I went in after him, with the skillet cocked and ready in case he made to get up. But he didn't look like there was a whole lot of fight left in him right then. He was awake, at least partly awake, but his nose was just spouting blood and it seemed like I'd knocked out a few of his teeth. I wish I could tell you I was sorry or glad, but I didn't feel much of anything, really, just that high lonesome whistle in the blood I used to get when I took that Dilaudid. Susan was sitting on the floor against the wall, leaning down on her knees and sniveling. Her eyes were red but she didn't have any bruises where they showed. He never did hit her on the face, that was the kind he was. There was a big crack coming down the wall behind her and I remember thinking it probably wouldn't be too much longer before it worked through to my side.

"I'm going to pack and drive over to Norfolk," I told her. I hadn't thought of it till I spoke but just then it came to me as the thing I would do. "You can ride along with me if you want to. With your looks you could make enough money serving drinks to the sailors to buy that Quik-Sak and blow it up."

She didn't say anything, just raised her head up and stared at me kind of bug-eyed. And after a minute I turned around and went out. It didn't take me any time at all to get ready. All I had was two boxes of kitchen stuff and a suitcase and another box of clothes. The sheets and blankets I just yanked off the bed and stuffed in the trunk in one big wad. I didn't care a damn about that furniture, I would have lit it on fire for a dare.

When I was done I stuck my head back into the other apartment. The door was still open like I had left it. What was she doing but kneeling down over that son of a bitch and trying to clean his face off with a washrag. I noticed he was making a funny sound when he breathed, and his nose was still bleeding pretty quick, so I thought maybe I had broke it. Well, I can't say that worried me much.

"Come on now if you're coming, girl," I said.

She looked up at me, not telling me one word, just giving me a stare out of those big cow eyes of hers like I was the one had been beating on her that whole winter through. And I saw then that they were both stuck in their groove and that she would not be the one to step out of it. So I pulled back out of the doorway and went on down the steps to my car.

I was speeding down the road to Norfolk, doing seventy, seventy-five. I'd have liked to go faster if the car had been up to it. It didn't matter to me that I didn't have any brakes. Anybody wanted to keep out of a wreck had better just keep the hell out of my way. I can't say I felt sorry for busting that guy, though I didn't enjoy the thought of it either. I just didn't know what difference it had made, and chances were it had made none at all. Kind of a funny thing, when you thought about it that way. It was the second time in my life I'd hurt somebody bad, and the other time I hadn't meant to do it at all. This time I'd known what I was doing for sure, but I still didn't know what I'd done.

Reading as a Writer

1. How does this story open? What's the sense of imbalance that keeps you reading?

2. How does Bell sustain suspense throughout the piece?

3. What are some of the conflicts in the story? Were they resolved? If so, how?

MARY YUKARI WATERS

Aftermath

IN IMAMIYA PARK the boys are playing dodge-ball, a new American game. Their voices float indistinctly on the soft summer evening. Behind them tall poplars rise up through the low-lying dusk, intercepting the last of the sun's rays, which dazzle the leaves with white and gold.

Makiko can hardly believe her son, Toshi, belongs with these older boys. Seven years old! Once his growth had seemed commensurate with the passage of time. These last few years, however, with the war and surrender, the changes have come too fast, skimming her consciousness like skipped pebbles over water.

Makiko is grateful the war is over. But she cannot ignore a niggling sense that Japan's surrender has spawned a new threat more subtle, more diffuse. She can barely articulate it, even to herself; feels unmoored, buffeted among invisible forces that surge up all around her. Her son's thin body, as if caught up in these energies, is rapidly lengthening. Look! Within that circle in the dirt he is dodging, he is feinting; his body twists with an unfamiliar grace, foreshadowing that of a young man.

Toshi's growth is abetted by a new lunch program at school, subsidized by the American government, which has switched, with dizzying speed, from enemy to ally. Each day now, her son comes home with alien food in his stomach: bread, cheese, bottled milk. Last week, in the pocket of his shorts, Makiko found a cube of condensed peanut butter (an American dessert, Toshi explained) that he had meant to save for later. It was coated with lint from his pocket, which he brushed off, ignoring her plea to "get rid of that filthy thing."

Each day now, Toshi comes home with questions she cannot answer: Who was Magellan? How do you say "my name is Toshi" in English? How do you play baseball?

Makiko shows him the ball games her own mother taught her. She bounces an imaginary ball, chanting a ditty passed down from the Edo Period:

> *yellow topknots*
> *of the Portuguese wives*
>
> *spiraled like seashells*
> *and stuck atop their heads*
>
> *hold one up, to your ear*
> *shake it up and down*
>
> *one little shrunken brain*
> *is rattling inside*

In the old days, she tells him, they used to put something inside the rubber balls—maybe a scrap of iron, she wasn't sure—that made a rattling noise. Toshi, too old now for this sort of amusement, sighs with impatience.

Just four years ago, Toshi's head had been too big for his body—endearingly out of proportion, like the head of a stuffed animal. Even then he had a manly, square-jawed face, not unlike that of a certain city council candidate displayed on election posters at the time. "Mr. Magistrate," her husband, Yoshitsune, nicknamed the boy. Before he went off to war, Yoshitsune and their son had developed a little routine. "Oyi, Toshi! Are you a man?" Yoshitsune would prompt in his droll tone, using the word *otoko*, with its connotations of male bravery, strength, and honor. He asked this question several times a day, often before neighbors and friends.

"Hai, Father! I am a man!" little Toshi would cry, stiffening at soldierly attention as he had been coached, trembling with eagerness to please. His short legs, splayed out from the knees as if buckling under the weight of his head, were still dimpled with baby fat.

"Maaa! An excellent, manly answer!" the grown-ups praised, through peals of laughter.

Makiko had laughed too, a faint constriction in her throat, for recently Yoshitsune had remarked to her, "When I'm out fighting in the Pacific, that's how I'm going to remember him." After that she began watching their child closely, trying to memorize what Yoshitsune was memorizing. Later, when her husband was gone, it comforted her to think that the same images swam into both their minds at night. Even today, Toshi's three-year-old figure is vivid in her mind. On the other hand, she has not fully absorbed the war years, still shrinks from those memories and all that has followed.

Foreigners, for instance, are now a familiar sight. American Army jeeps with beefy red arms dangling out the windows roar down Kagane Boulevard, the main thoroughfare just east of Toshi's school. "Keep your young women indoors," the neighbors say. Makiko has watched an occasional soldier offering chocolates or peanuts to little children, squatting down to their level, holding out the treat—it seems to her they all have hairy arms—as if to a timid cat. Just yesterday Toshi came home, smiling broadly and carrying chocolates—not one square but three. Bile had surged up in Makiko's throat, and before she knew it, she had struck them right out of his hand and onto the kitchen floor. "How could you!" she choked as Toshi, stunned, burst into sobs. "How could you?! Your father, those men killed your *father*!"

This evening Makiko has come to the park with a small box of caramels, bought on the black market with some of the money she was hoarding to buy winter yarn. "In the future," she will tell him, "if you want something so badly, you come to me. Ne? Not to them."

On a bench in the toddlers' section, now deserted, she waits for her son to finish his game with the other boys. All the other mothers have gone home to cook dinner. The playground equipment has not been maintained since the beginning of the war. The swing set is peeling with rust; the free-standing animals—the ram, the pig, the rooster—rest on broken-down springs, and their carnival paint has washed away, exposing more rusted steel.

Ara maaa! Her Toshi has finally been hit! Makiko feels a mother's pang. He is crossing the line to the other side now, carrying the ball. Makiko notes the ease with which the fallen one seems to switch roles in this game, heaving the ball at his former teammates without the slightest trace of allegiance.

This year, Makiko is allowing Toshi to light the incense each evening before the family altar. He seems to enjoy prayer time much more now that he can use matches. She also regularly changes which photograph of her husband is displayed beside the miniature gong. This month's photograph shows Yoshitsune in a long cotton *yukata*,[1] smoking under the ginkgo tree in the garden. Sometimes, in place of a photograph, she displays an old letter or one of his silk scent bags, still fragrant after a bit of massaging. The trick is to keep Toshi interested, to present his father in the light of constant renewal.

"Just talk to him inside your mind," she tells her son. "He wants to know what you're learning in school, what games you're playing. Just like any other father, ne? Don't leave him behind, don't ignore him, just because he's dead." She wonders if Toshi secretly considers his father a burden, making demands from the altar, like a cripple from a wheelchair.

"Your father's very handsome in this picture, ne?" she says tonight. Within the lacquered frame, her son's father glances up from lighting a cigarette, a bemused half smile on his face, as if he is waiting to make a wry comment.

Toshi nods absently. Frowning, he slashes at the matchbox with the expert flourish of a second-grade boy. The match rips into flames.

"Answer properly! You're not a little baby anymore."

"Hai, Mother." Toshi sighs with a weary, accommodating air, squaring his shoulders in a semblance of respectful attention. Makiko remembers with sorrow the big head, the splayed legs of her baby boy.

It amazes her that Toshi has no memory of the routine he once performed with his father. "What *do* you remember of him?" she prods every so often, hoping to dislodge some new memory. But all that Toshi remembers of his father is being carried on one arm before a sunny window.

"Maaa, what a wonderful memory!" Makiko encourages him each time. "It must have been a very happy moment!"

When would this have taken place: which year, which month? Would even Yoshitsune have remembered it, this throw-away moment that, inexplicably, has outlasted all the others in their son's mind? She tries conjuring it up, as if the memory is her own. For some reason she imagines autumn, the season Yoshitsune sailed away: October 1942. How the afternoon sun would seep in through the nursery window, golden, almost amber, advancing with the slow, viscous quality of Tendai honey, overtaking sluggish dust motes and even sound. She wishes Toshi could remember the old view from that upstairs window: a sea of gray-tiled roofs drowsing in the autumn haze, as yet unravaged by the fires of war.

1. Japanese summer garment.

"I'm done," Toshi says.

"What! Already? Are you sure?"

"Hai, Mother." Already heading for the dining room, where supper lies waiting on the low table, he slides back the shoji door in such a hurry that it grates on its grooves. Makiko considers calling him back—his prayers are getting shorter and shorter—but the incident with the chocolates is still too recent for another reprimand.

She follows him into the dining room. "A man who forgets his past," she quotes as she scoops rice into his bowl, "stays at the level of an animal." Toshi meets her eyes with a guilty, resentful glance. "Go on," she says blandly, "eat it while it's hot."

Toshi falls to. In order to supplement their meager rice ration, Makiko continues to mix in chopped *kabura* radishes—which at least resemble rice in color—as she did during the war. Sometimes she switches to chopped turnips. At first, before the rationing became strict, Toshi would hunch over his rice bowl with his chopsticks, fastidiously picking out one bit of vegetable after another and discarding it onto another plate. Now, he eats with gusto. It cuts her, the things he has grown used to. As a grown man he will reminisce over all the wrong things, things that should never have been a part of his childhood: this shameful pauper food; blocks of peanut paste covered with lint; enemy soldiers amusing themselves by tossing chocolate and peanuts to children.

Later, Toshi ventures a question. Makiko has noticed that nighttime—the black emptiness outside, the hovering silence—still cows him a little, stripping him of his daytime cockiness. After his goodnight bow, Toshi remains kneeling in bowing position on the tatami floor. He says, "I was thinking, Mama, about how I'm seven—and how I only remember things that happened after I was three. So that means I've forgotten a whole half of my life. Right?"

"That's right," Makiko says. He is looking up at her, his brows puckered in a look of doleful concentration that reminds her of his younger days. "But it's perfectly normal, Toshi-kun. It's to be expected."

He is still thinking. "So when I get older," he says, "am I going to keep on forgetting? Am I going to forget you, too?"

Makiko reaches out and strokes his prickly crew cut. "From this age on," she says, "you're going to remember everything, Toshi-kun. Nothing more will ever be lost."

In the middle of the night, Makiko awakes from a dream in which her husband, Yoshitsune, is hitting her with a fly-swatter. She lies paralyzed under her futon, outrage buzzing in her chest. Details from the dream wash back into her mind: Yoshitsune's smile, distant and amused; the insolent way he wielded the swatter, as if she were hardly worth the effort.

A blue sheet of moonlight slips in through the space between two sliding panels.

In the first year or two after Yoshitsune's death, this sort of thing would happen often, and not always in the form of dreams. There were times—but hardly ever anymore; why tonight?—when, in the middle of washing the dishes or sweeping the alley, some small injustice from her past, long forgotten, would rise up in Makiko's mind, blotting out all else till her heart beat hard and fast. Like that time, scarcely a month after their wedding, when Yoshitsune had run into his old girlfriend at Nanjin Station and made such a fuss: his absurd, rapt gaze; the intimate timbre of his voice as he inquired after her welfare.

And there was the time—the only time in their entire marriage—when Yoshitsune had grabbed Makiko by the shoulders and shaken her hard. He'd let go immediately, but not before she felt the anger in his powerful hands and her throat had choked up with fear. That, too, was early on in the marriage, before Makiko learned to tolerate his sending sizable sums of money home to his mother each month.

What is to be done with such memories?

They get scattered, left behind. Over these past few years, more pleasant recollections have taken the lead, informing all the rest, like a flock of birds, heading as one body along an altered course of nostalgia.

She has tried so hard to remain true to the past. But the weight of her need must have been too great: her need to be comforted, her need to provide a legacy for a small, fatherless boy. Tonight she senses how far beneath the surface her own past has sunk, its outline distorted by deceptively clear waters.

Toshi has been counting the days till Tanabata Day. A small festival is being held at the riverbank—the first one since the war. It will be a meager affair, of course nothing like it used to be: no goldfish scooping, no soba noodles, no fancy fireworks. However, according to the housewives at the open-air market, there will be a limited number of sparklers (the nicest kind anyway, Makiko tells her son) and traditional corn grilled with soy sauce, which can be purchased out of each family's ration allowance.

Because of a recent after-dark incident near Kubota Temple involving an American soldier and a young girl, Makiko's younger brother has come by this evening to accompany them to the festival. Noboru is a second-year student at the local university.

"Ne, Big Sister! Are you ready yet?" he keeps calling from the living room. Makiko is inspecting Toshi's nails and the back of his collar.

"Big Sister," Noboru says, looking up as Makiko finally appears in the doorway, "your house is too immaculate, I get nervous every time I come here!" He is sitting stiffly on a floor cushion, sipping homemade persimmon tea.

"Well," Makiko answers, "I hate filth." She tugs down her knee-length dress. She has switched, like most women, to Western dresses—they require less fabric—but it makes her irritable, having to expose her bare calves in public.

"Aaa," says young Noboru from his floor cushion, "but I, for one, am fascinated by it. The idea of it, I mean. What's that old saying—'Nothing grows in a sterile pond'? Just think, Big Sister, of the things that come out of filth. A lotus, for example. Or a pearl. Just think: a pearl's nothing more than a grain of dirt covered up by oyster fluid! And life itself, Big Sister, billions of years ago—taking shape for the first time in the primordial muck!"

"Maa maa, Nobo-kun." She sighs, double-checking her handbag for coin purse, ration tickets, and handkerchief. "You seem to be learning some very interesting concepts at the university."

Toshi is waiting by the front door in shorts and a collared shirt, impatiently rolling the panel open and then shut, open and then shut.

Finally, they are on their way, strolling down the narrow alley in the still, muggy evening. The setting sun angles down on the east side of the alley, casting a pink and orange glow on the charred wooden lattices where shadows reach, like long heads of snails, from the slightest of protrusions. In the shadowed side of the alley, one of the buck-toothed Yarnada daughters ladles water from a bucket onto the asphalt around her door, pausing, with a good-evening bow, to let them pass. The water, colliding with warm asphalt, has burst into a smell of many layers: asphalt, earth, scorched wood, tangy dragon's beard moss over a mellower base of tree foliage; prayer incense and tatami straw, coming from the Yamadas' half-open door; and mixed in with it all, some scent far back from Makiko's own childhood that falls just short of definition.

"We Japanese," Noboru is saying, "must reinvent ourselves." There are, he tells her, many such discussions now at the university. "We must change to fit the modern world," he says. "We mustn't allow ourselves to remain an occupied nation." He talks of the new constitution, of the new trade agreements. Makiko has little knowledge of politics. She is amused—disquieted, too—by this academic young man, who before the war was a mere boy loping past her window with a butterfly net over his shoulder.

"Fundamental shifts . . . ," Noboru is saying, " . . . outdated pyramidal structures." Lately he has taken to wearing a hair pomade with an acrid metallic scent. It seems to suggest fervor, fundamental shifts.

"Toshi-kun!" Makiko calls. "Don't go too far." The boy stops running. He walks, taking each new step in exaggerated slow motion.

"So much change!" she says to Noboru as she tugs at her cotton dress. "And so fast. Other countries had centuries to do it in."

"Soh soh, Big Sister!" Noboru says. "Soh soh. But we have no choice, that's a fact. You jettison from a sinking ship if you want to survive."

The pair approach Mr. Watanabe, watering his potted morning glories in the twilight. Holding his watering can in one hand, the old man gives them a genteel bow over his cane. "Yoshitsune-san," he murmurs politely, "Makiko-san." He then turns back to his morning glories, bending over them with the tenderness of a mother with a newborn.

"Poor Watanabe-san, ne," Noboru whispers. "He gets more and more confused every time we see him."

Yes, poor Mr. Watanabe, Makiko thinks. Bit by bit he is being pulled back in, like a slowing planet, toward some core, some necessary center of his past. Laden with memory, his mind will never catch up to Noboru's new constitution or those new trade agreements, or even the implications of that billboard with English letters—instructions for arriving soldiers?—rising above the blackened rooftops and blocking his view of the Tendai hills.

Oddly, Mr. Watanabe's mistake has triggered a memory from the past: Makiko is strolling with her husband this summer evening. For one heartbeat she experiences exactly how things used to be—that feel of commonplace existence, before later events imposed their nostalgia—with a stab of physical recognition, impossible to call up again. Then it is gone, like the gleam of a fish, having stirred up all the waters around her.

They walk on in silence. "Toshi-kun!" she calls out again. "Slow down." Toshi pauses, waiting for them; he swings at the air with an imaginary bat. "Striku! Striku!" he hisses.

It occurs to Makiko that this war has suspended them for too long in an artificial, unsustainable state of solidarity. For a while, everyone had clung together in the bomb shelter off Nijiya Street, thinking the same thoughts, breathing in the same damp earth and the same warm, uneasy currents made by bodies at close range. But that is over now.

Makiko thinks of her future. She is not so old. She is still full of life and momentum. There is no doubt that she will pass through this period and on into whatever lies beyond it, but at a gradually slowing pace; a part of her, she knows, will lag behind in the honeyed light of prewar years.

"Toshi-kun!" she cries. "Wait!" Her son is racing ahead, his long shadow sweeping the sunlit fence as sparrows flutter up from charred palings.

At her first glimpse of the festival, Makiko's stomach sinks. Although she has come to this festival for Toshi's sake only—she herself having no interest in children's festivals, not having attended a Tanabata Night fair since her own teenage years—she is nonetheless taken unawares by the difference between the bright, colorful booths of her childhood and what now stands before her: four poles in the earth, supporting a crude black canopy made from some kind of industrial tarpaulin. A few tattered red paper lanterns, probably dug out from someone's attic, hang forlornly from the corners. Under this cover, corn is roasting on makeshift grills made from oil barrels split lengthwise. It puts Makiko in mind of a refugee tent, the kind she associates with undeveloped countries somewhere in Southeast Asia, where natives and stray dogs alike mill about waiting to be fed. The shock of this impression, coming as it does at this unguarded moment, awakens anew the shame of defeat.

"Ohhh-i!" Toshi yells out to one of his friends, and almost scampers off into the crowd before Makiko grabs him.

"Well," Makiko says, turning to her younger brother.

"That's the spirit!" Noboru says heartily, surveying the crowd. "Fall seven times, get up eight! Banzai! Banzai, for national rebuilding!" He proclaims this partly for Makiko's benefit and partly for that of a pretty young girl who is approaching them, no doubt a classmate of his. She has short hair with a permanent wave, like that of an American movie actress.

Standing in line with the young couple and a fidgety Toshi, Makiko wonders if the time will ever come when she can see a postwar substitute without the shadow of its former version.

But now, despite herself, she is distracted by the nearness of the corn, sizzling and crackling as the soy sauce and sugar drip into the flames. Her mouth waters. And when she finally takes her first bite, she is amazed to find it tastes exactly the way it did in her childhood, burnt outside and chewy inside. The surprise and relief of it bring tears to her eyes, and she chews vigorously to hide the sudden twisting of her features.

"This corn is so *good*, ne, Mama?" Toshi keeps saying, looking up from his rationed four centimeters of corncob. "This sure tastes *good*, ne?" The joy on his face, caught in the red glow of paper lanterns, is like a tableau.

"Yes, it's good," she says with pride, as if this is her own creation, her own legacy that she is handing down. "We ate food like this when your father was alive." she watches her son gnawing off the last of the kernels, sucking out the soy sauce from the cob. She hands him her own ration, from which she has taken but one bite.

"What a greedy piglet," Noboru teases, pretending to box his nephew's ears. Then he turns serious, remembering the girl beside him with the permanent wave. He is impressing her with his knowledge of astronomy. "Do you know which stars represent the separated lovers in that Tanabata legend?" he asks.

"I remember my father once pointing them out to me," the girl says. They are both gazing up at the sky, even though it is too early for stars. The girl gives a long sigh. "I've always loved that story," she says. "It's so sad and romantic, how once a year on Tanabata Night they're allowed to cross the gulf of the Milky Way, just for a few minutes, and be reunited again."

"The Western names for those stars," Noboru murmurs to her, "are Altair and Vega."

Later that night Makiko stands outside on her veranda, fanning herself with a paper *uchiwa*.[2] Toshi is already asleep. The night garden is muggy; the mosquitoes are out in full force. She can hear their ominous whine from the hydrangea bush, in between the rasping of crickets, but they no longer target her as they did in her youth. She is thinner now, her skin harder from the sun, her blood watered down from all the rationing.

What a nice festival it turned out to be. More somber than in the old days, yet with remnants of its old charm. With the coming of the dark, the tent's harsh outlines had melted away and the red lanterns seemed to glow brighter. Shadowy forms gathered at the river's edge: adults bending over their children, helping them to hold out sparklers over the glassy water. The sparklers sputtered softly in the dark, shedding white flakes of light. Makiko had watched from a distance; Toshi was old enough, he had insisted, to do it by himself. She had remarked to Noboru how there is something in everyone that responds to fireworks: so fleeting, so lovely in the dark.

Right now the stars are out, although the surrounding rooftops obscure most of the night sky except for a full moon. She had noticed the moon earlier, at dusk, opaque and insubstantial. Now, through shifting moisture in the air, it glows bright and strong, awash with light, pulsing with light.

Surely tonight's festival owed its luster to all that lay beneath, to all those other evenings of her past that emit a lingering phosphorescence through tonight's surface.

2. Traditional Japanese handicraft.

Which long-ago evenings exactly? . . . but they are slowly losing shape, dissolving within her consciousness.

Perhaps Toshi will remember this night. Perhaps it will rise up again, once he is grown, via some smell, some glint of light, bringing indefinable texture and emotion to a future summer evening. As will his memory of being carried by his father before an open window, or a time when he prayed before his father's picture.

Reading as a Writer

1. How does the story open? What about this opening made you want to keep reading?
2. What is the plot of this piece? Is it based on traditional conflict, or is there something else that drives the plot?
3. Why does Waters use present tense to tell the story? How does that impact the effect the story has on you?
4. How does the story fulfill the contract with the reader established in the opening and provide emotional satisfaction by the end of the piece?

CHAPTER TWELVE

What's This Story Really About?
True Emotions, Sensory Events

Sooner or later, we need to take a step back from our writing and ask the big question: What's the meaning of this story? Yes, it's about a boy going to visit his dying uncle; but on a deeper, emotional level, what's it really about?

In many textbooks this is called *theme,* but I thought we'd avoid using that word because (again) it has us thinking in terms of abstractions: love or beauty or death rather than the particulars of the highly specific situations we have chosen to creatively investigate. And of course, no story that is worth its weight in words can be easily paraphrased—we would never want to be able to easily sum up what a piece is about just like that. That would indicate a major problem with the piece: a lack of complexity, depth, and resonance—all the things that make a creative piece worth reading.

In this chapter we'll first review the precept that all writing must exist on two levels: in the sensory world, and in a world that embraces a complex emotional and intellectual subtext. Then we will talk about what you can do to join these two equally important aspects together. We'll try some exercises that will help us understand how to do this successfully. Finally, two readings illustrate this particular aspect of writing creatively.

Many Different Answers to the Same Question

Trying to figure out the meaning of a piece can be a difficult challenge. For example, with "Emergency" by Denis Johnson (pp. 13–21), you could correctly answer the question "What is this story about?" with any number of responses. It's a story about two men who take drugs and go for a joyride in the country. It's a story about redemption. It's a story about longing for a time that has been lost forever. It's a story about friendship. It's a story about a guy who continually messes up. And so forth.

Nothing except the text itself can give someone a full understanding of what stories like this are "about." As Flannery O'Connor says:

> Some people have the notion that you read the story and then climb out of it into the meaning, but for the fiction writer himself the whole story is the meaning, because it is an experience, not an abstraction.
>   —FLANNERY O'CONNOR, *Mystery and Manners*

Because it is an experience, it must exist in *this* world, the world of the five senses. But it must also have resonance at a deeper emotional level. Thus the dual nature of creative writing is what this chapter addresses.

Writing about What Matters

In a way, we're back to what we were talking about in Chapter 2: the need to write about what matters. If a subject doesn't resonate for us personally, if we don't find it irresistibly interesting, then the result will be utter dullness for the reader, no matter how skillfully we render things on the page.

Things to write about come from many places: images, overheard conversations, memories, stories told to you by others, and so on. Something moves you, intrigues you. There is mystery there for you, something worth exploring. That "something" should be very, very specific. Not abstract, not theoretical, not general. And that something must do three things:

1. It must resonate with true emotion *for you*.

2. It must remain active and mysterious and complex *even after* you've successfully gotten it on the page.

3. It must be rendered *with the five senses*.

As we learned in Chapter 3, when discussing literary images, and in Chapter 8, when discussing dialogue, writing always exists on two levels:

1. What happens in the world of the senses (plot, storyline, words spoken)

2. What is really going on (emotional and intellectual subtext)

Sometimes the first aspect is "given" to us. With very little or no tweaking, we can make a story work simply by writing down something that actually happened. The meaning of the events is perfectly intelligible to whoever reads it; the emotional subtext is magically tied to the events of the piece. This *does* happen.

But more frequently, that simply doesn't work. We wonder, "Why doesn't this thing that happened to me carry the emotional weight I want it to when I relate it to others? I'm telling the story just as it happened to me, yet people don't seem to 'get' it." This can happen because of a problem in marrying the surface world of the piece with the subtext: you haven't successfully *transferred* the emotional and intellectual complexity of the intended subtext onto the sensory-based objects and events themselves.

This is the opposite of abstraction. To *abstract* something is to dissociate it from a particular object. In other words, you move away from the very particular scene of a mother interacting with her truculent daughter and extrapolate "mother love." That's the reverse of what we do in writing; we are talking about the act of *associa- tion,* about the skill and talent required to associate complex meaning with sensory objects, behaviors, and events.

Transference: Borrowing from Freud

A key part of Sigmund Freud's theory of psychoanalysis had to do with the idea of *transference.* The idea is that we commonly take emotions that we are feeling about one thing and transfer them onto other things. For example, we feel angry but can't bear to acknowledge that anger. So we transfer that emotion onto other people and get the inexplicable feeling that they are mad *at us.* In the psychoanalytic relation- ship, emotions transferred in such an undeserving way onto the analyst would give clues as to what the patient was feeling inside.

This is exactly what we do in writing. We take emotional meaning and *transfer* it onto people, places, or things. Thus with Little Red Riding Hood, a walk through the woods becomes much more than just a simple walk through the woods—it becomes one filled with emotional as well as physical danger and the potential loss of innocence.

We use the narrative skills we've learned about in this book (description, scene, narrative, dialogue, etc.) to effect a *transformation* so that the importance and truth of the event are transferred to the page. Our goal is to render the emotional truth of the original experience.

So there are actually three steps to the writing process:

1. We **notice something** that deserves to be written about.

2. We **discover** the emotional heart of our material through writing (remember moving from "triggering" to "real" subject, from Chapter 2).

3. We **render** our material in such a way that the emotion or truth is apparent (we are transferring or attaching concrete sensory details to correspond with emotions).

In this way, we get at both what has happened (what has been observed, witnessed, reacted to), and what it "means" (the emotional subtext).

In fiction, of course, we make up things when we do this. (In nonfiction, we would stick to the facts.) But in both cases, we must accomplish the same thing: attach meaning and emotions to sensory objects.

"We Are Made of Dust"

If this sounds familiar, that's because in a way we're back to where we were at the beginning of Chapter 3: focusing on concrete details. Without the details—without remembering, as Flannery O'Connor admonished us, that "we are made of dust"— our work is theoretical, abstract, empty, and devoid of interest.

That's because you can't attach an emotion to an abstraction or an intellectual idea. It won't work. Emotions need to be attached to things of this world: things as mundane as tables and chairs and trees and flowers. Innocuous things—until we've imbued them with the power of our imagination.

What these images should (must) be: the outward manifestation of interior movement, or emotions. Not just physical objects, but truth. In the passage below we see how physical details like new linen and flowers carry emotional weight; these objects have come to mean much more than just their physical attributes:

> When he was shown to his sitting room on the eighth floor, he saw at a glance that everything was as it should be; there was but one detail in his mental picture that the place did not realize, so he rang for the bell boy and sent him down for flowers. He moved about nervously until the boy returned, putting away his new linen and fingering it delightedly as he did so. When the flowers came, he put them hastily into water, and then tumbled into a hot bath. Presently, he came out of his white bathroom, resplendent in his new silk underwear, and playing with the tassels of his red robe. The snow was whirling so fiercely outside his windows that he could scarcely see across the street; but within, the air was deliciously soft and fragrant. He put the violets and jonquils on the table beside the couch, and threw himself down with a long sigh, covering himself with a Roman blanket. He was thoroughly tired; he had been in such haste, he had stood up to such a strain, covered so much ground in the last twenty-four hours, that he wanted to think about how it had all come about. Lulled by the sound of the wind, the warm air, and the cool fragrance of the flowers, he sank into deep, drowsy retrospection.   —WILLA CATHER, "Paul's Case"

We want emotions to be forever and unalterably linked to those objects and events we choose. A key thing to remember is that popular fiction, in many cases, is all about the surface events: who marries whom, who makes money, who kills, who dies, and so on. However, I've seen much "serious" but poorly written fiction that's all emotional subtext: the writer feels so intensely and wants to cram so much *feeling* into a piece, but forgets that we are made of dust and require things of the sensory world to carry our meaning. What we want is a marriage of the two.

The Road to Universality

It's one of the contradictions of writing, this need for specificity. Especially when we want to make a difference, we want to matter, we want everyone to feel the universality of what we are saying, we don't want it just to apply to this particular situation, we don't want it to be *just* a story about a girl fly-fishing with her grandfather, but something more, something that brings meaning to others.

Here's an example in which the author renders the house where the narrator's mother grew up. Although it is unmistakably the house of the narrator's mother, and no other house, still there is universality about it; it gives us a sense that we, too, have been there and understand the emotional undertones of the place:

In this house there were many rooms. Although I have been there, although I have seen the house with my own eyes, I still don't know how many. Parts of it were closed off, or so it seemed; there were back staircases. Passages led else-where. Five children lived in it, two parents, a hired man, and a hired girl, whose name and faces kept changing. The structure of the house was hierarchi-cal, with my grandfather at the top, but its secret life—the life of pie crusts, clean sheets, the box of rags in the linen closet, the loaves in the oven—was female. The house, and all through it, the air was heavy with things that were known but not spoken. Like a hollow log, a drum, a church, it amplified, so that conversations whispered in it sixty years ago can be half-heard even today.

—MARGARET ATWOOD, "Significant Moments"

But It's the Truth!

It's very common, in a creative writing workshop, to hear the criticism that a piece is not believable. People express skepticism about coincidences, character behavior, plot twists, or other aspects of a story that has been put up for discussion. And a common response to this sort of criticism is, "But it really happened this way!"

How can things that really happened be less believable than other, made-up events?

The answer is simple: the piece has not been rendered in a way that makes it believable to readers. For example, in "Emergency" by Denis Johnson (pp. 13–21), a whole slew of events must converge for the main character to find himself in the emotional space he's in by the end of the story. There are the drugs he's consumed, of course. His sleepless state. The successful "operation" his drug-addled friend per-forms in the emergency room. Getting lost in the snowstorm. Rescuing (and then killing) the baby rabbits. His current longing—for the story is told from some point in the distant future—for this simpler, happier time in his life.

You could argue that without any of these events, or emotional preparations, the moment of reckoning for him would not be credible. Certainly it would not have the emotional weight it does.

Making Things Carry More Emotional Weight than They Logically Should

We should always keep in mind what Robert Stone said: to paraphrase, our job as writers is to push the reader out of his or her space, and occupy it ourselves.

Be very aggressive. Push. Occupy. Writing is an aggressive business. "I am going to make you feel what I want you to feel." "You may never have been lost in the woods and stalked by wolves, but by God I will make you feel as though you have had this experience." Not necessarily agree with, not necessarily enjoy, not neces-sarily understand completely, but *experience*.

Sometimes we're lucky. The surface events are so wonderful (or so awful) that they carry all the weight we need. But most of the time, we have to tinker. We have to choose. We have to edit, rearrange. Sometimes we exaggerate or lie or make things up; if we do that enough, we call it fiction.

But here's the important part: The surface events can be faked. The underlying subtext cannot. It must ring true emotionally. Of course, anyone who has survived their teens probably has enough material—emotional material, that is—to write. Loss. Love. Yearning. Loneliness. Joy. We've all felt that. "Attaching" the right surface details takes skill, ingenuity, even talent. But it's this—subtext—that is the heart of what we try to do.

Writing can fail on either, or both, levels:

- Our readers may not believe the physical events. ("That's implausible. Too much of a coincidence, or blatantly untrue; for example, I know how birds mate, and that's wrong.")

- Our readers may not be convinced by the subtext. As we said above, "But this is *true*" misses the point entirely. "But it's true, I knew a woman who just suddenly packed her bags and left her husband and five children and moved to Tibet." "It's true, there was a guy, without any warning, who killed everyone in his office." That "truth" doesn't matter if the material hasn't been rendered on the page skillfully enough to *convince*.

Here are some examples of writing in which emotional subtext has been masterfully linked to concrete details in fiction:

> I began to walk very quickly, then stopped because the light was different. A green light. I had reached the forest and you cannot mistake the forest. It is hostile. The path was overgrown but it was possible to follow it. I went on without looking at the tall trees on either side. Once I stepped over a fallen log swarming with white ants. How can one discover truth? I thought and that thought led me nowhere. No one would tell me the truth. Not my father nor Richard Mason, certainly not the girl I had married. I stood still, so sure I was being watched that I looked over my shoulder. Nothing but the trees and the green light under the trees. A track was just visible and I went on, glancing from side to side and sometimes quickly behind me. This was why I stubbed my foot on a stone and nearly fell. The stone I had tripped on was not a boulder but part of the paved road. There had been a paved road through this forest. The track led to a large clear space. Here were the ruins of a stone house and round the ruins rose trees that had grown to an incredible height. At the back of the ruins a wild orange tree covered with fruit, the leaves a dark green. A beautiful place. And calm—so calm that it seemed foolish to think or plan. What had I to think about, and how could I possibly plan?   —JEAN RHYS, *Wide Sargasso Sea*

In this novel a trip through the forest becomes much more than just a walk through a forest. It becomes something strange and exotic, an almost druglike experience that induces in the narrator a sense of rootlessness and hopelessness that is quite out of keeping with his personality.

After that, I wanted a drink, so the second work was over, I headed for the bar. But I couldn't step in the door of The Blue and The Gold. It stank. I found myself walking east again until the dirty bodega shone like a star from the corner of Avenue C just like it did that night with Punkette. I bought a beer and sat on a milk crate in the back drinking it in the store while the Puerto Rican woman on the register watched TV. I don't exactly understand Spanish, but you get used to hearing it and I could tell what was going on because the emotions were so huge. Men and women in fabulous costumes were fretting, threatening, falling passionately in and out of love. The characters yelled and screamed and cried and danced around. They felt everything very deeply. American TV actors just stare at each other and move their mouths. Sitting there watching those people on Channel 47 let it all out, I learned something very personal. I learned that sometimes a person's real feelings are so painful they have to pretend just to get by.

In the back of the store they had three shelves filled with devotional candles covered with drawings of the saints. I bought one for Santa Barbara and lit it right there. The woman didn't blink. People probably made novenas on the spot every day, next to the cans of Goya beans. On the back of the candle was written *O Dios! Aparta de mi lado esos malvados.* Oh God! Keep the wicked away from me.

I had to laugh at myself, going to all the trouble of praying and then only asking for less of something. I didn't want more of anything, not money or love or sex. I was praying to Saint Barbara simply to take some of the pain away.

—SARAH SCHULMAN, *After Delores*

On one level this passage is just about a walk to a local store and a brief glimpse of a television show. But there's also much longing and yearning infused into this piece, much sadness and loss that has been inextricably tied to the concrete sensory events in the story.

The sight of cigarettes and nitrites piled up on the glass ashtray made me want to empty it, to clean it, get it to sparkle, get it immaculate—and get a cigarette and light up. I did all that; now the ashtray is as full as it was.

It is getting dark outside; in this room it's getting late. I have cleaned the glasses by the bed, and am about to drink what is left of the tequila. I want the bottle out of the room, away from the bed. This is a small matter, I admit, but I do not like liquor bottles in bedrooms. It is not that I have rules against drinking in bed; on the contrary, I have taken many drinks to bed. But what I take is the drink—the liquor in the glass. To make another drink, I leave the bed; I put on a robe and take the glass to the bottle, in another room. Unless I have cleared some messy evenings from my mind, I can claim truthfully that taking a liquor bottle into a bedroom is something I have never done, and which I, unlike Nicholas, would be incapable of doing.   —CHRISTOPHER COE, *I Look Divine*

This passage shows how something as simple as a bottle in the bedroom can carry tremendous emotional weight. It's just a bottle, but in this passage it becomes a moral issue: the narrator would never take a bottle to the bedroom—he would take the drink, but not a bottle. The bottle has taken on more weight than it logically should, and that reveals something about this narrator, about his situation.

EXERCISES

Exercise 1: Getting an Image to Spill Its Secrets

GOAL: To illustrate the complexity of the transference we do all the time onto everyday objects.

1. Think quickly, without straining, and notice the first image that comes to mind.

2. Write down this image (it can be a moving image, hence an event rather than an object) in great detail. Don't try to explain; just get the image down on paper.

3. Write down all the emotions the image "tells" you.

The following passage was contributed by Jan Ellison:

I had just turned twenty-one, and I'd taken a taxi over to Park Lane from the boarding house in Victoria, where I'd been renting a room.

The building had a doorman. He insisted on carrying my pack up, though I hadn't wanted him to, because then I was afraid I would need to tip him. I did tip him; I pressed a pound coin into his palm and he nodded and left me alone.

The room was more an oversized hotel room than a flat. There was a bathroom, cold white tile, a heavy curtain pulled across the bathtub, gold fixtures, a glass bowl with tiny soaps wrapped in cellophane. There was a kitchenette, stainless steel appliances, gray granite counters. There were a few stiff chairs with floral printed cushions and elaborately carved wooden legs. Chairs I knew I would never sit in.

Across the far wall was a bank of drapes—gold velvet. Luxurious. Oppressive. There was a bed—enormous, with a red and gold spread that looked like a tapestry, pillows stacked against the headboard that would need to be removed before the bed could be used. Before I could sleep there—before Graham and I could lie there together. That was the point of all this—that we would lie there together in the mornings, before work began. And then when we were done we would stay together all day; he would not have to leave me as he had done the first time. He didn't like to leave me, he'd said.

I opened my backpack, put my clothes in the clean empty drawers, stacked my books and notebooks on the bedside table. I went to the window and pulled back the drapes, and there was the city beneath me, the gray buildings, the wide paved roads and the roundabouts. There was London as the last of the day's light drained from the sky and the few white billowing clouds collected it—pink, lavender, then a final flame of orange and it was almost night. I stood and watched as the lights went on, as the sky darkened. What I felt seemed so familiar it was as if I'd predicted it, as if I'd reached for it—a longing for the blue room I'd given up, a feeling that I'd stepped into someone else's life, a whole new kind of loneliness, the kind I imagined might belong to someone much older than I was then.

Emotions suggested by the image: Opulence of a distancing source. Self-doubt. Is this the right step? An optimistic beginning; guilt. Something secretive. Strength in details. Controlling little things to empower larger emotions. Out of placeness in the room. Either an adventure or a sacrifice. This is what it takes to get into this relationship.

Exercise 2: What I Lost

GOAL: To show transference at work (an object taking on more meaning than it logically should).

1. Think about a time when you lost something and were inexplicably upset about it. That is, the emotion was out of proportion to the thing lost (the lost object should not be valuable financially or emotionally, but something more mundane, so that the sense of being bereft should be a bit of a mystery).

2. Write down the story, concentrating on concrete details and immersing the reader in the experience rather than just summarizing it.

The following passage was written by Teresa Heger:

The damn key hangs in the garage on a rusted old nail. It's slyly hidden under a green plastic dustbin that is about forty years old. To get to the key you have to move about thirty ancient brooms, rakes, and hoes, push aside a hundred-foot coil of old greasy rope, and brush away layers of spiderwebs and dust and god knows what else. But when I go back home, they always insist I use that key, the spare key.

Don't lose it! Where's the key? Did you remember to put back the key? Don't go back to California with the key! When I once suggested I make a copy of the key, the idea was met with horror. What if I lost it? What if someone stole it? What if someone broke in because I *lost the key?* Looking around my parents' house, I could only think that a little theft might be a blessing to clear out some of their useless stuff that was—well—everywhere. In fact, I wondered if I should just start giving out copies of the key at garage sales and other events where junk collectors gather. But I gave in. No copy was made and I continued to fight the garage and the brooms and the dustbin and the spiders to get to the damn spare key.

And then one night—the dread event occurred. Alright. I'll admit it. I took the damn key and I had too much to drink. I went to an old high school buddy's house and we drank Pabst Blue Ribbon and watched reruns of Saturday Night Live and talked about the good old bad days and so on and so forth. So when I got home around midnight, the backfiring of the old Dodge Dart (as old as the dustbin and the key and the old brooms, etc.) must have announced my arrival to everyone in a twelve-block vicinity. But not my parents—no lights were on in the house.

   And that's when it happened. No key. No key in my pockets, my gloves, my purse, my wallet. Frantic searching in the subzero cold under the car produced nothing. No key on the car seat or under the car seat or behind the seat. No key in the ashtray. No key anywhere. I sat in the car and like a naturalized Californian I visualized that key, I imagined its steely coldness in my hand and I willed it to come to me. No luck. No key. Finally I had to pound on the door, our family dog that no longer remembers me barking furiously, and wait until my stepmother came to the door, muttering smugly—happily, really—swearing she knew that I was going to lose that damn key.

The following passage was written by Mary Petrosky:

After I'd asked him the third time if he'd seen the curved blue dish (with the delicate flowers painted on it) I'm sure the painter was convinced I was accusing him of stealing it. I unwrapped all the items I'd removed from the china cabinet before we shimmied it away from the wall—the square crystal candlesticks, the pewter and glass steins, the tiny ceramic bud vases my husband's grandmother had brought over from Germany in the 1920s, the china box with the boater from that Monet painting . . . everything was accounted for except the blue dish.

   I searched the garbage cans, the one in the kitchen, the two in the garage, pawing through paper towels sticky with gravy, cat puke, a rotting chicken carcass, the clingy green strings of cucumber peel. But there was no sign of the dish, not a fragment of its pearly sides or the azure that filled its belly.

   I asked the painter again if he had seen it. This time he wouldn't answer. He finished up in the next two days and I didn't bother to call him back when I noticed that the baseboards in the dining room were still half white.

READINGS

FREDERICK BUSCH

Ralph the Duck

I WOKE UP AT 5:25 because the dog was vomiting. I carried seventy-five pounds of heaving golden retriever to the door and poured him onto the silver, moonlit snow. "Good boy," I said because he'd done his only trick. Outside he retched, and I went back up, passing the sofa on which Fanny lay. I tiptoed with enough weight on my toes to let her know how considerate I was while she was deserting me. She blinked her eyes. I swear I heard her blink her eyes. Whenever I tell her that I hear her blink her eyes, she tells me I'm lying; but I can hear the damp slap of lash after I have made her weep.

In bed and warm again, noting the red digital numbers (5:29) and certain that I wouldn't sleep, I didn't. I read a book about men who kill each other for pay or for their honor. I forget which, and so did they. It was 5:45, the alarm would buzz at 6:00, and I would make a pot of coffee and start the wood stove; I would call Fanny and pour her coffee into her mug; I would apologize because I always did, and then she would forgive me if I hadn't been too awful—I didn't think I'd been that bad—and we would stagger through the day, exhausted but pretty sure we were all right, and we'd sleep that night, probably after sex, and then we'd awaken in the same bed to the alarm at 6:00, or the dog, if he returned to the frozen deer carcass he'd been eating in the forest on our land. He loved what made him sick. The alarm went off, I got into jeans and woolen socks and a sweatshirt, and I went downstairs to let the dog in. He'd be hungry, of course.

I was the oldest college student in America, I thought. But of course I wasn't. There were always ancient women with their parchment for skin who graduated at seventy-nine from places like Barnard and the University of Georgia. I was only forty-two, and I hardly qualified as a student. I patrolled the college at night in a Bronco with a leaky exhaust system, and I went from room to room in the classroom buildings, kicking out students who were studying or humping in chairs—they'd do it anywhere—and answering emergency calls with my little blue light winking on top of the truck. I didn't carry a gun or a billy, but I had a flashlight that took six batteries and I'd used it twice on some of my overprivileged northeastern-playboy part-time classmates. On Tuesdays and Thursdays I would awaken at 6:00 with my wife, and I'd do my home-work, and work around the house, and go to school at 11:30 to sit there for an hour and a half while thirty-five stomachs growled with hunger and boredom, and this guy gave instruction about books. Because I was on the staff, the college let me take a course for nothing every term. I was getting educated, in a kind of slow-motion way—it would have taken me something like fifteen or sixteen years to graduate, and I would no doubt get an F in gym and have to repeat—and there were times when I respected myself for it. Fanny often did, and that was fair incentive.

I am not unintelligent. *You are not an unintelligent writer,* my professor wrote on my paper about Nathaniel Hawthorne. We had to read short stories, I and the other stu-dents, and then we had to write little essays about them. I told how I saw Kafka and Hawthorne in similar light, and I was not unintelligent, he said. He ran into me at dusk one time, when I answered a call about a dead battery and found out it was him. I jumped his Buick from the Bronco's battery, and he was looking me over, I could tell, while I clamped onto the terminals and cranked it up. He was a tall, handsome guy who never wore a suit. He wore khakis and sweaters, loafers or sneaks, and he was always talking to the female students with the brightest hair and best builds. But he couldn't get a Buick going on an ice-cold night, and he didn't know enough to look for cells going bad. I told him he was going to need a new battery and he looked me over the way men sometimes do with other men who fix their cars for them.

"Vietnam?"

I said, "Too old."

"Not at the beginning. Not if you were an adviser. So-called. Or one of the Phoenix Project fellas?"

I was wearing a watch cap made of navy wool and an old Marine fatigue jacket. Slick characters like my professor like it if you're a killer or at least a onetime middleweight fighter. I smiled like I knew something. "Take it easy," I said, and I went back to the truck to swing around the cemetery at the top of the campus. They'd been known to screw in down-filled sleeping bags on horizontal stones up there, and the dean of students didn't want anybody dying of frostbite while joined at the hip to a matriculating fellow resident of our northeastern camp for the overindulged.

He blinked his high beams at me as I went. "You are not an unintelligent driver," I said.

Fanny had left me a bowl of something with sausages and sauerkraut and potatoes, and the dog hadn't eaten too much more than his fair share. He watched me eat his leftovers and then make myself a king-sized drink composed of sourmash whiskey and ice. In our back room, which is on the northern end of the house, and cold for sitting in that close to dawn, I sat and watched the texture of the sky change. It was going to snow, and I wanted to see the storm come up the valley. I woke up that way, sitting in the rocker with its loose right arm, holding a watery drink, and thinking right away of the girl I'd convinced to go back inside. She'd been standing outside her dormitory, looking up at a window that was dark in the midst of all those lighted panes—they never turned a light off, and often left the faucets run half the night—crying onto her bathrobe. She was barefoot in shoe-pacs, the brown ones so many of them wore unlaced, and for all I know she was naked under the robe. She was beautiful, I thought, and she was somebody's redheaded daughter, standing in a quadrangle how many miles from home weeping.

"He doesn't love anyone," the kid told me. "He doesn't love his wife—I mean his ex-wife. And he doesn't love the ex-wife before that, or the one before that. And you know what? He doesn't love me. I don't know anyone who *does*!"

"It isn't your fault if he isn't smart enough to love you," I said, steering her toward the truck.

She stopped. She turned. "You know him?"

I couldn't help it. I hugged her hard, and she let me, and then she stepped back, and of course I let her go. "Don't you *touch* me! Is this sexual harassment? Do you know the rules? Isn't this sexual harassment?"

"I'm sorry," I said at the door to the truck. "But I think I have to be able to give you a grade before it counts as harassment."

She got in. I told her we were driving to the dean of students' house. She smelled like marijuana and something very sweet, maybe one of those coffee-with-cream liqueurs you don't buy unless you hate to drink.

As the heat of the truck struck her, she started going kind of clay-gray-green, and I reached across her to open the window.

"You touched my breast!" she said.

"It's the smallest one I've touched all night, I'm afraid."

She leaned out the window and gave her rendition of my dog.

But in my rocker, waking up, at whatever time in the morning in my silent house, I thought of her as someone's child. Which made me think of ours, of course. I went for more ice, and I started on a wet breakfast. At the door of the dean of students' house, she'd turned her chalky face to me and asked, "What grade would you give me, then?"

*   *   *

It was a week composed of two teachers locked out of their offices late at night, a Toyota with a flat and no spare, an attempted rape on a senior girl walking home from the library, a major fight outside a fraternity house (broken wrist and significant concussion), and variations on breaking-and-entering. I was scolded by the director of nonacademic services for embracing a student who was drunk; I told him to keep his job, but he called me back because I was right to hug her, he said, and also wrong, but what the hell, and would I please stay. I thought of the fringe benefits—graduation in only sixteen years—so I went back to work.

My professor assigned a story called "A Rose for Emily," and I wrote him a paper about the mechanics of corpse fucking, and how, since she clearly couldn't screw her dead boyfriend, she was keeping his rotten body in bed because she truly loved him. I called the paper "True Love." He gave me a B and wrote *See me, pls.* In his office after class, his feet up on his desk, he trimmed a cigar with a giant folding knife he kept in his drawer.

"You got to clean the hole out," he said, "or they don't draw."

"I don't smoke," I said.

"Bad habit. Real *habit*, though. I started in smoking 'em in Georgia, in the service. My C.O. smoked 'em. We collaborated on a brothel inspection one time, and we ended up smoking these with a couple of women." He waggled his eyebrows at me, now that his malehood was established.

"Were the women smoking them too?"

He snorted laughter through his nose while the greasy smoke came curling off his thin, dry lips. "They were pretty smoky, I'll tell ya!" Then he propped his feet—he was wearing cowboy boots that day—and he sat forward. "It's a little hard to explain. But—hell. You just don't say *fuck* when you write an essay for a college prof. Okay?" Like a scoutmaster with a kid he'd caught in the outhouse jerking off: "All right? You don't wanna do that."

"Did it shock you?"

"Fuck, no, it didn't shock me. I just told you. It violates certain proprieties."

"But if I'm writing it to you, like a letter—"

"You're writing it for posterity. For some mythical reader someplace, not just me. You're making a *statement*."

"Right. My statement said how hard it must be for a woman to fuck with a corpse."

"And a point worth making. I said so. Here."

"But you said I shouldn't say it."

"No, Listen. Just because you're talking about fucking, you don't have to say *fuck*. Does that make it any clearer?"

"No."

"I wish you'd lied to me just now," he said.

I nodded. I did too.

"Where'd you do your service?" he asked.

"Baltimore. Baltimore, Maryland."

"What's in Baltimore?"

"Railroads. I liaised on freight runs of army matériel. I killed a couple of bums on the rod with my bare hands, though."

He snorted again, but I could see how disappointed he was. He'd been banking on my having been a murderer. Interesting guy in one of my classes, he must have told some terrific woman at an overpriced meal: I just *know* the guy was a rubout special-ist in the Nam, he had to have said. I figured I should come to work wearing my fatigue jacket and a red bandana tied around my head. Say "Man" to him a couple of times, hang a fist in the air for grief and solidarity, and look terribly worn, exhausted by experiences he was fairly certain that he envied me. His dungarees were ironed, I noticed.

On Saturday we went back to the campus because Fanny wanted to see a movie called *The Seven Samurai*. I fell asleep, and I'm afraid I snored. She let me sleep until the auditorium was almost empty. Then she kissed me awake. "Who was screaming in my dream?" I asked her.

"Kurosawa," she said.

"Who?"

"Ask your professor friend."

I looked around, but he wasn't there. "Not an un-weird man," I said.

We went home and cleaned up after the dog and put him out. We drank a little Spanish brandy and went upstairs and made love. I was fairly premature, you might say, but one way and another by the time we fell asleep we were glad to be there with each other, and glad that it was Sunday coming up the valley toward us, and nobody with it. The dog was howling at another dog someplace, or at the moon, or maybe just his moon-thrown shadow on the snow. I did not strangle him when I opened the back door and he limped happily past me and stumbled up the stairs. I followed him into our bedroom and groaned for just being satisfied as I got into bed. You'll notice I didn't say fuck.

He stopped me in the hall after class on a Thursday, and asked me How's it goin, just one of the kickers drinking sour beer and eating pickled eggs and watching the tube in a country bar. How's it goin. I nodded. I wanted a grade from the man, and I did want to learn about expressing myself. I nodded and made what I thought was a smile. He'd let his mustache grow out and his hair grow longer. He was starting to wear dark shirts with lighter ties. I thought he looked like someone in *The Godfather*. He still wore those light little loafers or his high-heeled cowboy boots. His corduroy pants looked baggy. I guess he wanted them to look that way. He motioned me to the wall of the hallway, and he looked and said, "How about the Baltimore stuff?"

I said, "Yeah?"

"Was that really true?" He was almost blinking, he wanted so much for me to be a damaged Vietnam vet just looking for a bell tower to climb into and start firing from. The college didn't have a bell tower you could get up into, though I'd once spent an ugly hour chasing a drunken ATO down from the roof of the observatory. "You were just clocking through boxcars in Baltimore?"

I said, "Nah."

"I thought so!" He gave a kind of sigh.

"I killed people," I said.

"You know, I could have sworn you did," he said.

I nodded, and he nodded back. I'd made him so happy.

The assignment was to write something to influence somebody. He called it Rhetoric and Persuasion. We read an essay by George Orwell and "A Modest Proposal" by Jonathan Swift. I liked the Orwell better, but I wasn't comfortable with it. He talked about "niggers," and I felt him saying it two ways.

I wrote "Ralph the Duck."

Once upon a time, there was a duck named Ralph who didn't have any feathers on either wing. So when the cold wind blew, Ralph said, Brr, and shivered and shook.

What's the matter? Ralph's mommy asked.

I'm cold, Ralph said.

Oh, the mommy said. Here. I'll keep you warm.

So she spread her big, feathery wings, and hugged Ralph tight, and when the cold wind blew, Ralph was warm and snuggly, and fell fast asleep.

The next Thursday, he was wearing canvas pants and hiking boots. He mentioned kind of casually to some of the girls in the class how whenever there was a storm he wore his Lake District walking outfit. He had a big, hairy sweater on. I kept waiting for him to make a noise like a mountain goat. But the girls seemed to like it. His boots made a creaky squeak on the linoleum of the hall when he caught up with me after class.

"As I told you," he said, "it isn't unappealing. It's just—not a college theme."

"Right," I said. "Okay. You want me to do it over?"

"No," he said. "Not at all. The D will remain your grade. But I'll read something else if you want to write it."

"This'll be fine," I said.

"Did you understand the assignment?"

"Write something to influence someone—Rhetoric and Persuasion."

We were at his office door and the redheaded kid who had gotten sick in my truck was waiting for him. She looked at me like one of us was in the wrong place, which struck me as accurate enough. He was interested in getting into his office with the redhead, but he remembered to turn around and flash me a grin he seemed to think he was known for.

Instead of going on shift a few hours after class, the way I'm supposed to, I told my supervisor I was sick, and I went home. Fanny was frightened when I came in, because I don't get sick and I don't miss work. She looked at my face and she grew sad. I kissed her hello and went upstairs to change. I always used to change my clothes when I was a kid, as soon as I came home from school. I put on jeans and a flannel shirt and thick wool socks, and I made myself a dark drink of sourmash. Fanny poured herself some wine and came into the cold northern room a few minutes later. I was sitting in the rocker, looking over the valley. The wind was lining up a lot of rows of cloud so that the sky looked like a baked trout when you lift the skin off. "It'll snow," I said to her.

She sat on the old sofa and waited. After a while, she said, "I wonder why they always call it a mackerel sky?"

"Good eating, mackerel," I said.

Fanny said, "Shit! You're never that laconic unless you feel crazy. What's wrong? Who'd you punch out at the playground?"

"We had to write a composition," I said.

"Did he like it?"

"He gave me a D."

"Well, you're familiar enough with D's. I never saw you get this low over a grade."

"I wrote about Ralph the Duck."

She said, "You did?" She said, "Honey." She came over and stood beside the rocker and leaned into me and hugged my head and neck. "Honey," she said. "Honey."

It was the worst of the winter's storms, and one of the worst in years. That afternoon they closed the college, which they almost never do. But the roads were jammed with snow over ice, and now it was freezing rain on top of that, and the only people working at the school that night were the operator who took emergency calls and me. Everyone else had gone home except the students, and most of them were inside. The ones who weren't were drunk, and I kept on sending them in and telling them to act like grown-ups. A number of them said they were, and I really couldn't argue. I had the bright beams on, the defroster set high, the little blue light winking, and a thermos of sourmash and hot coffee that I sipped from every time I had to get out of the truck or every time I realized how cold all that wetness was out there.

About eight o'clock, as the rain was turning back to snow and the cold was worse, the roads impossible, just as I was done helping a country sander on the edge of the campus pull a panel truck out of a snowbank, I got the emergency call from the college operator. We had a student missing. The roommates thought the kid was heading for the quarry. This meant I had to get the Bronco up on a narrow road above the campus, above the old cemetery, into all kinds of woods and rough track that I figured would be choked with ice and snow. Any kid up there would really have to want to be there, and I couldn't go in on foot, because you'd only want to be there on account of drugs, booze, or craziness, and either way I'd be needing blankets and heat, and then a fast ride down to the hospital in town. So I dropped into four-wheel drive to get me up the hill above the campus, bucking snow and sliding on ice, putting all the heater's warmth up onto the windshield because I couldn't see much more than swarming snow. My feet were still cold from the tow job, and it didn't seem to matter that I had on heavy socks and insulated boots I'd coated with water-proofing. I shivered, and I thought of Ralph the Duck.

I had to grind the rest of the way, from the cemetery, in four-wheel low, and in spite of the cold I was smoking my gearbox by the time I was close enough to the quarry—they really did take a lot of rocks for the campus buildings from there—to see I'd have to make my way on foot to where she was. It was a kind of scooped-out shape, maybe four or five stories high, where she stood—well, wobbled is more like it. She was as chalky as she'd been the last time, and her red hair didn't catch the light anymore. It just lay on her like something that had died on top of her head. She was in a white nightgown that was plastered to her body. She had her arms crossed as if she wanted to be warm. She swayed, kind of, in front of the big, dark, scooped-out rock face, where the trees and brush had been cleared for trucks and earthmovers. She looked tiny against all the darkness. From where I stood, I could see the snow driving down in front of the lights I'd left on, but I couldn't see it near her. All it looked like around her was dark. She was shaking with the cold, and she was crying.

I had a blanket with me, and I shoved it down the front of my coat to keep it dry for her, and because I was so cold. I waved. I stood in the lights and I waved. I don't know what she saw—a big shadow, maybe. I surely didn't reassure her, because when she saw me she backed up, until she was near the face of the quarry. She couldn't go any farther.

I called, "Hello! I brought a blanket. Are you cold? I thought you might want a blanket."

Her roommates had told the operator about pills, so I didn't bring her the coffee laced with mash. I figured I didn't have all that much time, anyway, to get her down and pumped out. The booze with whatever pills she'd taken would make her die that much faster.

I hated that word. Die. It made me furious with her. I heard myself seething when I breathed. I pulled my scarf and collar up above my mouth. I didn't want her to see how close I might come to wanting to kill her because she wanted to die.

I called, "Remember me?"

I was closer now. I could see the purple mottling of her skin. I didn't know if I was cold or dying. It probably didn't matter much to distinguish between them right now, I thought. That made me smile. I felt the smile, and I pulled the scarf down so she could look at it. She didn't seem awfully reassured.

"You're the sexual harassment guy," she said. She said it very slowly. Her lips were clumsy. It was like looking at a ventriloquist's dummy.

"I gave you an A," I said.

"When?"

"It's a joke," I said. "You don't want me making jokes. You want me to give you a nice warm blanket, though. And then you want me to take you home."

She leaned against the rock face when I approached. I pulled the blanket out then zipped my jacket back up. The snow had stopped, I realized, and that wasn't really a very good sign. It felt like an arctic cold descending in its place. I held the blanket out to her, but she only looked at it.

"You'll just have to turn me in," I said. "I'm gonna hug you again."

She screamed, "No more! I don't want any more hugs!"

But she kept her arms on her chest, and I wrapped the blanket around her and stuffed a piece into each of her tight, small fists. I didn't know what to do for her feet. Finally, I got down on my haunches in front of her. She crouched down too, protecting herself.

"No," I said. "No. You're fine."

I took off the woolen mittens I'd been wearing. Mittens keep you warmer than gloves because they trap your hand's heat around the fingers and palms at once. Fanny had knitted them for me. I put a mitten as far onto each of her feet as I could. She let me. She was going to collapse, I thought.

"Now, let's go home," I said. "Let's get you better."

With her funny, stiff lips, she said, "I've been very self-indulgent and weird and I'm sorry. But I'd really like to die." She sounded so reasonable that I found myself nodding in agreement as she spoke.

"You can't just die," I said.

"Aren't I dying already? I took all of them," and then she giggled like a child, which of course is what she was. "I borrowed different ones from other people's rooms. See, this isn't some teenage cry for like help. Understand? I'm seriously interested in death and I have to like stay out here a little longer and fall asleep. All right?"

"You can't do that," I said. "You ever hear of Vietnam?"

"I saw that movie," she said. "With the opera in it? *Apocalypse*? Whatever."

"I was there!" I said. "I killed people! I helped to kill them! And when they die, you see their bones later on. You dream about their bones and blood on the ends of the splintered ones, and this kind of mucous stuff coming out of their eyes. You probably heard of guys having dreams like that, didn't you? Whacked-out Vietnam vets? That's me, see? So I'm telling you, I know about dead people and their eyeballs and everything falling out. And people keep dreaming about the dead people they knew, see? You can't make people dream about you like that! It isn't fair!"

"You dream about me?" She was ready to go. She was ready to fall down, and I was going to lift her up and get her to the truck.

"I will," I said. "If you die."

"I want you to," she said. Her lips were hardly moving now. Her eyes were closed. "I want you all to."

I dropped my shoulder and put it into her waist and picked her up and carried her down to the Bronco. She was talking, but not a lot, and her voice leaked down my back. I jammed her into the truck and wrapped the blanket around her better and then put another one down around her feet. I strapped her in with the seat belt. She was shaking, and her eyes were closed and her mouth open. She was breathing. I checked that twice, once when I strapped her in, and then again when I strapped myself in and backed hard into a sapling and took it down. I got us into first gear, held the clutch in, leaned over to listen for breathing, heard it—shallow panting, like a kid asleep on your lap for a nap—and then I put the gear in and howled down the hillside on what I thought might be the road.

We passed the cemetery. I told her that was a good sign. She didn't respond. I found myself panting too, as if we were breathing for each other. It made me dizzy, but I couldn't stop. We passed the highest dorm, and I dropped the truck into four-wheel high. The cab smelled like burnt oil and hot metal. We were past the chapel now, and the observatory, the president's house, then the bookstore. I had the blue light winking and the V-6 roaring, and I drove on the edge of out-of-control, sensing the skids just before I slid into them, and getting back out of them as I needed to. I took a little fender off once, and a bit of the corner of a classroom building, but I worked us back on course, and all I needed to do now was negotiate the sharp left turn around the Administration Building past the library, then floor it for the straight run to the town's main street and then the hospital.

I was panting into the mike, and the operator kept saying, "Say again?"

I made myself slow down some, and I said we'd need stomach pumping, and to get the names of the pills from her friends in the dorm, and I'd be there in less than five or we were crumpled up someplace and dead.

"Roger," the radio said. "Roger all that." My throat tightened and tears came into my eyes. They were helping us, they'd told me: Roger.

I said to the girl, whose head was slumped and whose face looked too blue all through its whiteness, "You know, I had a girl once. My wife, Fanny. She and I had a small girl one time."

I reached over and touched her cheek. It was cold. The truck swerved, and I got my hands on the wheel. I'd made the turn past the Ad Building using just my left. "I can do it in the dark," I sang to no tune I'd ever learned. "I can do it with one hand." I said to her, "We had a girl child, very small. Now, I do *not* want you dying."

I came to the campus gates doing fifty on the ice and snow, smoking the engine, grinding the clutch, and I bounced off a wrought iron fence to give me the curve going left that I needed. On a pool table, it would have been a bank shot worth applause. The town cop picked me up and got out ahead of me and let the street have all the lights and noise I could want. We banged up to the emergency room entrance and I was out and at the other door before the cop on duty, Elmo St. John, could loosen his seat belt. I loosened hers, and I carried her into the lobby of the ER. They had a gurney, and doctors, and they took her away from me. I tried to talk to them, but they made me sit down and do my shaking on a dirty sofa decorated with drawings of little spinning wheels. Somebody brought me hot coffee, I think it was Elmo, but I couldn't hold it.

"They won't," he kept saying to me. "They won't."

"What?"

"You just been sitting there for a minute and a half like St. Vitus dancing, telling me, Don't let her die. Don't let her die."

"Oh."

"You all *right*?"

"How about the kid?"

"They'll tell us soon."

"She better be all right."

"That's right."

"She—somebody's gonna have to tell me plenty if she isn't."

"That's right."

"She better not die this time," I guess I said.

Fanny came downstairs to look for me. I was at the northern windows, looking through the mullions down the valley to the faint red line along the mounds and little peaks of the ridge beyond the valley. The sun was going to come up, and I was looking for it.

Fanny stood behind me. I could hear her. I could smell her hair and the sleep on her. The crimson line widened, and I squinted at it. I heard the dog limp in behind her, catching up. He panted and I knew why his panting sounded familiar. She put her hands on my shoulders and arms. I made muscles to impress her with, and then I let them go, and let my head drop down until my chin was on my chest.

"I didn't think you'd be able to sleep after that," Fanny said.

"I brought enough adrenaline home to run a football team."

"But you hate being a hero, huh? You're hiding in here because somebody's going to call, or come over, and want to talk to you—her parents for shooting sure, sooner or later. Or is that supposed to be part of the service up at the playground? Saving their suicidal daughters. Almost dying to find them in the woods and driving too fast for any weather, much less what we had last night. Getting their babies home. The bastards." She was crying. I knew she would be, sooner or later. I could hear the soft sound of her lashes. She sniffed and I could feel her arm move as she felt for the tissues on the coffee table.

"I have them over here," I said. "On the windowsill."

"Yes." She blew her nose, and the dog thumped his tail. He seemed to think it one of Fanny's finer tricks, and he had wagged for her for thirteen years whenever she'd done it. "Well, you're going to have to talk to them."

"I will," I said. "I will." The sun was in our sky now, climbing. We had built the room so we could watch it climb. "I think that jackass with the smile, my prof? She showed up a lot at his office, the last few weeks. He called her 'my advisee,' you know? The way those guys sound about what they're achieving by getting up and shaving and going to work and saying the same thing every day? Every year? Well, she was his advisee, I bet. He was shoving home the old advice."

"She'll be okay," Fanny said. "Her parents will take her home and love her up and get her some help." She began to cry again, then she stopped. She blew her nose, and the dog's tail thumped. She kept a hand between my shoulder and my neck. "So tell me what you'll tell a waiting world. How'd you talk her out?"

"Well, I didn't, really. I got up close and picked her up and carried her is all."

"You didn't say *any*thing?"

"Sure I did. Kid's standing in the snow outside of a lot of pills, you're gonna say something."

"So what'd you *say*?"

"I told her stories," I said. "I did Rhetoric and Persuasion."

Fanny said, "Then you go in early on Thursday, you go in half an hour early, and you get that guy to jack up your grade."

Reading as a Writer

1. Point out several places where emotion has been successfully transferred onto sense-based events in the story. How does Busch accomplish this?

2. What are some of the images that work to best effect to establish the mood of the piece?

3. What is this story ultimately about?

STACEY RICHTER

My Date with Satan

MY DATE WITH SATAN COMMENCED at the Sanrio store near Union Square where we went to browse through two stories of miniature Japanese school supplies and grooming accessories. Satan seemed nervous. "All the light," he said, "I don't like all the light." It's true the Sanrio store has a wide glass facade, glass doors, and a Plexiglas staircase to better illuminate the many rows of miniature Hello Kitty and Ahiru No Pekkle trinkets—endless, perfectly arranged rows of tiny colored pencils, mite-sized plastic address books, barrettes as small as aspirin—a thousand diminutive products to lodge in a thousand dinky airways. What do you think of that, Satan? What do you think of little kiddies choking on Sanrio brand Keroppi-Frog pencil erasers? Satan liked that very much and set to cackling and browsing and didn't seem so nervous once he had something evil to rest his mind on.

I voyaged deep into the Hello Kitty aisle and stared into Kitty's pert Liza Minnelli eyes as they gazed back at me from a giant cat-shaped plastic display case, the only large object in the room. Inside its belly was tier upon tier of Hello Kitty dolls, arrayed like a scientific model of parasites invading a host. The display reminded me of a documentary I'd seen about a shrine in Japan stocked with ceramic cats with their paws raised—entreating, liquid-eyed cats. Suppliants would bring offerings of tuna and pray to Buddha for mercy on the souls of their lost pets. They'd burn incense in hope of drawing their cats home safely. This struck me as wildly funny and I went up to

Satan, who was reading Sanrio product literature by the register, to tell him about the shrine in Japan for wayward cats.

Satan was laughing maniacally. "Look here." he said, thrusting a magazine at me. "There's this interview with the lady who invented all these Sanrio characters, and the guy asks her, 'To what do you attribute the success of your creation Hello Kitty?' and the lady replies, 'She has no mouth you see.'"

He threw back his head and laughed some more.

A crowd of children had started to gather around Satan and me, pointing at my hair, which I had done up in braids entwined with wire so they stuck out of my head at right angles like my namesake, Pippi Longstocking, or PipiLngstck as I am known onscreen. Also, I was wearing a pinafore over a white smock and Buster Brown shoes; these may have attracted the children as well. Satan appeared more kosher in terms of what is acceptable in San Francisco. He was wearing a black trench coat, a black silky shirt, Gap jeans, and black Reeboks—he looked dorky, to tell the truth, like a brooding loser outcast guy. His Paul McCartney bowl cut was the clincher. Still, there's nothing I love better than loser outcast guys, as I'd told Satan when I first met him in LE CHATEAU, brooding in the corner, trying to get someone to notice him.

"You're exactly the kind of guy I would have had a crush on in high school," I said. He threw bits of chalk at me for the next twenty minutes. Not actually throwing, as we were communicating in a computer chat room, LE CHATEAU, the SM meeting place, but rather, periodically typing in the phrase: *"Lobbing another piece of chalk at PipiLngstck's head."* And I'd type back, *"Ouch, Satan, that hurts. You're a very bad boy!"* Then Satan would throw a notebook at me. So I'd say, *"Satan, do you have to be taken outside and spanked?"* And Satan would type back, *"Oh, I love you, PipiLngstck."* I'd say, *"I don't want LOVE from such a nasty boy. I want OBEDIENCE!!!"*

Then he'd ignore me for a while while other people in LE CHATEAU, Domin8U, sub-Boy, or LaraLee tried to pick me up. *"Are you brooding, Satan?"* I'd ask. Satan would make weak excuses for his behavior, saying stuff like, *"Forgive me, dove, it's the solitude, the incessant solitude, that has made me this way."* Occasionally he'd lapse into stilted, romantic-medieval blather: *"PipiLngstck, I see you bearing down upon me in a flowing robe, thighs flashing; a dagger in your hand. You strike for my neck and leave me tattered, bleeding, devastated."*

"You're not one of those geeks who likes Renaissance fairs, are you, Stan?" (If you want to get Satan really mad, call him Stan.)

"A geek for love."

Then I shoved Satan into a private room, where no one else on the system could see what we typed, and told him exactly what I was doing to him, blow by blow.

*   *   *

I was hoping for something wholesome on my date with Satan; maybe not exactly wholesome, but I was wearing a stiff, white Playtex bra like somebody's second-grade teacher might wear and I wanted to bring Satan to the Sanrio store so we could look at all the miniature products in their ingenious packaging arranged so perfectly and orderly on the shelf, all the edges lining up. All of it was so cute and perky it

stirred up some kind of answering violence in me, the violence of white cotton underwear, of Catholic schoolgirls, of PipiLngstck and cookies and milk. I told Satan how
there's a saying in Japan—people might say this of an infant or a baby animal—*he's so
cute I want to hit him on the head with a hammer*. Satan *really* liked that. He said he knew
all about that. When he laughed he looked pretty damn cute himself. His hair was too
long and falling into his eyes; there was some baby fat left around his chin even
though he claimed to be twenty-five, same as me. He was jumping around the store
totally hyper, pointing at Hello Kitty and going, "BAM," like he was braining her and
chanting: "She has no mouth, you see."

"Chill, Satan, they'll kick us out."

"Fair lady, who cares?" Satan leered and I thought he was going to kiss me. I took
a giant step backward. Even though I'd done everything I could think of to him in private rooms on the computer, I didn't think it proper for him to kiss me just yet. We
still had a lot to learn about each other. He'd made *that* pitifully clear on the phone
when he'd said that his idea of a perfect date was to drink a couple of beers while
watching *The Lost Boys* with a lassie in latex pants slumped next to him on the couch.
My dream date, on the other hand, involved the perky sterility of the Sanrio store.

"She has no mouth, you see," Satan said, again. "No mouth, no expression. She
could be feeling anything, that's what the lady said, though I'm not convinced Kitty
is a lassie. There seems to be no indication down there"—he flipped the doll over—
"so that little Timmy can imagine Kitty is smiling, crying, or smoking crack! Whatever so pleases him, to match his very own mood!" He leapt across the aisle and
knocked a Spottie Dottie dental hygiene set onto the floor. "The secret of success. No
mouth!"

I dragged Satan out of there with the sales staff (whose duty it was to be peppy in
all circumstances) looking pissed off. We walked up Stockton toward the Chinatown
tunnel. We had a plan to go to Satan's favorite dim sum shop. The whole date was
very organized. While we waited to cross the street, Satan reached into his coat and
pulled out a stuffed Hello Kitty doll. "For you, dove."

"For me? You stole this for me?"

I was wearing eyeliner. He was wearing eyeliner too.

At the dim sum take-out shop Satan ordered nothing but those long, slimy noodles in
beef sauce that have the same heft and texture as a human tongue. I ordered a variety
of items, including pork buns and shrimp balls. Satan snorted when I said "pork
buns." By then, I noticed, I was starting to get sick of him.

We took our food outside and sat on the sidewalk with our shoes in the gutter.
"For you, dove," Satan said, pulling a pair of chopsticks out of his pocket.

I watched him suck noodles into his mouth. "All one thing, isn't that a little, uh,
extreme? For a meal intended as a series of appetizers?"

Satan shifted his food into his cheek. "I have an attraction to extremes, fair Pippi."

"Oh, yeah. I second that."

"If it's not extreme," he continued, "I mean, what's the point?" He stared into
crates of cabbage and unripe mangos overflowing onto the sidewalk. "When you eat

on the street in Chinatown," Satan observed, "people look at you like you're a dog eating out of the gutter."

It was true, I noticed, people did shoot us dirty looks, but I was used to it. All the bosses I'd ever had seemed to regard me as disposable tissue that typed: ordering me around, snickering behind my back, seeming more amazed when I did a job well than when I did one badly. Maybe it was my unusual personal appearance—the fact that I drew freckles on my cheeks with eyeliner or daubed teardrops under my eyes with mascara, or that my braids stuck out at right angles from my head; or maybe it was the short skirts, white bobby socks, and cardigan sweaters I often wore. Or my high, little-girl voice. I don't know. It seemed like there were plenty of people in San Francisco who dressed artistically, you'd think even people with power would get over it. But I was forced to suffer indignities. At one office, before I quit to become a temp, I was told to sign a ten-point CODE OF BEHAVIOR or else CLEAN OUT MY DESK. These points included: no toothbrushing in common areas, no cavorting in skirts short enough to reveal undergarments, no wearing of little stuffed birds in the hair.

All I wanted was to look sweet and wholesome. I wanted to have some sort of access to the land of puppies and bunnies and things that are good and simple and true. I wanted the goodness to seep inside me so I would be good and simple and true myself. This way I could keep everything in order; I could be sad at certain times and happy at others. Some nights I dreamed I was throwing live kittens at moving cars, choking with rage. When I woke up I'd still feel out-of-sorts, so I might go into the bathroom before work and draw on a grin, or add big eyelashes and spot my cheeks with roses. That would mean I was happy. Or draw on tears—then I was sad again. It all had a linear cause and effect that calmed me and made me a better worker, in my opinion.

"Satan, are you cold?" The afternoon was mild, but Satan hunched on the curb with the collar of his trench coat turned up, sucking noodles into his mouth.

"The chill is within my soul, lady."

It was sort of disturbing to watch him eat. He wasn't very good with the chopsticks. "Now that you've met me, Satan, what do you think?"

He eyed me coolly. He wasn't as eager in real life as he was onscreen. In fact, he was kind of arrogant. "I think you're pretty."

"I told you I was pretty."

"Computers lie."

"Computers don't lie. People using computers lie."

"Guns don't kill people, people kill people."

"You're real snappy, Satan. A real snappy guy. Aren't you going to ask me if I like you?"

"No." He grinned that sassy grin. "I can tell you like me."

I squealed and grabbed him by the hair. He was right.

At that point, I knew about one thing for sure about Satan: he was a geek. He had the queer, stylized diction, the mannered exterior, the inability to make eye contact, that screamed of geekdom. Geek! He was, I decided, one of those guys who had been obsessed with role-playing games like Dungeons and Dragons in high school; misfits shamed into lives of fantasy by the scarlet bubbles of acne percolating across their faces. They had to take on the role of Sir Quidball or Fatemaster or The Lad Ambrose and pretend to seize the opal from the high tower or something if they were ever going to be able to converse with another human being. But now all those guys need is a computer and a modem and they can just log on and avoid showing their faces altogether.

I thought it was nice. Someone could type: *"I'm grinding my pelvis into your face and yanking up on your hair,"* into a keyboard, and everyone would get hard and wet and come or whatever in the privacy of their own homes. I really hate it when people, usually the older generation, say how technology is depersonalizing and makes us into machines and the future is dank and scary. I mean, first of all, I see plenty of people in real life, and secondly, it's not like people on the computer are fake. They're out there. I knew Satan as the sweet boy who licked my boots and called me Mistress of the Doves. When he found out we both lived in the Bay Area, he was beside himself with excitement.

"Please," he typed, *"if I could feast my eyes on you but once fair lady, all my existence would be complete."*

"I don't know, Satan," I typed back, *"it could spoil everthing."*

"Lady, I think about you day and night," he replied. *"It doesn't seem like there would be any point in getting up in the mroning, or that my pathetic life would be worth living at all, if I missed the chance to touch you, even once."*

So there we were, on a date, dating. My date with Satan.

We went back to his place. "His place" isn't the term, exactly, because "due to unusual circumstances where my presence and my responsibility are often unexpectedly required," as he put it, Satan lived at home with his mother and sister.

"Mom's out today," he said, as we climbed the stairs. "And sister's always out."

It was a deluxe apartment on the top story of a Victorian in North Beach, a very fancy address. He led me into a big open room with a view of the bay and the Golden Gate, all that tourist stuff. They had a piano with a bowl of real fruit on it. Satan hunched over it and started to play "Some Enchanted Evening."

"Nice pad, Satan." I had an urge to defile the place.

"Yes, my sweet, I call it home. Come, allow me to escort you on the grand tour."

Satan began to lead me around the apartment. He showed me the kitchen, the balcony, the den, and then his room. I knew Satan was a respectable guy with a job as a programmer at some hot shit firm in Berkeley but, well, I guess I wasn't surprised to see he lived with his mom with only one place as a refuge—his room. It was all decked out with Star Trek posters, shelves of William Gibson and Anne Rice books, a slick computer with every available peripheral. We made a loop and ended up back in the front room. Satan stopped on a little step below me and looked at me with hungry, velvet eyes. I grabbed his chin and kissed him hard on the mouth. He sank to his knees and began lapping at my ankles.

I have no idea why I elicit this from men. Every boy I've ever known has wanted to put on an apron and high heels in my honor and scrub my sink with Comet, or wear a collar with a leash threaded through his nipple rings and have me pull him around the floor. They want to be turned over my knees with their pants pulled down and be spanked, paddled, and whipped. They want to lick my boots and roll over on their backs and pee on themselves like cowed beta wolves. There seems to be something about me. I have a markedly little-girl style I admit. I've been told I look like a little lost orphan by bus drivers, store clerks, and ticket vendors. There must be some kind of magnetic attraction in this, to be flailed at by a full-grown girl in a pink romper. Maybe they think I can't really hurt them.

I'll confess I don't really mind. I mean, I kind of enjoy it, and it seems to mean so much to them. It's like they open their souls, they get so sweet and vulnerable. I don't have to do anything really. Half the time they don't ask for anything from me. I just stand there and say, "You slut, you love it," or whatever seems right, and they tell me all their secrets. They weep and say they love me.

In this case Satan and I had already practiced on the screen so I knew exactly what kind of scenes were flitting through his mind. I was composing a list in my head of things I was going to do to him, there on the stairs with Satan groveling at my feet, when a little girl about six years old pounced into the room chased by a woman.

"Shit," said Satan, standing up. "What'd you have to bring her in here for?"

"You try and stop her," said the woman. She dropped to her knees and started to crawl toward the little girl.

The girl jumped into the center of the room. One blue eye looked at me while the other wandered up the wall. She was pretty I thought, with wild, blue-black hair and little hands balled up in fists. She had on a sequined body suit with a stiff ruffle pouching out around her waist, like a ballet costume.

"She's so cute," I said. "A little fairy thing. What is she, your sister?"

"Yeah," Satan said quietly.

"Well, she's cute."

"She can't help it," Satan said. "Let's go into my room."

The little girl stared ahead with glassy eyes. "Are you a real little girl?" I asked.

"Are you a real little girl?" she said back.

"Or are you a fairy?"

"Or are you a fairy?"

"I'm the Queen of the fairies," I told her, bending closer, "and I want to know if you're one of us."

"If you're one of us." She looked at me with vacant panic.

"I get it, it's a game. What's your name, honey?"

The little girl stared at me, but it felt like she was looking through my head.

"Her name is Ivy," the woman said. She had a fancy haircut and a young face but she seemed so annoyed and responsible that I thought she must be an employee.

"She's a doll. I want one."

"Can we get her out of here?" Satan was nervous. He began to edge toward the little girl from the side while the woman—the maid I guess—snuck up from behind. As soon as he was within reach the girl began to scream.

"Fuck!" yelled Satan.

"My God, what did you do to her?"

"I didn't do anything to her," he said, in a weary voice, "she's just like this. There isn't really anything to do to her."

The girl sat on the floor and started doing something that looked like she was shooing invisible flies off her nose, over and over.

"Come on, Pippi. Nancy's supposed to be taking care of her anyway."

When we started to leave the room the little girl began to scream again; piercing, vicious, cat snarls.

"Please," the lady said, "please?" She gave Satan a long, pathetic, entreating look. "If I have to deal with this all day, they'll have to put *me* in an institution."

"No way," Satan said. "I have a guest."

Long, rhythmic shrieks issued from the little girl. The lady sank to the floor.

Satan dragged himself to the piano. "You owe me, Nancy. You owe me big." He made some curlicues up in the high notes. "And now, ladies and gentlemen," he addressed the back of the piano, a classy baby grand, "a serenade to the diminutive tyrant of the household." Satan's head drooped and his hair fell over his face. He played a slow, mournful introduction, buried under Ivy's wails, then began to sing: *"Mommy's blue"*—oh! a Billie Holiday song!—" . . . *because her little girl is going on three . . ."* He had a low, trembling voice, *"but Miss Amanda she's as proud as can be . . ."*

Satan was swaying, his eyelids drooping, looking so natural and self-conscious at once I felt like running out of the room. It all seemed so, I don't know—complicated. Instead I looked at the little girl, the delightful little Ivy-girl, shrieking now in raspy hiccups. The music seemed to relax her. Her hands uncurled and she focused on my knees, staggering toward them, arms extended in front of her like a baby version of Frankenstein, aiming directly for the Hello Kitty hanging out of my hand.

"She wants my doll."

"Oh God," Satan said, but he kept playing.

"Just let her have it," the woman implored.

"No!" Satan jumped up. "She'll fuck with it!"

The little girl began screaming anew. What vocal cords! The glass in the window frames rattled. Satan resumed playing and she quieted. Ivy began pulling on Hello Kitty's leg.

"Just give it to her," he told me, "the little fascist. Otherwise we'll be here forever. You can't believe her endurance. Sorry. I'm really sorry."

Satan played on. I handed the girl the doll and she set upon it, tearing its belly along the sharp edge of the coffee table, ripping a big gash in Kitty's stomach with a methodical violence, a strange mixture of purpose and detachment.

"You're a big girl now . . ." Satan sang, as Ivy, with muffled gasps, pulled spun stuffing out of Kitty's body cavity and tossed it onto the floor.

"God, why is she doing that?"

"Ivy has a thing about dolls," Satan said, his fingers moving across the keys. "She has to get inside of them. She thinks there's something in there."

"We think she's looking for their feelings. People with her disorder have trouble with emotions."

"What's wrong with her?"

"She's autistic," said the woman.

"Oh. Will she always be like that?"

"I don't know," she said. "No one really knows."

Ivy had calmed down—she was flinging bits of fiber into the air and watching them descend through the light, enraptured. The woman was able to pick her up and carry her from the room. My Kitty lay deflated, her polyester feelings strung out across the hardwood floor.

"I regret the interruption," Satan said. "Accept my apologies. And now, my dear, allow me to escort you into the inner sanctuary."

Satan was striped with gaffer's tape and he wanted me to rip it off. When I kissed him and ran my hands under his shirt I discovered the plastic slickness of the tape encasing him like armor. I removed his clothes to discover he was crosshatched on his chest and buttocks and thighs.

"Jesus, Satan, that's going to make you yelp."

"Fair princess, to feel pain at your hands is but the greatest pleasure." He was spread out on top of his bed, trembling, surrounded by computers and high school banners and a big poster of a blond lady riding a horse through a Day-Glo medieval forest.

"Well, you might flinch. We'll have to prevent that," I said, and began to tie Satan to the posts of his bed with laundry I picked off the carpet. My braids kept getting in the way so I twisted them together behind my neck. "You look so cute, I want to hit you on the head with a hammer."

"Don't make me wait," said Satan, a catch in his voice, so I hopped astride him and tore one leg of a chest-sized X off his skin, a clean rip from nipple to belly.

He screamed.

I turned over the tape and examined the hairs embedded in it. It had left a tender pink swath across Satan's chest. Dots of blood welled from his pores.

"That looks pretty rough, kiddo. Are you up for this? Maybe we should start a little slower."

"Don't turn pussy on me now," he said. I told him he was asking for it and pulled off the other half of the X.

Satan screamed. He had quite a hard-on. "We'll see who's a pussy now," I said, working methodically, tearing the smaller sections of tape off his thighs and legs rhythmically. He eventually stopped screaming and simply lay there trembling.

"I'm completely at your mercy. I'm yours. Do with me as you will. Rip me open. I am like one of Ivy's dolls if you so desire, my lady."

I wrapped my hand around his thing.

He said, "I love you."

"Yeah, I know."

"No really, I love you really. God, I can't believe this is happening. I feel like we've known each other forever."

I slid his penis into my mouth and he actually kept talking:

"It's just a computer, I know, but it's so real. I can tell so much about you by what you write. You don't know how many times I've pictured you here with me. Ferris. My real name is Ferris. What's your real name?"

I relaxed my lips and let my teeth scrape against him. Whenever a guy gets all earnest and yearning like that, my enthusiasm for sex just clots. Sometimes I think they go out of their way to disgust me. I gave his penis one last gnaw and spat it out.

"I don't have a real name." I took a flap of silver tape without much stick left to it and put it over my mouth. "I have no mouth, you see."

"Hey, please, come on. I love you. I'd be on my knees if I weren't tied up. I'd kiss your feet. I mean," his eyes filmed over, "I really love you. So tell me your real name? I'm begging?"

My eyes trailed across the pink and trembling figure of Satan, bound. Ferris, now he'd want me to call him *Ferris*. I don't know why this always has to happen to me. Guys always reach the point where they want me to take out my braids, wipe off my makeup, dress like other girls, "real girls," they say. They want me to tell them my name, my address, my social security number; they want to open me up like a package and crawl around inside and find out exactly what's wrong with me and fix it and love it and I don't know why the hell they don't lay off. I don't know where they get off thinking I'm going to give up all my secrets, hand my life up over to some guy, a stupid guy, who doesn't even have his own apartment. Who lives with his mother.

"You know what, Ferris?" I said cheerfully. "Fuck you."

His face fell. "Oh God, what did I do?"

Because there isn't any problem until they think there's a problem. There isn't any problem until they want to know what's inside me and then the problem is *they are all fucked up.* If they want a piece of me, I figure they must be empty to start with, right? Once they get started, where will it end? Before you know it I'll be married and living in the suburbs, fretting over carpet stains. I'll be one of those hollowed-out zombie wives, filling up a grocery cart, dimly wondering how I ever let some guy lure me into his little dream life. I've found the only thing to do in these cases is to leave. PipiLngstck is an expert in the delicate art of cutting her losses.

I left him on the bed, tied up and gunked with white adhesive residue. He had a decent chance, I decided, of working himself free before anyone (i.e., his mom) found him.

"Pippi," he whimpered, "you're leaving? Will I see you again on-line?"

Some guys, I've found, are like that: the colder Pipi-Lngstck is to them, the more they think they have to have her.

On my way out, I decided to try to find the baby girl. I just wanted to say goodbye. I couldn't get over how adorable she looked in her princess dress, tearing up my Kitty doll in a trance. I poked around until I found her, alone in a room, staring at the pink and blue wallpaper like it was television. The water was running in the bathroom. She was so precious. Why was I always the one to leave empty-handed? I wrapped my arm around her little waist and dragged her with me down the stairs.

Reading as a Writer

1. How long does it take to get your bearings and understand what is happening in this piece? How does the delay add to the emotional subtext of the story?

2. How do the concrete details anchor this piece and make it convincing?

3. Does Richter succeed in rendering meaning that is accessible to a wide audience?

CHAPTER THIRTEEN

Learning to Fail Better
On Revision

Revision can be one of the most exciting and rewarding aspects of creating fiction. There is nothing some writers like more than taking a raw piece of work and reworking and polishing it to make it shine. Indeed, some people breathe a sigh of relief when the first rough draft is done and they can get to the revision process. The hardest work, that of generating a raw draft, is finished; now they can concentrate on figuring out what the story is really about, and getting it to fulfill its promise.

There's no magic bullet or panacea for revision. Every person's revision process, like his or her writing process, is different. What we do in this chapter is provide you with a flexible model for revision that has worked well for many writing students. But it's not the only way. There are many different paths by which to effectively reimagine or reinvent a piece of creative writing, and this model cannot hope to cover all of them. What this model *does* do is provide an adjunct or alternative to the conventional "workshop" method of helping students with revision that is used in so many writing courses around the country.

In this chapter we first review some wise words from established writers on what happens and what it feels like to have completed an early draft. Next we talk about the workshop method for giving and receiving criticism on early drafts of stories, and we discuss its benefits as well as its drawbacks. Then we go over the various stages of the creative process: although nothing could be more individual than each writer's process for generating creative work, some things can be said about the general stages that most creative work passes through and the kind of feedback that is most helpful at each stage.

Finally, we review a number of types of exercises that can be useful in what I call the "anti-workshop" method of revision. The main difference between this exercise section and the exercises found in the rest of the book is that these are supposed to teach you how to devise your own exercises so you can continue writing and revising on your own, even after your class or writing workshop has finished.

Advice for Writers from Writers

Perhaps there's no better way to feel relieved and reassured about this thing called creative writing than to read what some of the masters have said about the revision process. Below you'll find quotations from some of our most accomplished writers as to what it feels like to have finished an early draft.

> There's not much that I like better than to take a story that I've had around the house for a while and work it over again. It's the same with the poems I write. I'm in no hurry to send something off just after I write it, and I sometimes keep it around the house for months doing this or that to it, taking this out and putting that in. It doesn't take that long to do the first draft of the story, that usually happens in one sitting, but it does take a while to do the various versions of the story. I've done as many as twenty or thirty drafts of a story. Never less than ten or twelve drafts. It's instructive, and heartening both, to look at the early drafts of great writers. I'm thinking of the photographs of galleys belonging to Tolstoy, to name one writer who loved to revise. I mean, I don't know if he loved it or not, but he did a great deal of it. He was always revising, right down to the time of page proofs. He went through and rewrote *War and Peace* eight times and was still making corrections in the galleys. Things like this should hearten every writer whose first drafts are dreadful, like mine are.
>
> —RAYMOND CARVER

> What I tend to do is not so much pick at a thing but sit down and rewrite it completely. Both for *A Single Man* and *A Meeting by the River* I wrote three entire drafts. After making notes on one draft I'd sit down and rewrite it again from the beginning. I've found that's much better than patching and amputating things. One has to rethink the thing completely. They say D. H. Lawrence used to write second drafts and never look at the first.   —CHRISTOPHER ISHERWOOD

> First drafts are for learning what your novel or story is about. Revision is working with that knowledge to enlarge and enhance an idea, *to reform it*. D. H. Lawrence, for instance, did seven or eight drafts of *The Rainbow*. The first draft is the most uncertain—where you need the guts, the ability to accept the imperfect until it is better. Revision is one of the true pleasures of writing. "The men and things of today are wont to lie fairer and truer in tomorrow's memory," Thoreau said.   —BERNARD MALAMUD

> Progress does seem to come so very heavily disguised as chaos.
>
> —JOYCE GRENFELL

> All of us have failed to match our dream of perfection. I rate us on the basis of our splendid failure to do the impossible. If I could write all my work again, I'm convinced I could do it better. This is the healthiest condition for an artist. That's why he keeps working, trying again: he believes each time that this time he will do it, bring it off. Of course he won't.   —WILLIAM FAULKNER

Perfection Is Our Enemy

The biggest problem many writers (beginning and otherwise) face is that they are seeking perfection. They want what they write to be smooth and polished and meaningful and affecting from the very first word, and unfortunately that is simply not to be (or not very often). This desire to excel right from the starting gate can have serious consequences. It significantly raises the odds that a writer will freeze and/or go abstract, rather than focusing on the small telling details that will eventually lead to riveting and important material. Anne Lamott discusses this with good humor and grace in "Shitty First Drafts" (pp. 455–458), and the fact is that if you can convince yourself to sit down and write something shitty every day, you'll get a lot more done than if you are determined to write the Great American Novel or short story in flawless, unedited prose.

The Workshop Method

You may be using this book in conjunction with a workshop class. If not, perhaps you have heard about workshops and wondered how they work. The way workshops are conducted is fairly straightforward: a group of students meets, usually once a week, with an instructor or workshop coordinator. Students provide their colleagues with copies of a piece of work, giving them enough time to read it and comment on the text itself as well as provide a summary report of what they think. Then the class meets together, and everyone discusses the piece in question: what works, what doesn't work, what needs to be further developed, and so on.

The results of a workshop can be magical, or brutal, or extraordinarily helpful, or ludicrously unhelpful, or all of the above. It depends on who is in the class, who is leading the workshop (the experience and personality and skill level of the instructor matter enormously), and the particular story being discussed.

In some workshops, the feedback is supposed to be provided along some carefully structured lines: for example, if you are "up" you submit a list of questions to the class, which will be answered within the course of the discussion. In other workshops, what happens is a sort of freeform debate that can range all over the map. In any case, the goal is the same: to provide you (the writer) with sufficient information about your piece so that you can return to it and begin revising it to make it better.

Proponents of the workshop method say that it's the best way to obtain a thorough and productive reading of your work. During the most traditional workshops, if you're "up" you are supposed to remain silent throughout the discussion; no matter how misguided or mistaken you think the group is about your piece, you must keep your opinion to yourself until the discussion has been concluded. The idea behind this (and it's a valid one, in many ways) is that, since under most circumstances you wouldn't be there to "defend" or otherwise interpret your work for readers (if the piece were published in a magazine or as part of a book, for example), the more closely the class can replicate a fresh and unbiased reading of the work, the better for you.

And when it works, it works well. You may get valuable information about your work from classmates who respect you and honor your intentions, and you can take the feedback home with you to work productively on the next draft.

However, there are many drawbacks to the workshop method. Problems can occur when there are personality clashes within the workshop, or when certain students are arrogant or disrespectful of one another's work. Some instructors, too, don't do a good job of monitoring and controlling discussion, which can get stalled in unproductive ways. Finally, there's the inclination of the group to want to enforce its aesthetics on the individual. And, as Madison Smartt Bell says, the workshop method has no way of rewarding success:

> It sounds almost idyllic: a happy community of cooperating artists. But there are snakes in the garden.
>
> I was aware of the first pitfall before I ever came to Iowa. Fiction workshops are inherently almost incapable of recognizing *success*. The fiction workshop is designed to be a fault-finding mechanism; its purpose is to diagnose and prescribe. The inert force of this proposition works on all the members, and the teacher too. Whenever I pick up a student manuscript and read a few pages without defect, I start to get very nervous. Because my *job* is to find those flaws. If I *don't* find flaws, I will have *failed*. It takes a wrenching sort of effort to perform the inner *volte-face* that lets me change from a hostile to an enthusiastic critic and start rooting for the story to succeed. [. . .]
>
> At Iowa, I began to recognize some other hazards of the workshop method of which I'd been previously unaware. At Iowa, the students were very diligent about annotating each manuscript and writing an overarching commentary at the end—each student producing a separate version of the instructor's work (and some of them were already teaching undergraduate workshops). When the classroom discussion was finished, these fourteen annotated copies would be handed over to the unfortunate author, along with mine. My heart misgave me every time I watched the student (victim) gather them up, and an inner voice whispered, *Please, when you get home, just burn those things.*
>
> But of course they didn't do that. It would be idiotic if they had. After all, this was the criticism they'd come to receive—they'd paid for it, worked for it, striven for it. I found out through private conversations that many of these students, if not all, would indeed spread out the fifteen different annotated copies and try somehow to incorporate *all* the commentary into a revision of the work.
>
> The results of this kind of revision were often very disheartening. I'd get second drafts that very likely had less obvious flaws than the first, but also a whole lot less interest. These revisions tended to live up to commonly heard, contemptuous descriptions of workshop work being well-tooled, inoffensive, unexceptional, and rather dull.   —MADISON SMARTT BELL, *Narrative Design*

Jane Smiley, who also teaches MFA workshops, found that a traditional workshop didn't work for her students, who got combative and overly critical of each other's work while eagerly looking for approval from the teacher, rather than learning from the discussion and deciding what *they* thought. Here she talks about her method for conducting workshops these days, which she calls her "fiction writing boot camp":

> Well, the first draft they turn in they're usually pretty proud of, and they think of it as fairly polished. And with the first story always, no matter how hard I've prepared them and no matter how hard they've tried not to, what they're really seeking is praise. They want for the impossible thing to happen, for me and the class to say, "This is great, you don't have to do any more drafts, just send it off now and it'll get published, I guarantee it." In my experience the first drafts are fairly short, fairly polished, and with some problem in them that seems fairly minimal. Let's say the section that's supposed to be the climax will be confusing. So we'll talk about that and we'll say that the person has to clear up the confusing parts of the climax for next week. But usually that involves all sorts of other things, too, like a more careful defining of the characters, or making the rising action move more slowly and clearly. It ends up requiring a kind of narrative restructuring just to make the climax less confusing.
>
> As soon as they open up this box of the first draft, which is in, what shall we say, a state of *faux* completion, then the whole thing starts to fall apart. And the second draft is often a mess, because they are trying to bring in or explore elements that aren't in balance anymore. They're usually disappointed with the second draft; there's more to it but it's more of a mess, too. The third draft is better but still in a state of "uncontrol." But often by the time we've talked about the third draft we're all saying, "Aha!" and what we're saying "Aha" about is that we as readers feel that we finally understand what the author is getting at, and the author finally understands where *he's* going, too. Usually then they feel a certain amount of self-confidence about going on to the fourth draft, and it's really much better and more complete but often still unfinished. So they say they want to do a fifth draft, and I say, "No you have to go to the next story."   —JANE SMILEY, "A Conversation with Jane Smiley"

Other teachers have found individual ways to deal with the pitfalls and problems of the workshop method. My personal misgivings about the process are that I feel that the interests of the individual and the group are diametrically opposed. Workshops are great for the students who are critiquing the manuscript in question: they get to sharpen their critical claws and dissect a piece in a way that can be very helpful for their own analytical abilities—they can then take the skills they learn from criticizing their colleagues' work and apply it to their own.

But it's not necessarily a good thing if you're the writer whose work is under discussion. First, it can be very discouraging to have each and every flaw pointed out—and not even pointed out, but eagerly discussed and denounced. A teacher meeting with a student on an individual basis wouldn't necessarily redline everything, but would instead focus on a few things—things that student would be able to "hear" without becoming discouraged. All too often, in a workshop the teacher's role becomes one of defending a student against an over-eager throng of well-meaning but ultimately ruthless lynchers.

Second, the kind of advice parceled out during workshops isn't always appropriate for the stage that a work is in. You may be trying something new that doesn't work—yet. But a workshop may well decide that a section that isn't working simply needs to be removed. "Take it out!" is a common phrase heard in workshops. Yet the passage in question, when refined, could become a critical part of the story. Just because it isn't working now doesn't mean it won't work in the next draft, or the next, or the next.

Third, students in a workshop, unsure of what to say about a piece, frequently ask for "more." They want more of the mother, of the dog, of the reason that the boy threw away the toy that was so important to him. Sometimes they have a legitimate point: there is a gap in the story, and some additional development is needed before the piece is complete. But, in my experience, this request for more information can often result in overkill: by asking for more, critics force the writer into tipping the balance between a delicately wrought piece of work and one that has everything spelled out too neatly or obviously.

The net result: after a workshop, you can go home with too many voices in your head, which can pollute the revision process. As Madison Smartt Bell says in *Narrative Design,* all too often the next draft of the piece is tepid, watered down, and has lost its force. People—often with the best intentions—want to remake a story in their own image, and it can be difficult to shake the impression that their comments leave.

Undue Influence: A Cautionary Tale

Two of the readings at the end of this chapter provide a cautionary tale about the dangers of relying too much on other people while revising your work. These readings have to do with the work of Raymond Carver, especially the work that he generated when working with his longtime friend and editor, Gordon Lish. Indeed, it has been suggested that Carver's celebrated minimalism might well have been more Lish's doing than a reflection of Carver's own aesthetic predilections; the two stories show two different treatments of the same material. As you'll see, when given a chance, Carver rewrote one of his stories to reflect a more open, less minimal version of the prose: compare "The Bath" (pp. 458–463) and "A Small, Good Thing" (pp. 463–480) to see how the two versions play out.

This should be a cautionary tale to all of us. Although we might have strong opinions about someone else's work, we must always be respectful of their vision and intentions, and never assume that we have the answer to someone else's creative challenges. I tell my students that they need to approach a workshop critique carrying two equally strong but contradictory thoughts in their heads: to be open to criticism and ready to receive whatever they can learn from the discussion, and to retain the option of telling people to go to hell if the advice doesn't make sense. Unless you can somehow navigate between these two ways of thinking about criticism, a workshop will be of little or no use to you—and might even cause some harm.

The Developmental Stages of a Creative Work

It's important to understand that the creative process is not linear. You don't move seamlessly from initial concept, to first draft, to revision, to copyediting, to publishing. There are all sorts of reversals, returns, retreats. Sometimes a piece is magically done after just one or two revisions, but more often it takes a lot more than that. Sometimes it's necessary to tear up the latest draft and return to the original source of the material. Sometimes it's necessary to rethink a whole piece even after the twentieth revision.

Still, there *are* some things you can say about the stages of a creative work. Just as Richard Hugo talks about writing one's way from the "triggering" to the "real" subject (p. 35), we can talk in a general way about the various stages that a creative work goes through to get from the initial idea to the final draft.

Stage 1: Initial generating: The piece is being messily generated, as per the "triggering" subject we discussed in Chapter 2. This stage eventually leads to the first (rough) draft. What's the best help that you can provide a colleague with at this stage? Merely an "attaboy" or "attagirl." "Yes, you're writing, and there's something of interest there. Keep going!"

Stage 2: Creative revisioning (drafts 1 through 20+): Although a first draft has been generated, the piece is still usually under "deep" creative construction that often requires complete rewriting of the point of view, the setting, the scenes, the characters, the plot, and so on. During this stage the writer is gradually working your way from the "triggering" into the "real" subject. What's the best help that you can provide a colleague with at this stage? Exercise-based revision suggestions (see below).

Stage 3: Constructive revisioning (drafts 2 through 20+): The piece has solidified and can now be examined, and critiqued, as a whole piece, rather than as something that is still under primary construction. This is where a traditional workshop is the most helpful, by providing feedback on character development, plot, scene versus narrative—all the things that can be discussed safely once a piece has started to "jell." Prior to this stage, however, a workshop can frequently do more harm than good.

Stage 4: Copyediting: The piece is done, and now it needs to be examined for wordsmithing, grammar, awkward syntax—anything that detracts from a smooth, polished read.

One of the worst things you can do to a piece is to assume it's more complete than it is. And one of the most critical problems with the workshop method is that a

workshop is generally best for critiquing manuscripts that have entered the constructive revisioning stage—which, in other words, are pretty far along. Are the
characters believable? Is the plot working? Is the narrative rich and evocative? Do
we have the right scenes, dramatized correctly? All these things can be examined
once a piece has solidified.

Yet a good many stories are shown to workshops prior to this stage. They are critiqued as though they are more finished than they actually are. And nothing can be
more damaging to a piece than to have it "frozen" in place before it is ready. What's
critical is that a piece stays "fluid" for as long as necessary to ensure that all the relevant material has been fully explored.

"Hot Spots" and Other Noteworthy Aspects of an Early Draft

What can we do if a piece is not yet at the constructive revisioning stage? One of the
most helpful things we can do when reading an earlier draft by a colleague or student—one that is still in the creative revisioning stage, for example—is to point out
what's interesting, or what seem like "hot spots" in the text. You're not assuming
that all the scenes are in place, or that the characters or relationships have jelled, or
that the plot has solidified. Rather, you are merely indicating to the writer the places
in the text where you felt a quickening of interest, or, conversely, those places that
seem to have the most potential, even though they have yet to be fully developed.

The point is not to help a fellow writer "Band-Aid" together a piece by glossing
over defects or superficially mending holes, but to encourage deep, creative revision
by helping the writer question where the heart of a piece really is.

An Exercise-Based Approach to Deep Revision

In addition to pointing out "hot spots," the single most helpful way I've found to
help students is what I call the anti-workshop, or an exercise-based approach to
deep revision. Rather than directly telling a student writer what to do to a piece, I
suggest exercises to be done "in the margins." The exercises may result in text that
never becomes part of the story directly, but it will inform the writer's understanding of the work nonetheless.

For example, say that the relationship between two characters—a mother and a
daughter—is undeveloped. A workshop would point this out—and probably make
recommendations on how it could be fixed. But an exercise-based approach to deep
revision doesn't presume to tell you, the writer, what to do (or not to do). Instead,
your colleagues would suggest exercises that would "explode" open the piece in
order to give you a greater understanding of the relationship between the two characters and help you understand what to do next—even if the actual results of the
exercise never make it into the story.

The point isn't to put a Band-Aid on the story at a weak spot, but instead to put a
metaphorical stick of dynamite there, to explode the piece in a way that teaches you

more, and more interesting, things about the piece than you were previously aware of. The goal: to trick you into pushing your material in fresh and surprising directions—by thinking small. (Thinking "big" when attempting revision can cause you to panic and get blocked; it also often results in contrived and labored prose.) Not incidentally, this approach eliminates the danger that the critic tries to rewrite the story in his or her own image. An exercise-based approach to deep revision enables the writer to go back into the piece and explore and learn for himself or herself.

For example, one exercise suggestion could be for you to write five vignettes of the last five times the mother and daughter disagreed. Or, conversely, the last five times the mother and daughter *agreed* about something. By writing out these things, you will learn more about the relationship and more about the situation of the story. You might even learn how to fix the problem of the undeveloped relationship, or at least see your way to the next step. This is what an exercise-based approach to revision is all about: helping you see what can be done next without dictating such "fixes" to you.

There are all sorts of exercises that one can do when working "in the margins." The important thing is to remember that much of what you generate with these types of device may not end up in the piece itself. But you'll almost certainly learn something about your material, and you might even—if you're lucky—get onto something exciting. And you shouldn't be alarmed if your piece ends up messier and less coherent than when you began. That's usually a good thing: the point of exercise-based revision isn't to copyedit, but to *explore*.

A Word about Constraints

Contrary to what you might think, absolute freedom isn't always beneficial to creativity. Instead, what psychologists and scientists are finding is that *constraints*, or limits in choices, are often more conducive to creativity than the blank page or empty computer screen.

"The more constraints one imposes, the more one frees oneself of the chains that shackle the spirit," wrote Igor Stravinsky, the composer, talking about this phenomenon. Which, of course, is what we do when we do exercises: we're imposing certain constraints on our ability to write. Instead of being told, "Write about anything," we're being told to write within a very particular context, one with constraints all around it.

OULIPO is an entire movement based on this concept of constraints. Standing for the Ouvroir de Littérature Potentielle, or Workshop of Potential Literature, OULIPO is a group of writers and mathematicians whose members include Raymond Queneau, François Le Lionnais, Claude Berge, Georges Perec, and Italo Calvino. The idea behind OULIPO is to generate new works of literature based on puzzles and formulas—and constraints. For example, one of the most famous works to come out of the OULIPO movement is a novel by Georges Perec that was written completely without the letter "e." Other OULIPO constraints include writing a piece based on only the letters that make up your name, or by randomly choosing words out of a book. Any method that limits a writer's choices involves constraints, and constraints can be very conducive to creativity.

Constraints are important when it comes to exercise-based revision also, because we're not advocating total freedom. We're not saying, "Do anything at this point to open up the text." We're usually giving some very specific instructions with the idea they will induce, not inhibit, the creative spark.

EXERCISES

As a way to categorize the various types of exercises you can use during the revision process, I have come up with four broad categories of constraint: analytical/mechanical, creative, research-based, and chance-based. Examples of each type are listed below. The goal of this section is to inspire you to build your own exercises, rather than depending on exercises from others. The more adept you are at creating constraint-based writing activities, the closer you are to being able to tackle the revision process on your own.

Analytical / Mechanical Exercises

These kinds of exercise are precisely that: they analyze. These are good to do when your creative juices are running a little low and you want to do something, even if it starts out being mechanical. Because that's what happens with these analytical exercises: they start out slow and methodical, but very often they lead to creative inspiration, which is of course the point. Remember, this is not an exclusive list: there are many mechanical things you can do to a manuscript to jump-start a productive revision session.

- Retype the story (or a section of the story). The simple act of going over the piece word by word will spark new ideas.

- Highlight all forms of "to have" and "to be." By replacing them with more active verbs, you can often see where this piece lacks movement or energy.

- Highlight all "-ing" verbs. Then check each sentence for awkward syntax or unnecessary verbiage. Again, this is usually a sign of a deeper problem, such as imprecise rendering of a key image or action.

- Highlight all abstractions or generalities. Question whether the section has been adequately grounded in concrete sensory detail.

- Examine all imagery (any object, person, or place described using one or more of the senses). Is it *precise* enough? Does it push the reader toward an inevitable (and complex) emotional response? If not, focus and intensify.

- Highlight all metaphors and similes. Make sure they *add something* to the story. Also make sure you're not over-relying on them. Telling us what something is *like* before telling us what it *is* is often a sign you're having difficulty rendering something complex (an emotion or interaction) precisely on the page.

- Read out loud and listen to the rhythm of the language. If you stumble, highlight the sentence.
- Put the damn thing away for six months.

Creative Exercises

Most of the exercises in this book are creative. These are the ones that attempt to get the creative process going, to promote ideas and inspiration. There's literally no end to the creative exercises you can come up with: all of them involve constraints of some kind, and constraints are good for creativity. Some of my favorite creative exercises are list-making ones, such as Things I Was Taught / Things I Was Not Taught (p. 38) and Sins of Commission, Sins of Omission (p. 339). Or generating a handful of "moments" that fulfill a particular requirement, such as "the last five times this character felt rage" or "the last five times she made a mistake." Here are just a few of the creative constraints you can use to open up a piece for revision:

- Change the point of view of the piece and rewrite. See what you learn.
- Change the tense (from past to present, or vice versa).
- Introduce a new character who summarizes what happens in his or her own words.
- Write about an event in your character's past without which the current situation couldn't exist.
- Write about the current situation from the point of view of a character looking back from ten years in the future.
- Make a list of the things that *won't* happen to the characters as a result of this scene (situation) being enacted.
- Describe physical aspects of the scene in great detail: the setting, the characters, the clothes, the food. Do this obsessively. Do not worry about whether it is *interesting.*
- Describe a number of unrelated events occurring nearby as this scene unfolds.
- Describe a number of unrelated events occurring *far away* as this scene unfolds.
- Describe a prediction made in the past that this scene fulfills.
- Change the setting to an unlikely place: for example, from Paris to Milwaukee. Adjust all details accordingly.
- Describe the scene as each character would describe it in his or her diary, without editing.
- Rewrite the scene as a "family legend" narrated by the child of one of the characters.
- If narrative, rewrite as scene.

- If scene, rewrite as narrative.
- Do any sort of "listing" exercise you can think up to learn about a character, place, or dramatic event.

Research-Based Exercises

Another category of exercises requires the writer to go out into the world and gather additional information. Established writers often use research to help spark creative ideas. Again, this is just a representative sample—this list could go on and on. Anything that you can research at the library or on the Internet is fair game.

- Find out ten facts about the place in which your story is set that you didn't know before.
- Interview a person whose profession is being used in the story, and find out ten things about what the person does that you didn't know before.
- Research five recipes that the people in the story were eating (or could have been eating).
- Find out ten things that were happening in the world at the same time as the story (they don't necessarily have to be in the story; in fact, it's better if they're not).
- Interview five people about what they would do if one of the events of the piece befell them.
- Research the kind of music that would have been playing on the radio at the time the piece is set.
- Learn ten facts about the religion of one of the characters in your piece.
- Research the type of salary and subsequent budget that your main character has.
- Find out what was in the newspaper the day the events in the piece transpired.

Chance-Based Exercises

Chance-based exercises are based on events that can't be predicted but are randomly generated or happened upon. Chance-based exercises are exciting and interesting because they open you up to possibilities that would never have occurred to you logically.

- Go to your bookshelf and pick out the third book from the right. Open to the third chapter; write down the first, third, seventh, and ninth words in the chapter; and write several paragraphs for your piece based on that combination of words.
- Take a walk around the block. Make whatever happens (or doesn't happen), or whatever you observe, the basis for a freewrite that you can include in your piece.
- Make a list of all the things that happened to you this week that surprised you. Do a freewrite on one of them that might be relevant to your piece.

- Go out to a café or other place where you can hear people talking. Write down a conversation you hear and then do a freewrite based on it.

- Turn on the radio to a music channel and wait until the fifth song comes on. Do a freewrite based on your associations with the song.

- Roll a die. Whatever number you get, take that many steps outside your door and do a freewrite based on what you immediately see.

- Do a freewrite based on the third phone call you get in a given day (if it's a telemarketer, so be it).

- Turn to page 6 (or page 10, or whatever) of your local newspaper and do a freewrite based on one of the articles you find there.

- Flip a coin. If you get heads, go someplace you wouldn't ordinarily go and do a freewrite based on what happens to you there. If you get tails, go to a familiar place and ditto.

Revision Example

The following texts constitute three versions of the same story, by Jan Ellison, so you can see the extent of a true revision. First is the germ of the story, which is very short, very succinct, less than 1,000 words; following that is the first draft of the "real" story; and then, finally, the finished story as it was published in the *New England Review*. You can see how some scenes are the same and some descriptions are the same, but by the final draft it's a completely different story, expanded, fully developed. The names of the characters have been changed, and we now have the sense of a narrator with a current life of her own (husband, kids) looking back on her life.

"Germ" of Story (written in response to an exercise)

When I think of Jamie today, I see him in a staggering, energetic drunk, delivering to me the gift of a tall potted plant. He said nothing, only stumbled into my apartment, placed the plant in the center of the room and left without closing the door. He was back in ten minutes with another. Then another, and another, all the time saying nothing, only smiling a wild, hilarious smile. He was stealing the plants from the lobby of the hotel across the street. I laughed and accepted his gifts. Finally he tripped and fell and passed out in the middle of the living room, amidst a modest forest of green. I curled up next to his heavy brown body, my hands in his white-blond hair, and we slept. In the morning he was gone. That was his way. But I knew where to find him. Him and Freddie. Because always, there was Freddie, too.

Jamie and Freddie shared a room the size of a walk-in closet, in a stale, dank apartment in King's Cross, on a street where all the squalor of Sydney collected, where the wasted young whores swayed, in doorways, to and fro, to and fro, where the bars were, where we drank every night. Jamie and Freddie drank martinis and at first I pretended to but I couldn't get to like them so I drank draught beer in pints. We always sat at the bar. They played Bob Dylan on the jukebox and time seemed different, not at all important. Afterward, I slept with Jamie on his mattress on the floor. We rustled and rubbed and sneaked silent orgasms with half our clothes on, and always there was the sound of Freddie's breathing across the room, on the mattress against the other wall, in the room no bigger than a walk-in closet.

When I think of myself at that time I see a picture they took of me—passed out drunk in my black gauze dress, on Jamie's mattress on the floor. My black hair is splayed out behind me on a stained pillow with no case, and they have placed a six-pack of beer next to my head and a pack of cigarettes on my belly. I don't know now what they meant by that; whether it meant they mocked me or loved me. At the time I didn't care; I was one of them; I was a part of it; I belonged.

We were drunk every night and the thing I regret now is not that it went on so long but that it didn't go long or wild enough. I shook off my hangover each morning and left them to go home to my apartment, to shower and change and go off to my typing job, while they slept the morning away, their sweet bodies heavy and still, and woke at noon for a beer. That is what I missed, and what can't be gotten back now, not now with two small children and one on the way and a house—a house about which people say, oh, it's so beautiful, did you pick out all the colors yourself?

My friends, the ones I'd traveled to Australia with, said: "You can't keep doing this. You're getting ugly. You're not yourself. You're drunk every night and you didn't show up for our dinner party." It was something they'd agreed upon, to face me across the coffee table in their pristine living room in their pristine apartment in the complex with a security punchpad at the gate. Their warning worked on me like white noise; mostly I ignored it, but once in awhile it broke through and worked its way into the hilarity of that time, making me pause and wonder. The fun we had felt like happiness, it did, and I was not prepared to give it up. So I kept going out to the bars to find Jamie and Freddie, and when the bars closed I sprinted or stumbled or was carried back to their apartment where I slept on the damp mattress with Jamie, curled into his large sweet body. Always there was Freddie, on the mattress at the other end of the room, breathing.

Only one night it happened that I was there with Freddie, on the other mattress, just sitting, and then we were kissing, this one deep long-remembered kiss, our tongues and our fingers filled up with booze, the memory of that kiss, too, filled up with booze, petrified under half a dozen martinis and ten pints of beer. So it goes on, that kiss, the one that either he or I ended because there was Jamie, on his mattress against the other wall, in the room that was no bigger than a walk-in closet, in a dank apartment in King's Cross, where all the squalor of Sydney gathered for the long, long party, there was Jamie, saying "Hey," at first, laughing, then "Hey," louder, more confused, then "Hey!" a third time, until we stopped. Stopping it was an act of will, an act against nature. I can feel it still, the drag of his lips on mine, the intention of that kiss to go on to its reckless conclusion. Freddie whispered something afterwards, some incoherent words that I remembered then and that I wish I could remember now.

In the morning the kiss was not remembered. At least we never spoke of it. Still, I imagine it to be the moment I lost them, the moment that the trip north, the drunk trip in the rusted green van they bought for a thousand dollars, up through Queensland and the Gold Coast to the hot wastelands around Darwin, before the van gave out, it seemed the moment it was decided that the trip would belong in their memories but not in mine, except as an emptiness.

First Draft: working title "Jimmy and Ray"

I met Jimmy on a bus tour on the east coast of New Zealand in a great rain storm. He and his best friend Ray were on a bus tour south, I was on the same tour but headed north, and we ended up in the same tiny bar in the same tiny town in this tremendous storm. I had ridden alone that morning on a rented bicycle three miles along a dirt path to the glacier and on the way back it began to rain. I headed straight into the bar without stopping to fix up my hair and there they were drinking martinis at eleven o'clock in the morning. Jimmy was tall and fair-haired with clear innocent eyes and a lovely face. Ray was smaller and darker and not at all handsome. He had a look of distrust about him, but he shared with Jimmy a Southern drawl that seemed inviting and I went right up behind them and ordered a drink. Jimmy moved over to make a place between them and that was the beginning. We drank for two hours and watched the rain and once in a while my knee would knock up against Jimmy's beneath the bar. Then my bus was going north and theirs was going south and I almost changed directions and went with them but I thought the better of it. What with Jimmy being the one I wanted to knock knees with and Ray being the one I wanted to talk to I thought I better get back on my bus and go north.

It was October when I bumped into them again. I walked into a bar in Sydney, where I'd been living for a few months, and there they were drinking martinis.

"You again," Ray said.

"Have a drink!" Jimmy bellowed out. They were already drunk and in good spirits.

We drank until the bars closed, then Jimmy walked me home and stayed the night on the couch. He was like that, a true Southern gentleman, even after eight straight hours of drinking. My roommates didn't like a guy passed out on the couch so after that we passed out at the flat in King's Cross that he shared with Ray and a half dozen other guys and their backpacks. There was always someone sleeping on the couch there and nobody cared.

It was easy to love Jimmy because he expected nothing and because we were always with Ray and we were always drunk or on our way there. There was no requirement to make conversation or to get to know each other in some essential way, only the necessity of showing up at the bar, where he would be drinking with Ray, and Bob Dylan would be on the jukebox and I could slide in between them and order a beer on their tab. They put everything on one of their father's credit cards and the bills were paid back home.

We got drunk in the bars all over King's Cross and Wooloomooloo and Circular Quay and when it got really hot in December, we celebrated with a case of beer and a ferry ride over to Manly for a long day at the beach. At dusk we played frisbee and watched the sea go from green to indigo to black and then when it was very dark and we were very drunk we went for a last hilarious swim in huge waves that ought to have scared me but that did not. That whole time was like that; I ought to have been afraid, or worried about my health or my safety or my reputation, but I was not. I was safe and drunk and happy and what I regret was not the time we wasted but that it all ended too soon.

We caught the last ferry home and stumbled back to their flat, arms linked with me in the middle, and I slept with Jimmy on his mattress on the floor. We rustled and rubbed and sneaked silent orgasms with half our clothes on, and there was the sound of Ray's breathing a few feet away, on the mattress against the other wall, in the room no bigger than a walk-in closet. Laid end-to-end the two mattresses covered the whole floor. There was a poster of Faye Dunaway and Mickey Rourke in *Barfly* on one wall; there were clothes strewn about and a half a bottle of whiskey and that was all.

Jimmy was a drinker without angst, without remorse, without resolutions. I loved his sweet brown skin and his large lumbering frame and I loved not loving him, not needing to imagine a future with him. I knew almost nothing about him, only that he grew up in the South, in Raleigh, that his parents had a summer house on the beach, that he went to college close to home and joined a fraternity and did lots of drugs. I knew that he was a drinker like me, a drinker who would always say what the hell and have another. Later, it would work that way for me with babies, so that one after another they came, every two years, until my house filled up with little bodies, and still it would seem a good idea to have another, if only to experience one last time that perfectly clean smell, that absolute sense of ownership, that soft head under my chin in the dead of night.

Jimmy was a staggering, energetic drunk. One night, just after we'd met again in Sydney, he stumbled into my apartment and delivered to me the gift of a tall potted plant. He said nothing, only placed the plant in the center of the room and left without closing the door. He was back in ten minutes with another. Then another and another. Sweat broke out on his forehead. He said nothing, only smiled a wild, hilarious smile. He was stealing the plants from the lobby of the hotel across the street. I laughed and accepted his gifts. Finally he tripped and fell and passed out in the middle of the living room amidst the greenery. I curled into his big brown body and we slept. In the morning he was gone, but I knew where to find him.

Jimmy knew something about being kind to women. He held doors open for me; he made me drink a glass of milk before bed to stave off the hangover; he tucked the sheet around me if I passed out first.

Sometimes he was the one to pass out first.

I wanna get drunk, he'd yell, knocking his head against the wall when Ray and I had dragged him home from the bars.

Lay down, I'd say, you're already drunk.

Am I? he'd say with a grin full of straight white teeth.

Then he'd fall down on the bed and close his blue, bloodshot eyes and go to sleep.

I never asked what he studied in college, or what he planned to do when the trip was over, or whether he had ever been in love.

It was Ray I wanted to understand; it was Ray who'd been damaged. Ray was dark and swarthy and all his features seemed bunched up into the middle of his face. He lived right on the edge of ugly but to talk to him was to know something about danger and privilege and heartbreak; to talk to him was to want to heal him or win him. When he was drunk he talked to me about Annalee, Annalee the beauty, with red hair down to her butt riding around in her yellow convertible in the fall. She always drove, he said, Always. Annalee had a cocaine habit; she stole money from him and then left him for her mother's boyfriend. But when he spoke about her it was with reverence; he had not forgiven her but he had not yet given her up. Something about that made me want to make him see other women in the world; it made me want to make him see me.

In March, when the rains began again, Jimmy and Ray made plans for a trip north. They bought a rusted green van with a bed in the back, and though I'd been there with them all through that raucous, timeless summer, in the flat and in the bars and on the beach and on the dirty mattress at the end of that room that was no more than a walk-in closet, with Jimmy and his sweet brown belly and his clear blue eyes and his gentle talk, with Ray at the other end of the room snoring like only a drunk can snore; even though I'd been right in the center of all that, somehow it became clear that I would not be going on the trip north. The bed in the back of the van could only sleep two.

"There's the front seat," I finally said.

Jimmy said, "Ah, c'mon Cath." His voice was soft with apology.

Ray said, "No fuckin' way. It's a guy thing."

I stuck my tongue out at him and he smiled.

The day they left was gray and rainy, like all the days that followed. We stood on the sidewalk while they piled their backpacks and their tent and an arsenal of booze in the van. Jimmy came and stood behind me. His hands were warm on the back of my neck. I was trying to think of something flip to say.

"Well, see ya," I said, and it came out angry. I gave him a hug, but not a kiss and I didn't give Ray a good-bye at all. I walked off before they got in the van so I wouldn't be the girl standing on the wet sidewalk waving good-bye.

I told myself: It was because I was broke and they were tired of buying my drinks. It was because they imagined the women they would meet on the open road, Australian women with darling accents, blond hair, skin still brown from summer. It was because I had played the game badly, had pretended for too long that I didn't want to go on the trip, that I didn't have the money, that I had to work. Right up to that last morning, I expected them to change their minds, to say Ah, c'mon Cath, get your stuff, as if my invitation had simply been overlooked.

But there was also this: There was one deep long-remembered kiss on the wrong side of the room on the wrong dirty threadbare mattress, with Ray.

This is what I remember about the night it happened: Jimmy wears a T-shirt over his big shoulders. The T-shirt is barely hanging on his body and I remember something about that, that we ripped it during the party at the flat that night, not in a rage or a passion but just because there had been a tiny hole, just above his right nipple, and I began to tear and it tore and tore and everyone joined in and then someone poured a beer over our heads. We didn't take offense, nobody did, not ever during all those months. At some point in the night my roommates came by; three lovely girls with bare muscular calves, short skirts, high heels. When they arrived, for some reason I had a paper bag over my head. They stayed only a few minutes, time for one gin and tonic each, then they headed off to a club to go dancing, leaving the boys cheated and me relieved.

Somehow at the end of the night I was sitting cross-legged on Ray's mattress, facing him and that poster of Mickey Rourke. I was watching Mickey for a sign. Then the tips of my fingers were touching the tips of Ray's on both hands, then we were leaning into each other, then we were kissing, this one long boozy necessary kiss. Jimmy said "Hey," at first with laughter in his voice, then "Hey," louder, then "Hey!" a third time, and this time he was standing over us yelling so we stopped. Stopping it was like the pain of coming up out of a deep, dreamless sleep when your baby cries in the night. Ray whispered something to me as we pulled away from each other, some words that I understood and cherished and then forgot and that I can never get back.

In the morning, neither of them remembered. At least it was never mentioned. Still, I imagine it to be the moment I lost them, the moment that the trip north—the drunk trip in the green van they bought for a thousand dollars, up through Queensland and the Gold Coast, all the way up to the hot wastelands around Darwin and then on down along the west coast—it seemed to be the moment that the trip around the whole of Australia in a rusted green van became a thing that would take place without me.

Final Story; published in New England Review

JAN ELLISON

The Company of Men

FOR A FEW YEARS I HAD IN MY POSSESSION two rain slickers that smelled of whiskey and cigarettes and aftershave. They were cherry-red and lined with fleece, and I kept them in a cardboard box on a shelf above the toilet in the tiny apartment where I lived alone. Then when I was about to be married and I wanted to be rid of so many failings, so many unhelpful habits and longings, when I believed the past could no longer inform me, I threw the slickers into the Goodwill pile and lost them forever. Now what is left is a single photo I return to now and then, of two young men in bright red coats hitchhiking under a darkened sky.

I met them first on my last full day in New Zealand, after I'd rented a bike and ridden three miles up a dirt path to touch my fingers to a glacier. It began to rain, and by mid-morning when I got back down to the village, I was soaked through to my bra. My bus for Christchurch wasn't leaving until one, and across from the bus depot was a pub. Inside there was a fire in the fireplace and two young men—Jimmy and Ray—standing at the bar in their rain slickers drinking martinis. Ray was stocky and dark, with a sunken torso, small eyes, and a huge, humped nose. His hair was thin and black above a high, smooth forehead, and all his features seemed bunched up in the middle of his face. Jimmy was taller and fair, with square shoulders and fine blue eyes.

His hair curled at his ears and at the nape of his sunburned neck. There was something loopy, almost accidental about the way Jimmy stood in his frame, as if he were blind to the effect his size and good looks might have—the effect they were having—on a wet girl standing in the doorway of a bar seven thousand miles from home.

I'd been traveling alone for a year, since I finished college, through Europe and India and Southeast Asia, and I'd just spent a month at the northernmost tip of the North Island picking tomatoes in the sun for minimum wage, eating cheese sandwiches, and sleeping alone in a pitch-black room of empty bunks. It came to me suddenly as I stood in the doorway of the bar that I was sick of the struggle in it—sick of crouching in the sun, sick of taking it all in, of making notes on yellow legal pads, of stumping across rock and snow in my boots and across sand and kelp and coral and wet grass in my worn-down Tevas. It was not exactly loneliness I wanted to banish as I crossed the bar toward them but a kind of self-imposed austerity, a compulsion to justify the experience, to tear meaning from it, to bring something home. It was the days of weighty, maturing experiences strung together one after another in what seemed to me then a long stretch without a flirtation, a debate, a convergence—a black-out drunk.

Jimmy and Ray had just graduated from the University of North Carolina and they were on a tour of New Zealand and Australia and maybe Bali or Kathmandu. Under their rain slickers, they dressed the way they must have dressed back home, in jeans and leather loafers and button-down shirts, and they drawled when they talked. They addressed me as *y'all*, which made me feel oddly important, as if I carried with me the authority of a secret entourage. We drank five fast rounds together while the rain beat the window and the mud slid off the hill outside into a great brown puddle. In the distance were the white tips of the glacier rising up out of a black mass of cloud.

While we drank, Jimmy rested his hand against the small of my back and Ray told me about his girl back home—a redhead who'd stolen his money and broken his heart. When it was time for me to go—when the exhaust was shooting from the back of the bus and the faces of passengers began to appear in the windows behind the drenching rain—the wish to stay had hardened into longing. But I had a half-price ticket to Sydney in the morning and my tourist visa was about to expire.

"Y'all need to stay and drink with us," Jimmy said, as I stood and dropped a twenty on the bar. He picked it up and stuck it in the back pocket of my jeans. He downed his martini, put the toothpick between his teeth, and leaned in toward me, so close I could feel his boozy breath in my eyelashes. I slipped off the olive and held it between my teeth, then passed it back to him in an almost-kiss.

"You're still wet," he said. He slipped off his rain slicker.

"Don't give her that, you loser," Ray said.

"Easy boy," Jimmy said. Then he shrugged and slipped the coat back over his own shoulders. I stuck my tongue out at Ray and walked from the bar into the rain and got on the bus.

Everywhere in Sydney I saw people I knew. I'd step out of an underground station into the sun, and there would be a girl from my freshman dorm, sitting at a bus stop, or the married man I'd been with in London the year before, ducking into a cab. My arm would shoot into the air to flag them down, then when they turned toward me, the people I knew vanished into the puzzled faces of strangers. The idea of going home was always with me, but there were good reasons not to. My father had moved out again, before I'd left, and I suspected this time it was for good. "At some point things have to be admitted," was what he'd said, not to my mother but to me. I knew I was making it easy for him, staying away, giving up the cause, but the time and distance had muted my sense of responsibility. It had lulled me into believing my mother might be only heartsick and sad, not despairing, not desperate.

I moved into a flat with three German girls who'd been backpacking around the world together for a year. They hardly spoke English and that made it easy; there was no pretending we would take up as friends. I signed up at a temp agency—one that didn't check work visas and paid in cash every Friday. The agency found me a six-month assignment, typing for an insurance company in the city. The work was dull but the money was good and I buckled into it. In my spare time I renewed my long-standing self-improvement campaign. I quit smoking and stayed out of the bars; I worked on my typing speed; I wrote down words I didn't know on yellow legal pads and looked them up in the dictionary in the library on my way home. From the library I'd walk through the park, past the pub at Woolloomooloo and up over the hill to King's Cross. I'd buy myself a falafel and sit at the fountain in the square, watching the hookers in the doorways, the backpackers and tourists and solitary businessmen moving in and out of the strip joints and clubs, the restaurants and shops and seedy bars.

I was taken up in the change of seasons, the shift from the misty rains of May into the flat gray cold of what was summer back home. Then the holidays approached and the days began to lengthen and grow hot and expectant. On the last day of my typing job, I took the long way home through the park and stopped at the railing overlooking Sydney Harbor. The Opera House glowed white and magnificent in the distance, the water glistened, and a full blue moon floated low in the sky. I was filled up with a vast emptiness, a glorious freedom, and as always I was careful to stay there and treasure it, to take it all in. But what can you do with a feeling like that? It was like other solitary moments during those years of traveling—it was the Himalayas at dusk after a cold day walking alone, it was the deck of a freighter on the Adriatic Sea at sunrise, it was Paris under a velvet snowfall. It was manufactured and overly private and tiresome. The other murkier moments meant more, finally, the dramas that began for the most part in bars, when the swirling motion of the evening would straighten itself and alight on a human form and there was suddenly the possibility not just of desire, and of being desired, but of a story of poverty or addiction or betrayal. There was the promise of some new knowledge—the shape of an ear, the smell of musk—or a shift in one's view of oneself in the world.

I started walking again, fast now through the park, and when I got to the bar at Woolloomooloo I went right in, sat down on an empty stool, and ordered myself a pint. Bob Dylan was on the jukebox. I sang along to "Like a Rolling Stone" and ran my hands over the smooth wood of the bar. I thought I heard my name, but I was done with phantoms and I kept my head steady. I cupped my beer between my hands. Then there was the heat of a body behind me, and sudden hands on my shoulders, and I turned and it was Jimmy.

"Hey, Catherine," he said. He took the seat on one side of me and Ray took the seat on the other. I turned toward Ray. He looked at me deadpan and stuck out his tongue. I stuck out mine and we both laughed, as if this was the way we'd greeted each other every Friday night for a decade. It encouraged me, Ray's laughter, but it unnerved me, too. He was so ugly, so private, until his face was thrown open with that laugh. Then he was all teeth and bright eyes, his forehead wrinkling like linen. What I learned, though, was that he could close down again in an instant and make me wonder what I'd done.

Jimmy opened a tab on Ray's dad's card and ordered us all martinis, and we started drinking hard and fast. Ray began to talk.

"So this girl, Jasmine, back in Raleigh. The reason we're here?" He said it like a question. "Her house was next to mine growing up. Jimmy's was three doors down. She was just punky, a tomboy. Then she lets her hair grow out and she has these green eyes that look like contacts. Junior year in high school, she gets a '67 Mustang convertible for her birthday and we paint it up for her. Yellow like she asked for."

"'Yellow like ladyslipper,' was what she said."

"She was into flowers and shit," Jimmy said.

"Yeah, but only yellow," Ray said. "She planted up her whole front yard with them—roses and tulips and whatever. They even wrote it up in the paper, with her picture and all in a yellow dress. Then she went off to Brown and her mom sold the house and we didn't see her for a while. Until bingo. She turns up last summer on the Cape, and she's still got the car. Jimmy was down in Miami working on a boat so it was just me and Jasmine, staying up all night doing coke, driving around in the Mustang. And in the back seat she's got all these pots she made on a potting wheel in school, like dozens of them, all planted up with yellow flowers."

Ray stared straight ahead as he talked, at the orderly rows of bottles lined up on the bar. He paused and took a swig of his martini.

"So what happened?" I said.

"Well so she transfers to Carolina, right, for senior year? And we spend the whole year pretty much together, and we're talking about moving to New York after graduation. I was dealing, so I knew I could get us an apartment and everything. Then right after finals, she takes five thousand bucks out of the stash in my room and splits. She just drives her car out to California and hooks up with some professor dude—he's ancient, like forty, and he's gotten a job out there—and the way I find out about the whole deal is she sends me a postcard."

"My God, there must have been signs," I said to Ray. "To just take off and leave like that."

"Maybe. But I never had times like that with anybody," Ray said.

"Except me," Jimmy said.

"Even you, Jimmy my boy."

I'd been listening to Ray with my elbows up on the bar and my chin in my hand, with the intensity that can come over you when you've had a lot to drink. His story seemed strange and sad and unforgettable. While Ray talked, Jimmy kept the drinks coming and he let the back of his hand fall against my arm on the bar. He let his thigh rub against my knee beneath it. This seemed to be the arrangement. With the drinks and the roving hands and the sweet eyes and the good looks, Jimmy's role was to draw people to the two of them, and Ray's—with his stories and his mournful eyes—was to keep them there. He would keep us there until finally we could not bear to hear the story again, then Jimmy would rescue us, with a drink or a song or a wild run in the dark through the park.

"Fucking A!" Jimmy said now from the jukebox. He slapped his hands against the glass and dropped in some coins. Neil Young's "Sugar Mountain" came on and he came and sat close beside me and Ray stopped talking while Jimmy and I sang. The song was suddenly something that was ours alone—we both knew every single line—and Ray would not join in. When we pressed him he said, "I don't sing," as if singing were a habit he'd long since outgrown.

Jimmy and I sang it over and over, and after a while Ray and his story seemed to recede until there was only Jimmy and me and those lyrics and the smoky blue glory of the bar. My final memory of that first night is of standing at the jukebox at last call, trying hard to fit a quarter into the slot so we could sing that song one last time. The next morning, I woke up fully dressed under the covers with my shoes placed neatly next to the bed. There was no obvious evidence of intimacy—no chafing or fluids or foreign smells. There wasn't a phone number either, nothing inked on my palm or scribbled on a napkin and tucked into my sock. I spent the day sleeping off my hangover and waking from time to time to wonder how I might track them down—Jimmy and Ray—I didn't know their last names. When I finally got up and showered, it was late afternoon, and the German girls were watching TV. I started a letter to my mother. I wrote things I knew she'd like; I'd saved some money, I was getting along with my roommates, I was enjoying the neighborhood—all the shops, the square, the outdoor cafés. She didn't need to know that it was the seedy heart of the red light district, that the streets were lined with drug dealers and prostitutes and strip joints and bars. I started a letter to my father and crumpled it up and threw it away. It was the first of many letters to him that I started and never finished, or finished and never sent. I was afraid to lose the closeness we'd had, but contact with him seemed duplicitous—an encouragement or even a betrayal.

At six o'clock, Jimmy lumbered in through the open door of the apartment with a tall potted plant held against his chest. The trunk was flung over his shoulder and the branches swept along the carpet behind him. He dropped the plant to the ground, spilling potting soil onto the worn white shag. His eyes were closed to half slits and there was a look of deep concentration on his face. He seemed especially large in the narrow white room and his cheeks were full of color beside the pale German girls, who carefully moved their eyes from the television set to him.

"What are you doing there, sir?" I said.

" 'Liverin' you a *gif*," he said, and he walked out the door. I went to the window and watched him. He staggered across the street into the lobby of the old Rex Hotel and emerged again with a plant under each arm. Then he was back in the apartment to deliver them, and still the Germans said nothing. When he left again, they began to murmur amongst themselves, and when he returned with two more plants, they smiled at him and then at me and they actually laughed.

He made a dozen trips, each time pinching a plant or two without anyone seeming to notice and dropping them heavily in the center of our living room floor. Finally he sat down hard on a bare patch of carpet, crossed his legs Indian style, and gave me a triumphant grin made up of perfect white teeth. Then he closed his eyes and his body tipped backward and his head landed on the ground with a thump.

He was too heavy to move. All we could do was straighten his legs and lay his arms over his chest. Later, when the German girls had gone to sleep, I brought out a pillow and blanket and lay down next to him. His shirt was pulled up out of his jeans and I put my palm on his stomach and touched the fuzzy blond hairs around his belly button. His stomach was not exactly fat, but it was not so firm as to suggest vanity or self-discipline, two qualities that at that time I found unpleasant in a man. I ran the back of my hand over his sunburned cheek. He smelled of booze and smoke and the kind of aftershave frat boys wore in college. It was a smell that reminded me of fast, haphazard sex.

I curled into him, into the sheer size of his body. There was heat in the places where our bodies touched and the moment seemed simple and absolutely complete. It stayed that way between us. I never knew what he thought about most things, whether he had grave opinions about the economy or the nature of men or the existence of God. The things he knew about—football, sailboats, the business of manufacturing heavy equipment—couldn't power a conversation between us. We were rarely alone and we were almost always drunk, so there was never a requirement to get to know each other in an essential way; there was no imagined future. We were free of the heaviness I had so much of in college and later, when you announce to yourself and the world that you've met someone special and then you must stay the course.

You must whisper into the night and you must embrace his terrible flaws—the dandruff at his temples, his tendency to speak rudely to waitresses, his inclination to overdress.

With Jimmy it was simply about putting "Sugar Mountain" on the jukebox and letting our thighs touch under the bar. It was about talking to Ray and drinking and letting time pass without clutching it or measuring it. It wasn't about ideas; it was about the weight and heat of a body against your own. I felt something like it again when I held my firstborn in my arms. The simple physical fact of her moved me—her button chin and the fleshy lobe of ear, her head smooth and blond as sand, her milky breath against my face.

After that first night, the Germans moved the plants onto the balcony of the apartment, and with muted hand gestures and apologetic smiles, made it clear they'd prefer it if Jimmy didn't make a habit of passing out on our living room floor. So we took to passing out at the flat just off the square that Jimmy shared with Ray and a half-dozen other backpackers—mostly Kiwis on summer holidays—who came and went. I was happy in that scrappy flat—the stained green sofa, the tiny kitchenette stocked with beer and tomatoes and sometimes an avocado or a lime, the walk-in closet where Jimmy and Ray slept on bare mattresses that, laid end-to-end, reached the entire length of the room. There was a collection of empty whiskey bottles in one corner, two fishing poles in the other, and their open backpacks in the center, overflowing with clothes. Taped to the wall over Jimmy's bed were photos of their trip so far; Jimmy and Ray in wet underwear beside a lake in the sun, Jimmy and Ray climbing a mountain trail in their loafers, Jimmy and Ray in their rain slickers, hitchhiking under a darkened sky.

We got drunk every night, mostly in the Cross, sometimes down at Woolloomooloo or The Rocks. We'd sleep until noon and then head out for lunch and start drinking all over again. I had enough money saved that I could have picked up a round or two from time to time, but they never once let me. The drinks were charged to one of their fathers' cards, and the bills were taken care of back home.

Jimmy was a drinker without angst or moderation. He always said yes to the next one, and I was the same. It was not exactly that we set out to get drunk. It was that there was always the idea of that first drink in our minds, and when that one was gone, there was the idea of the next. Later it would work that way for me with babies, so that despite the burdens in it—the chaos and worry, the sleeplessness, the unqualified loss of freedom—when one child was weaned I was ready for the next, for the sweetness of a small hot body against my chest.

Ray was different. He got drunk when he set out to, did not when he did not intend to, and was often sober enough to remember the night and report back in the morning.

"Jesus, you puked on my fucking shoes," he'd say to Jimmy, or "You hit the bartender in the eye with a paper airplane."

"Did I?" Jimmy would ask me, grinning.

"Not that I remember," I'd say, which was most always true.

When I was drunkest, Jimmy would get me onto the mattress, cover me in a blue sheet, and tuck it tight around me. He knew something about being kind to women. He opened doors for me, he held my hair out of my face when I threw up, he made me drink a glass of milk before bed. And when Jimmy was first to get bad at the bars, Ray and I would each take an arm over our shoulders and drag him home. He'd stand on the mattress with his shoulder propped against the wall and yell, "I wanna get drunk."

"Lay down," Ray would order. "You're already drunk."

"Am I?" Jimmy would say. Then he'd sink down and close his bloodshot eyes and sleep for fourteen hours straight. It was a routine they knew by heart, and I sensed that Ray took a deep pleasure in keeping Jimmy safe in the world. I never asked Jimmy what he studied in college, or what he planned to do when the trip was over, or whether he'd ever been in love. It was Ray I wanted to understand. Ray lived right on the edge of ugly but to talk to him was to want to heal him or win him. At the bars, sometimes he ignored me, or coldly put up with me as if I were a wart he might some-day burn away. Other times he sat up close and talked to me about Jasmine, telling me the same stories over and over again. For years I carried around a picture in my head of Jasmine driving fast along a coast road in her yellow convertible, her red hair flying out behind her, her back seat filled with flowers. It was a picture that could bring on a tightness in my chest, a vague longing to be an original, a girl who could win love absolutely and then walk away. When Ray spoke of her it was with rever-ence and regret; he had not forgiven her but he had not given her up either. Some-thing about that made me want to make him see other women in the world; it made me want to make him see me.

On Christmas Day we planned a picnic on the beach. We took the ferry over to Manly early in the morning when the beach was empty and the air was still damp. Ray went off to the boardwalk and came back with three dozen clams in a bucket and a gallon jug of red wine. He opened the clams with his pocketknife and we ate them one after another, washing them down with wine straight from the bottle. By noon the beach was packed and it was so hot you couldn't walk on the sand. Ray went off again and came back with bread and cheese, peaches, pistachios, and a case of Victo-ria Bitter. Later, the German girls came by, pale and strong in their one-piece suits, and the Kiwis arrived with another case of beer. We assembled for a game of foot-ball—gridiron, the Kiwis called it—American style.

I can still feel myself in that day, my stomach flat and brown in an orange bikini, my hair wet down my back, the way I could sense my own ribs under my skin. The sun was hot on my head as I bent for the snap, ready to sprint after the ball. I didn't catch a single pass, and Ray traded me for one of the German girls who caught one and scored. But I didn't care. With every drink I became more beautiful in my own mind and the day grew more perfect. Later I would throw up over the railing of the ferry in the wind. I would pass out on the couch in the flat with a cigarette in my hand and burn a hole in the upholstery, and I would find, in the morning, dark spots of sunburn high on my cheeks that took years of creams and gels to take away. But in the place in my memory where that day lives on, nothing was damaged. Nothing was lost.

By dusk everyone else had gone and I sat between Jimmy and Ray under the changing sky and watched the water go from green to indigo to an oily black. In the half-dark, we staggered into the huge surf. I dove, stayed low to the sand and let the waves beat in my ears and sweep over me. I went through every wave, and I never ran out of breath. I might have been afraid out there in the waves, but I wasn't. That whole time was like that; I might have been worried about my health or my reputation or my safety but I never was. I was protected and drunk and happy, and if there is room for regret it is not for the time we wasted but that it ended too soon. In February, when the Kiwis were leaving Sydney to go back home, Jimmy and Ray threw them a going-away party in the flat. I imagined later that it was the night I lost them, the night that the trip around Australia in the green van—up through Queensland and the Gold Coast to the hot wastelands of Darwin and the white beaches of Perth— became a journey that would take place without me.

What I remember about that night is Jimmy with a threadbare undershirt over his square shoulders and how we ripped it, not in a rage or a passion but because there'd been a tiny hole above the right nipple, and I began to tear and everyone joined in and then someone poured a beer over our heads. At some point in the night the German girls came by—three steady girls with thick calves, short skirts, and high heels. I remember that when they arrived I had a paper bag over my head; someone had cut holes in it so I could see and breathe.

When almost everyone had gone and I was edging toward a blackout, I found myself in the walk-in closet on the wrong side of the room on the wrong mattress— with Ray. We were sitting cross-legged, facing each other, our knees touching, and Ray was holding a fishing pole across his lap. Then he was reaching his fingers out toward me and as I raised mine to meet them, he looked right at me, he leaned in toward me, and we were caught up in a kiss. It was gentle at first, almost a question, then it grew more urgent, until his lips against mine were hard and necessary. Jimmy was suddenly standing over us. *Hey!* he said, laughing at first like it was a joke he might have been in on. Then *hey!* again, then *hey!* a third time, loudly, with his hand pressing the ball of my shoulder away from Ray. So we stopped. Ray whispered something to me as we pulled away from each other, some words that I understood and cherished and then forgot—and that I can never get back.

I woke the next day on the mattress next to Jimmy. The afternoon sun filtered in through the doorway and fell on his face. The circles under his eyes were purple as dusk, and he seemed impossibly dear, the more so because I was afraid I'd lost him. At the same time, there was a small, stubborn part of me that wanted Ray to acknowledge the thing that had happened between us, that wanted him to make it happen again. It was a part of me I had not yet begun to understand—the part in the habit of expecting attention from men under the most extraordinary circumstances. Not just the first glow of desire, of glossy hair and full lips, but the whole messy miracle of love. It was not that I wanted the entrapments that come along with love, or that I would promise to offer it in return. It was that I believed that once a man knew me, he would see how different I was from an everyday girl—how forthright and clever and secretly kind—and he would find me indispensable.

It was a habit that persisted through heartbreak and havoc, through years of evidence to the contrary. Then I was married, and there were glimmers of it sometimes—at the pool where my son takes his swimming lessons, at the grocery store when a bagboy pushed my extra cart to the car—but for the most part I became convinced I'd outgrown it. Then on a hot night in August we threw a dinner party for friends. The kids were at my in-laws for a long-awaited overnight, and afterward, when the wives had kissed me and thanked me and gone home to relieve babysitters, and the other husbands—three men I've known for a decade—had assembled for a game of poker, I sat down in the chair left empty by my husband who had promptly passed out on the couch. One arm was flung across his face and the other hung over the back of the sofa, so that from where I sat I could see his long fingers dangling there, I could see his clean, clipped nails.

The game progressed. There was bluffing and folding. There was whiskey and chain-smoking and there were outrageous bets scribbled onto cocktail napkins. There were forearms—handsome, hairy, manly extremities brushing against mine on the tabletop as we handled the cards. Then all at once there was a knee pressed purposefully against my thigh beneath the table. There were brown eyes intent on my face and breath hot against my ear. And beyond that, where my husband's arm had been, was only the back of the couch. There was no sign of the formidable wrist, the sturdy thumb, the callused, well-loved palm. There was no further sign of my husband in the room at all. I was on my own in the company of men with the makings of a straight in my hand, ace high. Desire was thumping in my chest and the instinct to win, to go forward with abandon, was shooting through me, across the back of my neck and down between my legs.

At the same time—reaching me through the fog of scotch and cards and sex—was the power of my own house. There was the china waiting to be put back in the hutch. There was the cabinet door threatening to come off its hinge and a stack of catalogues to sort and toss. There was the phone, the bulletin board, the family calendar—the command center of our domestic life. Down the hall were my children's rooms, their mattresses and pillows encased in special covers to keep the dust mites at bay. Those rooms where each night I checked breathing and the temperatures of foreheads, where I kissed the gentle dip between cheeks and ears.

The question that persists, that pursues me even now, is whether it was only the card I was dealt—the seven of spades—that saved me. That freed me to shift my legs into open space, to lay my cards down on the table in a fold, and with an unlikely pinch of resolve, take my leave.

Jimmy got a two-week job down at Rushcutter's Bay scraping the underside of a yacht. When he was working that first week, I imagined him there, drinking a Coke in the sun. On Friday, I bought two sandwiches and a six-pack and made my way down to the boat yard. The day was warm and bright and the bay was dotted with sails. Jimmy was there and so was Ray. They were fishing. They weren't sitting close to each other and they weren't talking, but there was something between them, something silent and male, both a history and a future, and I almost turned around and left.

"Hey," Jimmy said, when he saw me. He glanced at Ray.

"I brought beers," I said.

"We never drink when we fish," Ray said. There was a silence. Then he laughed and took two beers. He popped one open for Jimmy and one for himself. "They're biting today. That's damned sure," he said.

I opened myself a beer and sat down on the dock next to Jimmy. The wood was gray and splintered, the water green with moss. We sat in silence for a while and then Ray's line began to move. I stood up as they did, as Ray reeled in his line, a fish slick and panicked at the end of it. Jimmy picked the pliers out of the bait box and worked the hook out, while Ray held the fish and then dropped it in the bucket with three others. There was nothing for me to do but stand and watch.

They finished their beers and began to pack up their fishing gear.

"That Kiwi band's playing at Woolloomooloo a week from Saturday," I said to Ray.

Ray looked at Jimmy then, and something passed between them, something that had already been decided.

"We're gonna be heading north, actually," Jimmy said. "We got a van and all." His face was soft with apology as he said it, and I might imagine now that he touched my cheek or took my hand in his. But he did not. He knocked his elbow against mine and punched me gently in the arm. We were like that together sober—clumsy and halting and overtaken by silences it was Ray's job to fill. But Ray had already turned and was walking up the hill home.

The day they left, the sky came down low and dark. They had their rain slickers on. I was coatless and cold. Ray loaded the arsenal of booze they'd assembled for the trip into the back of the van while Jimmy and I stood on the sidewalk and watched.

"I could sleep in the front seat," I said finally.

"No fucking way," Ray said from the back of the van.

"Ah, c'mon Cath," Jimmy said. He cocked his head to the side and turned his lips down in a pout. Then he took off his slicker and laid it over my shoulders. It had started to rain.

Ray came and stood next to Jimmy. For one long minute, he looked right at me and the lines of his face softened. My nose began to tingle with emotion and I had to look away. He walked toward me, slipped his rain slicker off his shoulders and laid it over me, so that I was wearing both coats, one on top of the other. I didn't know then what he meant by it, and I don't know now, but I hope he meant that I was forgiven—for my secret greed, for wanting to be so universally loved.

When they'd heaved their backpacks into the van and closed the doors and waved and were gone, I stood alone for a moment on the sidewalk in the rain, excessively dry under two rain slickers—cherry-red and lined with fleece. Then I walked up to the flat and let myself in and surveyed the closet that had been their room. They'd left the photos behind and I peeled one off the wall, slipped it into my pocket, and headed out into the rain. I started walking in the opposite direction of home, in and out of weather, into parts of the city I'd never been before, with my hands first in the pockets of one coat, then in the pockets of the other. As I walked, I thought about them hard—Jimmy and Ray—going over each episode in my mind, weighing and measuring, considering cause and effect. Not in an effort to shed the loss but to savor it, to shape it, to give it permanence.

READINGS

ANNE LAMOTT

Shitty First Drafts

NOW, PRACTICALLY EVEN BETTER NEWS than that of short assignments is the idea of shitty first drafts. All good writers write them. This is how they end up with good second drafts and terrific third drafts. People tend to look at successful writers, writers who are getting their books published and maybe even doing well financially, and think that they sit down at their desks every morning feeling like a million dollars, feeling great about who they are and how much talent they have and what a great story they have to tell; that they take in a few deep breaths, push back their sleeves, roll their necks a few times to get all the cricks out, and dive in, typing fully formed passages as fast as a court reporter. But this is just the fantasy of the uninitiated. I know some very great writers, writers you love who write beautifully and have made a great deal of money, and not *one* of them sits down routinely feeling wildly enthusiastic and confident. Not one of them writes elegant first drafts. All right, one of them does, but we do not like her very much. We do not think that she has a rich inner life or that God likes her or can even stand her. (Although when I mentioned this to my priest friend Tom, he said you can safely assume you've created God in your own image when it turns out that God hates all the same people you do.)

Very few writers really know what they are doing until they've done it. Nor do they go about their business feeling dewy and thrilled. They do not type a few stiff warm-up sentences and then find themselves bounding along like huskies across the snow. One writer I know tells me that he sits down every morning and says to himself nicely, "It's not like you don't have a choice, because you do—you can either type or kill yourself." We all often feel like we are pulling teeth, even those writers whose prose ends up being the most natural and fluid. The right words and sentences just do not come pouring out like ticker tape most of the time. Now, Muriel Spark is said to have felt that she was taking dictation from God every morning—sitting there, one supposes, plugged into a Dictaphone, typing away, humming. But this is a very hostile and aggressive position. One might hope for bad things to rain down on a person like this.

For me and most of the other writers I know, writing is not rapturous. In fact, the only way I can get anything written at all is to write really, really shitty first drafts.

The first draft is the child's draft, where you let it all pour out and then let it romp all over the place, knowing that no one is going to see it and that you can shape it later. You just let this childlike part of you channel whatever voices and visions come through and onto the page. If one of the characters wants to say, "Well, so what, Mr. Poopy Pants?" you let her. No one is going to see it. If the kid wants to get into really sentimental, weepy, emotional territory, you let him. Just get it all down on paper, because there may be something great in those six crazy pages that you would never have gotten to by more rational, grown-up means. There may be something in the very last line of the very last paragraph on page six that you just love, that is so beautiful or wild that you now know what you're supposed to be writing about, more or less, or in what direction you might go—but there was no way to get to this without first getting through the first five and a half pages.

I used to write food reviews for *California* magazine before it folded. (My writing food reviews had nothing to do with the magazine folding, although every single review did cause a couple of canceled subscriptions. Some readers took umbrage at my comparing mounds of vegetable puree with various ex-presidents' brains.) These reviews always took two days to write. First I'd go to a restaurant several times with a few opinionated, articulate friends in tow. I'd sit there writing down everything anyone said that was at all interesting or funny. Then on the following Monday I'd sit down at my desk with my notes, and try to write the review. Even after I'd been doing this for years, panic would set in. I'd try to write a lead, but instead I'd write a couple of dreadful sentences, xx them out, try again, xx everything out, and then feel despair and worry settle on my chest like an x-ray apron. It's over, I'd think, calmly. I'm not going to be able to get the magic to work this time. I'm ruined. I'm through. I'm toast. Maybe, I'd think, I can get my old job back as a clerk-typist. But probably not. I'd get up and study my teeth in the mirror for a while. Then I'd stop, remember to breathe, make a few phone calls, hit the kitchen and chow down. Eventually I'd go back and sit down at my desk, and sigh for the next ten minutes. Finally I would pick up my one-inch picture frame, stare into it as if for the answer, and every time the answer would come: all I had to do was to write a really shitty first draft of, say, the opening paragraph. And no one was going to see it.

So I'd start writing without reining myself in. It was almost just typing, just making my fingers move. And the writing would be *terrible*. I'd write a lead paragraph that was a whole page, even though the entire review could only be three pages long, and then I'd start writing up descriptions of the food, one dish at a time, bird by bird, and the critics would be sitting on my shoulders, commenting like cartoon characters. They'd be pretending to snore, or rolling their eyes at my overwrought descriptions, no matter how hard I tried to tone those descriptions down, no matter how conscious I was of what a friend said to me gently in my early days of restaurant reviewing. "Annie," she said, "it is just a piece of *chicken*. It is just a bit of *cake*."

But because by then I had been writing for so long, I would eventually let myself trust the process—sort of, more or less. I'd write a first draft that was maybe twice as long as it should be, with a self-indulgent and boring beginning, stupefying descriptions of the meal, lots of quotes from my black-humored friends that made them sound more like the Manson girls than food lovers, and no ending to speak of. The whole thing would be so long and incoherent and hideous that for the rest of the day I'd obsess about getting creamed by a car before I could write a decent second draft. I'd worry that people would read what I'd written and believe that the accident had really been a suicide, that I had panicked because my talent was waning and my mind was shot.

The next day, though, I'd sit down, go through it all with a colored pen, take out everything I possibly could, find a new lead somewhere on the second page, figure out a kicky place to end it, and then write a second draft. It always turned out fine, sometimes even funny and weird and helpful. I'd go over it one more time and mail it in.

Then, a month later, when it was time for another review, the whole process would start again, complete with the fears that people would find my first draft before I could rewrite it.

Almost all good writing begins with terrible first efforts. You need to start somewhere. Start by getting something—anything—down on paper. A friend of mine says that the first draft is the down draft—you just get it down. The second draft is the up draft—you fix it up. You try to say what you have to say more accurately. And the third draft is the dental draft, where you check every tooth, to see if it's loose or cramped or decayed, or even, God help us, healthy.

What I've learned to do when I sit down to work on a shitty first draft is to quiet the voices in my head. First there's the vinegar-lipped Reader Lady, who says primly, "Well, *that's* not very interesting, is it?" And there's the emaciated German male who writes these Orwellian memos detailing your thought crimes. And there are your parents, agonizing over your lack of loyalty and discretion; and there's William Burroughs, dozing off or shooting up because he finds you as bold and articulate as a houseplant; and so on. And there are also the dogs: let's not forget the dogs, the dogs in their pen who will surely hurtle and snarl their way out if you ever *stop* writing, because writing is, for some of us, the latch that keeps the door of the pen closed, keeps those crazy ravenous dogs contained.

Quieting these voices is at least half the battle I fight daily. But this is better than it used to be. It used to be 87 percent. Left to its own devices, my mind spends much of its time having conversations with people who aren't there. I walk along defending myself to people, or exchanging repartee with them, or rationalizing my behavior, or seducing them with gossip, or pretending I'm on their TV talk show or whatever. I speed or run an aging yellow light or don't come to a full stop, and one nanosecond later am explaining to imaginary cops exactly why I had to do what I did, or insisting that I did not in fact do it.

I happened to mention this to a hypnotist I saw many years ago, and he looked at me very nicely. At first I thought he was feeling around on the floor for the silent alarm button, but then he gave me the following exercise, which I still use to this day.

Close your eyes and get quiet for a minute, until the chatter starts up. Then isolate one of the voices and imagine the person speaking as a mouse. Pick it up by the tail and drop it into a mason jar. Then isolate another voice, pick it up by the tail, drop it in the jar. And so on. Drop in any high-maintenance parental units, drop in any contractors, lawyers, colleagues, children, anyone who is whining in your head. Then put the lid on, and watch all these mouse people clawing at the glass, jabbering away, trying to make you feel like shit because you won't do what they want—won't give them more money, won't be more successful, won't see them more often. Then imagine that there is a volume-control button on the bottle. Turn it all the way up for a minute, and listen to the stream of angry, neglected, guilt-mongering voices. Then turn it all the way down and watch the frantic mice lunge at the glass, trying to get to you. Leave it down, and get back to your shitty first draft.

A writer friend of mine suggests opening the jar and shooting them all in the head. But I think he's a little angry, and I'm sure nothing like this would ever occur to you.

Reading as a Writer

1. Can you identify with Lamott's experience of her writing process? If so, in what ways?

2. After you've finished a first draft, how do you feel? Relieved? Anxious? Do you always know what to do next? If not, how do you figure it out?

3. At the end of the essay, Lamott describes an exercise she uses to "quiet the voices" of doubt and distraction that prevent her from writing. What techniques or methods do you use to help focus on writing (and revising), if any?

RAYMOND CARVER

The Bath

SATURDAY AFTERNOON THE MOTHER DROVE to the bakery in the shopping center. After looking through a loose-leaf binder with photographs of cakes taped onto the pages, she ordered chocolate, the child's favorite. The cake she chose was decorated with a spaceship and a launching pad under a sprinkling of white stars. The name SCOTTY would be iced on in green as if it were the name of the spaceship.

The baker listened thoughtfully when the mother told him Scotty would be eight years old. He was an older man, this baker, and he wore a curious apron, a heavy thing with loops that went under his arms and around his back and then crossed in front again where they were tied in a very thick knot. He kept wiping his hands on the front of the apron as he listened to the woman, his wet eyes examining her lips as she studied the samples and talked.

He let her take her time. He was in no hurry.

The mother decided on the spaceship cake, and then she gave the baker her name and her telephone number. The cake would be ready Monday morning, in plenty of time for the party Monday afternoon. This was all the baker was willing to say. No pleasantries, just this small exchange, the barest information, nothing that was not necessary.

Monday morning, the boy was walking to school. He was in the company of another boy, the two boys passing a bag of potato chips back and forth between them. The birthday boy was trying to trick the other boy into telling what he was going to give in the way of a present.

At an intersection, without looking, the birthday boy stepped off the curb, and was promptly knocked down by a car. He fell on his side, his head in the gutter, his legs in the road moving as if he were climbing a wall.

The other boy stood holding the potato chips. He was wondering if he should finish the rest or continue on to school.

The birthday boy did not cry. But neither did he wish to talk anymore. He would not answer when the other boy asked what it felt like to be hit by a car. The birthday boy got up and turned back for home, at which time the other boy waved good-bye and headed off for school.

The birthday boy told his mother what had happened. They sat together on the sofa. She held his hands in her lap. This is what she was doing when the boy pulled his hands away and lay down on his back.

Of course, the birthday party never happened. The birthday boy was in the hospital instead. The mother sat by the bed. She was waiting for the boy to wake up. The father hurried over from his office. He sat next to the mother. So now the both of them waited for the boy to wake up. They waited for hours, and then the father went home to take a bath.

The man drove home from the hospital. He drove the streets faster than he should. It had been a good life till now. There had been work, fatherhood, family. The man had been lucky and happy. But fear made him want a bath.

He pulled into the driveway. He sat in the car trying to make his legs work. The child had been hit by a car and he was in the hospital, but he was going to be all right. The man got out of the car and went up to the door. The dog was barking and the telephone was ringing. It kept ringing while the man unlocked the door and felt the wall for the light switch.

He picked up the receiver. He said, "I just got in the door!"

"There's a cake that wasn't picked up."

This is what the voice on the other end said.

"What are you saying?" the father said.

"The cake," the voice said. "Sixteen dollars."

The husband held the receiver against his ear, trying to understand. He said, "I don't know anything about it."

"Don't hand me that," the voice said.

The husband hung up the telephone. He went into the kitchen and poured himself some whiskey. He called the hospital.

The child's condition remained the same.

While the water ran into the tub, the man lathered his face and shaved. He was in the tub when he heard the telephone again. He got himself out and hurried through the house, saying, "Stupid, stupid," because he wouldn't be doing this if he'd stayed where he was in the hospital. He picked up the receiver and shouted, "Hello!"

The voice said, "It's ready."

The father got back to the hospital after midnight. The wife was sitting in the chair by the bed. She looked up at the husband and then she looked back at the child. From an apparatus over the bed hung a bottle with a tube running from the bottle to the child.

"What's this?" the father said.

"Glucose," the mother said.

The husband put his hand to the back of the woman's head.

"He's going to wake up," the man said.

"I know," the woman said.

In a little while the man said, "Go home and let me take over."

She shook her head. "No," she said.

"Really," he said. "Go home for a while. You don't have to worry. He's sleeping, is all."

A nurse pushed open the door. She nodded to them as she went to the bed. She took the left arm out from under the covers and put her fingers on the wrist. She put the arm back under the covers and wrote on the clipboard attached to the bed.

"How is he?" the mother said.

"Stable," the nurse said. Then she said, "Doctor will be in again shortly."

"I was saying maybe she'd want to go home and get a little rest," the man said. "After the doctor comes."

"She could do that," the nurse said.

The woman said, "We'll see what the doctor says." She brought her hand up to her eyes and leaned her head forward.

The nurse said, "Of course."

The father gazed at his son, the small chest inflating and deflating under the covers. He felt more fear now. He began shaking his head. He talked to himself like this. The child is fine. Instead of sleeping at home, he's doing it here. Sleep is the same wherever you do it.

The doctor came in. He shook hands with the man. The woman got up from the chair.

"Ann," the doctor said and nodded. The doctor said, "Let's just see how he's doing." He moved to the bed and touched the boy's wrist. He peeled back an eyelid and then the other. He turned back the covers and listened to the heart. He pressed his fingers here and there on the body. He went to the end of the bed and studied the chart. He noted the time, scribbled on the chart, and then he considered the mother and the father.

This doctor was a handsome man. His skin was moist and tan. He wore a three-piece suit, a vivid tie, and on his shirt were cufflinks.

The mother was talking to herself like this. He has just come from somewhere with an audience. They gave him a special medal.

The doctor said, "Nothing to shout about, but nothing to worry about. He should wake up pretty soon." The doctor looked at the boy again. "We'll know more after the tests are in."

"Oh, no," the mother said.

The doctor said, "Sometimes you see this."

The father said, "You wouldn't call this a coma, then?"

The father waited and looked at the doctor.

"No, I don't want to call it that," the doctor said. "He's sleeping. It's restorative. The body is doing what it has to do."

"It's a coma," the mother said. "A kind of coma."

The doctor said, "I wouldn't call it that."

He took the woman's hands and patted them. He shook hands with the husband.

*   *   *

The woman put her fingers on the child's forehead and kept them there for a while. "At least he doesn't have a fever," she said. Then she said, "I don't know. Feel his head."

The man put his fingers on the boy's forehead. The man said, "I think he's supposed to feel this way."

The woman stood there awhile longer, working her lip with her teeth. Then she moved to her chair and sat down.

The husband sat in the chair beside her. He wanted to say something else. But there was no saying what it should be. He took her hand and put it in his lap. This made him feel better. It made him feel he was saying something. They sat like that for a while, watching the boy, not talking. From time to time he squeezed her hand until she took it away.

"I've been praying," she said.

"Me too," the father said. "I've been praying too."

A nurse came back in and checked the flow from the bottle.

A doctor came in and said what his name was. This doctor was wearing loafers.

"We're going to take him downstairs for more pictures," he said. "And we want to do a scan."

"A scan?" the mother said. She stood between this new doctor and the bed.

"It's nothing," he said.

"My God," she said.

Two orderlies came in. They wheeled a thing like a bed. They unhooked the boy from the tube and slid him over onto the thing with wheels.

It was after sunup when they brought the birthday boy back out. The mother and father followed the orderlies into the elevator and up to the room. Once more the parents took up their places next to the bed.

They waited all day. The boy did not wake up. The doctor came again and examined the boy again and left after saying the same things again. Nurses came in. Doctors came in. A technician came in and took blood.

"I don't understand this," the mother said to the technician.

"Doctor's orders," the technician said.

The mother went to the window and looked out at the parking lot. Cars with their lights on were driving in and out. She stood at the window with her hands on the sill. She was talking to herself like this. We're into something now, something hard.

She was afraid.

She saw a car stop and a woman in a long coat get into it. She made believe she was that woman. She made believe she was driving away from here to someplace else.

The doctor came in. He looked tanned and healthier than ever. He went to the bed and examined the boy. He said, "His signs are fine. Everything's good."

The mother said, "But he's sleeping."

"Yes," the doctor said.

The husband said, "She's tired. She's starved."

The doctor said, "She should rest. She should eat. Ann," the doctor said.

"Thank you," the husband said.

He shook hands with the doctor and the doctor patted their shoulders and left.

"I suppose one of us should go home and check on things," the man said. "The dog needs to be fed."

"Call the neighbors," the wife said. "Someone will feed him if you ask them to."

She tried to think who. She closed her eyes and tried to think anything at all. After a time she said, "Maybe I'll do it. Maybe if I'm not here watching, he'll wake up. Maybe it's because I'm watching that he won't."

"That could be it," the husband said.

"I'll go home and take a bath and put on something clean," the woman said.

"I think you should do that," the man said.

She picked up her purse. He helped her into her coat. She moved to the door, and looked back. She looked at the child, and then she looked at the father. The husband nodded and smiled.

She went past the nurses' station and down to the end of the corridor, where she turned and saw a little waiting room, a family in there, all sitting in wicker chairs, a man in a khaki shirt, a baseball cap pushed back on his head, a large woman wearing a housedress, slippers, a girl in jeans, hair in dozens of kinky braids, the table littered with flimsy wrappers and styrofoam and coffee sticks and packets of salt and pepper.

"Nelson," the woman said. "Is it about Nelson?"

The woman's eyes widened.

"Tell me now, lady," the woman said. "Is it about Nelson?"

The woman was trying to get up from her chair. But the man had his hand closed over her arm.

"Here, here," the man said.

"I'm sorry," the mother said. "I'm looking for the elevator. My son is in the hospital. I can't find the elevator."

"Elevator is down that way," the man said, and he aimed a finger in the right direction.

"My son was hit by a car," the mother said. "But he's going to be alright. He's in shock now, but it might be some kind of coma too. That's what worries us, the coma part, I'm going out for a little while. Maybe I'll take a bath. But my husband is with him. He's watching. There's a chance everything will change when I'm gone. My name is Ann Weiss."

The man shifted in his chair. He shook his head.

He said, "Our Nelson."

She pulled into the driveway. The dog ran out from behind the house. He ran in circles on the grass. She closed her eyes and leaned her head against the wheel. She listened to the ticking of the engine.

She got out of the car and went to the door. She turned on lights and put on water for tea. She opened a can and fed the dog. She sat down on the sofa with her tea.

The telephone rang.

"Yes!" she said. "Hello!" she said.

"Mrs. Weiss," a man's voice said.

"Yes," she said. "This is Mrs. Weiss. Is it about Scotty?" she said.

"Scotty," the voice said. "It is about Scotty," the voice said. "It has to do with Scotty, yes."

Reading as a Writer

1. Why would this story be considered a "minimalist" story? (Hint: What is kept to a minimum in it?)

2. What are some of the details that are supposed to give us hints to what is going on?

3. Do you miss having more "telling," or narrative, in this story?

RAYMOND CARVER

A Small, Good Thing

SATURDAY AFTERNOON SHE DROVE to the bakery in the shopping center. After looking through a loose-leaf binder with photographs of cakes taped onto the pages, she ordered chocolate, the child's favorite. The cake she chose was decorated with a space ship and launching pad under a sprinkling of white stars, and a planet made of red frosting at the other end. His name, SCOTTY, would be in green letters beneath the planet. The baker, who was an older man with a thick neck, listened without saying anything when she told him the child would be eight years old next Monday. The baker wore a white apron that looked like a smock. Straps cut under his arms, went around in back and then to the front again, where they were secured under his heavy waist. He wiped his hands on his apron as he listened to her. He kept his eyes down on the photographs and let her talk. He let her take her time. He'd just come to work and he'd be there all night, baking, and he was in no real hurry.

She gave the baker her name, Ann Weiss, and her telephone number. The cake would be ready on Monday morning, just out of the oven, in plenty of time for the child's party that afternoon. The baker was not jolly. There were no pleasantries between them, just the minimum exchange of words, the necessary information. He made her feel uncomfortable, and she didn't like that. While he was bent over the counter with the pencil in his hand, she studied his coarse features and wondered if he'd ever done anything else with his life besides be a baker. She was a mother and thirty-three years old, and it seemed to her that everyone, especially someone the baker's age—a man old enough to be her father—must have children who'd gone through this special time of cakes and birthday parties. There must be that between them, she thought. But he was abrupt with her—not rude, just abrupt. She gave up trying to make friends with him. She looked into the back of the bakery and could see a long, heavy wooden table with aluminum pie pans stacked at one end; and beside the table a metal container filled with empty racks. There was an enormous oven. A radio was playing country-Western music.

The baker finished printing the information on the special order card and closed up the binder. He looked at her and said, "Monday morning." She thanked him and drove home.

On Monday morning, the birthday boy was walking to school with another boy. They were passing a bag of potato chips back and forth and the birthday boy was trying to find out what his friend intended to give him for his birthday that afternoon. Without looking, the birthday boy stepped off the curb at an intersection and was immediately knocked down by a car. He fell on his side with his head in the gutter and his legs out in the road. His eyes were closed, but his legs moved back and forth as if he were trying to climb over something. His friend dropped the potato chips and started to cry. The car had gone a hundred feet or so and stopped in the middle of the road. The man in the driver's seat looked back over his shoulder. He waited until the boy got unsteadily to his feet. The boy wobbled a little. He looked dazed, but okay. The driver put the car into gear and drove away.

The birthday boy didn't cry, but he didn't have anything to say about anything either. He wouldn't answer when his friend asked him what it felt like to be hit by a car. He walked home, and his friend went on to school. But after the birthday boy was inside his house and was telling his mother about it—she sitting beside him on the sofa, holding his hands in her lap, saying, "Scotty, honey, are you sure you feel all right, baby?" thinking she would call the doctor anyway—he suddenly lay back on the sofa, closed his eyes, and went limp. When she couldn't wake him up, she hurried to the telephone and called her husband at work. Howard told her to remain calm, remain calm, and then he called an ambulance for the child and left for the hospital himself.

Of course, the birthday party was canceled. The child was in the hospital with a mild concussion and suffering from shock. There'd been vomiting, and his lungs had taken in fluid which needed pumping out that afternoon. Now he simply seemed to be in a very deep sleep—but no coma, Dr. Francis had emphasized, no coma, when he saw the alarm in the parents' eyes. At eleven o'clock that night, when the boy seemed to be resting comfortably enough after the many X-rays and the lab work, and it was just a matter of his waking up and coming around, Howard left the hospital. He and Ann had been at the hospital with the child since that afternoon, and he was going home for a short while to bathe and change clothes. "I'll be back in an hour," he said. She nodded. "It's fine," she said. "I'll be right here." He kissed her on the forehead, and they touched hands. She sat in the chair beside the bed and looked at the child. She was waiting for him to wake up and be all right. Then she could begin to relax.

Howard drove home from the hospital. He took the wet, dark streets very fast, then caught himself and slowed down. Until now, his life had gone smoothly and to his satisfaction—college, marriage, another year of college for the advanced degree in business, a junior partnership in an investment firm. Fatherhood. He was happy and, so far, lucky—he knew that. His parents were still living, his brothers and his sister were established, his friends from college had gone out to take their places in the world. So far, he had kept away from any real harm, from those forces he knew existed and that could cripple or bring down a man if the luck went bad, if things suddenly turned. He pulled into the driveway and parked. His left leg began to tremble. He sat in the car for a minute and tried to deal with the present situation in a rational manner. Scotty had been hit by a car and was in the hospital, but he was going to be all right. Howard closed his eyes and ran his hand over his face. He got out of the car and went up to the front door. The dog was barking inside the house. The telephone rang and rang while he unlocked the door and fumbled for the light switch. He shouldn't have left the hospital, he shouldn't have. "Goddamn it!" he said. He picked up the receiver and said, "I just walked in the door!"

"There's a cake here that wasn't picked up," the voice on the other end of the line said.

"What are you saying?" Howard asked.

"A cake," the voice said. "A sixteen-dollar cake."

Howard held the receiver against his ear, trying to understand. "I don't know anything about a cake," he said. "Jesus, what are you talking about?"

"Don't hand me that," the voice said.

Howard hung up the telephone. He went into the kitchen and poured himself some whiskey. He called the hospital. But the child's condition remained the same; he was still sleeping and nothing had changed there. While water poured into the tub, Howard lathered his face and shaved. He'd just stretched out in the tub and closed his eyes when the telephone rang again. He hauled himself out, grabbed a towel, and hurried through the house, saying, "Stupid, stupid," for having left the hospital. But when he picked up the receiver and shouted, "Hello!" there was no sound at the other end of the line. Then the caller hung up.

He arrived back at the hospital a little after midnight. Ann still sat in the chair beside the bed. She looked up at Howard, and then she looked back at the child. The child's eyes stayed closed, the head was still wrapped in bandages. His breathing was quiet and regular. From an apparatus over the bed hung a bottle of glucose with a tube running from the bottle to the boy's arm.

"How is he?" Howard said. "What's all this?" waving at the glucose and the tube.

"Dr. Francis's orders," she said. "He needs nourishment. He needs to keep up his strength. Why doesn't he wake up, Howard? I don't understand, if he's all right."

Howard put his hand against the back of her head. He ran his fingers through her hair. "He's going to be all right. He'll wake up in a little while. Dr. Francis knows what's what."

After a time, he said, "Maybe you should go home and get some rest. I'll stay here. Just don't put up with this creep who keeps calling. Hang up right away."

"Who's calling?" she asked.

"I don't know who, just somebody with nothing better to do than call up people. You go on now."

She shook her head. "No," she said, "I'm fine."

"Really," he said. "Go home for a while, and then come back and spell me in the morning. It'll be all right. What did Dr. Francis say? He said Scotty's going to be all right. We don't have to worry. He's just sleeping now, that's all."

A nurse pushed the door open. She nodded at them as she went to the bedside. She took the left arm out from under the covers and put her fingers on the wrist, found the pulse, then consulted her watch. In a little while, she put the arm back under the covers and moved to the foot of the bed, where she wrote something on a clipboard attached to the bed.

"How is he?" Ann said. Howard's hand was a weight on her shoulder. She was aware of the pressure from his fingers.

"He's stable," the nurse said. Then she said, "Doctor will be in again shortly. Doctor's back in the hospital. He's making rounds right now."

"I was saying maybe she'd want to go home and get a little rest," Howard said. "After the doctor comes," he said.

"She could do that," the nurse said. "I think you should both feel free to do that, if you wish." The nurse was a big Scandinavian woman with blond hair. There was the trace of an accent in her speech.

"We'll see what the doctor says," Ann said. "I want to talk to the doctor. I don't think he should keep sleeping like this. I don't think that's a good sign." She brought her hand up to her eyes and let her head come forward a little. Howard's grip tightened on her shoulder, and then his hand moved up to her neck, where his fingers began to knead the muscles there.

"Dr. Francis will be here in a few minutes," the nurse said. Then she left the room.

Howard gazed at his son for a time, the small chest quietly rising and falling under the covers. For the first time since the terrible minutes after Ann's telephone call to him at his office, he felt a genuine fear starting in his limbs. He began shaking his head. Scotty was fine, but instead of sleeping at home in his own bed, he was in a hospital bed with bandages around his head and a tube in his arm. But this help was what he needed right now.

Dr. Francis came in and shook hands with Howard, though they'd just seen each other a few hours before. Ann got up from the chair. "Doctor?"

"Ann," he said and nodded. "Let's just first see how he's doing," the doctor said. He moved to the side of the bed and took the boy's pulse. He peeled back one eyelid and then the other. Howard and Ann stood beside the doctor and watched. Then the doctor turned back the covers and listened to the boy's heart and lungs with his stethoscope. He pressed his fingers here and there on the abdomen. When he was finished, he went to the end of the bed and studied the chart. He noted the time, scribbled something on the chart, and then looked at Howard and Ann.

"Doctor, how is he?" Howard said. "What's the matter with him exactly?"

"Why doesn't he wake up?" Ann said.

The doctor was a handsome, big-shouldered man with a tanned face. He wore a three-piece blue suit, a striped tie, and ivory cufflinks. His gray hair was combed along the sides of his head, and he looked as if he had just come from a concert. "He's all right," the doctor said. "Nothing to shout about, he could be better, I think. But he's all right. Still, I wish he'd wake up. He should wake up pretty soon." The doctor looked at the boy again. "We'll know some more in a couple of hours, after the results of a few more tests are in. But he's all right, believe me, except for the hairline fracture of the skull. He does have that."

"Oh, no," Ann said.

"And a bit of a concussion, as I said before. Of course, you know he's in shock," the doctor said. "Sometimes you see this in shock cases. This sleeping."

"But he's out of any real danger?" Howard said. "You said before he's not in a coma. You wouldn't call this a coma, then—would you, doctor?" Howard waited. He looked at the doctor.

"No, I don't want to call it a coma," the doctor said and glanced over at the boy once more. "He's just in a very deep sleep. It's a restorative measure the body is taking on its own. He's out of any real danger, I'd say that for certain, yes. But we'll know more when he wakes up and the other tests are in," the doctor said.

"It's a coma," Ann said. "Of sorts."

"It's not a coma yet, not exactly," the doctor said. "I wouldn't want to call it coma. Not yet, anyway. He's suffered shock. In shock cases, this kind of reaction is common enough; it's a temporary reaction to bodily trauma. Coma. Well, coma is a deep, prolonged unconsciousness, something that could go on for days, or weeks even. Scotty's not in that area, not as far as we can tell. I'm certain his condition will show improvement by morning. I'm betting that it will. We'll know more when he wakes up, which shouldn't be long now. Of course, you may do as you like, stay here or go home for a time. But by all means feel free to leave the hospital for a while if you want. This is not easy, I know." The doctor gazed at the boy again, watching him, and then he turned to Ann and said, "You try not to worry, little mother. Believe me, we're doing all that can be done. It's just a question of a little more time now." He nodded at her, shook hands with Howard again, and then he left the room.

Ann put her hand over the child's forehead. "At least he doesn't have a fever," she said. Then she said, "My God, he feels so cold, though. Howard? Is he supposed to feel like this? Feel his head."

Howard touched the child's temples. His own breathing had slowed. "I think he's supposed to feel this way right now," he said. "He's in shock, remember? That's what the doctors said. The doctor was just in here. He would have said something if Scotty wasn't okay."

Ann stood there a while longer, working her lip with her teeth. Then she moved over to her chair and sat down.

Howard sat in the chair next to her chair. They looked at each other. He wanted to say something else and reassure her, but he was afraid, too. He took her hand and put it in his lap, and this made him feel better, her hand being there. He picked up her hand and squeezed it. Then he just held her hand. They sat like that for a while, watching the boy and not talking. From time to time, he squeezed her hand. Finally, she took her hand away.

"I've been praying," she said.

He nodded.

She said, "I almost thought I'd forgotten how, but it came back to me. All I had to do was close my eyes and say, 'Please God, help us—help Scotty,' and then the rest was easy. The words were right there. Maybe if you prayed, too," she said to him.

"I've already prayed," he said. "I prayed this afternoon—yesterday afternoon, I mean—after you called, while I was driving to the hospital. I've been praying," he said.

"That's good," she said. For the first time, she felt they were together in it, this trouble. She realized with a start that, until now, it had only been happening to her and to Scotty. She hadn't let Howard into it, though he was there and needed all along. She felt glad to be his wife.

The same nurse came in and took the boy's pulse again and checked the flow from the bottle hanging above the bed.

In an hour, another doctor came in. He said his name was Parsons, from Radiology. He had a bushy mustache. He was wearing loafers, a Western shirt, and a pair of jeans.

"We're going to take him downstairs for more pictures," he told them. "We need to do some more pictures, and we want to do a scan."

"What's that?" Ann said. "A scan?" She stood between this new doctor and the bed. "I thought you'd already taken all your X-rays."

"I'm afraid we need some more," he said. "Nothing to be alarmed about. We just need some more pictures, and we want to do a brain scan on him."

"My God," Ann said.

"It's perfectly normal procedure in cases like this," this new doctor said. "We just need to find out for sure why he isn't back awake yet. It's normal medical procedure, and nothing to be alarmed about. We'll be taking him down in a few minutes," this doctor said.

In a little while, two orderlies came into the room with a gurney. They were black-haired, dark-complexioned men in white uniforms, and they said a few words to each other in a foreign tongue as they unhooked the boy from the tube and moved him from his bed to the gurney. Then they wheeled him from the room. Howard and Ann got on the same elevator. Ann gazed at the child. She closed her eyes as the elevator began its descent. The orderlies stood at either end of the gurney without saying anything, though once one of the men made a comment to the other in their own language, and the other man nodded slowly in response.

Later that morning, just as the sun was beginning to lighten the windows in the waiting room outside the X-ray department, they brought the boy out and moved him back up to his room. Howard and Ann rode up on the elevator with him once more, and once more they took up their places beside the bed.

They waited all day, but still the boy did not wake up. Occasionally, one of them would leave the room to go downstairs to the cafeteria to drink coffee and then, as if suddenly remembering and feeling guilty, get up from the table and hurry back to the room. Dr. Francis came again that afternoon and examined the boy once more and then left after telling them he was coming along and could wake up at any minute now. Nurses, different nurses from the night before, came in from time to time. Then a young woman from the lab knocked and entered the room. She wore white slacks and a white blouse and carried a little tray of things which she put on the stand beside the bed. Without a word to them, she took blood from the boy's arm. Howard closed his eyes as the woman found the right place on the boy's arm and pushed the needle in.

"I don't understand this," Ann said to the woman.

"Doctor's orders," the young woman said. "I do what I'm told. They say draw that one, I draw. What's wrong with him, anyway?" she said. "He's a sweetie."

"He was hit by a car," Howard said. "A hit-and-run."

The young woman shook her head and looked again at the boy. Then she took her tray and left the room.

"Why won't he wake up?" Ann said. "Howard? I want some answers from these people."

Howard didn't say anything. He sat down again in the chair and crossed one leg over the other. He rubbed his face. He looked at his son and then he settled back in the chair, closed his eyes, and went to sleep.

Ann walked to the window and looked out at the parking lot. It was night, and cars were driving into and out of the parking lot with their lights on. She stood at the window with her hands gripping the sill, and knew in her heart that they were into something now, something hard. She was afraid, and her teeth began to chatter until she tightened her jaws. She saw a big car stop in front of the hospital and someone, a woman in a long coat, get into the car. She wished she were that woman and somebody, anybody, was driving her away from here to somewhere else, a place where she would find Scotty waiting for her when she stepped out of the car, ready to say *Mom* and let her gather him in her arms.

In a little while, Howard woke up. He looked at the boy again. Then he got up from the chair, stretched, and went over to stand beside her at the window. They both stared out at the parking lot. They didn't say anything. But they seemed to feel each other's insides now, as though the worry had made them transparent in a perfectly natural way.

The door opened and Dr. Francis came in. He was wearing a different suit and tie this time. His gray hair was combed along the sides of his head, and he looked as if he had just shaved. He went straight to the bed and examined the boy. "He ought to have come around by now. There's just no good reason for this," he said. "But I can tell you we're all convinced he's out of any danger. We'll just feel better when he wakes up. There's no reason, absolutely none, why he shouldn't come around. Very soon. Oh, he'll have himself a dilly of a headache when he does, you can count on that. But all of his signs are fine. They're as normal as can be."

"It is a coma, then?" Ann said.

The doctor rubbed his smooth cheek. "We'll call it that for the time being, until he wakes up. But you must be worn out. This is hard. I know this is hard. Feel free to go out for a bite," he said. "It would do you good. I'll put a nurse in here while you're gone if you'll feel better about going. Go and have yourselves something to eat."

"I couldn't eat anything," Ann said.

"Do what you need to do, of course," the doctor said. "Anyway, I wanted to tell you that all the signs are good, the tests are negative, nothing showed up at all, and just as soon as he wakes up he'll be over the hill."

"Thank you, doctor," Howard said. He shook hands with the doctor again. The doctor patted Howard's shoulder and went out.

"I suppose one of us should go home and check on things," Howard said. "Slug needs to be fed, for one thing."

"Call one of the neighbors," Ann said. "Call the Morgans. Anyone will feed a dog if you ask them to."

"All right," Howard said. After a while, he said, "Honey, why don't you do it? Why don't you go home and check on things, and then come back? It'll do you good. I'll be right here with him. Seriously," he said. "We need to keep up our strength on this. We'll want to be here for a while even after he wakes up."

"Why don't *you* go?" she said. "Feed Slug. Feed yourself."

"I already went," he said. "I was gone for exactly an hour and fifteen minutes. You go home for an hour and freshen up. Then come back."

She tried to think about it, but she was too tired. She closed her eyes and tried to think about it again. After a time, she said, "Maybe I will go home for a few minutes. Maybe if I'm not just sitting right here watching him every second, he'll wake up and be all right. You know? Maybe he'll wake up if I'm not here. I'll go home and take a bath and put on clean clothes. I'll feed Slug. Then I'll come back."

"I'll be right here," he said. "You go on home, honey. I'll keep an eye on things here." His eyes were bloodshot and small, as if he'd been drinking for a long time. His clothes were rumpled. His beard had come out again. She touched his face; and then she took her hand back. She understood he wanted to be by himself for a while, not have to talk or share his worry for a time. She picked her purse up from the night-stand, and he helped her into her coat.

"I won't be gone long," she said.

"Just sit and rest for a little while when you get home," he said. "Eat something. Take a bath. After you get out of the bath, just sit for a while and rest. It'll do you a world of good, you'll see. Then come back," he said. "Let's try not to worry. You heard what Dr. Francis said."

She stood in her coat for a minute trying to recall the doctor's exact words, looking for any nuances, any hint of something behind his words other than what he had said. She tried to remember if his expression had changed any when he bent over to exam-ine the child. She remembered the way his features had composed themselves as he rolled back the child's eyelids and then listened to his breathing.

She went to the door, where she turned and looked back. She looked at the child, and then she looked at the father. Howard nodded. She stepped out of the room and pulled the door closed behind her.

She went past the nurses' station and down to the end of the corridor, looking for the elevator. At the end of the corridor, she turned to her right and entered a little waiting room where a Negro family sat in wicker chairs. There was a middle-aged man in a khaki shirt and pants, a baseball cap pushed back on his head. A large woman wearing a housedress and slippers was slumped in one of the chairs. A teenaged girl in jeans, hair done in dozens of little braids, lay stretched out in one of the chairs smoking a cigarette, her legs crossed at the ankles. The family swung their eyes to Ann as she entered the room. The little table was littered with hamburger wrappers and Styrofoam cups.

"Franklin," the large woman said as she roused herself. "Is it about Franklin?" Her eyes widened. "Tell me now, lady," the woman said. "Is it about Franklin?" She was trying to rise from her chair, but the man had closed his hand over her arm.

"Here, here," he said. "Evelyn."

"I'm sorry," Ann said. "I'm looking for the elevator. My son is in the hospital, and now I can't find the elevator."

"Elevator is down that way, turn left," the man said as he aimed a finger.

The girl drew on her cigarette and stared at Ann. Her eyes were narrowed to slits, and her broad lips parted slowly as she let the smoke escape. The Negro woman let her head fall on her shoulder and looked away from Ann, no longer interested.

"My son was hit by a car," Ann said to the man. She seemed to need to explain her-self. "He has a concussion and a little skull fracture, but he's going to be all right. He's in shock now, but it might be some kind of coma, too. That's what really worries us, the coma part. I'm going out for a little while, but my husband is with him. Maybe he'll wake up while I'm gone."

"That's too bad," the man said and shifted in the chair. He shook his head. He looked down at the table, and then he looked back at Ann. She was still standing there. He said, "Our Franklin, he's on the operating table. Somebody cut him. Tried to kill him. There was a fight where he was at. At this party. They say he was just standing and watching. Not bothering nobody. But that don't mean nothing these days. Now he's on the operating table. We're just hoping and praying, that's all we can do now." He gazed at her steadily.

Ann looked at the girl again, who was still watching her, and at the older woman, who kept her head down, but whose eyes were now closed. Ann saw the lips moving silently, making words. She had an urge to ask what those words were. She wanted to talk more with these people who were in the same kind of waiting she was in. She was afraid, and they were afraid. They had that in common. She would have liked to have said something else about the accident, told them more about Scotty, that it had happened on the day of his birthday, Monday, and that he was still unconscious. Yet she didn't know how to begin. She stood looking at them without saying anything more.

She went down the corridor the man had indicated and found the elevator. She waited a minute in front of the closed doors, still wondering if she was doing the right thing. Then she put out her finger and touched the button.

She pulled into the driveway and cut the engine. She closed her eyes and leaned her head against the wheel for a minute. She listened to the ticking sounds the engine made as it began to cool. Then she got out of the car. She could hear the dog barking inside the house. She went to the front door, which was unlocked. She went inside and turned on lights and put on a kettle of water for tea. She opened some dogfood and fed Slug on the back porch. The dog ate in hungry little smacks. It kept running into the kitchen to see that she was going to stay. As she sat down on the sofa with her tea, the telephone rang.

"Yes!" she said as she answered. "Hello!"

"Mrs. Weiss," a man's voice said. It was five o'clock in the morning, and she thought she could hear machinery or equipment of some kind in the background.

"Yes, yes! What is it?" she said. "This is Mrs. Weiss. This is she. What is it, please?" She listened to whatever it was in the background. "Is it Scotty, for Christ's sake?"

"Scotty," the man's voice said. "It's about Scotty, yes. It has to do with Scotty, that problem. Have you forgotten about Scotty?" the man said. Then he hung up.

She dialed the hospital's number and asked for the third floor. She demanded information about her son from the nurse who answered the telephone. Then she asked to speak to her husband. It was, she said, an emergency.

She waited, turning the telephone cord in her fingers. She closed her eyes and felt sick at her stomach. She would have to make herself eat. Slug came in from the back porch and lay down near her feet. He wagged his tail. She pulled at his ear while he licked her fingers. Howard was on the line.

"Somebody just called here," she said. She twisted the telephone cord. "He said it was about Scotty," she cried.

"Scotty's fine," Howard told her. "I mean, he's still sleeping. There's been no change. The nurse has been in twice since you've been gone. A nurse or else a doctor. He's all right."

"This man called. He said it was about Scotty," she told him.

"Honey, you rest for a little while, you need the rest. It must be that same caller I had. Just forget it. Come back down here after you've rested. Then we'll have breakfast or something."

"Breakfast," she said. "I don't want any breakfast."

"You know what I mean," he said. "Juice, something. I don't know. I don't know anything, Ann. Jesus, I'm not hungry, either. Ann, it's hard to talk now. I'm standing here at the desk. Dr. Francis is coming again at eight o'clock this morning. He's going to have something to tell us then, something more definite. That's what one of the nurses said. She didn't know any more than that. Ann? Honey, maybe we'll know something more then. At eight o'clock. Come back here before eight. Meanwhile, I'm right here and Scotty's all right. He's still the same," he added.

"I was drinking a cup of tea," she said, "when the telephone rang. They said it was about Scotty. There was a noise in the background. Was there a noise in the background on that call you had, Howard?"

"I don't remember," he said. "Maybe the driver of the car, maybe he's a psychopath and found out about Scotty somehow. But I'm here with him. Just rest like you were going to do. Take a bath and come back by seven or so, and we'll talk to the doctor together when he gets here. It's going to be all right, honey. I'm here, and there are doctors and nurses around. They say his condition is stable."

"I'm scared to death," she said.

She ran water, undressed, and got into the tub. She washed and dried quickly, not taking the time to wash her hair. She put on clean underwear, wool slacks, and a sweater. She went into the living room, where the dog looked up at her and let its tail thump once against the floor. It was just starting to get light outside when she went out to the car.

She drove into the parking lot of the hospital and found a space close to the front door. She felt she was in some obscure way responsible for what had happened to the child. She let her thoughts move to the Negro family. She remembered the name Franklin and the table that was covered with hamburger papers, and the teenaged girl staring at her as she drew on her cigarette. "Don't have children," she told the girl's image as she entered the front door of the hospital. "For God's sake, don't."

She took the elevator up to the third floor with two nurses who were just going on duty. It was Wednesday morning, a few minutes before seven. There was a page for a Dr. Madison as the elevator doors slid open on the third floor. She got off behind the nurses, who turned in the other direction and continued the conversation she had interrupted when she'd gotten into the elevator. She walked down the corridor to the little alcove where the Negro family had been waiting. They were gone now, but the chairs were scattered in such a way that it looked as if people had just jumped up from them the minute before. The tabletop was cluttered with the same cups and papers, the ashtray was filled with cigarette butts.

She stopped at the nurses' station. A nurse was standing behind the counter, brushing her hair and yawning.

"There was a Negro boy in surgery last night," Ann said. "Franklin was his name. His family was in the waiting room. I'd like to inquire about his condition."

A nurse who was sitting at a desk behind the counter looked up from a chart in front of her. The telephone buzzed and she picked up the receiver, but she kept her eyes on Ann.

"He passed away," said the nurse at the counter. The nurse held the hairbrush and kept looking at her. "Are you a friend of the family or what?"

"I met the family last night," Ann said. "My own son is in the hospital. I guess he's in shock. We don't know for sure what's wrong. I just wondered about Franklin, that's all. Thank you." She moved down the corridor. Elevator doors the same color as the walls slid open and a gaunt, bald man in white pants and white canvas shoes pulled a heavy cart off the elevator. She hadn't noticed these doors last night. The man wheeled the cart out into the corridor and stopped in front of the room nearest the elevator and consulted a clipboard. Then he reached down and slid a tray out of the cart. He rapped lightly on the door and entered the room. She could smell the unpleasant odors of warm food as she passed the cart. She hurried on without looking at any of the nurses and pushed open the door to the child's room.

Howard was standing at the window with his hands behind his back. He turned around as she came in.

"How is he?" she said. She went over to the bed. She dropped her purse on the floor beside the nightstand. It seemed to her she had been gone a long time. She touched the child's face. "Howard?"

"Dr. Francis was here a little while ago," Howard said. She looked at him closely and thought his shoulders were bunched a little.

"I thought he wasn't coming until eight o'clock this morning," she said quickly.

"There was another doctor with him. A neurologist."

"A neurologist," she said.

Howard nodded. His shoulders were bunching, she could see that. "What'd they say, Howard? For Christ's sake, what'd they say? What is it?"

"They said they're going to take him down and run more tests on him, Ann. They think they're going to operate, honey. Honey, they *are* going to operate. They can't figure out why he won't wake up. It's more than just shock or concussion, they know that much now. It's in his skull, the fracture, it has something, something to do with that, they think. So they're going to operate. I tried to call you, but I guess you'd already left the house."

"Oh, God," she said. "Oh, please, Howard, please," she said, taking his arms.

"Look!" Howard said. "Scotty! Look, Ann!" He turned her toward the bed.

The boy had opened his eyes, then closed them. He opened them again now. The eyes stared straight ahead for a minute, then moved slowly in his head until they rested on Howard and Ann, then traveled away again.

"Scotty," his mother said, moving to the bed.

"Hey, Scott," his father said. "Hey, son."

They leaned over the bed. Howard took the child's hand in his hands and began to pat and squeeze the hand. Ann bent over the body and kissed his forehead again and again. She put her hands on either side of his face. "Scotty, honey, it's Mommy and Daddy," she said. "Scotty?"

The boy looked at them, but without any sign of recognition. Then his mouth opened, his eyes scrunched closed, and he howled until he had no more air in his lungs. His face seemed to relax and soften then. His lips parted as his last breath was puffed through his throat and exhaled gently through the clenched teeth.

*　　*　　*

The doctors called it a hidden occlusion and said it was a one-in-a-million circumstance. Maybe if it could have been detected somehow and surgery undertaken immediately, they could have saved him. But more than likely not. In any case, what would they have been looking for? Nothing had shown up in the tests or in the X-rays.

Dr. Francis was shaken. "I can't tell you how badly I feel. I'm so very sorry, I can't tell you," he said as he led them into the doctors' lounge. There was a doctor sitting in a chair with his legs hooked over the back of another chair, watching an early-morning TV show. He was wearing a green delivery-room outfit, loose green pants and green blouse, and a green cap that covered his hair. He looked at Howard and Ann and then looked at Dr. Francis. He got to his feet and turned off the set and went out of the room. Dr. Francis guided Ann to the sofa, sat down beside her, and began to talk in a low, consoling voice. At one point, he leaned over and embraced her. She could feel his chest rising and falling evenly against her shoulder. She kept her eyes open and let him hold her. Howard went into the bathroom, but he left the door open. After a violent fit of weeping, he ran water and washed his face. Then he came out and sat down at the little table that held a telephone. He looked at the telephone as though deciding what to do first. He made some calls. After a time, Dr. Francis used the telephone.

"Is there anything else I can do for the moment?" he asked them.

Howard shook his head. Ann stared at Dr. Francis as if unable to comprehend his words.

The doctor walked them to the hospital's front door. People were entering and leaving the hospital. It was eleven o'clock in the morning. Ann was aware of how slowly, almost reluctantly, she moved her feet. It seemed to her that Dr. Francis was making them leave when she felt they should stay, when it would be more the right thing to do to stay. She gazed out into the parking lot and then turned around and looked back at the front of the hospital. She began shaking her head. "No, no," she said. "I can't leave him here, no." She heard herself say that and thought how unfair it was that the only words that came out were the sort of words used on TV shows where people were stunned by violent or sudden deaths. She wanted her words to be her own. "No," she said, and for some reason the memory of the Negro woman's head lolling on the woman's shoulder came to her. "No," she said again.

"I'll be talking to you later in the day," the doctor was saying to Howard. "There are still some things that have to be done, things that have to be cleared up to our satisfaction. Some things that need explaining."

"An autopsy," Howard said.

Dr. Francis nodded.

"I understand," Howard said. Then he said, "Oh, Jesus. No, I don't understand, doctor. I can't, I can't. I just can't."

Dr. Francis put his arm around Howard's shoulders. "I'm sorry. God, how I'm sorry." He let go of Howard's shoulders and held out his hand. Howard looked at the hand, and then he took it. Dr. Francis put his arms around Ann once more. He seemed full of some goodness she didn't understand. She let her head rest on his shoulder, but her eyes stayed open. She kept looking at the hospital. As they drove out of the parking lot, she looked back at the hospital.

At home, she sat on the sofa with her hands in her coat pockets. Howard closed the door to the child's room. He got the coffee-maker going and then he found an empty box. He had thought to pick up some of the child's things that were scattered around the living room. But instead he sat down beside her on the sofa, pushed the box to one side, and leaned forward, arms between his knees. He began to weep. She pulled his head over into her lap and patted his shoulder. "He's gone," she said. She kept patting his shoulder. Over his sobs, she could hear the coffee-maker hissing in the kitchen. "There, there," she said tenderly. "Howard, he's gone. He's gone and now we'll have to get used to that. To being alone."

In a little while, Howard got up and began moving aimlessly around the room with the box, not putting anything into it, but collecting some things together on the floor at one end of the sofa. She continued to sit with her hands in her coat pockets. Howard put the box down and brought coffee into the living room. Later, Ann made calls to relatives. After each call had been placed and the party had answered, Ann would blurt out a few words and cry for a minute. Then she would quietly explain, in a measured voice, what had happened and tell them about arrangements. Howard took the box out to the garage, where he saw the child's bicycle. He dropped the box and sat down on the pavement beside the bicycle. He took hold of the bicycle awkwardly so that it leaned against his chest. He held it, the rubber pedal sticking into his chest. He gave the wheel a turn.

Ann hung up the telephone after talking to her sister. She was looking up another number when the telephone rang. She picked it up on the first ring.

"Hello," she said, and she heard something in the background, a humming noise. "Hello!" she said. "For God's sake," she said. "Who is this? What is it you want?"

"Your Scotty, I got him ready for you," the man's voice said. "Did you forget him?"

"You evil bastard!" she shouted into the receiver. "How can you do this, you evil son of a bitch?"

"Scotty," the man said. "Have you forgotten about Scotty?" Then the man hung up on her.

Howard heard the shouting and came in to find her with her head on her arms over the table, weeping. He picked up the receiver and listened to the dial tone.

Much later, just before midnight, after they had dealt with many things, the telephone rang again.

"You answer it," she said. "Howard, it's him, I know." They were sitting at the kitchen table with coffee in front of them. Howard had a small glass of whiskey beside his cup. He answered on the third ring.

"Hello," he said. "Who is this? Hello! Hello!" The line went dead. "He hung up," Howard said. "Whoever it was."

"It was him," she said. "That bastard. I'd like to kill him," she said. "I'd like to shoot him and watch him kick," she said.

"Ann, my God," he said.

"Could you hear anything?" she said. "In the background? A noise, machinery, something humming?"

"Nothing, really. Nothing like that," he said. "There wasn't much time. I think there was some radio music. Yes, there was a radio going, that's all I could tell. I don't know what in God's name is going on," he said.

She shook her head. "If I could, could get my hands on him." It came to her then. She knew who it was. Scotty, the cake, the telephone number. She pushed the chair away from the table and got up. "Drive me down to the shopping center," she said. "Howard."

"What are you saying?"

"The shopping center. I know who it is who's calling. I know who it is. It's the baker, the son-of-a-bitching baker, Howard. I had him bake a cake for Scotty's birthday. That's who's calling. That's who has the number and keeps calling us. To harass us about that cake. The baker, that bastard."

They drove down to the shopping center. The sky was clear and stars were out. It was cold, and they ran the heater in the car. They parked in front of the bakery. All of the shops and stores were closed, but there were cars at the far end of the lot in front of the movie theater. The bakery windows were dark, but when they looked through the glass they could see a light in the back room and, now and then, a big man in an apron moving in and out of the white, even light. Through the glass, she could see the display cases and some little tables with chairs. She tried the door. She rapped on the glass. But if the baker heard them, he gave no sign. He didn't look in their direction.

They drove around behind the bakery and parked. They got out of the car. There was a lighted window too high up for them to see inside. A sign near the back door said the pantry bakery, special orders. She could hear faintly a radio playing inside and something creak—an oven door as it was pulled down? She knocked on the door and waited. Then she knocked again, louder. The radio was turned down and there was a scraping sound now, the distinct sound of something, a drawer, being pulled open and then closed.

Someone unlocked the door and opened it. The baker stood in the light and peered out at them. "I'm closed for business," he said. "What do you want at this hour? It's midnight. Are you drunk or something?"

She stepped into the light that fell through the open door. He blinked his heavy eyelids as he recognized her. "It's you," he said.

"It's me," she said. "Scotty's mother. This is Scotty's father. We'd like to come in."

The baker said, "I'm busy now. I have work to do."

She had stepped inside the doorway anyway. Howard came in behind her. The baker moved back. "It smells like a bakery in here. Doesn't it smell like a bakery in here, Howard?"

"What do you want?" the baker said. "Maybe you want your cake? That's it, you decided you want your cake. You ordered a cake, didn't you?"

"You're pretty smart for a baker," she said. "Howard, this is the man who's been calling us." She clenched her fists. She stared at him fiercely. There was a deep burning inside her, an anger that made her feel larger than herself, larger than either of these men.

"Just a minute here," the baker said. "You want to pick up your three-day-old cake? That it? I don't want to argue with you, lady. There it sits over there, getting stale. I'll give it to you for half of what I quoted you. No. You want it? You can have it. It's no good to me, no good to anyone now. It cost me time and money to make that cake. If you want it, okay, if you don't, that's okay, too. I have to get back to work." He looked at them and rolled his tongue behind his teeth.

"More cakes," she said. She knew she was in control of it, of what was increasing in her. She was calm.

"Lady, I work sixteen hours a day in this place to earn a living," the baker said. He wiped his hands on his apron. "I work night and day in here, trying to make ends meet." A look crossed Ann's face that made the baker move back and say, "No trouble, now." He reached to the counter and picked up a rolling pin with his right hand and began to tap it against the palm of his other hand. "You want the cake or not? I have to get back to work. Bakers work at night," he said again. His eyes were small, mean-looking, she thought, nearly lost in the bristly flesh around his cheeks. His neck was thick with fat.

"I know bakers work at night," Ann said. "They make phone calls at night, too. You bastard," she said.

The baker continued to tap the rolling pin against his hand. He glanced at Howard. "Careful, careful," he said to Howard.

"My son's dead," she said with a cold, even finality. "He was hit by a car Monday morning. We've been waiting with him until he died. But, of course, you couldn't be expected to know that, could you? Bakers can't know everything—can they, Mr. Baker? But he's dead. He's dead, you bastard!" Just as suddenly as it had welled in her, the anger dwindled, gave way to something else, a dizzy feeling of nausea. She leaned against the wooden table that was sprinkled with flour, put her hands over her face, and began to cry, her shoulders rocking back and forth. "It isn't fair," she said. "It isn't, isn't fair."

Howard put his hand at the small of her back and looked at the baker "Shame on you," Howard said to him. "Shame."

The baker put the rolling pin back on the counter. He undid his apron and threw it on the counter. He looked at them, and then he shook his head slowly. He pulled a chair out from under the card table that held papers and receipts, an adding machine, and a telephone directory. "Please sit down," he said. "Let me get you a chair," he said to Howard. "Sit down now, please." The baker went into the front of the shop and returned with two little wrought-iron chairs. "Please sit down, you people."

Ann wiped her eyes and looked at the baker. "I wanted to kill you," she said. "I wanted you dead."

The baker had cleared a space for them at the table. He shoved the adding machine to one side, along with the stacks of notepaper and receipts. He pushed the telephone directory onto the floor, where it landed with a thud. Howard and Ann sat down and pulled their chairs up to the table. The baker sat down, too.

"Let me say how sorry I am," the baker said, putting his elbows on the table. "God alone knows how sorry. Listen to me. I'm just a baker. I don't claim to be anything else. Maybe once, maybe years ago, I was a different kind of human being. I've forgotten, I don't know for sure. But I'm not any longer, if I ever was. Now I'm just a baker. That don't excuse my doing what I did, I know. But I'm deeply sorry. I'm sorry for your son, and sorry for my part in this," the baker said. He spread his hands out on the table and turned them over to reveal his palms. "I don't have any children myself, so I can only imagine what you must be feeling. All I can say to you now is that I'm sorry. Forgive me, if you can," the baker said. "I'm not an evil man, I don't think. Not evil, like you said on the phone. You got to understand what it comes down to is I don't know how to act anymore, it would seem. Please," the man said, "let me ask you if you can find it in your hearts to forgive me?"

It was warm inside the bakery. Howard stood up from the table and took off his coat. He helped Ann from her coat. The baker looked at them for a minute and then nodded and got up from the table. He went to the oven and turned off some switches. He found cups and poured coffee from an electric coffee-maker. He put a carton of cream on the table, and a bowl of sugar.

"You probably need to eat something," the baker said. "I hope you'll eat some of my hot rolls. You have to eat and keep going. Eating is a small, good thing in a time like this," he said.

He served them warm cinnamon rolls just out of the oven, the icing still runny. He put butter on the table and knives to spread the butter. Then the baker sat down at the table with them. He waited. He waited until they each took a roll from the platter and began to eat. "It's good to eat something," he said, watching them. "There's more. Eat up. Eat all you want. There's all the rolls in the world in here."

They ate rolls and drank coffee. Ann was suddenly hungry, and the rolls were warm and sweet. She ate three of them, which pleased the baker. Then he began to talk. They listened carefully. Although they were tired and in anguish, they listened to what the baker had to say. They nodded when the baker began to speak of loneliness, and of the sense of doubt and limitation that had come to him in his middle years. He told them what it was like to be childless all these years. To repeat the days with the ovens endlessly full and endlessly empty. The party food, the celebrations he'd worked over. Icing knuckle-deep. The tiny wedding couples stuck into cakes. Hundreds of them, no, thousands by now. Birthdays. Just imagine all those candles burning. He had a necessary trade. He was a baker. He was glad he wasn't a florist. It was better to be feeding people. This was a better smell anytime than flowers.

"Smell this," the baker said, breaking open a dark loaf. "It's a heavy bread, but rich." They smelled it, then he had them taste it. It had the taste of molasses and coarse grains. They listened to him. They ate what they could. They swallowed the dark bread. It was like daylight under the fluorescent trays of light. They talked on into the early morning, the high, pale cast of light in the windows, and they did not think of leaving.

Reading as a Writer

1. Point out some of the differences between "The Bath" and this story.

2. What are some of the most effective passages that "tell," or narrate, part of the story?

3. What are some of the more effective descriptions that appear in this story that are missing from "The Bath"?

4. How is the ultimate effect of this story different from that of "The Bath"? What are the emotions that you take away from it, as compared to how you felt about "The Bath"?

CHAPTER 14

Getting Published
A Guide to Starting Out

So YOU'VE WRITTEN WHAT YOU CONSIDER—and what your classmates and friends tell you—is a good story. You've done everything you can think of to polish your final draft (for now, anyway—never underestimate a writer's ability to go back and tinker with even published work!). You're beginning to think about publishing, but you're not sure what's next: in this chapter we'll discuss a few guidelines on how to get started publishing in literary magazines.

The Lowdown on Literary Magazines

Literary magazines are a world unto themselves. Don't expect to find them on the magazine rack at the drugstore or even at most bookstores. It takes a certain kind of literary bookstore to carry these publications, which tend to be expensive, with price tags of $6 to $10 for often painfully thin paperback booklets. Even independent bookstores dedicated to the local literary scene are loathe to carry more than the top-selling literary magazines, which usually have small circulations.

Another thing you should know about literary magazines is that there are literally hundreds of literary magazines, each with its own voice, mission, and focus. Some only publish stories or essays from a certain geographic region, such as the South-west, or New York. Others focus on a particular demographic: stories and essays with a feminist, gay, or lesbian slant, for example. Some will only publish experimental, postmodern pieces; others stick to more traditional work. There is a rich landscape of publications out there—both print and online—so before you attempt to publish anything you'll want to do some research and familiarize yourself with the marketplace.

You'll also want to keep in mind that literary magazines are utterly swamped with submissions. Most of them are run by very small core staffs—usually an editor, or maybe two, and a couple of interns (if they're lucky). Many of them are run by grad-uate students in college English or creative writing programs, and the volume of unsolicited stories they receive is staggering. It's not unusual for them to get hundreds, if not more than a thousand, submissions for any given issue, and most literary magazines are only published quarterly or semi-annually, which means there aren't many slots for pieces in a given year. Indeed, if you saw the number of manuscripts sitting on a typical editor's desk (or, more commonly, starting on the floor and reaching above the level of the desktop) you'd realize how very difficult it is to have your manuscript picked out of this "slush pile" and earmarked for publication.

Given these factors, how difficult is it to get published? Very. The sheer volume of submissions ensures that. Unless you have a personal relationship with an editor or have been solicited to submit your work you should be prepared for rejection—lots of it. But I encourage you to think of rejection letters as badges of courage: you're putting your work out there—and risking disappointment—to get an audience for your work. And that's not an easy thing to do.

Another important thing to understand about publishing in a literary journal is that you won't get paid very much even if your story is chosen. Some magazines may give you a $25 or $50 honorarium, but mostly your compensation comes in the form of pride of authorship and three or four copies of the magazine your work appears in.

Preparing Your Manuscript

Given the volume of submissions they face, editors usually have a limited amount of time to spend doing an initial read of a story, so the presentation of your manuscript is critical. You should prepare it with exquisite care. Always use a plain, easily read-able typeface with a reasonable font size—usually a 12-point font. Proofread *care-fully* for typos and misspellings. Careless mistakes will turn off editors no matter how good your story is. Number the pages, and put your name and the title of the piece in the header of each page. On the first page of the manuscript, make sure you list the title of the piece, and your name, address, phone number, and email address. Be sure to follow any additional instructions in the submission guidelines of the par-ticular magazine.

Choosing Your Target Publications— and Following Directions Carefully

So how do you decide which publications to send your work to? It requires a fair amount of thought—and research. After all, each literary magazine has its own per-sonality. And editors frequently complain that writers don't bother to check out the focus of a particular publication before deluging them with submissions. Thus jour-nals that would never consider a science fiction story routinely receive such pieces, while magazines that are specifically devoted to medical fiction get coming-of-age stories. So the first rule of thumb is: know your publication.

But how do you do that if literary journals are hard to find? First, check your local independent bookstore and your library, though these are unlikely to carry any but the most popular titles—the ones for which there is the fiercest competition for placement.

One resource that many writers use to find journals for which their work is a good fit is *Novel & Short Story Writer's Market*. Although it lists book publishers as well as magazines, it contains an exhaustive roundup of the top literary magazines, containing contact information, editors' names, addresses, payment terms, submission guidelines, and frequently a blurb from the editor saying what the magazine is looking for. Since this book is republished every year, the information in it is reasonably up to date—which is important, because the editorial turnover at literary magazines is notoriously high.

Another terrific resource is *The Literary Press and Magazine Directory*, a publication put out by Council of Literary Magazines and Presses (CLMP) (www.clmp.org). This invaluable book lists all the major literary magazines, both print and online, and provides tips from editors on how to submit to your best advantage, along with addresses, names, and details about each publication. *The International Directory of Little Magazines and Small Presses* and *The Directory of Small Press / Magazine Editors & Publishers* are also useful resources, both published by Dustbooks (www.dustbooks.com).

Many writers simply use the latest collection of *The Best American Short Stories*, which is published yearly. Each volume has a list of literary magazines (along with addresses) at the back of the book, from which the top one hundred nominees for the year's best stories are taken.

Many literary magazines have their own websites from which you can order magazines and download the author guidelines. (Some will even accept submissions via email.) A good place to go for links to all the major (and many of the more obscure) literary magazines is NewPages.com (www.newpages.com/npguides/litmags.htm), which provides links that take you directly to the magazines' websites.

Poets and Writers magazine also has an extensive online link library to literary magazines (www.pw.org/links_pages/Literary_Magazines/). You might consider getting a subscription to *Poets and Writers*; it lists contests, grants, awards, and calls for submissions by new literary magazines. It also has helpful articles on how to get an agent and other aspects of making your way as a literary writer in a world that can be tough to navigate.

Regardless of where you get your basic information, it's critical to actually *read* an issue or two of the magazines you target. You can order issues of the publications directly from the magazines, and determine whether they represent a good fit for your work. How can you tell? The first clue is whether they publish stories or essays that resemble your own in style, theme, or content. A second clue is whether they publish pieces that you find yourself responding to. If you like the work featured by a particular publication, chances are better that the editors will like yours, too.

Be aware that one of the biggest complaints from editors of literary magazines is that writers don't bother to read the submission guidelines. Many literary magazines—especially the ones published by universities—have some very specific times of the year that they accept submissions. Others are adamant about manuscript formatting, word limits, or how many pieces can be submitted simultaneously. Read the submissions guidelines *carefully* before sending your manuscript anywhere.

Sending It Off

Each manuscript you send should have a cover letter, which can't be too brief. Think of it as just a knock on the door of the literary magazine. You want to be polite, but not waste the time of the editor, who will, after all, be judging the story on its own merits. This is not the place to talk about what *you* think is strong about the piece, or where the inspiration for it came from, or anything else other than the title of the piece, and (if necessary) a brief, one-sentence description of what it's about.

As far as your credentials are concerned, there is no need to provide a résumé or talk about where you attended (or are attending) college or your extracurricular activities. If you've been published before, briefly state when and where. If you've won any literary prizes, list them. (Don't bother to mention any that you won in high school or earlier.) It is okay to request feedback, but your letter should be extremely succinct. See p. 485 for an example of a cover letter you might send when submitting a manuscript in hard copy.

If you are sending your submission through the U.S. Postal Service, use an $8\frac{1}{2} \times 11$-inch flat envelope. (Don't try to squeeze your manuscript into a regular letter-sized envelope.) Make sure to include a self-addressed stamped envelope. If the magazine accepts online submissions, write your cover letter as the body of an email message and attach your story in a Microsoft Word or text file.

Simultaneous Submissions

The debate is ongoing about whether simultaneous submissions—sending a piece to more than one publication at once—are acceptable. Editors would prefer that you send your piece to them and only to them, giving them the first right of refusal. But given the realities of the publishing world—and the fact that it can take anywhere from three months to a year before you hear back from a particular magazine—from the writer's perspective, multiple submissions are absolutely necessary if you hope to get published within your lifetime.

Most writers I know have some system: they submit to five publications at a time, or seven, or even ten; they make careful note of what they send and where, along with dates sent and rejection received. And they keep sending them out until they get an acceptance.

Of course, if you *do* send out multiple submissions of a piece, and it gets accepted by one publication, you should immediately send letters to the other publications

JOAN SMITH
42 SOUTH MAIN STREET
CHAMPAIGN, IL 61820
PHONE: 255.111.1112   FAX: 255.511.1112   EMAIL: JSMITH@WRITER.COM

April 21, 2008

Editor
Tin House Magazine
1515 SE Division Street
Portland, OR 97202

Dear Sir or Madam,

   Please consider my story "Singing" for publication in *Tin House*. I have
published the story "At the Bay" in the *New Yorker,* and have received an O. Henry
Award for the story "The Oboe Player."
   Any feedback you could provide would be appreciated.

Yours sincerely,

Joan Smith

---

telling them your story is no longer available. (That's another reason why it's important to keep careful records of where you sent a piece and when.)

Patience, Patience

Now comes the hard part: waiting. *Endless* waiting. With very few exceptions, you
can expect to wait months before you get a reply to your submission. I know writers
who have waited more than a year for a response to a submission. And keep in mind
that it does *not* do you any good (and it may do you a great deal of harm) to call the
editor of the magazine and ask whether he or she has read your story yet. Patience
is the watchword here, which is another reason to consider multiple submissions:
your waiting will be less painful if you know that there are multiple editors considering your work.

All Rejections Are Not Equal

Then come the rejections. Steel yourself in advance: rejection is inevitable, no matter what your fantasies might be of instant recognition and success. Even prize-winning stories get rejected—often multiple times—before they're finally published. Realize that the finest writers in the world have received more than their ample share of rejection, and take heart.

It's also important to recognize that not all rejections are equal. You'll probably get a standard rejection form letter, without so much as a signature on it, for most of your submissions. But every once in a while there might be a scrawled note on the side, signed by a reader or editor. Best of all are the personal letters that, although they reject the story in question, ask you to try again. Occasionally (although this is increasingly rare) an editor will actually provide feedback on the strengths or weaknesses of a piece. Those kinds of responses, although technically still rejections, should give you hope: someone has picked your work out of the thousands of submissions in the slush pile and thought enough of it to give you personal encouragement. You should take it in that spirit.

Success!

Sometimes there is good news. You'll get a response from an editor saying that the magazine wants to publish your piece. Such moments are truly worth savoring, especially if it's your first time to be picked up by a literary magazine. The editor may have suggestions for changes, and whether you make those changes are up to you, though sometimes the editor will say, in effect, that publication is dependent on certain revisions.

Publishing: A Case History

Here's the publishing story of Jan Ellison, the writer featured in Chapter 13 whose story "The Company of Men" progressed from an exercise, to a short short story, to a fully developed piece that first won a college fiction writing contest, was subsequently published in the *New England Review,* and, finally, won an O. Henry Award.

> After several years of writing and revising, when I thought "The Company of Men" might be finished at last, I submitted it to San Francisco State University's annual short story contest. The contest was judged by Ann Cummins that year and the story won first prize.
>
> Armed with the award, I crafted my cover letters and mailed the story off to *The New Yorker* and *Atlantic Monthly.* I never did receive a reply from *The New Yorker,* but just a few weeks after I'd sent the story, a letter came in the mail from C. Michael Curtis at *The Atlantic.* "You write with feeling," he wrote, "but 'The Company of Men' is awfully ruminative, and internalized. We're not drawn to it, I'm sorry to say, but try us again." Although I ought to have been

pleased to have received a personal communication from Mr. Curtis, the phrase "we're not drawn to it" got under my skin. And I was annoyed by his use of a comma after the word ruminative; it seemed to me an excessive and misplaced emphasis. But I went back to the story and made some changes, editing out sentences and phrases that seemed most guilty of being "ruminative, and internalized." I continued rewriting for a few more months, tweaking a sentence here, a comma there, deleting scenes and then putting them back again. Then my fourth child was born and I put the story aside altogether. A full year passed before I sent it out again, this time to a list of more than two dozen journals I had compiled from a fairly obsessive analysis of recent *Best American* and *O. Henry Prize* short story collections.

Mostly, I received the usual rejection slips. A half a dozen journals sent me the "try us again" slip, and a handful sent personal notes. The manuscript editor at *The Sun*, who had sent me a note about another of my stories, wrote that she continued to admire and enjoy my work, and that she was sorry they couldn't use it. There was one from *Missouri Review,* a hand-written "Please try us again!" which for some reason I found especially encouraging. A guest editor at *Michigan Quarterly Review* wrote me a very nice letter saying that they had almost taken the story but had not been able to reach consensus. *Five Points* wrote: "Nice writing, but we won't be publishing it."

I had collected fifty or sixty rejections by then on the three stories I'd been sending out, and at that point it began to seem to me that holding out hope was no longer productive. I made the decision that I would keep at it until I hit one hundred rejections, then I would buckle down and write my novel, not in order to publish it but for my own entertainment, or more truthfully, to maintain some measure of sanity amidst the chaos of my domestic life.

Then after having had the story for seven months, Carolyn Kuebler, the managing editor at *New England Review,* left a message on my cell phone saying that they wanted to publish "The Company of Men" in their Fall issue. I played Carolyn's message over and over again, not quite able to believe it was real. *NER* took the story almost as-is, and after some debate decided to leave the title alone as well.

The story was still out at a few places, and I was delighted to be able to write the editors letters of withdrawal. Even then, I received rejection slips from two of these journals, so that all in all, the story was turned down by twenty-seven publications. The issue of *NER* in which the story appeared finally arrived on my doorstep one morning in late November, six months after it had been accepted, two years after I began submitting it and a full five years from the time I put my first ideas for it down on paper.

—Jan Ellison

Anthology

OF

Stories

Donald Barthelme

Me and Miss Mandible

13 September

MISS MANDIBLE WANTS to make love to me but she hesitates because I am officially a child; I am, according to the records, according to the gradebook on her desk, according to the card index in the principal's office, eleven years old. There is a misconception here, one that I haven't quite managed to get cleared up yet. I am in fact thirty-five, I've been in the Army, I am six feet one, I have hair in the appropriate places, my voice is a baritone, I know very well what to do with Miss Mandible if she ever makes up her mind.

In the meantime we are studying common fractions. I could, of course, answer all the questions, or at least most of them (there are things I don't remember). But I prefer to sit in this too-small seat with the desktop cramping my thighs and examine the life around me. There are thirty-two in the class, which is launched every morning with the pledge of allegiance to the flag. My own allegiance, at the moment, is divided between Miss Mandible and Sue Ann Brownly, who sits across the aisle from me all day long and is, like Miss Mandible, a fool for love. Of the two I prefer, today, Sue Ann; although between eleven and eleven and a half (she refuses to reveal her exact age) she is clearly a woman, with a woman's disguised aggression and a woman's peculiar contradictions.

15 September

Happily our geography text, which contains maps of all the principal land-masses of the world, is large enough to conceal my clandestine journal-keeping, accomplished in an ordinary black composition book. Every day I must wait until Geography to put down such thoughts as I may have had during the morning about my situation and my fellows. I have tried writing at other times and it does not work. Either the teacher is walking up and down the aisles (during this period, luckily, she sticks close to the map rack in the front of the room) or Bobby Vanderbilt, who sits behind me, is punching me in the kidneys and wanting to know what I am doing. Vanderbilt, I have found out from certain desultory conversations on the playground, is hung up on sports cars, a veteran consumer of *Road & Track*. This explains the continual roaring sounds which seem to emanate from his desk: he is reproducing a record album called *Sounds of Sebring*.

19 September

Only I, at times (only at times), understand that somehow a mistake has been made, that I am in a place where I don't belong. It may be that Miss Mandible also knows this, at some level, but for reasons not fully understood by me she is going along with the game. When I was first assigned to this room I wanted to protest, the error seemed obvious, the stupidest principal could have seen it; but I have come to believe it was deliberate, that I have been betrayed again.

Now it seems to make little difference. This life-role is as interesting as my former life-role, which was that of a claims adjuster for the Great Northern Insurance Company, a position which compelled me to spend my time amid the debris of our civilization: rumpled fenders, roofless sheds, gutted warehouses, smashed arms and legs. After ten years of this one has a tendency to see the world as a vast junkyard, looking at a man and seeing only his (potentially) mangled parts, entering a house only to trace the path of the inevitable fire. Therefore when I was installed here, only I knew an error had been made. I countenanced it, I was shrewd; I was aware that there might well be some kind of advantage to be gained from what seemed a disaster. The role of The Adjuster teaches one much.

22 September

I am being solicited for the volleyball team. I decline, refusing to take unfair profit from my height.

23 September

Every morning the roll is called: Bestvina, Bokenfohr, Broan, Brownly, Cone, Coyle, Crecelius, Darin, Durbin, Geiger, Guiswite, Heckler, Jacobs, Kleinschmidt, Lay, Logan, Masei, Mitgag, Pfeilsticker. It is like the litany chanted in the dim miserable dawns of Texas by the cadre sergeant of our basic training company.

In the Army, too, I was ever so slightly awry. It took me a fantastically long time to realize what the others grasped almost at once: that much of what we were doing was absolutely pointless, to no purpose. I kept wondering why. Then something happened that proposed a new question. One day we were commanded to whitewash, from the ground to the topmost leaves, all of the trees in our training area. The corporal who relayed the order was nervous and apologetic. Later an off-duty captain sauntered by and watched us, white-splashed and totally weary, strung out among the freakish shapes we had created. He walked away swearing. I understood the principle (orders are orders), but I wondered: Who decides?

29 September

Sue Ann is a wonder. Yesterday she viciously kicked my ankle for not paying attention when she was attempting to pass me a note during History. It is swollen still. But Miss Mandible was watching me, there was nothing I could do. Oddly enough Sue Ann reminds me of the wife I had in my former role, while Miss Mandible seems to be a child. She watches me constantly, trying to keep sexual significance out of her look: I am afraid the other children have noticed. I have already heard, on that ghostly frequency that is the medium of classroom communication, the words *"Teacher's pet!"*

2 October

Sometimes I speculate on the exact nature of the conspiracy which brought me here. At times I believe it was instigated by my wife of former days, whose name was . . . I am only pretending to forget. I know her name very well, as well as I know the name of my former motor oil (Quaker State) or my old Army serial number (US 54109268). Her name was Brenda.

7 October

Today I tiptoed up to Miss Mandible's desk (when there was no one else in the room) and examined its surface. Miss Mandible is a clean-desk teacher, I discovered. There was nothing except her gradebook (the one in which I exist as a sixth-grader) and a text, which was open at a page headed *Making the Processes Meaningful.* I read: "Many pupils enjoy working fractions when they understand what they are doing. They have confidence in their ability to take the right steps and to obtain correct answers. However, to give the subject full social significance, it is necessary that many realistic situations requiring the processes be found. Many interesting and lifelike problems involving the use of fractions should be solved . . ."

8 October

I am not irritated by the feeling of having been through all this before. Things are done differently now. The children, moreover, are in some ways different from those who accompanied me on my first voyage through the elementary schools: *"They have confidence in their ability to take the right steps and to obtain correct answers."* This is surely true. When Bobby Vanderbilt, who sits behind me and has the great tactical advantage of being able to maneuver in my disproportionate shadow, wishes to bust a classmate in the mouth he first asks Miss Mandible to lower the blind, saying that the sun hurts his eyes. When she does so, *bip!* My generation would never have been able to con authority so easily.

13 October

I misread a clue. Do not misunderstand me: it was a tragedy only from the point of view of the authorities. I conceived that it was my duty to obtain satisfaction for the injured, for an elderly lady (not even one of our policy-holders, but a claimant against Big Ben Transfer & Storage, Inc.) from the company. The settlement was $165,000; the claim, I still believe, was just. But without my encouragement Mrs. Bichek would never have had the self-love to prize her injury so highly. The company paid, but its faith in me, in my efficacy in the role, was broken. Henry Goodykind, the district manager, expressed this thought in a few not altogether unsympathetic words, and told me at the same time that I was to have a new role. The next thing I knew I was here, at Horace Greeley Elementary, under the lubricious eye of Miss Mandible.

17 October

Today we are to have a fire drill. I know this because I am a Fire Marshal, not only for our room but for the entire right wing of the second floor. This distinction, which was awarded shortly after my arrival, is interpreted by some as another mark of my some-what dubious relations with our teacher. My armband, which is red and decorated with white felt letters reading FIRE, sits on the little shelf under my desk, next to the brown paper bag containing the lunch I carefully make for myself each morning. One of the advantages of packing my own lunch (I have no one to pack it for me) is that I am able to fill it with things I enjoy. The peanut butter sandwiches that my mother made in my former existence, many years ago, have been banished in favor of ham and cheese. I have found that my diet has mysteriously adjusted to my new situation; I no longer drink, for instance, and when I smoke, it is in the boys' john, like every-body else. When school is out I hardly smoke at all. It is only in the matter of sex that I feel my own true age; this is apparently something that, once learned, can never be forgotten. I live in fear that Miss Mandible will one day keep me after school, and when we are alone, create a compromising situation. To avoid this I have become a model pupil: another reason for the pronounced dislike I have encountered in certain quarters. But I cannot deny that I am singed by those long glances from the vicinity of the chalkboard; Miss Mandible is in many ways, notably about the bust, a very tasty piece.

24 October

There are isolated challenges to my largeness, to my dimly realized position in the class as Gulliver. Most of my classmates are polite about this matter, as they would be if I had only one eye, or wasted, metal-wrapped legs. I am viewed as a mutation of some sort but essentially a peer. However Harry Broan, whose father has made him-self rich manufacturing the Broan Bathroom Vent (with which Harry is frequently reproached; he is always being asked how things are in Ventsville), today inquired if I wanted to fight. An interested group of his followers had gathered to observe this suicidal undertaking. I replied that I didn't feel quite up to it, for which he was obviously grateful. We are now friends forever. He has given me to understand pri-vately that he can get me all the bathroom vents I will ever need, at a ridiculously modest figure.

25 October

"Many interesting and lifelike problems involving the use of fractions should be solved . . ."
The theorists fail to realize that everything that is either interesting or lifelike in the

classroom proceeds from what they would probably call interpersonal relations: Sue Ann Brownly kicking me in the ankle. How lifelike, how womanlike, is her tender solicitude after the deed! Her pride in my newly acquired limp is transparent; everyone knows that she has set her mark upon me, that it is a victory in her unequal struggle with Miss Mandible for my great, overgrown heart. Even Miss Mandible knows, and counters in perhaps the only way she can, with sarcasm. "Are you wounded, Joseph?" Conflagrations smolder behind her eyelids, yearning for the Fire Marshal clouds her eyes. I mumble that I have bumped my leg.

30 October

I return again and again to the problem of my future.

4 November

The underground circulating library has brought me a copy of *Movie-TV Secrets*, the multicolor cover blazoned with the headline "Debbie's Date Insults Liz!" It is a gift from Frankie Randolph, a rather plain girl who until today has had not one word for me, passed on via Bobby Vanderbilt. I nod and smile over my shoulder in acknowledgment; Frankie hides her head under her desk. I have seen these magazines being passed around among the girls (sometimes one of the boys will condescend to inspect a particularly lurid cover). Miss Mandible confiscates them whenever she finds one. I leaf through *Movie-TV Secrets* and get an eyeful. "The exclusive picture on these pages isn't what it seems. We know how it looks and we know what the gossipers will do. So in the interests of a nice guy, we're publishing the facts first. Here's what really happened!" The picture shows a rising young movie idol in bed, pajama-ed and bleary-eyed, while an equally blowzy young woman looks startled beside him. I am happy to know that the picture is not really what it seems: it seems to be nothing less than divorce evidence.

What do these hipless eleven-year-olds think when they come across, in the same magazine, the full-page ad for Maurice de Paree, which features "Hip Helpers" or what appear to be padded rumps? ("A real undercover agent that adds appeal to those hips and derriere, both!") If they cannot decipher the language the illustrations leave nothing to the imagination. "Drive him frantic . . ." the copy continues. Perhaps this explains Bobby Vanderbilt's preoccupation with Lancias and Maseratis; it is a defense against being driven frantic.

Sue Ann has observed Frankie Randolph's overture, and catching my eye, she pulls from her satchel no less than seventeen of these magazines, thrusting them at me as if to prove that anything any of her rivals has to offer, she can top. I shuffle through them quickly, noting the broad editorial perspective:

"Debbie's Kids Are Crying"
"Eddie Asks Debbie: Will You?"
"The Nightmares Liz Has About Eddie!"
"The Things Debbie Can Tell About Eddie"

"The Private Life of Eddie and Liz"
"Debbie Gets Her Man Back?"
"A New Life for Liz"
"Love Is a Tricky Affair"
"Eddie's Taylor-Made Love Nest"
"How Liz Made a Man of Eddie"
"Are They Planning to Live Together?"
"Isn't It Time to Stop Kicking Debbie Around?"
"Debbie's Dilemma"
"Eddie Becomes a Father Again"
"Is Debbie Planning to Re-wed?"
"Can Liz Fulfill Herself?"
"Why Debbie Is Sick of Hollywood"

Who are these people, Debbie, Eddie, Liz, and how did they get themselves in such a terrible predicament? Sue Ann knows, I am sure; it is obvious that she has been studying their history as a guide to what she may expect when she is suddenly freed from this drab, flat classroom.

I am angry and I shove the magazines back at her with not even a whisper of thanks.

5 November

The sixth grade at Horace Greeley Elementary is a furnace of love, love, love. Today it is raining, but inside the air is heavy and tense with passion. Sue Ann is absent; I suspect that yesterday's exchange has driven her to her bed. Guilt hangs about me. She is not responsible, I know, for what she reads, for the models proposed to her by a venal publishing industry; I should not have been so harsh. Perhaps it is only the flu.

Nowhere have I encountered an atmosphere as charged with aborted sexuality as this. Miss Mandible is helpless; nothing goes right today. Amos Darin has been found drawing a dirty picture in the cloakroom. Sad and inaccurate, it was offered not as a sign of something else but as an act of love in itself. It has excited even those who have not seen it, even those who saw but understood only that it was dirty. The room buzzes with imperfectly comprehended titillation. Amos stands by the door, waiting to be taken to the principal's office. He wavers between fear and enjoyment of his temporary celebrity. From time to time Miss Mandible looks at me reproachfully; as if blaming me for the uproar. But I did not create this atmosphere, I am caught in it like all the others.

8 November

Everything is promised my classmates and me, most of all the future. We accept the outrageous assurances without blinking.

9 November

I have finally found the nerve to petition for a larger desk. At recess l can hardly walk; my legs do not wish to uncoil themselves. Miss Mandible says she will take it up with the custodian. She is worried about the excellence of my themes. Have I, she asks, been receiving help? For an instant I am on the brink of telling her my story. Something, however, warns me not to attempt it. Here I am safe. I have a place; I do not wish to entrust myself once more to the whimsy of authority. I resolve to make my themes less excellent in the future.

11 November

A ruined marriage, a ruined adjusting career, a grim interlude in the Army when I was almost not a person. This is the sum of my existence to date, a dismal total. Small wonder that re-education seemed my only hope. It is clear even to me that I need reworking in some fundamental way. How efficient is the society that provides thus for the salvage of its clinkers?

14 November

The distinction between children and adults, while probably useful for some purposes, is at bottom a specious one, I feel. There are only individual egos, crazy for love.

15 November

The custodian has informed Miss Mandible that our desks are all the correct size for sixth-graders, as specified by the Board of Estimate and furnished the schools by the Nu-Art Educational Supply Corporation of Englewood, California. He has pointed out that if the desk size is correct, then the pupil size must be incorrect. Miss Mandible, who has already arrived at this conclusion, refuses to press the matter further. I think I know why. An appeal to the administration might result in my removal from the class, in a transfer to some sort of setup for "exceptional children." This would be a disaster of the first magnitude. To sit in a room with child geniuses (or, more likely, children who are "retarded") would shrivel me in a week. Let my experience here be that of the common run, I say; let me be, please God, typical.

20 November

We read signs as promises. Miss Mandible understands by my great height, by my resonant vowels, that I will one day carry her off to bed. Sue Ann interprets these same signs to mean that I am unique among her male acquaintances, therefore most desirable, therefore her special property as is everything that is Most Desirable. If neither of these propositions works out then life has broken faith with them.

I myself, in my former existence, read the company motto ("Here to Help in Time of Need") as a description of the duty of the adjuster, drastically mislocating the company's deepest concerns. I believed that because I had obtained a wife who was made up of wife-signs (beauty, charm, softness, perfume, cookery) I had found love. Brenda, reading the same signs that have now misled Miss Mandible and Sue Ann Brownly, felt she had been promised that she would never be bored again. All of us, Miss Mandible, Sue Ann, myself, Brenda, Mr. Goodykind, still believe that the American flag betokens a kind of general righteousness.

But I say, looking about me in this incubator of future citizens, that signs are signs, and some of them are lies.

23 November

It may be that my experience as a child will save me after all. If only I can remain quietly in this classroom, making my notes while Napoleon plods through Russia in the droning voice of Harry Broan, reading aloud from our History text. All of the mysteries that perplexed me as an adult have their origins here. But Miss Mandible will not permit me to remain ungrown. Her hands rest on my shoulders too warmly, and for too long.

7 December

It is the pledges that this place makes to me, pledges that cannot be redeemed, that will confuse me later and make me feel I am not *getting anywhere*. Everything is presented as the result of some knowable process; if I wish to arrive at four I get there by way of two and two. If I wish to burn Moscow the route I must travel has already been marked out by another visitor. If, like Bobby Vanderbilt, I yearn for the wheel of the Lancia 2.4-liter coupé, I have only to go through the appropriate process, that is, get the money. And if it is money itself that I desire, I have only to *make* it. All of these goals are equally beautiful in the sight of the Board of Estimate; the proof is all around us, in the no-nonsense ugliness of this steel and glass building, in the straightline matter-of-factness with which Miss Mandible handles some of our less reputable wars. Who points out that arrangements sometimes slip, that errors are made, that signs are misread? *"They have confidence in their ability to take the right steps and to obtain correct answers."*

8 December

My enlightenment is proceeding wonderfully.

9 December

Disaster once again. Tomorrow I am to be sent to a doctor, for observation. Sue Ann Browrily caught Miss Mandible and me in the cloakroom, during recess, Miss Mandible's naked legs in a scissors around my waist. For a moment I thought Sue Ann was going to choke. She ran out of the room weeping, straight for the principal's office, certain now which of us was Debbie, which was Eddie, which Liz. I am sorry to be the cause of her disillusionment, but I know that she will recover. Miss Mandible is ruined but fulfilled. Although she will be charged with contributing to the delinquency of a minor, she seems at peace; *her* promise has been kept. She knows now that everything she has been told about life, about America, is true.

I have tried to convince the school authorities that I am a minor only in a very special sense, that I am in fact mostly to blame—but it does no good. They are as dense as ever. My contemporaries are astounded that I present myself as anything other than an innocent victim. Like the Old Guard marching through the Russian drifts, the class marches to the conclusion that truth is punishment.

Bobby Vanderbilt has given me his copy of *Sounds of Sebring*, in farewell.

RICK BASS

Wild Horses

KAREN WAS TWENTY-SIX. She had been engaged twice, married once. Her husband had run away with another woman after only six months. It still made her angry when she thought about it, which was not often.

The second man she had loved more, the most. He was the one she had been engaged to, but had not married. His name was Henry. He had drowned in the Mississippi the day before they were to be married. They never even found the body. He had a marker in the cemetery, but it was a sham. All her life, Karen had heard those stories about fiances dying the day before the wedding; and then it had happened to her.

Henry and some of his friends, including his best friend, Sydney Bean, had been sitting up on the old railroad trestle, the old highway that ran so far and across that river, above the wide muddiness. Louisiana and trees on one side; Mississippi and trees, and some farms, on the other side—the place from which they had come. There had been a full moon and no wind, and they had been sitting above the water, maybe a hundred feet above it, laughing, and drinking Psychos from the Daiquiri World over in Delta, Louisiana. The Psychos contained rum and Coca-Cola and various fruit juices and blue food coloring. They came in styrofoam cups the size of small trash cans, so large they had to be held with both hands. They had had too many of them: two, maybe three apiece.

Henry had stood up, beaten his chest like Tarzan, shouted, and then dived in. It had taken him forever, just to hit the water; the light from the moon was good, and they had been able to watch him, all the way down.

Sometimes Sydney Bean still came by to visit Karen. Sydney was gentle and sad, her own age, and he worked somewhere on a farm, out past Utica, back to the east, where he broke and sometimes trained horses.

Once a month—at the end of each month—Sydney would stay over on Karen's farm, and they would go into her big empty closet, and he would let her hit him: striking him with her fists, kicking him, kneeing him, slapping his face until his ears rang and his nose bled; slapping and swinging at him until she was crying and her hair was wild and in her eyes, and the palms of her hands hurt too much to hit him any more.

It built up, the ache and the anger in Karen; and then, hitting Sydney, it went away for a while. He was a good friend. But the trouble was that it always came back.

Sometimes Sydney would try to help her in other ways. He would tell her that someday she was going to have to realize that Henry would not be coming back. Not ever—not in any form—but to remember what she had had, to keep *that* from going away.

Sydney would stand there, in the closet, and let her strike him. But the rules were strict: she had to keep her mouth closed. He would not let her call him names while she was hitting him.

Though she wanted to.

After it was over, and she was crying, more drained than she had felt since the last time, sobbing, her feelings laid bare, Sydney would help her up. He would take her into the bedroom and towel her forehead with a cool washcloth. Karen would be crying in a child's gulping sobs, and he would brush her hair, hold her hand, even hold her against him, and pat her back while she moaned.

Farm sounds would come from the field, and when she looked out the window, she might see her neighbor, old Dr. Lynly, the vet, driving along in his ancient blue truck, moving along the bayou, down along the trees, with his dog, Buster, running alongside, barking; herding the cows together for vaccinations.

"I can still feel the hurt," Karen would tell Sydney sometimes, when Sydney came over, not to be beaten up, but to cook supper for her, or to just sit on the back porch with her, and to watch the fields.

Sydney would nod whenever Karen said that she still hurt, and he would study his hands.

"I could have grabbed him," he'd say, and then look up and out at the field some more. "I keep thinking that one of these years, I'm going to get a second chance." Sydney would shake his head again. "I think I could have grabbed him," he'd say.

"Or you could have dived in after him," Karen would say, hopefully, wistfully. "Maybe you could have dived in after him."

Her voice would trail off, and her face would be flat and weary.

On these occasions, Sydney Bean wanted the beatings to come once a week, or even daily. But they hurt, too, almost as much as the loss of his friend, and he said nothing. He still felt as if he owed Henry something. He didn't know what.

Sometimes, when he was down on his knees, and Karen was kicking him or elbowing him, he felt close to it—and he almost felt angry at Karen—but he could never catch the shape of it, only the feeling.

He wanted to know what was owed, so he could go on.

On his own farm, there were cattle down in the fields, and they would get lost, separated from one another, and would low all through the night. It was a sound like soft thunder in the night, before the rain comes, and he liked it.

He raised the cattle, and trained horses too: he saddle-broke the young ones that had never been ridden before, the one- and two-year-olds, the stallions, the wild mares. That pounding, and the evil, four-footed stamp-and-spin they went into when they could not shake him; when they began to do that, he knew he had them beaten. He charged $250 a horse, and sometimes it took him a month.

Old Dr. Lynly needed a helper, but couldn't pay much, and Sydney, who had done some business with the vet, helped Karen get the job. She needed something to do besides sitting around on her back porch, waiting for the end of each month.

Dr. Lynly was older than Karen had thought he would be, when she met him up close. He had that look to him that told her it might be the last year of his life. It wasn't so much any illness or feebleness or disability. It was just a finished look.

He and Buster—an Airedale, six years old—lived within the city limits of Vicksburg, down below the battlefield, hidden in one of the ravines—his house was up on blocks, the yard flooded with almost every rain—and in his yard, in various corrals and pens, were chickens, ducks, goats, sheep, ponies, horses, cows, and an ostrich. It was illegal to keep them as pets, and the city newspaper editor was after him to get rid of them, but Dr. Lynly claimed they were all being treated by his tiny clinic.

"You're keeping these animals too long, Doc," the editor told him. Dr. Lynly would pretend to be senile, and would pretend to think the editor was asking for a prescription, and would begin quoting various and random chemical names.

The Airedale minded Dr. Lynly exquisitely. He brought the paper, the slippers, he left the room on command, and he brought the chickens' eggs, daily, into the kitchen, making several trips for his and Dr. Lynly's breakfast. Dr. Lynly would have six eggs, fried for himself, and Buster would get a dozen or so, broken into his bowl raw. Any extras went into the refrigerator for Dr. Lynly to take on his rounds, though he no longer had many; only the very oldest people, who remembered him, and the very poorest, who knew he worked for free. They knew he would charge them only for the medicine.

Buster's coat was glossy from the eggs, and burnished, black and tan. His eyes, deep in the curls, were bright, sometimes like the brightest things in the world. He watched Dr. Lynly all the time.

Sometimes Karen watched Dr. Lynly play with Buster, bending down and swatting him in the chest, slapping his shoulders. She had thought it would be mostly kittens and lambs. Mostly, though, he told her, it would be the horses.

The strongest creatures were the ones that got the sickest, and their pain was unspeakable when they finally did yield to it. On the rounds with Dr. Lynly, Karen forgot to think about Henry at all. Though she was horrified by the pain, and almost wished it were hers, bearing it rather than watching it, when the horses suffered.

Once, when Sydney was with her, he had reached out and taken her hand in his. When she looked down and saw it, she had at first been puzzled, not recognizing what it was, and then repulsed, as if it were a giant slug: and she threw Sydney's hand off hers quickly, and ran into her room.

Sydney stayed out on the porch. It was heavy blue twilight and all the cattle down in the fields were feeding.

"I'm sorry," he called out. "But I can't bring him back!" He waited for her to answer, but could only hear her sobs. It had been three years, he thought.

He knew he was wrong to have caught her off-balance like that: but he was tired of her unhappiness, and frustrated that he could do nothing to end it. The sounds of her crying carried, and the cows down in the fields began to move closer, with interest. The light had dimmed, there were only dark shadows and pale lights, and a low gold thumbnail of a moon—a wet moon—came up over the ragged tear of trees by the bayou.

The beauty of the evening, being on Karen's back porch and in her life, when it should have been Henry, flooded Sydney with a sudden guilt. He had been fighting it, and holding it back, constantly: and then, suddenly, the quietness of the evening, and the stillness, released it.

He heard himself saying a crazy thing.

"I pushed him off, you know," he said, loudly enough so she could hear. "I finished my drink, and put both hands on his skinny-ass little shoulders, and said, 'Take a deep breath, Henry.' I just pushed him off," said Sydney.

It felt good, making up the lie. He was surprised at the relief he felt: it was as if he had control of the situation. It was like when he was on the horses, breaking them, trying to stay on.

Presently, Karen came back out with a small blue pistol, a .38, and she went down the steps and out to where he was standing; and she put it next to his head.

"Let's get in the truck," she said.

He knew where they were going.

The river was about ten miles away, and they drove slowly. There was fog flowing across the low parts of the road and through the fields and meadows like smoke, coming from the woods, and he was thinking about how cold and hard the water would be when he finally hit.

He felt as if he were already falling towards it, the way it had taken Henry forever to fall. But he didn't say anything, and though it didn't feel right, he wondered if perhaps it was this simple, as if this was what was owed after all.

They drove on, past the blue fields and the great spills of fog. The roofs of the hay barns were bright silver polished tin, under the little moon and stars. There were small lakes, cattle stock tanks, and steam rose from them.

They drove with the windows down; it was a hot night, full of flying bugs, and about two miles from the river, Karen told him to stop.

He pulled off to the side of the road, and wondered what she was going to do with his body. A cattle egret flew by, ghostly white and large, flying slowly, and Sydney was amazed that he had never recognized their beauty before, though he had seen millions. It flew right across their windshield, from across the road, and it startled both of them.

The radiator ticked.

"You didn't really push him off, did you?" Karen asked. She still had the pistol against his head, and had switched hands.

Like frost burning off the grass in a bright morning sun, there was in his mind a sudden, sugary, watery feeling—like something dissolving. She was not going to kill him after all.

"No," he said.

"But you could have saved him," she said, for the thousandth time.

"I could have reached out and grabbed him," Sydney agreed. He was going to live. He was going to get to keep feeling things, was going to get to keep seeing things.

He kept his hands in his lap, not wanting to alarm Karen, but his eyes moved all around as he looked for more egrets. He was eager to see another one.

Karen watched him for a while, still holding the pistol against him, and then turned it around and looked at the open barrel of it, cross-eyed, and held it there, right in her face, for several seconds. Then she reached out and put it in the glove box.

Sydney Bean was shuddering.

"Thank you," he said. "Thank you for not shooting yourself."

He put his head down on the steering wheel, in the moonlight, and shuddered again. There were crickets calling all around them. They sat like that for a long time, Sydney leaning against the wheel, and Karen sitting up straight, just looking out at the fields.

Then the cattle began to move up the hill towards them, thinking that Karen's old truck was the one that had come to feed them, and slowly, drifting up the hill from all over the fields, coming from out of the woods, and from their nearby resting spots on the sandbars along the little dry creek that ran down into the bayou—eventually, they all assembled around the truck, like schoolchildren.

They stood there in the moonlight, some with white faces like skulls, all about the same size, and chewed grass and watched the truck. One, bolder than the rest—a yearling black Angus—moved in close, bumped the grille of the truck with his nose, playing, and then leapt back again, scattering some of the others.

"How much would you say that one weighs?" Karen asked. "How much, Sydney?"

They drove the last two miles to the river slowly. It was about four a.m. The yearling cow was bleating and trying to break free; Sydney had tied him up with his belt, and with jumper cables and shoelaces, and an old shirt. His lip was bloody from where the calf had butted him.

But he had wrestled larger steers than that before.

They parked at the old bridge, the one across which the trains still ran. Farther downriver, they could see an occasional car, two round spots of headlight moving slowly and steadily across the new bridge, so far above the river, going very slowly. Sydney put his shoulders under the calf's belly and lifted it with his back and legs, and like a prisoner in the stock, he carried it out to the center of the bridge. Karen followed. It took about fifteen minutes to get there, and Sydney was trembling, dripping with sweat, when finally they gauged they had reached the middle. The deepest part.

They sat there, soothing the frightened calf, stroking its ears, patting its flanks, and waited for the sun to come up. When it did, pale orange behind the great steaminess of the trees and river below—the fog from the river and trees a gunmetal gray, the whole world washed in gray flatness, except for the fruit of the sun—they untied the calf, and pushed him over.

They watched him forever and forever, a black object and then a black spot against the great background of no-colored river, and then there was a tiny white splash, lost almost immediately in the river's current. Logs, which looked like twigs from up on the bridge, swept across the spot. Everything headed south, moving south, and there were no eddies, no pauses.

"I am halfway over him," Karen said.

And then, walking back, she said: "So that was really what it was like?"

She had a good appetite, and they stopped at the Waffle House and ate eggs and pancakes, and had sausage and biscuits and bacon and orange juice. She excused herself to go to the restroom, and when she came back out, her face was washed, her hair brushed and clean-looking. Sydney paid for the meal, and when they stepped outside, the morning was growing hot.

"I have to work today," Karen said, when they got back to her house. "We have to go see about a mule."

"Me, too," said Sydney. "I've got a stallion who thinks he's a bad-ass."

She studied him for a second, and felt like telling him to be careful, but didn't. Something was in her, a thing like hope stirring, and she felt guilty for it.

Sydney whistled, driving home, and tapped his hands on the steering wheel, though the radio did not work.

Dr. Lynly and Karen drove until the truck wouldn't go any farther, bogged down in the clay, and then they got out and walked. It was cool beneath all the big trees, and the forest seemed to be trying to press in on them. Dr. Lynly carried his heavy bag, stopping and switching arms frequently. Buster trotted slightly ahead, between the two of them, looking left and right, and up the road, and even up into the tops of the trees.

There was a sawmill, deep in the woods, where the delta's farmland in the northern part of the county settled at the river and then went into dark mystery; hardwoods, and muddy roads, then no roads. The men at the sawmill used mules to drag their trees to the cutting. There had never been money for bulldozers, or even tractors. The woods were quiet, and foreboding; it seemed to be a place without sound or light.

When they got near the sawmill, they could hear the sound of axes. Four men, shirtless, in muddy boots with the laces undone, were working on the biggest tree Karen had ever seen. It was a tree too big for chain saws. Had any of the men owned one, the tree would have ruined the saw.

One of the men kept swinging at the tree: putting his back into it, with rhythmic, stroking cuts. The other three stepped back, hitched their pants, and wiped their faces with their forearms.

The fourth man stopped cutting finally. There was no fat on him and he was pale, even standing in the beam of sunlight that was coming down through an opening in the trees—and he looked old; fifty, maybe, or sixty. Some of his fingers were missing.

"The mule'll be back in a minute," he said. He wasn't even breathing hard. "He's gone to bring a load up out of the bottom." He pointed with his ax, down into the swamp.

"We'll just wait," said Dr. Lynly. He bent back and tried to look up at the top of the trees. "Y'all just go right ahead with your cutting."

But the pale muscled man was already swinging again, and the other three, with another tug at their beltless pants, joined in: an odd, pausing drumbeat, as four successive whacks hit the tree; then four more again; and then, almost immediately, the cadence stretching out, growing irregular, as the older man chopped faster.

All around them were the soft pittings, like hail, of tree chips, raining into the bushes. One of the chips hit Buster in the nose, and he rubbed it with his paw, and turned and looked up at Dr. Lynly.

They heard the mule before they saw him: he was groaning, like a person. He was coming up the hill that led out of the swamp; he was coming towards them.

They could see the tops of small trees and saplings shaking as he dragged his load through them. Then they could see the tops of his ears; then his huge head, and after that they saw his chest. Veins raced against the chestnut thickness of it.

Then the tops of his legs.

Then his knee. Karen stared at it and then she started to tremble. She sat down in the mud, and hugged herself—the men stopped swinging, for just a moment—and Dr. Lynly had to help her up.

It was the mule's right knee that was injured, and it had swollen to the size of a basketball. It buckled, with every step he took, pulling the sled up the slick and muddy hill, but he kept his footing and he did not stop. Flies buzzed around the knee, around the infections, where the loggers had pierced the skin with nails and the ends of their knives, trying to drain the pus. Dried blood ran down in streaks to the mule's hoof, to the mud.

The sawlogs on the back of the sled smelled good, fresh. They smelled like they were still alive.

Dr. Lynly walked over to the mule and touched the knee. The mule closed his eyes and trembled slightly, as Karen had done, or even as if in ecstasy, at the chance to rest. The three younger men, plus the sledder, gathered around.

"We can't stop workin' him," the sledder said. "We can't shoot him, either. We've got to keep him alive. He's all we've got. If he dies, it's us that'll have to pull them logs up here."

A cedar moth, from the woods, passed over the mule's ears, fluttering blindly. It rested on the mule's forehead briefly, and then flew off. The mule did not open his eyes. Dr. Lynly frowned and rubbed his chin. Karen felt faint again, and leaned against the mule's sweaty back to keep from falling.

"You sure you've got to keep working him?" Dr. Lynly asked.

"Yes, sir."

The pale logger was still swinging: tiny chips flying in batches.

Dr. Lynly opened his bag. He took out a needle and rag, and a bottle of alcohol. He cleaned the mule's infections. The mule drooled a little when the needle went in, but did not open his eyes. The needle was slender, and it bent and flexed, and slowly Dr. Lynly drained the fluid.

Karen held onto the mule's wet back and vomited into the mud: both her hands on the mule as if she were being arrested against the hood of a car, and her feet spread out wide. The men gripped their axes awkwardly.

Dr. Lynly gave one of them a large plastic jug of pills.

"These will kill his pain," he said. "The knee will get big again, though. I'll be back out, to drain it again." He handed Karen a clean rag from his satchel, and led her away from the mule, away from the mess.

One of the ax men carried their satchel all the way back to the truck. Dr. Lynly let Karen get up into the truck first, and then Buster; then the ax man rocked and shoved, pushing on the hood of the truck as the tires spun, and helped them back it out of the mud: their payment for healing the mule. A smell of burning rubber and smoke hung in the trees after they left.

They didn't talk much. Dr. Lynly was thinking about the painkillers: how for a moment, he had almost given the death pills instead.

Karen was thinking how she would not let him pay her for that day's work. Also she was thinking about Sydney Bean: she would sit on the porch with him again, and maybe drink a beer and watch the fields.

He was sitting on the back porch, when she got in; he was on the wooden bench next to the hammock, and he had a tray set up for her with a pitcher of cold orange juice. There was froth in the pitcher, a light creamy foaminess from where he had been stirring it, and the ice cubes were circling around. Beads of condensation slid down the pitcher, rolling slowly, then quickly, like tears. She could feel her heart giving. The field was rich summer green, and then, past the field, the dark line of trees. A long string of cattle egrets flew past, headed down to their rookery in the swamp.

Sydney poured her a small glass of orange juice. He had a metal pail of cold water and a clean washcloth. It was hot on the back porch, even for evening. He helped her get into the hammock; then he wrung the washcloth out and put it across her forehead, her eyes. Sydney smelled as if he had just gotten out of the shower, and he was wearing clean white duckcloth pants and a bright blue shirt.

She felt dizzy, and leaned back in the hammock. The washcloth over her eyes felt so good. She sipped the orange juice, not looking at it, and licked the light foam of it from her lips. Owls were beginning to call, down in the swamp.

She felt as if she were younger, going back to a place, some place she had not been in a long time but could remember fondly. It felt like she was in love. She knew that she could not be, but that was what it felt like.

Sydney sat behind her and rubbed her temples.

It grew dark, and the moon came up.

"It was a rough day," she said, around ten o'clock.

But he just kept rubbing.

Around eleven o'clock, she dozed off, and he woke her, helped her from the hammock, and led her inside, not turning on any lights, and helped her get in bed.

Then he went back outside, locking the door behind him. He sat on the porch a little longer, watching the moon, so high above him, and then he drove home, slowly, cautiously, as ever. Accidents were everywhere; they could happen at any time, from any direction.

Sydney moved carefully, and tried to look ahead and be ready for the next one.

He really wanted her. He wanted her in his life. Sydney didn't know if the guilt was there for that—the wanting—or because he was alive, still seeing things, still feeling. He wanted someone in his life, and it didn't seem right to feel guilty about it. But he did.

Sometimes, at night, he would hear the horses running, thundering across the hard summer-baked flatness of his pasture, running wild—and he would imagine they were laughing at him for wasting his time feeling guilty, but it was a feeling he could not shake, could not ride down, and his sleep was often poor and restless.

Sydney often wondered if horses were even meant to be ridden at all.

It was always such a struggle.

The thing about the broncs, he realized—and he never realized it until they were rolling on top of him in the dust, or rubbing him off against a tree, or against the side of a barn, trying to break his leg—was that if the horses didn't get broken, tamed, they'd get wilder. There was nothing as wild as a horse that had never been broken. It just got meaner, each day.

So he held on. He bucked and spun and arched and twisted, shooting up and down with the mad horses' leaps; and when the horse tried to hurt itself, by running straight into something—a fence, a barn, the lake—he stayed on.

If there was, once in a blue moon, a horse not only stronger, but more stubborn than he, then he would have to destroy it.

The cattle were easy to work with, they would do anything for food, and once one did it, they would all follow; but working with the horses made him think ahead, and sometimes he wondered, in streaks and bits of paranoia, if perhaps all the horses in the world did not have some battle against him, and were destined, all of them, to pass through his corrals, each one testing him before he was allowed to stop.

Because like all bronc-busters, that was what Sydney someday allowed himself to consider and savor, in moments of rest: the day when he could stop. A run of successes. A string of wins so satisfying and continuous that it would seem—even though he would be sore, and tired—that a horse would never beat him again, and he would be convinced of it, and then he could quit.

Mornings in summers past, Henry used to come over, and sit on the railing and watch. He had been an elementary school teacher, and frail, almost anemic: but he had loved to watch Sydney Bean ride the horses. He taught only a few classes in the summers, and he would sip coffee and grade a few papers while Sydney and the horse fought out in the center.

Sometimes Henry had set a broken bone for Sydney—Sydney had shown him how—and other times Sydney, if he was alone, would set his own bones, if he even bothered with them. Then he would wrap them up and keep riding. Dr. Lynly had set some of his bones, on the bad breaks.

Sydney was feeling old, since Henry had drowned. Not so much in the mornings, when everything was new and cool, and had promise; but in the evenings, he could feel the crooked shapes of his bones, within him. He would drink beers, and watch his horses, and other people's horses in his pasture, as they ran. The horses never seemed to feel old, not even in the evenings, and he was jealous of them, of their strength.

He called Karen one weekend. "Come out and watch me break horses," he said.

He was feeling particularly sore and tired. For some reason he wanted her to see that he could always do it; that the horses were always broken. He wanted her to see what it looked like, and how it always turned out.

"Oh, I don't know," she said, after she had considered it. "I'm just so *tired*." It was a bad and crooked road, bumpy, from her house to his, and it took nearly an hour to drive it.

"I'll come get you . . . ?" he said. He wanted to shake her. But he said nothing; he nodded, and then remembered he was on the phone and said, "I understand."

She did let him sit on the porch with her, whenever he drove over to her farm. She had to have someone.

"Do you want to hit me?" he asked one evening, almost hopefully.

But she just shook her head sadly.

He saw that she was getting comfortable with her sorrow, was settling down into it, like an old way of life, and he wanted to shock her out of it, but felt paralyzed and mute, like the dumbest of animals.

Sydney stared at his crooked hands, with the scars from the cuts, made over the years by the fencing tools. Silently, he cursed all the many things he did not know. He could lift bales of hay. He could string barbed-wire fences. He could lift things. That was all he knew. He wished he were a chemist, an electrician, a poet, or a preacher. The things he had—what little of them there were—wouldn't help her.

She had never thought to ask how drunk Henry had been. Sydney thought that made a difference: whether you jumped off the bridge with one beer in you, or two, or a six-pack; or with a sea of purple Psychos rolling around in your stomach—but she never asked.

He admired her confidence, and doubted his ability to be as strong, as stubborn. She never considered that it might have been her fault, or Henry's; that some little spat might have prompted it, or general disillusionment.

It was his fault, Sydney's, square and simple, and she seemed comfortable, if not happy, with the fact.

Dr. Lynly treated horses, but he did not seem to love them, thought Karen.

"Stupid creatures," he would grumble, when they would not do as he wanted, when he was trying to doctor them. "Utter idiots." He and Buster and Karen would try to herd the horse into the trailer, or the corral, pulling on the reins and swatting the horse with green branches.

"Brickheads," Dr. Lynly would growl, pulling the reins and then walking around and slapping, feebly, the horse's flank. "Brickheads and fatheads." He had been loading horses for fifty years, and Karen would giggle, because the horses' stupidity always seemed to surprise, and then anger Dr. Lynly, and she thought it was sweet.

It was as if he had not yet really learned that that was how they always were.

But Karen had seen that right away. She knew that a lot of girls, and women, were infatuated with horses, in love with them even, for their great size and strength, and for their wildness—but Karen, as she saw more and more of the sick horses, the ailing ones, the ones most people did not see regularly, knew that all horses were dumb, simple and trusting, and that even the smartest ones could be made to do as they were told.

And they could be so dumb, so loyal, and so oblivious to pain. It was as if—even if they could feel it—they could never, ever acknowledge it.

It was sweet, she thought, and dumb.

Karen let Sydney rub her temples and brush her hair. She would go into the bathroom, and wash it while he sat on the porch. He had taken up whittling; one of the stallions had broken Sydney's leg by throwing him into a fence and then trampling him, and the leg was in a heavy cast. So Sydney had decided to take a break for a few days.

He had bought a whittling kit at the hardware store, and was going to try hard to learn how to do it. There were instructions. At kit had a square, light piece of balsa wood, almost the weight of nothing, and a plain curved whittling knife. There was a dotted outline in the shape of a duck's head on the balsa wood that showed what the shape of his finished work would be.

After he learned to whittle, Sydney wanted to learn to play the harmonica. That was next, after whittling.

He would hear the water running, and hear Karen splashing, as she put her head under the faucet and rinsed.

She would come out in her robe, drying her hair, and then would let him sit in the hammock with her and brush her hair. It was September, and the cottonwoods were tinging, were making the skies hazy, soft and frozen. Nothing seemed to move.

Her hair came down to the middle of her back. She had stopped cutting it. The robe was old and worn, the color of an old blue dish. Something about the shampoo she used reminded him of apples. She wore moccasins that had a shearling lining in them, and Sydney and Karen would rock in the hammock, slightly. Sometimes Karen would get up and bring out two Cokes from the refrigerator, and they would drink those.

"Be sure to clean up those shavings when you go," she told him. There were little balsa wood curls all over the porch. Her hair, almost dry, would be light and soft. "Be sure not to leave a mess when you go," she would say.

It would be dark then, Venus out beyond them.

"Yes," he said.

Before he left, she reached out from the hammock, and caught his hand. She squeezed it, and then let go.

He drove home slowly, thinking of Henry, and of how he had once taken Henry fishing for the first time. They had caught a catfish so large that it had scared Henry. They drank beers, and sat in the boat, and talked.

One of Sydney Bean's headlights faltered, on the drive home, then went out, and it took him an hour and a half to get home.

The days got cold and and brittle. It was hard, working with the horses: Sydney's leg hurt all the time. Sometimes the horse would leap, and come down with all four hooves bunched in close together, and the pain and shock of it would travel all the way up Sydney's leg and into his shoulder, and down into his wrists: the break was in his ankle.

He was sleeping past sun-up, some days, and was being thrown, now, nearly every day; sometimes several times in the same day.

There was always a strong wind. Rains began to blow in. It was cool, getting cold, crisp as apples, and it was the weather that in the summer everyone said they would be looking forward to. One night there was a frost, and a full moon.

On her back porch, sitting in the hammock by herself with a heavy blanket around her, Karen saw a stray balsa shaving caught between the cracks of her porch floor. It was white, in the moonlight—the whole porch was—and the field was blue—the cattle stood out in the moonlight like blue statues—and she almost called Sydney.

She even went as far as to get up and call information, to find out his number; it was that close.

But then the silence and absence of a thing—she presumed it was Henry, but did not know for sure what it was—closed in around her, and the field beyond her porch, like the inside of her heart, seemed to be deathly still—and she did not call.

She thought angrily, I can love who I want to love. But she was angry at Sydney Bean, for having tried to pull her so far out, into a place where she did not want to go.

She fell asleep in the hammock, and dreamed that Dr. Lynly was trying to wake her up, and was taking her blood pressure, feeling her forehead, and, craziest of all, swatting at her with green branches.

She awoke from the dream, and decided to call him after all. Sydney answered the phone as if he, too, had been awake.

"Hello?" he said. She could tell by the true questioning in his voice that he did not get many phone calls.

"Hello," said Karen. "I just—wanted to call, and tell you hello." She paused; almost a falter, "And that I feel better. That I feel good, I mean. That's all.

"Well," said Sydney Bean. "Well, good. I mean, great."

"That's all," said Karen. "Bye," she said.

"Good-bye," said Sydney.

On Thanksgiving Day, Karen and Dr. Lynly headed back out to the swamp, to check up on the loggers' mule. It was the hardest cold of the year, and there was bright ice on the bridges, and it was not thawing, even in the sun. The inside of Dr. Lynly's old truck was no warmer than the air outside. Buster, in his wooliness, lay across Karen to keep her warm.

They turned onto a gravel road, and started down into the swamp. Smoke, low and spreading, was all in the woods, like a fog. The men had little fires going all throughout the woods; they were each working on a different tree, and had small warming fires where they stood and shivered when resting.

Karen found herself looking for the pale ugly logger.

He was swinging the ax, but he only had one arm, he was swinging at the tree with one arm. The left arm was gone, and there was a sort of a sleeve over it, like a sock. The man was sweating, and a small boy stepped up and quickly toweled him dry each time the pale man stepped back to take a rest.

They stopped the truck and got out and walked up to him, and he stepped back—wet, already, again; the boy toweled him off, standing on a low stool and starting with the man's neck and shoulders, and then going down the great back—and the man told them that the mule was better but that if they wanted to see him, he was lower in the swamp.

They followed the little path towards the river. All around them were downed trees, and stumps, and stacks of logs, but the woods looked no different. The haze from the fires made it seem colder. Acorns popped under their feet.

About halfway down the road, they met the mule. He was coming back up towards them, and he was pulling a good load. A small boy was in front of him, holding out a carrot, only partially eaten. The mule's knee looked much better, though it was still a little swollen, and probably always would be.

The boy stopped, and let the mule take another bite of carrot, making him lean far forward in the trace. His great rubbery lips stretched and quavered, and then flapped, as he tried to get it, and then there was the crunch when he did.

They could smell the carrot as the mule ground it with his old teeth. It was a wild carrot, dug from the woods, and not very big: but it smelled good.

Karen had brought an apple and some sugar cubes, and she started forward to give them to the mule, but instead, handed them to the little boy, who ate the sugar cubes himself, and put the apple in his pocket.

The mule was wearing an old straw hat, and looked casual, out-of-place. The boy switched him, and he shut his eyes and started up: his chest swelled, tight and sweaty, to fit the dark soft stained leather harness, and the big load behind him started in motion, too.

Buster whined, as the mule went by.

It was spring again then, the month in which Henry had left them, and they were on the back porch. Karen had purchased a Clydesdale yearling, a great and huge animal, whose mane and fur she had shaved to keep it cool in the warming weather, and she had asked a little boy from a nearby farm with time on his hands to train it, in the afternoons. The horse was already gentled, but needed to be stronger. She was having the boy walk him around in the fields, pulling a makeshift sled of stones and tree stumps and old rotten bales of hay.

In the fall, when the Clydesdale was strong enough, she and Dr. Lynly were going to trailer it out to the swamp, and trade it for the mule.

Sydney Bean's leg had healed, been broken again, and was now healing once more. The stallion he was trying to break was showing signs of weakening. There was something in the whites of his eyes, Sydney thought, when he reared up, and he was not slamming himself into the barn—so it seemed to Sydney, anyway—with quite as much anger. Sydney thought that perhaps this coming summer would be the one in which he broke all of his horses, day after day, week after week.

They sat in the hammock and drank Cokes and nibbled radishes, celery, which Karen had washed and put on a little tray. They watched the boy, or one of his friends, his blue shirt a tiny spat against the treeline, as he followed the big dark form of the Clydesdale. The sky was a wide spread of crimson, all along the western trees, towards the river. They couldn't tell which of the local children it was, behind the big horse; it could have been any of them.

"I really miss him," said Sydney Bean. "I really hurt."

"I know," Karen said. She put her hand on Sydney's, and rested it there. "I will help you," she said.

Out in the field, a few cattle egrets fluttered and hopped behind the horse and boy. The great young draft horse lifted his thick legs high and free of the mud with each step, free from the mud made soft by the rains of spring, and slowly—they could tell—he was skidding the sled forward.

The egrets hopped and danced, following at a slight distance, but neither the boy nor the horse seemed to notice. They kept their heads down, and moved forward.

ANGELA CARTER

The Company of Wolves

ONE BEAST AND ONLY ONE howls in the woods by night.

The wolf is carnivore incarnate and he's as cunning as he is ferocious; once he's had a taste of flesh then nothing else will do.

At night, the eyes of wolves shine like candle flames, yellowish, reddish, but that is because the pupils of their eyes fatten on darkness and catch the light from your lantern to flash it back to you—red for danger; if a wolf's eyes reflect only moonlight, then they gleam a cold and unnatural green, a mineral, a piercing colour. If the benighted traveller spies those luminous, terrible sequins stitched suddenly on the black thickets, then he knows he must run, if fear has not struck him stock-still.

But those eyes are all you will be able to glimpse of the forest assassins as they cluster invisibly round your smell of meat as you go through the wood unwisely late.

They will be like shadows, they will be like wraiths, grey members of a congregation of nightmare; hark! his long, wavering howl . . . an aria of fear made audible.

The wolfsong is the sound of the rending you will suffer, in itself a murdering.

It is winter and cold weather. In this region of mountain and forest, there is now nothing for the wolves to eat. Goats and sheep are locked up in the byre, the deer departed for the remaining pasturage on the southern slopes—wolves grow lean and famished. There is so little flesh on them that you could count the starveling ribs through their pelts, if they gave you time before they pounced. Those slavering jaws; the lolling tongue; the rime of saliva on the grizzled chops—of all the teeming perils of the night and the forest, ghosts, hobgoblins, ogres that grill babies upon gridirons, witches that fatten their captives in cages for cannibal tables, the wolf is worst for he cannot listen to reason.

You are always in danger in the forest, where no people are. Step between the portals of the great pines where the shaggy branches tangle about you, trapping the unwary traveller in nets as if the vegetation itself were in a plot with the wolves who live there, as though the wicked trees go fishing on behalf of their friends—step between the gateposts of the forest with the greatest trepidation and infinite precautions, for if you stray from the path for one instant, the wolves will eat you. They are grey as famine, they are as unkind as plague.

The grave-eyed children of the sparse villages always carry knives with them when they go out to tend the little flocks of goats that provide the homesteads with acrid milk and rank, maggoty cheeses. Their knives are half as big as they are, the blades are sharpened daily.

But the wolves have ways of arriving at your own hearthside. We try and try but sometimes we cannot keep them out. There is no winter's night the cottager does not fear to see a lean, grey, famished snout questing under the door, and there was a woman once bitten in her own kitchen as she was straining the macaroni.

Fear and flee the wolf; for, worst of all, the wolf may be more than he seems.

There was a hunter once, near here, that trapped a wolf in a pit. This wolf had massacred the sheep and goats; eaten up a mad old man who used to live by himself in a hut halfway up the mountain and sing to Jesus all day; pounced on a girl looking after the sheep, but she made such a commotion that men came with rifles and scared him away and tried to track him into the forest but he was cunning and easily gave them the slip. So this hunter dug a pit and put a duck in it, for bait, all alive-oh; and he covered the pit with straw smeared with wolf dung. Quack, quack! went the duck and a wolf came slinking out of the forest, a big one, a heavy one, he weighed as much as a grown man and the straw gave way beneath him—into the pit he tumbled. The hunter jumped down after him, slit his throat, cut off all his paws for a trophy.

And then no wolf at all lay in front of the hunter but the bloody trunk of a man, headless, footless, dying, dead.

A witch from up the valley once turned an entire wedding party into wolves because the groom had settled on another girl. She used to order them to visit her, at night, from spite, and they would sit and howl around her cottage for her, serenading her with their misery.

Not so very long ago, a young woman in our village married a man who vanished clean away on her wedding night. The bed was made with new sheets and the bride lay down in it; the groom said, he was going out to relieve himself, insisted on it, for the sake of decency, and she drew the coverlet up to her chin and she lay there. And she waited and she waited and then she waited again—surely he's been gone a long time? Until she jumps up in bed and shrieks to hear a howling, coming on the wind from the forest.

That long-drawn, wavering howl has, for all its fearful resonance, some inherent sadness in it, as if the beasts would love to be less beastly if only they knew how and never cease to mourn their own condition. There is a vast melancholy in the canticles of the wolves, melancholy infinite as the forest, endless as these long nights of winter and yet that ghastly sadness, that mourning for their own, irremediable appetites, can never move the heart for not one phrase in it hints at the possibility of redemption; grace could not come to the wolf from its own despair, only through some external mediator, so that, sometimes, the beast will look as if he half welcomes the knife that despatches him.

The young woman's brothers searched the outhouses and the haystacks but never found any remains so the sensible girl dried her eyes and found herself another husband not too shy to piss into a pot who spent the nights indoors. She gave him a pair of bonny babies and all went right as a trivet until, one freezing night, the night of the solstice, the hinge of the year when things do not fit together as well as they should, the longest night, her first good man came home again.

A great thump on the door announced him as she was stirring the soup for the father of her children and she knew him the moment she lifted the latch to him although it was years since she'd worn black for him and now he was in rags and his hair hung down his back and never saw a comb, alive with lice.

"Here I am again, missus," he said. "Get me my bowl of cabbage and be quick about it."

Then her second husband came in with wood for the fire and when the first one saw she'd slept with another man and, worse, clapped his red eyes on her little children who'd crept into the kitchen to see what all the din was about, he shouted: "I wish I were a wolf again, to teach this whore a lesson!" So a wolf he instantly became and tore off the eldest boy's left foot before he was chopped up with the hatchet they used for chopping logs. But when the wolf lay bleeding and gasping its last, the pelt peeled off again and he was just as he had been, years ago, when he ran away from his marriage bed, so that she wept and her second husband beat her.

They say there's an ointment the Devil gives you that turns you into a wolf the minute you rub it on. Or, that he was bom feet first and had a wolf for his father and his torso is a man's but his legs and genitals are a wolf's. And he has a wolf's heart.

Seven years is a werewolf's natural span but if you burn his human clothing you condemn him to wolfishness for the rest of his life, so old wives hereabouts think it some protection to throw a hat or an apron at the werewolf, as if clothes made the man. Yet by the eyes, those phosphorescent eyes you know him in all his shapes; the eyes alone unchanged by metamorphosis.

Before he can become a wolf, the lycanthrope strips stark naked. If you spy a naked man among the pines, you must run as if the Devil were after you.

It is midwinter and the robin, the friend of man, sits on the handle of the gardener's spade and sings. It is the worst time in all the year for wolves but this strong-minded child insists she will go off through the wood. She is quite sure the wild beasts cannot harm her although, well-warned, she lays a carving knife in the basket her mother has packed with cheeses. There is a bottle of harsh liquor distilled from brambles; a batch of flat oatcakes baked on the hearthstone; a pot or two of jam. The flaxen-haired girl will take these delicious gifts to a reclusive grandmother so old the burden of her years is crushing her to death. Granny lives two hours' trudge through the winter woods; the child wraps herself up in her thick shawl, draws it over her head. She steps into her stout wooden shoes; she is dressed and ready and it is Christmas Eve. The malign door of the solstice still swings upon its hinges but she has been too much loved ever to feel scared.

Children do not stay young for long in this savage country. There are no toys for them to play with so they work hard and grow wise but this one, so pretty and the youngest of her family, a little late-comer, had been indulged by her mother and the grandmother who'd knitted her the red shawl that, today, has the ominous if brilliant look of blood on snow. Her breasts have just begun to swell; her hair is like lint, so fair it hardly makes a shadow on her pale forehead; her cheeks are an emblematic scarlet and white and she has just started her woman's bleeding, the clock inside her that will strike, henceforward, once a month.

She stands and moves within the invisible pentacle of her own virginity. She is an unbroken egg; she is a sealed vessel; she has inside her a magic space the entrance to which is shut tight with a plug of membrane; she is a closed system; she does not know how to shiver. She has her knife and she is afraid of nothing.

Her father might forbid her, if he were home, but he is away in the forest, gathering wood, and her mother cannot deny her.

The forest closed upon her like a pair of jaws.

There is always something to look at in the forest, even in the middle of winter— the huddled mounds of birds, succumbed to the lethargy of the season, heaped on the creaking boughs and too forlorn to sing; the bright frills of the winter fungi on the blotched bunks of the trees; the cuneiform slots of rabbits and deer, the herringbone tracks of the birds, a hare as lean as a rasher of bacon streaking across the path where the thin sunlight dapples the russet brakes of last year's bracken.

When she heard the freezing howl of a distant wolf, her practised hand sprang to the handle of her knife, but she saw no sign of a wolf at all, nor of a naked man, neither, but then she heard a clattering among the brushwood and there sprang on to the path a fully clothed one, a very handsome young one, in the green coat and wide-awake hat of a hunter, laden with carcasses of game birds. She had her hand on her knife at the first rustle of twigs but he laughed with a flash of white teeth when he saw her and made her a comic yet flattering little bow; she'd never seen such a fine fellow before, not among the rustic clowns of her native village. So on they went together, through the thickening light of the afternoon.

Soon they were laughing and joking like old friends. When he offered to carry her basket, she gave it to him although her knife was in it because he told her his rifle would protect them. As the day darkened, it began to snow again; she felt the first flakes settle on her eyelashes but now there was only half a mile to go and there would be a fire, and hot tea, and a welcome, a warm one, surely, for the dashing huntsman as well as for herself.

This young man had a remarkable object in his pocket. It was a compass. She looked at the little round glass face in the palm of his hand and watched the wavering needle with a vague wonder. He assured her this compass had taken him safely through the wood on his hunting trip because the needle always told him with perfect accuracy where the north was. She did not believe it; she knew she should never leave the path on the way through the wood or else she would be lost instantly. He laughed at her again; gleaming trails of spittle clung to his teeth. He said, if he plunged off the path into the forest that surrounded them, he could guarantee to arrive at her grandmother's house a good quarter of an hour before she did, plotting his way through the undergrowth with his compass, while she trudged the long way, along the winding path.

I don't believe you. Besides, aren't you afraid of the wolves?

He only tapped the gleaming butt of his rifle and grinned.

Is it a bet? he asked her. Shall we make a game of it? What will you give me if I get to your grandmother's house before you?

What would you like? she asked disingenuously.

A kiss.

Commonplaces of a rustic seduction; she lowered her eyes and blushed.

He went through the undergrowth and took her basket with him but she forgot to be afraid of the beasts, although now the moon was rising, for she wanted to dawdle on her way to make sure the handsome gentleman would win his wager.

Grandmother's house stood by itself a little way out of the village. The freshly falling snow blew in eddies about the kitchen garden and the young man stepped delicately up the snowy path to the door as if he were reluctant to get his feet wet, swinging his bundle of game and the girl's basket and humming a little tune to himself.

There is a faint trace of blood on his chin; he has been snacking on his catch.

He rapped upon the panels with his knuckles.

Aged and frail, granny is three-quarters succumbed to the mortality the ache in her bones promises her and almost ready to give in entirely. A boy came out from the village to build up her hearth for the night an how ago and the kitchen crackles with busy firelight. She has her Bible for company, she is a pious old woman. She is propped up on several pillows in the bed set into the wall peasant-fashion, wrapped up in the patchwork quilt she made before she was married, more years ago than she cares to remember. Two china spaniels with liver-coloured blotches on their coats and black noses sit on either side of the fireplace. There is a bright rug of woven rags on the pantiles. The grandfather clock ticks away her eroding time.

We keep the wolves outside by living well.

He rapped upon the panels with his hairy knuckles.

It is your granddaughter, he mimicked in a high soprano.

Lift up the latch and walk in, my darling.

You can tell them by their eyes, eyes of a beast of prey, nocturnal, devastating eyes as red as a wound; you can hurl your Bible at him and your apron after, granny, you thought that was a sure prophylactic against these infernal vermin . . . now call on Christ and his mother and all the angels in heaven to protect you but it won't do you any good.

His feral muzzle is sharp as a knife; he drops his golden burden of gnawed pheasant on the table and puts down your dear girl's basket, too. Oh, my God, what have you done with her?

Off with his disguise, that coat of forest-coloured cloth, the hat with the feather tucked into the ribbon; his matted hair streams down his white shirt and she can see the lice moving in it. The sticks in the hearth shift and hiss; night and the forest has come into the kitchen with darkness tangled in its hair.

He strips off his shirt. His skin is the colour and texture of vellum. A crisp stripe of hair runs down his belly, his nipples are ripe and dark as poison fruit but he's so thin you could count the ribs under his skin if only he gave you the time. He strips off his trousers and she can see how hairy his legs are. His genitals, huge. Ah! huge.

The last thing the old lady saw in all this world was a young man, eyes like cinders, naked as a stone, approaching her bed.

The wolf is carnivore incarnate.

When he had finished with her, he licked his chops and quickly dressed himself again, until he was just as he had been when he came through her door. He burned the inedible hair in the fireplace and wrapped the bones up in a napkin that he hid away under the bed in the wooden chest in which he found a clean pair of sheets. These he carefully put on the bed instead of the tell-tale stained ones he stowed away in the laundry basket. He plumped up the pillows and shook out the patchwork quilt, he picked up the Bible from the floor, closed it and laid it on the table. All was as it had been before except that grandmother was gone. The sticks twitched in the grate, the clock ticked and the young man sat patiently, deceitfully beside the bed in granny's nightcap.

Rat-a-tap-tap.

Who's there, he quavers in granny's antique falsetto.

Only your granddaughter.

So she came in, bringing with her a flurry of snow that melted in tears on the tiles, and perhaps she was a little disappointed to see only her grandmother sitting beside the fire. But then he flung off the blanket and sprang to the door, pressing his back against it so that she could not get out again.

The girl looked round the room and saw there was not even the indentation of a head on the smooth cheek of the pillow and how, for the first time she'd seen it so, the Bible lay closed on the table. The tick of the clock cracked like a whip. She wanted her knife from her basket but she did not dare reach for it because his eyes were fixed upon her—huge eyes that now seemed to shine with a unique, interior light, eyes the size of saucers, saucers full of Greek fire, diabolic phosphorescence.

What big eyes you have.

All the better to see you with.

No trace at all of the old woman except for a tuft of white hair that had caught in the bark of an unburned log. When the girl saw that, she knew she was in danger of death.

Where is my grandmother?

There's nobody here but we two, my darling.

Now a great howling rose up all around them, near, very near, as close as the kitchen garden, the howling of a multitude of wolves; she knew the worst wolves are hairy on the inside and she shivered, in spite of the scarlet shawl she pulled more closely round herself as if it could protect her although it was as red as the blood she must spill.

Who has come to sing us carols, she said.

Those are the voices of my brothers, darling; I love the company of wolves. Look out of the window and you'll see them.

Snow half-caked the lattice and she opened it to look into the garden. It was a white night of moon and snow; the blizzard whirled round the gaunt, grey beasts who squatted on their haunches among the rows of winter cabbage, pointing their sharp snouts to the moon and howling as if their hearts would break. Ten wolves; twenty wolves—so many wolves she could not count them, howling in concert as if demented or deranged. Their eyes reflected the light from the kitchen and shone like a hundred candles.

It is very cold, poor things, she said; no wonder they howl so.

She closed the window on the wolves' threnody and took off her scarlet shawl, the colour of poppies, the colour of sacrifices, the colour of her menses, and, since her fear did her no good, she ceased to be afraid.

What shall I do with my shawl?

Throw it on the fire, dear one. You won't need it again.

She bundled up her shawl and threw it on the blaze, which instantly consumed it. Then she drew her blouse over her head; her small breasts gleamed as if the snow had invaded the room.

What shall I do with my blouse?

Into the fire with it, too, my pet.

The thin muslin went flaring up the chimney like a magic bird and now off came her skirt, her woollen stockings, her shoes, and on to the fire they went, too, and were gone for good. The firelight shone through the edges of her skin; now she was clothed only in her untouched integument of flesh. This dazzling, naked she combed out her hair with her fingers; her hair looked white as the snow outside. Then went directly to the man with red eyes in whose unkempt mane the lice moved; she stood up on tip-toe and unbuttoned the collar of his shirt.

What big arms you have.

All the better to hug you with.

Every wolf in the world now howled a prothalamion outside the window as she freely gave the kiss she owed him.

What big teeth you have!

She saw how his jaw began to slaver and the room was full of the clamour of the forest's Liebestod[1] but the wise child never flinched, even when he answered:

All the better to eat you with.

The girl burst out laughing; she knew she was nobody's meat. She laughed at him full in the face, she ripped off his shirt for him and flung it into the fire, in the fiery wake of her discarded clothing. The flames danced like dead souls on Walpurgis-nacht[2] and the old bones under the bed set up a terrible clattering but she did not pay them any heed.

Carnivore incarnate, only immaculate flesh appeases him.

She will lay his fearful head on her lap and she will pick out the lice from his pelt and perhaps she will put the lice into her mouth and eat them, as he will bid her, as she would do in a savage marriage ceremony.

The blizzard will die down.

The blizzard died down, leaving the mountains as randomly covered with snow as if a blind woman had thrown a sheet over them, the upper branches of the forest pines limed, creaking, swollen with the fall.

Snowlight, moonlight, a confusion of paw-prints.

All silent, all still.

Midnight; and the clock strikes. It is Christmas Day, the werewolves' birthday, the door of the solstice stands wide open; let them all sink through.

See! sweet and sound she sleeps in granny's bed, between the paws of the tender wolf.

Barbara Gowdy

Disneyland

THE CHRISTMAS THAT LOUISE AND LINDA were twelve and Sandy was eleven, there was only one gift under the tree for each of them. Viewmasters for the twins and a beatnik doll with a string that you pulled to make it talk for Sandy. The three girls wept.

Their father let them go at it for a while, and then he sprang the surprise; he was taking them to Disneyland in a top-of-the-line trailer that slept five.

"When, Daddy? When?" the girls cried.

---

1. A love of death.
2. A witches' gathering that takes place on the eve of May Day.

"The summer. Maybe take a couple of extra weeks off work and drive down to Me-hi-co while we're at it. Eh, señorita?" He pulled the string on Sandy's doll.

"I'm hip, like uh, you know, beatnik," the doll said.

That was Christmas nineteen-sixty, and it was the next month that air-raid drills started in Glenn Mills Public School for when the Russians dropped the bomb. The principal made a speech in the gymnasium to all the students. If it ever suddenly got very light, he said, like a huge flashbulb going off in the sky, you were to cover your eyes with your hands and crouch under your desks until the teacher said it was safe to come out. Then, two by two, you were to file down to the cellar. You were not to try to run home.

"The hell with that," their father said when they told him. "You run home." He had decided to build a fallout shelter. He had a pamphlet that he'd sent away for called "Pioneers of Self-Defense" on how to do it.

As soon as the ground was soft enough, about the end of April, he had a man with a bulldozer dig a hole in the back yard. The next day another man in a truck delivered a pile of concrete blocks, and some pipes and boards and sheets of metal, and their father went right to work.

It took a month. Every minute that their father wasn't sleeping or working he was down in that hole; he even ate his meals there. He let Louise help, and she got pretty good at mixing mortar and hammering nails in the floorboards, as long as he didn't yell at her that she was doing it all wrong, which, if he stood over her shoulder, she did. But if he left her alone, she seemed to have a knack. In the morning she woke up yearning for the feel of the hammer in her hand, she dreamed about hammering all day at school. She wished she could do it when he wasn't around, and yet sometimes, when he wasn't mad or tired, she liked the fact that they worked as a team: she mixing the mortar, he setting the blocks; he sawing the boards, she nailing them down. He had to have everything perfect, and the longer she helped him the more she wanted everything to be perfect, too, the more she couldn't blame him for his tantrums. She wondered if he wished her brother was alive so he could help instead of her.

When the outside was done, the man came back with the bulldozer to shovel the earth back on the roof. Inside, Louise and her father built shelves and fold-up bunks and painted the walls canary-yellow, which was supposed to add a note of cheerfulness. Even though Louise said that she and her sisters never played hopscotch anymore, her father painted a hopscotch on the floor because the pamphlet said you should if you had kids.

He bought two weeks' worth of canned food, jugs for the water, candles, lanterns, paper plates, a chemical toilet, canned heat, a fire extinguisher and a camping stove. The rest of what the pamphlet said he should buy—bedding, Band-Aids, a transistor radio, a flashlight, batteries, board games, a shovel in case they had to dig themselves out from the house falling on top of them—they already had. A small library of books on nature and American history would prove useful and inspirational, the pamphlet said, but he said, did they know how much a book cost nowadays, and he carried down a box of his old *Life* magazines. He also brought down two cases of Canadian Club whiskey for their mother, and his World War Two gun.

Every three days the girls had to empty the water jugs and refill them using the hose, so that the supply would always be fresh. Their father started to have drills, but they were nothing like the ones at school, where the important thing was to stay calm. He would blow a whistle, sometimes in the middle of the night, and they all had to run like crazy to do their assigned tasks: Linda, shut and latch the windows and lock the front door; Louise, unscrew all the fuses in the fuse box and turn off the valve to the water heater; Sandy, shut off the furnace switch; their mother, just get herself to the cellar landing. Meanwhile he went on blowing the whistle and shouting, "Move it!" Then they charged out the back door to the shelter, which they entered in order of size, Sandy first, him last to pull the hatch shut. Down inside he shone the flashlight on his stopwatch and announced how long it had taken. He shone the light in their faces and told them how they could shave off those precious seconds. It was cold down there, and they shivered, especially at night in their pajamas and bare feet, or if it had been raining. Their mother asked how many more drills they had to do, and he said they had to keep at it until the bomb dropped—they had to be in top form.

"Well," she said. "Let's just hope it drops before winter. We'll catch our deaths, running out here all the time in the snow."

He slept in the shelter. He put in an electric outlet so he could listen to his Judy Garland records down there. The girls imagined him dancing with the shovel, smooching it: "How's about a little kiss, baby." They loved him being out of the house in the evenings. They could change the channels, say whatever they felt like, go to bed late. As long as their mother's coffee mug was filled with Canadian Club whiskey, she didn't care what happened.

The drills didn't stop though. The girls could go through them in their sleep, and sometimes did, waking up in the morning barely recalling that a few hours before they'd been flying around the house and out into the night. Often their mother didn't bother coming back up. She just fell onto one of the bunks and stayed there until morning. The girls could have too, their father said so. But they never would. When the light was off it was so black it was like being dead. Also there was a weird smell, which they thought came from where they'd buried Checkers, their puppy that hung itself one night trying to get in the basement window out of the cold, not knowing it couldn't jump in unless one of the girls had unhooked its chain, not knowing that they could only unhook its chain and cry, "Jump, Checkers!" when their father wasn't home.

At breakfast, the Saturday before the last week of school, their father announced that they were going down the bomb shelter for two weeks.

They didn't get it. Did he mean, have a drill every day for two weeks? No, he meant stay down for two weeks. Sleep there? they asked. Sleep there, he said, eat there, not come out for two whole weeks.

"Oh, my lord," their mother said quietly, dropping her spoon in her cereal.

"Watch TV down there?" Louise asked.

"No TV. We'll be living as if the bomb's dropped and all electricity is out."

"What if the phone rings?" Sandy asked.

"We'll tell everyone where we are beforehand."

"But won't you have to go to work?" Linda asked.

"Nope. I've got two weeks coming,"

They still didn't get it. "Two *more* weeks?" Louise asked.

"Two weeks," he said. "Two weeks is two weeks." He clapped his hands. "Okay, we'll be going down a week from today. So this Friday I want the sheets and blankets out on the line for an airing. I want the water changed. I want you all to have baths."

"But when are we going to Disneyland?" Linda asked.

"We're not," he said.

They weren't down the shelter an hour when Louise got her first period. It started after breakfast with cramps; gas pains is what she thought they were and she thought she must have to go number two, but she didn't want to smell up the place and didn't want them all listening. After a few minutes, though, she felt like she couldn't hold it—she sure couldn't hold it for two weeks—so she went behind the plywood partition and sat on the toilet.

In the shadowy lantern light her white underpants were dark. She touched them, felt wetness and held her fingers in front of her, toward the light in the corner. Her fingers were red.

A sound like someone yelling far away came out of her mouth. She was outside the shelter, in the yard, listening to herself calling under the lawn.

"What's the matter?" It was her father, standing in front of her. Linda and Sandy were behind him.

Louise pulled her pants up to her thighs. "Daddy," she said, frightened and shamed. She was on the toilet.

"What the hell are you making that noise for?" he said.

Linda came around him and blocked his view. "What's the matter?" she asked.

"I'm bleeding," Louise said, barely a whisper, but Linda heard.

"It's okay," Linda said to their father.

"What's the matter?" Sandy asked.

"She's just having a hard time going to the bathroom," Linda said, pushing Sandy away.

"Well, let's try to keep this kind of thing down," their father said, walking off. "We don't need a big production."

"I'm dying," Louise whispered to Linda.

"You moron," Linda whispered. "It's the curse."

"What?"

"Menstruation. You know."

"How do you know?"

"Well, what else? What a moron."

"Do you have it?"

"No," Linda said, as if she wouldn't be caught dead.

"How do you know then?"

"Because everybody knows. When you start bleeding down there, that's what it is."

Louise looked at the dark stain on her underpants. She was dripping blood into the toilet now. "What am I going to do?"

"Well, you use Kotex. But l guess there isn't any down here." She scanned the shelf beside the toilet. Band-Aids, toilet paper, Tums. "Just a sec." She poked her head around the end of the partition. "Mommy? Can you come here?"

"What's going on?" their father asked.

"Nothing. Mommy?"

Their mother's slippers flapped as she walked across the floor.

"Louise is menstruating," Linda whispered.

Their mother covered her mouth with both hands.

"Do we have any Kotex down here?" Linda asked.

Their mother shook her head. She turned around. "Jim," she said. "I'm just popping up to the house."

"What are you talking about?" he said. "There's radiation out there."

"Well, there isn't really."

"Yeah, but we have to act like there is or we ruin the whole exercise."

"Louise has started her period."

Silence. Louise shut her eyes.

"Jesus Christ," their father said.

"So I have to get her some napkins."

"She's really bleeding?" he asked.

"Well, yes."

"All right," he said. "We tear up a sheet." He took one off the shelf where the linen was and ripped it in half. "What d'ya think the pioneers did?" he said.

The rest of the morning Louise was allowed to lie on the bunk with her mother, who drank whiskey from her coffee mug and smoked. Louise curled up on her side with her head on her mother's shoulder. Her mother's neck smelled of Evening in Paris perfume. When her father wasn't looking, her mother let her have sips from her mug to ease the cramps. Her mother patted her head and said, "You're a young lady now," about every fifteen minutes.

Linda and Sandy had to stick to "The Regime." This was a chart that their father had written out on a piece of yellow Bristol board and nailed to the wall. The time of day was down one side, and what they were supposed to do was down the other. "Eight o'clock—rise; eight o'clock to eight fifteen—use toilet in the following order: Dad, Mom, Louise, Linda, Sandy." Et cetera. In front of some of the things they had to do were the initials "l.o." standing for "lights out" to save on candles and fuel. For instance, the singsong and afternoon exercises had an l.o. in front of them.

Ten-thirty to eleven-thirty in the morning was exercises with the lights on. For the first part, their father led Linda and Sandy in a march around and around the shelter, hollering, "Hup two three four! Left! Left!" By the end they both had to go to the bathroom. It seemed like one of the five of them was always on the toilet. And since you couldn't flush, there was no way of drowning out the noise. When their father had a pee before breakfast, it sounded like Niagara Falls.

The next exercise, after they used the toilet, was touching their toes twenty-five times. Then they had to do pushups. The floor was cold on their hands, and Linda and Sandy could only do a couple before their arms gave out.

"Five! Six! Seven!" their father went on counting. He clapped between each of his pushups, holding himself in the air for a second. His face darkened. He glared out of the corners of his eyes for the girls to keep on going. They did a few more, but it was just too hard.

He went on to fifty. Then he bounced up like a jack-in-the-box and shouted, "Stride jumps!"

They jumped facing him, stepping on each other's toes and hitting each other's hands because there wasn't enough room. His mouth was open in a circle and he gusted coffee-smelling breath at them. His eyes bulged, sweat streamed down his face. If they had seen a man on the street looking like he was, they'd have run away.

"Okay, play hopscotch," he said after the stride jumps.

"We need stones," Linda said.

"Play without 'em." He went over to the shelves and poured himself a glass of water. Linda asked if she could have one, she was dying of thirst.

"Wait till lunch," he said. "We have to ration."

"Come here," her mother whispered, crooking her finger, and when Linda went over she snuck her a sip from her mug. "We'll never get through this otherwise," she whispered.

Sandy came over for a sip, too. She'd tried it before, she knew it burned going down your throat and she didn't like it. But she liked this—sneaking drinks behind his back. Them against him.

"Come on," their father said, cranking the blower for fresh air. "Hopscotch!" So they returned to the middle of the floor and jumped up and down the squares. It was dumb playing without stones. It was dumb anyway, a kid's game.

He lay down on a bottom bunk and had a smoke. He kept checking the time, and after about a quarter of an hour announced that it was eleven-thirty and they could stop. Now what they had to do was sit at the foot of the one chair in the shelter—a pink-painted wooden chair that used to be in Linda and Louise's bedroom—while he went around putting out all the lights except for one candle, which he carried back to the chair. He sat down and blew the candle out. Sandy shut her eyes, opened them. There was no difference. She felt for Linda's hand.

"All right," he said. "What do you want to sing?" His voice seemed to come from all directions.

"Um," Linda said, but couldn't think of anything. "Um," she said again to hear her thin voice, like a pin of light in the black.

"It's a long way to Tipperary," he started singing. "Come on! Everybody! Sally, Louise."

"It's a long way to go," their mother sang from the bunk in her high shaky voice.

The girls joined in, softly at first, then louder and louder because he was yelling at them to.

Sandy squeezed Linda's fingers. She smelled Checkers. Every time the lights went out she suddenly smelled him. He was buried at the bottom of the yard. Was that behind her, where the air vent was? Down here she had no sense of direction, but the smell was so strong she thought the air vent must be right next to where he was. But why did he give off a smell only when it was pitch dark? She remembered that rhyme: "The worms crawl in, the worms crawl out, up your brain, and out your snout."

They sang "The British Grenadiers," "The Battle Hymn of the Republic," "Marching to Pretoria" and "You're a Sap Mister Jap," all at the top of their lungs. Then they switched to songs from Judy Garland movies, singing these quietly. Dulcet tones was what their father demanded for Judy Garland songs, even for "Ballin' the Jack" and "The Trolley Bus Song." They ended with "Somewhere over the Rainbow." Their father had a really good voice—it sounded even better in the dark, not seeing him singing—and at the last line of "Somewhere over the Rainbow," the line that goes, "Why oh why can't I?" where the girls and their mother knew to slow right down, his voice rose clear and smooth as a boy's before their softer, higher voices, making a sound in the blackness so sweet and beautiful that it surprised them all and they were quiet for a moment afterward.

Linda spoke first. "We're like stars," she said softly. She meant the stars in the sky.

"Look out, Broadway," their father said. He struck a match, lit the candle and looked at his watch. "Twelve on the dot. Lunch time."

He heated up two cans of spaghetti on the camping stove while Linda mixed up the powdered milk and spread margarine on slices of bread. They ate sitting on the edge of the bottom bunks. After one mouthful, Louise found she wasn't hungry. She gave her plate back to her father and went to the toilet to see if her rag needed changing.

It sure did. How could so much blood be coming out of her and she was still alive, she wondered. Her stomach didn't hurt any longer, but she was dizzy. Maybe that was the whiskey, though. What if it wasn't, what if she really was bleeding to death? He wouldn't believe her.

She unpinned the old rag, wrapped it in toilet paper and pinned on another from the ones on the shelf above the toilet. On the way back to the bed she opened the lid of the garbage pail and dropped the balled-up rag in. The pail was lined with polyethylene and there was a container of disinfectant on the floor for sprinkling inside. If she died, would he keep her down here for two weeks?

In the shelter the girls had jobs, even Sandy, who never did anything up in the house. Her job was washing the dishes. Their father said that she had to use the same dishwater for two days, so when she went to wash the lunch things, there were soggy Cheerios and Frosted Flakes swimming around. Now there were white snakes of spaghetti. She held the plates by the rim and tried to keep her hands out of the water.

The Regime said lunch and cleanup were to take one hour, but Sandy was done by twelve-forty.

"What'll we do until one?" Linda asked, sneaking a sip of her mother's whiskey. One o'clock to three o'clock was cards and board games.

Their father tapped his watch, frowning. "Well, I guess we can start the games early," he said. "But tomorrow we stretch lunch out. Eat slower. Talk. I want you all to think up topics of conversation."

He spread a blanket on the floor over the hopscotch and they sat in a circle. Their mother came over, too, although she never played games in the house. She said that she just couldn't get used to no TV. It was like losing one of your senses, she said, like not being able to see or hear. Their father reached across the floor for the Canadian Club and topped up her glass.

First they played cards. Rummy. Usually the girls hated playing cards with him. He yelled at them to hurry up and discard and then said, "Are you kidding" when they did. He yelled at them to hold their cards up—they were showing everyone their hand. He said they were lucky when they won, but when he won he said that it was 80 percent skill, 20 percent luck. He swore at his cards, he swore at them if they picked up a card he had been planning to. "It's only a game," he told them when they got upset or excited, but he would shout "Yes, Momma!" and slap his cards down. He would pace and swear. How the games usually ended was with him either sending them to bed or storming out of the house.

Today, though, maybe because their mother was playing or maybe because he couldn't storm out, he was nicer. He used his nice voice. It made the girls giggle. Everything he said and did, just picking up a card and looking at it, struck them as really funny.

Their mother smiled at them over the perfect fan of her cards. She kept winning, a surprise to the girls but not to her, and they realized that rummy must be something else, like sewing and tap dancing, that she was secretly good at.

"Mommy!" they cried, hugging her when she laid down her cards in neat rows, catching them all with mittfuls.

"Well, well," their father said, his smile stopping at the edges of his mouth. The girls laughed. "Settle down," he said nicely.

They were having a great time. It was fun down here. It was like being in a fort. They played hearts next, and their mother went on winning, going for all the cards twice and getting them.

Their father started pacing between deals. "There's something going on," he said, wagging his cigarette at the girls. "This is a trick on your old dad."

"No!" They laughed.

But he didn't believe them. He said that he wanted to play Scrabble, a game of every man for himself. Except that only four could play, so Sandy and their mother were a team. While he was getting the game off the shelf the girls had another sip of whiskey.

Their father went first and made the word "bounce." That broke them up. Their mother and Sandy made "tinkle," which was even funnier. Louise used the *b* to make "bust." They shrieked with laughter. Linda did "fuse" and they couldn't stand it, it seemed so funny.

"Settle down," their father said again. They saw the vein in his forehead come out and throb, a danger sign, but they couldn't stop laughing.

It was his turn. Using the *k*, he made "kidny."

"Okay," he said enthusiastically, starting to add up his score. "Double word—"

"What is it?" Linda asked.

"Kidney," he said. "An organ. Also a bean."

"But kidney's got an *e!*" she cried.

He frowned at the board. "No it doesn't."

"Well, it does," their mother said. "K-i-d-n-*e*-y."

"That's the British spelling." he said. "I'm using the American."

Their mother shook her head. "I think there's only the one way to spell it, Jim."

"Daddy, you can't spell," Sandy said tenderly. She couldn't spell either.

"Hey, you can make 'dinky'!" Linda said, rearranging his letters.

"Dinky!" Louise cried. They all three burst out laughing.

He hit Linda with a backhand across her mouth. She fell sideways, screaming. Louise and Sandy leaped up and ran to the wall. Their mother leaned over to get the whiskey bottle, and held it tight on the floor. He stood. He kicked the Scrabble board. It went shooting straight up, scattering letters, bent at the crease down the middle as if it would fly, then fell back to the floor, flat.

Linda, on her feet now, was making jumps at the roof, trying to grab the stairs, which you pulled down.

"The hatch is locked," their father said matter-of-factly.

"Let me out!" Linda screamed.

He looked at his watch. "Nap time," he said, and began putting out the lights.

Linda threw herself back on the floor. She cried that she was never going to get up. He stepped over her.

The others went to the bunks. There were two bunks on the end wall, which were Linda's and Louise's; one along the same wall as the toilets, which was Sandy's; and two on the wall across from that—their mother's and father's. Their father took a candle to his bunk, and after he'd climbed up and set the alarm he blew it out. Black. And then that smell. Linda imagined it was coming from under the shelter, beneath where she was lying. She started to shiver. The floor was cold and hard, and suddenly she was so tired. She began crawling to the end of the room, knowing where she was by her father's snores. She waved her hand in front of her. When it hit the bottom bunk, she laid her head on the edge, too weary to climb to the top or even to climb in with Louise. She fell into a dead sleep.

Louise was aware of her sister crawling across the floor. She felt the mattress go down—Linda's foot, she thought, but it didn't move. She touched it and felt hair.

"Linda," she whispered.

No answer.

"Get up." She shook Linda's head a little, then remembered her face might be sore. She laid her palm gently on Linda's mouth for a minute. She put her other hand under the covers, down her pants, to see if her rag was leaking. She couldn't tell. It felt kind of damp, though. If she leaked all over the bed, he'd kill her. But he'd kill her if she got up and lit a candle to see. She had meant to put on a new rag after the games. Her head throbbed. Also she felt sick to her stomach. Was that the curse? Why did she have the curse and Linda didn't? What if boys tried to get her pregnant? Boys smelled the blood. Boys stared at her. She saw them staring at her chest, and it frightened her how childish their faces went, as if they hadn't learned any rules or manners yet. Even on hot days she wore two undershirts and a sweater. She slept on her stomach so she wouldn't grow any bigger. She couldn't do that now because of feeling like she was going to bring up. How was anyone supposed to sleep down here anyway, with their father snoring his head off?

Under the covers, pressing the place where the sound came out of the mattress, Sandy pulled the doll's string over and over. She didn't like this doll. It had black straight hair, and she was too old for dolls. The only reason she'd brought it down was that their father said she could, so she thought she had to. It was stuck, saying, "Hey cool cat, let's jive." She didn't care what it said, as long as it kept talking. But when she pulled the string, in the second when it wasn't talking, the smell crept in. The smell was the worms eating. The way Checkers's head had flopped, like a puppet's, had made her think that that's what it was hanging there. A Checkers puppet that somebody had hung in the window. She had screamed, then laughed, then gone closer and screamed. She was afraid to ask their father to leave the candle burning. She was afraid to make him mad. "What's the matter with you?" he asked after he hit Louise or Linda, and she was the one who couldn't stop crying. He never hit her. She thought it was because she was the prettiest.

For some reason the alarm went off at ten after four instead of four o'clock, cutting into their exercise hour. He gave them only a minute each to use the toilet, Louise two minutes to change her rag. The blood hadn't leaked onto her sheets, but it had gone through to her underpants and made a spot on her blue corduroy pants. She would have to wear them like that all week. There was no laundry detergent down here, let alone extra water or a time on The Regime for doing a wash, and they had only been allowed to bring down one change of clothing, which they weren't supposed to put on until next Saturday.

Sandy begged for a drink of water and he let her have a sip. Linda wouldn't ask, but she drank a whole glass when he was peeing. She said she had a headache, and Sandy and Louise said, "Same here." Their mother let them have more whiskey.

Louise got out of exercises again by saying her stomach hurt. In the dark (afternoon exercises were lights out), she and her mother passed the mug back and forth, and pretty soon Louise's headache was gone.

Sandy clung to Linda's hand as they marched, and Linda only pretended to lift her knees and swing her free arm. She let Sandy go on holding her hand during touching toes, where the two of them only touched their knees, and during pushups, where they just lay on their stomachs making grunting and panting noises. During stride jumps they jumped up and down holding hands. Their father's sweat rained on them.

The next hour, "Pep Talk," was him telling stories of his hardships in the war: marching for three days on a broken ankle, eating a can of moldy peach halves, saving a wounded buddy under a barrage of Jerry fire—stories they'd heard a thousand times. Then there was supper and dishes, then two hours of "Free Time," which was either playing games quietly or reading. The girls played hearts with their mother and took a couple of sips from her mug. Linda also snuck puffs of her cigarette. Louise conked out on the floor. Their father lay on his bunk, smoking and reading his *Life* magazines, mostly aloud, making them stop their game and listen. At nine o'clock Louise had to wake up, and they changed into their pajamas, facing their bunks. He went behind the partition to change. Then they climbed into their beds and said, "Now I lay me down to sleep," all together. Then he blew the candle out. Instantly he started snoring. They smelled Checkers. Sandy wept.

"What is it, honey?" their mother said.

"I smell worms eating Checkers," she whimpered.

"That's just Daddy."

"No, it's a rotten smell," Louise said. "Don't you smell it?"

"It happens in the dark," Sandy said.

Their mother got up and lit the lantern in the corner by the toilet. "There," she said. The smell disappeared and they went to sleep. An hour or so later, when the alarm rang for their father to crank the blower, he wanted to know who had lit the lantern. Their mother said she had. The dark gave her that nightmare, she said. He turned around and looked at her. What nightmare? the girls wondered. He went back to bed, leaving the lantern burning. Every few hours the alarm went off for him to get up and crank the blower. One of the times, the lantern was out, and he put in more fuel and lit it again.

AMY HEMPEL

In the Cemetery Where Al Jolson Is Buried

For Jessica

TELL ME THINGS I WON'T MIND FORGETTING," she said. "Make it useless stuff or skip it."

I began. I told her insects fly through rain, missing every drop, never getting wet. I told her no one in America owned a tape recorder before Bing Crosby did. I told her the shape of the moon is like a banana—you see it looking full, you're seeing it end-on.

The camera made me self-conscious and I stopped. It was trained on us from a ceiling mount—the kind of camera banks use to photograph robbers. It played our image to the nurses down the hall in Intensive Care.

"Go on, girl," she said, "you get used to it."

I had my audience. I went on. Did she know that Tammy Wynette had changed her tune? Really. That now she sings "Stand By Your *Friends*"? Paul Anka did it too, I said. Does "You're Having *Our* Baby." He got sick of all that feminist bitching.

"What else?" she said. "Have you got something else?"

Oh yes. For her I would always have something else.

"Did you know when they taught the first chimp to talk, it lied? When they asked her who did it on the desk, she signed back Max, the janitor. And when they pressed her, she said she was sorry, that it was really the project director. But she was a mother, so I guess she had her reasons."

"Oh, that's good," she said. "A parable."

"There's more about the chimp," I said. "But it will break your heart."

"No thanks," she says, and scratches at her mask.

We look like good-guy outlaws. Good or bad, I am not used to the mask yet. I keep touching the warm spot where my breath, thank God, comes out. She is used to hers. She only ties the strings on top. The other ones—a pro by now—she lets hang loose.

We call this place the Marcus Welby Hospital. It's the white one with the palm trees under the opening credits of all those shows. A Hollywood hospital though in fact it is several miles west. Off camera, there is a beach across the street.

She introduces me to a nurse as "the Best Friend." The impersonal article is more intimate. It tells me that *they* are intimate, my friend and her nurse.

"I was telling her we used to drink Canada Dry Ginger Ale and pretend we were in Canada."

"That's how dumb *we* were," I say.

"You could be sisters," the nurse says.

So how come, I'll bet they are wondering, it took me so long to get to such a glamorous place? But do they ask?

They do not ask.

Two months, and how long is the drive?

The best I can explain it is this—I have a friend who worked one summer in a mortuary. He used to tell me stories. The one that really got to me was not the grisliest, but it's the one that did. A man wrecked his car on 101 going south. He did not lose consciousness. But his arm was taken down to the wet bone—and when he looked at it—it scared him to death. I mean, he died.

So I didn't dare look any closer. But now I'm doing it—and hoping I won't be scared to death.

She shakes out a summer-weight blanket, showing a leg you did not want to see. Except for that, you look at her and understand the law that requires *two* people to be with the body at all times.

"I thought of something," she says. "I thought of it last night. I think there is a real and present need here. You know," she says, "like for someone to do it for you when you can't do it yourself. You call them up whenever you want—like when push comes to shove."

She grabs the bedside phone and loops the cord around her neck.

"Hey," she says, "the End o' the Line."

She keeps on, giddy with something. But I don't know with what.

"The giveaway was the solarium," she says. "That's where Marcus Welby broke the news to his patients. Then here's the real doctor suggesting we talk in the solarium. So I knew I was going to die.

"I can't remember," she says, "what does Kübler-Ross say comes after Denial?"

It seems to me Anger must be next. Then Bargaining, Depression, and so on and so forth. But I keep my guesses to myself.

"The only thing is," she says, "is where's Resurrection? God knows I want to do it by the book. But she left out Resurrection."

She laughs, and I cling to the sound the way someone dangling above a ravine holds fast to the thrown rope.

We could have cried then, but when we didn't, we couldn't.

"Tell me," she says, "about that chimp with the talking hands. What do they do when the thing ends and the chimp says, 'I don't want to go back to the zoo'?"

When I don't say anything, she says, "O.K.—then tell me another animal story! I like animal stories. But not a sick one—I don't want to know about all the Seeing Eye dogs going blind."

No, I would not tell her a sick one.

"How about the hearing-ear dogs?" I say. "They're not going deaf, but they are getting very judgmental. For instance, there's this golden retriever in Jersey, he wakes up the deaf mother and drags her into the daughter's room because the kid has got a flashlight and is reading under the covers."

"Oh, you're killing me," she says. "Yes, you're definitely killing me."

"They say the smart dog obeys, but the smarter dog knows when to *disobey*."

"Yes," she says, "the smarter *anything* knows when to disobey. Now, for example."

She is flirting with the Good Doctor, who has just appeared. Unlike the Bad Doctor, who checks the I.V. drip before saying good morning, the Good Doctor says things like "God didn't give epileptics a fair shake." He awards himself points for the cripples he could have hit in the parking lot. Because the Good Doctor is a little in love with her he says maybe a year. He pulls a chair up to her bed and suggests I might like to spend an hour on the beach.

"Bring me something back," she says. "Anything from the beach. Or the gift shop. Taste is no object."

The Doctor slowly draws the curtain around her bed.

"Wait!" she cries.

I look in at her.

"Anything," she says, "except a magazine subscription."

The doctor turns away.

I watch her mouth laugh.

What seems dangerous often is not—black snakes, for example, or clear-air turbulence. While things that just lie there, like this beach, are loaded with jeopardy. A yellow dust rising from the ground, the heat that ripens melons overnight—this is earthquake weather. You can sit here braiding the fringe on your towel and the sand will all of a sudden suck down like an hourglass. The air roars. In the cheap apartments onshore, bathtubs fill themselves and gardens roll up and over like green waves. If nothing happens, the dust will drift and the heat deepen till fear turns to desire. Nevres like that are only brought off by catastrophe.

"It never happens when you're thinking about it," she observed once.

"Earthquake, earthquake, earthquake," she said.

"Earthquake, earthquake, earthquake," I said.

Like the aviaphobe who keeps the plane aloft with prayer, we kept it up till an aftershock cracked the ceiling.

That was after the big one in '72. We were in college; our dormitory was five miles from the epicenter. When the ride was over and my jabbering pulse began to slow, she served five parts champagne to one part orange juice and joked about living in Ocean View, Kansas. I offered to drive her to Hawaii on the new world psychics predicted would surface the next time, or the next.

I could not say that now—next. *Whose* next? she could ask.

Was I the only one who noticed that the experts had stopped saying *if* and now spoke of *when*? Of course not; the fearful ran to thousands. We watched the traffic of Japanese beetles for deviation. Deviation might mean more natural violence.

I wanted her to be afraid with me, but she said, "I don't know. I'm just not."

She was afraid of nothing, not even of flying.

I have this dream before a flight where we buckle in and the plane moves down the runway. It takes off at thirty-five miles an hour, and then we're airborne, skimming on tree tops. Still, we arrive in New York on time. It is so pleasant. One night I flew to Moscow this way.

She flew with me once. That time she flew with me she ate macadamia nuts while the wings bounced. She knows the wing tips can bend thirty feet up and thirty feet down without coming off. She believes it. She trusts the laws of aerodynamics. My mind stampedes. I can almost accept that a battleship floats and everybody knows steel sinks.

I see fear in her now and am not going to try to talk her out of it. She is right to be afraid.

After a quake, the six o'clock news airs a film clip of first-graders yelling at the broken playground per their teacher's instructions.

"*Bad* earth!" they shout, because anger is stronger than fear.

But the beach is standing still today. Everyone on it is tranquilized, numb or asleep. Teenaged girls rub coconut oil on each other's hard-to-reach places. They smell like macaroons. They pry open compacts like clamshells; mirrors catch the sun and throw a spray of white rays across glazed shoulders. The girls arrange their wet hair with silk flowers the way they learned in *Seventeen*. They pose.

A formation of low-riders pulls over to watch with a six-pack. They get vocal when the girls check their tan lines. When the beer is gone, so are they—flexing their cars on up the boulevard.

Above this aggressive health are the twin wrought-iron terraces, painted flamingo pink, of the Palm Royale. Someone dies there every time the sheets are changed. There's an ambulance in the driveway, so the remaining residents line the balconies, rocking and not talking, one-upped.

The ocean they stare at is dangerous, and not just the undertow. You can almost see the slapping tails of sand sharks keeping cruising bodies alive.

If she looked, she could see this, some of it, from her window. She would be the first to say how little it takes to make a thing all wrong.

There was a second bed in the room when I returned. For two beats I didn't get it. Then it hit me like an open coffin.

She wants every minute, I thought. She wants my life.

"You missed Gussie," she said.

Gussie is her parents' 300-pound narcoleptic maid. Her attacks often come at the ironing board. The pillowcases in that family are all bordered with scorch.

"It's a hard trip for her," I said. "How is she?"

"Well, she didn't fall asleep, if that's what you mean. Gussie's great—you know what she said? She said, 'Darlin' just keep prayin', down on your knees.' "

She shrugged, "See anybody good?"

"No," I said, "just the new Charlie's Angel. And I saw Cher's car down near the Arcade."

"Cher's car is worth *three* Charlie's Angels," she said. "What else am I missing?"

"It's earthquake weather," I told her.

"The best thing to do about earthquakes," she said, "is not to live in California."

"That's useful," I said. "You sound like Reverend Ike: 'The best thing to do for the poor is not be one of them.' "

We're crazy about Reverend Ike.

I noticed her face was bloated.

"You know," she said, "I feel like hell. I'm about to stop having fun."

"The ancients have a saying," I said. " 'There are times when the wolves are silent; there are times when the moon howls.' "

"What's that, Navajo?"

"Palm Royale lobby graffiti," I said. "I bought a paper there. I'll read to you."

"Even though I care about nothing?" she said.

I turned to page three, to a UPI filler datelined Mexico City. I read her "Man Robs Bank with Chicken," about a man who bought a barbecued chicken at a stand down the block from a bank. Passing the bank, he got the idea. He walked in and approached a teller. He pointed the brown paper bag at her and she handed over the day's receipts. It was the smell of barbecue sauce that eventually led to his capture.

The story made her hungry, she said, so I took the elevator down six floors to the cafeteria and brought back all the ice cream she wanted. We lay side by side, adjustable beds cranked up for optimal TV viewing, littering the sheets with Good Humor wrappers, picking toasted almonds out of the gauze. We were Lucy and Ethel, Mary and Rhoda in extremis. The blinds were closed to keep light off the screen.

We watched a movie starring men we used to think we wanted to sleep with. Hers was a tough cop out to stop mine, a vicious rapist who went after cocktail waitresses.

"This is a good movie," she said, when snipers felled them both.

I missed her already; my straight man, my diary.

A Filipino nurse tiptoed in and gave her an injection. She removed the pile of Popsicle sticks from the nightstand—enough to splint a small animal.

The injection made us sleepy—me in the way I picked up her inflection till her mother couldn't tell us apart on the phone. We slept.

I dreamed she was a decorator, come to furnish my house. She worked in secret, singing to herself. When she finished, she guided me proudly to the door. "How do you like it?" she asked, easing me inside.

Every beam and sill and shelf and knob was draped in black bunting with streamers and black crepe looped around darkened mirrors.

"I have to go home," I said when she woke up.

She thought I meant home to her house in the Canyon, and I had to say, No, *home*, home. I twisted my hands in the hackneyed fashion of people in pain. I was supposed to offer something. The Best Friend. I could not even offer to come back.

I felt weak and small and failed. Also exhilarated. I had a convertible in the parking lot. Once out of that room, I would drive it too fast down the coast highway through the crab-smelling air. A stop in Malibu for sangria. The music in the place would be sexy and loud. They would serve papaya and shrimp and watermelon ice. After dinner I would pick up beach boys. I would shimmer with life, buzz with heat, vibrate with health, stay up all night with one and then the other.

Without a word, she yanked off her mask and threw it on the floor. She kicked at the blankets and moved to the door. She must have hated having to pause for breath and balance before slamming out of Isolation, and out of the second room, the one where you scrub and tie on the white masks.

A voice shouted her name in alarm, and people ran down the corridor. The Good Doctor was paged over the intercom. I opened the door and the nurse at the station stared hard, as if this flight had been my idea.

"Where is she?" I asked, and they nodded to the supply closet.

I looked in. Two nurses were kneeling beside her on the floor, talking to her in low voices. One held a mask over her nose and mouth, the other rubbed her back in slow circles. The nurses glanced up to see if I was the doctor, and when they saw I wasn't, they went back to what they were doing.

"There, there, honey," they cooed.

On the morning she was moved to the cemetery, the one where Al Jolson is buried, I enrolled in a Fear of Flying class. "What is your worst fear?" the instructor asked, and I answered, "That I will finish this course and still be afraid."

I sleep with a glass of water on the nightstand so I can see by its level if the coastal earth is trembling or if the shaking is still me.

What do I remember? I remember only the useless things I hear—that Bob Dylan's mother invented Wite-out, that twenty-three people must be in a room before there is a fifty-fifty chance two will have the same birthdate. Who cares whether or not it's true? In my head there are bath towels swaddling this stuff. Nothing else seeps through.

I review those things that will figure in the retelling: a kiss through surgical gauze, the pale hand correcting the position of the wig. I noted these gestures as they happened, not in any retrospect. Though I don't know why looking *back* should show us more than looking *at*. It is just possible I will say I stayed the night. And who is there that can say I did not?

Nothing else gets through until I think of the chimp, the one with the talking hands.

In the course of the experiment, that chimp had a baby. Imaging how her trainers must have thrilled when the mother, without prompting, began to sign to the newborn. Baby, drink milk. Baby, play ball. And when the baby died, the mother stood over the body, her wrinkled hands moving with animal grace, forming again and again the words, Baby, come hug, Baby, come hug, fluent now in the language of grief.

JAMES ALAN MCPHERSON

A Loaf of Bread

IT WAS ONE OF THOSE obscene situations, pedestrian to most people, but invested with meaning for a few poor folk whose lives are usually spent outside the imaginations of their fellow citizens. A grocer named Harold Green was caught red-handed selling to one group of people the very same goods he sold at lower prices at similar outlets in better neighborhoods. He had been doing this for many years, and at first he could not understand the outrage heaped upon bum. He acted only from habit, he insisted, and had nothing personal against the people whom he served. They were his neighbors. Many of them be had carried on the cuff during hard times. Yet, through some mysterious access to a television station, the poor folk were now empowered to make grand denunciations of the grocer. Green's children now saw their father's business being picketed on the Monday evening news.

No one could question the fact that the grocer had been overcharging the people. On the news even the reporter grimaced distastefully while reading the statistics. His expression said, "It is my job to report the news, but sometimes even I must disassociate myself from it to protect my honor." This, at least, was the impression the grocer's children seemed to bring away from the television. Their father's name had not been mentioned, but there was a close-up of his store with angry black people, and a few outraged whites, marching in groups of three in front of it. There was also a close-up of his name. After seeing this, they were in no mood to watch cartoons. At the dinner table, disturbed by his children's silence, Harold Green felt compelled to say, "I am not a dishonest man." Then he felt ashamed. The children, a boy and his older sister, immediately left the table, leaving Green alone with his wife. "Ruth. I am not dishonest," he repeated to her.

Ruth Green did not say anything. She knew, and her husband did not, that the outraged people had also picketed the school attended by their children. They had threatened to return each day until Green lowered his prices. When they called her at home to report this, she had promised she would talk with him. Since she could not tell him this, she waited for an opening. She looked at her husband across the table.

"I did not make the world," Green began, recognizing at once the seriousness in her stare. "My father came to this country with nothing but his shirt. He was exploited for as long as he couldn't help himself. He did not protest or picket. He put himself in a position to play by the rules he had learned." He waited for his wife to answer, and when she did not, he tried again. "I did not make this world," he repeated. "I only make my way in it. Such people as these, they do not know enough to not be exploited. If not me, there would be a Greek, a Chinaman, maybe an Arab or a smart one of their own kind. Believe me, I deal with them. Then is something in their styles that lacks the patience to run a concern such as mine. If I closed down, take my word on it, someone else would do what has to be done."

But Ruth Green was not thinking of his leaving. Her mind was on other matters. Her children had cried when they came home early from school. She had no special feeling for the people who picketed, but she did not like to see her children cry. She had kissed them generously, then sworn them to silence. "One day this week," she told her husband, "you will give free, for eight hours, anything your customers come in to buy. There will be no publicity, except what they spread by word of mouth. No matter what they say to you, no matter what they take, you will remain silent." She stared deeply into him for what she knew was there. "If you refuse, you have seen the last of your children and myself."

Her husband grunted. Then he leaned toward her. "I will not knuckle under," he said. "I will *not* give!"

"We shall see," his wife told him.

The black pickets, for the most part, had at first been frightened by the audacity of their undertaking. They were peasants whose minds had long before become resigned to their fate as victims. None of them, before now, had thought to challenge this. But now, when they watched themselves on television, they hardly recognized the faces they saw beneath the hoisted banners and placards. Instead of reflecting the meekness they all felt, the faces looked angry. The close-ups looked especially intimidating. Several of the first pickets, maids who worked in the suburbs, reported that their employers, seeing the activity on the afternoon news, had begun treating them with new respect. One woman, midway through the weather report, called around the neighborhood to disclose that her employer had that very day given her a new china plate for her meals. The paper plates, on which all previous meals had been served, had been thrown into the wastebasket. One recipient of this call, a middle-aged woman known for her bashfulness and humility, rejoined that her husband, a sheet-metal worker, had only a few hours before been called "Mister" by his supervisor, a white man with a passionate hatred of color. She added the tale of a neighbor down the street, a widow-woman named Murphy, who had at first been reluctant to join the picket; this woman now was insisting it should be made a daily event. Such talk as this circulated among the people who had been instrumental in raising the issue. As news of their victory leaked into the ears of others who had not participated, they received all through the night calls from strangers requesting verification, offering advice, and vowing support. Such strangers listened, and then volunteered stories about indignities inflicted on them by city officials, policemen, other grocers. In this way, over a period of hours, the community became even more incensed and restless than it had been at the time of the initial picket.

Soon, the man who had set events in motion found himself a hero. His name was Nelson Reed, and all his adult life he had been employed as an assembly-line worker. He was a steady husband, the father of three children, and a deacon in the Baptist church. All his life he had trusted in God and gotten along. But now something in him capitulated to the reality that came suddenly into focus. "I was wrong," he told people who called him. "The onliest thing that matters in this world is *money*. And when was the last time you seen a picture of Jesus on a dollar bill?" This line, which he repeated over and over, caused a few callers to laugh nervously, but not without some affirmation that this was indeed the way things were. Many said they had known it all along. Others argued that although it was certainly true, it was one thing to live without money and quite another to live without faith. But still most callers laughed and said, "You right. You *know* I know you right. Ain't it the truth, though?" Only a few people, among them Nelson Reed's wife, said nothing and looked very sad.

Why they looked sad, however, they would not communicate. And anyone observing their troubled faces would have to trust his own intuition. It is known that Reed's wife, Betty, measured all events against the fullness of her own experience. She was skeptical of everything. Brought to the church after a number of years of living openly with a jazz musician, she had embraced religion when she married Nelson Reed. But though she no longer believed completely in the world, she nonetheless had not fully embraced God. There was something in the nature of Christ's swift rise that had always bothered her, and something in the blood and vengeance of the Old Testament that was mellowing and refreshing. But she had never communicated these thoughts to anyone, especially her husband. Instead, she smiled vacantly while others professed leaps of faith, remained silent when friends spoke fiercely of their convictions. The presence of this vacuum in her contributed to her personal mystery; people said she was beautiful, although she was not outwardly so. Perhaps it was because she wished to protect this inner beauty that she did not smile now, and looked extremely sad, listening to her husband on the telephone.

Nelson Reed had no reason to be sad. He seemed to grow more energized and talkative as the days passed. He was invited by an alderman, on the Tuesday after the initial picket, to tell his story on a local television talk show. He sweated heavily under the hot white lights and attempted to be philosophical. "I notice," the host said to him, "that you are not angry at this exploitative treatment. What, Mr. Reed, is the source of your calm?" The assembly-line worker looked unabashedly into the camera and said, "I have always believed in *Justice* with a capital *J*. I was raised up from a baby believin' that God ain't gonna let nobody go *too* far. See, in *my* mind God is in charge of *all* the capital letters in the alphabet of this world. It say in the Scripture He is Alpha and Omega, the first and the last. He is just about the *onliest* capitalizer they is." Both Reed and the alderman laughed. "Now, when *men* start to capitalize, they gets *greedy*. They put a little *j* in *joy* and a littler one in *justice*. They raise up a big *G* in *Greed* and a big *E* in *Evil*. Well, soon as they commence to put a little *g* in *god*, you can expect some kind of reaction. The Savior will just raise up the *H* in *Hell* and go on from there. And that's just what I'm doin', giving these sharpies *HELL* with a big *H*." The talk show host laughed along with Nelson Reed and the alderman. After the taping they drank coffee in the back room of the studio and talked about the sad shape of the world.

Three days before he was to comply with his wife's request, Green, the grocer, saw this talk show on television while at home. The words of Nelson Reed sent a chill through him. Though Reed had attempted to be philosophical, Green did not perceive the statement in this light. Instead, he saw a vindictive-looking black man seated between an ambitious alderman and a smug talk-show host. He saw them chatting comfortably about the nature of evil. The cameraman had shot mostly close-ups, and Green could see the set in Nelson Reed's jaw. The color of Reed's face was maddening. When his children came into the den, the grocer was in a sweat. Before he could think, he had shouted at them and struck the button turning off the set. The two children rushed from the room screaming. Ruth Green ran in from the kitchen. She knew why he was upset because she had received a call about the show; but she said nothing and pretended ignorance. Her children's school had been picketed that day, as it had the day before. But both children were still forbidden to speak of this to their father.

"Where do they get so much power?" Green said to his wife. "Two days ago, nobody would have cared. Now, everywhere, even in my home, I am condemned as a rascal. And what do I own? An airline? A multinational? Half of South America? *No!* I own three stores, one of which happens to be in a certain neighborhood inhabited by people who cost me money to run it." He sighed and sat upright on the sofa, his chubby legs spread wide. "A cab driver has a meter that clicks as he goes along. I pay extra for insurance, iron bars, pilfering by customers and employees. Nothing clicks. But when I add a little overhead to my prices, suddenly everything clicks. But for someone else. When was there last such a world?" He pressed the palms of both hands to his temples, suggesting a bombardment of brain-stinging sounds.

This gesture evoked no response from Ruth Green. She remained standing by the door, looking steadily at him. She said, "To protect yourself, I would not stock any more fresh cuts of meat in the store until after the giveaway on Saturday. Also, I would not tell it to the employees until after the first customer of the day has begun to check out. But I would urge you to hire several security guards to close the door promptly at seven-thirty, as is usual." She wanted to say much more than this, but did not. Instead she watched him. He was looking at the blank gray television screen, his palms still pressed against his ears. "In case you need to hear again," she continued in a weighty tone of voice, "I said two days ago, and I say again now, that if you fail to do this you will not see your children again for many years."

He twisted his head and looked up at her. "What is the color of these people?" he asked.

"Black," his wife said.

"And what is the name of my children?"

"Green."

The grocer smiled. "There is your answer," he told his wife. "Green is the only color I am interested in."

His wife did not smile. "Insufficient," she said.

"The world is mad!" he moaned. "But it is a point of sanity with me to not bend. I will not bend." He crossed his legs and pressed one hand firmly atop his knee. *"I will not bend,"* he said.

"We will see," his wife said.

Nelson Reed, after the television interview, became the acknowledged leader of the disgruntled neighbors. At first a number of them met in the kitchen at his house; then, as space was lacking for curious newcomers, a mass meeting was held on Thursday in an abandoned theater. Him wife and three children sat in the front row. Behind them sat the widow Murphy, Lloyd Dukes, Tyrone Brown, Les Jones—those who had joined him on the first picket line. Behind these sat people who bought occasionally at the store, people who lived on the fringes of the neighborhood, people from other neighborhoods come to investigate the problem, and the merely curious. The middle rows were occupied by a few people from the suburbs, those who had seen the talk show and whose outrage at the grocer proved much more powerful than their fear of black people. In the rear of the theater crowded aging, old-style leftists, somber students, cynical young black men with angry grudges to explain with inarticulate gestures. Leaning against the walls, huddled near the doors at the rear, tape-recorder-bearing social scientists looked as detached and serene as bookies at the track. Here and there, in this diverse crowd, a politician stationed himself, pumping hands vigorously and pressing his palms gently against the shoulders of elderly people. Other visitors passed out leaflets, buttons, glossy color prints of men who promoted causes, the familiar and obscure. There was a hubbub of voices, a blend of the strident and the playful, the outraged and the reverent, lending an undercurrent of ominous energy to the assembly.

Nelson Reed spoke from a platform on the stage, standing before a yellowed, shredded screen that had once reflected the images of matinee idols. "I don't mind sayin' that I have always been a sucker," he told the crowd. "All my life I have been a sucker for the words of Jesus. Being a natural-born fool, I just ain't never had the *sense* to learn no better. Even right today, while the whole world is sayin' wrong is right and up is down, I'm so dumb I'm *still* steady believin' what is wrote in the Good Book . . ."

From the audience, especially the front rows, came a chorus singing, "Preach!"

"I have no doubt," he continued in a low baritone, "that it's true what is writ in the Good Book: 'The last shall be first and the first shall be last.' I don't know about y'all, but I have *always* been the last. I never wanted to be the first, but sometimes it look like the world get so bad that them that's holdin' onto the tree of life is the onliest ones left when God commence to blowin' dead leafs off the branches."

"Now you preaching," someone called.

In the rear of the theater a white student shouted an awkward "Amen."

Nelson Reed began walking across the stage to occupy the major part of his nervous energy. But to those in the audience, who now hung on his every word, it looked as though he strutted. "All my life," he said, "I have claimed to be a man without earnin' the right to call myself that. You know, the *average* man ain't really a man. The average man is a *boot-licker*. In fact, the *average* man would *run away* if he found hisself standing alone facin' down a adversary. I have done that *too many a time* in my life. But *not no more*. Better to be *once* was than *never* was a man. I will tell you tonight, there is somethin' *wrong* in being average. *I intend to stand up!* Now, if your average man that ain't really a man stand up, two things gonna happen: *One*, he g'on bust through all the weights that been place on his head, and, *two*, he g'on feel a lot of pain. But that same hurt is what make things fall in place. That, and gettin' your hands on one of these slick four-flushers tight enough so's you can squeeze him and say, 'No *more!*' You do that, you g'on hurt some, but *you won't be average no more* . . ."

"No *more!*" a few people in the front rows repeated.

"I say *no more!*" Nelson Reed shouted.

"*No more! No more! No more!*" The chant rustled through the crowd like the rhythm of an autumn wind against a shedding tree.

Then people laughed and chattered in celebration.

As for the grocer, from the evening of the television interview he had begun to make plans. Unknown to his wife, he cloistered himself several times with his brother-in-law, an insurance salesman, and plotted a course. He had no intention of tossing steaks to the crowd. "And why should I, Tommy?" he asked his wife's brother, a lean, bald-headed man named Thomas. "I don't cheat anyone. I have never cheated anyone. The businesses I run are always on the up-and-up. So why should I pay?"

"Quite so," the brother-in-law said, chewing an unlit cigarillo. "The world has gone crazy. Next they will say that people in my business are responsible for prolonging life. I have found that people who refuse to believe in death refuse also to believe in the harshness of life. I sell well by saying that death is a long happiness. I show people the realities of life and compare this to a funeral with dignity, *and* the promise of a bundle for every loved one salted away. When they look around hard at life, they usually buy."

"So?" asked Green. Thomas was a college graduate with a penchant for philosophy.

"So," Thomas answered. "You must fight to show these people the reality of both your situation and theirs. How would it be if you visited one of their meetings and chalked out, on a blackboard, the dollars and cents of your operation? Explain your overhead, your security fees, all the additional expenses. If you treat them with respect, they might understand."

Green frowned. "That I would never do," he said. "It would be admission of a certain guilt."

The brother-in-law smiled, but only with one corner of his month. "Then you have something to feel guilty about?" be asked.

The grocer frowned at him. *"Nothing!"* he said with great emphasis.

"So?" Thomas said.

This first meeting between the grocer and his brother-in-law took place on Thursday, in a crowded barroom.

At the second meeting, in a luncheonette, it was agreed that the grocer should speak privately with the leader of the group, Nelson Reed. The meeting at which this was agreed took place on Friday afternoon. After accepting this advice from Thomas, the grocer resigned himself to explain to Reed, in as finite detail as possible, the economic structure of his operation. He vowed to suppress no information. He would explain everything: inventories, markups, sale items, inflation, balance sheets, specialty items, overhead, and that mysterious item called profit. This last item, promising to be the most difficult to explain, Green and his brother-in-law debated over for several hours. They agreed first of all that a man should not work for free, then they agreed that it was unethical to ruthlessly exploit. From these parameters, they staked out an area between fifteen and forty percent, and agreed that someplace between these two borders lay an amount of return that could be called fair. This was easy, but then Thomas introduced the factor of circumstance. He questioned whether the fact that one serviced a risky area justified the earning of profits, closer to the forty-percent edge of the scale. Green was unsure. Thomas smiled. "Here is a case that will point out an analogy," he said, licking a cigarillo. "I read in the papers that a family wants to sell an electric stove. I call the home and the man says fifty dollars. I ask to come out and inspect the merchandise. When I arrive I see they are poor, have already bought a new stove that is connected, and are selling the old one for fifty dollars because they want it out of the place. The electric stove is in good condition, worth much more than fifty. But because I see what I see I offer forty-five."

Green, for some reason, wrote down this figure on the back of the sales slip for the coffee they were drinking.

The brother-in-law smiled. He chewed his cigarillo. "The man agrees to take forty-five dollars, saying he has had no other calls. I look at the stove again and see a spot of rust. I say I will give him forty dollars. He agrees to this, on condition that I myself haul it away. I say I will haul it away if he comes down to thirty. You, of course, see where I am going."

The grocer nodded. "The circumstances of his situation, his need to get rid of the stove quickly, placed him in a position where he has little room to bargain?"

"Yes," Thomas answered. "So? Is it ethical, Harry?"

Harold Green frowned. He had never liked his brother-in-law, and now he thought the insurance agent was being crafty. "But," he answered, "this man does not *have* to sell! It is his choice whether to wait for other ealls. It is not the fault of the buyer that the seller is in a hurry. It is the right of the buyer to get what he wants at the lowest price possible. That is the rule. That has *always* been the rule. And the reverse of it applies to the seller as well."

"Yes," Thomas said, sipping coffee from the Styrofoam cup. "But suppose that in addition to his hurry to sell, the owner was also of a weak soul. There are, after all, many such people." He smiled. "Suppose he placed no value on the money?"

"Then," Green answered, "your example is academic. Here we are not talking about real life. One man lives by the code, one man does not. Who is there free enough to make a judgment?" He laughed. "Now you see," he told his brother-in-law. "Much more than a few dollars are at stake. If this one buyer is to be condemned, then so are most people in the history of the world. An examination of history provides the only answer to your question. This code will be here tomorrow, long after the ones who do not honor it are not."

They argued fiercely late into the afternoon, the brother-in-law leaning heavily on his readings. When they parted, a little before 5:00 p.m., nothing had been resolved.

Neither was much resolved during the meeting between Green and Nelson Reed. Reached at home by the grocer in the early evening, the leader of the group spoke coldly at first, but consented finally to meet his adversary at a nearby drugstore for coffee and a talk. They met at the lunch counter, shook hands awkwardly, and sat for a few minutes discussing the weather. Then the grocer pulled two gray ledgers from his briefcase. "You have for years come into my place," he told the man. "In my memory I have always treated you well. Now our relationship has come to this." He slid the books along the counter until they touched Nelson Reed's arm.

Reed opened the top book and flipped the thick green pages with his thumb. He did not examine the figures. "All I know," he said, "is over at your place a can of soup cost me fifty-five cents, and two miles away at your other store for white folks you chargin' thirty-nine cents." He said this with the calm authority of an outraged soul. A quality of condescension tinged with pity crept into his gaze.

The grocer drummed his fingers on the counter top. He twisted his head and looked away, toward shelves containing cosmetics, laxatives, toothpaste. His eyes lingered on a poster of a woman's apple red lips and milk white teeth. The rest of the face was missing.

"Ain't no use to hide," Nelson Reed said, as to a child. "*I* know you wrong, *you* know you wrong, and before I finish, *everybody in this city* g'on know you wrong. God don't *like* ugly." He closed his eyes and gripped the cup of coffee. Then he swung his head suddenly and faced the grocer again. "Man, why you want to *do* people that way?" he asked. "We human, same as you."

"Before *God!*" Green exclaimed, looking squarely into the face of Nelson Reed. "Before God!" he said again. *"I am not an evil man!"* These last words sounded more like a moan as he tightened the muscles in his throat to lower the sound of his voice. He tossed his left shoulder as if adjusting the sleeve of his coat, or as if throwing off some unwanted weight. Then he peered along the counter top. No one was watching. At the end of the counter the waitress was scrubbing the coffee urn. "Look at these figures, please," he said to Reed.

The man did not drop his gaze. His eyes remained fixed on the grocer's face.

"All right," Green said. "Don't look. I'll tell you what is in these books, believe me if you want. I work twelve hours a day, one day off per week, running my business in three stores. I am not a wealthy person. In one place, in the area you call white, I get by barely by smiling lustily at old ladies, stocking gourmet stuff on the chance I will build a reputation as a quality store. The two clerks there cheat me; there is nothing I can do. In this business you must be friendly with everybody. The second place is on the other side of town, in a neighborhood as poor as this one. I get out there seldom. The profits are not worth the gas. I use the loss there as a write-off against some other properties." He paused. "Do you understand write-off?" he asked Nelson Reed.

"Naw," the man said.

Harold Green laughed. "What does it matter?" he said in a tone of voice intended for himself alone. "In this area I will admit I make a profit, but it is not so much as you think. But I do not make a profit here because the people are black. I make a profit because a profit is here to be made. I invest more here in window bars, theft losses, insurance, spoilage; I deserve to make more here than at the other places." He looked, almost imploringly, at the man seated next to him. "You don't accept this as the right of a man in business?"

Reed grunted. "Did the bear shit in the woods?" he said.

Again Green laughed. He gulped his coffee awkwardly, as if eager to go. Yet his motions slowed once he had set his coffee cup down on the blue plastic saucer. "Place yourself in *my* situation," he said, his voice high and tentative. "If *you* were running my store in this neighborhood, what would be *your* position? Say on a profit scale of fifteen to forty percent, at what point in between would you draw the line?"

Nelson Reed thought. He sipped his coffee and seemed to chew the liquid. "Fifteen to forty?" he repeated,

"Yes."

"I'm a churchgoin' man," he said. "Closer to fifteen than to forty."

"How close?"

Nelson Reed thought. "In church you tithe ten percent."

"In restaurants you tip fifteen," the grocer said quickly.

"All right," Reed said. "Over fifteen."

"How much over?"

Nelson Reed thought.

"Twenty, thirty, thirty-five?" Green chanted, leaning closer to Reed.

Still the man thought.

"Forty? Maybe even forty-five or fifty?" the grocer breathed in Reed's ear. "In the supermarkets, you know, they have more subtle ways of accomplishing such feats."

Reed slapped his coffee cup with the back of his right hand. The brown liquid swirled across the counter top, wetting the books. *"Damn this!"* he shouted.

Startled, Green rose from his stooL

Nelson Reed was trembling. "I ain't *you*," he said in a deep baritone. "I ain't the *supermarket* neither. All I is is a poor man that works *too* hard to see his pay slip through his fingers like rainwater. All I know is you done *cheat* me, you done *cheat* everybody in the neighborhood, and we organized now to get some of it *back!*" Then he stood and faced the grocer. "My daddy sharecropped down in Mississippi and bought in the company store. He owed them twenty-three years when be died. I paid off five of them years and then ran away to up here. Now, I'm a deacon in the Baptist church. I raised my kids the way my daddy raise me and don't bother nobody. Now come to find out, after all my runnin', they done lift that *same company store* up out of Mississippi and slip it down on us here! Well, my daddy was a *fighter*, and if he hadn't owed all them years he would of raise him some hell. Me, I'm steady my daddy's child, plus I got seniority in my union. I'm a free man. Buddy, don't you know *I'm gonna raise me some hell!*"

Harold Green reached for a paper napkin to sop the coffee soaking into his books.

Nelson Reed threw a dollar on top of the books and walked away.

"I *will not* do it!" Harold Green said to his wife that same evening. They were in the bathroom of their home. Bending over the face bowl, she was washing her hair with a towel draped around her neck. The grocer stood by the door, looking in at her. "I will not bankrupt myself tomorrow," he said.

"I've been thinking about it, too," Ruth Green said, shaking her wet hair. "You'll do it, Harry."

"Why should I?" he asked. "You won't leave. You know it was a bluff. I've waited this long for you to calm down. Tomorrow is Saturday. This week has been a hard one. Tonight let's be realistic."

"Of course you'll do it," Ruth Green said. She said it the way she would say "Have some toast." She said, "You'll do it because you want to see your children grow up."

"And for what other reason?" he asked.

She pulled the towel tighter around her neck. "Because you are at heart a moral man."

He grinned painfully. "If I am, why should I have to prove it to *them*?"

"Not them," Ruth Green said, freezing her movements and looking in the mirror. "Certainly not them. By no means them. They have absolutely nothing to do with this."

"Who, then?" he asked, moving from the door into the room. "Who else should I prove something to?"

His wife was crying. But her entire face was wet. The tears moved secretly down her face.

"Who else?" Harold Green asked.

It was almost 11:00 p.m. and the children were in bed. They had also cried when they came home from school. Ruth Green said, "For yourself, Harry. For the love that lives inside your heart."

All night the grocer thought about this.

Nelson Reed also slept little that Friday night. When be returned home from the drugstore, he reported to his wife as much of the conversation as he could remember. At first he had joked about the exchange between himself and the grocer, but as more details returned to his conscious mind he grew solemn and then bitter. "He ask me to put myself in *his* place," Reed told his wife. "Can you imagine that kind of gumption? I never cheated nobody in my life. All my life I have lived on Bible principles. I am a deacon in the church. I have work all my life for other folks and I don't even own the house I live in." He paced up and down the kitchen, his big arms flapping loosely at his sides. Betty Reed sat at the table, watching. "This here's a low-down, ass-kicking world," he said. "I swear to God it is! All my life I have lived on principle and I ain't got a dime in the bank. Betty," he turned suddenly toward her, "don't you think I'm a fool?"

"Mr. Reed," she said. "Let's go on to bed."

But he would not go to bed. Instead, he took the fifth of bourbon from the cabinet under the sink and poured himself a shot. His wife refused to join him. Reed drained the glass of whiskey, and then another, while he resumed pacing the kitchen floor. He slapped his hands against his sides. "*I* think I'm a fool," he said. "Ain't got a dime in the bank, ain't got a pot to *pee* in or a wall to pitch it over, and that there *cheat* ask me to put myself inside *his* shoes. Hell, I can't even *afford* the kind of shoes he wears." He stopped pacing and looked at his wife.

"Mr. Reed," she whispered, "tomorrow ain't a work day. Let's go to bed."

Nelson Reed laughed, the bitterness in his voice rattling his wife. "The *hell* I will!" he said.

He strode to the yellow telephone on the wall beside the sink and began to dial. The first call was to Lloyd Dukes, a neighbor two blocks away and a lieutenant in the organization. Dukes was not at home. The second Call was to McElroy's Bar on the corner of 65th and Carroll, where Stanley Harper, another of the lieutenants, worked as a bartender. It was Harper who spread the word, among those men at the bar, that the organization would picket the grocer's store the following morning. And all through the night, in the bedroom of their house, Betty Reed was awakened by telephone calls coming from Lester Jones, Nat Lucas, Mrs. Tyrone Brown, the widow-woman named Murphy, all coordinating the time when they would march in a group against the store owned by Harold Green. Betty Reed's heart beat loudly beneath the covers as she listened to the bitterness and rage in her husband's voice. On several occasions, hearing him declare himself a fool, she pressed the pillow against her eyes and cried.

The grocer opened later than usual this Saturday morning, but still it was early enough to make him one of the first walkers in the neighborhood. He parked his car one block from the store and strolled to work. There were no birds singing. The sky in this area was not blue. It was smog-smutted and gray, seeming on the verge of a light rain. The street, as always, was littered with cans, papers, bits of broken glass. As always the garbage cans overflowed. The morning breeze plastered a sheet of newspaper playfully around the sides of a rusted garbage can. For some reason, using his right foot, he loosened the paper and stood watching it slide into the street and down the block. The movement made him feel good. He whistled while unlocking the bars shielding the windows and door of his store. When he had unlocked the main door he stepped in quickly and threw a switch to the right of the jamb, before the shrill sound of the alarm could shatter his mood. Then he switched on the lights. Everything was as it had been the night before. He had already telephoned his two employees and given them the day off. He busied himself doing the usual things— hauling milk and vegetables from the cooler, putting cash in the till—not thinking about the silence of his wife, or the look her eyes, only an hour before when he left home. He had determined, at some point while driving through the city, that today it would be business as usual. But he expected very few customers.

The first customer of the day was Mrs. Nelson Reed. She came in around 9:30 a.m. and wandered about the store. He watched her from the checkout counter. She seemed uncertain of what she wanted to buy. She kept glancing at him down the center aisle. His suspicions aroused, he said finally, "Yes, may I help you, Mrs. Reed?" His words caused her to jerk, as if some devious thought had been perceived going through her mind. She reached over quickly and lifted a loaf of whole wheat bread from the rack and walked with it to the counter. She looked at him and smiled. The smile was a broad, shy one, that rare kind of smile one sees on virgin girls when they first confess love to themselves. Betty Reed was a woman of about forty-five. For some reason he could not comprehend, this gesture touched him. When she pulled a dollar from her purse and laid it on the counter, an impulse, from no place he could locate with his mind, seized control of his tongue. "Free," he told Betty Reed. She paused, then pushed the dollar toward him with a firm and determined thrust of her arm. "Free," he heard himself saying strongly, his right palm spread and meeting her thrust with absolute force. She clutched the loaf of bread, and walked out of his store.

The next customer, a little girl, arriving well after 10:30 a.m., selected a candy bar from the rack beside the counter. "Free," Green said cheerfully. The little girl left the candy on the counter and ran out of the store.

At 11:15 a.m. a wino came in looking desperate enough to sell his soul. The grocer watched him only for an instant. Then he went to the wine counter and selected a half gallon of medium-grade red wine. He shoved the jug into the belly of the wino, the man's sour breath bathing his face. "Free," the grocer said. "But you must not drink it in here."

He felt good about the entire world, watching the wino through the window gulping the wine and looking guiltily around.

At 11:25 a.m. the pickets arrived.

Two dozen people, men and women, young and old, crowded the pavement in front of his store. Their signs, placards, and voices denounced him as a parasite. The grocer laughed inside himself. He felt lighthearted and wild, like a man drugged. He rushed to the meat counter and pulled a long roll of brown wrapping paper from the rack, tearing it neatly with a quick shift of his body resembling a dance step practiced fervently in his youth. He laid the paper on the chopping block and with the black-inked, felt-tipped marker scrawled, in giant letters, the word FREE. This he took to the window and pasted in place with many strands of Scotch tape. He was laughing wildly. "Free!" he shouted from behind the brown paper. "Free! Free! Free! Free! Free! Free!" He rushed to the door, pushed his head out, and screamed to the confused crowd, "*Free!*" Then he ran back to the counter and stood behind it, like a soldier at attention.

They came in slowly.

Nelson Reed entered first, working his right foot across the dirty tile as if tracking a squiggling worm. The others followed: Lloyd Dukes dragging a placard, Mr. and Mrs. Tyrone Brown, Stanley Harper walking with his fists clenched, Lester Jones with three of his children, Nat Lucas looking sheepish and detached, a clutch of winos, several bashful nuns, ironic-smiling teenagers and a few students. Bringing up the rear was a bearded social scientist holding a tape recorder to his chest "Free!" the grocer screamed. He threw up his arms in a gesture that embraced, or dismissed, the entire store. "*All free!*" he shouted. He was grinning with the grace of a madman.

The winos began grabbing first. They stripped the shelf of wine in a matter of seconds. Then they fled, dropping bottles on the tile in their wake. The others, stepping quickly through this liquid, soon congealed it into a sticky, bloodlike consistency. The young men went for the cigarettes and luncheon meats and beer. One of them had the prescience to grab a sack from the counter, while the others loaded their arms swiftly, hugging cartons and packages of cold cuts like long-lost friends. The students joined them, less for greed than for the thrill of the experience. The two nuns backed toward the door. As for the older people, men and women, they stood at first as if stuck to the wine-smeared floor. Then Stanley Harper, the bartender, shouted, "The man said *free*, y'all heard him." He paused. "Didn't you say *free* now?" he called to the grocer.

"I said free," Harold Green answered, his temples pounding.

A cheer went up. The older people began grabbing, as if the secret lusts of a lifetime had suddenly seized command of their arms and eyes. They grabbed toilet tissue, cold cuts, pickles, sardines, boxes of raisins, boxes of starch, cans of soup, tins of tuna fish and salmon, bottles of spices, cans of boned chicken, slippery cans of olive oil. Here a man, Lester Jones, burdened himself with several heads of lettuce, while his wife, in another aisle, shouted for him to drop those small items and concentrate on the gourmet section. She herself took imported sardines, wheat crackers, bottles of candied pickles, herring, anchovies, imported olives, French wafers, an ancient, half-rusted can of pâté, stocked, by mistake, from the inventory of another store. Others packed their arms with detergents, hams, chocolate-coated cereal, whole chickens with hanging asses, wedges of bologna and salami like squashed footballs, chunks of cheeses, yellow and white, shriveled onions, and green peppers. Mrs. Tyrone Brown hung a curve of pepperoni around her neck and seemed to take on instant dignity, much like a person of noble birth in possession now of a long sought-after gem.

Another woman, the widow Murphy, stuffed tomatoes into her bosom, holding a half-chewed lemon in her mouth. The more enterprising fought desperately over the three rusted shopping carts, and the victors wheeled these along the narrow aisles, sweeping into them bulk items—beer in six-packs, sacks of sugar, flour, glass bottles of syrup, toilet cleanser, sugar cookies, prune, apple and tomato juices—while others endeavored to snatch the carts from them. There were several fistfights and much cursing. The grocer, standing behind the counter, hummed and rang his cash register like a madman.

Nelson Reed, the first into the store, followed the nuns out, empty-handed.

In less than half an hour the others had stripped the store and vanished in many directions up and down the block. But still more people came, those late in hearing the news. And when they saw the shelves were bare, they cursed soberly and chased those few stragglers still bearing away goods. Soon only the grocer and the social scientist remained, the latter stationed at the door with his tape recorder sucking in leftover sounds. Then he too slipped away up the block.

By 12:10 p.m. the grocer was leaning against the counter, trying to make his mind slow down. Not a man given to drink during work hours, he nonetheless took a swallow from a bottle of wine, a dusty bottle from beneath the wine shelf, somehow overlooked by the winos. Somewhat recovered, he was preparing to remember what he should do next when he glanced toward a figure at the door. Nelson Reed was standing there, watching him.

"All gone," Harold Green said. "My friend, Mr. Reed, there is no more." Still the man stood in the doorway, peering into the store.

The grocer waved his arms about the empty room. Not a display case had a single item standing. "All gone," he said again, as if addressing a stupid child. "There is nothing left to get. You, my friend, have come back too late for a second load. I am cleaned out."

Nelson Reed stepped into the store and strode toward the counter. He moved through wine-stained flour, lettuce leaves, red, green, and blue labels, bits and pieces of broken glass. He walked toward the counter.

"All day," the grocer laughed, not quite hysterically now, "all day long I have not made a single cent of profit. The entire day was a loss. This store, like the others, is *bleeding* me." He waved his arms about the room in a magnificent gesture of uncaring loss. "Now do you understand?" he said. "Now will you put yourself in my shoes? I have nothing here. Come, now, Mr. Reed, would it not be so bad a thing to walk in my shoes?"

"Mr. Green," Nelson Reed said coldly. "My wife bought a loaf of bread in here this mornin'. She forgot to pay you. I, myself, have come here to pay you your money."

"Oh," the grocer said.

"I think it was brown bread. Don't that cost more than white?"

The two men looked away from each other, but not at anything in the store.

"In my store, yes," Harold Green said. He rang the register with the most casual movement of his finger. The register read fifty-five cents.

Nelson Reed held out a dollar.

"And two cents tax," the grocer said.

The man held out the dollar.

"After all," Harold Green said. "We are all, after all, Mr. Reed, in debt to the government."

He rang the register again. It read fifty-seven cents.

Nelson Reed held out a dollar.

Rick Moody

Boys

BOYS ENTER THE HOUSE, boys enter the house. Boys, and with them the ideas of boys (ideas leaden, reductive, inflexible), enter the house. Boys, two of them, wound into hospital packaging, boys with infant pattern baldness, slung in the arms of parents, boys dreaming of breasts, enter the house. Twin boys, kettles on the boil, boys in hideous vinyl knapsacks that young couples from Edison, NJ, wear on their shirt fronts, knapsacks coated with baby saliva and staphylococcus and milk vomit, enter the house. Two boys, one striking the other with a rubberized hot dog, enter the house. Two boys, one of them striking the other with a willow switch about the head and shoulders, the other crying, enter the house. Boys enter the house, speaking nonsense. Boys enter the house, calling for Mother. On a Sunday, in May, a day one might nearly describe as *perfect*, an ice cream truck comes slowly down the lane, chimes inducing salivation, and children run after it, not long after which boys dig a hole in the backyard and bury their younger sister's dolls *two feet down*, so that she will never find these dolls and these dolls will *rot in hell*, after which boys enter the house. Boys, trailing after their father like he is the Second Goddamned Coming of Christ Goddamned Almighty, enter the house, repair to the basement to watch baseball. Boys enter the house, site of devastation, and repair immediately to the kitchen, where they mix lighter fluid, vanilla pudding, drain-opening lye, balsamic vinegar, blue food coloring, calamine lotion, cottage cheese, ants, a plastic lizard that one of them received in his Xmas stocking, tacks, leftover mashed potatoes, Spam, frozen lima beans, and chocolate syrup in a medium-sized saucepan and heat over a low flame until thick, afterwards transferring the contents of this saucepan into a Pyrex lasagna dish, baking the Pyrex lasagna dish in the oven for nineteen minutes before attempting to persuade their sister that she should *eat the mixture*; later they smash three family heirlooms (the last, a glass egg, *intentionally*) in a two-and-a-half hour stretch, whereupon they are sent to their bedroom, until freed, in each case thirteen minutes after. Boys enter the house, starchy in pressed shirts and flannel pants that *itch so bad*, fresh from Sunday School instruction, blond and brown locks (respectively) plastered down, but even so with a number of cowlicks protruding at odd angles, disconsolate and humbled, uncertain if boyish things—such as shooting at the neighbor's dog with a pump action bb gun and gagging the fat boy up the street with a bandanna and showing their shriveled boy-penises to their younger sister—are exempted from the commandment to *Love the Lord thy God with all thy heart and with all thy soul, and with all thy might, and thy neighbor as thyself.* Boys enter the house in baseball gear (only one of the boys can hit): in their spikes, in mismatched tube socks that smell like Stilton cheese. Boys enter the house in soccer gear. Boys enter the house carrying skates. Boys enter the house with lacrosse sticks, and, soon after, tossing a lacrosse ball lightly in the living room they destroy a lamp. One boy enters the house sporting basketball clothes, the other wearing jeans and a sweatshirt. One boy enters the house bleeding profusely and is taken out to get stitches, the other watches. Boys enter the house at the end of term carrying report cards, sneak around the house like spies of foreign nationality, looking for a place to hide the report cards for the time being (under the toaster? in a medicine cabinet?). One boy with a black eye enters the house, one boy without. Boys with acne enter the house and squeeze and prod large skin blemishes in front of their sister. Boys with acne treatment products hidden about their persons enter the house. Boys, standing just up the street, sneak cigarettes behind a willow in the Elys' yard, wave smoke away from their natural fibers, hack terribly, experience nausea, then enter the house. Boys call each other *retard, homo, geek*, and, later, *Neckless Thug, Theater Fag*, and enter the house exchanging further epithets. Boys enter the house with nose hair clippers, chase sister around the house threatening to depilate her eyebrows. She cries. Boys attempt to induce girls to whom they would not have spoken only six or eight months prior to enter the house with them. Boys enter the house with girls efflorescent and homely, and attempt to induce girls to sneak into their bedroom, as they still share a single bedroom; girls refuse. Boys enter the house, go to separate bedrooms. Boys, with their father (an arm around each of them), enter the house, but of the monologue preceding and succeeding this entrance, not a syllable is preserved. Boys enter the house having masturbated in a variety of locales. Boys enter the house having masturbated in train station bathrooms, in forests, in beach houses, in football bleachers at night under the stars, in cars (under a blanket), in the shower, backstage, on a plane, the boys masturbate constantly, identically, three times a day in some cases, desire like a madness upon them, at the mere sound of certain words, words that sound like other words, *interrogative* reminding them of *intercourse, beast* reminding them of *breast, sects* reminding them of *sex*, and so forth, the boys are not very smart yet, and, as they enter the house, they feel, as always, immense shame at the scale of this *self-abusive cogitation*, seeing a classmate, seeing a billboard, seeing a fire hydrant, seeing things that should not induce thoughts of masturbation (their sister, e.g.) and then thinking of masturbation anyway. Boys enter the house, go to their rooms, remove sexually explicit magazines from hidden stashes, put on loud music, feel despair. Boys enter the house worried; they argue. The boys are ugly, they are failures, they will never be loved, they enter the house. Boys enter the house and kiss their mother, who feels differently, now they have outgrown her. Boys enter the house, kiss their mother, she explains the seriousness of their sister's difficulty, *her diagnosis.* Boys enter the house, having attempted to locate the spot in their yard where the dolls were buried, eight or nine years prior, without success; they go to their sister's room, sit by her bed. Boys enter the house and tell their completely bald sister jokes about baldness. Boys hold either hand of their sister, laying aside differences, having trudged grimly into the house. Boys skip school, enter house, hold vigil. Boys enter the house after their parents have both gone off to work, sit with their sister and with their sister's nurse. Boys enter the house carrying cases of beer. Boys enter the house, very worried now, didn't know more worry was possible. Boys enter the house carrying controlled substances, neither having told the other that he is carrying a controlled substance, though an intoxicated posture seems appropriate under the circumstances. Boys enter the house *weeping* and hear weeping around them. Boys enter the house, embarrassed, silent, anguished, keening, afflicted, angry, woeful, *griefstricken*. Boys enter the house on vacation, each clasps the hand of the other with genuine warmth, the one wearing dark colors and having shaved a portion of his head, the other having grown his hair out longish and wearing, uncharacteristically, a tie-dyed shirt. Boys enter the house on vacation and argue bitterly about politics (other subjects are no longer discussed), one boy supporting the Maoist insurgency in a certain Southeast Asian country, one believing that *to change the system you need to work inside it*; one boy threatens to *beat the living shit out of the other*, refuses crème brûlée, though it is created by his mother in order to keep the peace. One boy writes home and thereby enters the house only through a mail slot: he argues that the other boy is *crypto-fascist*, believing that *the market can seek its own level on questions of ethics and morals*; boys enter the house on vacation and announce future professions; boys enter the house on vacation and change their minds about professions; boys enter the house on vacation and one boy brings home a *sweetheart*, but throws a tantrum when it is suggested that the *sweetheart* will have to retire on the folding bed in the basement; the other boy, having no *sweetheart*, is distant and withdrawn, preferring to talk late into the night about family members gone from this world. Boys enter the house several weeks apart. Boys enter the house on days of heavy rain. Boys enter the house, in different calendar years, and upon entering, the boys seem to do nothing but compose manifestos, for the benefit of parents; they follow their mother around the place, having fashioned their manifestos in celebration of brand-new independence: *Mom, I like to lie in bed late into the morning watching game shows*, or, *I'm never going to date anyone but artists from now on, mad girls, dreamers, practicers of black magic*, or *A man should eat bologna, sliced meats are important*, or, *An American should bowl at least once a year*, but these manifestos apply only for brief spells after which they are reversed or discarded. Boys don't enter the house, at all, except as ghostly afterimages of younger selves, fleeting images of sneakers dashing up a staircase; soggy towels on the floor of the bathroom; blue jeans coiled like asps in the basin of the washing machine; boys as an absence of boys, blissful at first, you put a thing down on a spot, put this book down, come back later, *it's still there*; you buy a box of cookies, eat three, later three are missing. Nevertheless, when boys next enter the house, which they ultimately must do, it's a relief, even if it's only in preparation for weddings of acquaintances from boyhood, one boy has a beard, neatly trimmed, the other has rakish sideburns, one boy wears a hat, the other boy thinks hats are ridiculous, one boy wears khakis pleated at the waist, the other wears denim, but each changes into his suit (one suit fits well, one is a little tight), as though suits are *the* liminary marker of adulthood. Boys enter the house after the wedding and they are slapping each other on the back and yelling at anyone who will listen, *It's a party!* One boy enters the house, carried by friends, having been arrested (after the wedding) for driving while intoxicated, complexion ashen; the other boy tries to keep his mouth shut: the car is on its side in a ditch, the car has the top half of a tree broken over its bonnet, the car has struck another car which has in turn struck a third, *Everyone will have seen.* One boy misses his brother horribly, misses the past, misses a time worth being nostalgic over, *a time that never existed*, back when they set their sister's playhouse on fire; the other boy avoids all mention of that time; each of them is once the boy who enters the house alone, missing the other, each is devoted and each callous, and each plays his part on the telephone, over the course of months. Boys enter the house with fishing gear, according to prearranged date and time, arguing about whether to use *lures* or *live bait*, in order to meet their father for the *fishing adventure*, after which boys enter the house again, almost immediately, with live bait, having settled the question; boys boast of having caught fish in the past, though no fish has ever been caught: *Remember when the blues were biting?* Boys enter the house carrying their father, slumped. Happens so fast. Boys rush into the house leading EMTs to the couch in the living room where the body lies, boys enter the house, boys enter the house, boys enter the house. Boys hold open the threshold, awesome threshold that has welcomed them when they haven't even been able to welcome themselves, that threshold which welcomed them when they *had* to be taken in, here is its tarnished knocker, here is its euphonious bell, here's where the boys had to sand the door down because it never would hang right in the frame, here are the scuff-marks from when boys were on the wrong side of the door *demanding*, here's where there were once milk bottles for the milkman, here's where the newspaper always landed, here's the mail slot, here's the light on the front step, illuminated, here's where the boys are standing, as that beloved man is carried out. Boys, no longer boys, exit.

ALICE MUNRO

Save the Reaper

THE GAME EVE WAS PLAYING with her daughter Sophie's children was almost the same one that she had played with Sophie on long, dull car trips when Sophie was a little girl. Then the game was spies—now it was aliens. Sophie's children were in the back seat. Daisy was barely three and could not understand what was going on. Philip was seven, and in control. He was the one who picked the car they were to follow, in which there were newly arrived space travelers on their way to the secret headquarters, the invaders' lair. The aliens got their directions from the signals sent by plausible-looking people in other cars, or from somebody standing by a mailbox or even riding a tractor in a field. Many aliens had already arrived on Earth and been translated—this was Philip's word—so that anybody might be one: gas-station attendants or women pushing baby carriages or even the babies riding in the carriages.

Eve ventured to say that they might have to switch from following one vehicle to following another, because some were only decoys, not heading for the hideaway at all but leading you astray.

"No, that isn't it," said Philip. "What they do, they suck the people out of one car into another car, just in case anybody is following. They go into different people all the time, and the people never know what was in them."

"Really?" Eve said. "So how do we know which car?"

"The code's on the license plate," Philip said.

He sat as far forward as he could with his seat belt on, tapping his teeth sometimes in urgent concentration and making light whistling noises as he cautioned her.

"Uh-uh, watch out here," he said. "I think you're going to have to turn around. Yeah. Yeah. I think this may be it."

They had been following a white Mazda and were now, apparently, to follow an old green pickup truck, a Ford. Eve said, "Are you sure?"

"Sure."

What Eve had originally planned was to have the headquarters turn out to be in the village store that sold ice cream. But Philip had taken charge so thoroughly that now it was hard to manage the outcome. The pickup truck was turning off the paved country road onto a graveled side road. It was a decrepit truck with no topper, its body eaten by rust—it would not be going far. Home to some farm, most likely. They might not meet another vehicle to switch to before the destination was reached.

"You're positive this is it?" said Eve. "It's only one man by himself, you know. I thought they never traveled alone."

"The dog," said Philip.

For there was a dog riding in the open back of the truck, running back and forth from one side to the other as if there were events to be kept track of everywhere.

"The dog's one too."

Eve had come home from the village the day before laden with provisions. The village store was actually a classy supermarket these days. You could find almost anything—coffee, wine, rye bread without caraway seeds because Philip hated caraway, a ripe melon, fresh shrimp for Sophie, the dark cherries they all loved though Daisy had to be watched with the stones, a tub of chocolate-fudge ice cream, and all the regular things to keep them going for another week.

Sophie was clearing up the children's lunch. "Oh," she cried. "Oh, what'll we do with all that stuff?"

Ian had phoned, she said. Ian had phoned to say he was flying in to Toronto tomorrow. Work on his book had progressed more quickly than he had expected, so he had changed his plans. Instead of waiting for the three weeks to be up, he was coming tomorrow to collect Sophie and the children and take them on a little trip. He wanted to go to Quebec City. He had never been there, and he thought the children should see the part of Canada where people spoke French.

"He got lonesome," Philip said.

Sophie laughed. She said, "Yes. He got lonesome for us."

Twelve days, Eve thought. Twelve days had passed of the three weeks. She had had to take the house for a month. It was a cramped little house, fixed up on the cheap for summer rental. Eve's idea had been to get a lakeside cottage for the holiday— Sophie and Philip's first visit with her in nearly five years and Daisy's first ever. She had settled on this stretch of the Lake Huron shore because her parents used to bring her here, with her brother, when they were children. Things had changed—the cottages were all like suburban houses, and the rents were out of sight. This house, half a mile inland from the rocky, unfavored north end of the usable beach, had been the best she could manage. It stood in the middle of a cornfield. She had told the children what her father had once told her—that at night you could hear the corn growing. When she took the sheets off the line she had to shake out the corn bugs.

Sophie said that she and Ian and the children would drive to Quebec City in the rented car, then drive straight back to the Toronto airport, where the car was to be turned in. No mention of Eve's going along. There wasn't room in the rented car. But couldn't she have taken her own car? Ian could take the children, if he was so lonesome for them, give Sophie a rest. Eve and Sophie could ride together, as they used to in the summer, traveling to towns they had never seen before, where Eve had got parts in various summer-theater productions.

That was ridiculous. Eve's car was nine years old and in no condition to make a long trip. And it was Sophie Ian had got lonesome for—you could tell that by her warm, averted face.

"Well, that's wonderful," Eve said. "That he's got along so well with his book."

"It is," said Sophie. She always had an air of careful detachment when she spoke of Ian's book, and when Eve asked what it was about she had merely said. "Urban geography." Perhaps this was the correct behavior for academic wives—Eve had never known any.

"Anyway, you'll get some time by yourself," Sophie said. "After all this circus."

Maybe they'd had a tiff, thought Eve. This whole visit might have been tactical. Sophie might have taken the children off just to show him something. Planning holidays without him, to prove to herself that she could do it.

And the burning question was, who did the phoning?

"Why don't you leave the children here?" she said. "Just while you drive to the airport? Then drive back and pick them up and take off. That way, you'd have a little time alone, and a little time alone with Ian. It'll be hell with them at the airport."

"I'm tempted," Sophie said.

So in the end that was what she did.

Now Eve had to wonder if she herself had planned that change so that she could question Philip, which she must not do.

("Wasn't it a big surprise when your dad phoned from California?"

"He didn't phone. My mom phoned him."

"Did she? Oh, I didn't know. What did she say?"

"She said, 'I can't stand it here, I'm sick of it, let's figure out some plan to get me away.'")

When Sophie had called from California to say that she and Ian were getting married, Eve had asked her if it wouldn't be smarter just to live together first.

She had not thought Ian was any sort of contender—not so serious, even, as the Irish boy who had passed through a couple of years before, leaving Sophie pregnant with Philip, who initially looked a lot like Samuel Beckett.

"Oh, no," Sophie said. "Ian's weird, he doesn't believe in that."

And from then until now it had not been feasible for Eve to get to California. Invitations to visit had not been all that urgent, or even specific. Sophie had walked out of Eve's household a girl student with a toddling son—a winter-pale girl, harassed but high-spirited—and come back a self-contained full-bodied married woman with two children, a creamed-coffee skin, and lilac crescents of a permanent mild fatigue beneath her eyes. Also with a certain aversion to memories of the life she'd shared with Eve, of her blithe childhood (as Eve recalled it) or her adventurous days as a young mother. During this visit they had maintained a pleasant puttering routine of morning chores, beach afternoons, wine and movies when the children were in bed. And had avoided what seemed to be some mysterious disagreement or irreparable change of heart.

When Eve was a child staying in the village with her brother and her parents, they didn't have a car—it was wartime, they had come here on the train. The woman who ran the hotel was friends with Eve's mother, and they would be invited along when she drove to the country to buy corn or raspberries or tomatoes. Sometimes they would stop to have tea and look at the old dishes and bits of furniture for sale in some enterprising farm woman's front parlor. Eve's father preferred to stay behind and play checkers with some of the other men on the beach, while her brother watched them or went swimming unsupervised—he was older. The old hotel with its verandas extending over the sand was gone now, and the railway station with its flowerbeds spelling out the name of the village. The railway tracks, too. Instead, there was a fake old-fashioned mall with the satisfactory new supermarket and boutiques for leisure wear and country crafts.

When Eve was quite small and wore a great hair bow on top of her head, she was fond of these country expeditions. She ate tiny jam tarts and cakes whose frosting was stiff on top and soft underneath, topped with a bleeding maraschino cherry. She was not allowed to touch the dishes or the lace-and-satin pincushions or the sallow-looking old dolls, and the women's conversations passed over her head with a temporary and mildly depressing effect, like the inevitable clouds. But she enjoyed riding in the back seat, imagining herself on horseback or in a royal coach. Later on she refused to go. She began to hate trailing along with her mother and being identified as her mother's daughter. My daughter Eva. How richly condescending, and mistakenly possessive, that voice sounded in her ears. (She herself would use it, or some version of it, for years as a staple in some of her broadest, least accomplished acting.) She also detested her mother's habit of wearing large hats and gloves in the country, and sheer dresses on which there were raised flowers, like scabs. The oxford shoes, on the other hand—worn to favor her mother's corns—appeared embarrassingly stout and shabby. "What did you hate most about your mother?" was a game that Eve played with her friends in her first years free of home. "Corsets," one girl would say, and another said, "Wet aprons." Hairnets. Fat arms. Bible quotations. The way she sang "Danny Boy," Eve always said. Her corns.

She had forgotten all about this game until recently. The thought of it now was like touching a bad tooth.

Ahead of them the truck slowed and, without signaling, turned into a long tree-lined lane. Eve said, "I can't follow them any farther, Philip. That truck just belongs to some farmer who's headed home."

Philip said, "You're wrong. We have to." Eve drove on all the same, but as she passed the lane she noticed the gateposts. They were unusual, being shaped something like crude minarets and decorated with whitewashed pebbles and bits of colored glass. Neither one of them was straight, and they were half hidden by goldenrod and wild carrot, so that they had lost all reality as gateposts and looked instead like abandoned stage props from some gaudy operetta. The minute Eve saw them she remembered something else—a whitewashed outdoor wall in which pictures were set. The pictures were stiff, fantastic, childish scenes. Churches with spires, castles with towers, square houses with square, lopsided yellow windows. Triangular Christmas trees and tropical-colored birds half as big as the trees, a fat horse with dinky legs and burning red eyes, curly blue rivers of unvarying width, like lengths of ribbon, a moon and drunken stars and fat sunflowers nodding over the roofs of houses. All this made of pieces of colored glass set into cement, or plaster. She had seen it, and it wasn't in any public place. It was out in the country, and she was with her mother. The shape of her mother loomed in front of the wall—she was talking to an old farmer. He might only have been her mother's age, of course, and just looked old to Eve.

They went to look at odd things on those trips; they didn't just look at antiques. They had gone to see a shrub cut to resemble a bear, and an orchard of dwarf apple trees.

She didn't remember the gateposts at all, but it seemed to her that they could not have belonged to any other place. She backed the car up and swung around into the narrow track beneath the trees. The trees were heavy old Scotch pines, probably dangerous—you could see dangling dead and half-dead branches, and branches that had already blown or fallen down were lying in the grass and weeds on either side of the track. The car rocked back and forth in the ruts, and it seemed that Daisy approved of this motion. She began to make an accompanying noise: "Whoppy. Whoppy. Whoppy."

Here was something Daisy might remember—all she might remember—of this day. The arched trees, the sudden shadow, the interesting motion of the car. Maybe the white faces of the wild carrot that brushed at the windows. The sense of Philip beside her—his incomprehensible serious excitement, the tingling of his childish voice brought under unnatural control. A much vaguer sense of Eve—bare, freckly, sun-wrinkled arms, gray-blond frizzy curls held back by a black hair band. Maybe a smell. Not of cigarettes anymore, or of the touted creams and cosmetics on which Eve had once spent so much of her money. Old skin? Garlic? Wine? Mouthwash? Eve might be dead when Daisy remembered this. Daisy and Philip might be estranged. Eve had not spoken to her own brother for three years. Not since he said to her on the phone, "You shouldn't have become an actress if you weren't equipped to make a better go of it."

There wasn't any sign of a house ahead, but through a gap in the trees the skeleton of a barn rose up, walls gone, beams intact, roof whole but flopping to one side like a funny hat. There seemed to be pieces of machinery, old cars, or trucks scattered around it, in the sea of flowering weeds. Eve didn't have much leisure to look—she was busy controlling the car on this rough track. The green truck had disappeared ahead of her—how far could it have gone? Then she saw that the lane curved. It curved, and they left the shade of the pines and were out in the sunlight. The same sea foam of wild carrot, the same impression of rusting junk strewn about, a high wild hedge to one side, and there was the house, finally, behind it. A big house, two stories of yellowish gray brick, an attic story of wood, its dormer windows stuffed with dirty foam rubber. One of the lower windows shone with the tinfoil that covered it on the inside.

She had come to the wrong place. She had no memory of this house. There was no wall here around mowed grass. Saplings grew up at random in the weeds.

The truck was parked ahead of her. And ahead of that she could see a patch of cleared ground where gravel had been spread and where she could have turned the car around. But she couldn't get past the truck to do that. She had to stop too. She wondered if the man in the truck had stopped where he had on purpose, so that she would have to explain herself. He was now getting out of the truck in a leisurely way. Without looking at her, he released the dog, which had been running back and forth and barking with a great deal of angry spirit. Once on the ground, it continued to bark but didn't leave the man's side. The man wore a cap that shaded his face, so that Eve could not see his expression. He stood by the truck looking at them, not yet deciding to come any closer.

Eve unbuckled her seat belt.

"Don't get out," Philip said in a shrill voice. "Stay in the car. Turn around. Drive away."

"I can't," said Eve. "It's all right. That dog's just a yapper—he won't hurt me."

"Don't get out."

She should never have let the game get so far out of control. Philip was too excitable. "This isn't part of the game," she said. "He's just a man."

"I know," said Philip. "But don't get out."

"Stop that," said Eve, and got out and shut the door.

"Hi," she said. "I'm sorry. I made a mistake. I thought this was somewhere else."

The man said something like "Hey."

"I was actually looking for another place," Eve said. "It was a place I came to once when I was a little girl. There was a wall with pictures on it all made with pieces of broken glass. A cement wall, I think, whitewashed. When I saw those pillars by the road, I thought this must be it. You must have thought we were following you. It sounds so silly."

She heard the car door open. Philip got out, dragging Daisy behind him. Eve thought he had come to be close to her, and she put out her arm to welcome him. But he detached himself from Daisy and circled round Eve and spoke to the man. He had been almost hysterical a moment before, but now he said in a challenging way, "Is your dog friendly?"

"She won't hurt you," the man said. "Long as I'm here, she's okay. She gets in a tear because she's really a pup. She's still a pup."

He was a small man, no taller than Eve. He was wearing jeans and one of those open vests of colorful weave, made in Peru or Guatemala. Gold chains and medallions sparkled on his hairless, tanned, and muscular chest. When he spoke, he threw his head back and Eve could see that his face was older than his body. Some front teeth were missing.

"We won't bother you anymore," she said. "Philip, I was just telling this man we drove down this road looking for a place I came to when I was a little girl, and there were pictures made of colored glass set in a wall. But I made a mistake, this isn't the place."

"What's her name?" said Philip.

"Trixie," the man said, and on hearing her name the dog jumped up and bumped his arm. He swatted her down. "I don't know about no pictures. I don't live here. Harold, he's the one would know."

"It's all right," said Eve, and hoisted Daisy up on her hip. "If you could just move the truck ahead, then I could turn around."

"I don't know no pictures. See, if they was in the front part of the house I never would've saw them because Harold, like, he's got the front part of the house shut off."

"No, they were outside," said Eve. "It doesn't matter. This was years and years ago."

"Yeah. Yeah. Yeah." the man said, warming to the conversation. "You come in and get Harold to tell you about it. You know Harold? He's who owns it here. Mary, she owns it like, but Harold he put her in the Home, so now he does. It wasn't his fault—she had to go there." He reached into the truck and took out two cases of beer. "I just had to go to town. Harold sent me into town. You go on. You go in. Harold be glad to see you."

"Here, Trixie," Philip said sternly. Eve didn't believe he even cared about dogs—he was just asserting himself.

The dog came yelping and bounding around them. Daisy squealed with fright and pleasure—she was the one who was more of an animal lover—and somehow they were all en route to the house, Eve carryng Daisy and Philip and Trixie scrambling around her up some earthen bumps that had once been porch steps. The man came close behind them, smelling of the beer that he must have been drinking in the truck.

"Open it up, go ahead in," he said. "Make your way through. You don't mind it's got a little untidy here? Mary's in the Home, nobody to keep it organized like it used to be."

Massive disorder was what they had to make their way through—the kind that takes years to accumulate. The bottom layer of it was made up of chairs and tables and couches and perhaps a stove or two, with old bedclothes and newspapers and window shades and dead potted plants and ends of lumber and empty bottles and broken lighting fixtures and curtain rods piled on top of that, up to the ceiling in some places, blocking nearly all the light from outside. To make up for that, a light was burning by the inside door.

The man shifted the beer and got that door open, and shouted for Harold. It was hard to tell what sort of room they were in now—there were kitchen cupboards with the doors open, some cans on the shelves, but there were also a couple of cots with bare mattresses and rumpled blankets. The windows were so successfully covered up with furniture or hanging quilts that you couldn't tell where they were, and the smell was that of a junk store, a plugged sink, or maybe a plugged toilet, of cooking and grease and cigarettes and human sweat and dog mess and unremoved garbage.

Nobody answered the shouts. Eve turned around—there was room to turn around here, as there hadn't been on the porch—and said, "I don't think we should." But Trixie got in her way and the man ducked round her to bang on another door.

"Here he is," he said, still at the top of his voice, though he had opened the door. "Here's Harold, in here." At the same time, Trixie rushed forward and another man's voice said, "Fuck. Get that dog out of here."

"Lady here wants to see some pictures," the little man said. Trixie whined in pain—somebody had kicked her. Eve had no choice but to go on into the room.

This was a dining room. There was a heavy old dining room table and substantial chairs. Three men were sitting, playing cards. The fourth man had got up to kick the dog. The temperature in the room was about ninety degrees.

"Shut the door, there's a draft," one of the men at the table said.

The little man hauled Trixie out from under the table and threw her into the outer room, then closed the door behind Eve and the children.

"Christ. Fuck," said the man who had got up. His chest and arms were so heavily tattooed that he seemed to have purple or bluish skin. He shook one foot as if it hurt. Perhaps he had also kicked a table leg when he kicked Trixie.

Sitting with his back to the door was a young man with sharp shoulders and a delicate neck. At least Eve assumed he was young, because he wore his hair in dyed golden spikes and had gold rings in his ears. He didn't turn around. The man across from him was as old as Eve herself, and had a shaved head, a tidy gray beard, and bloodshot blue eyes. He looked at Eve without any friendliness but with some intelligence or comprehension, and in this he was unlike the tattooed man, who had looked at her as if she were some kind of hallucination that he had decided to ignore.

At the end of the table, in the host's or the father's chair, sat the man who had given the order to close the door but who hadn't looked up or otherwise paid any attention to the interruption. He was a large-boned, fat, pale man with sweaty brown curls, and as far as Eve could tell, he was entirely naked. The tattooed man and the blond man were wearing jeans, and the gray-bearded man was wearing jeans and a checked shirt buttoned up to the neck and a string tie. There were glasses and bottles on the table. The man in the host's chair—he must be Harold—and the gray-bearded man were drinking whiskey. The other two were drinking beer.

"I told her maybe there was pictures in the front, but she couldn't go in there, you got that shut up," the little man said.

Harold said, "You shut up."

Eve said, "I'm really sorry." There seemed to be nothing to do but go into her spiel, enlarging it to include staying at the village hotel as a little girl, drives with her mother, the pictures in the wall, her memory of them today, the gateposts, her obvious mistake, her apologies. She spoke directly to the graybeard, since he seemed to be the only one willing to listen or capable of understanding her. Her arm and shoulder ached from the weight of Daisy and from the tension that had got hold of her entire body. Yet she was thinking how she would describe this—she'd say it was like finding yourself in the middle of a Pinter play. Or like all her nightmares of a stolid, silent, hostile audience.

The graybeard spoke when she could not think of any further charming or apologetic thing to say. He said, "I don't know. You'll have to ask Harold. Hey. Hey, Harold. Do you know anything about some pictures made out of broken glass?"

"Tell her when she was riding around looking at pictures I wasn't even born yet," said Harold, without looking up.

"You're out of luck, lady," said the graybeard.

The tattooed man whistled. "Hey you," he said to Philip. "Hey, kid. Can you play the piano?"

There was a piano behind Harold's chair. There was no stool or bench—Harold himself taking up most of the room between the piano and the table—and inappropriate things, such as plates and overcoats, were piled on top of it, as they were on every surface in the house.

"No," said Eve quickly. "No, he can't."

"I'm asking him," the tattooed man said. "Can you play a tune?"

"Let him alone," the graybeard said.

"Just asking if he can play a tune, what's the matter with that?"

"Let him alone."

"You see, I can't move until somebody moves the truck," Eve said.

She thought, There is a smell of semen in this room.

"If you could just move—" she said, turning and expecting to find the little man behind her. She stopped when she saw he wasn't there, he wasn't in the room at all, he had got out without her knowing when. What if he had locked the door?

She put her hand on the knob and it turned. The door opened with a little difficulty and a scramble on the other side. The little man had been crouched right there, listening. She went out without speaking to him, out through the kitchen, Philip trotting along beside her like the meekest little boy in the world. Along the narrow pathway in the porch, through the junk, and when they reached the open air she sucked it in, not having taken a real breath for a long time.

"You ought to go along down the road, ask down at Harold's cousin's place," the little man's voice came after her. "They got a nice place. They got a new house, she keeps it beautiful. They'll show you pictures or anything you want, they'll make you welcome. They'll sit you down and feed you, they don't let nobody go away empty."

He couldn't have been crouched against the door all the time, because he had moved the truck. Or somebody had. It had disappeared altogether, been driven away to some shed or parking spot out of sight.

"Thanks for telling me," Eve said. She got Daisy buckled in. Philip was buckling himself in, without having to be reminded. Trixie appeared from somewhere and walked around the car in a disconsolate way, sniffing at the tires.

Eve got in and closed the door, put her sweating hand on the key. The car started, she pulled ahead, onto the gravel—a space that was surrounded by thick bushes, berry bushes, she supposed, and old lilacs, as well as weeds. In places, these bushes had been flattened by piles of old tires and bottles and tin cans. It was hard to believe that things had been thrown out of that house, considering all that was left in it, but apparently they had. And as Eve swung the car around she saw, revealed by this flattening, some fragment of a wall, to which bits of whitewash still clung. She thought she could see pieces of glass embedded there, glinting.

She didn't slow down to look. She hoped Philip hadn't noticed. She got the car pointed toward the lane and drove past the dirt steps leading to the porch. The little man stood there waving with both arms, and Trixie was wagging her tail, sufficiently roused from her scared docility to bark farewell and chase them partway down the lane. The chase was only a formality, she could have caught up with them if she'd wanted to. Eve had to slow down at once when she hit the ruts.

She was driving so slowly that it was possible—easy—for a figure to rise up out of the tall weeds on the passenger side of the car and open the door, which Eve had not thought of locking, and jump in.

It was the blond boy who had been sitting at the table, the one whose face she had never seen.

"Don't be scared. Don't be scared, anybody. I just wondered if I could hitch a ride with you guys, okay?"

It wasn't a man or a boy. It was a young girl. A girl now wearing a dirty sort of undershirt.

"Okay," Eve said. She had just managed to hold the car in the track.

"I couldn't ask you back in the house," the girl said. "I went in the bathroom and got out the window and run out here. They probably don't even know I'm gone yet. They're boiled." She grabbed a handful of the undershirt, which was much too large for her, and sniffed at it. "Stinks," she said. "I just grabbed this of Harold's was in the bathroom. Stinks."

Eve left the ruts, the darkness of the lane, and turned onto the ordinary road. "Jesus, I'm glad to get out of there." the girl said. "I didn't know nothing about what

I was getting into. I didn't know even how I got there. It was night. It wasn't no place for me. You know what I mean?"

"They seemed pretty drunk, all right." Eve said.

"Yeah. Well, I'm sorry if I scared you."

"That's okay."

"If I hadn't've jumped in I thought you wouldn't stop for me. Would you?"

"I don't know," said Eve. "I guess I would have if it got through to me you were a girl. I didn't really get a look at you before."

"Yeah, I don't look like much now. I look like shit now. I'm not saying I don't like to party. I like to party. But there's party and there's party, you know what I mean?"

She turned in the seat and looked at Eve so steadily that Eve had to take her eyes off the road for a moment and look back. And what she saw was that this girl was much drunker than she sounded. Her dark-brown eyes were glazed but wide open, rounded with effort, and they had the imploring yet distant expression that drunks' eyes get—a kind of last-ditch insistence on fooling you. Her skin was blotched in some places and ashy in others, her whole face crumpled with the effects of a mighty binge. She was a natural brunette—the gold spikes were intentionally and provoca-tively dark at the roots—and pretty enough, if you disregarded her present dinginess, to make you wonder how she had ever got mixed up with Harold and his crew. Her shoulders were broad for a girl and her chest lean—her way of living and the style of the times must have taken ten or fifteen pounds off her—but she wasn't tall, and she really wasn't boyish. Her true inclination was to be a cuddly chunky girl, a darling dumpling.

"Herb was crazy bringing you in there like that," she said. "He's got a screw loose, Herb."

Eve said, "I gathered that."

"I don't know what he does around there, I guess he works for Harold. I don't think Harold uses him too good, neither."

Eve had never believed herself to be attracted to women in a sexual way, and her idea of attractiveness in another woman had never been this soiled and wayward charm. But perhaps the girl did not believe this possible—she must be so used to appealing to people. At any rate, she slid her hand along Eve's bare thigh, just getting a little way beyond the hem of her shorts. It was a practiced move, drunk as she was. To spread the fingers, to grasp flesh on the first try, would have been too much. A practiced, automatically hopeful move, yet so lacking in any true, strong, squirmy, comradely lust that Eve felt the hand might just as easily have fallen short and caressed the car upholstery instead.

"I'm okay," the girl said, and her voice, like the hand, struggled to put herself and Eve on a new level of intimacy. "You know what I mean? You understand me. Okay?"

"Of course," Eve said brightly, and the hand trailed away, its whore's courtesy fin-ished. But it had not failed altogether. Blatant and halfhearted as it was, it had been enough to set some old wires twitching. And the fact that it could be effective in any way filled Eve with misgiving, flung a shadow from this moment over all the rowdy and impulsive, as well as all the hopeful and serious, the more or less unrepented-of, couplings of her life. Not a real flare-up of shame, a sense of sin—just a shadow. What a joke on her, if she started to hanker now after a purer past and a cleaner slate.

No. It was possible that she just hankered after love.

Sophie's father was from Kerala, in the south of India. Eve had met him, and spent her whole time with him, on a train going from Vancouver to Toronto. He was a young doctor studying in Canada on a fellowship. He had a wife already, and a baby daughter, at home in India.

The train trip took three days. There was a half-hour stop in Calgary. Eve and the doctor ran around looking for a drugstore where they could buy condoms. They didn't find one. By the time they got to Winnipeg, where the train stopped for a full hour, it was too late. In fact, Eve always said, when she told their story, by the time they left the Calgary city limits it was probably too late.

He was traveling in the day coach—his school fellowship was not generous. But Eve had splurged and got herself a roomette. It was this extravagance—a last-minute decision—it was the convenience and privacy of the roomette that was responsible, Eve said, for the existence of Sophie and the greatest change in her, Eve's, life. That, and the fact that you couldn't get condoms anywhere around the Calgary station, not for love or money.

In Toronto, she waved goodbye to her lover from Kerala, as you would wave to any train acquaintance, because she was met there by the man who was at that time the serious interest and the main trouble in her life. The whole three days had been underscored by the swaying and rocking of the train—their motions were never just what they contrived themselves, and perhaps for that reason seemed guiltless, irresistible. Their feelings and conversations must have been affected too. Eve remembered these as sweet and generous, never solemn or desperate.

She told Sophie his Christian name—Thomas, after the saint. Until she met him, Eve had never heard about the ancient Christians in southern India. For a while, when she was in her teens, Sophie had taken an interest in Kerala. She brought home books from the library and took to going to parties in a sari. She talked about looking her father up when she got older. The fact that she knew his first name and his special study—diseases of the blood—seemed to her possibly enough. Eve stressed to her the size of the population of India and the chance that he had not even stayed there. What she could not bring herself to explain was how incidental, how nearly unimaginable, the existence of Sophie would be, necessarily, in her father's life. Fortunately, the idea faded, and Sophie gave up wearing the sari when all those dramatic ethnic costumes became too commonplace. The only time she mentioned her father, later on, was when she was carrying Philip and making jokes about keeping up the family tradition of fly-by fathers.

Eve said to the girl, "Where is it you want to go?"

The girl jerked backward, facing the road. "Where are you going?" she said. "You live around here?" The blurred, tired tones of seduction had changed, as no doubt they would after sex, into a tone of exhausted contempt and vague threat or challenge.

"There's a bus goes through the village," Eve said. "It stops at the gas station. I've seen the sign."

"Yeah, but just one thing," the girl said. "I got no money. See, I got away from there in such a hurry I never got to collect my money. So what use would it be me getting on a bus without no money?"

The thing to do was not to recognize a threat. Tell her that she could hitchhike if she had no money. It wasn't likely that she had a gun in her jeans. She just wanted to sound as if she might have one.

But a knife?

The girl turned for the first time to look into the back seat.

"You kids okay back there?" she said.

No answer.

"They're cute," she said. "They shy with strangers?"

How stupid to think about sex when the reality, the danger, was elsewhere.

Eve's purse was on the floor of the car in front of the girl's feet. She didn't know how much money was in it. Sixty, seventy dollars. Hardly more. If she offered money for a ticket, the girl would name an expensive destination. Montreal. Or at least Toronto. If she said, "Just take what's there," the girl would see capitulation. She would sense Eve's fear and might try to push further. What was the best she could do? Steal the car? If she left Eve and the children beside the road, the police would be after her in a hurry. If she left them dead in some thicket, she might get farther. Or if she took them along while she needed them, a knife against Eve's side or a child's throat.

Such things happen. But not as often as in the movies. Such things don't often happen.

Eve turned onto the county road, which was fairly busy. Why did that make her feel better? Safety there was an illusion. She could be driving along the highway in the midst of the day's traffic, taking herself and the children to their deaths.

The girl said, "Where's this road go?"

"It goes out to the main highway."

"Let's drive out there."

"That's where I'm driving," Eve said.

"Which way's the highway go?"

"It goes north to Owen Sound or up to Tobermory, where you get the boat. Or south to—I don't know. But it joins another highway that would get you to Sarnia. Or London. Or Detroit or Toronto if you keep going."

Nothing more was said until they reached the highway. Eve turned onto it and said, "This is it."

"Which way you heading now?"

Couldn't she tell by the sun?

"I'm heading north," Eve said.

"That the way you live, then?"

"I'm going to the village. I'm going to stop for gas."

"You got gas," the girl said. "You got over half a tank."

That was stupid. Eve should have said groceries.

Beside her the girl let out a long groan of decision, maybe of relinquishment.

"You know," she said. "You know, I might as well get out here if I'm going to hitch a ride. Get a ride here as easy as anyplace."

Eve pulled over onto the gravel. Relief was turning into something like shame. What was it like to be drunk, wasted, with no money, at the side of the road?

"Which way you said we're going?"

"North," Eve told her again.

"Which way you said to Sarnia?"

"South. Just cross the road, the cars'll be headed south. Watch out for the traffic."

"Sure," the girl said. Her voice was already distant, she was calculating new chances. She was half out of the car as she said, "See you." And into the back seat, "See you guys. Be good."

"Wait," Eve said. She leaned over and felt in her purse for her wallet, and took out a twenty-dollar bill. She got out of the car and went round to where the girl was waiting. "Here," she said. "This'll help you."

"Yeah, thanks," the girl said, stuffing the bill in her pocket, her eyes on the road.

"Listen," said Eve. "If you're stranded, I'll tell you where my house is. It's about two miles north of the village, and the village is about half a mile north of here. North. This way. It's all by itself in the middle of a field. It's got one ordinary window on one side of the front door and a funny-looking little window on the other. That's where they put in the bathroom."

"Yeah," the girl said.

"It's just that I thought, if you don't get a ride—"

"Okay," the girl said. "Sure."

When they had started driving again, Philip said, "Yuck. She smelled like vomit."

A little farther on he said, "She didn't even know you should look at the sun to tell directions. She was stupid. Wasn't she?"

"I guess so," Eve said.

"Yuck. I never ever saw anybody so stupid."

As they went through the village, he asked if they could stop for ice cream cones. Eve said no.

"There's so many people stopping for ice cream it's hard to find a place to park," she said. "We've got scads of ice cream at home."

"You shouldn't say 'home,'" said Philip. "It's just where we're staying. You should say 'the house.'"

The big hay rolls in a field to the east of the highway were facing ends on into the sun, so tightly packed they looked like shields or gongs or faces of Aztec metal. Past that was a field of pale soft gold. Barley.

"That's called barley, that gold stuff with the tails on it," she said to Philip.

"I know," he said.

"The tails are called beards sometimes." She began to recite, "But the reapers, reaping early, in among the bearded barley—"

Daisy said, "What does mean pearly?"

Philip said, "Bar-ley."

"Only reapers, reaping early," Eve said. She tried to remember. "Save the reapers, reaping early—"

That was the one she liked best. Save the reaper.

Sophie and Ian had bought corn at a roadside stand. It was for dinner. Plans had changed—they weren't leaving until morning. And they had bought a bottle of gin and some limes. Ian made the drinks while Eve and Sophie sat husking the corn.

"Two dozen. That's crazy," Eve said.

"Wait and see," said Sophie. "Ian loves corn."

Ian bowed when he presented Eve with her drink, and after she had tasted it she said, "This is most heavenly."

Ian wasn't much as she had remembered or pictured him. He was not tall, Teutonic, humorless. He was a slim fair-haired man of medium height, quick-moving, companionable. Sophie was less assured, more eager in all she said and did, than she had seemed in the last two weeks. But happier too.

Eve told her story. She began with the checkerboard on the beach, the vanished hotel, the drives into the country. It included her mother's city-lady outfits, her sheer dresses and matching slips, but not the older Eve's feelings of repugnance. And the things they went to see—the dwarf orchard, the shelf of old dolls, the marvelous pictures made of colored glass.

"They were a little like Chagall?" Eve said.

Ian said, "Yep, even us urban geographers know about Chagall."

"Sor-ry," Eve said. Both laughed.

Now the gateposts, the sudden memory, the dark lane and ruined barn and rusted machinery, the house a shambles.

"The owner was in there playing cards with his friends," Eve said. "He didn't know anything about it. Didn't know or didn't care. And my God, it could have been sixty years ago, think of that."

Sophie said, "Oh, Mom. What a shame." She was glowing with relief to see Ian and Eve getting on so well together.

(She's not so awful, couldn't we stay one night?)

"Are you sure it was even the right place?" she said.

"Maybe not," said Eve. "Maybe not."

She would not mention the fragment of wall she had seen beyond the bushes. Why bother, when there were so many things she thought it best not to mention? First, the game that she had got Philip playing, overexciting him. And nearly everything about Harold and his companions. Everything, every single thing about the girl who had jumped into the car.

There are people who carry decency and optimism around with them, who seem to cleanse every atmosphere they settle in, and you can't tell such people things, it is too disruptive. Ian struck Eve as being one of those people, in spite of his present graciousness, and Sophie as being someone who thanked her lucky stars that she had found him. Eve could say that the house had smelled vile, and that the owner and his friends looked boozy and disreputable, but not that Harold was naked and never that she herself had been afraid. And never what she had been afraid of.

Philip was in charge of gathering up the cornhusks and carrying them outside to throw them along the edge of the field. Occasionally Daisy picked up a few on her own and took them off to be distributed around the house. Philip had added nothing to Eve's story and had not seemed to be concerned with the telling of it. But once it was told, and Ian (interested in bringing this local anecdote into line with his professional studies) was asking Eve what she knew about the breakup of older patterns of village and rural life, about the spread of what was called agribusiness, Philip did look up from the stooping and crawling he was doing around the adults' feet. He looked at Eve—a flat look, a moment of conspiratorial blankness, a buried smile, that passed before there could be any demand for recognition of it. It seemed to mean that, however much or little he knew, he knew about the importance of keeping things to yourself. Eve got a jolt from that. She wished to deny that she was in any way responsible for it, but she couldn't disclaim it.

If the girl came looking for her, they would all still be here. Then Eve's carefulness would go for nothing.

The girl wouldn't come. Much better offers would turn up before she'd stood ten minutes by the highway. More dangerous offers, perhaps, but more interesting, likely to be more profitable.

The girl wouldn't come. Unless she found some homeless, heartless wastrel her own age. (I know where there's a place we can stay, if we can get rid of the old lady.)

Not tonight but tomorrow night, Eve would lie down in this hollowed-out house, its board walls like a paper shell around her. She would will herself to grow light, free of consequence, and hope to go to sleep with nothing in her head but the deep, live rustle of the corn.

PETER ORNER

The Raft

MY GRANDFATHER, WHO LOST his short-term memory sometime during the first Eisenhower administration, calls me into his study because he wants to tell me the story he's never told anybody before, again. My grandmother, from her perch at her beauty table, with the oval mirror circled by little bulbs I used to love to unscrew, shouts, "Oh, for God's sake, Seymour. We're meeting the Dewoskins at Twin Orchards at seven-thirty. Must you go back to the South Pacific?"

My grandfather slams the door and motions me to the chair in front of his desk. I'll be thirteen in two weeks. "There's something I want to tell you, son," he says. "Something I've never told anybody. You think you're ready? You think you've got the gumption?"

"I think so."

"Think so?"

"I know so, sir. I know I've got the gumption."

He sits down at his desk and rips open an envelope with a gleaming letter opener in the shape of a miniature gold sword. "So, you want to know?"

"Very much."

"Well then, stand up, sailor."

My grandfather's study is carpeted with white shag, which feels woolly against my bare feet. I twist my toes in it. Many cactuses are also in the room. My grandfather often encourages me to touch their prickers to demonstrate how tough an old boy a plant can be. My grandfather captained a destroyer during World War II.

"It was late," he says. "Someone knocked on my stateroom door. I leaped up. In those days I slept in uniform—shoes too." My grandfather smiles. His face is so perfectly round that his smile looks like a gash in a basketball. I smile back.

"Don't smile," he says. "Just because I'm smiling, don't assume I couldn't kill you right now. Know that about a man."

"Oh, Seymour, *my God*," my grandmother protests through the door. "Isn't he supposed to be at summer camp, anyway? Call his mother."

He looks straight at me and snarls at her, "Another word out of you, ensign, and I'll have you thrown in the brig, and you won't see Beanie Dewoskin till V-J Day."

"I'll make coffee," my grandmother says.

"It was late," I say. "Someone knocked."

"Two knocks," he says. "And by the time he raised his knuckle for the third, I'd opened the door. 'A message from the watch, sir. A boat, sir, three miles due north. Very small, sir. Could be an enemy boat, sir; then again, it might not be. Hard to tell, sir.' I told the boy to can it. Some messengers don't know when to take a breath and let you think. They think if you aren't saying anything, you want to hear more, which is never true. Remember that. I went up to the bridge. 'Wait,' I told them. 'Wait till we can see it. And ready the torpedoes,' I told them, or something like that. I forget the lingo."

"The torpedoes?" I say.

"Yes," he says. "The torpedoes. I couldn't see it clearly, but the chance that it wasn't a hostile boat was slim. You see what I'm driving at?"

"I do, sir."

"No, you don't, sailor."

"No, I don't," I say. "Don't at all."

"We'd been warned in a communiqué from the admiral to be on high alert for kamikaze flotillas. Do you have any idea what a kamikaze flotilla is?"

"Basically," I say, "it hits the side of your boat, and whango."

"You being smart with me? You think this isn't life and death we're talking about here?"

"Sorry, sir."

"So I waited. It took about a half-hour on auxiliary power for us to get within a quarter mile of the thing—then I could see it with the search."

My grandfather pauses and then opens his right-hand desk drawer, where he keeps a safety-locked pistol and a stack of tattered pornographic comic books. They are strange books. In the cartoons men with long penises with hats on the ends of them and hair growing up the sides, so that to me they look like pickles, chase women with skirts raised over their heads and tattoos on their asses that say things like "Uncle Sam's my Daddy" and "I never kissed a Kaiser." He whacks the drawer shut and brings his hands together in front of his face, movng his thumbs around as if he's getting ready either to pray or to thumb-wrestle.

"Japs," he says. "Naked Japs on a raft. A raftload of naked Jap sailors. Today the bleedyhearts would probably call them refugees, but back then we didn't call them anything but Japs. Looked like they'd been floating for days. They turned their backs to the light, so all we could see was their backsides, skin and bone fighting it out and the bone winning."

I step back. I want to sit down but I don't. He stands and leans over his desk, examines my face. Then he points at the door and murmurs, "Phyllis doesn't know." On a phone-message pad he scrawls "BLEW IT UP" in capital letters. He whispers, "I gave the order." He comes around the desk and motions to his closet. "We can talk in there," he says, and I follow him into his warren of suits. My grandfather has long ago moved all his clothes out of my grandmother's packed-to-the-gills closets. He leaves the light off. In the crack of sun beneath the door I can see my grandfather's shoes and white socks. He's wearing shorts. He was working on his putting in the driveway.

"At ease, sailor," he says, and I kneel down amid the suits and dangling ties and belts. And I see now that it's not how many times you hear a story but where you hear it that matters. I've heard this before, but this is the first time I've been in a closet alone with my grandfather.

"Why?" I say. "Why, if you knew it wasn't—"

"Why?" he says, not as if he's repeating my question but as if he really doesn't know. He sighs. Then, still whispering even though we're in the closet, he says, "Some men would lie to you. They'd say it's war. I won't lie to you. It had zero to do with war and everything to do with the uniform I was wearing. Because my job was to make decisions. Besides, what the hell would I have done with a boatload of naked Japanese? There was a war on."

"But you just said—"

"Listen, my job. Just because men like me made the world safe for men like your father to be cowards doesn't mean you won't ever blow up any civilians. Because you will. I do it once a week at the bank." He places a stumpy, powerful hand on my shoulder. "*Comprende?*"

"Never," I breathe.

"Good," he says, and we are standing in the dark and looking at each other and the story is the same and different—like last time except this time his tears come so fast they're like lather. He blows his nose into his hand. I reach and offer him the sleeve of one of his tweed jackets. "I'll let myself out," he says, and leaves me in the confessional, shutting the door behind him.

I don't imagine anything, not even a hand that feels like a fish yanking my ankle. Another door opens. "Seymour? Seymour?" my grandmother says. "Where's the kid?"

TOBIAS WOLFF

Bullet in the Brain

ANDERS COULDN'T GET TO THE BANK until just before it closed, so of course the line was endless and he got stuck behind two women whose loud, stupid conversation put him in a murderous temper. He was never in the best of tempers anyway, Anders—a book critic known for the weary, elegant savagery with which he dispatched almost everything he reviewed.

With the line still doubled around the rope, one of the tellers stuck a "POSITION CLOSED" sign in her window and walked to the back of the bank, where she leaned against a desk and began to pass the time with a man shuffling papers. The women in front of Anders broke off their conversation and watched the teller with hatred. "Oh, that's nice," one of them said. She turned to Anders and added, confident of his accord, "One of those little human touches that keep us coming back for more."

Anders had conceived his own towering hatred of the teller, but he immediately turned it on the presumptuous crybaby in front of him. "Damned unfair," he said. "Tragic, really. If they're not chopping off the wrong leg, or bombing your ancestral village, they're closing their positions."

She stood her ground. "I didn't say it was tragic," she said. "I just think it's a pretty lousy way to treat your customers."

"Unforgivable," Anders said. "Heaven will take note."

She sucked in her cheeks but stared past him and said nothing. Anders saw that the other woman, her friend, was looking in the same direction. And then the tellers stopped what they were doing, and the customers slowly turned, and silence came over the bank. Two men wearing black ski masks and blue business suits were standing to the side of the door. One of them had a pistol pressed against the guard's neck. The guard's eyes were closed, and his lips were moving. The other man had a sawed-off shotgun. "Keep your big mouth shut!" the man with the pistol said, though no one had spoken a word. "One of you tellers hits the alarm, you're all dead meat. Got it?"

The tellers nodded.

"Oh, bravo," Anders said. "*Dead meat.*" He turned to the woman in front of him. "Great script, eh? The stern, brass-knuckled poetry of the dangerous classes."

She looked at him with drowning eyes.

The man with the shotgun pushed the guard to his knees. He handed the shotgun to his partner and yanked the guard's wrists up behind his back and locked them together with a pair of handcuffs. He toppled him onto the floor with a kick between the shoulder blades. Then he took his shotgun back and went over to the security gate at the end of the counter. He was short and heavy and moved with peculiar slowness, even torpor. "Buzz him in," his partner said. The man with the shotgun opened the gate and sauntered along the line of tellers, handing each of them a Hefty bag. When he came to the empty position he looked over at the man with the pistol, who said, "Whose slot is that?"

Anders watched the teller. She put her hand to her throat and turned to the man she'd been talking to. He nodded. "Mine," she said.

"Then get your ugly ass in gear and fill that bag."

"There you go," Anders said to the woman in front of him. "Justice is done."

"Hey! Bright boy! Did I tell you to talk?"

"No," Anders said.

"Then shut your trap."

"Did you hear that?" Anders said. " 'Bright boy.' Right out of 'The Killers.' "

"Please be quiet," the woman said.

"Hey, you deaf or what?" The man with the pistol walked over to Anders. He poked the weapon into Anders' gut. "You think I'm playing games?"

"No," Anders said, but the barrel tickled like a stiff finger and he had to fight back the titters. He did this by making himself stare into the man's eyes, which were clearly visible behind the holes in the mask: pale blue and rawly red-rimmed. The man's left eyelid kept twitching. He breathed out a piercing, ammoniac smell that shocked Anders more than anything that had happened, and he was beginning to develop a sense of unease when the man prodded him again with the pistol.

"You like me, bright boy?" he said. "You want to suck my dick?"

"No," Anders said.

"Then stop looking at me."

Anders fixed his gaze on the man's shiny wing-tip shoes.

"Not down there. Up there." He stuck the pistol under Anders' chin and pushed it upward until Anders was looking at the ceiling.

Anders had never paid much attention to that part of the bank, a pompous old building with marble floors and counters and pillars, and gilt scrollwork over the tellers' cages. The domed ceiling had been decorated with mythological figures whose fleshy, toga-draped ugliness Anders had taken in at a glance many years earlier and afterward declined to notice. Now he had no choice but to scrutinize the painter's work. It was even worse than he remembered, and all of it executed with the utmost gravity. The artist had a few tricks up his sleeve and used them again and again—a certain rosy blush on the underside of the clouds, a coy backward glance on the faces of the cupids and fauns. The ceiling was crowded with various dramas, but the one that caught Anders' eye was Zeus and Europa—portrayed, in this rendition, as a bull ogling a cow from behind a haystack. To make the cow sexy, the painter had canted her hips suggestively and given her long, droopy eyelashes through which she gazed back at the bull with sultry welcome. The bull wore a smirk and his eyebrows were arched. If there'd been a bubble coming out of his mouth, it would have said, "Hubba hubba."

"What's so funny, bright boy?"

"Nothing."

"You think I'm comical? You think I'm some kind of clown?"

"No."

"You think you can fuck with me?"

"No."

"Fuck with me again, you're history. *Capiche?*"

Anders burst out laughing. He covered his mouth with both hands and said, "I'm sorry, I'm sorry," then snorted helplessly through his fingers and said, "*Capiche*—oh, God, *capiche*," and at that the man with the pistol raised the pistol and shot Anders right in the head.

The bullet smashed Anders' skull and ploughed through his brain and exited behind his right ear, scattering shards of bone into the cerebral cortex, the corpus callosum, back toward the basal ganglia, and down into the thalamus. But before all this occurred, the first appearance of the bullet in the cerebrum set off a crackling chain of iron transports and neuro-transmissions. Because of their peculiar origin these traced a peculiar pattern, flukishly calling to life a summer afternoon some forty years past, and long since lost to memory. After striking the cranium the bullet was moving at 900 feet per second, a pathetically sluggish, glacial pace compared to the synaptic lightning that flashed around it. Once in the brain, that is, the bullet came under the mediation of brain time, which gave Anders plenty of leisure to contemplate the scene that, in a phrase he would have abhorred, "passed before his eyes."

It is worth noting what Anders did not remember, given what he did remember. He did not remember his first lover, Sherry, or what he had most madly loved about her, before it came to irritate him—her unembarrassed carnality, and especially the cordial way she had with his unit; which she called Mr. Mole, as in, "Uh-oh, looks like Mr. Mole wants to play," and, "let's hide Mr. Mole!" Anders did not remember his wife, whom he had also loved before she exhausted him with her predictability, or his daughter, now a sullen professor of economics at Dartmouth. He did not remember standing just outside his daughter's door as she lectured her bear about his naughtiness and described the truly appalling punishments Paws would receive unless he changed his ways. He did not remember a single line of the hundreds of poems he had committed to memory in his youth so that he could give himself the shivers at will—not "Silent, upon a peak in Darien," or "My God, I heard this day," or "All my pretty ones? Did you say all? O hell-kite! All?" None of these did he remember; not one. Anders did not remember his dying mother saying of his father, "I should have stabbed him in his sleep."

He did not remember Professor Josephs telling his class how Athenian prisoners in Sicily had been released if they could recite Aeschylus, and then reciting Aeschylus himself, right there, in the Greek. Anders did not remember how his eyes had burned at those sounds. He did not remember the surprise of seeing a college classmate's name on the jacket of a novel not long after they graduated, or the respect he had felt after reading the book. He did not remember the pleasure of giving respect.

Nor did Anders remember seeing a woman leap to her death from the building opposite his own just days after his daughter was born. He did not remember shouting, "Lord have mercy!" He did not remember deliberately crashing his father's car into a tree, or having his ribs kicked in by three policemen at an anti-war rally, or waking himself up with laughter. He did not remember when he began to regard the heap of books on his desk with boredom and dread, or when he grew angry at writers for writing them. He did not remember when everything began to remind him of something else.

This is what he remembered. Heat. A baseball field. Yellow grass, the whirr of insects, himself leaning against a tree as the boys of the neighborhood gather for a pickup game. He looks on as the others argue the relative genius of Mantle and Mays. They have been worrying this subject all summer, and it has become tedious to Anders: an oppression, like the heat.

Then the last two boys arrive, Coyle and a cousin of his from Mississippi. Anders has never met Coyle's cousin before and will never see him again. He says hi with the rest but takes no further notice of him until they've chosen sides and someone asks the cousin what position he wants to play. "Shortstop," the boy says. "Short's the best position they is." Anders turns and looks at him. He wants to hear Coyle's cousin repeat what he's just said, but he knows better than to ask. The others will think he's being a jerk, ragging the kid for his grammar. But that isn't it, not at all—it's that Anders is strangely roused, elated, by those final two words, their pure unexpectedness and their music. He takes the field in a trance, repeating them to himself.

The bullet is already in the brain; it won't be outrun forever, or charmed to a halt. In the end it will do its work and leave the troubled skull behind, dragging its comet's tail of memory and hope and talent and love into the marble hall of commerce. That can't be helped. But for now Anders can still make time. Time for the shadows to lengthen on the grass, time for the tethered dog to bark at the flying ball, time for the boy in right field to smack his sweat-blackened mitt and softly chant, *They is, they is, they is.*

Authors

James Baldwin

Born in 1924 in Harlem, James Baldwin said that he began plotting novels "at about the time I learned to read." At age twenty-one he was waiting tables in Greenwich Village and working on his first novel, *Go Tell It on the Mountain* (1953), and on the basis of that work-in-progress was awarded a Saxton Fellowship. At the age of twenty-four, with encouragement from fellow African American writer Richard Wright, Baldwin moved to France, where he finished and published his first novel in 1954. He then wrote *Giovanni's Room* (1956) and *Another Country* (1961), in which he openly discussed and explored his homosexuality.

He published the bestselling *The Fire Next Time* in 1963, just as the fledgling civil rights movement was getting under way. Baldwin's acclaimed short story collection *Going to Meet the Man* was published in 1965.

About his approach to writing, Baldwin once said, "One writes out of one thing only—one's own experience. Everything depends on how relentlessly one forces from this experience the last drop, sweet or bitter, it can possibly give. This is the only real concern of the artist, to recreate out of the disorder of life that order which is art."

Toni Cade Bambara

Toni Cade Bambara was born in Harlem in 1939 and spent her childhood there. Originally named Miltona Mirkin Cade, Bambara changed her name when she was five years old. She graduated from Queen's College with a BA in theater arts / English in 1960 and went on to earn a master's degree in English at the same institution. She taught writing at City College of New York between 1965 and 1969 and began writing both fiction and nonfiction that was heavily influenced by the civil rights and feminist movements. During that time she published a highly acclaimed anthology of fiction, nonfiction, and poetry entitled *The Black Woman* (1970). In 1970, Bambara began teaching at Rutgers University, and in 1971 she published another anthology, *Tales and Stories for Black Folks*. In 1972 Bambara released her first book of short stories, *Gorilla, My Love*, which included the story "My Man Bovanne." In 1977, she published another book of short fiction, *The Sea Birds Are Still Alive*.

Despite her stated fondness for the short story over the novel, in 1980 she published *The Salt Eaters,* her first novel. She then switched her medium to film and in 1986 won an Academy Award for her documentary *The Bombing of Osage Avenue.* Bambara died of cancer in 1995. Two of her books have been published posthumously: *Deep Sightings and Rescue Missions: Fiction, Essays, and Conversations* (1996) and *Those Bones Are Not My Child* (1999).

In "What It Is I Think I'm Doing Anyhow," Bambara wrote, "Writing is one of the ways I practice the commitment to explore bodies of knowledge for the usable wisdoms they yield."

Donald Barthelme

A writer that Thomas Pynchon has called "notoriously uncategorizable," Donald Barthelme was born in 1931. He began publishing stories and poetry in 1948, while he was still in high school; later, while attending the University of Houston, he edited the campus newspaper and wrote film criticism for the *Houston Post.* Barthelme was drafted in 1953, and after completing his tour of duty in 1955 he accepted a job as director of the Contemporary Arts Museum in Houston. He left that position in 1962 and moved to New York to be managing editor of an arts review called *Location.* He published his first story in *Harper's* in 1961 before publishing his first *New Yorker* story, "L'Lapse." He wrote fiction almost exclusively for that publication for the next twenty years. His short fiction can be found in *Forty Stories* (1987) and *Sixty Stories* (1981), the latter of which won the PEN/Faulkner Award for fiction in 1981.

Barthelme had one daughter, for whom he wrote a children's story, *The Slightly Irregular Fire Engine, or the Hithering Thithering Djinn* (1971), which won the National Book Award in 1972. Toward the end of his life, Barthelme accepted a position as a professor at the University of Houston. His last major publication during his life was the novel *Paradise* (1986). He died in 1989 of cancer. Posthumous publications include *The Teachings of Don B* (1992) and *The King* (1990).

Barthelme once wrote, "The only forms I trust are fragments." A *New York Times Magazine* article published in 1970 titled "Freaked Out on Barthelme" said, "Almost all his stories, and in particular the later ones, are collages. Thus if you come away from one of his works confused, terribly aware of it as a jumble of images and ideas, you will have caught his basic drift." Barthelme himself said that the "principle of collage is the central principle of all art in the twentieth century."

Rick Bass

Rick Bass was born in Fort Worth, Texas, in 1958. The son of a geologist, he was always interested in the natural world, and he earned an undergraduate degree in geology at Utah State University in 1979. After graduation he moved to Mississippi, where he worked as an oil and gas geologist. He began writing stories on his lunch break, and after he read Jim Harrison's *Legends of the Fall* he quit to devote all his time to writing. Bass received the PEN/Nelson Algren Award in 1988 for his first short story, "The Watch." Bass currently lives in Montana, where, in addition to his writing, he works on environmental causes.

Bass is the author of twenty-one books, including *Where the Sea Used to Be* (1998), which won the James Jones Fellowship Award, and *Colter: The True Story of the Best Dog I Ever Had* (2000). His stories have been awarded the Pushcart Prize and the O. Henry Award and have been collected in several editions of *The Best American Short Stories.*

About his writing process, Bass once said, "Writers are guilty of overanalyzing or delighting in the technical part of a great story in the same way that a chef eating a great meal delights in knowing all the flavors and marveling at the way they all work together. But ultimately what makes a great story for the reader is the physical and emotional reactions it produces. It's that simple and that complex."

Madison Smartt Bell

Born in 1957 in Tennessee, Madison Smartt Bell earned his BA from Princeton in 1979 and an MA from Hollins College in 1981. He has taught in various creative writing programs, including the Iowa Writers' Workshop and the Johns Hopkins University Writing Seminars. He is currently head of the Goucher College Creative Program, where he has taught since 1984.

Bell's novels include *Waiting for the End of the World* (1985), *The Year of Silence* (1987), *Save Me* (1993), and *Soldier's Joy* (1989), which received the Lillian Smith Award in 1989. *All Souls' Rising* (1995), his eighth novel and the first in his Haitian Revolutionary trilogy, was a finalist for the 1995 National Book Award and the 1996 PEN/Faulkner Award, and winner of the 1996 Anisfield-Wolf Award for the best book of the year dealing with matters of race; *Master of the Crossroads* (2000) and *The Stone That the Builder Refused* (2004) are the final novels in the trilogy. His novel *Anything Goes* was published in 2002.

Bell's nonfiction includes *History of the Owen School: From Its Early Origins to 1984* (1985), *Narrative Design: A Writer's Guide to Structure* (1997), and *Narrative Design: Working with Imagination, Craft, and Form* (2000). His short fiction includes *Zero db and Other Stories* (1987) and *Barking Man and Other Stories* (1990).

As he makes clear in his book *Narrative Design,* Smartt Bell doesn't believe there is any single way to write a story. In an essay he wrote for the Goucher College Website, he said, "I tell students, 'You have read short stories in your lives. Go write one.' Then I see what they do. There is no one method."

Amy Bloom

Born in 1953, Amy Bloom was originally determined to be an actor, and she earned undergraduate degrees in theatre and political science. After marrying and having three children, Bloom went back to school and earned a social work degree, which led to her work as a psychotherapist. After ten years of practicing psychotherapy, Bloom turned to writing and almost immediately found success with her short fiction. Her first published story, "Love Is Not a Pie," was selected for *The Best American Short Stories 1991.* In 1993 she published her acclaimed short story collection *Come to Me,* which was selected as a finalist for both the National Book Award and The Los Angeles Times Fiction Award. Her other works include *Love Invents Us* (1998), a novel, and another collection of short stories, *A Blind Man Can See How Much I Love You* (2001), which was nominated for the National Book Critics Circle Award.

About her writing process, Bloom once said, "When I write fiction, I close my eyes and type. I pretend I have no parents, no spouse and no children. I tell myself that no one will ever read what I've written, that everyone will understand the conventions of fiction and know that the schizophrenic sister, the indifferent mother, the adulterous lovers are not me and not mine."

Frederick Busch

Frederick Busch was born in Brooklyn in 1941 and graduated from Columbia University in 1967. He published his first book, *I Wanted a Year without Fall*, in 1971, and he's since written more than twenty-five books, including *Don't Tell Anyone* (2000), *The Night Inspector* (1999), *The Children in the Woods* (1994), *Invisible Mending* (1984), and *Girls* (1997). Busch has won awards from the American Academy of Arts and Letters and is a recipient of the PEN/Malamud Award for short fiction. He has also been awarded the National Jewish Book Award, a Guggenheim fellowship, a grant from the National Endowment for the Arts, and a James Merrill fellowship.

In addition to his fiction, Busch has authored a number of books on writing: *Letters to a Fiction Writer* (1999), *A Dangerous Profession* (1998), and *When People Publish* (1986). He taught creative writing to undergraduates at Colgate University and retired three years before his death in 2006.

When asked for his advice to beginning writers, Busch said, "The most important component you can develop is energy, to get up at 5:30 in the morning. It's hard work, brutally hard work. And it's frustrating and you fail most of the time. Most of what a serious fiction writer does is fail. But in spite of rejection by yourself, your editors, agents, and readers—the first novel I published was the fourth I wrote—you have to keep going. That's the hardest part."

Robert Olen Butler

Robert Olen Butler was born in 1945 in Granite City, Illinois. He earned a BS in theatre from Northwestern University in 1967 and an MA in playwriting from the University of Iowa in 1969. Drafted into the army in 1969, he served in Vietnam until 1972. During his time there, he became fluent in Vietnamese and worked as an interpreter. Upon returning to the United States, he began writing fiction while he worked at a series of odd jobs to support himself, eventually working for trade publications such as *Electronic News* and *Energy User News*.

Although his first published novel, *The Alleys of Eden* (1981), was rejected twenty-one times before it was finally published, it was eventually nominated for a number of literary prizes. In 1982 Butler published *Sun Dogs*, which made use of his Vietnam experiences. His collection of short stories, *A Good Scent from a Strange Mountain* (1992), was awarded the 1993 Pulitzer Prize for fiction. Butler has also received a Guggenheim fellowship in fiction and an NEA grant, as well as the Richard and Linda Rosenthal Award from the American Academy of Arts and Letters. He currently teaches creative writing at Florida State University.

Butler said about the "literary artist" that "she does not know, before the work begins, what it is she sees about the world. She has in her unconscious, in her dreamspace, an inchoate sense of order behind the apparent chaos of life, and she must create this object in order to understand what that order is. It's as much an act of exploration as it is an act of expression."

Angela Carter

Angela Carter was born in 1940 in Eastbourne, Sussex, and attended Bristol University, where she studied medieval literature. After graduating, Carter stayed in Bristol, where she wrote her first books. These have become known as the Bristol trilogy: *Shadow Dance* (1966), *Several Perceptions* (1968), and *Love* (1971). Carter later was a teacher of writing at Sheffield University in England and at Brown University and the Iowa Writers' Workshop. She died of cancer in 1992.

Carter is known for her purposely grotesque work in novels like *The Infernal Desire Machines of Doctor Hoffman* (1972) and *The Passion of New Eve* (1977). Her early work also includes two collections of short stories: *Fireworks: Nine Profane Pieces* (1974) and *The Bloody Chamber and Other Stories* (1979). The latter, a collection of radical revisions of classic fairy tales such as "Red Riding Hood," "Bluebeard," and "Sleeping Beauty," made her famous in the United States. Her other novels include *The Magic Toyshop* (1967) and *Nights of the Circus* (1984).

Critics often describe Carter's writing style as "magic realism," but she herself did not like being labeled in this way. In a *New York Times* interview she said, "It's more realism than not. I can't define it until after it's done except that it is definitely fiction."

Raymond Carver

Raymond Carver was born in 1938 in Clatskanie, Oregon, and grew up in Yakima, Washington. He married after graduating from high school and had two children before he was twenty. While holding a number of jobs to support his family, Carver enrolled briefly in 1958 at Chico State College, in California, where he was highly influenced by a creative writing class taught by John Gardner. In 1963 he received his BA from Humboldt State College. His family life was turbulent, marked by alcoholism and marital squabbling, but by the age of forty he was widely considered to be one of the most talented writers of the time.

Carver's first collection of stories, *Will You Please Be Quiet Please* (1976), was nominated for the National Book Award in 1976. Four more collections of stories and five books of poetry followed. Carver was a Guggenheim Fellow in 1979 and was twice awarded grants from the National Endowment for the Arts. He was also awarded the Mildred and Harold Strauss Living Award and, in 1985, *Poetry* magazine's Levinson Prize. In 1988 he was elected to the American Academy and Institute of Arts and Letters and was awarded an honorary Doctorate of Letters from the University of Hartford. He received a Brandeis Citation for fiction in 1988, shortly before his death from cancer later that year.

About writing, Carver once wrote in an essay that "it's possible, in a poem or short story, to write about commonplace things and objects using commonplace but precise language, and to endow those things—a chair, a window, a curtain, a fork, a stone, a woman's earring—with immense, even startling power. It is possible to write a line of seemingly innocuous dialogue and have it send a chill along the reader's spine."

Dan Chaon

Dan Chaon is the author of *Fitting End and Other Stories* (1995), *You Remind Me of Me* (2004), and *Among the Missing* (2001), which was a finalist for the National Book Award. Chaon's short stories have won the Pushcart Prize and O. Henry Award and have been published in a number of journals and anthologies. He is a professor of creative writing at Oberlin College.

On his approach to writing, Chaon said in an interview in *The Believer*, "I think that the way I write stories is by instinct. You have some basic ideas—a character, or an image, or a situation that sounds compelling—and then you just feel your way around until you find the edges of your story. It's like going into a dark room . . . you stumble around until you find the walls and then inch your way to the light switch."

Anton Chekhov

Born in 1860 in Taganrog, Russia, the son of a grocer and the grandson of a serf, Anton Chekhov wrote his first stories while he was a medical student at Moscow University. His first literary works were humorous sketches of Moscow life that he published in minor magazines under the pen name Antosha Chekhonte. By 1882 he was a regular contributor to a number of humorous journals.

Chekhov published his first two collections of stories in 1886 and 1887, and by 1888 he was placing his stories in the more literary and respected journals in Moscow. He has since been acknowledged as one of the world's greatest storytellers, writing more than eight hundred stories that have broadly influenced the global writing community. Chekhov died of tuberculosis in a hotel bedroom in the German spa of Badenweiler in 1904.

Although criticized during his lifetime for focusing on trivialities instead of addressing important social issues, Chekhov chose to render what he saw in the world, without judgment. About this kind of criticism, Chekhov said, "You abuse me for objectivity, calling it indifference to good and evil, lack of ideals and ideas, and so on. You would have me, when I describe horse thieves, say, 'Stealing horses is an evil.' But that has been known for ages without my saying so. Let the jury judge them; it's my job simply to show what sort of people they are."

Sandra Cisneros

Born in Chicago in 1954, Sandra Cisneros grew up as the only girl in a household with six brothers. In 1976 she graduated with a BA in English from Loyola University of Chicago, after which she attended the Iowa Writers' Workshop.

After earning her MA at the University of Iowa, Cisneros returned to her native Chicago and worked at various jobs, many of them involving the Chicano community; she also returned to Loyola University as an administrative assistant. Her first book, *The House on Mango Street*, was published in 1984 and won the Before Columbus Foundation's American Book Award. Cisneros has twice won fellowships from the National Endowment for the Arts—one for poetry—and published her first book of poetry, *My Wicked, Wicked Ways*, in 1987. Her collection of short stories *Woman Hollering Creek* (1991) won the PEN Center West Award for Best Fiction of 1991 and was selected as a noteworthy book of the year by the *New York Times* and the *American Library Journal.* In 1995 Cisneros won a MacArthur Foundation Fellowship.

Cisneros once wrote, "If I were asked what it is I write about, I would have to say I write about those ghosts inside that haunt me, that will not let me sleep, of that which even memory does not like to mention."

Michael Cunningham

Michael Cunningham grew up in southern California and earned a BA from Stanford University in 1975. After college he traveled and worked at odd jobs while continuing to write, and eventually he attended the Iowa Writers' Workshop, graduating in 1980. His work began to be published in the *Atlantic Monthly* and other magazines while he was still in graduate school. In 1984 Cunningham published his first novel, *Golden State.* Although it received favorable reviews by critics, Cunningham himself was not pleased with the novel, saying in an interview with *Other Voices,* "I'm so much more interested in some kind of grand ambitious failure than I am in someone's modest little success that achieves its modest little aims. I felt that I had written a book like that, and I wasn't happy about it."

After graduation, Cunningham found employment as a secretary at the Carnegie Corporation while he worked on his second novel, *A Home at the End of the World* (1990). His best-selling 1998 novel, *The Hours,* based upon Virginia Woolf's *Mrs. Dalloway,* won the Pulitzer Prizer and the PEN/Faulkner award and was chosen as a Best Book of 1998 by the *New York Times* and the *Los Angeles Times.*

In addition to publishing short stories in major publications including the *New Yorker* magazine and *Paris Review,* Cunningham has written creative nonfiction articles for publications such as *Esquire, Vogue, Out,* and the *New York Times.* He's won numerous awards, including fellowships from the Whiting and Guggenhiem foundations. He currently lives in New York City.

Junot Díaz

Junot Díaz was born in 1968 in Santo Domingo, in the Dominican Republic, where he lived until he immigrated to the United States with his family at age six. He received his BA from Rutgers University and an MFA in creative writing from Cornell. His stories have been published in *Story* magazine, the *New Yorker* magazine, and *Paris Review.* His works include the short story collection *Drown* (1996) and the novel *The Brief Wondrous Life of Oscar Wao* (2007).

A recipient of a 1999 Guggenhiem fellowship, Díaz is a professor of creative writing at Syracuse University. Among the writers who have most influenced his work, Díaz includes Sandra Cisneros, Toni Morrison, and Denis Johnson, among others.

About his writing process, Díaz said in an interview, "Nothing takes the joy out for me like planning."

Barbara Gowdy

Barbara Gowdy was born in Windsor, Ontario, in 1950, but she moved to Toronto when she was four and grew up in the suburban town of Don Mills. She attended York University and the Royal Conservatory of Music and was involved in theatre until the 1980s, when she decided to pursue a career as a writer.

Her first novel, *Through the Green Valley*, was published in 1988, but Gowdy didn't receive critical recognition for her work until her second book, *Falling Angels*, was published in 1989. Her other books include a short story collection, *We So Seldom Look on Love* (1992), *Mister Sandman* (1995), and *The White Bone* (1999), which was nominated for the Giller Prize.

Stories by Gowdy have been included in a number of anthologies, including *The Best American Short Stories* (1989), *The New Oxford Book of Canadian Short Stories in English* (1995), and the *Penguin Anthology of Stories by Canadian Women* (1998). Gowdy has been a finalist for several literary awards, including the Trillium Award for *We So Seldom Look on Love* and the Trillium Award, the Giller Prize, and the Governor General's Award for *Mister Sandman*. In 1996 she was awarded the Marian Engel Award, which recognizes the complete body of work by a Canadian woman writer.

Gowdy's advice to beginning writers is to "read everything, especially the classics and poetry. Eavesdrop on real conversations. Don't watch too much TV, nobody talks like TV people do. Don't ever be too attached to anything you've written; you are the vehicle for the word, not its creator. Write what you're obsessed by."

Ron Hansen

Ron Hansen was born in 1947 in Omaha, Nebraska. After earning his BA in English from Creighton University, he spent two years in the army during the Vietnam War. He then earned his MFA from the University of Iowa and in 1979 published his first novel, *Desperados*. He is the author of five other novels: *Mariette in Ecstasy* (1991), *The Assassination of Jesse James by the Coward Robert Ford* (1983), *Atticus* (1996; it was a finalist for the 1996 National Book Award), *Hitler's Niece* (1999), and *Isn't It Romantic* (2003). His book of short stories, *Nebraska* (1989), earned him an award from the American Academy and National Institute of Arts and Letters. A book of essays called *A Stay against Confusion: Essays on Faith and Fiction* was published in 2001.

Among his many honors are a Guggenhiem Foundation grant, an Award in Literature from the American Academy and National Institute of Arts and Letters, two grants from the National Endowment for the Arts, and a three-year fellowship from the Lyndhurst Foundation. Hansen currently teaches English at the University of Santa Clara in California.

In an article in *Publishers Weekly*, Hansen said, "For me, the process of writing is the joy of writing. It's the putting down individual sentences, making them fit together, making the story interesting. Once you've completed a book, you realize how ramshackle a thing writing a novel is. You've somehow made it seem like it was always coherent. That's the satisfying aspect of writing, the really affirming thing about it."

Ernest Hemingway

Hemingway was born in 1899 in Oak Park, Illinois. The son of a doctor, he did not attend college. Instead, upon graduating from high school at age seventeen, he went to work as a reporter for the Kansas City *Star*. After the United States entered World War I, Hemingway volunteered for an ambulance unit in the Italian army. Serving at the front, he was wounded before he was nineteen and earned a decoration by the Italian government. He returned to the United States and continued to practice journalism, but soon he contrived to be sent back to Europe to cover European events. He eventually settled in Paris and became a core member of a group of expatriate American writers that included Gertrude Stein.

His first book, *In Our Time* (1925), was quickly followed up with *The Sun Also Rises* (1926), which he published to great success. His other novels include *A Farewell to Arms* (1929), *For Whom the Bell Tolls* (1940), and *The Old Man and the Sea* (1952). Hemingway has become celebrated for his stripped-down prose style, minimalist dialogue, and understatement. His short stories were published in numerous magazines and collected in *Men without Women* (1927) and *The Fifth Column and the First Forty-Nine Stories* (1938).

He explained his writing style as having to do with the "iceberg theory," according to which seven-eighths of a story could take place underwater as long as the writer possessed the relevant knowledge of situation and character. If any omission was due to ignorance on the part of the writer, Hemingway said, the omission would be felt by the reader.

Amy Hempel

Amy Hempel was born in 1951 in Chicago. As a teenager she moved to California, then attended a number of universities before deciding to be a writer and moving to New York City. There she attended Columbia University and studied with Gordon Lish, whose minimalist style greatly influenced her own.

In 1985 she published her first story collection, *Reasons to Live*, which won the Commonwealth Club of California Silver Medal. She is also the author of the collection *At the Gates of the Animal Kingdom* (1990), the novella *Tumble Home* (1997), and more recently, *The Dog of the Marriage* (2005). She also co-edited the anthology *Unleashed: Poems by Writer's Dogs* (1995) with Jim Shepard. Her stories have appeared in *Harper's*, *Vanity Fair*, *GQ*, and many other magazines, and they have been anthologized in *The Best American Short Stories*, *The Pushcart Prize XI*, and *The Norton Anthology of Short Fiction*, among others. Her nonfiction has appeared in such magazines as *Esquire*, *Elle*, *Vanity Fair*, the *New York Times Magazine*, and *Bomb*.

Hempel has won several literary awards for her work, including the Hobson Award and a Guggenheim fellowship. She has taught at a number of colleges and is currently a faculty member in the Graduate Writing Program at Bennington College in Vermont.

"I am really interested in resilience," Hempel told an interviewer. "Dr. Christiaan Barnard said, 'Suffering isn't ennobling, recovery is.'"

Denis Johnson

Denis Johnson was born in 1949 in Munich, West Germany. The son of an American diplomat, he had lived in Tokyo, Washington, D.C., Manila, and Munich by the time he was eighteen. He received a BA from the University of Iowa in 1971 and attended the Iowa Writers' Workshop. When he was nineteen, his first collection of poetry, *The Incognito Lounge*, was selected for the 1982 National Poetry Series. His works include the story collection *Jesus' Son* (1992) and the novels *Angels* (1983), *Fiskadora* (1985), *The Stars at*

Noon (1986), *Resuscitation of a Hanged Man* (1991), *Already Dead: A California Gothic* (1997), and *The Name of the World* (2000). Johnson has been awarded a number of NEA fellowships, a fellowship from the Fine Arts Work Center in Provincetown, Massachusetts, and a Whiting Writers Award for excellence in fiction and poetry. His work has appeared in *Paris Review*, the *New Yorker* magazine, and *McSweeney's*. In 2001 a collection of his creative nonfiction pieces, *Seek: Reports from the Edges of America and Beyond*, was published. He currently lives in northern Idaho.

About his writing process, Johnson has said, "I really enjoy writing novels. It's like the ocean. You can just build a boat and take off. I can't understand why anybody would criticize anything that ends up being a novel because you've arrived to the other shore, you've made it alive. Maybe you started off for Africa and ended up in Spain, but so what?"

Anne Lamott

Born in San Francisco in 1954, writer and essayist Anne Lamott has taught at the University of California at Davis and at writing conferences across the country. She is the subject of a 1999 documentary by Academy Award–winning filmmaker Freida Mock, *Bird by Bird with Annie.*

Lamott is the author of the national bestsellers *Traveling Mercies* (1999), *Bird by Bird* (1994), *Operating Instructions* (1993), and *Plan B: Further Thoughts on Faith* (2005), as well as six novels, including *Blue Shoe* (2002), *Hard Laughter* (1980), *Crooked Little Heart* (1997), and *Rosie* (1983). Her collection of essays *Grace (Eventually): Thoughts on Faith* was published in 2007. Lamott's column in *Salon* magazine, "Word by Word," was voted the Best of the Web by *Newsweek* magazine. A past recipient of a Guggenheim fellowship, she lives in Northern California with her son.

Gabriel García Márquez

Gabriel García Márquez was born in 1928 in the small town of Aracataca in Colombia. The oldest of twelve children, Márquez attended a Jesuit high school and originally studied law at the University of Bogotá, but he abandoned those studies in favor of journalism. Since going abroad on assignment in 1954, he has largely lived in self-imposed exile from his native country.

García Márquez's best-known work may be *One Hundred Years of Solitude*, which was published in 1967 to international acclaim. His other novels include *Chronicle of a Death Foretold* (1981), *Love in the Time of Cholera* (1985), *The General in His Labyrinth* (1989), and *Memories of My Melancholy Whores* (2004). The first volume of anticipated three-volume autobiography, *Living to Tell the Tale*, was published in Spanish in 2002 and translated into English in 2003. In 1982 García Márquez won the Nobel Prize for Literature.

Márquez believed that the fantastical is a critical aspect of mankind's everyday reality. He has said, "Fiction was invented the day Jonas arrived home and told his wife that he was three days late because he'd been swallowed by a whale."

James Alan McPherson

James Alan McPherson was born in 1943 in Savannah, Georgia. He was educated at Morgan State University, Morris Brown College, Harvard Law School, the University of

Iowa's Writers' Workshop, and Yale Law School. Now a professor of English at the University of Iowa, McPherson has also taught at the University of California, Santa Cruz, and at Harvard; he has lectured in Japan at Meiji University and Chiba University.

McPherson's short stories and essays have appeared in dozens of periodicals, and he has won numerous prizes for his writing, including a Guggenheim fellowship in 1973 and a Pulitzer Prize in 1978 for his novel *Elbow Room* (1977). In 2000 John Updike included McPherson's story "Gold Coast" in *The Best American Short Stories of the Century*.

Rick Moody

Born in 1961, Rick Moody earned his BA from Brown University in 1983 and his MFA from Columbia University in 1986. He worked as an editor at Farrar, Strauss and Giroux prior to becoming a published novelist.

Moody has won the Pushcart Editors' Book Award, a PEN American Center Award, and a Guggenheim fellowship. A prolific writer, his books include *Garden State* (1997), *The Ice Storm* (1994), *Ring of Brightest Angels around Heaven: A Novella and Stories* (1995), *Joyful Noise: The New Testament Revisited* (1997), *Demonology* (2001), and *The Black Veil* (2002). His short stories have appeared in the *New Yorker* magazine, *Esquire*, *Paris Review*, and *Harper's*.

About his work, Moody has said, "I think literature is best when it's voicing what we would prefer not to talk about. . . . Literature is about interior states and emotional states, about what people think that they don't always say to their neighbors. I'm drawn magnetically with my tangled long sentences to those spots people don't want to talk about."

Bharati Mukherjee

Bharati Mukherjee was born in Calcutta in 1940 to an upper-class family. When she was eight, the family moved to London, returning to India when she was eleven. Mukherjee earned her BA from the University of Calcutta in 1959 and her MA from the University of Baroda in 1961. She came to the United States to earn her doctorate at the University of Iowa, then moved to Canada, where she wrote her novels *The Tiger's Daughter* (1972) and *Wife* (1975). Mukherjee settled permanently in the United States in 1980, eventually becoming an American citizen. She was a professor of English at the City University of New York from 1987 to 1990, and since 1990 she has been a professor of English at the University of California, Berkeley.

Mukherjee's books include *Darkness* (1985), *The Middleman and Other Stories* (1988), *Jasmine* (1989), *The Holder of the World* (1993), and *Leave It to Me* (1997), as well as two works of nonfiction co-authored with her husband, Clark Blaise: *The Sorrow and the Terror* (1987) and *Days and Nights in Calcutta* (1977).

Mukherjee has been recognized for her rendering of complex cultural clashes experienced by North American immigrants who find themselves in unfamiliar settings. When asked by an online interviewer why she had chosen the life of a writer over one in politics, she said, "I live my most real life through writing."

Alice Munro

Alice Munro was born in 1931 in Wingham, Ontario, and grew up on a farm in a rural community near Lake Huron. At fifteen she decided she would soon write a great novel, "but I thought perhaps I wasn't ready so I would write a short story in the meantime," she said. She began publishing her stories when she was a student at the University of Western Ontario, which she attended for two years before leaving in 1951.

Munro has won three Governor General's Awards in Canada for *Dance of the Happy Hour* (1968), *Who Do You Think You Are?* (1978), and *The Progress of Love* (1986). Her other books include *Lives of Girls and Women* (1971), *Something I've Been Meaning to Tell You* (1974), *Open Secrets* (1994), *The Love of a Good Woman* (1998), and *Hateship, Friendship, Courtship, Loveship, Marriage* (2001). Munro cites as her major influence Eudora Welty, Carson McCullers, Katherine Anne Porter, Flannery O'Connor, James Agee, Peter Taylor, William Trevor, Edna O'Brien, and Richard Ford.

In her essay "What Is Real?" Munro wrote, "I don't take up a story and follow it as if it were a road, taking me somewhere, with views and neat diversions along the way. I go into it, and move back and forth and settle here and there, stay in it for a while. It's more like a house. Everybody knows what a house does, how it encloses space and makes connections between one enclosed space and another and presents what is outside in a new way. This is the nearest I can come to explaining what a story does for me, and what I want my stories to do for other people."

Joyce Carol Oates

Joyce Carol Oates was born in 1938 in Lockport, New York. She earned a BA in English from Syracuse University in 1960 and an MA from the University of Wisconsin in 1961. She is currently a professor of English at Princeton University. Oates's first book, the short-story collection *By the North Gate*, was published in 1963. Her first novel, *With Shuddering Fall*, was published in 1966. Her novel *them* (1969) received the National Book Award.

Oates has published nearly seventy-five books of fiction, poetry, and literary criticism. Her many novels include *A Garden of Earthly Delights* (1967, rev. ed. 2003), *Expensive People* (1968), *Wonderland* (1971), *Because It Is Bitter, and Because It Is My Heart* (1990), *What I Lived For* (1994), *Blonde* (2000), and *The Gravedigger's Daughter* (2007).

Her collections include *Heat and Other Stories* (1991), *Haunted: Tales of the Grotesque* (1994), *Will You Always Love Me and Other Stories* (1996), *Faithless: Tales of Transgression* (2001), and *Wild Nights* (2008). In 1996 Oates received the PEN/Malamud Prize for "a lifetime of literary achievement."

In an essay for the *New York Times*, Oates described the importance of running to her writing process. "Stories come to us as wraiths requiring precise embodiments. Running seems to allow me, ideally, an expanded consciousness in which I can envision what I'm writing as a film or a dream. I rarely invent at the typewriter but recall what I've experienced. I don't use a word processor but write in longhand, at considerable length. By the time I come to type out my writing formally, I've envisioned it repeatedly. I've never thought of writing as the mere arrangement of words on the page but as the attempted embodiment of a vision: a complex of emotions, raw experience."

Tim O'Brien

Tim O'Brien was born in 1946 in Austin, Minnesota, and earned his BA in political science at Macalester College. He was drafted upon graduating, and served in the Vietnam

War as an infantry foot soldier. He rose to the rank of sergeant and was awarded the Purple Heart. After returning from Vietnam, O'Brien enrolled in graduate school at Harvard to get a PhD in government, but after a stint as an intern at the *Washington Post* he left to become a full-time newspaper reporter.

O'Brien's career as a reporter transitioned to fiction writing after the 1973 publication of his memoir, *If I Die in a Combat Zone, Box Me Up and Send Me Home.* His other books include *Northern Lights* (1975); *Going after Cacciato* (1978), which won the National Book Award; *The Things They Carried* (1990), which was a finalist for the Pulitzer Prize; and *July, July* (2002).

O'Brien's short stories have appeared in *Esquire, Harper's, Atlantic, Playboy, GQ,* and the *New Yorker* magazine, and in several editions of *The O. Henry Prize Stories, The Pushcart Prize,* and *The Best American Short Stories.* O'Brien has been awarded fellowships from the Guggenheim Foundation and the National Endowment for the Arts.

O'Brien has said, "A good piece of fiction, in my view, does not offer solutions. Good stories deal with our moral struggles, our uncertainties, our dreams, our blunders, our contradictions, our endless quest for understanding. Good stories do not resolve the mysteries of the human spirit but rather describe and expand upon those mysteries."

Flannery O'Connor

Born in 1925 in Savannah, Georgia, the only child of deeply religious Catholic parents, Flannery O'Connor attended Georgia State College for Women, where she published stories and edited the literary magazine. After being awarded a scholarship to the Iowa Writers' Workshop, O'Connor earned her MFA in fiction in 1946. In 1947 her thesis story collection, *The Geranium,* won the Rinehart-Iowa Fiction Award, providing her with $750 and an option on her first novel, which she titled *Wise Blood* (1952). When *Wise Blood* was published to largely bad reviews, O'Connor returned to the short story form, which won her three O. Henry awards. In 1950 she was diagnosed with lupus, and she returned to Milledgeville, Georgia, to live with her mother on a 500-acre farm, where she lived for the rest of her life.

O'Connor won a number of grants and fellowships from such institutions as the National Institute of Arts and Letters and the Ford Foundation. Though she published just thirty-one stories, she had a reputation as a major writer by the end of the 1950s. She produced little fiction in the last years of life because of her failing health but she traveled and gave lectures, many of which were collected and published in 1969 in the book *Mystery and Manners.* Her *Complete Stories* (1971) won National Book Award for fiction in 1972.

Peter Orner

Peter Orner was born in Chicago in 1968 and graduated from the University of Michigan in 1990. After teaching in Namibia in the early 1990s, Orner received a law degree from Northeastern University and later an MFA from the Iowa Writers' Workshop. His work has been published in *Atlantic Monthly, Paris Review, McSweeny's,* and the *Southern Review,* among others. Set in Namibia, his novel, *The Second Coming of Mavala Shikongo* (2006) was a finalist for the Los Angeles Times Book Prize and won the Bard Fiction Prize.

His short story collection, *Esther Stories* (2001), was awarded the Rome Prize from the American Academy of Arts and Letters, as well as the Goldberg Prize for Jewish Fiction, and was a finalist for the PEN Hemingway Award. His stories have been anthologized in *The Best American Short Stories* and two editions of *The Pushcart Prize*. He has also been awarded fellowships from the Guggenheim and Lannan foundations. Currently, he is a professor of writing at San Francisco State University.

When asked about his favorite part of the writing process in an online interview, Orner said, "There are mornings when I literally lose time. When I look up and see that I've been sitting there for hours without knowing it—those days are the best."

ZZ Packer

ZZ Packer was born in Chicago in 1973 and grew up in Atlanta and Louisville, Kentucky. She attended Yale, Johns Hopkins University, and the Iowa Writers' Workshop, where she received her MFA in 1999. She was awarded a Guggenheim fellowship in fiction as well as a Wallace Stegner Fellowship at Stanford University, where she was also a Jones Lecturer. She currently lives in San Francisco.

Packer's short stories have been published in the *New Yorker* magazine, *Best American Short Stories 2000*, *Harper's*, and *Story* magazine, and in the anthology *25 and Under: Fiction*. Her collection *Drinking Coffee Elsewhere* was published in 2003.

Packer's advice for unpublished writers is to "plan for success and expect failure." On submitting work for publication, she said in an online interview, "I never expected anything to get taken, so when stories did start getting taken, I was always pleasantly surprised."

Francine Prose

Born in 1947 in Brooklyn, Francine Prose earned her BA at Radcliffe College in 1968. She has won a Guggenheim fellowship, a Fulbright grant, a Pushcart Prize, and the PEN Translation Prize. She is the author of more than twenty books, including thirteen books of fiction, among them *Bigfoot Dreams* (1986), *Household Saints* (1981), *Hunters and Gatherers* (1995), *Primitive People* (1992), and *Guided Tours of Hell* (1997). Her novel *Blue Angel* (2000) was a finalist for the National Book Award, and her book of creative nonfiction, *The Lives of the Muses: Nine Women and the Artists They Inspired* (2002), was a national bestseller and a New York Times Notable Book. Her short fiction and essays have appeared in the *New York Times*, the *New Yorker* magazine, *Atlantic Monthly*, *GQ*, and *Paris Review*; she is also a contributing editor at *Harper's* and writes about art for the *Wall Street Journal*. She has taught at the Iowa Writers' Workshop, the Sewanee Writers' Conference, and Johns Hopkins University. She lives in New York City.

About teaching in writing programs, Prose once said, "You can certainly teach people to edit their own work. You can teach people to pay attention to language. But you can't teach talent. Who knows what that is? The irony is that the really gifted ones don't need you at all and probably shouldn't be there."

Stacey Richter

Born in 1965 in Phoenix, Stacey Richter has won numerous Pushcart prizes and a National Prize for Fiction for her short stories. Her first story collection, *My Date with*

Satan (1999), was named a New York Times Notable Book. She regularly publishes in *Tin House, Zoetrope: All-Story,* and other literary journals. Her most recent book is *Twin Studies: Stories* (2007).

About her tendency to start her stories with striking, often shocking, opening lines, Richter has written, "I like things to start well. It is important to me. I think the first page or first paragraph should contain everything that's in the story thematically, and lots of times when I read a story I love I go back and read the first page again."

Akhil Sharma

Born in 1971 in Delhi, India, Akhil Sharma moved to New Jersey at the age of eight. He studied creative writing as an undergrad at Princeton before earning his BA in public policy. He then attended law school, later working as an investment banker in New York.

Sharma has had work published in both *Best American Short Stories* and *O. Henry Prize Stories,* as well as in the *Atlantic* and the *New Yorker* magazine. He was the recipient of a Wallace Stegner Fellowship from Stanford University. His first novel, *An Obedient Father* (2000), won the PEN/Hemingway Award.

When asked how he achieves the effects he wants in writing, Sharma said, "I wait a lot. I pause and revise. I try to be honest—I try to be very, very honest. If something feels false, I'll wait years for the right image to come to me. There are other techniques, like putting the noun and the verb near the center of a sentence, but those other things are probably the most important."

Mary Yukari Waters

Born in 1965 in Kyoto, Japan, Mary Yukari Waters is the daughter of a homemaker and a physicist. She moved to northern California at the age of nine, and after studying business in college, she worked as a certified public accountant before earning her MFA from the University of California, Irvine in 2002. She started to write fiction in her early thirties. Waters has won a Pushcart Prize, an O. Henry Award, and a grant from the National Endowment for the Arts. Her work has been published in numerous literary magazines. Waters's debut short story collection, *The Laws of Evening,* was published in 2003.

Regarding the late start of her writing career, Waters said in an interview, "Writing wasn't a hobby; I didn't even write my first story until I was almost thirty and happened to enroll in a night class on a whim. I hope others will keep in mind that it's never too late in life to discover a hidden interest or talent, and that once you discover it, it's never too late to pursue it."

John Edgar Wideman

John Edgar Wideman was born in 1951 in Washington, D.C., but he grew up in Pittsburgh, Pennsylvania. He attended the University of Pennsylvania on a scholarship and was a successful athlete even as he was winning creative writing contests for his fiction. Upon graduating in 1963, Wideman won a Rhodes scholarship that allowed him to study at Oxford University. He is currently a professor of English at the University of Massachusetts, Amherst.

Wideman wrote his first novel, *A Glance Away* (1967), while attending the Writer's Workshop at the University of Iowa. His other novels include *Two Cities* (1998), *The*

Lynchers (1973), *Sent for You Yesterday* (1983), *Philadelphia Fire* (2005), and *The Cattle Killing* (1996). He is the author of the memoir *Brothers and Keepers* (1984), and his short story collections include *Fever* (1989), *The Stories of John Edgar Wideman* (1992), and *All Stories are True* (1993).

Wideman is the only two-time recipient of the PEN/Faulkner Award for fiction. His other awards include the Rea Award for the short story (1990), the American Book Award for Fiction (1990), the Lannan Literary Fellowship for Fiction (1991), and the MacArthur Award (1993).

On his inspiration for writing, Wideman once said, "I've always been drawn to the craft of language. The classical Greeks, Ralph Ellison, Norman Mailer. And I've learned from the oral tradition—listening to my mother's stories, from the music of the blues, from slave narrations, from the magic of a preacher. I value the world. I respond to it as a writer."

Tobias Wolff

Born in 1945 in Birmingham, Alabama, Tobias Wolff grew up in the Skagit River Valley of Washington State. He spent four years in the army, including a tour of duty in Vietnam that ended in 1968. After graduating from Oxford University in 1972, Wolff held a number of jobs until he was awarded a writing fellowship at Stanford University in 1975. His first novel, *Ugly Rumors*, was published in 1975, and although his first two collections of short stories, *In the Garden of North American Martyrs* (1981) and *Back in the World* (1985), were both well received, it was *This Boy's Life* (1989), a memoir about growing up with a restless mother and an absent father, that made Wolff famous. He has since published *In Pharaoh's Army: Memoirs of the Lost War* (1994), a memoir of his experiences in Vietnam; *The Night in Question* (1996), another collection of short stories; and the novels *The Barracks Thief* (1984), which won the 1985 PEN/Faulkner Award; and *Old School* (2003).

Wolff has received numerous other awards, including the Los Angeles Times Book Prize, the Academy Award in Literature from the American Academy of Arts and Letters, two National Endowment for the Arts fellowships, a Guggenheim fellowship, and three O. Henry awards. He currently teaches at Stanford.

About the difference between short stories and novels, Wolff said, "I believe that the short story is as different a form from the novel as poetry is, and the best stories seem to me to be perhaps closer in spirit to poetry than to novels. They have to be; there just can't be any kind of relaxation of the narrative. Everything has to be pulling weight in a short story for it to be really of the first order. And you can't do that with a novel. A novel invites digression and a little relaxation of the grip because a reader can't endure being held that tightly in hand for so long a time."

Glossary

ABSTRACT Possessing qualities apart from those of an object. Referring to intangible attributes, like love, death, happiness, rather than concrete ones, like frog, desk, or chair.

ATMOSPHERE The mood of a piece, related to setting. It can include everything from descriptions of place, to weather, to time of day.

BACKSTORY The history of a character or characters as relevant to the present events of a story.

CHARACTER An imagined person. Considered one of the key ingredients of fiction.

CHARACTER-BASED FICTION Fiction that focuses on characters and the human condition rather than on examinations of the nature of writing or fictional processes.

CLICHÉ An overused, familiar phrase, often of figurative language, that has lost its ability to convey meaning due to excessive use.

CLIMAX The moment when all the conflict in a story culminates in a crisis point, after which the action falls and things in the narrative are resolved.

COMPLICATION That aspect of plot that creates tension and sustains the reader's interest, frequently leading to a climax, or epiphany. Often used as a synonym for conflict.

CONCEIT An extended comparison of two very unlike things that generally requires elaboration and explanation to be fully understood.

CONCRETE Referring to particular objects, people, or events rendered with one or more of the five senses. The opposite of abstract.

CONFLICT Tension arising from opposing forces; considered necessary by some to sustain a reader's interest. Others feel that this word doesn't adequately describe all the nuanced ways in which a writer can hold the reader's attention.

CONVENTION An accepted means of expression within a particular form.

CRISIS The point of highest tension in a narrative. The moment after which the conflict in the narrative comes to a resolution. Also known as the climax.

DEAD METAPHOR A metaphor that has been so overused that it has been absorbed into our language; the comparison is no longer fresh or surprising. For example, "he ran for office" no longer evokes the image of someone actually running.

DENOUEMENT The falling action, following a climax or crisis, after which things in a narrative are resolved.

DIALOGUE Words spoken between two or more characters in a scene.

DISTANCE The sense of how close the narrator is to the characters or the action in a narrative.

EPIPHANY A literary revelation, or lifting of appearances in order to reveal meaning and truth. A moment of realization by a character, or the reader, or both.

EXPOSITION Explanation, usually through narration, of information essential to the story.

FALLING ACTION Denouement, or the wrapping up of loose ends that follows the climax or crisis of a narrative.

FICTION Imagined events presented as if true in a narrative. Can be a novel, a novella, or a short story.

FLASHBACK Scene of a prior event juxtaposed against a current scene. Usually triggered by a current event or by a character's memory.

IMAGE Anything that has been rendered by any one (or more) of the five senses. Images are the building blocks of fiction.

IRONY An apparent contradiction or incongruity that dissembles or hides a "truth," not to deceive, but to achieve an effect. In *dramatic irony*, the reader knows something the character doesn't.

MELODRAMA Extravagant theatricality, and action dominating over characterization. From the Greek *melo*, for song; melodrama originally referred to any drama that was set to music.

METAFICTION Fiction that examines fictional processes, conventions, or craft. Frequently the text is self-referential, or self-conscious in the sense that the characters (or narrators) are aware that they are in the middle of writing a fictional work. John Barth's "Lost in the Funhouse" is an example.

METAPHOR A direct comparison of two unlike things. "The dog days of August" is a metaphor.

NARRATION The events and characters that constitute a story.

NARRATOR The character or voice that is telling the story. Can be first person, second person, or third person (see point of view).

OMNISCIENT NARRATOR A godlike intelligence that knows everything about the universe of the story or novel.

PERSONIFICATION The technique of giving human traits to natural objects.

PLOT The series of events or actions that make up the story, arranged in a specific order, and told in a particular way by a narrator.

Point of view The perspective from which the events of the story are narrated. Can be first person, second person, or third person.

Resolution The point at which the story's elements come together in an emotionally satisfying way.

Rising Action In a traditional story or novel, those plot points that steadily increase the tension of a piece until it reaches its climax.

Scene A dramatic episode in a story that takes place between specific characters in a particular setting.

Scènes à Faire French for "scenes to make." A legal term referring to scenes or parts of the plot that are conventionally expected in treatments of a particular topic.

Sentimentality An excess of sentiment, or feeling, that hasn't been "earned" by a story or novel. A clichéd or overly familiar rendering of events or circumstances rather than a rendition that is fresh and surprising.

Setting The location and time in which a story or novel occurs. The physical surroundings, as described by a narrator.

Short story A work of prose with no minimum length and (usually) not exceeding 20,000 words.

Simile A comparison of two unlike things, using "like" or "as." "My love is like a red red rose" and "She had a face as round and as innocent as a cabbage" are similes.

Stereotype A clichéd or stock character familiar to the reader through a standard set of traits. The prostitute with the heart of gold and the browbeaten husband are two examples of stock characters that appear in fiction.

Style The distinctive techniques or methods used by a writer to approach elements like point of view, syntax, and imagery that contribute to his or her unique voice.

Subtext Meaning that is implied rather than stated. All text has a subtext—the meaning that lies beneath the actual words.

Suspense Sense of apprehension, or feeling that something of dramatic importance is about to happen. The state of being uncertain, unresolved.

Symbol A concrete object or image that has a meaning beyond its literal sense, or that stands for something beyond itself. The white whale in *Moby-Dick* stands for something forbidden that mankind should not attempt to pursue or possess.

Tension The juxtaposition of two opposing forces.

Voice The specific way that a writer expresses himself or herself in writing, depending on decisions he or she makes about style, technique, and the material he or she chooses to explore.

Bibliography

Alvarez, Julia. "The Rudy Elmenhurst Story." In *How the Garcia Girls Lost Their Accents.* Chapel Hill, NC: Algonquin Books, 1991.

Anderson, Sherwood. "Death in the Woods." In *Winesburg, Ohio.* New York: Bantam, 1995.

———. "Hands." In *Winesburg, Ohio.* New York: Bantam, 1995.

Atwood, Margaret. "Significant Moments in the Life of My Mother." In *Bluebeard's Egg.* Toronto: McClelland & Stewart Bantam, 1983.

Austen, Jane. *Pride and Prejudice.* New York: Penguin, 1996.

Baldwin, James. "Sonny's Blues." In *Going to Meet the Man.* New York: Dial Press, 1965.

Bambara, Toni Cade. "My Man Bovanne." In *Gorilla, My Love.* New York: Vintage, 1992.

Barrie, James. *Peter Pan.* New York: Henry Holt, 1987.

———. *Peter Pan.* New York: Oxford University Press, 1995.

Barthelme, Donald. "Me and Miss Mandible." In *Sixty Stories.* New York: Penguin, 2003.

———. "Not Knowing." In *Not-Knowing: The Essays and Interviews of Donald Barthelme.* New York: Vintage, 1999.

———. "The Sandman." In *Sixty Stories.* New York: Penguin, 2003.

Bass, Rick. "An Oilman's Notebook." In *Oil Notes.* Dallas: Southern Methodist University Press, 1995.

———. "Wild Horses." In *The Watch.* New York: W. W. Norton, 1989.

Baxter, Charles. "Against Epiphanies." In *Burning Down the House: Essays on Fiction.* St. Paul, MN: Graywolf Press, 1997.

———. "On Defamiliarization." In *Burning Down the House: Essays on Fiction.* St. Paul, MN: Graywolf Press, 1997.

Beattie, Ann. "The Cinderella Waltz." In *The Burning House.* New York: Vintage, 1995.

———. "Find and Replace." In *Follies: New Stories.* New York: Scribner, 2005.

Beckett, Samuel. "Krapp's Last Tape." In *Krapp's Last Tape, and Other Dramatic Pieces.* New York: Grove Press, 1957.

Bell, Madison Smartt. "Customs of the Country." In *Barking Man and Other Stories.* New York: Ticknor and Fields, 1990.

———. *Narrative Design: A Writer's Guide to Structure.* New York: W. W. Norton, 1997.

Berriault, Gina. "Who Is It Can Tell Me Who I Am?" In *Women in Their Beds.* Washington, DC: Counterpoint, 1996.

Bishop, Elizabeth. "Letter to NY (for Louise Crane)." In *The Complete Poems: 1927–1979.* New York: Farrar, Straus & Giroux, 1983.

Bloom, Amy. "Silver Water." In *Come to Me.* New York: HarperPerennial, 1993.

Bowles, Jane. *Two Serious Ladies.* 1943. In *My Sister's Hand in Mine: The Collected Works of Jane Bowles.* New York: Farrar, Straus & Giroux, 1966.

Boyle, T. Coraghessan. "Friendly Skies." In *After the Plague and Other Stories.* New York: Viking Penguin, 2001.

Burgess, Anthony. *A Clockwork Orange.* New York: W. W. Norton, 1962.

Busch, Frederick. "Ralph the Duck." In *Absent Friends.* New York: Alfred A. Knopf, 1989.

Butler, Robert Olen. "A Good Scent from a Strange Mountain." In *A Good Scent from a Strange Mountain.* New York: Henry Holt, 1992.

Carter, Angela. "The Company of Wolves." In *The Bloody Chamber.* New York: Penguin, 1990.

Carver, Raymond. "The Bath." In *What We Talk about When We Talk about Love.* New York: Alfred A. Knopf, 1981.

———. "Cathedral." In *Cathedral.* New York: Alfred A. Knopf, 1983.

———. *Fires.* New York: Vintage, 1989.

———. "A Small, Good Thing." In *Cathedral.* New York: Alfred A. Knopf, 1983.

Cather, Willa. "Paul's Case: A Study in Temperament." In *The Troll Garden,* edited by James Woodress. Lincoln: University of Nebraska Press, 2000.

Chaon, Dan. "The Bees." In *McSweeney's Mammoth Treasury of Thrilling Tales,* edited by Michael Chabon. New York: Vintage, 2003.

Cheever, John. "Interview with John Cheever." *Paris Review* 67, Fall 1976.

———. "The Swimmer." In *The Stories of John Cheever.* New York: Alfred A. Knopf, 1978.

———. "The Wrysons." In *The Stories of John Cheever.* New York: Alfred A. Knopf, 1978.

Chekhov, Anton. "The Lady with the Little Dog." In *Stories,* translated by Richard Pevear and Larissa Volokhonsky. New York: Bantam, 2001.

Cisneros, Sandra. "Woman Hollering Creek." In *Woman Hollering Creek and Other Stories.* New York: Random House, 1991.

Coe, Christopher. *I Look Divine.* New York: Random House, 1998.

Costello, Mark. "Murphy's Xmas." In *The Murphy Stories.* Champaign, IL: Illini Books, 1973.

Crane, Stephen. "The Open Boat." In *The Open Boat and Other Stories.* New York: Doubleday & McClure, 1898.

Cunningham, Michael. "White Angel." In *A Home at the End of the World.* New York: Farrar, Straus & Giroux, 1990.

Davies, Robertson. *Fifth Business.* New York: Penguin, 1977.

DeMarinis, Rick. *The Art and the Craft of the Short Story.* Cincinnati, OH: Story Press Books, 2000.

Díaz, Junot. "Fiesta, 1980." In *Drown.* New York: Riverhead Books, 1996.

———. "The Sun, the Moon, the Stars." In *The Best American Short Stories 1999,* edited by Katrina Kenison and Amy Tan. Boston: Houghton Mifflin, 1999.

———. "Ysrael." In *Drown.* New York: Riverhead Books, 1996.

Dixon, Stephen. *Interstate.* New York: Owl Books, 1997.

Drabble, Margaret. *The Waterfall.* New York: Random House, 1969.

Dubus, Andre. "A Father's Story." In *Selected Stories.* Boston: David R. Godine, 1988.

Dybek, Stuart. "Pet Milk." In *Coast of Chicago.* New York: Alfred A. Knopf, 1990.

———. "We Didn't." In *I Sailed with Magellan.* New York: Picador, 2003.

Ellison, Jan. "The Company of Men." *New England Review* 26, no. 4, 2005.

Ellison, Ralph. *Invisible Man.* New York: Random House, 1947.

———. "King of the Bingo Game." *Tomorrow,* November 1944.

Erdrich, Louise. *Four Souls: A Novel.* New York: HarperCollins, 2004.

Eugenides, Jeffrey. *The Virgin Suicides.* New York: Warner Books, 1994.

Faulkner, William. *As I Lay Dying.* New York: Vintage, 1991.

———. "A Rose for Emily." In *The Collected Stories.* New York: Vintage, 1977.

———. *The Sound and the Fury.* New York: Vintage, 1991.

Fitzgerald, F. Scott. *The Great Gatsby.* New York: Scribner, 2003.

Flaubert, Gustave. "A Simple Heart." In *Three Tales,* translated by Robert Baldick. London: Penguin, 1961.

Ford, Richard. "Rock Springs." In *Rock Springs.* New York: Grove / Atlantic, 1987.

Forster, E. M. *Aspects of the Novel.* Orlando, FL: Harcourt, 1927.

———. *Howards End.* New York: Alfred A. Knopf, 1921.

Friend, Tad. "Copy Cats." *New Yorker,* September 14, 1998.

Gallant, Mavis. "Bernadette." In *My Heart Is Broken.* New York: Random House, 1964.

Gardner, John. *The Art of Fiction.* New York: Alfred A. Knopf, 1984.

Gass, William. "In the Heart of the Heart of the Country." In *In the Heart of the Heart of the Country and Other Stories.* Boston: David R. Godine, 1984.

Gawande, Atul. "Final Cut." *New Yorker,* March 19, 2001.

Glaspell, Susan. "A Jury of Her Peers." In *The Best Short Stories of 1917,* edited by Edward J. O'Brien. Boston: Small, Maynard, 1918.

Godshalk, C. S. "The Wizard." *Agni* 28, 1989.

Gowdy, Barbara. "Disneyland." In *Falling Angels.* New York: Soho Press, 1989.

Grant, Annette. "Interview with John Cheever." *Paris Review* 67, Fall 1976.

Hanna, Barry. "Testimony of Pilot." In *Airships.* New York: Grove / Atlantic, 1970.

Hansen, Ron. "Nebraska." In *Nebraska: Stories.* New York: Grove / Atlantic, 1989.

Hass, Robert. *20th Century Pleasures.* New York: HarperCollins, 1984.

Hemingway, Ernest. "Hills Like White Elephants." In *Men without Women.* New York: Scribner, 1927.

Hempel, Amy. "In the Cemetery Where Al Jolson Is Buried." In *Reasons to Live.* New York: Alfred A. Knopf, 1985.

Hugo, Richard. *The Triggering Town.* New York: W. W. Norton, 1979.

Isherwood, Christopher. "Goodbye to Berlin." In *Berlin Stories*. New York: New Directions, 1963.

James, Henry. "The Art of Fiction." *Longman's Magazine* 4 (Sept. 1884). Reprinted in *Partial Portraits*. New York: Macmillan, 1888.

———. "Four Meetings." In *Complete Stories: 1874–1884*. New York: Literary Classics of the United States, 1999.

Johnson, Denis. "Dirty Wedding." In *Jesus' Son*. New York: Farrar, Straus & Giroux, 1992.

———. "Emergency." In *Jesus' Son*. New York: Farrar, Straus & Giroux, 1992.

Joyce, James. "Araby." In *Dubliners*. New York: Penguin, 2000.

Kafka, Franz. "The Metamorphosis." In *The Metamorphosis*, translated and edited by Stanley Corngold. New York: Bantam, 1972.

Kennedy, William. *Ironweed*. New York: Viking Penguin, 1983.

Kesey, Ken. *One Flew over the Cuckoo's Nest*. New York: Viking, 1962.

Kincaid, Jamaica. "Girl." In *At the Bottom of the River*. New York: Farrar, Straus & Giroux, 1983.

Kingsolver, Barbara. *Animal Dreams*. New York: HarperCollins, 1990.

Kittredge, William. "Redneck Secrets." In *Owning It All*. St. Paul, MN: Graywolf Press, 2002.

Kotzwinkle, William. "Follow the Eagle." In *Elephant Bangs Train*. New York: Equinox, 1974.

Lamott, Anne. "Shitty First Drafts." In *Bird by Bird: Some Instructions on Writing and Life*. New York: Pantheon, 1994.

Larkin, Philip. "The Pleasure Principle." In *Required Writing: Miscellaneous Pieces 1955–1982*. Ann Arbor: University of Michigan Press, 1999.

Leavitt, David. "Territory." In *Family Dancing*. Boston: Houghton Mifflin, 1984.

Le Guin, Ursula K. "The New Atlantis." In *The Blind Geometer / The New Atlantis* (Tor Double Novel, No. 13). Stuttgart, Germany: Tor Books, 1989.

Lessing, Doris. "A Sunrise on the Veld." In *African Stories*. New York: Simon & Schuster, 1951.

Macauley, Robie, and George Lanning. *Technique in Fiction*. 2nd ed. New York: St. Martin's Press, 1990.

Madden, David. "No Trace." In *The Shadow Knows*. Baton Rouge: Louisiana State University Press, 1970.

Mamet, David. "The Museum of Science and Industry Story." In *Five Television Plays*. New York: Grove Press, 1990.

Mansfield, Katherine. "Bliss." In *Bliss and Other Stories*. Hertfordshire, Great Britain: Wordsworth, 1998.

———. "Daughters of the Late Colonel." In *The Garden Party, and Other Stories*. New York: Alfred A. Knopf, 1922.

Márquez, Gabriel García. "A Very Old Man with Enormous Wings." In *Leaf Storm and Other Stories*, translated by Gregory Rabassa. New York: Harper Collins, 2003.

Matthiessen, Peter. *Far Tortuga: A Novel*. New York: Vintage, 1988.

Maxwell, William. "The Thistles in Sweden." In *All the Days and Nights: The Collected Stories of William Maxwell.* New York: Alfred A. Knopf, 1995.

McConkey, James. *Court of Memory.* Boston: Nonpareil Books, 1993.

McInerney, Jay. *Bright Lights, Big City.* New York: Vintage, 1984.

McMurtry, Larry. *Terms of Endearment.* New York: Simon & Schuster, 1975.

McPherson, James Alan. "A Loaf of Bread." In *Elbow Room.* New York: Little, Brown and Company, 1977.

Michaels, Leonard. "Journal Entries: 1976–1987." In *Our Private Lives: Journals, Notebooks, and Diaries,* edited by Daniel Halpern. New York: Ecco Press, 1988.

Milosz, Czeslaw. "In a Parish." Translated by Robert Haas. In *New and Collected Poems.* New York: HarperCollins, 2001.

Moody, Rick. "Boys." In *Demonology.* New York: Little, Brown and Company, 2001.

Moore, Lorrie. "How to Be a Writer." In *Self-Help.* New York: Alfred A. Knopf, 1985.

Mukherjee, Bharati. "The Management of Grief." In *The Middleman and Other Stories.* New York: Grove Press, 1988.

———. "The Tenant." In *The Middleman and Other Stories.* New York: Grove Press, 1988.

Munro, Alice. "Save the Reaper." In *The Love of a Good Woman.* New York: Vintage, 1999.

———. "Wild Swans." In *The Beggar Maid: Stories of Flo and Rose.* New York: Alfred A. Knopf, 1977.

Nabokov, Vladimir. *Lolita.* London: Everyman, 1992.

Nelson, Antonya. "Naked Ladies." In *Family Terrorists.* New York: Scribner, 1996.

Neubauer, Alexander. "A Conversation with Jane Smiley." In *Conversations on Writing Fiction: Interviews with Thirteen Distinguished Teachers of Fiction Writing in America.* New York: HarperPerennial, 1994.

Oates, Joyce Carol. Introduction to *The Oxford Book of American Short Stories.* New York: Oxford University Press, 1994.

———. "Where Are You Going, Where Have You Been?" In *Where Are You Going, Where Have You Been? Stories of Young America.* Greenwich, CT: Fawcett, 1974.

O'Brien, Tim. "The Things They Carried." In *The Things They Carried.* Boston: Houghton Mifflin, 1990.

O'Connor, Flannery. "Everything That Rises Must Converge." In *Everything That Rises Must Converge.* New York: Farrar, Straus & Giroux, 1965.

———. "Writing Short Stories." In *Mystery and Manners: Occasional Prose,* edited by Sally and Robert Fitzgerald. New York: Farrar, Straus & Giroux, 1969.

O'Hara, Frank. "Why I Am Not a Painter." In *The Collected Poems of Frank O'Hara,* edited by Donald Allen. New York: Alfred A. Knopf, 1979.

Olds, Sharon. "Forty-One, Alone, No Gerbil." In *The Wellspring.* New York: Alfred A. Knopf, 1996.

Ondaatje, Michael. *The English Patient.* New York: Alfred A. Knopf, 1992.

———. *Running in the Family.* New York: Vintage, 1993.

———. "7 or 8 Things I Know about Her—A Stolen Biography." In *The Cinnamon Peeler.* New York: Alfred A. Knopf, 1989.

Orner, Peter. "The Raft." In *Esther Stories.* New York: Mariner Books, 2001.

Packer, ZZ. "Brownies." In *Drinking Coffee Elsewhere.* New York: Riverhead Books, 2003.

Paley, Grace. "A Conversation with My Father." In *Enormous Changes at the Last Minute.* New York: Farrar, Straus & Giroux, 1974.

———. "Mother." In *Later the Same Day.* New York: Farrar, Straus & Giroux, 1985.

Phillips, Jayne Anne. "Souvenir." In *Black Tickets.* New York: Delacorte Press, 1979.

Plath, Sylvia. "Tulips." In *The Collected Poems,* edited by Ted Hughes. New York: Harper-Collins, 1981.

Prose, Francine. "What Makes a Short Story?" In *On Writing Short Stories,* edited by Tom Bailey. New York: Oxford University Press, 1999.

Proulx, Annie. "Brokeback Mountain." In *Close Range: Wyoming Stories.* New York: Scribner, 2000.

———. *The Shipping News.* New York: Touchstone Books, 1994.

Rhys, Jean. *Wide Sargasso Sea.* New York: W. W. Norton, 1966.

Richards, I. M. *Practical Criticism: A Study of Literary Judgement.* Orlando, FL: Harcourt, Brace, 1929.

Richter, Stacey. "My Date with Satan." In *My Date with Satan.* New York: Scribner, 1999.

Schulman, Sarah. *After Delores.* New York: New American Library, 1989.

Scott, Paul. "Method: The Mystery and the Mechanics." In *On Writing and the Novel.* London: William Morrow, 1987.

Shakespeare, William. *The Complete Sonnets and Poems,* edited by Colin Burrow. New York: Oxford University Press, 2002.

———. *Hamlet.* New York: Washington Square Press, 2003.

Sharma, Akhil. "Surrounded by Sleep." *New Yorker,* December 13, 2001.

Shelton, Richard. "The Stones." In *Selected Poems 1969–1981.* Pittsburgh: University of Pittsburgh Press, 1982.

Shepard, Jim. "I Know Myself Real Well. That's the Problem." In *Bringing the Devil to His Knees: The Craft of Fiction and the Writing Life,* edited by Charles Baxter and Peter Turchi. Ann Arbor: University of Michigan Press, 2004.

Smiley, Jane. "A Conversation with Jane Smiley." In Alexander Neubauer, *Conversations on Writing Fiction: Interviews with Thirteen Distinguished Teachers of Fiction Writing in America.* New York: HarperPerennial, 1994.

———. *A Thousand Acres.* New York: Alfred A. Knopf, 1991.

Spark, Muriel. *A Far Cry from Kensington.* New York: New Directions, 2000.

Stone, Robert. "Helping." In *Bear and His Daughter.* Boston: Houghton Mifflin, 1997.

Tan, Amy. *The Joy Luck Club.* New York: Penguin Putnam, 1989.

Tolstoy, Leo. *Anna Karenina.* Translated by Constance Garnett. New York: Random House, 1965.

Waters, Mary Yukari. "Aftermath." In *The Laws of Evening.* New York: Scribner, 2003.

Weldon, Fay. *Remember Me.* London: Hodder & Stoughton, 1976.

Wideman, John Edgar. "Fever." In *Fever.* New York: Henry Holt, 1989.

Williams, Joy. "Taking Care." In *Taking Care.* New York: Random House, 1982.

Wolff, Tobias. "Bullet in the Brain." In *The Night in Question.* New York: Knopf, 1996.

———. "The Rich Brother." In *Back in the World.* Boston: Houghton Mifflin, 1985.

———. "What Is a Short Short?" In *Sudden Fiction: American Short Short Stories,* edited by Robert Shapard and James Thomas. Layton, UT: Gibbs M. Smith, 1986.

Woolf, Virginia. *The Years.* Orlando, FL: Harcourt, Brace, 1937.

Wright, C. D. "Scratch Music." In *Steal Away: Selected and New Poems.* Port Townsend, WA: Copper Canyon Press, 2002.

Permissions

Index

ABCDE formula, 106, 371
abstraction
  defined, 62, 398, 591
  generalization vs., 62–63
  specificity vs., 62
  transference vs., 398–99
action
  character revealed through, 331–32
  falling, 99, 592
  in openings, 371–72
  plot points and, 333
  rising, 99, 593
  as showing, 148
After Delores (Schulman), 403
"Aftermath" (Waters), 388–96
"Against Epiphanies" (Baxter), 103
Alexander v. Haley, 287
Alvarez, Julia, 333–34
American Heritage Dictionary, The, 96, 147, 150
analysis, as telling, 148
Andersen, Hans Christian, 110
Anderson, Sherwood, 32, 331, 332
Animal Dreams (Kingsolver), 239–40
Anna Karenina (Tolstoy), 337
"A & P" (Updike), 102, 114, 116
"Araby" (Joyce), 102
Aristotle, 97, 102
Art and the Craft of the Short Story, The
    (DeMarinis), 106–7
Art of Fiction, The (Gardner), 64–65, 203, 282,
    373
"Art of Fiction, The" (James), 98
As I Lay Dying (Faulkner), 5

Aspects of the Novel (Forster), 3, 278–79, 283,
    367–68
Atlantic Monthly, 486
atmosphere, 591
attention to detail
  crowding out the reader, 68–69
  exercises, 75–78
  generalizations vs., 62, 66–68
  imagery, 63–66, 73–75
  metaphors, 69–72
  sensory experience and, 69, 399–400
  symbols, 72–73
  thinking small, 61–63
attribution of dialogue, 260
Atwood, Margaret, 401
Austen, Jane, 197–98

Babel, Isaac, 109
backstory, 148, 334, 591
Baldwin, James
  about, 575
  "Sonny's Blues," 114, 115, 116, 284–86, 290–312
Bambara, Toni Cade, 273–77, 575–76
Barrie, J. M., 154–56
Barth, John, 281
Barthelme, Donald
  about, 576
  Carver and, 31
  "Me and Miss Mandible," 491–99
  metafiction and, 281
  "Not Knowing," 105
  "Sandman, The," 195
  on short stories, 96

Bass, Rick
    about, 576–77
    "Oilman's Notebook, An," 37–38
    "Wild Horses," 499–512
"Bath, The" (Carver), 432, 458–63
Baxter, Charles, 103, 283–84
Beattie, Ann, 31, 328
Beckett, Samuel, 63, 117
"Bees, The" (Chaon), 220–33
Bell, Madison Smartt
    about, 577
    "Customs of the Country," 376–88
    Narrative Design, 101–2, 430
Berge, Claude, 435
Berriault, Gina, 330
Best American Short Stories, The, 483
"Bezhin Meadow" (Turgenev), 111
Bishop, Elizabeth, 3–4
"Bliss" (Mansfield), 200–201
Bloom, Amy, 21–28, 261, 577–78
Borges, Jorge Luis, 96, 281
Boswell, Robert, 109
Bowles, Jane, 201–2
Boyle, T. Coraghessan, 336
"Boys" (Moody), 549–52
Bright Lights, Big City (McInerney), 195
"Brokeback Mountain" (Proulx), 5
Brontë, Emily, 112
"Brownies" (Packer), 163–78
"Bullet in the Brain" (T. Wolff), 570–73
Burgess, Anthony, 263
Busch, Frederick, 406–17, 578
Butler, Robert Olen, 243–52, 578–79
Byron, Lord, 70

California magazine, 456
Calvino, Italo, 281, 435
Carter, Angela
    about, 579
    "Company of Wolves, The," 196, 330,
        512–19
Carver, Raymond
    about, 579
    "Bath, The," 432, 458–63
    "Cathedral," 113, 114, 116, 372
    Fires, 31, 367
    on revision process, 428, 432
    "Small, Good Thing, A," 330, 432, 463–80
"Cathedral" (Carver), 113, 114, 116, 372
Cather, Willa, 105–6, 400

causality, in plot, 279–80, 286
change
    in narrative distance, 202–5
    necessity in short stories, 104–5
Chaon, Dan, 220–33, 580
character-based fiction, 281, 591
characters
    addressed by narrators, 195–96
    complexity of, 329
    consistency in, 329
    defined, 591
    exercises for, 338–40
    flat vs. round, 326–28
    imagination of, 334–35
    methods for defining, 329–33
    in openings, 368
    plot and, 282, 333–35
    relationships between, 336–38
    revealed through dialogue, 261
    showing relationships, 257
    specificity in, 328–29
    thoughts and emotions of, 198
    wants and needs, 335–36
    See also point of view
Cheever, John
    Carver and, 31
    "Goodbye, My Brother," 115
    on plot, 284
    "Wrysons, The," 201
Chekhov, Anton
    about, 580
    Gorki and, 10
    "In the Ravine," 114
    "Lady with the Little Dog, The," 101, 111,
        114, 116, 118, 208–20, 327
    Maugham on, 110
    on openings, 369
    on short stories, 96, 113
    writing advice, 69
Ciardi, John, 3
"Cinderella Waltz, The" (Beattie), 328
Cisneros, Sandra
    about, 580–81
    Woman Hollering Creek, 53–60
clichés
    defined, 591
    in metaphors, 71
    in plots, 287–88
    in similes, 71
climax, 99, 591

"clock," 148, 153
Clockwork Orange, A (Burgess), 263
Cochrell, Christie, 12–13, 108
Coe, Christopher, 403
Coleridge, Samuel Taylor, 238–39
commentary, as telling, 148
"Company of Men, The" (Ellison), 444–55, 486, 487
"Company of Wolves, The" (Carter), 196, 330, 512–19
complexity, of characters, 329
complications, 591
    See also conflict
conceit, 591
concreteness, 62, 591
    See also specificity
conflict
    conflict-crisis-resolution model, 98–100
    defined, 591
    plot and, 282–84
conflict-crisis-resolution model, 98–102
Conrad, Joseph, 97, 109
consistency, in characters, 329
constraints, creativity and, 435–36
convention
    defined, 106, 591
    in point of view, 236, 238
"Conversation with Jane Smiley, A" (Smiley), 431
"Conversation with My Father, A" (Paley), 337
convincing nature, of characters, 327
"Copy Cats" (Friend), 287–88
copyediting, 433
Costello, Mark, 70, 371
Council of Literary Magazines and Presses, 483
craft, inspiration vs., 1–3
Crane, Stephen, 199
creativity
    Barthelme on, 105
    constraints and, 435–36
    craft vs. inspiration, 1–3
    developmental stages, 433–34
    Picasso on, 2
Crichton, Michael, 287
crisis
    conflict-crisis-resolution model, 98–100
    defined, 591
"Crossing Into Poland" (Babel), 109
Cunningham, Michael, 313–25, 581
Curtis, C. Michael, 486

"Customs of the Country" (Bell), 376–88
Czyzewski, Carl, 242–43

"Darkness of Love, The" (Boswell), 109
"Daughters of the Late Colonel" (Mansfield), 104–5, 111
Davies, Robertson, 71
dead metaphors, 70, 592
"Death in the Woods" (Anderson), 332
DeMarinis, Rick, 106–7
de Maupassant, Guy, 328
denouement, 592
detail. *See* attention to detail
dialect, in dialogue, 265–66
dialogue
    attribution of, 260
    character revealed through, 331
    characters revealed through, 261
    defined, 592
    dialect in, 265–66
    exercises for, 267–69
    gesture and, 260–61
    grammatical correctness in, 263
    misusing, 258–60
    placeholders for, 266–67
    sensory experience and, 264
    as showing, 148
    silence and, 262–63
    specificity in, 258
    subtext in, 264–65
    uses for, 257–58
Díaz, Junot, 137–46, 333, 581
Dickinson, Emily, 117
direct observers, narrators as, 196–200
Directory of Small Press / Magazine Editors & Publishers, The, 483
"Dirty Wedding" (Johnson), 204–5
disbelief, willing suspension of, 239
discovery
    exercises for, 38–40
    Hugo on, 35–36
    interesting others, 36–37
    mysteries around us, 33–34
    of natural voice, 10–11
    obsession and, 37–38
    of real subjects, 35–36
    surprising yourself, 36–37
    transference and, 399
    writing about what you don't know, 32–33
    writing about what you know, 30–32

"Disneyland" (Gowdy), 519–29
distance
    defined, 592
    in point of view, 200–202
    shifting, 202–5
Dixon, Stephen, 334
drafts
    hot spots in, 434
    perfection and, 429
    writers on, 428
dramatization. *See* showing
Dubus, Andre, 328–29
Dybek, Stuart, 65, 283

early drafts. *See* drafts
Elkin, Stanley, 31
Ellison, Jan
    "Company of Men, The," 444–55, 486, 487
    getting published, 486–87
    revision example, 439–44
    on sensory experience, 404–5
Ellison, Ralph
    Invisible Man, 266
    "King of the Bingo Game," 369
"Emergency" (Johnson), 13–21, 282, 397, 401
emotions
    of characters, 198
    exercises for, 404–6
    specificity and, 400–401
    as telling, 148
    transferring, 398–99
    writing about what matters, 398–99
    See also sensory experience
environment, character revealed through, 330
epiphany
    as culmination of story, 102–4
    defined, 102, 592
Erdrich, Louise, 369
Eugenides, Jeffrey, 194
Euripides, 366
"Everything That Rises Must Converge" (O'Connor),
        99–100, 113–14, 116, 159, 178–89, 335
exercises
    for attention to detail, 75–78
    for characters, 338–40
    for dialogue, 267–69
    for discovery, 38–40
    for emotions, 404–6
    for epiphany, 107–8
    for exploring material, 11–12

    for narration, 161–63
    for noticing things, 12–13
    for openings, 374–76
    for plot, 288–90
    for point of view, 206–8
    for reliability of narrators, 241–43
    for revisions, 436–39
    for sensory experience, 404–6
    for short stories, 107–9
    for showing, 161–63
    for transference, 404–6
experience. *See* sensory experience
explanation, as telling, 148
exposition, 99, 592
    See also openings

falling action, 99, 592
Far Cry from Kensington, A (Spark), 10–11
Far Tortuga (Matthiessen), 266
"Father's Story, A" (Dubus), 328–29
Faulkner, William
    Carver and, 31
    As I Lay Dying, 5
    on revision process, 428
    "Rose For Emily, A," 194
    Sound and the Fury, The, 235–36
feelings. *See* emotions
Fever (Wideman), 118–37
fiction
    character-based, 281, 591
    conflict-crisis-resolution model, 98–100
    defined, 3, 592
    embodying mystery, 33–34
    metafiction, 281
    See also good writing
Fields, Bert, 287
"*Fiesta, 1980*" (Díaz), 137–46
Fifth Business (Davies), 71
Fires (Carver), 31, 367
first drafts. *See* drafts
"First Love" (Beckett), 117
first person narrators
    about, 191–94
    choosing point of view, 203–4
    detached, 191–92
    directly involved, 191, 193
    inverted, 194–95
    reliability of, 234–38
first person observer, 191–92
Fitzgerald, F. Scott, 191–93

Five Points publication, 487
flashbacks, 334, 592
Flaubert, Gustave, 280–81, 328
Fleming, Alexander, 62
"Follow the Eagle" (Kotzwinkle), 283
Ford, Richard, 331
Forster, E. M.
    Aspects of the Novel, 3, 278–79, 283, 367–68
    Howards End, 36, 200
    story as term, 284
"Forty-One, Alone, No Gerbil" (Olds), 30–31
"Four Meetings" (James), 368
Freitag triangle, 98–102
Freud, Sigmund, 399
Friend, Tad, 287–88
"Friendly Skies" (Boyle), 336
"Friend of My Youth" (Munro), 115
Fuentes, Carlos, 36

Gallant, Mavis, 96
Garcia, John, 208
García Márquez, Gabriel, 252–56, 584
Gardner, John, 64–65, 203, 282, 373
Garrett, George, 70
Gass, William, 70, 101
generalization
    abstraction vs., 62–63
    attention to detail vs., 62, 66–68
    defined, 62
    See also abstraction
gesture, dialogue and, 260–61
getting published
    case history, 486–87
    literary magazines, 481–82
    manuscript preparation, 482
    patience waiting, 485
    rejections, 486
    selecting target publications, 482–84
    simultaneous submissions, 484–85
"Girl" (Kincaid), 283
Glaspell, Susan, 371
Godshalk, C. S., 369–70
Goethe, 66, 98
"Goodbye, My Brother" (Cheever), 115
"Goodbye to Berlin" (Isherwood), 9
"Good Scent from a Strange Mountain, A"
    (Butler), 243–52
good writing
    avoiding "writerly" voice, 10–11
    as convincing, 3–4

    Forster on, 3
    noticing things, 9
    O'Connor on, 4
    resisting paraphrase, 4–5
    sentiment vs. sentimentality, 5–9
    as surprising, 3–4
Gorki, Maxim, 10
Gowdy, Barbara, 519–29, 581–82
grammar, in dialogue, 263
Great Gatsby, The (Fitzgerald), 191–93
"Greatness Strikes Where It Pleases"
    (Gustafsson), 115
Grenfell, Joyce, 428
Grimm, Brothers, 110
Gustafsson, Lars, 115

"hack mind," 65
Haley, Alex, 287
Hamlet (Shakespeare), 1, 65
Hanafee, James, 339–40
"Hands" (Anderson), 331
Hanna, Barry, 65–66
Hansen, Ron, 78, 92–95, 582
"*Harper's* Index, May 2006," 75–78
Hass, Robert, 33, 63
"Heart of Darkness" (Conrad), 97, 109
"Heavenly Flame" (Tolstaya), 115
Heger, Teresa, 405–6
"Helping" (Stone), 148–50, 150–52, 153
Hemingway, Ernest
    about, 582–83
    Carver and, 31
    "Hills Like White Elephants," 112, 115,
        153–54, 159, 198, 202, 260–61, 269–72
Hempel, Amy, 191, 529–35, 583
"Hills Like White Elephants" (Hemingway),
        112, 115, 153–54, 159, 198, 202, 260–61,
        269–72
history, as telling, 148
Horace, 369
hot spots, in drafts, 434
Howards End (Forster), 36, 200
"How to Discover What You Have to Say: A
    Talk to Students" (Skinner), 36
how vs. why, 280–81
Hugo, Richard, 35, 62, 433
Huxley, Aldous, 32

"I Know Myself Real Well. That's the Problem"
    (Shepard), 103

I Look Divine (Coe), 403
"Images" (Hass), 63
images / imagery
    as creative source, 73–75
    defined, 63, 592
    within literary context, 63–64
    working on two levels, 64–66
imagination, of characters, 334–35
imbalance, in openings, 368–69
in medias res, 369
In Search of Lost Time (Proust), 112
inspiration, craft vs., 1–3
*International Directory of Little Magazines and
    Small Presses, The,* 483
interpretation, objectivity vs., 152–53
Interstate (Dixon), 334
"In the Cemetery Where Al Jolson Is Buried"
    (Hempel), 191, 529–35
"In the Heart of the Heart of the Country"
    (Gass), 101
"In the Parish" (Milosz), 33
"In the Ravine" (Chekhov), 114
Invisible Man (Ellison), 266
Ironweed (Kennedy), 240–41
irony, 592
Irving, John, 31
Isherwood, Christopher, 9, 428
"I Stand Here Ironing" (Olsen), 115

James, Henry
    "Art of Fiction, The," 98
    "Four Meetings," 368
    on short stories, 96, 110
Jamison, Susan, 374
Johnson, Denis
    about, 583–84
    "Dirty Wedding," 204–5
    "Emergency," 13–21, 282, 397, 401
    simile example, 70
Joyce, James, 72, 102
Joy Luck Club, The (Tan), 335
"Judgment, The" (Kafka), 114
Jurassic Park (Crichton), 287
"Jury of Her Peers, A" (Glaspell), 371

Kafka, Franz, 114, 238–39, 336
Kennedy, William, 240–41
Kenyon, Jane, 32
Kesey, Ken, 237
Kilhearn, Thomas, 375

Kincaid, Jamaica, 283
"King of the Bingo Game" (Ellison), 369
Kingsolver, Barbara, 239–40
Kotzwinkle, William, 283
"Krapp's Last Tape" (Beckett), 63
Kuebler, Carolyn, 487

Ladies Night (play), 287
"Lady with the Little Dog, The" (Chekhov),
    101, 111, 113, 114, 116, 118, 208–20, 327
Lamott, Anne, 429, 455–58, 584
Lanning, George, 258, 367
Larkin, Philip, 37
Lawrence, D. H., 428
Leavitt, David, 198–99
left-brain thinking, 2
Le Guin, Ursula K., 337–38, 368
Le Lionnais, François, 435
Lessing, Doris, 373
"Letter to NY (for Louise Crane)" (Bishop), 3–4
L'Heureux, John, 104, 148
linear vs. modular stories, 101–2
Lish, Gordon, 432
literary magazines
    getting published, 481–82
    rejections from, 486
    simultaneous submissions, 484–85
    websites, 483
Literary Press and Magazine Directory, The, 483
"Loaf of Bread, A" (McPherson), 535–49
Lolita (Nabokov), 150, 156

Macauley, Robie, 258, 367
McInerney, Jay, 195
McMurtry, Larry, 8
McPherson, James Alan, 535–49, 584
Madden, David, 370
Malamud, Bernard, 428
Mamet, David, 262
"Management of Grief, The" (Mukherjee),
    353–65, 373
Mansfield, Katherine
    "Bliss," 200–201
    "Daughters of the Late Colonel," 104–5,
        111
    "Prelude," 115
manuscript preparation, 482
"Marquise of O., The" (von Kleist), 116
Marvin, Steve, 108–9, 206–7
Matthews, Brander, 97

Matthiessen, Peter, 266
Maugham, Somerset, 110
"Mauser" (Erdrich), 369
Maxwell, William, 64
"Me and Miss Mandible" (Barthelme), 491–99
meaning
    defined, 397
    subtext and, 593
Meeting by the River, A (Isherwood), 428
melodrama, 6, 592
Melville, Herman, 72
Merriam-Webster's Collegiate Dictionary, 3, 63,
        106, 373
metafiction, 281, 592
"Metamorphosis, The" (Kafka), 114, 238–39,
        336
metaphors
    clichéd, 71
    dead, 70, 592
    defined, 69–70, 592
    personification and, 72
    shock value, 70
    similes vs., 70
    usage recommendations, 72
"Method: The Mystery and the Mechanics"
        (Scott), 73–74
Michigan Quarterly Review, 487
middle, starting in, 369–71
Milosz, Czeslaw, 33
Missouri Review, 487
Moby-Dick (Melville), 72
modular vs. linear stories, 101–2
Moody, Rick, 549–52, 585
"Mother" (Paley), 74–75, 101
Mrs. Dalloway (Woolf), 112
Mukherjee, Bharati
    about, 585
    "Management of Grief, The," 353–65, 373
    "Tenant, The," 332–33
Munro, Alice
    about, 585–86
    "Friend of My Youth," 115
    "Save the Reaper," 552–67
    on short stories, 96
    "Wild Swans," 372–73
"Murphy's Xmas" (Costello), 371
"Museum of Science and Industry Story, The"
        (Mamet), 262
"My Date with Satan" (Richter), 417–26
"My Man Bovanne" (Bambara), 273–77

mystery
    in openings, 367
    of our position on earth, 33–34
    writing process as, 105
Mystery and Manners (O'Connor), 33, 62, 398

Nabokov, Vladimir, 150, 156
"Naked Ladies" (Nelson), 68
narration (telling)
    changing point of view, 206–7
    common advice, 148–50
    defined, 147, 150, 592
    exercises for, 161–63
    importance of, 154–56
    interpretation and, 152
    manipulating time, 148, 153
    objectivity and, 152–53
    "show, not tell" advice, 148–52, 156–57
    showing-telling continuum, 157–60
    traditional uses of, 153–54
Narrative Design (Bell), 101–2, 430
narrators
    attitude in, 200
    defined, 190, 592
    exercises for, 241–43
    first person, 191–94
    omniscient, 196–202, 204, 592
    reliability of, 234–41
    second person, 194–96
    shifts in distance, 202–5
    in short stories, 198
    third person, 196–200
    See also point of view
Nebraska (Hansen), 78, 92–95
needs of characters, 335–36
Nelson, Antonya, 68
"New Atlantis, The" (Le Guin), 337–38
New England Review, 439, 444, 486, 487
New Yorker, The, 486
1984 (Orwell), 288
noticing things, 9, 12–13
not knowing. See discovery
"Not Knowing" (Barthelme), 105
"No Trace" (Madden), 370
Novel & Short Story Writer's Market, 483

Oates, Joyce Carol
    about, 586
    on short stories, 97, 98
    "Where Are You Going, Where Have You
        Been?", 40–53, 98, 202–3, 286–87, 327

objectivity
   interpretation vs., 152–53
   showing story, 148
O'Brien, Tim
   about, 586–87
   "Things They Carried, The," 79–92, 100, 103,
      114, 116
observers
   first person, 191–92
   third person, 196–200
obsession, as a virtue, 37–38
O'Connor, Flannery
   about, 587
   Carver and, 31
   "Everything That Rises Must Converge,"
      99–100, 113–14, 116, 159, 178–89, 335
   Mystery and Manners, 33, 62, 398
   on short stories, 97
   simile example, 70
   third person narrators, 200
   "we are made of dust," 399
   writing advice, 4, 34, 62
   "Writing Short Stories," 105
O'Connor, Mary, 375
O'Hara, Frank, 35–36
"Oilman's Notebook, An" (Bass), 37–38
Olds, Sharon, 30–31
Olsen, Tillie, 115
omniscient narrators
   about, 196–200
   advantages, 204
   defined, 592
   examples, 201–2
Ondaatje, Michael, 340–42
"On Defamiliarization" (Baxter), 283–84
One Flew Over the Cuckoo's Nest (Kesey), 237
"Open Boat, The" (Crane), 199
openings
   action in, 371–72
   beginning with inaction, 372–73
   characteristics of good, 367–68
   as contract with reader, 366–67
   exercises for, 374–76
   imbalance in, 368–69
   starting in the middle, 369–71
   suspense in, 373–74
Orner, Peter, 567–70, 587–88
Orwell, George, 288
OULIPO, 435–36

Oxford Book of American Short Stories, The, 97
Ozick, Cynthia, 31, 109

Packer, ZZ, 163–78, 588
Paley, Grace
   "Conversation with My Father, A," 337
   "Mother," 74–75, 101
   on plot, 278
   on short stories, 96
paraphrase, resisting, 4–5, 98, 279
Paris Review, 284
"Paul's Case" (Cather), 400
Perec, Georges, 435
personification, 72, 592
Peter Pan (novella) (Barrie), 154–55
Peter Pan (play) (Barrie), 155–56
"Pet Milk" (Dybek), 283
Petrosky, Mary, 406
Pevear, Richard, 208
Phillips, Jayne Anne, 283
Philpott, Jenna, 163, 341–42
physical settings, in openings, 368
Picasso, Pablo, 2
"Pit and the Pendulum, The" (Poe), 113
placeholders, for dialogue, 266–67
Plath, Sylvia, 70
"Pleasure Principle, The" (Larkin), 37
plot
   causality in, 279–80, 286
   character-based, 282
   characters and, 333–35
   clichés in, 287–88
   conflict and, 282–84
   defined, 279, 592
   exercises for, 288–90
   resisting paraphrase, 279
   scènes à faire in, 287–88
plot points
   analyzing, 284–87
   creating by acting, 333
   creating by reacting, 333–34
Poe, Edgar Allan
   "Pit and the Pendulum, The," 113
   on short stories, 97
   on single effect, 112, 117
poetry
   Ciardi on, 3
   Dickinson on, 117
Poets and Writers magazine, 483

point of view
    choosing, 203–5
    common problems, 205–6
    conventions in, 236, 238
    defined, 190, 593
    distance in, 200–202
    exercises for, 206–8, 241–43
    first person, 191–94
    reliability of, 234–38
    second person, 194–96
    shifts in distance, 202–5
    third person, 196–200, 200–202
Practical Criticism (Richards), 6–7
"Prelude" (Mansfield), 115
Pride and Prejudice (Austen), 197–98
Pritchett, V. S., 113
Prose, Francine
    about, 588
    "What Makes a Short Story?" 96, 97, 109–18,
        279
Proulx, E. Annie, 5, 158–59
Proust, Marcel, 112
publishing, guide to. *See* getting published

Queneau, Raymond, 435

Rabassa, Gregory, 252
"Raft, The" (Orner), 567–70
Rainbow, The (Lawrence), 428
Raj Quartet, The (Scott), 73
"Ralph the Duck" (Busch), 406–17
reaction of characters, 148, 333–34
rejections, 486
relationships between characters, 257, 336–38
reliability
    exercises for, 241–43
    of first person narrators, 234–38
remembering, plot and, 334
Remember Me (Weldon), 264–65
rendering
    attention to detail and, 78
    solving vs., 280–81
resolution
    conflict-crisis-resolution model, 98–100
    defined, 99, 593
reversal, in short stories, 104–5
revision
    advice from writers, 428
    analytical / mechanical exercises for, 436–37

chance-based exercises for, 438–39
    constraints, 435–36
    creative exercises for, 437–38
    depending on others, 432–33
    developmental stages, 433–34
    Ellison example, 439–44
    exercise-based approach to, 434–35
    exercises for, 436–39
    hot spots in early drafts, 434
    research-based exercises for, 438
    seeking perfection, 429
    workshop method of, 429–32
Rhys, Jean, 402
Richards, I. M., 6–7
Richter, Stacey, 417–26, 588–89
right-brain thinking, 2
rising action, 99, 593
"Rock Springs" (Ford), 331
Roots (Haley), 287
"Rose For Emily, A" (Faulkner), 194
Roth, Philip, 283
"Rudy Elmenhurst Story, The" (Alvarez),
    333–34

"Sandman, The" (Barthelme), 195
"Sanitarium Under the Sign of the Hour Glass"
    (Schulz), 116
satisfaction, unit of, 98
"Save the Reaper" (Munro), 552–67
scènes à faire, 287–88, 593
Schoen, Steven, 96
Schulman, Sarah, 403
Schulz, Bruno, 116
Scott, Paul, 73–74
"Scratch Music" (Wright), 160
second person narrators
    about, 194–96
    addressing characters, 195–96
    addressing readers, 196
    inverted first person, 194–95
sensory experience
    attention to detail and, 69
    being aggressive with, 401–4
    detail and, 399–400
    dialogue and, 264
    exercises for, 404–6
    writing about what matters, 398–99
    See also emotions
sentiment, 5–9

sentimentality, 5–9

settings, 593

"7 or 8 Things I Know about Her—A Stolen Biography" (Ondaatje), 340–42

Shakespeare, William
  Hamlet, 1, 65
  metaphor example, 70
  sentimentality and, 7
  Sonnet 130, 7
  "sound and fury," 236

Sharma, Akhil, 342–53, 589

"Shawl, The" (Ozick), 109

Shelton, Richard, 193–94

Shepard, Jim, 103

Shipping News, The (Proulx), 158–59

"Shitty First Drafts" (Lamott), 429, 455–58

short stories
  ABCDE formula, 106, 371
  becoming slaves to theory, 105–7
  conflict-crisis-resolution model, 98–102
  defined, 96–98, 593
  earthquake model, 101
  epiphanies, 102
  linear vs. modular, 101–2
  narrators in, 198
  necessity of change in, 104–5
  Prose on, 96, 97, 109–18
  resisting paraphrase, 98
  reversal in, 104–5

Short Story, The (Matthews), 97

showing
  common advice, 148–50
  defined, 147
  exercises for, 161–63
  objectivity and, 152–53
  "show, not tell" advice, 148–52, 156–57
  showing-telling continuum, 157–60

"Significant Moments" (Atwood), 401

silence, in dialogue, 262–63

"Silver Water" (Bloom), 21–28, 261

similes
  clichéd, 71
  defined, 69–70, 593
  metaphors vs., 70

"Simple Heart, A" (Flaubert), 280–81

simultaneous submissions, 484–85

single effect, 112, 117

Single Man, A (Isherwood), 428

Skinner, B. F., 36

"Small, Good Thing, A" (Carver), 330, 432, 463–80

Smiley, Jane, 157–58, 431

Sonnet 130 (Shakespeare), 7

"Sonny's Blues" (Baldwin), 114, 115, 116, 284–86, 290–312

Sound and the Fury, The (Faulkner), 235–36

"Souvenir" (Phillips), 283

Spark, Muriel, 10–11, 455

specificity
  abstraction vs., 62
  in characters, 328–29
  defined, 62
  in dialogue, 258
  sensory experience and, 400–401

stereotypes, 327, 593

stock responses, 7

Stone, Robert
  "Helping," 148–50, 150–52, 153
  writing advice, 36–37, 68, 401

"Stones, The" (Shelton), 193–94

stories. *See* short stories

Stuart, Perry, 242

style, 593

subjects, triggering vs. real, 35–36, 62, 433

submissions, simultaneous, 484–85

subtext
  character revealed through, 331
  defined, 593
  transference of, 398–99

summary. *See* narration

"Sun, the Moon, the Stars, The" (Díaz), 333

"Sunrise on the Veld, A" (Lessing), 373

surprise, in characters, 327

"Surrounded by Sleep" (Sharma), 342–53

suspense, in stories, 373–74, 593

suspension of disbelief, 238–39

symbols, 72, 73, 593

"Taking Care" (Williams), 332

Tan, Amy, 335

Technique in Fiction (Lanning and Macauley), 258, 367

telling. *See* narration

"Tenant, The" (Mukherjee), 332–33

tension, 593
  See also conflict

Terms of Endearment (McMurtry), 8

"Territory" (Leavitt), 198–99

"Testimony of Pilot" (Hanna), 65–66
Texts and Pretexts (Huxley), 32
The Full Monty (film), 287
theme. *See* meaning
"Things They Carried, The" (O'Brien), 79–92, 100, 103, 114, 116
thinking / thoughts
    of characters, 198, 332–33
    modes of, 2
    as telling, 148
third person narrators
    about, 196–200
    attitude in, 200
    as direct observers, 196–200
    intimate, 200
    limited, 197, 201, 204
    omniscient, 196–202, 204, 592
"Thistles in Sweden, The" (Maxwell), 64
Thomas, Steven, 11–12
Thousand Acres, A (Smiley), 157–58
"Three Hermits, The" (Tolstoy), 110
time, manipulating, 148, 153
Tolstaya, Tatiana, 115
Tolstoy, Leo, 110, 337
tone, in openings, 368
Towson, Jane, 375–76
transference
    abstraction vs., 398–99
    emotional, 398–99
    exercises for, 404–6
triggering subjects, 35–36, 62, 433
Triggering Town, The (Hugo), 35, 62
Tsui, Daniel, 268–69
"Tulips" (Plath), 70
Turgenev, Ivan, 111
Turin, Janis, 12
Two Serious Ladies (Bowles), 201–2

Unger, Cybele, 268
unit of satisfaction, 98
Updike, John
    "A & P," 102, 114, 116
    Carver and, 31

"Very Old Man with Enormous Wings, A" (García Márquez), 252–56
Virgin Suicides, The (Eugenides), 194

voice
    defined, 593
    "writerly" vs. natural, 10–11
Volokhonsky, Larissa, 208
von Kleist, Heinrich, 116

wants / needs of characters, 335–36
Waters, Mary Yukari, 388–96, 589
"We Didn't" (Dybek), 65
Weldon, Fay, 264–65
Welty, Eudora, 32
Wharton, Edith, 96
"What Makes a Short Story?" (Prose), 96, 97, 109–18, 279
"Where Are You Going, Where Have You Been?" (Oates), 40–53, 98, 202–3, 286–87, 327
"White Angel" (Cunningham), 313–25
"Who Is It Can Tell Me Who I Am?" (Berriault), 330
"Why I Am Not a Painter" (O'Hara), 35–36
why vs. how, 280–81
Wideman, John Edgar, 118–37, 589–90
Wide Sargasso Sea (Rhys), 402
"Wild Horses" (Bass), 499–512
"Wild Swans" (Munro), 372–73
Williams, Joy, 332
Winesburg, Ohio (Anderson), 32
"Wizard, The" (Godshalk), 369–70
Wolff, Geoffrey, 367
Wolff, Tobias, 34, 570–73, 590
Woman Hollering Creek (Cisneros), 53–60
Wood, Paul, 161–62
Wood, Susan, 78
Woolf, Virginia
    Mrs. Dalloway, 112
    writing advice, 61
    Years, The, 68
workshop method for revision, 429–32
World According to Garp, The (Irving), 31
Wright, C. D., 160
writing. *See* good writing
"Writing Short Stories" (O'Connor), 105
"Wrysons, The" (Cheever), 201
Wuthering Heights (Brontë), 112

Years, The (Woolf), 68